FUNDAMENTALS
OF JAVA

Comprehensive Course

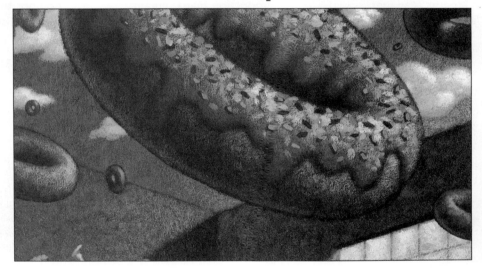

Lambert and Osborne

THOMSON

COURSE TECHNOLOGY

Australia • Canada • Mexico • Singapore • Spain • United Kingdom • United States

THOMSON
COURSE TECHNOLOGY

Fundamentals of Java, Comprehensive Course
by Lambert and Osborne

Senior Vice President, School SMG
Chris Elkhill

Managing Editor
Chris Katsaropolous

Sr. Product Manager
Dave Lafferty

Associate Product Manager
Jodi Dreissig

Marketing Manager
Kim Ryttel

Development
Custom Editorial Productions Inc.

Director of Production
Patty Stephan

Production Management
Custom Editorial Productions Inc.

Print Buyer
Denise Sandler

Cover Design
Abby Scholz

Illustrator
Paul Vismara

Compositor
GEX Publishing Services

Printer
Banta—Menasha

How to Use This Book

What makes a good computer instructional text? Sound pedagogy and the most current, complete materials. Not only will you find an inviting layout, but also many features to enhance learning.

Objectives— Objectives are listed at the beginning of each lesson, along with a suggested time for completion of the lesson. This allows you to look ahead to what you will be learning and to pace your work.

Exercises—Preceded by a topic discussion, these exercises are the "hands-on practice" part of the lesson. These may be written questions or practice writing short code segments.

A SAMPLE LESSON

LESSON X

OBJECTIVES

Estimated Time: 1.5 hours

VOCABULARY

Hot Tip

*E*XERCISE 1.1

FIGURE 1-4
Go To tab

Find and Replace

Find | Replace | Go To

Go to what:
Page
Section
Line
Bookmark
Comment
Footnote
Endnote

Enter page number:
5

Enter + and – to move relative to the current location.
Example: +4 will move forward four items.

Close | Previous | Go To

2

Marginal Boxes— These boxes provide additional information for Hot Tips, Notes, Warnings, Net Tips, fun facts (Did You Know?), Computer Concepts, Extra for Experts activities, and Thinking About Technology ideas.

Vocabulary—Terms identified in boldface throughout the lesson and summarized at the end.

Enhanced Screen Shots—Screen shots now come to life on each page with color and depth.

How to Use This Book

Summary—At the end of each lesson, you will find a summary to prepare you to complete the end-of-lesson activities.

Vocabulary/Review Questions—Review material at the end of each lesson and each unit enables you to prepare for assessment of the content presented.

Lesson Projects—End-of-lesson hands-on application of what has been learned in the lesson allows you to actually apply the techniques covered.

Critical Thinking Activities—Each lesson gives you an opportunity to apply creative analysis and use the Help system to solve problems.

End-of-Unit Projects—End-of-unit hands-on application of concepts learned in the unit provides opportunity for a comprehensive review.

Lesson **X** Unit Sample   Intro Excel   3

SUMMARY

VOCABULARY *Review*

REVIEW *Questions*

PROJECTS

CRITICAL *Thinking*

REVIEW *Questions*

PROJECTS

SCANS

SCANS—(Secretary's Commission on Achieving Necessary Skills)—The U.S. Department of Labor has identified the school-to-careers competencies.

Appendices—Appendices will vary, but focus on topics such as certification, concepts, operating systems, and other additional information.

PREFACE

This text is intended for a complete course in programming and problem solving. The book covers the material of typical Computer Science 1 and Computer Science 2 courses at the undergraduate level, but it is intended for the high school audience. The book is Advanced Placement (AP)-compliant for the A and AB levels, covering all of the required subset of Java™ for both levels.

We present seven major aspects of computing, some in stand-alone lessons and others spread across several lessons:

1. **Programming Basics.** This deals with the basic ideas of problem solving with computers, including primitive data types, control structures, methods, and algorithm analysis.

2. **Object-Oriented Programming.** OOP is today's dominant programming paradigm. All the essentials of this subject are covered.

3. **Data and Information Processing.** Fundamental data structures are discussed. These include strings, arrays, files, lists, stacks, queues, trees, sets, and maps. The general concept of abstract data type is introduced, and the difference between abstraction and implementation is illustrated.

4. **Software Development Life Cycle.** Rather than isolate software development techniques in one or two lessons, the book deals with them throughout in the context of numerous case studies.

5. **Graphical User Interfaces and Event-Driven Programming.** Many books at this level restrict themselves to character-based terminal I/O. The reason is simple. Graphical user interfaces and event-driven programming usually are considered too complex for beginning students. In this book, we circumvent the complexity barrier and show how to develop programs with graphical user interfaces with the same ease as their terminal-based counterparts.

6. **Graphics.** Problem solving with simple graphics is explored. This includes drawing basic geometric shapes, representing data graphically, and implementing a rudimentary sketching program.

7. **Web Basics.** The programming of Web pages with HTML and applets is introduced.

Focus on Fundamental Computer Science Topics

There seem to be two types of introductory Java textbooks. The first emphasizes basic problem solving and programming techniques, and the second emphasizes language features. This book takes the former approach and introduces Java features as they are needed to support programming concepts. In this way, all the AP-required syntax is covered without allowing the book to be syntax driven. Some additional and more advanced Java features, not part of the AP requirement, are covered in Lessons 19 through 22 and Appendix B.

Methods and Objects, Early or Late?

Occasionally, people argue about whether methods and objects should be introduced early or late in the first course. In Java, even the simplest program involves both, so the problem really becomes one of how to introduce these concepts in a clear and meaningful manner from the outset. Starting with the first program, we show how to instantiate and send messages to objects. The book's early lessons (2 through 4) focus on the use of objects, arithmetic expressions, control constructs, and algorithms in the context of short, simple programs. As programs become more complex, it becomes advantageous to decompose them into cooperating components. With this end in mind, Lesson 5 shows how to develop systems of cooperating classes and methods. Thus, we take a pragmatic rather than an ideological approach to the question of when to introduce methods and objects with complete confidence that students will master both by the end of the course.

Revisiting Control Structures, Classes, and Arrays

Years of teaching experience have demonstrated that beginning programming students have the most difficulty with control structures, classes, and arrays. In this text, we have sought to soften the blow by introducing these ideas in two steps. First, a lesson gives an initial overview of a topic using the most basic features in simple but realistic applications. A follow-up lesson then revisits the topic to fill in and refine the details.

Two Approaches to Data Structures

There are two approaches usually taken to data structures, that of the client who uses them and that of the implementer who writes their code. Courses that emphasize the first approach tend to be application oriented. Modern languages such as Java tend to support this approach well by providing a large set of classes for such data structures as lists and sets. However, some data structures, for example, queues and binary search trees, are not provided, so instructors must provide add-ons or require students to implement them. Over the past few years, the AP testing association has taken this approach, providing the so-called "AP classes" when necessary.

Courses that emphasize data structure implementation tend to use it as a vehicle for discussing space/time complexity tradeoffs and as an entry point for examining broad concepts such as memory management and algorithm design. Unfortunately, students who are expected to implement a list interface with arrays, linked structures, and iterators are likely to get bogged down in hundreds of lines of code and never see an application.

This text straddles both of these approaches to data structures. We provide introductory lessons on the interfaces and applications of each data structure and then follow-up lessons on implementations. Moreover, each implementation is presented as a prototype or trimmed-down version that allows students to explore its essential features and the space/time trade-offs without getting bogged down in details.

Input and Output Styles

The AP test requires simple standard terminal output but no input. A realistic first course will need some form of input, if only from the keyboard. We provide easy to use open source toolkits for terminal I/O, GUI-based I/O, and simple graphics. From the perspective of the AP requirements, however, all this material on I/O is optional and should be fitted into the course only as time allows. It is the authors' experience that I/O adds interest without being overly burdensome; however, on some programming projects instructors reasonably may prefer to provide all or most of the interface-related code. In general, students and instructors are free to choose the I/O style that suits their needs and interests.

Lessons 2 through 6 use terminal I/O and demonstrate standard terminal-based interface techniques such as how to write query-based and menu-driven programs. After that, instructors have the choice of asking students to write terminal-based or GUI-based programs. Terminal input is based on the `TerminalIO` package, which is an extension of the standard stream classes. Later in the book, we show how to use these standard stream classes directly.

The early lessons also provide the option of using a `TurtleGraphics` package that allows students to draw images without worrying about Java's complex painting mechanisms. Again, later in the book, we take students through the significant details. The book uses turtle graphics because they provide an engaging context for illustrating the use of objects.

GUIs usually are considered beyond the scope of an introductory Java course. This book uses a package called `BreezySwing` that allows students to develop GUIs with the same ease as terminal-based interfaces. `BreezySwing` extends Java's Abstract Windowing Toolkit (AWT) and Swing in a manner that hides most of the underlying complexities from the beginning programmer. Using `BreezySwing`, students write event-driven programs with realistic graphical user interfaces, but without becoming entangled in numerous and difficult details.

People sometimes argue that students need to know how to develop GUIs the real way—that is, using AWT and Swing—and of course they are correct; however, the first course is probably not the right place to master this material. In the meantime, `BreezySwing` provides a useful introduction to GUI-based programming. It is easy to learn and use, and it provides a bridge to AWT and Swing. For those who are interested and highly motivated, Lesson 22 explains the details of using AWT and Swing. After mastering Lesson 22, students are ready to abandon `BreezySwing` and undertake full-fledged Java GUI development with all its power and complexity.

All of the I/O packages are available on the CD accompanying this book and from the Web site *http://www.wlu.edu/~lambertk/hsjava/*. The Web site is the preferred source because it contains the latest release of `BreezySwing` together with online documentation and other related materials. An online tutorial that introduces the use of the packages is also available from the Web site.

Case Studies, the Software Life Cycle, and Comments

The book contains numerous case studies. These are complete Java programs ranging from the simple to the substantial. To emphasize the importance and usefulness of the software development life cycle, case studies are presented in the framework of a user request followed by analysis, design, and implementation, with well-defined tasks performed at each stage. Some case studies are carried through several lessons or extended in end-of-lesson programming projects.

Programming consists of more than just writing code, so we encourage students to submit an analysis and design as part of major programming assignments. We also believe that code should be properly commented, and for purposes of illustration, we include comments in selected examples of the code in the book.

Exercises

The book contains several different types of exercises. Most sections end with exercise questions that reinforce the reading by asking basic questions about the material in the section. Each lesson ends with a set of review exercises. All lessons except the first one include programming projects of varying degrees of difficulty. Finally, each lesson has a critical thinking activity that allows the student to reflect on a major topic covered in the lesson.

Special Features

Scattered throughout the book are short essays called Special Features. These present historical and social aspects of computing, including computer ethics and security

Alternative Paths Through the Book

The AP A-level material is covered in the first 11 lessons of the book. The AB-only material is covered in Lessons 12 through 18. Lessons 19 through 22 cover optional material not included in the AP course requirements. It is possible to cover some of this optional material early.

■ Those who want to do applets early can insert Lesson 21 between Lessons 3 and 4.

■ Those who want to do graphics early can jump ahead to Lesson 19 after finishing Lesson 7.

■ Information about files, introduced in Lesson 20, can be presented after Lesson 7.

Again, Lesson 22 is intended only for those who want to explore GUI-based development in detail and shows how to make the transition from `BreezySwing` to AWT and Swing.

We have tried to produce a high-quality text, but should you encounter any errors, please report them to *klambert@wlu.edu*. A listing of errata, should they exist, and other information about the book will be posted on the Web site *http://www.wlu.edu/~lambertk/hsjava/*.

Acknowledgments

We would like to thank the following reviewers for their time and efforts:

Kathleen Weaver
Hillcrest High School
Dallas, TX

Lisa Brock
Pine Crest School
Fort Lauderdale, FL

Karen Harris-Sweetman
Sumter High School
Sumter, SC

Michelle Hansen
Davenport University, Kalamazoo Campus
Kalamazoo, MI

Tom Krawczewicz
DeMatha Catholic High School
Hyattsville, MD

Yvonne Leonard
Coastal Community College
Jacksonville, NC

Neil Reger
Buckhannon-Upshur High School
Buckhannon, WV

Geni Slaughter
Green Hope High School
Morrisville, NC

We would like to thank the individuals at Course Technology who helped to assure that the content of all data and solution files used for this text were correct and accurate: Alex White and Vitaly Davidovich.

In addition several individuals contributed material to the *Instructor Resource Kit*:

Lori Hunt—Instructor Manual, Instructor Lesson Plans, and Student Lesson Plans

Michael Bjerkness—Testbank

Charlene Cestroni—PowerPoint Presentations

We would also like to thank several other people whose work made this book possible:

Rose Marie Kuebbing
Developmental Editor
Custom Editorial Productions Inc.

Megan Smith-Creed
Production Editor
Custom Editorial Productions Inc.

Dave Lafferty
Senior Product Manager SWCE
Course Technology

Dedication

To David, Carol, Ashley, Kris, Steve, Sarah, and John

Kenneth A. Lambert
Lexington, VA

Martin Osborne
Bellingham, Washington

TABLE OF CONTENTS

UNIT 2 THE NEXT STEP WITH JAVA

UNIT 3 ARRAYS, RECURSION, AND COMPLEXITY

UNIT 4 USING ABSTRACT DATA TYPES

UNIT 5 IMPLEMENTING ABSTRACT DATA TYPES

UNIT 6 GRAPHICS, FILES, APPLETS, AND SWING

GETTING STARTED WITH JAVA

Unit 1

🕑 **Estimated Time for Unit: 12.5 hrs.**

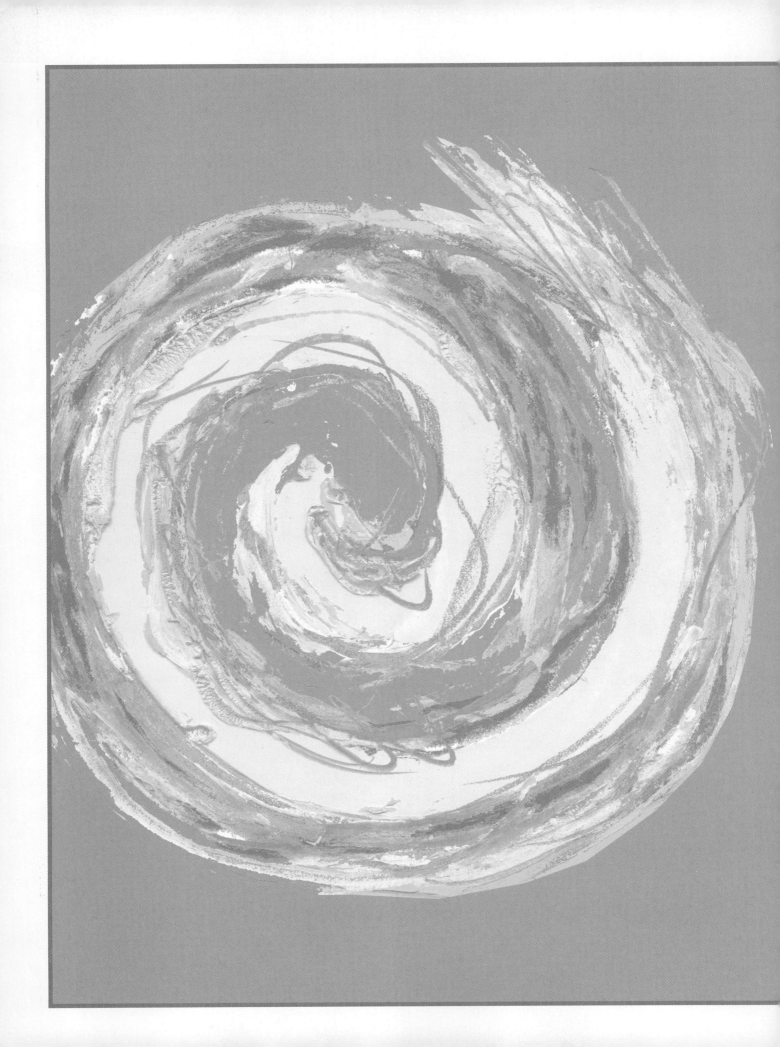

BACKGROUND

OBJECTIVES

Upon completion of this lesson, you should be able to:

- Give a brief history of computers.

- Describe how hardware and software make up computer architecture.

- Understand the binary representation of data and programs in computers.

- Discuss the evolution of programming languages.

- Describe the software development process.

- Discuss the fundamental concepts of object-oriented programming.

Estimated Time: 2 hours

VOCABULARY

application software

bit

byte

central processing unit (CPU)

hardware

information hiding

object-oriented programming

primary memory

secondary memory

software

software development life cycle (SDLC)

system software

waterfall model

This is the only lesson in the book that is not about the details of writing Java programs. This lesson discusses computing in general, hardware and software, the representation of information in binary (i.e., as 0s and 1s), and general concepts of object-oriented programming. All this material will give you a broad understanding of computing and a foundation for your study of programming.

1.1 History of Computers

ENIAC, or Electronic Numerical Integrator and Computer, built in the late 1940s, was one of the world's first computers. It was a large stand-alone machine that filled a room and used more electricity than all the houses on an average city block. ENIAC contained hundreds of miles of wire and thousands of heat-producing vacuum tubes. The mean time between failures was less than an hour, yet because of its fantastic speed when compared to hand-operated electromechanical calculators, it was immensely useful.

In the early 1950s, IBM sold its first business computer. At the time, it was estimated that the world would never need more than 10 such machines. By comparison, however, its awesome computational power was a mere 1/800 of the typical 800-megahertz Pentium personal computer purchased for about $1000 in 2000. Today, there are hundreds of millions of computers in the world, most of which are PCs. There are also billions of computers embedded in everyday products such as hand-held calculators, cars, refrigerators, and soon even clothing.

These first computers could perform only a single task at a time, and input and output were handled by such primitive means as punch cards and paper tape.

In the 1960s, time-sharing computers, costing hundreds of thousands and even millions of dollars, became popular at organizations large enough to afford them. These computers were powerful enough for 30 people to work on them simultaneously—and each felt as if he or she were the sole user. Each person sat at a teletype connected by wire to the computer. By making a connection through the telephone system, teletypes could even be placed at a great distance from the computer. The teletype was a primitive device by today's standards. It looked like an electric typewriter with a large roll of paper attached. Keystrokes entered at the keyboard were transmitted to the computer, which then echoed them back on the roll of paper. In addition, output from the computer's programs was printed on this roll.

In the 1970s, people began to see the advantage of connecting computers in networks, and the wonders of e-mail and file transfers were born.

In the 1980s, PCs appeared in great numbers, and soon after, local area networks of interconnected PCs became popular. These networks allowed a local group of PCs to communicate and share such resources as disk drives and printers with each other and with large centralized multiuser computers.

The 1990s saw an explosion in computer use. Hundreds of millions of computers appeared on many desktops and in many homes. And most of them are connected through the Internet (Figure 1-1).

FIGURE 1-1
An interconnected world of computers

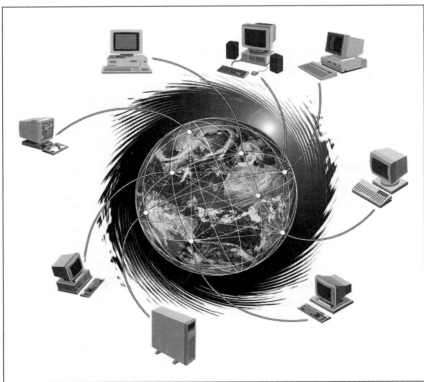

And the common language of all these computers is fast becoming Java™.

1.2 Computer Hardware and Software

Computers can be viewed as machines that process information. They consist of two primary components: hardware and software. *Hardware* consists of the physical devices that you see on your desktop, and *software* consists of the programs that give the hardware useful functionality. The main business of this book, which is programming, concerns software. But before diving into programming, let us take a moment to consider some of the major hardware and software components of a typical PC.

Bits and Bytes

It is difficult to discuss computers without referring to bits and bytes. A *bit* or *binary digit*, is the smallest unit of information processed by a computer and consists of a single 0 or 1. A *byte* consists of eight adjacent bits. The capacity of computer memory and storage devices is usually expressed in bytes.

Computer Hardware

As illustrated in Figure 1-2, a PC consists of six major subsystems.

FIGURE 1-2
A PC's six major subsystems

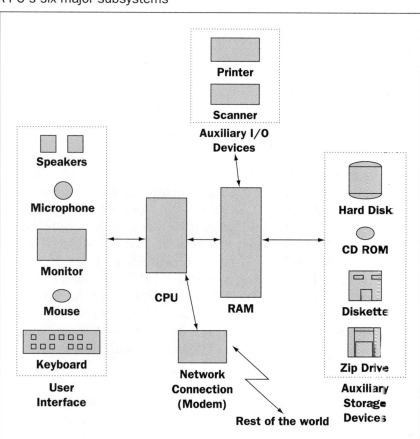

Listed in order from outside and most visible to inside and most hidden, these are as follow:

- The user interface, which supports moment-to-moment communication between a user and the computer

- Auxiliary I/O devices such as printers and scanners

- Auxiliary storage devices for long-term storage of data and programs

- A network connection for connecting to the Internet and thus the rest of the world

- Internal memory, or RAM, for momentary storage of data and programs

- The all important CPU, or central processing unit

Now we explore each of these subsystems in greater detail.

User Interface

The user interface consists of several devices familiar to everyone who has used a PC. In this book, we assume that our readers have already acquired basic computer literacy and have performed common tasks such as using a word processor or surfing the Internet. The keyboard and mouse are a computer's most frequently used input devices, and the monitor or screen is the principal output device. Also useful, but less common, are a microphone for input and speakers for output.

Auxiliary I/O Devices

Computers have not yet produced a paper-free world, so we frequently rely on the output from printers. Scanners are most commonly used to enter images, but in conjunction with appropriate software they can also be used to enter text. In case you have not already guessed, I/O stands for input/output. Numerous other I/O devices are available for special applications, such as joysticks for games.

Auxiliary Storage Devices

The computer's operating system, the applications we buy, and the documents we write are all stored on devices collectively referred to as auxiliary storage or *secondary memory*. The current capacity of these devices is incredibly large and continues to increase rapidly. In 2001, as these words are being written, *hard disks* typically store tens of billions of bytes of information, or gigabytes (Gbytes) as they are commonly called. In addition to hard disks, which are permanently encased within computers, there are several *portable storage media*. Most computer software is now purchased on *CD-ROMs*. CD stands for compact disk and ROM for read-only memory. The term *ROM* is becoming somewhat misleading in this context as PCs are increasingly being equipped with CD devices that can read and write. Most CDs have a capacity of about 600 million bytes (megabytes or Mbytes), enough for an hour of music or a typical PC software package. Currently, CDs are being supplanted by *DVDs*, which have about 10 times a CD's capacity. *Zip drives* with a capacity of 100 to 200 Mbytes are the most convenient portable storage device, but diskettes with a capacity of a mere 1 Mbyte are still widely used. Both support input and output and are used primarily for transporting data between computers that are not interconnected and for making backup copies of crucial computer files.

Network Connection

A network connection is now an essential part of every PC, connecting it to all the resources of the Internet. For home computer users, a modem has long been the most widely used connection device. Modem stands for modulator-demodulator and refers to the fact that the device converts the digital information (0s and 1s) of the computer to an analog form suitable for transmission on phone lines and vice versa. Of course, as phone technology becomes increasingly digital, the term *modem* is fast becoming a misnomer. Other devices for connecting to the Internet include cable modems, which use TV cable rather than a phone connection, and Ethernet cards, which attach directly to local area networks and from there to the Internet.

Internal Memory

Although auxiliary storage devices have great capacity, access to their information is relatively slow in comparison to the speed of a computer's central processing unit. For this reason, computers include high-speed internal memory, also called *random access memory (RAM)* or *primary memory*. The contents of RAM are lost every time the computer is turned off, but when the computer is running, RAM is loaded from auxiliary storage with needed programs and data. Because a byte of RAM costs about 100 times as much as a byte of hard disk storage, PCs usually contain only about 32 to 128 Mbytes of RAM. Consequently, RAM is often unable to simultaneously hold all the programs and data a person might be using during a computer session. To deal with this situation, the computer swaps programs and data backward and forward between RAM and the hard disk as necessary. Swapping takes time and slows down the apparent speed of the computer from the user's perspective. Often the cheapest way to improve a computer's performance is to install more RAM.

Another smaller piece of internal memory is called **ROM**—short for *read-only memory*. This memory is usually reserved for critical system programs that are used when the computer starts up and that are retained when the computer is shut down.

Central Processing Unit

The *central processing unit (CPU)* does the work of the computer. Given the amazing range of complex tasks performed by computers, one might imagine that the CPU is intrinsically very complex, but such is not the case. In fact, the basic functions performed by the CPU consist of the everyday arithmetic operations of addition, subtraction, multiplication, and division together with some comparison and I/O operations. The complexity lies in the programs that direct the CPU's operations rather than in the CPU itself, and it is the programmer's job to determine how to translate a complex task into an enormous series of simple operations, which the computer then executes at blinding speed. One of the authors of this book, Martin Osborne, uses a computer that operates at 800 million cycles per second (800 MHz), and during each cycle, the CPU executes all or part of a basic operation.

Perhaps we have gone too far in downplaying the complexity of the CPU. To be fair, it too is highly complex—not in terms of the basic operations it performs, but rather in terms of how it achieves its incredible speed. This speed is achieved by packing several million transistors onto a silicon chip roughly the size of a postage stamp. Since 1955, when transistors were first used in computers, hardware engineers have been doubling the speed of computers about every 18 months, principally by increasing the number of transistors on computer chips. This phenomenon is commonly known as Moore's Law. However, basic laws of physics guarantee that the process of miniaturization that allows ever greater numbers of transistors to be packed onto a single chip will soon end. How soon this will be, no one knows.

The *transistor*, the basic building block of the CPU and RAM, is a simple device that can be in one of two states—ON, conducting electricity, or OFF, not conducting electricity. All the information in a computer—programs and data—is expressed in terms of these ONs and OFFs, or 1s and 0s as they are more conveniently called. From this perspective, RAM is merely a large array of 1s and 0s, and the CPU is merely a device for transforming patterns of 1s and 0s into other patterns of 1s and 0s.

To complete our discussion of the CPU, we describe a typical sequence of events that occurs when a program is executed, or run:

1. The program and data are loaded from disk into separate regions of RAM.

2. The CPU copies the program's first instruction from RAM into a decoding unit.

3. The CPU decodes the instruction and sends it to the Arithmetic and Logic Unit (ALU) for execution; for instance, it may add a number at one location in RAM to one at another location and store the result at a third location.

4. The CPU determines the location of the next instruction and repeats the process of copy, decode, and execute until the end of the program is reached.

5. After the program has finished executing, the data portion of RAM contains the results of the computation performed by the program.

Needless to say, this description has been greatly simplified. We have, for instance, completely ignored all issues related to input and output; however, the description provides a view of the computational process that will help you understand what follows.

Computer Software

Computer hardware processes complex patterns of electronic states or 0s and 1s. Computer software transforms these patterns, allowing them to be viewed as text, images, and so forth. Software is generally divided into two broad categories—system software and application software.

System Software

System software supports the basic operations of a computer and allows human users to transfer information to and from the computer. This software includes

- The operating system, especially the file system for transferring information to and from disk and schedulers for running multiple programs concurrently

- Communications software for connecting to other computers and the Internet

- Compilers for translating user programs into executable form

- The user interface subsystem, which manages the look and feel of the computer, including the operation of the keyboard, the mouse, and a screen full of overlapping windows

Application Software

Application software allows human users to accomplish specialized tasks. Examples of types of application software include

- Word processors

- Spreadsheets

- Database systems

- Other programs we write

EXERCISE 1.2

1. What is the difference between a bit and a byte?

2. Name two input devices and two output devices.

3. What is the purpose of auxiliary storage devices?

4. What is RAM and how is it used?

5. Discuss the differences between hardware and software.

1.3 Binary Representation of Information and Computer Memory

As we saw in the previous section, computer memory stores patterns of electronic signals, which the CPU manipulates and transforms into other patterns. These patterns in turn can be viewed as strings of binary digits or bits. Programs and data are both stored in memory, and there is no discernible difference between program instructions and data; they are both just sequences of 0s and 1s. To determine what a sequence of bits represents, we must know the context. We now examine how different types of information are represented in binary notation.

Integers

We normally represent numbers in decimal (base 10) notation, whereas the computer uses binary (base 2) notation. Our addiction to base 10 is a physiological accident (10 fingers rather than 8, 12, or some other number). The computer's dependence on base 2 is due to the on/off nature of electric current.

To understand base 2, we begin by taking a closer look at the more familiar base 10. What do we really mean when we write a number such as 5403? We are saying that the number consists of 5 thousands, 4 hundreds, 0 tens, and 3 ones, or expressed differently:

$$(5 * 10^3) + (4 * 10^2) + (0 * 10^1) + (3 * 10^0)$$

In this expression, each term consists of a power of 10 times a coefficient between 0 and 9. In a similar manner, we can write expressions involving powers of 2 and coefficients between 0 and 1. For instance, let us analyze the meaning of 10011_2, where the subscript 2 indicates that we are using a base of 2:

$$10011_2 = (1 * 2^4) + (0 * 2^3) + (0 * 2^2) + (1 * 2^1) + (1 * 2^0)$$
$$= 16 + 0 + 0 + 2 + 1 = 19$$
$$= (1 * 10^1) + (9 * 10^0)$$

The inclusion of the base as a subscript at the end of a number helps us avoid possible confusion. Here are four numbers that contain the same digits but have different bases and thus different values:

$$1101101_{16}$$
$$1101101_{10}$$

1101101_8

1101101_2

Computer scientists use bases 2 (*binary*), 8 (*octal*), and 16 (*hexadecimal*) extensively. Base 16 presents the dilemma of how to represent digits beyond 9. The accepted convention is to use the letters A through F, corresponding to 10 through 15. For example:

$$3BC4_{16} = (3 * 16^3) + (11 * 16^2) + (12 * 16^1) + (4 * 16^0)$$
$$= (3 * 4096) + (11 * 256) + (12 * 16) + 4$$
$$= 15300_{10}$$

As you can see from these examples, the next time you are negotiating your salary with an employer, you might allow the employer to choose the digits as long as she allows you to pick the base. In closing, Table 1-1 shows some base 10 numbers and their equivalents in base 2.

TABLE 1-1
Some base 10 numbers and their base 2 equivalents

BASE 10	BASE 2
0	0
1	1
2	10
3	11
4	100
5	101
6	110
7	111
43	101011

Floating-Point Numbers

Numbers with a fractional part, such as 354.98, are called *floating-point numbers*. They are a bit trickier to represent in binary than integers. One way is to use the *mantissa/exponent notation* in which the number is rewritten as a value between 0 and 1, inclusive ($0 \leq x < 1$), times a power of 10. For example

$$354.98_{10} = 0.35498_{10} * 10^3$$

where the mantissa is 35498, and the exponent is 3, or the number of places the decimal has moved. Similarly, in base 2

$$10001.001_2 = 0.10001001_2 * 2^5$$

with a mantissa of 10001001 and exponent of $5_{10} = 101_2$. In this way we can represent any floating-point number by two separate sequences of bits, with one sequence for the mantissa and the other for the exponent.

Characters and Strings

To process text, computers must represent characters such as letters, digits, and other symbols on a keyboard. There are many encoding schemes for characters. One popular scheme is called **ASCII** (**American Standard for Information Interchange**). In this scheme, each character is represented as a pattern of 8 bits or a byte.

In binary notation, byte values can range from 0000 0000 to 1111 1111, allowing for 256 possibilities. These are more than enough for the characters

- A...Z

- a...b

- 0...9

- +, -, *, /, etc.

- And various unprintable characters such as carriage return, line feed, a ringing bell, and command characters

Table 1-2 shows some characters and their corresponding ASCII bit patterns.

> **Computer Concepts**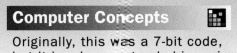
>
> Many computers follow the slightly different IEEE standard in which the mantissa contains one digit before the decimal or binary point. In binary, the mantissa's leading 1 is then suppressed.

> **Computer Concepts**
>
> Originally, this was a 7-bit code, but it has been extended in various ways to 8 bits.

TABLE 1-2
Some characters and their corresponding ASCII bit patterns

CHARACTER	BIT PATTERN	CHARACTER	BIT PATTERN	CHARACTER	BIT PATTERN
A	0100 0001	a	0110 0001	0	0011 0000
B	0100 0010	b	0110 0010	1	0011 0001
...	...	...	...	...	..
Z	0101 1010	z	0111 1010	9	0011 1001

Java, however, uses a scheme called **Unicode** rather than ASCII. In this scheme, each character is represented by a pattern of 16 bits, ranging from 0000 0000 0000 0000 to 1111 1111 1111 1111. Unicode allows for 65,536 possibilities and can represent many alphabets simultaneously. Within Unicode, the patterns 0000 0000 0000 0000 to 0000 0000 1111 1111 duplicate the ASCII encoding scheme.

Strings are another type of data used in text processing. Strings are sequences of characters, such as "The cat sat on the mat." The computer encodes each character in ASCII or Unicode and strings them together.

Images

Representing images in a computer is a straightforward task. For example, consider a black-and-white picture. To represent this image, we superimpose a fine grid on the image, or for better resolution, an even finer grid. If a grid cell, or **pixel**, contains black, we encode it as 0;

otherwise, we encode it as 1. Color images are encoded in a similar manner but use several bits to represent the color value of each pixel. This is done in terms of the color's composition as a mixture of varying intensities of red, green, and blue. Typically, 8 bits are used to represent each intensity for a total of 24 bits or 16,777,126 (the number of possible sequences of 24 bits) color values per pixel.

> ### Did You Know?
>
> The sampling rate of 44,000 times a second is not arbitrary, but corresponds to the number of samples required to reproduce accurate sounds with a frequency of up to 22,000 cycles per second. Sounds above that frequency are of more interest to dogs, bats, and dolphins than people.

Sound

We can digitize sound as follows:

- For each stereo channel, every 1/44,000 of a second measure the amplitude of the sound on a scale of 0 to 65,535.

- Convert this number to binary using 16 bits.

Thus, 1 hour of stereo music requires

```
              1 hour    60 minutes   60 seconds   44,000 samples   16 bits
2 channels *  ------ *  ---------- * ----------- * ---------------- * ------
              channel   hour         minute        second            sample
= 5,068,800,000 bits
= 633,600,000 bytes
```

which is the capacity of a standard CD.

Program Instructions

Program instructions are represented as a sequence of bits in RAM. For instance, on some hypothetical computer, the instruction to add two numbers already located in RAM and store their sum at some third location in RAM might be represented as follows:

```
0000 1001 / 0100 0000 / 0100 0010 / 0100 0100
```

where

- The first group of 8 bits represents the ADD command and is called the operation code, or opcode for short
- The second group of 8 bits represents the location (64_{10}) in memory of the first operand
- The third group of 8 bits represents the location (66_{10}) in memory of the second operand
- The fourth group of 8 bits represents the location (68_{10}) at which to store the sum

In other words, add the number at location 64 to the number at location 66 and store the sum at location 68.

Computer Memory

We can envision a computer's memory as a gigantic sequence of bytes. A byte's location in memory is called its *address*. Addresses are numbered from 0 to 1 less than the number of bytes of memory installed on that computer, say, 32M - 1, where M stands for *megabyte*.

A group of contiguous bytes can represent a number, a string, a picture, a chunk of sound, a program instruction, or whatever, as determined by context. For example, let us consider the meaning of the two bytes starting at location 3 in Figure 1-3.

FIGURE 1-3
A 32-Mbyte RAM

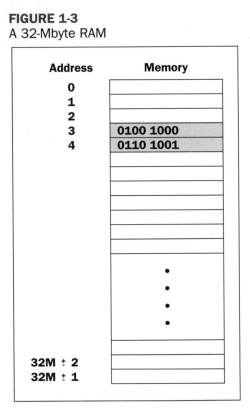

The several possible meanings include these:

■ If it is a string, then the meaning is "Hi".

■ If it is a binary encoded integer, then the meaning is 18537_{10}.

■ If it is a program instruction, then it might mean ADD, depending on the type of computer.

EXERCISE 1.3

1. Translate 11100011_2 to a base 10 number.

2. Translate $45B_{16}$ to a base 10 number.

3. What is the difference between Unicode and ASCII?

4. Assume that 4 bits are used to represent the intensities of red, green, and blue. How many total colors are possible in this scheme?

5. An old-fashioned computer has just 16 bits available to represent an address of a memory location. How many total memory locations can be addressed in this machine?

COMPUTER ETHICS

COMPUTER ETHICS: THE ACM CODE OF ETHICS

The Association for Computing Machinery (ACM) is the flagship organization for computing professionals. The ACM supports publications of research results and new trends in computer science, sponsors conferences and professional meetings, and provides standards for computer scientists as professionals. The standards concerning the conduct and professional responsibility of computer scientists have been published in the ACM Code of Ethics. The code is intended as a basis for ethical decision making and for judging the merits of complaints about violations of professional ethical standards.

The code lists several general moral imperatives for computer professionals:

- Contribute to society and human well-being.
- Avoid harm to others.
- Be honest and trustworthy.
- Be fair and take action not to discriminate.
- Honor property rights including copyrights and patents.
- Give proper credit for intellectual property.
- Respect the privacy of others.
- Honor confidentiality.

The code also lists several more specific professional responsibilities:

- Strive to achieve the highest quality, effectiveness, and dignity in both the process and products of professional work.
- Acquire and maintain professional competence.
- Know and respect existing laws pertaining to professional work.
- Accept and provide appropriate professional review.
- Give comprehensive and thorough evaluations of computer systems and their impacts, including analysis of possible risks.
- Honor contracts, agreements, and assigned responsibilities.
- Improve public understanding of computing and its consequences.
- Access computing and communication resources only when authorized to do so.

In addition to these principles, the code offers a set of guidelines to provide professionals with explanations of various issues contained in the principles. The complete text of the ACM Code of Ethics is available at the ACM's Web site, http://www.acm.org.

1.4 Programming Languages

Question: "If a program is just some very long pattern of electronic states in a computer's memory, then what is the best way to write a program?" The history of computing provides several answers to this question in the form of generations of programming languages.

Generation 1 (Late 1940s to Early 1950s)—Machine Languages

Early on, when computers were new on this earth, they were very expensive, and programs were very short. Programmers toggled switches on the front of the computer to enter programs and data directly into RAM in the form of 0s and 1s. Later, devices were developed to read the 0s and 1s into memory from punched cards and paper tape. There were several problems with this machine language coding technique:

- Coding was error prone (entering just a single 0 or 1 incorrectly was enough to make a program run improperly or not at all).

- Coding was tedious and slow.

- It was extremely difficult to modify programs.

- It was nearly impossible for one person to decipher another's program.

- A program was not portable to a different type of computer because each type had its own unique machine language.

Needless to say, this technique is no longer used!

Generation 2 (Early 1950s to Present)—Assembly Languages

Instead of the binary notation of machine language, assembly language uses mnemonic symbols to represent instructions and data. For instance, here is a machine language instruction followed by its assembly language equivalent:

```
0011 1001 / 1111 0110 / 1111 1000 / 1111 1010
ADD         A,           B,           C
```

meaning

1. Add the number at memory location 246, which we refer to as A

2. To the number at memory location 248, which we refer to as B

3. And store the result at memory location 250, which we refer to as C

Each *assembly language* instruction corresponds exactly to one machine language instruction. The standard procedure for using assembly language consists of several steps:

1. Write the program in assembly language.

2. Translate the program into a machine language program—this is done by a computer program called an *assembler*.

3. Load and run the machine language program—this is done by another program called a *loader*.

When compared to machine language, assembly language is

- More programmer friendly

- Still unacceptably (by today's standards) tedious to use, difficult to modify, and so forth

- No more portable because each type of computer still has its own unique assembly language

Assembly language is used as little as possible by programmers today, although sometimes it is used when memory or processing speed are at a premium. Thus, every student of computer science probably learns at least one assembly language.

Generation 3 (Mid-1950s to Present)—High-Level Languages

Early examples of *high-level languages* are FORTRAN and COBOL, which are still in widespread use. Later examples are BASIC, C, and Pascal. Recent examples include Smalltalk, C++, and Java. All these languages are designed to be human friendly—easy to write, easy to read, and easy to understand—at least when compared to assembly language. For example, all high-level languages support the use of algebraic notation, such as the expression $x + (y * z)$.

Each instruction in a high-level language corresponds to many instructions in machine language. Translation to machine language is done by a program called a *compiler*. Generally, a program written in a high-level language is portable, but must be recompiled for each different type of computer on which it is going to run. Java is a notable exception because it is a high-level language that does not need to be recompiled for each type of computer. We will learn more about this in Lesson 2. The vast majority of software written today is written in high-level languages.

*E*XERCISE 1.4

1. State two of the difficulties of programming with machine language.

2. State two features of assembly language.

3. What is a loader and what is it used for?

4. State one difference between a high-level language and assembly language.

1.5 The Software Development Process

High-level programming languages help programmers write high-quality software in much the same sense as good tools help carpenters build high-quality houses, but there is much more to programming than writing lines of code, just as there is more to building houses than pounding nails. The "more" consists of organization and planning and various diagrammatic conventions for expressing those plans. To this end, computer scientists have developed a view of the software development process known as the *software development life cycle (SDLC)*. We now present a particular version of this life cycle called the *waterfall model*.

The waterfall model consists of several phases:

1. **Customer request**—In this phase, the programmers receive a broad statement of a problem that is potentially amenable to a computerized solution. This step is also called the *user requirements phase*.

2. **Analysis**—The programmers determine what the program will do. This is sometimes viewed as a process of clarifying the specifications for the problem.

3. **Design**—The programmers determine how the program will do its task.

4. **Implementation**—The programmers write the program. This step is also called the *coding phase*.

5. **Integration**—Large programs have many parts. In the integration phase, these parts are brought together into a smoothly functioning whole, usually not an easy task.

6. **Maintenance**—Programs usually have a long life; a life span of 5 to 15 years is common for software. During this time, requirements change and minor or major modifications must be made.

The interaction between the phases is shown in Figure 1-4. Note that the figure resembles a waterfall, in which the results of each phase flow down to the next. A mistake detected in one phase often requires the developer to back up and redo some of the work in the previous phase. Modifications made during maintenance also require backing up to earlier phases.

FIGURE 1-4
The waterfall model of the software development life cycle

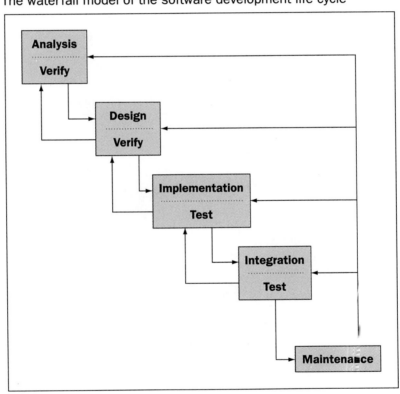

Programs rarely work as hoped the first time they are run; hence, they should be subjected to extensive and careful testing. Many people think that testing is an activity that applies only to the implementation and integration phases; however, the outputs of each phase should be scrutinized carefully. In fact mistakes found early are much less expensive to correct than those found late.

Figure 1-5 illustrates some relative costs of repairing mistakes when found in different phases.

FIGURE 1-5
Relative costs of repairing mistakes when found in different phases

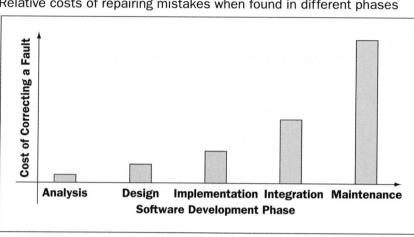

Finally, the cost of developing software is not spread equally over the phases. The percentages shown in Figure 1-6 are typical.

FIGURE 1-6
Percentage of total cost incurred in each phase of the development process

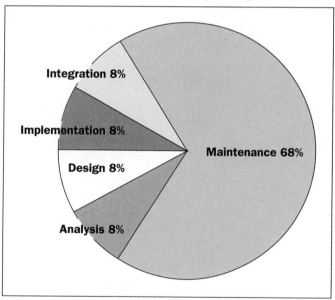

Most people probably think that implementation takes the most time and therefore costs the most. However, maintenance is, in fact, the most expensive aspect of software development. The cost of maintenance can be reduced by careful analysis, design, and implementation.

As you read this book and begin to sharpen your programming skills, you should remember two points:

1. There is more to software development than hacking out code.

Hot Tip

For a thorough discussion of the software development process and software engineering in general, see Stephen R. Schach, *Software Engineering with Java* (Chicago: Irwin, 1997).

2. If you want to reduce the overall cost of software development, write programs that are easy to maintain. This requires thorough analysis, careful design, and good coding style. We will have more to say about coding style throughout the book.

*E*XERCISE 1.5

1. What happens during the analysis and design phases of the software development process?

2. Which phase of the software development process incurs the highest cost to developers?

3. How does the waterfall model of software development work?

4. In which phase of the software development process is the detection and correction of errors the least expensive?

1.6 Basic Concepts of Object-Oriented Programming

The high-level programming languages mentioned earlier fall into two major groups, and these two groups utilize two different approaches to programming. The first group, consisting of the older languages (COBOL, FORTRAN, BASIC, C, and Pascal), uses what is called a *procedural approach*. Inadequacies in the procedural approach led to the development of the *object-oriented approach* and to several newer languages (Smalltalk, C++, and Java). There is little point in trying to explain the differences between these approaches in an introductory programming text, but suffice it to say that everyone considers the object-oriented approach to be the superior of the two. There are also several other approaches to programming, but that too is a topic for a more advanced text.

Most programs in the real world contain hundreds of thousands of lines of code. Writing such programs is a highly complex task that can only be accomplished by breaking the code into communicating components. This is an application of the well-known principle of "divide and conquer" that has been applied successfully to many human endeavors. There are various strategies for subdividing a program, and these depend on the type of programming language used. We now give an overview of the process in the context of *object-oriented programming* (OOP)—that is, programming with objects. Along the way, we introduce fundamental OOP concepts, such as class, inheritance, and polymorphism. Each of these concepts is also discussed in greater detail later in the book. For best results, reread this section as you encounter each concept for a second time.

We proceed by way of an extended analogy in an attempt to associate something already familiar with something new. Like all analogies, this one is imperfect but ideally useful. Imagine that it is your task to plan an expedition in search of the lost treasure of Palbor. How familiar can this be, you ask? Well, that depends on your taste in books, movies, and video games. Your overall approach might consist of the following steps:

1. **Planning.** You determine the different types of team members needed, including leaders, pathfinders, porters, and trail engineers. You then define the responsibilities of each member in terms of

   ■ A list of the resources used—these include the materials and knowledge needed by each member

   ■ The rules of behavior followed—these define how the team member behaves and responds in various situations.

   Finally, you decide how many of each type will be needed.

2. **Execution.** You recruit the team members and assemble them at the starting point, send the team on its way, and sit back and wait for the outcome. (There is no sense in endangering your own life too.)

3. **Outcome.** If the planning was done well, you will be rich; otherwise, prepare for disappointment.

How does this analogy relate to OOP? We give the answer in Table 1-3 below. On the left side of the table we describe various aspects of the expedition and on the right side are listed corresponding aspects of object-oriented programming. Do not expect to understand all the new terms now. We explore them with many other examples in the rest of this book.

TABLE 1-3
Expedition analogy to OOP

THE WORLD OF THE EXPEDITION	THE WORLD OF OOP
The trip must be planned.	Computer software is created in a process called ***programming***.
The team is composed of different types of team members, and each type is characterized by its list of resources and rules of behavior.	A program is comprised of different types of software components called ***classes***. A class defines or describes a list of data resources called *instance variables* and rules of behavior called ***methods***. Combining the description of resources and behaviors into a single software entity is called ***encapsulation***.
First the trip must be planned. Then it must be set in motion.	First a program must be written. Then it must be run, or executed.
When the expedition is in progress, the team is composed of individual members and not types. Each member is, of course, an instance of a particular type.	An executing program is composed of interacting objects, and each object's resources (instance variables) and rules of behavior (methods) are described in a particular class. An object is said to be an instance of the class that describes its resources and behavior.
At the beginning of the expedition, team members must be recruited.	While a program is executing, it creates, or instantiates, objects as needed.
Team members working together accomplish the mission of the expedition. They do this by asking each other for services.	Objects working together accomplish the mission of the program. They do this by asking each other for services or, in the language of OOP, by sending messages to each other.
When a team member receives a request for service, she follows the instructions in a corresponding rule of behavior.	When an object receives a message, it refers to its class to find a corresponding rule or method to execute.
If someone who is not a pathfinder wants to know where north is, she does not need to know anything about compasses. She merely asks one of the pathfinders, who are well-known providers of this service. Even if she did ask a pathfinder for his compass, he would refuse. Thus, team members tell others about the services they provide but never anything about the resources they use to provide these services.	If an object A needs a service that it cannot provide for itself, then A requests the service from some well-known provider B. However, A knows nothing of B's data resources and never asks for access to them. This principle of providing access to services but not to data resources is called ***information hiding***.

TABLE 1-3 (continued)
Expedition analogy to OOP

THE WORLD OF THE EXPEDITION	THE WORLD OF OOP
The expedition includes general-purpose trail engineers plus two specialized subtypes. All trail engineers share common skills, but some specialize in bridge building and others in clearing landslides. Thus, there is a hierarchy of engineers.	Classes are organized into a hierarchy also. The class at the root, or base, of the hierarchy defines methods and instance variables that are shared by its subclasses, those below it in the hierarchy. Each subclass then defines additional methods and instance variables. This process of sharing is called *inheritance*.

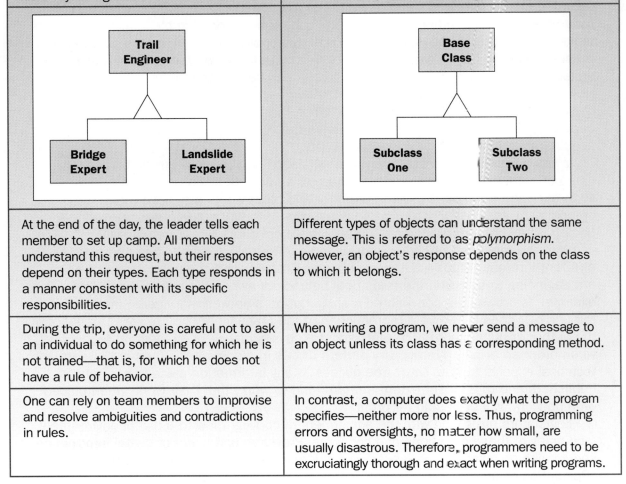

THE WORLD OF THE EXPEDITION	THE WORLD OF OOP
At the end of the day, the leader tells each member to set up camp. All members understand this request, but their responses depend on their types. Each type responds in a manner consistent with its specific responsibilities.	Different types of objects can understand the same message. This is referred to as *polymorphism*. However, an object's response depends on the class to which it belongs.
During the trip, everyone is careful not to ask an individual to do something for which he is not trained—that is, for which he does not have a rule of behavior.	When writing a program, we never send a message to an object unless its class has a corresponding method.
One can rely on team members to improvise and resolve ambiguities and contradictions in rules.	In contrast, a computer does exactly what the program specifies—neither more nor less. Thus, programming errors and oversights, no matter how small, are usually disastrous. Therefore, programmers need to be excruciatingly thorough and exact when writing programs.

EXERCISE 1.6

1. In what way is programming like planning?

2. An object-oriented program is a set of objects that interact by sending messages to each other. Explain.

3. What is a class and how does it relate to objects in an object-oriented program?

4. Explain the concept of inheritance with an example.

5. Explain the concept of information hiding with an example.

COMPUTER ETHICS

COMPUTER ETHICS: COPYRIGHT, INTELLECTUAL PROPERTY, AND DIGITAL INFORMATION

For hundreds of years, copyright law has existed to regulate the use of intellectual property. At stake are the rights of authors and publishers to a return on their investment in works of the intellect, which include printed matter (books, articles, etc.), recorded music, film, and video. More recently, copyright law has been extended to include software and other forms of digital information. For example, copyright law protects the software on the disk included with this book. This prohibits the purchaser from reproducing the software for sale or free distribution to others. If the software is stolen or "pirated" in this way, the perpetrator can be prosecuted and punished by law. However, copyright law also allows for "fair use"—the purchaser may make backup copies of the software for personal use. When the purchaser sells the software to another user, the seller thereby relinquishes the right to use it, and the new purchaser acquires this right.

When governments design copyright legislation, governments try to balance the rights of authors and publishers to a return on their work against the rights of the public to fair use. In the case of printed matter and other works that have a physical embodiment, the meaning of fair use is usually clear. Without fair use, borrowing a book from a library or playing a CD at a high school dance would be unlawful.

With the rapid rise of digital information and its easy transmission on networks, different interest groups—authors, publishers, users, and computer professionals— are beginning to question the traditional balance of ownership rights and fair use. For example, is browsing a copyrighted manuscript on a network service an instance of fair use? Or does it involve a reproduction of the manuscript that violates the rights of the author or publisher? Is the manuscript a physical piece of intellectual property when browsed or just a temporary pattern of bits in a computer's memory? Users and technical experts tend to favor free access to any information placed on a network. Publishers and to a lesser extent authors tend to worry that their work, when placed on a network, will be resold for profit.

Legislators struggling with the adjustment of copyright law to a digital environment face many of these questions and concerns. Providers and users of digital information should also be aware of the issues. For a detailed discussion, see Pamela Samuelson, "Regulation of Technologies to Protect Copyrighted Works," *Communications of the ACM*, Vol. 39, No. 7 (July 1996), 17–22.

SUMMARY

In this lesson, you learned:

■ The modern computer age began in the late 1940s with the development of ENIAC. Business computing became practical in the 1950s, and time-sharing computers advanced computing in large organizations in the 1960s and 1970s The 1980s saw the development and first widespread sales of personal computers, and the 1990s saw personal computers connected in networks.

■ Modern computers consist of two primary components: hardware and software. Computer hardware is the physical component of the system. Computer software consists of programs that enable us to use the hardware.

■ All information used by a computer is represented in binary form. This information includes numbers, text, images, sound, and program instructions.

■ Programming languages have been developed in the course of three generations: generation 1 is machine language, generation 2 is assembly language, and generation 3 is high-level language.

■ The software development process consists of several standard phases: customer request, analysis, design, implementation, integration, and maintenance.

■ Object-oriented programming is a style of programming that can lead to better quality software. Breaking code into easily handled components simplifies the job of writing a large program.

VOCABULARY *Review*

Define the following terms:

application software	information hiding	software development life
bit	object-oriented programming	cycle (SDLC)
byte	primary memory	system software
central processing unit (CPU)	secondary memory	waterfall model
hardware	software	

REVIEW *Questions*

WRITTEN QUESTIONS

Write a brief answer to the following questions.

1. What are the three major hardware components of a computer?

2. Name three input devices.

3. Name two output devices.

4. What is the difference between application software and system software?

5. Name a first generation programming language, a second generation programming language, and a third generation programming language.

FILL IN THE BLANK

Complete the following sentences by writing the correct word or words in the blanks provided.

1. All information used by a computer is represented using _____ notation.

2. The _____ phase of the software life cycle is also called the coding phase.

3. Over half of the cost of developing software goes to the _____ phase of the software life cycle.

4. ACM stands for _____.

5. Copyright law is designed to give fair use to the public and to protect the rights of _____ and _____.

PROJECTS

PROJECT 1-1

Take some time to become familiar with the architecture of the computer you will use for this course. Describe your hardware and software using the following guidelines:

■ What hardware components make up your system?

■ How much memory does your system have?

■ What are the specifications of your CPU? (Do you know its speed and what kind of micro-processor it has?)

■ What operating system are you using? What version of that operating system is your computer currently running?

■ What major software applications are loaded on your system?

CRITICAL *Thinking*

You have just written some software that you would like to sell. Your friend suggests that you copyright your software. Discuss why this might be a good idea.

FIRST JAVA PROGRAMS

OBJECTIVES

Upon completion of this lesson, you should be able to:

- Discuss why Java is an important programming language.

- Explain the Java virtual machine and byte code.

- Choose a user interface style.

- Describe the structure of a simple Java program.

- Write a simple program.

- Edit, compile, and run a program using a Java development environment.

- Format a program to give a pleasing, consistent appearance.

- Understand compile-time errors.

- Write a simple turtle graphics program.

Estimated Time: 3.5 hours

VOCABULARY

applet

assignment operator

byte code

DOS development environment

graphical user interface (GUI)

hacking

integrated development environment (IDE)

Java virtual machine (JVM)

just-in-time compilation (JIT)

parameter

source code

statement

terminal I/O interface

turtle graphics

variable

Programs are written in programming languages, and the language used in this book is Java. This lesson gets you up and running with a couple of simple Java programs. We show how to write these first programs, compile them, and run them. In the process, you will become acquainted with a Java programming environment, the structure of a simple Java program, and the basic ideas of variables, input and output statements, and sending messages to objects.

2.1 Why Java?

Java is the fastest growing programming language in the world. Companies such as IBM and Sun have adopted Java as their major application development language. There are several reasons for this.

First, Java is a modern object-oriented programming language. The designers of Java spent much time studying the features of classical object-oriented languages such as Smalltalk and C++

and made a successful effort to incorporate the good features of these languages and omit the less desirable ones.

Second, Java is secure, robust, and portable. That is, the Java language

- Enables the construction of virus-free, tamper-free systems (secure)
- Supports the development of programs that do not overwrite memory (robust)
- Yields programs that can be run on different types of computers without change (portable)

These features make Java ideally suited to develop distributed, network-based applications, which is an area of ever increasing importance.

Third, Java supports the use of advanced programming concepts such as threads. A *thread* is a process that can run concurrently with other processes. For example, a single Java application might consist of two threads. One thread transfers an image from one machine to another across a network while the other thread simultaneously interacts with the user.

Fourth and finally, Java bears a superficial resemblance to C++, which is currently the world's most popular industrial strength programming language. Thus, it is easy for a C++ programmer to learn Java and for a Java programmer to learn C++. Compared to C++, however, Java is easier to use and learn, less error prone, more portable, and better suited to the Internet.

On the negative side, Java runs more slowly than most modern programming languages because it is interpreted. To understand this last point we must now turn our attention to the Java virtual machine and byte code.

EXERCISE 2.1

1. What is a portable program?

2. Describe two features of Java that make it a better language than C++.

3. What is a thread? Describe how threads might be used in a program.

2.2 The Java Virtual Machine and Byte Code

Compilers usually translate a higher-level language into the machine language of a particular type of computer. However, the Java compiler translates Java not into machine language, but into a pseudomachine language called Java *byte code*. Byte code is the machine language for an imaginary Java computer. To run Java byte code on a particular computer, you must install a *Java virtual machine* (JVM) on that computer.

A JVM is a program that behaves like a computer. Such a program is called an *interpreter*. An interpreter has several advantages as well as some disadvantages. The main disadvantage of an interpreter is that a program pretending to be a computer runs programs more slowly than an actual computer. Java virtual machines are getting faster every day, however. For instance, some JVMs translate byte code instructions into machine language when they are first encountered—called *just-in-time compilation* (JIT)—so that the next time the instruction is encountered it is executed as fast machine code rather than being interpreted as slow byte code. Also, new computer chips are being developed that implement a JVM directly in hardware, thus avoiding the performance penalty.

The main advantage of an interpreter is that any computer can run it. Thus, Java byte code is highly portable. For instance, many of the pages you download on the Web contain small Java programs already translated into byte code. These are called *applets*, and they are run in a JVM that is incorporated into your Web browser. These applets range from the decorative (displaying a comical animated character on the Web page) to the practical (displaying a continuous stream of stock market quotes).

Because Java programs run inside a virtual machine, it is possible to limit their capabilities. Thus, ideally, you never have to worry about a Java applet infecting your computer with a virus, erasing the files on your hard drive, or stealing sensitive information and sending it across the Internet to a competitor. In practice, however, computer hackers have successfully penetrated Java's security mechanisms in the past and may succeed again

> **Thinking about Technology**
>
> For a discussion of the current impact of Java, see "The Java Factor," *Communications of the ACM,* Volume 41, No. 6 (June 1998): 34–76.

in the future. But all things considered, Java applets really are very secure and security weaknesses are repaired as soon as they become known.

*E*XERCISE 2.2

1. What does JVM stand for?

2. What is byte code? Describe how the JVM uses byte code.

3. What is an applet? Describe how applets are used.

2.3 Choosing a User Interface Style

Before writing our first program, we must make a difficult decision. What type of user interface do we want to use? There are two choices: the *graphical user interface* (GUI), familiar to all PC users, and the less common *terminal I/O interface*. Figure 2-1 illustrates both in the context of a program that converts degrees Fahrenheit to degrees Celsius. The graphical interface on the left is familiar and comfortable. The user enters a number in the first box, clicks the command button, and the program displays the answer in the second box. The terminal-based interface on the right begins by displaying the prompt "Enter degrees Fahrenheit:". The user then enters a number and presses the Enter key. The program responds by displaying the answer.

FIGURE 2-1
Two interfaces for a temperature conversion program

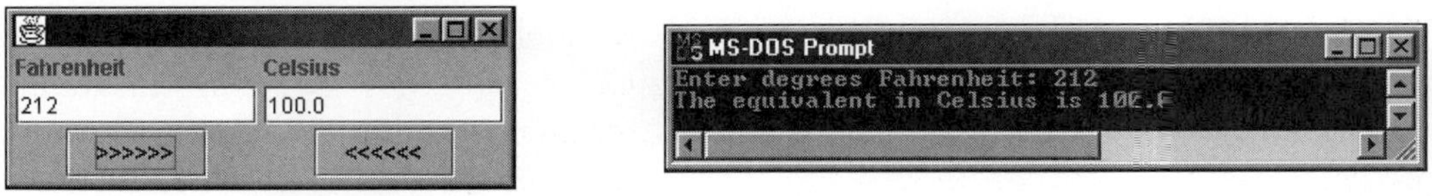

We begin with terminal I/O and in Lesson 7 make a swift and easy transition to GUIs. Thereafter you can choose the style you consider most suitable to the problem at hand. In the long run, you will discover that this book's core material is independent of interface issues. There are three reasons for beginning with terminal I/O. First, in Java and many other languages, a terminal interface is easier to implement than a GUI, although in other languages, such as Visual BASIC, the opposite is true. Second, there are programming situations that require terminal I/O rather than a GUI, so familiarity with the techniques of terminal-oriented programming is important. Third, terminal-oriented programs are similar in structure to programs that process files of sequentially organized data, and what we learn here will be transferable to that setting.

2.4 Hello World

In conformance with a long and honorable tradition dating back to the early days of the language C, a textbook's first program often does nothing more than display the words "Hello World" in a terminal window. Actually, as you can see in Figure 2-2, we could not resist adding a few embellishments. In case you have not guessed, the imagery is the words "Hello World" rising like steam from the cup of hot Java.

FIGURE 2-2
Hello World

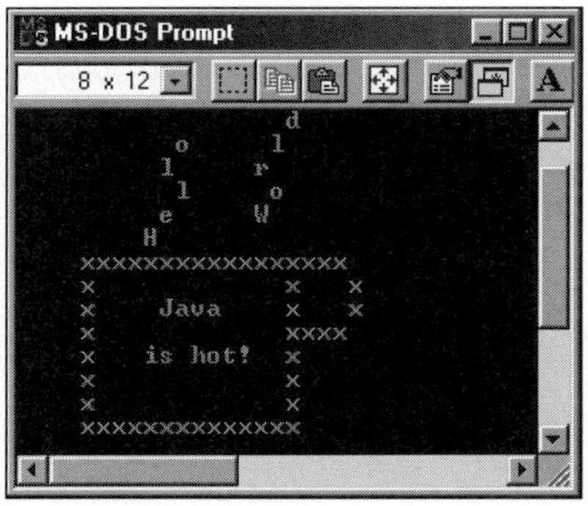

The Source Code

Just as a recipe is a sequence of instructions for a chef, a program is a sequence of instructions for a computer. And just as a recipe does nothing until executed by a chef, so a program does nothing until executed by a computer. With that in mind, the following is the bulk of the instructions, or *source code*, for our HelloWorld program:

```
System.out.println("                    d        ");
System.out.println("             o      l        ");
System.out.println("          l       r          ");
System.out.println("          l          o       ");
System.out.println("        e        W           ");
System.out.println("        H                    ");
System.out.println("     xxxxxxxxxxxxxxxx         ");
System.out.println("     x            x   x       ");
System.out.println("     x    Java    x   x       ");
System.out.println("     x            xxxx        ");
System.out.println("     x  is hot!  x            ");
System.out.println("     x            x           ");
System.out.println("     x            x           ");
System.out.println("     xxxxxxxxxxxxx            ");
```

The Explanation

In this code

- `System.out` is the name of an object that knows how to display or print characters in a terminal window.

- `println` is the name of the message being sent to the `System.out` object.

- The strings enclosed in quotation marks contain the characters to be printed.

- Semicolons (;) mark the end of each *statement* or sentence in the program.

As mentioned at the end of Lesson 1, an object-oriented program accomplishes its tasks by sending messages to objects. In this program, a `System.out` object responds to a `println` message by printing a string of characters in the terminal window. The string of characters that appears between the parentheses following the message is called a *parameter*. Some messages require several parameters, separated from each other by commas, whereas other messages have no parameters. The "ln" in the message `println` stands for "line" and indicates that the `System.out` object should advance to the beginning of the next line after printing a string.

Sending messages to objects always takes the form

```
<name of object>.<name of message>(<parameters>)
```

The period (.) between the object's name and the message's name is called a *method selector operator*. The period between the words "System" and "out" is not a method selector operator. For now you can just think of it as part of the object's name.

The Larger Framework

The program as presented so far is not complete. It must be embedded in a larger framework defined by several additional lines of code. No attempt will be made to explain this code until a later lesson, but fortunately, it can be reused with little change from one program to the next. Following then is the complete program with the new lines shown in blue:

```
public class HelloWorld {
    public static void main(String [] args) {
        System.out.println("                    d          ");
        System.out.println("              o     l          ");
        System.out.println("           l     r             ");
        System.out.println("           l        o          ");
        System.out.println("          e     W              ");
        System.out.println("         H                     ");
        System.out.println("     xxxxxxxxxxxxxxxxx          ");
        System.out.println("     x               x   x      ");
        System.out.println("     x      Java      x   x     ");
        System.out.println("     x               xxxx       ");
        System.out.println("     x   is hot!  x             ");
        System.out.println("     x               x          ");
        System.out.println("     x               x          ");
        System.out.println("     xxxxxxxxxxxxxx             ");
    }
}
```

To reuse the framework, replace `HelloWorld` with the name of another program:

```
public class <name of program> {
    public static void main(String [] args) {
        . . . put the source code here . . .
    }
}
```

In this text, we write the name of the program (and any other class name) in a larger font so you can easily pick it out from the rest of the code.

EXERCISE 2.4

1. Give a short definition of "program."

2. What is the effect of the message `println`?

3. Describe how to use the `System.out` object.

4. Write a sequence of statements to display your name, address, and phone number in the terminal window.

2.5 Edit, Compile, and Execute

In the preceding section, we presented the source code for our first program. Now we discuss how to enter it into a computer and run it. There are three steps:

1. **Edit.** In the first step, the programmer uses a word processor or editor to enter the source code into the computer and save it in a text file. The name of the text file must match the name of the program with the extension `.java` added, as in `HelloWorld.java`.

2. **Compile.** In the second step, the programmer invokes the Java language compiler to translate the source code into Java byte code. In this example, the compiler translates source code in the file `HelloWorld.java` to byte code in the file `HelloWorld.class`. The extension for a byte code file is always `.class`.

3. **Execute.** In the third step, the programmer instructs the JVM to load the byte code into memory and execute it. At this point the user and the program can interact, with the user entering data and the program displaying instructions and results.

Figure 2-3 illustrates the steps. The ovals represent the processes edit, compile, and execute. The names of the files `HelloWorld.java` and `HelloWorld.class` are shown between parallel lines.

FIGURE 2-3
Editing, compiling, and running a program

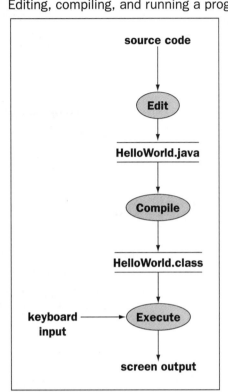

Development Environments

The details involved in editing, compiling, and running a program vary with the development environment being used. Some common development environments available to Java programmers include the following:

■ UNIX using a standard text editor with command line activation of the compiler and the JVM.

■ Various versions of Microsoft Windows and NT using Notepad for the editor with command line activation of the compiler and the JVM from inside a command or DOS window. We call this the *DOS development environment.*

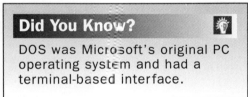

Did You Know?

DOS was Microsoft's original PC operating system and had a terminal-based interface.

■ Windows, NT, or MacOS using an *integrated development environment* (IDE) such as Symantec's Visual Café, Microsoft's Visual J++, or Borland's JBuilder.

The first two options are free and merely require you to download and install the Java software development kit (JDK) as described in Appendix A. The third option, an integrated development environment, costs money, but it has the advantage of combining an editor, a Java compiler, a debugger, and a JVM in a manner intended to increase programmer productivity. IDEs take time to master, however, and they can obscure fundamental details of the edit, compile, run sequence.

As we cannot possibly discuss all of these environments simultaneously, we will give our instructions in terms of the DOS development environment; however, the installation and use of the major alternatives are presented in our supplemental materials on the book's Web site (the URL is in Appendix A).

> **Thinking about Technology** 🧑
>
> Needless to say, people argue heatedly about whether or not IDEs should be used in introductory programming classes.

Preparing Your Development Environment

Before writing your first program, you must install a Java development environment on your computer, and you must install the software package that accompanies this book. Guidelines for doing this are presented in Appendix A.

Step-by-Step Instructions

We are now ready to present step-by-step instructions for editing, compiling, and running the HelloWorld program. After reading what follows, read the supplemental material for an explanation that matches the development environment on your computer.

Step 1. Use Windows Explorer to create the directory in which you intend to work (for instance, C:\Javafiles). Open a terminal window by selecting **MS-DOS Prompt** (or something similar) from the **Start/Programs** or **Start/Programs/Accessories** menu. In the terminal window, use the **cd** command to move to the working directory as illustrated in Figure 2-4.

FIGURE 2-4
Using the cd command to move to the working directory

```
MS-DOS Prompt                        _ □ ×
C:\>cd Javafiles
C:\Javafiles>_
```

Step 2. Open the Notepad editor and create the file `HelloWorld.java` by typing the text as shown in Figure 2-5.

FIGURE 2-5
Activating Notepad to edit the program

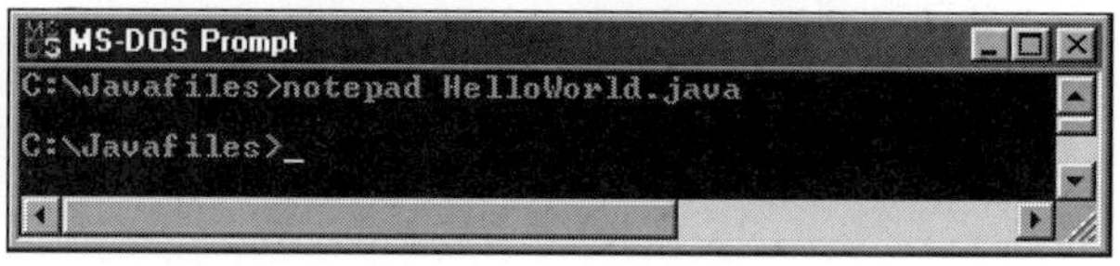

```
MS-DOS Prompt                        _ □ ×
C:\Javafiles>notepad HelloWorld.java
C:\Javafiles>_
```

Once Notepad opens, type in the lines of code for the program. Figure 2-6 shows the Notepad window after the program has been entered.

FIGURE 2-6
The program as typed into Notepad

```
HelloWorld.java - Notepad
File  Edit  Search  Help
public class HelloWorld {
    public static void main(String [] args) {
        System.out.println("               d           ");
        System.out.println("          o      l          ");
        System.out.println("          l    r            ");
        System.out.println("          l      o          ");
        System.out.println("          e      W          ");
        System.out.println("          H                 ");
        System.out.println("     xxxxxxxxxxxxxxxxx       ");
        System.out.println("     x            x    x     ");
        System.out.println("     x    Java    x    x     ");
        System.out.println("     x            xxxx       ");
        System.out.println("     x  is hot!   x          ");
        System.out.println("     x            x          ");
        System.out.println("     x            x          ");
        System.out.println("     xxxxxxxxxxxxx           ");
    }
}
```

Step 3. Save the file and switch back to the terminal window and comple the program by typing `javac HelloWorld.java`. The DOS prompt returns when the compilation is complete.

Step 4. Run the program by typing `java HelloWorld`. Figure 2-7 illustrates this step as well as the previous step.

FIGURE 2-7
Compiling and running the program

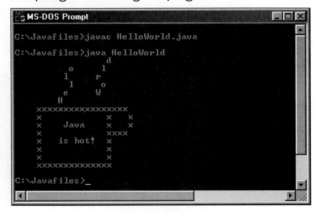

Compile-Time Errors

It is inevitable that we will make typographical errors when we edit programs, and the compiler will nearly always detect them. Mistakes detected by the compiler are called *syntax errors* or *compile-time errors*. To illustrate these, we modify the program so that it includes two errors. After reading this subsection, read the supplemental material that matches your development environment.

Warning

In some development environments, the terminal window disappears immediately after the JVM executes the program's last instruction. We will show you how to overcome this problem later in the lesson when we present a temperature conversion program.

For the first error, on line 3, we misspell `println` as `prinrln`. For the second, we omit the semi-colon at the end of line 9. Figure 2-8 shows the program with the errors as it appears in Notepad.

FIGURE 2-8
The program with compile-time errors on lines 3 and 9

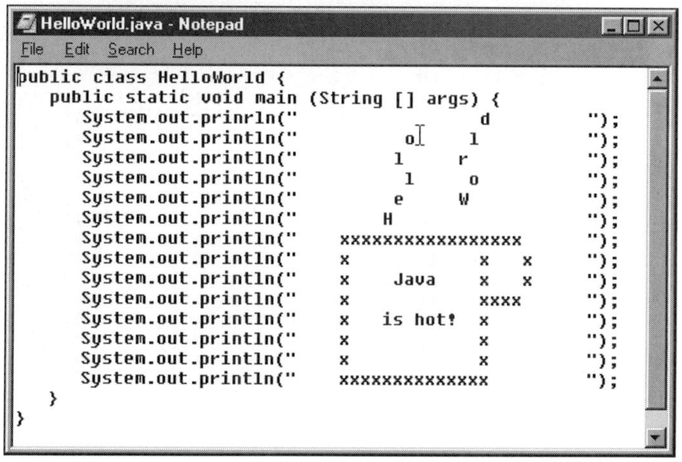

When the program is compiled, the compiler prints a list of errors in the terminal window as shown in Figure 2-9. The first error message is easy to understand. It refers to line 9 and says that a semicolon is missing. The second message, which refers to line 3, is somewhat difficult to understand. It says that the symbol for method `prinrln` cannot be resolved within the class `java.io.PrintStream`. In fact, the object `System.out` is a member of this class and the program has attempted to send a message that the class does not recognize. Unfortunately, some error messages may be difficult to decipher, but at least they indicate where the compiler encountered text it could not translate into byte code.

FIGURE 2-9
The compiler's error messages

Readability

Programs typically have a long life and are usually maintained by many people other than their original authors. For this reason, if for no other, it is extremely important to write programs that are highly readable. The main factor affecting a program's readability is its layout. Indentation, the inclusion of blank lines and spaces, and other typographical considerations make the difference between an intelligible program and an incomprehensible mess. Interestingly, the compiler completely ignores a program's format, provided that there are no line breaks in the middle of words or quoted strings. Throughout the book, we attempt to format our programs in a pleasing and consistent manner, and you should strive to do the same. For your enjoyment the following example is a very unreadable but completely functional rendering of the HelloWorld program:

```
public class
     HelloWorld
{public static void main (String [] args) {System.out.println(
"              d            ");System.out.println
       ("         o    l           ");
System.out.println("          l      r            ");
 System.   out
.println("        l        o          ")
; System.out.println("          e    W              ");System.out
.println("       H                  ");System.out.println
("    xxxxxxxxxxxxxxxxx         ");System.out.println(
"   x             x   x      ")
;System.out.println("     x     Java    x    x      ");
     System.out.println("       x                 xxxx          ");
          System.out.println("     x   is hot!   x             " );
System.out.println("      x                x            ");
     System.out.println("     x                x             ");
          System.out.println("     xxxxxxxxxxxxxx                ");  }
```

COMPUTER ETHICS: INTRUSIVE HACKING

Hacking is a term whose use goes back to the early days of computing. In its original sense, a "hack" is a programmer who exhibits rare problem-solving ability and commands the respect of other programmers. The culture of hackers began in the late 1950s at the MIT computer science labs. These programmers, many of them students and later professionals and teachers in the field, regarded hacking as an accomplishment along the lines of Olympic gymnastics. These programmers even advocated a "hacker ethic," which stated, among other things, that hackers should respect the privacy of others and distribute their software for free. For a narrative of the early tradition of hacking, see Steven Levy, *Hackers: Heroes of the Computer Revolution* (Garden City, NY: Anchor Press/Doubleday, 1984).

Unfortunately, the practice of hacking has changed over the years, and the term has acquired darker connotations. Programmers who break into computer systems in an unauthorized way are called hackers, whether their intent is just to impress their peers or to cause actual harm. Students and professionals who lack a disciplined approach to programming are also called hackers. An excellent account of the most famous case of intrusive hacking can be found in Clifford Stoll, *The Cuckoo's Egg: Tracking Through the Maze of Computer Espionage* (New York: Doubleday, 1989).

EXERCISE 2.5

1. Name the three steps in writing and running a program.

2. What are compile-time errors?

3. Find the compile-time errors in the following statements:
   a. System.out.println("Here is an error);
   b. System.out.println("Here is another error";

4. Why is readability a desirable characteristic of a program?

2.6 Temperature Conversion

We now present code for the temperature conversion program illustrated earlier in the lesson. To refresh your memory we show the interface again in Figure 2-10. This program is fundamentally more interesting than the HelloWorld program because it reads user inputs and performs computations. Despite its brevity and simplicity, the program demonstrates several important concepts.

FIGURE 2-10
Interface for the temperature conversion program

```
MS-DOS Prompt
Enter degrees Fahrenheit: 212
The equivalent in Celsius is 100.0
```

The Source Code

The program's source code is

```java
import TerminalIO.KeyboardReader;

public class Convert {
   public static void main(String [] args) {
      KeyboardReader reader = new KeyboardReader();
      double fahrenheit;
      double celsius;

      System.out.print("Enter degrees Fahrenheit: ");
      fahrenheit = reader.readDouble();

      celsius = (fahrenheit - 32.0) * 5.0 / 9.0;

      System.out.print("The equivalent in Celsius is ");
      System.out.println(celsius);

      reader.pause();
   }
}
```

The Explanation

Following is a line-by-line explanation of the portions of the program shown in black.

```
import TerminalIO.KeyboardReader;
```

The program's first line of code is an **import statement.** The program must read inputs entered at the keyboard, and this functionality is provided by something called a keyboard reader object. Such objects are instances of the class `KeyboardReader`. In this line of code, we are telling the compiler where to find complete specifications for the class. The period that appears in this statement is NOT a method selector.

```
KeyboardReader reader = new KeyboardReader();
```

In this statement, we instantiate or create a `KeyboardReader` object. We have arbitrarily decided to call the object `reader`. The name suggests what the object does, so it is a good choice. As mentioned in Lesson 1, an object is always an instance of a class and must be created, or instantiated, before being used. In general, instantiation is done like this:

```
SomeClass someObject = new SomeClass();
```

```
double fahrenheit;
double celsius;
```

In these statements, we declare that the program will use two numeric variables called `fahrenheit` and `celsius`. A numeric **variable** names a location in RAM in which a number can be stored. The number is usually referred to as the variable's **value.** During the course of a program, a variable's value can change, but its name remains constant. The variables in this program are of type `double`, which means they will contain only floating-point numbers. It is customary, though not required, to begin variable names with a lowercase letter, thus 'fahrenheit" rather than "Fahrenheit." We are allowed to declare as many variables as we want in a program, and we can name them pretty much as we please. Restrictions are explained in Lesson 3.

```
System.out.print("Enter degrees Fahrenheit: ");
```

This statement is similar to those we saw in the HelloWorld program, but there is a minor difference. The message here is `print` rather than `println`. A `print` message positions the cursor immediately after the last character printed rather than moving it to the beginning of the next line.

```
fahrenheit = reader.readDouble();
```

In this statement, the `reader` object responds to the message `readDouble` by waiting for the user to type a number and then press Enter, at which point the `reader` object returns the number to the program. The number is then assigned to the variable `fahrenheit` by means of the **assignment operator** (=). The number entered by the user is now stored in the variable. Note that although the `readDouble` message has no parameters, the parentheses are still required. As the user types at the keyboard, the characters are automatically echoed in the terminal window, but not until the user presses Enter does this input become available to the program.

```
celsius = (fahrenheit - 32.0) * 5.0 / 9.0;
```

In this statement, the expression to the right of the assignment operator (=) is evaluated, and then the resulting value is stored in memory at location `celsius`. Statements utilizing an assignment operator are called *assignment statements*. When the computer evaluates the expression, it uses the value stored in the variable `fahrenheit`. Notice that all the numbers (32.0, 5.0, and 9.0) contain a decimal point. In Java, some unexpected rules govern what happens when integers and floating-point numbers are mixed in an expression, so until we discuss the rules in Lesson 3, we will not mix integers and floating-point numbers. In the expression, as in algebra, the following symbols are used:

* *   indicates the multiplication operator
* /   indicates the division operator
* -   indicates the subtraction operator

Of course, there is another common operator, namely + for *addition*. Notice the use of parentheses in the previous expression. In Java, as in algebra, multiplication and division are done before addition and subtraction unless parentheses are used to change the order of the computations, or in other words multiplication and division have higher precedence than addition and subtraction.

```
System.out.print("The equivalent in Celsius is ");
```

Here the `System.out` object prints the string "The equivalent in Celsius is ". The cursor is positioned after the last character in preparation for the next line of code.

```
System.out.println(celsius);
```

Here the `System.out` object prints the value of the variable `celsius`. The parameter for a `print` or `println` message can be a string in quotation marks, a variable, or even an expression. When a variable is used, the variable's value is printed, not its name. When an expression is used, the expression is evaluated before its value is printed.

```
reader.pause();
```

This statement is optional and is needed only in some development environments. The statement's purpose is to prevent the terminal window from disappearing immediately after the JVM executes the program's last statement. We discussed this problem when presenting the HelloWorld program. Sending the `pause` message to the `reader` object displays the string "Press Enter to continue . . ." in the terminal window, after which the program pauses until the user presses Enter.

Variables and Objects

Figure 2-11 depicts the variables and objects used in the program. All of these exist in the computer's memory while the program is running. The variables `fahrenheit` and `celsius` each hold a single floating-point number. At any given instant, the value stored in a variable depends on the effect of the preceding lines of code. The variables `reader` and `System.out` are very different than the variables `fahrenheit` and `celsius`. Instead of holding numbers, they hold references to objects. The arrows in the figure are intended to suggest this fact. During the course of the program, we think of the `reader` variable as being the name of an object. As the figure indicates, we know nothing about what lies inside the `reader` object (information hiding), but we do know that it responds to the message `readDouble`. `System.out` also names an object, but one that is never declared in our programs. How this can be so is explained in a later lesson. The `System.out` object responds to the messages `print` and `println`. One of the really significant facts about object-oriented programming is that we can use objects without having the least idea of their internal workings. Likewise, we can design objects for others to use without telling them anything about the implementation details.

FIGURE 2-11
Variables and objects used in the temperature conversion program

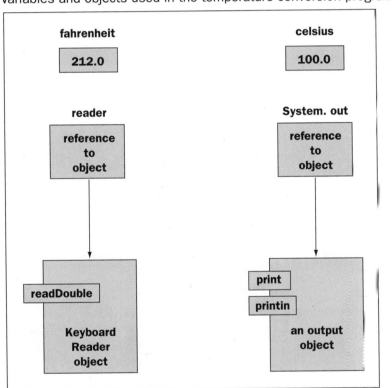

EXERCISE 2.6

1. What is a variable in a program and how is it used?

2. Describe the role of the assignment (=) operator in a program.

3. What is a `KeyboardReader` object?

EXERCISE 2.6 Continued

4. Explain the difference between a variable of type `double` and a variable of type `KeyboardReader`.

5. Describe the difference between `print` and `println` and give an appropriate example of the use of each.

2.7 Turtle Graphics

Turtle graphics provide a simple and enjoyable way to draw pictures in a window and give us an opportunity to send lots of messages to an object. Turtle graphics were originally developed as part of the children's programming language Logo created by Seymour Papert and his colleagues at MIT in the late 1960s. The name suggests the way in which we can think about the drawing process. Imagine a turtle crawling on a piece of paper with a pen tied to its tail. Commands direct the turtle as it moves across the paper and tell it to lift or lower its tail, turn some number of degrees left or right, and move a specified distance. Whenever the tail is down, the pen drags along the paper leaving a trail. In this manner it is possible to "program" the turtle to draw pictures ranging from the simple to the complex.

Java comes with a large array of classes that support graphics operations. In the early lessons of this book, we illustrate graphics operations by providing a nonstandard package called `TurtleGraphics`. A complete description of the classes in this package appears in Appendix H. Toward the end of this book, we show how to write graphics programs using the more complex features available in Java.

The Messages

In Java, we dispense with the turtle and focus on the pen, which is an instance of the class `StandardPen` (later we will encounter some other not-so-standard pens). Drawing is done in a window. We command a pen by sending it messages such as those shown in Table 2-1.

TABLE 2-1
Pen messages

PEN MESSAGE	WHAT IT DOES
`home()`	The pen jumps to the center of the graphics window without drawing and points north.
`setDirection(degrees)`	The pen points in the indicated direction. Due east corresponds to 0 degrees, north to 90 degrees, west to 180 degrees, and south to 270 degrees. Because there are 360 degrees in a circle, setting the direction to 400 would be equivalent to 400 − 360 or 40 and setting it to −30 would be equivalent to 360 − 30 or 330.
`turn(degrees)`	The pen adds the indicated degrees to its current direction. Positive degrees correspond to turning counterclockwise. The degrees can be an integer or floating-point number.
`down()`	The pen lowers itself to the drawing surface.
`up()`	The pen raises itself from the drawing surface.

TABLE 2-1 (continued)
Pen messages

PEN MESSAGE	WHAT IT DOES
move(distance)	The pen moves the specified distance in the current direction. The distance can be an integer or floating-point number and is measured in pixels (picture elements). The size of a pixel depends on the monitor's resolution. For instance, when we say that a monitor's resolution is 800 by 600, we mean that the monitor is 800 pixels wide and 600 pixels high.

Initially a pen is

■ In the center of the graphics window

■ In the down position

■ Pointing north

Drawing a Square

The following example is a program that draws a square, 50 pixels on a side, at the center of the graphics window:

```
import TurtleGraphics.StandardPen;

public class DrawSquare {
    public static void main(String [] args) {

        // Instantiate a pen object
        StandardPen pen = new StandardPen();

        // Lift the pen, move it to the square's top left corner,
        // and lower it again
        pen.up();
        pen.move(25);
        pen.turn(90); pen.move(25);
        pen.down();

        // Draw the square
        pen.turn(90); pen.move(50);
        pen.turn(90); pen.move(50);
        pen.turn(90); pen.move(50);
        pen.turn(90); pen.move(50);
    }
}
```

Everything following "//" at the beginning of a line in the program is treated as a comment. Comments make a program easier to understand; they are not programming instructions, however, and the compiler ignores them completely. The import statement at the beginning of the program tells the compiler and linker where to find the specification for the StandardPen class.

Figure 2-12 shows the graphics window after the program has completed execution. If the window is resized, the square is automatically redrawn in the center of the window without rerunning the program. The window can be closed in the usual manner.

FIGURE 2-12
A square drawn at the center of a graphics window

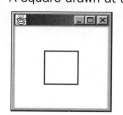

for Loops

The DrawSquare program is easily modified to draw a regular polygon with any number of sides; however, imagine how tedious it would be to repeat the statements needed to draw a polygon with 100 sides. The code might look something like this:

```
pen.turn(3.6); pen.move(1.6);
pen.turn(3.6); pen.move(1.6);
pen.turn(3.6); pen.move(1.6);
pen.turn(3.6); pen.move(1.6);
. . . etc . . .
```

Figure 2-13 shows the result of running this code, which, given the size of the figure and the resolution of the typical monitor, looks like a circle with a radius of about 25 pixels.

FIGURE 2-13
A regular polygon with 100 sides

Fortunately, Java provides a mechanism for repeating a group of statements any number of times. It is called a for loop. In this lesson, we introduce the simplest form of this statement, and we ask you to use it without worrying about the details. In Lesson 4, we will explain it fully. The following then is a for loop for drawing our 100 sided regular polygon:

```
int i;                              ← declaration of the loop control variable
. . .
for (i = 1; i <= 100; i++){         ← loop control
   pen.turn(3.6);                   ← loop body
   pen.move(1.6);                   ← loop body
}                                   ← loop end
```

To change the number of times the loop body is executed, we merely replace 100 with a different positive integer. The complete program looks like this:

```java
import TurtleGraphics.StandardPen;

public class Draw100gon {
    public static void main(String [] args) {
        int i;

        // Instantiate a pen object
        StandardPen pen = new StandardPen();

        // Lift the pen, move it to the top of the circle,
        // and lower it again
        pen.up();
        pen.move(25);
        pen.turn(90); pen.move(0.8);
        pen.down();

        // Draw the 100gon
        for (i = 1; i <= 100; i++){
            pen.turn(3.6);
            pen.move(1.6);
        }
    }
}
```

In later lessons, we show other aspects of turtle graphics, such as changing the color and line width of a pen and using pens of different types.

EXERCISE 2.7

1. What figures are drawn by each of the following snippets of code and where will they be located in the graphics window?

   a. ```java
   pen.home();
   pen.down();
   pen.move(60);
   pen.turn(180);
   pen.up();
   pen.move(30);
   pen.turn(90);
   pen.move(30);
   ```

   b. ```java
   pen.home();
   pen.down();
   int i;
   for (i = 1; i <= 3; i++){
       pen.move(30);
       pen.turn(60);
   }
   ```

EXERCISE 2.7 Continued

2. Write a `for` loop that prints your name a dozen times.

3. Show that if a regular polygon of 100 sides is used to approximate a circle with a radius of 25 pixels, then the turn amount should be 3.6 degrees and the sides should be approximately 1.6 pixels long.

SUMMARY

In this lesson, you learned:

- Java is the fastest growing programming language in the world. It is secure, robust, and portable. And it is similar to C++, the world's most popular programming language.

- The Java compiler translates Java into a pseudomachine language called Java byte code. Byte code can be run on any computer that has a Java virtual machine installed. The Java virtual machine (JVM) is a program that behaves like a computer—an interpreter.

- Java programs include variables, arithmetic expressions, statements, objects, messages, and methods.

- Three basic steps in the coding process are editing, compiling, and running a program using a Java development environment. Programmers should pay attention to a program's format to ensure readability.

- Java programs accomplish many tasks by sending messages to objects. Examples are sending text to the terminal window for output and receiving input data from the keyboard.

- There are several user interfaces styles, among them terminal based and graphical based.

- Turtle graphics provides an easy way of writing programs that draw images.

VOCABULARY *Review*

Define the following terms:

applet	hacking	parameter
assignment operator	integrated development	source code
byte code	environment (IDE)	statement
DOS development	Java virtual machine (JVM)	terminal I/O interface
environment	just-in-time compilation	turtle graphics
graphical user interface (GUI)	(JIT)	variable

REVIEW *Questions*

WRITTEN QUESTIONS

Write a brief answer to the following questions.

1. List three reasons why Java is an important programming language.

2. What is byte code?

3. What is the JVM?

4. List two objects that are used for terminal input and output in Java programs.

5. Give examples of two compile-time errors.

6. What steps must be followed to run a Java program?

7. State the purpose of a program comment.

8.   What is the purpose of an import statement in a Java program?

FILL IN THE BLANK

Complete the following sentences by writing the correct word or words in the blanks provided.

1.   Two user interface styles are _____ and _____ .

2.   The message _Println_ is used to output data to the terminal window.

3.   The message _Keyboard Reader_ is used to input an integer from the keyboard.

4.   A(n) _variable_ names a place where data can be stored in a Java program.

5.   A(n) _Assignment Statement_ stores the value of the expression in the variable.

6.   Programs manipulate objects by sending them _messages_ .

PROJECTS

Beginning with this lesson, we conclude each lesson with a set of programming problems and activities. We want to emphasize that programming is not just coding. Thus, a complete solution to each exercise in this section would include not just a set of **.java** and **.class** files for the program but also a report that covers the analysis, design, and results of testing the program. Ideally, you would do analysis and design before coding, and perhaps turn in this work for review before coding proceeds. How this is done depends on the size of the class and the time available to the instructor. In any case, when you see the words "write a program that . . .," you should at least pause to reflect on the nature of the problem before coding the solution. For example, your analysis might consist of a description of how the program would be used.

PROJECT 2-1

Write a program that displays your name, address, and telephone number.

PROJECT 2-2

A yield sign encloses the word YIELD within a triangle. Write a program that displays a yield sign (use stars to represent the sides of the triangle).

PROJECT 2-3

Write a program that takes as input a number of kilometers and prints the corresponding number of nautical miles. You may rely on the following items of information:

■ A kilometer represents 1/10,000 of the distance between the North Pole and the equator.

■ There are 90 degrees, containing 60 minutes of arc each, between the North Pole and the equator.

■ A nautical mile is 1 minute of an arc.

PROJECT 2-4

Write a program that calculates and prints the number of minutes in a year.

PROJECT 2-5

An object's momentum is its mass multiplied by its velocity. Write a program that expects an object's mass (in kilograms) and velocity (in meters per second) as inputs and prints its momentum.

PROJECT 2-6

The Müller-Lyer illusion is caused by an image that consists of two parallel line segments. One line segment looks like an arrow with two heads, and the other line segment looks like an arrow with two tails. Although the line segments are of exactly the same length, they appear to be unequal (see Figure 2-14). Write a turtle graphics program that illustrates this illusion.

FIGURE 2-14
The Müller-Lyer illusion

PROJECT 2-7

Modify the program of Project 2-6 so that it draws two new vertical line segments. Each of the new line segments should connect the end points of the two parallel line segments that cause the Müller-Lyer illusion. Does the illusion go away when you display the new figure?

CRITICAL *Thinking*

You have an idea for a program that will help the local pizza shop handle takeout orders. Your friend suggests an interview with the shop's owner to discuss her user requirements before you get started on the program. Explain why this is a good suggestion and list the questions you would ask the owner to help you determine the user requirements.

SYNTAX, ERRORS, AND DEBUGGING

To use a programming language, one must become familiar with its vocabulary and the rules for forming grammatically correct statements. You must also know how to construct meaningful statements and statements that express the programmer's intent. Errors of form, meaning, and intent are possible, so finally one must know how to detect these errors and correct them. This lesson discusses the basic elements of the Java language in detail and explores how to find and correct errors in programs.

3.1 Language Elements

Before writing code in any programming language, we need to be aware of some basic language elements. Every natural language, such as English, Japanese, and German, has its own vocabulary, syntax, and semantics. Programming languages also have these three elements.

Vocabulary is the set of all of the words and symbols in the language. Table 3-1 illustrates some examples taken from Java:

TABLE 3-1
Some Java vocabulary

TYPE OF ELEMENT	EXAMPLES
arithmetic operators	+ – * /
assignment operator	=
numeric literals	5.73 9
programmer defined variable names	fahrenheit celsius

Syntax consists of the rules for combining words into sentences, or *statements*, as they are more usually called in programming languages. Following are two typical syntax rules in Java:

1. In an expression, the arithmetic operators for multiply and divide must not be adjacent. Thus,

   (f - 32) * / 9

   is invalid.

2. In an expression, left and right parentheses must occur in matching pairs. Thus,

)f - 32(* 5 / 9

   and

   f - 32) * 5 / 9

   are both invalid.

Semantics define the rules for interpreting the meaning of statements. For example, the expression

   (f - 32.0) * 5.0 / 9.0

means "go into the parentheses first, subtract 32.0 from the variable quantity indicated by f, then multiply the result by 5.0, and finally divide the whole thing by 9.0."

Programming versus Natural Languages

Despite their similarities, programming languages and natural languages differ in three important ways: size, rigidity, and literalness.

Size

Programming languages have small vocabularies and a simple syntax and semantics when compared to natural languages. Thus, their basic elements are not hard to learn.

Rigidity

In a programming language one must get the syntax absolutely correct, whereas an ungrammatical English sentence is usually comprehensible. This strict requirement of correctness often makes writing programs difficult for beginners, though no more difficult than writing grammatically correct sentences in English or any other natural language.

Literalness

Third, when we give a friend instructions in English, we can be a little vague, relying on the friend to fill in the details. In a programming language, we must be exhaustively thorough. Computers follow instructions in a very literal manner. They do exactly what they are told, neither more nor less. When people blame problems on computer errors, they should more accurately blame sloppy programming. This last difference is the one that makes programming difficult even for experienced programmers.

Although programming languages are simpler than human languages, the task of writing programs is challenging. It is difficult to express complex ideas using the limited syntax and semantics of a programming language.

EXERCISE 3.1

1. What is the vocabulary of a language? Give an example of an item in the vocabulary of Java.

2. Give an example of a syntax rule in Java.

3. What does the expression (x + y) * z mean?

4. Describe two differences between programming languages and natural languages.

3.2 Basic Java Syntax and Semantics

Having seen several Java programs in Lesson 2, we are ready for a more formal presentation of the language's basic elements. Some points have already been touched on in Lesson 2, but others are new.

Data Types

In Lesson 1, we showed that many types of information can be represented in computer memory as patterns of 0s and 1s, and as far as we know, so can information of every type. In this book, however, we are less ambitious and restrict our attention to just a few types of data. These fall into two main categories. The first category consists of what Java calls *primitive data types* and includes numbers (both integer and floating-point), characters (such as "A," "B," and "C"), and Booleans (restricted to the logical values true and false). The second category consists of objects, for instance, keyboard readers and pens. Strings are also in this second category.

Syntax

Java's syntax for manipulating primitive data types differs distinctly from the syntax for manipulating objects. Primitive data types are combined in expressions involving operators such as addition and multiplication. Objects, on the other hand, are sent messages. In addition, objects must be instantiated before use, and there is no comparable requirement for primitive data types.

Actually, this concise picture is confused slightly by strings, which on the one hand are objects and are sent messages, but on the other hand do not need to be instantiated and can be combined using something called the *concatenation operator.*

Numbers

We close this subsection with a few details concerning the primitive data types for representing numbers, or *numeric data types*, as they are called for short. Java includes six numeric data types, but we will restrict ourselves to just two. These are `int` (for integer) and `double` (for floating-point numbers—numbers with decimals). The range of values available with these two data types is shown in Table 3-2.

TABLE 3-2
Some Java numeric data types

TYPE	STORAGE REQUIREMENTS	RANGE
`int`	4 bytes	–2,147,483,648 to 2,147,483,647
`double`	8 bytes	–1.79769313486231570E+308 to 1.79769313486231570E+308

The other numeric data types are `short`, `long`, `byte`, and `float`. The data types for Booleans and characters will be discussed in Lessons 6 and 7, respectively.

Numeric calculations are a central part of most, though not all, programs, so we will become very familiar with the numeric data types. Programs that manipulate numeric data types often share a common format: input numeric data, perform calculations, output numeric results. The temperature conversion program in Lesson 2 adhered to this format.

> **Extra for Experts**
>
> For more information about data types, see Appendix B.

*E*XERCISE 3.2

1. What is the difference between `double` and `int` data types?

2. How does the syntax for manipulating numeric data types and objects differ?

Literals

Literals are items in a program whose values do not change. They are restricted to the primitive data types and strings. Examples from the conversion program in Lesson 2 include the numbers 5.0 and 9.0 and the string "Enter degrees Fahrenheit: ". Table 3-3 gives other examples of numeric literals (note that numeric literals never contain commas).

TABLE 3-3
Examples of numeric literals

EXAMPLE	DATA TYPE
51	an integer
–31444843	a negative integer
3.14	a floating-point number (double)
5.301E5	a floating-point number equivalent to $5.301 * 10^5$, or 530,100
5.301E–5	a floating-point number equivalent to $5.301 * 10^{-5}$, or 0.00005301 (double)

The last two examples in Table 3-3 are written in what is called *exponential* or *scientific notation* and are expressed as a decimal number followed by a power of ten. The letter "E" can be written in upper- or lowercase.

EXERCISE 3.2 Continued

3. Convert the following floating-point numbers to exponential notation:
   a. 23.5
   b. 0.046

4. Convert the following numbers from exponential notation to floating-point notation:
   a. 32.21E4
   b. 55.6E–3

5. Give two examples of string literals.

Variables and Their Declarations

A variable is an item whose value can change during the execution of a program. A variable can be thought of as a named location or cell in the computer's memory. Changing the value of a variable is equivalent to replacing the value that was in the cell with another value (Figure 3-1). For instance, at one point in a program, we might set the value of the variable `fahrenheit` to 78.5. Later in the program, we could set the variable to another value such as -23.7. When we do this, the new value replaces the old one.

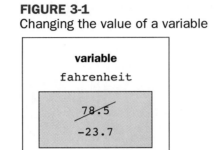

FIGURE 3-1
Changing the value of a variable

Although the value of a variable can change, the type of data it contains cannot, or in other words, during the course of a program, a specific variable can hold only one type of data. For instance, if it initially holds an integer, then it can never hold a floating-pointing number, and if it initially holds a reference to a pen, it can never hold a reference to a keyboard reader.

Declarations

Before using a variable for the first time, the program must declare its type. This is done in a *variable declaration statement*, as illustrated in the following code:

```
int age;
double celsius;
String name;
KeyboardReader reader;
```

The type appears on the left and the variable's name on the right. Frequently, we will speak of a *variable's type*, meaning the type indicator that appears on the left. Thus, we will say that `celsius` is a double.

It is permitted to declare several variables in a single declaration and simultaneously to assign them initial values. For instance, the following code segment initializes the variables z, q, pi, name, and reader:

```
int x, y, z = 7;
double p, q = 1.41, pi = 3.14, t;
String name = "Bill Jones";
KeyboardReader reader = new KeyboardReader();
```

The last statement declares the object variable `reader`, instantiates or creates a `KeyboardReader` object, and finally assigns the object to the variable. Instantiation takes the form

```
new <name of class>()
```

Constants

Occasionally, when initializing a variable, we want to specify that its value cannot change thereafter. This seems somewhat contradictory but is sometimes useful, as we shall see later. The next example illustrates how to do this:

> **Note** ☑
>
> The format for object instantiation is slightly more general than shown here, as will be explained in Lesson 5.

```
final double SALES_TAX_RATE = 7.85;
```

The keyword here is "`final`" and a variable declared in this way is called a *constant*. It is customary to write the names of constants in uppercase. Any attempt to change the value of a constant after it is initialized is flagged by the compiler as an error.

EXERCISE 3.2 Continued

6. Why is a variable called a variable?

7. Return to the programs in Lesson 2 and find an example of each of the different types of variables. Which of the types listed in this subsection are not included?

8. Declare a floating-point variable called `payRate` and simultaneously initialize it to $35.67.

9. Declare three integer variables (`a`, `b`, `c`) in a single declaration and simultaneously initialize `b` to `4`.

10. Give two examples of data that cannot be stored in a variable of type `int`.

11. There are approximately 2.2 pounds in a kilogram. Name and declare a constant to represent this value.

Assignment Statements

An assignment statement has the following form:

```
<variable> = <expression>;
```

where the value of the expression on the right is assigned to the variable on the left. For instance

```
double celsius, fahrenheit;
String name;
StandardPen pen;
. . .
fahrenheit = reader.readDouble();
celsius = (Fahrenheit - 32.0) * 5.0 / 9.0;
name = "Bill Smith";
pen = new StandardPen();
```

Arithmetic Expressions

An *arithmetic expression* consists of operands and operators combined in a manner familiar from algebra. The usual rules apply:

■ Multiplication and division are evaluated before addition and subtraction; that is, multiplication and division have higher precedence than addition and subtraction.

■ Operators of equal precedence are evaluated from left to right.

■ Parentheses can be used to change the order of evaluation.

Unlike in algebra, multiplication must be indicated explicitly: thus, a * b cannot be written as ab. Binary operators are placed between their operands (a * b, for example), whereas unary operators are placed before their operands (-a, for example). Table 3-4 shows several operands from the conversion program in Lesson 2, and Table 3-5 shows some common operators and their precedence.

TABLE 3-4
Examples of operands

TYPE	EXAMPLE
Literals	32.0 5.0 9.0
Variables	fahrenheit celsius
Parenthesized expressions	(fahrenheit - 32.0)

TABLE 3-5
Common operators and their precedence

OPERATOR	SYMBOL	PRECEDENCE (FROM HIGHEST TO LOWEST)	ASSOCIATION
Grouping	( )	1	Not applicable
Method selector	.	2	Left to right
Unary plus	+	3	Not applicable
Unary minus	–	3	Not applicable
Instantiation	new	3	Right to left
Cast	(double)	3	Right to left
	(int)		
Multiplication	*	4	Left to right

TABLE 3-5 (continued)
Common operators and their precedence

OPERATOR	SYMBOL	PRECEDENCE (FROM HIGHEST TO LOWEST)	ASSOCIATION
Division	/	4	Left to right
Remainder or modulus	%	4	Left to right
Addition	+	5	Left to right
Subtraction	-	5	Left to right
Assignment	=	10	Right to left

Division

Several points concerning operators need explanation. First, the semantics of division are different for integer and floating-point operands. Thus

5.0 / 2.0	yields	2.5
5 / 2	yields	2 (a quotient in which the fractional portion of the answer is simply dropped)

Modulus

The operator % yields the remainder obtained when one number is divided by another. Thus

9 % 5	yields	4
9.3 % 5.1	yields	4.2

Precedence

When evaluating an expression, Java applies operators of higher precedence before those of lower precedence unless overridden by parentheses. The highest precedence is 1.

3 + 5 * 3	yields	18
-3 + 5 * 3	yields	12
+3 + 5 * 3	yields	18 (use of unary + is uncommon)
3 + 5 * -3	yields	-12
3 + 5 * +3	yields	18 (use of unary + is uncommon)
(3 + 5) * 3	yields	24
3 + 5 % 3	yields	5
(3 + 5) % 3	yields	2

Association

The column labeled "Association" in Table 3-5 indicates the order in which to perform operations of equal precedence. Thus

18 - 3 - 4	yields 11
18 / 3 * 4	yields 24
18 % 3 * 4	yields 0
a = b = 7;	assigns 7 to b and then b to a

More Examples

Some more examples of expressions and their values are shown in Table 3-6. In this table, we see the application of two fairly obvious rules governing the use of parentheses:

1. Parentheses must occur in matching pairs.

2. Parenthetical expressions may be nested but must not overlap.

TABLE 3-6
Examples of expressions and their values

EXPRESSION	SAME AS	VALUE
3 + 4 - 5	7 - 5	2
3 + (4 - 5)	3 + (-1)	2
3 + 4 * 5	3 + 20	23
(3 + 4) * 5	7 * 5	35
8 / 2 + 6	4 + 6	10
8 / (2 + 6)	8 / 8	1
10 - 3 - 4 - 1	7 - 4 - 1	2
10 - (3 - 4 - 1)	10 - (-2)	12
(15 + 9) / (3 + 1)	24 / 4	6
15 + 9 / 3 + 1	15 + 3 + 1	19
(15 + 9) / ((3 + 1) * 2)	24 / (4 * 2) 24 / 8	3
(15 + 9) / (3 + 1) * 2	24 / 4 * 2 6 * 2	12

EXERCISE 3.2 Continued

12. Assume that the integer variable x is 5 and the integer variable y is 10. Give the values of the following expressions:
a. x + y * 2
b. x – y + 2
c. (x + y) * 2
d. y % x

13. Find the syntax errors in the following expressions:
a. a - * b + c
b. – (a + b) * c)
c. ()

Mixed-Mode Arithmetic

When working with a handheld calculator, we do not give much thought to the fact that we intermix integers and floating-point numbers. This is called *mixed-mode arithmetic*. For instance, if a circle has radius 3, we compute the area as follows:

```
3.14 * 3 * 3
```

In Java, when there is a binary operation on operands of different numeric types, the less inclusive type (int) is temporarily and automatically converted to the more inclusive type (double) before the operation is performed. Thus, in

```
double d;
d = 5.0 / 2;
```

the value of d is computed as 5.0/2.0, yielding 2.5. However, problems can arise when using mixed-mode arithmetic. For instance

```
3 / 2 * 5.0        yields        1 * 5.0        yields        5.0
```

whereas

```
3 / 2.0 * 5        yields        1.5 * 5        yields        7.5
```

Mixed-mode assignments are also allowed, provided the variable on the left is of a more inclusive type than the expression on the right. Otherwise, a syntax error occurs, as shown in the following code segment:

```
double d;
int i;

i = 45;        ← OK, because we assign an int to an int.
d = i;         ← OK, because d is more inclusive than i. The value 45.0 is stored in d.
i = d;         ← Syntax error because i is less inclusive than d.
```

EXERCISE 3.2 Continued

14. Assume that x is 4.5 and y is 2. Write the values of the following expressions:
   a. x / y
   b. y / x
   c. x % y

15. Assume that x and y are of type `double` and z is of type `int`. For each of the following assignment statements, state which are valid and which produce syntax errors:
   a. x = z
   b. x = y * z
   c. z = x + y

Casting to `int` and `double`

The difficulties associated with mixed-mode arithmetic can be circumvented using a technique called *casting*, which allows one data type to be explicitly converted to another. For instance, consider the following example:

```
int i;
double d;

i = (int)3.14;          ← i equals 3, truncation toward 0
d = (double)5 / 4;      ← d equals 1.25
```

The cast operator, either `(int)` or `(double)`, appears immediately before the expression it is supposed to convert. The `(int)` cast simply throws away the digits after the decimal point, which has the effect of truncation toward 0.

Precedence

The cast operator has high precedence (see Table 3-5) and must be used with care, as illustrated in the following code:

```
double x, y;

x = (double)5 / 4;       ← x equals 5.0 / 4 equals 1.25
y = (double)(5 / 4);     ← y equals (double)(1) equals 1.0
```

Rounding

The cast operator is useful for rounding floating-point numbers to the nearest integer:

```
int m, n;
double x, y;

x = . . . ;              ← some positive value is assigned to x
m = (int)(x + 0.5);

y = - . . .;             ← some negative value is assigned to y
n = (int)(x - 0.5);
```

EXERCISE 3.2 Continued

16. Assume that x is of type `double` and y is of type `int`. Also assume that x is 4.5 and y is 2. Write the values of the following expressions:

a. `(int) x * y`

b. `(int) (x * y)`

> **Extra for Experts**
>
> Other numeric casts such as `(char)` and `(float)` are discussed in Appendix B.

17. Assume that x is of type `double` and y is of type `int`. Write a statement that assigns the value contained in x to y after rounding this value to the nearest whole number.

String Expressions and Methods

Strings are used in programs in a variety of ways. As already seen, they can be used as literals or assigned to variables. Now we will see that they can be combined in expressions using the concatenation operator, and they also can be sent messages.

Simple Concatenation

The concatenation operator uses the plus symbol (+). Following is an example:

```
String firstName,                             // declare four string
       lastName,                              // variables
       fullName,
       lastThenFirst;

firstName = "Bill";                           // initialize firstName
lastName = "Smith";                           // initialize lastName

fullName = firstName + " " + lastName;        // yields "Bill Smith"
lastThenFirst = lastName + ", " + firstName;  // yields "Smith, Bill"
```

Concatenating Strings and Numbers

Strings also can be concatenated to numbers. When this occurs, the number is automatically converted to a string before the concatenation operator is applied:

```
String message;
int x = 20, y = 35;

message = "Bill sold " + x + " and Sylvia sold " + y + " subscriptions.";
// yields "Bill sold 20 and Sylvia sold 35 subscriptions."
```

Precedence of Concatenation

The concatenation operator has the same precedence as addition, which can lead to unexpected results:

```
"number " + 3 + 4      → "number 3" + 4    → "number 34"
"number " + (3 + 4)    → "number " + 7     → "number 7"
"number " + 3 * 4      → "number " + 12    → "number 12"
3 + 4 + " number"      → 7 + "number"      → "7 number"
```

Escape Character

String literals are delimited by quotation marks ("..."), which presents a dilemma when quotation marks are supposed to appear inside a string. Placing a special character before the quotation mark, indicating the quotation mark is to be taken literally and not as a delimiter, solves the problem. This special character, also called the *escape character*, is a back slash (\).

```
message = "As the train left the station, " +
          "the conductor yelled, \"All aboard.\"";
```

Other Uses for the Escape Character

The escape character also is used when including other special characters in string literals. The sequence backslash-t (\t) indicates a tab character, and backslash-n (\n) a newline character. These special sequences involving the backslash character are called *escape sequences*. The following code gives an example of the use of escape sequences followed by the output generated by the code:

Extra for Experts

There are several other escape sequences, but we omit them from this discussion (see Appendix B for further details).

Code

```
System.out.print ("The room was full of animals: \n" +
                  "\tdogs,\n\tcats, and\n\tchimpanzees.\n";
```

Output

```
The room was full of animals:
      dogs,
      cats, and
      chimpanzees.
```

Escaping the Escape Character

In solving one problem, we have introduced another. The backslash is the designated escape character, but sometimes a string must contain a backslash. This is accomplished by placing two backslashes in sequence:

```
path = "C:\\Java\\Ch3.doc";        ← yields the string C:\Java\Ch3.doc
```

The `length` Method

Strings are objects and implement several methods. In this lesson, we consider only the `length` method and defer discussions of others until Lessons 6 and 10 (for users of the Introductory and Comprehensive texts). A string returns its length in response to a `length` message:

```
String theString;
int theLength;

theString = "The cat sat on the mat.";
theLength = theString.length();          ← yields 23
```

EXERCISE 3.2 Continued

18. Assume that x refers to the string "Wizard" and y refers to the string "Java". Write the values of the following expressions:

a. y + x

b. y + y.length() + x

c. y + "\n" + x + "\n"

19. Declare a variable of type string called myInfo and initialize it to your name, address, and telephone number. Each item of information in this string should be followed by a newline character.

Methods, Messages, and Signatures

Classes implement methods, and objects are instances of classes. An object can respond to a message only if its class implements a corresponding method. To correspond the method must have the same name as the message. Thus a pen object responds to the move message, because the StandardPen class defines a move method.

Messages are sometimes accompanied by parameters and sometimes not:

```
pen.down();          // No parameters expected
pen.move(50.5);      // One parameter expected
```

The parameters included when a message is sent must match exactly in number and type the parameters expected by the method. For instance, the move method expects a single parameter of type double.

```
double d = 24.6;

pen.move(d);           // Perfect! A parameter of type double is expected.
pen.move(2.0 * d);     // Perfect! The expression yields a double.
pen.move(4);           // Fine! Integers can stand in for doubles.
pen.move();            // Error! A parameter is needed.
pen.move(6.7, 3.4);    // Error! One parameter only please.
pen.move("far");       // Error! A string parameter is NOT acceptable.
```

Some methods return a value and others do not. The StandardPen methods do not return a value; however, the method readDouble in class KeyboardReader does:

```
KeyboardReader reader = new KeyboardReader();
double x;

x = reader.readDouble();  // Returns the number entered by the user.
```

To use a method successfully we must know

■ What type of value it returns

■ Its name

■ The number and type of the parameters it expects

Together this information is called the method's *signature*, and from now on, when we introduce a new class, we will make a point of listing method signatures together with brief descriptions of what the methods do. Following are two examples, the first from class KeyboardReader and the second from class StandardPen:

`double readDouble()`   Returns a double entered by the user at the keyboard.

`void move(double distance)` Moves the indicated distance in the pen's current direction.

The word void indicates that the method does not return a value.

EXERCISE 3.2 Continued

20. What is the difference between a message and a method?

21. Describe the purpose of each item of information that appears in a method's signature.

22. Turn to Appendix H and make a list of all the methods implemented by the classes KeyboardReader and StandardPen.

> **Extra for Experts**
>
> Appendix H contains signatures and descriptions for all the methods in the classes KeyboardReader and StandardPen as well as those from several other classes.

User-Defined Symbols

Variable and program names are examples of user-defined symbols. We will see other examples later in the book. We now explain the rules for forming or naming user-defined symbols. These names must consist of a letter followed by a sequence of letters and/or digits. Letters are defined to be

- A .. Z
- a .. z
- _ and $
- Symbols that denote letters in several languages other than English

Digits are the characters 0 .. 9. Names are case sensitive; thus, celsius and Celsius are different names.

Some words cannot be employed as user-defined symbols. These words are called *keywords* or *reserved words* because they have special meaning in Java. Table 3-7 shows a list of Java's reserved words. You will encounter most of them by the end of the book. These words are case sensitive also, thus "import" is a reserved word but "Import" and "IMPORT" are not.

TABLE 3-7
Java's reserved words

abstract	double	int	static
boolean	else	interface	super
break	extends	long	switch
byte	final	native	synchronized
case	finally	new	this
catch	float	null	throw
char	for	package	throws
class	goto	private	transient
const	if	protected	try
continue	implements	public	void
default	import	return	volatile
do	instanceof	short	while

Here are examples of valid and invalid variable names:

Valid Names   surfaceArea3   _$_$$$

Invalid Names   3rdPayment   pay.rate   abstract

The first invalid name begins with a digit. The second invalid name contains a period. The third invalid name is a reserved word.

Well-chosen variable names greatly increase a program's readability and maintainability; consequently, it is considered good programming practice to use meaningful names such as

radius   rather than   r

taxableIncome   rather than   ti

When forming a compound variable name, programmers usually capitalize the first letter of each word except the first. For instance:

taxableIncome   rather than

taxableincome   or

TAXABLEINCOME   or

TaxableIncome

On the other hand, all the words in a program's name typically begin with a capital letter: for instance, ComputeEmployeePayroll. Finally, constant names usually are all uppercase. The goal of these rules and of all stylistic conventions is to produce programs that are easier to understand and maintain.

EXERCISE 3.2 Continued

23. State whether each of the following are valid or invalid user-defined symbols in Java:
  a. pricePerSquareInch
  b. student2
  c. 2GuysFromLexington
  d. PI
  e. allDone?

24. Write names for the following items that follow good programming practice:
  a. A variable that represents the diameter of a circle.
  b. A constant that represents the standard deduction for an income tax return.
  c. A method that draws a rectangle.

Packages and the `import` statement

Programmers seldom write programs from scratch. Instead they rely heavily on code written by many other programmers, most of whom they will never meet. Fortunately, Java provides a mechanism called a *package* that makes it easy for programmers to share code. Having written a class or group of classes that provide some generally useful service, a programmer can collect the classes together in a package. Other programmers who want to use the service can then import classes from the package. The programs in Lesson 2 illustrated the use of packages called `TerminalIO` and `TurtleGraphics`. The Java programming environment typically includes a large number of standard packages, some of which we will use in the subsequent lessons. These packages are standard because we expect to find them in every Java programming environment. The packages `TerminalIO` and `TurtleGraphics`, on the other hand, are nonstandard and were created by the authors to support users of this and other textbooks they have written; however, the packages and all their source code are freely available to anyone who wishes to use or modify them.

When using a package, a programmer imports the desired class or classes. The general form of an `import` statement is

```
import x.y.z;
```

where

■ x is the overall name of the package.

■ y is the name of a subsection within the package.

■ z is the name of a particular class in the subsection.

It is possible to import all the classes within a subsection at once; however, we will not usually do so. The statement to import all the classes with a subsection looks like this:

```
import x.y.*;
```

In general, a package can have any number of subsections, including zero, which is the case for the nonstandard packages used in this book, and each subsection can in turn have any number of sub-subsections, etc. When used, a star (*) can appear only at the lowest level. The star is used to make available all of the classes in a package.

EXERCISE 3.2 Continued

25. Describe the role of the items x, y, and z in the statement import x.y.z;.

26. What happens when the computer executes the statement import x.y.*;?

27. Assume that a program needs to use the class Format, which is included in the package BreezySwing. Show two ways to import this class with Java import statements.

3.3 Terminal I/O for Different Data Types

Objects support terminal input and output. An instance of the class KeyboardReader supports input and the object System.out supports output. The latter object is an instance of the class PrintStream. This class, together with a number of others, is available to Java programmers without specifying their names in import statements. Although System.out is an instance of the class PrintStream, do not try to instantiate this class until you become familiar with working in Java files.

Table 3-8 summarizes the methods in class KeyboardReader. The object System.out understands two messages, print and println. Both messages expect a single parameter, which can be of any type, including an object; however, we will postpone using an object as a parameter until Lesson 5.

TABLE 3-8
Methods in class KeyboardReader

SIGNATURE	DESCRIPTION
char readChar()	Returns the first character in the input line, even if it is a space.
double readDouble()	Returns the first double in the input line. Leading and trailing spaces are ignored.
int readInt()	Returns the first integer in the input line. Leading and trailing spaces are ignored.
String readLine()	Returns the input line, including leading and trailing spaces.
void pause()	Returns once the user presses Enter.

The following program illustrates the major features of terminal I/O, except for the readChar method, which is discussed in Lesson 7:

```
import TerminalIO.KeyboardReader;

public class TestTerminalIO {
    public static void main (String [] args) {
        KeyboardReader reader = new KeyboardReader();
        String name;
        int age;
        double weight;
```

```
System.out.print ("Enter your name (a string): ");
name = reader.readLine();

System.out.print ("Enter your age (an integer): ");
age = reader.readInt();

System.out.print ("Enter your weight (a double): ");
weight = reader.readDouble();

System.out.println ("Greetings " + name +
                    ". You are " + age +
                    " years old and you weigh " + weight +
                    " pounds.");
        reader.pause();
    }
}
```

When the program encounters an input statement—for instance, `reader.readInt();`—it pauses and waits for the user to press Enter, at which point the `reader` object processes the user's input. For the previous program, the interaction with the user looks something like this, where the user's input is shown in bold and the use of the Enter key is shown in italics:

```
Enter your name (a string): Carole JonesEnter
Enter your age (an integer): 45Enter
Enter your weight (a double): 130.6Enter
Greetings Carole Jones. You are 45 years old and you weigh 130.6 pounds.

Press Enter to continue . . .
```

*E*XERCISE 3.3

1. Write code segments that perform the following tasks:
   a. Prompt the user for an hourly wage and read the wage into a `double` variable `wage`.
   b. Prompt the user for a Social Security number and read this value into the `string` variable `ssn`.

2. What is the purpose of the method `pause()`?

3.4 Comments

When we first write a program, we are completely familiar with all its nuances; however, six months later, when we or someone else has to modify it, the code that was once so clear often seems confusing and mysterious. There is, however, a technique for dealing with this situation. The remedy is to include comments in the code. *Comments* are explanatory sentences inserted in a program in such a manner that the compiler ignores them. There are two styles for indicating comments:

■ End of line comments: These include all of the text following a double slash (`//`) on any given line; in other words, this style is best for just one line of comment.

■ Multiline comments: These include all of the text between an opening /* and a closing */.

The following code segment illustrates the use of both kinds of comments:

```
/* This code segment illustrates the
use of assignment statements and comments */

a = 3;          // assign 3 to variable a
b = 4;          // assign 4 to variable b
c = a + b;      // add the number in variable a
                //    to the number in variable b
                //    and assign the result, 7, to variable c
c = c * 3;      // multiply the number in variable c by 3
                //    and assign the result, 21, to variable c
```

Although this code segment illustrates the mechanics of how to include comments in a program, it gives a misleading idea of when to use them. The main purpose of comments is to make a program more readable and thus easier to maintain. With this end in mind, we usually

■ Begin a program with a statement of its purpose and other information that would help orient a programmer called on to modify the program at some future date.

■ Accompany a variable declaration with a comment that explains the variable's purpose.

■ Precede major segments of code with brief comments that explain their purpose.

■ Include comments to explain the workings of complex or tricky sections of code.

The case study in the next section follows these guidelines and illustrates a reasonable and helpful level of comments. Because the programs in this book usually are accompanied by an extensive discussion of what they do, we sometimes include few or no comments; however, the programs you write always should be well commented.

Too many comments are as harmful as too few, because over time, the burden of maintaining the comments becomes excessive. No matter how many comments are included in a program, future programmers must still read and understand the region of code they intended to modify. Common sense usually leads to a reasonable balance. We always will avoid comments that do nothing more than restate the obvious. For instance, the next comment is completely pointless:

```
a = 3;      // assign 3 to variable a. Duh!
```

The best-written programs are self-documenting; that is, the reader can understand the code from the symbols used and from the structure and overall organization of the program.

EXERCISE 3.4

1. Describe the difference between an end-of-line comment and a multiline comment.

2. State two rules of thumb for writing appropriate comments in a program.

Case Study 1: Income Tax Calculator

It is now time to write a program that illustrates some of the concepts we have been presenting. We do this in the context of a case study that adheres to the software development life cycle discussed in Lesson 1. This life cycle approach may seem overly elaborate for small programs, but it scales up well when programs become larger.

Each year nearly everyone with an income faces the unpleasant task of computing his or her income tax return. If only it could be done as easily as suggested in this case study.

Request

Write a program that computes a person's income tax.

Analysis

Here is the relevant tax law (mythical in nature):

■ There is a flat tax rate of 20%.

■ There is a $10,000 standard deduction.

■ There is a $2000 additional deduction for each dependent.

■ Gross income must be entered to the nearest penny.

■ The income tax is expressed as a decimal number.

The user inputs are the gross income and number of dependents. The program calculates the income tax based on the inputs and the tax law and then displays the income tax. Figure 3-2 shows the proposed terminal interface. Characters in bold indicate user inputs. The program prints the rest. The inclusion of an interface at this point is a good idea because it allows the customer and the programmer to discuss the intended program's behavior in a context understandable to both.

FIGURE 3-2
Interface for the income tax calculator

```
Enter the gross income: 50000.50
Enter the number of dependents: 4
The income tax is $6400.1
```

Design

During analysis, we specify what a program is going to do, and during design we describe how it is going to do it. This involves writing the algorithm used by the program. *Webster's New Collegiate Dictionary* defines an **algorithm** as "a step-by-step procedure for solving a problem or accomplishing some end." A recipe in a cookbook is a good example of an algorithm. Program algorithms are often written in a somewhat stylized version of English called **pseudocode**. Following is the pseudocode for our income tax program:

```
read grossIncome
read numDependents
compute taxableIncome = grossIncome - 10000 - 2000 * numDependents
compute incomeTax = taxableIncome * 0.20
print incomeTax
```

Although there are no precise rules governing the syntax of pseudocode, you should strive to describe the essential elements of the program in a clear and concise manner. Over time, you will develop a style that suits you.

Implementation

Given the preceding pseudocode, an experienced programmer now would find it easy to write the corresponding Java program. For a beginner, on the other hand, writing the code is the most difficult part of the process. Following is the program:

```
/*IncomeTaxCalculator.java
Compute a person's income tax.
1. Significant constants
       tax rate
       standard deduction
       deduction per dependent
2. The inputs are
       gross income
       number of dependents
3. Computations:
       net income = gross income - the standard deduction -
                    a deduction for each dependent
       income tax = is a fixed percentage of the net income
4. The outputs are
       the income tax
*/


import TerminalIO.KeyboardReader;

public class IncomeTaxCalculator {
    public static void main (String [] args) {

        // Constants
        final double TAX_RATE = 0.20;
        final double STANDARD_DEDUCTION = 10000.0;
        final double DEPENDENT_DEDUCTION = 2000.0;

        KeyboardReader reader = new KeyboardReader();

        double grossIncome;          // the gross income (input)
        int    numDependents;        // the number of dependents (input)
        double taxableIncome;        // the taxable income (calculated)
        double incomeTax;            // the income tax (calculated and
                                     // output)


        // Request the inputs
        System.out.print ("Enter the gross income: ");
        grossIncome = reader.readDouble();
        System.out.print ("Enter the number of dependents: ");
        numDependents = reader.readInt();
```

```
        // Compute the income tax
        taxableIncome = grossIncome - STANDARD_DEDUCTION -
                        DEPENDENT_DEDUCTION * numDependents;
        incomeTax = taxableIncome * TAX_RATE;

        // Display the income tax
        System.out.println ("The income tax is $" + incomeTax);
    }
}
```

Notice that we have used mixed-mode arithmetic, but in a manner that does not produce any undesired effects.

COMPUTER ETHICS

COMPUTER VIRUSES

A *virus* is a computer program that can replicate itself and move from computer to computer. Some programmers of viruses intend no harm; they just want to demonstrate their prowess by creating viruses that go undetected. Other programmers of viruses intend harm by causing system crashes, corruption of data, or hardware failures.

Viruses migrate by attaching themselves to normal programs, and then become active again when these programs are launched. Early viruses were easily detected if one had detection software. This software examined portions of each program on the suspect computer and could repair infected programs.

Viruses and virus detectors have coevolved through the years, however, and both kinds of software have become very sophisticated. Viruses now hide themselves better than they used to; virus detectors can no longer just examine pieces of data stored in memory to reveal the presence or absence of a virus. Researchers have recently developed a method of running a program that might contain a virus to see whether or not the virus becomes active. The suspect program runs in a "safe" environment that protects the computer from any potential harm. As you can imagine, this process takes time and costs money. For an overview of the history of viruses and the new detection technology, see Carey Nactenberg, "Computer Virus-Antivirus Coevolution," *Communications of the ACM*, Volume 40, No. 1 (January 1997): 46–51.

3.5 Programming Errors

According to an old saying, we learn from our mistakes, which is fortunate because most people find it almost impossible to write even simple programs without making numerous mistakes. These mistakes, or errors, are of three types: syntax errors, run-time errors, and logic errors.

The Three Types of Errors

Syntax errors, as we learned in Lesson 2, occur when we violate a syntax rule, no matter how minor. These errors are detected at compile time. For instance, if a semicolon is missing at the end of a statement or if a variable is used before it is declared, the compiler is unable to translate the program into byte code. The good news is that when the Java compiler finds a syntax error, it prints an error message, and we can make the needed correction. The bad news, as we saw previously, is that the error messages are often quite cryptic. Knowing that there is a syntax error at a particular point in a program, however, is usually a sufficient clue for finding the error.

Run-time errors occur when we ask the computer to do something that it considers illegal, such as dividing by 0. For example, suppose that the symbols x and y are variables. Then the expression x/y is syntactically correct, so the compiler does not complain. However, when the expression is evaluated during execution of the program, the meaning of the expression depends on the values contained in the variables. If the variable y has the value 0, then the expression cannot be evaluated. The good news is that the Java run-time environment will print a message telling us the nature of the error and where it was encountered. Once again, the bad news is that the error message might be hard to understand.

Logic errors (also called *design errors* or *bugs*) occur when we fail to express ourselves accurately. For instance, in every day life, we might give someone the instruction to turn left when what we really meant to say is to turn right. In this example

- The instruction is phrased properly, and thus the syntax is correct.

- The instruction is meaningful, and thus the semantics are valid.

- But the instruction does not do what we intended, and thus is logically incorrect.

The bad news is that programming environments do not detect logic errors automatically. The good news is that this text offers useful tips on how to prevent logic errors and how to detect them when they occur.

Now let's look at examples of each of these types of errors.

Illustration of Syntax Errors

We have already seen examples of syntax errors in Lesson 2; however, seeing a few more will be helpful. The following is a listing of the income tax calculator program with the addition of two syntax errors. See if you can spot them. The line numbers are not part of the program but are intended to facilitate the discussion that follows the listing.

```
1    import TerminalIO.KeyboardReader;
2
3    public class IncomeTaxCalculator {
4        public static void main (String [] args) {
5
6            final double TAX_RATE = 0.20;
```

```
 7            final double STANDARD_DEDUCTION = 10000.0;
 8            final double DEPENDENT_DEDUCTION = 2000.0;
 9
10            KeyboardReader reader = new KeyboardReader();
11
12            double grossIncome;
13            int  numDependents;
14            double taxableIncome;
15            double incomeTax;
16
17            System.out.print ("Enter the gross income: ");
18            grossIncome = reader.readDouble();
19            System.out.print ("Enter the number of dependents: ");
20            numDependents = reader.readInt();
21
22            taxableIncome = grossincome - STANDARD_DEDUCTION -
23                       DEPENDENT_DEDUCTION * numDependents;
24            incomeTax = taxableIncome * TAX_RATE
25
26            System.out.println ("The income tax is $" + incomeTax);
27      }
28 }
```

Just in case you could not spot them, the errors in the code are

- In line 22, where `grossIncome` has been misspelled as `grossincome` (remember Java is case sensitive)

- In line 24, where the semicolon is missing at the end of the line

When the program is compiled, the terminal window contains the following error messages. We could show a snapshot of the window, but we think the following plain text is more readable:

```
C:\IncomeTaxCalculator.java:22: Undefined variable: grossincome
      taxableIncome = grossincome - STANDARD_DEDUCTION -
                      ^
C:\IncomeTaxCalculator.java:24: Invalid type expression.
      incomeTax = taxableIncome * TAX_RATE
                ^
C:\IncomeTaxCalculator.java:26: Invalid declaration.
      System.out.println ("The income tax is $" + incomeTax);
                        ^

3 errors
```

Error 1: The compiler says that line 22 contains an undefined variable called `grossincome`. This is just what we expected. As you can see, a copy of line 22 is printed for our further edification with a carat mark (^) immediately under the word that contains the error.

Error 2: The compiler says that line 24 contains an invalid type expression. This message makes no sense, and the carat mark is under an equal sign. However, when we look at the line, we notice that a semicolon is missing from the end. At least the compiler realizes something is wrong with this line.

Error 3: The compiler says that line 26 contains an invalid declaration. Sorry, but this is not so. This line is fine. However, when the compiler is thrown off balance by a syntax error, it often spits out misleading error messages for several lines thereafter.

The corrective action is to go back into the editor, fix all the errors that make sense, save the file, and compile again. You may need to repeat this process a number of times until the compiler stops finding syntax errors.

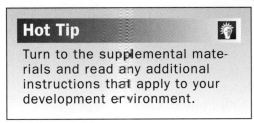

Hot Tip

Turn to the supplemental materials and read any additional instructions that apply to your development environment.

Illustration of Run-time Errors

There are a variety of run-time errors. We now present several of the most basic. We will encounter others later in the book.

Division by Integer Zero

For our first run-time error, we write a small program that attempts to perform division by 0. As is well known, division by 0 is not a well-defined operation and should be avoided. Nonetheless, we must ask what happens if we accidentally write a program that does it. Following then is a trivial program that illustrates the situation:

```
public class DivideByIntegerZero {
    public static void main (String [] args) {
        int i, j = 0;
        i = 3 / j;
        System.out.println ("The value of i is " + i);
    }
}
```

When we attempt to run this program, execution stops prematurely, and the following error message is displayed:

```
Exception in thread "main" java.lang.ArithmeticException: / by zero
        at DivideByIntegerZero.main(DivideByIntegerZero.java:4)
```

In this circumstance, we say that the JVM has thrown an *exception*. The message indicates the nature of the problem, "ArithmeticException: / by zero," and its location in Line 4 of method main.

Division by Floating-Point Zero

Interestingly, the JVM responds rather differently when the division involves a floating-point rather than an integer 0. Consider the following nearly identical program:

```
public class DivideByFloatingPointZero {
    public static void main (String [] args) {
        double i, j = 0.0;
        i = 3.0 / j;
        System.out.println ("The value of i is " + i);
        System.out.println ("10 / i equals " + 10 / i);
    }
}
```

The program now runs to completion, and the output is

```
The value of i is Infinity
10 / i equals 0.0
```

In other words, the value of the variable i is considered to be Infinity, which is to say it falls outside the range of a double, and if we now divide another number by i, we obtain 0.

Null Pointer Exception

Not all run-time errors involve arithmetic. Variables frequently represent objects. Sending a message to such a variable before the corresponding object has been instantiated causes a null pointer exception. Fortunately, many compilers detect the possibility of this error before it arises; however, later in this book the problem will occur in situations that the compiler cannot detect. Following is an example program together with the accompanying compiler error message:

The Program

```
import TerminalIO.KeyboardReader;

public class Test {
   public static void main (String [] args) {
      KeyboardReader reader;
      int age;
      age = reader.readInt();
   }
}
```

The Compiler Error Message

```
C:\Test.java:7: Variable reader may not have been initialized.
      age = reader.readInt();
                 ^
1 error
```

In this code, the compiler says that the variable reader may not have been initialized. If that's true (and in this case, it is), the attempt to send a message to it at run time will cause an error. The reason the variable is not initialized is that no value has been assigned to it with an assignment statement.

No Such Method Error

Following is a final, and rather puzzling, example of a run-time error. You might not notice it, even after you examine the program and the error message.

The Program

```
public class PuzzlingRuntimeError {
   public static void Main (String [] args) {
      System.out.println ("Hello World!");
   }
}
```

The Run-time Error Message

```
Exception in thread "main" java.lang.NoSuchMethodError: main
```

Have you spotted the problem? The word main has been misspelled as Main. Remember that Java is case sensitive, and computers are exasperatingly literalminded. They never try to guess what you meant to say, so every mistake, no matter how small, is significant.

Illustration of Logic Errors

Incorrect output is the most obvious indication that there is a logic error in a program. For instance, suppose our temperature conversion program converts 212.0 degrees Fahrenheit to 100.06 instead of 100.0 degrees Celsius. The error is small, but we notice it. And if we do not, our customers, for whom we have written the program, surely will. We caused the problem by incorrectly using 31.9 instead of 32 in the following statement:

```
celsius = (Fahrenheit  - 31.9) * 5.0 / 9.0;
```

Test Data

Errors of this sort are usually found by running a program with test data for which we already know the correct output. We then compare the program's output with the expected results. If there is a difference, we reexamine the program's logic to determine why the program is not behaving as expected.

But how many tests must we perform on a program before we can feel confident that it contains no more logic errors? Sometimes the fundamental nature of a program provides an answer. Perhaps your mathematical skills are sufficiently fresh to recognize that the statement

```
celsius = (fahrenheit  - 32.0) * 5.0 / 9.0;
```

is actually the equation of a line. Because two points determine a line, if the program works correctly for two temperatures, it should work correctly for all. In general, however, it is difficult to determine how many tests are enough. But we often can break down the data into categories and test one number in each, the assumption being that if the program works correctly for one number in a category, it will work correctly for all the other numbers in the same category. Careful choice of categories then becomes crucial.

Desk Checking

We can also reduce the number of logic errors in a program by rereading the code carefully after we have written it. This is called *desk checking* and is best done when the mind is fresh. It is even possible to use mathematical techniques to prove that a program or segment of a program is free of logic errors. Because programming requires exhausting and excruciating attention to detail, avoid programming for long stretches of time or when tired, a rule you will break frequently unless you manage your time well.

Usually, we never can be certain that a program is error free, and after making a reasonable but large number of tests, we release the program for distribution and wait anxiously for the complaints. If we release too soon, the number of errors will be so high that we will lose credibility and customers, but if we wait too long, the competition will beat us to the market.

EXERCISE 3.5

1. At what point in the program development process are syntax errors, run-time errors, and logic errors detected?

2. Give an example of a run-time error and explain why the computer cannot catch it earlier in the program development process.

3. State the type of error (compile-time, run-time, or logic) that occurs in each of the following pieces of code:
a. x = y / 0
b. x + y = z
c. area = length + width

3.6 Debugging

After we have established that a program contains a logic error, or *bug* as it is more affectionately called, we still have the problem of finding it. Sometimes the nature of a bug suggests its general location in a program. We then can reread this section of the program carefully with the hope of spotting the error. Unfortunately, the bug often is not located where we expect to find it, and even if it is, we will probably miss it. After all, we thought we were writing the program correctly in the first place, so when we reread it, we tend to see what we were trying to say rather than what we actually said.

Programmers, as a consequence, are frequently forced to resort to a rather tedious, but powerful, technique for finding bugs. We add to the program extra lines of code that print the values of selected variables in the terminal window. Of course, we add these lines where we anticipate they will do the most good—that is, preceding and perhaps following the places in the program where we think the bug is mostly likely located. We then run the program again, and from the extra output, we can determine if any of the variables deviate from their expected values. If one of them does, then we know the bug is close by, but if none do, we must try again at a different point in the program. A variable's value is printed in the terminal window as follows:

```
System.out.println ("<some message>" + <variable name>);
```

Now let us try to find a bug that has been secretly inserted into the temperature conversion program. Suppose the program behaves as shown in Figure 3-3. Something is seriously wrong. The program claims that 212 degrees Fahrenheit converts to 41.1 degrees Celsius instead of the expected 100.

FIGURE 3-3
Incorrect output from the temperature conversion program

Perhaps we can find the problem by checking the value of fahrenheit just before celsius is calculated. The needed code looks like this:

```
System.out.println ("fahrenheit = " + fahrenheit);   ← This is the
    debugging code
celsius = (Fahrenheit  - 32.0) * 5.0 / 9.0;
```

When we run the program again with the debugging code included, we get the following output:

```
Enter degrees Fahrenheit: 212
Fahrenheit = 106.0
The equivalent in Celsius is 41.111111111111114
```

We entered 212, but for some reason, the program says the value of fahrenheit is 106. Perhaps we should look at the surrounding code and see if we can spot the error. Here is the relevant code:

```
. . .
System.out.print ("Enter degrees Fahrenheit: ");
fahrenheit = reader.readDouble() / 2.0;
System.out.println ("fahrenheit = " + fahrenheit);
celsius = (fahrenheit - 32.0) * 5.0 / 9.0;
. . .
```

Ah, there is the error. It looks as if the value entered by the user is divided by 2 just before it is assigned to the variable fahrenheit. Devious, but we cannot be deceived for long.

EXERCISE 3.6

1. Describe how one can modify code so that the cause of a logic error can be discovered.

2. The following program contains a logic error. Describe where to insert the appropriate debugging statements to help locate the error:

> **Hot Tip**
>
> Now you can turn to the supplemental material and read additional information related to debugging in your development environment.

```
import TerminalIO.*;

public class AreaTriangle{

    public static void main(String [] args){

        double base, height;
        KeyboardReader reader = new KeyboardReader();

        System.out.print("Enter the base of the triangle: ");
        base = reader.readDouble();
        System.out.print("Enter the height of the triangle: ");
        height = reader.readDouble();
        area = base + height / 2;
        System.out.println("The area is " + area);
    }
}
```

Case Study 2: Count the Angels

Computers have been applied to many complex problems, from predicting the weather, to controlling nuclear power plants, to playing the best chess in the world. Now this case study extends computing into the realm of metaphysics. Although this case study is fanciful and humorous, it illustrates important issues regarding analysis and design. During analysis and design we deliberately introduce several subtle errors, which during implementation we incorporate into the program, yet the program runs perfectly and gives no hint that there are underlying problems. As you read the case study, see if you can spot the errors. At the end we will point out what they are and make some general comments about the software development process.

Request

Write a program that determines how many angels can dance on the head of a pin.

Analysis

To solve this problem, we first consulted several prominent theologians. From them we learned that the pertinent factors are the size of the pinhead, the space occupied by a single angel, and the overlap between adjacent angels. Although angels are incorporeal beings, there are limits to the amount of overlap they can tolerate. Also, no region of space is ever occupied by three angels simultaneously. This seems somewhat confusing. On further questioning, the experts explained that angels have what one might call an overlap factor. If, for instance, this factor is 30 percent, then

■ An angel can share at most 30 percent of it space with other angels.

■ 70 percent of its space cannot be shared.

■ Within any shared region, only two angels can overlap.

The inputs to the program are now fairly obvious: the radius of the pinhead, the space occupied by an angel, and the overlap factor. Based on these inputs, program will calculate

■ The area of pinhead = πr^2.

■ Nonoverlapping space required by an angel = space occupied by an angel * (1 − overlap factor).

■ Number of angels on pinhead = area of pinhead / nonoverlapping space required by an angel.

■ The proposed interface is shown in Figure 3-4.

FIGURE 3-4
Proposed interface for the count angels program

```
Enter the radius in millimeters: 10
Enter the space occupied by an angel in square micrometers: 0.0001
Enter the overlap factor: 0.75
The number of angels = 1.256E7
```

Design

Our rather crude estimate for π is 3.14. Obviously, more accurate estimates yield more accurate calculations of the area. Later we will see how Java itself can provide an excellent estimate. Following is the pseudocode for the count angels program:

```
read radius
read angelSpace
read overlapFactor
area = 3.14 * radius * radius
nonOverlapSpace = angelSpace * (1.0 - overlapFactor)
numberAngels = area / nonOverlapSpace
print numberAngels
```

Implementation

The code is a straightforward translation of the pseudocode into Java. Comments are included.

```
/*CountAngels.java
Count the number of angels that can dance on the head of a pin.
1. The user inputs are
        The radius of the pinhead
        The space occupied by an angel
        The allowed overlap between angels subject to the restriction
        that no space can simultaneously be occupied by more than two
2. The program computes
        The area of the pinhead based on its radius
        The amount of nonoverlapping space required by an angel
        The number of angels based on the preceding two values
3. The program ends by printing the number of angels.
*/

import TerminalIO.*;

public class CountAngels {
    public static void main (String [] args) {

        KeyboardReader reader = new KeyboardReader();

        double radius;            //Radius of the pinhead in millimeters
        double angelSpace;        //Space occupied by an angel
                                  //in square micrometers
        double overlapFactor;     //Allowed overlap between angels from 0 to 1
        double area;              //Area of the pinhead in square millimeters
        double nonOverlapSpace;   //Non overlapping space required by an angel
        double numberAngels;      //Number of angels that can dance on the
                                  //pinhead

        //Get user inputs
        System.out.print ("Enter the radius in millimeters: ");
        radius = reader.readDouble();
        System.out.print
            ("Enter the space occupied by an angel in square micrometers: ");
```

```
        angelSpace = reader.readDouble();
        System.out.print ("Enter the overlap factor: ");
        overlapFactor = reader.readDouble();

        //Perform calculations
        area = 3.14 * radius * radius;
        nonOverlapSpace = angelSpace * (1.0 - overlapFactor);
        numberAngels = area / nonOverlapSpace;

        //Print results
        System.out.print ("The number of angels = " + numberAngels);
    }
}
```

Discussion

So what were the mysterious errors we mentioned and what is their general significance? There were three errors, two during analysis and one during design.

First Analysis Error

During analysis we did not consider the shape of the region occupied by an angel, overlapping or otherwise. To appreciate the significance of our oversight, consider the problem of placing as many pennies as possible on a plate without overlap. Because there are gaps between the pennies, the answer is not obtained by dividing the area of the plate by the area of a penny. Even if two pennies are allowed to overlap by some amount, there are still gaps. Thus our solution is correct only if angels can mold their shapes to eliminate all empty spaces. Unfortunately, we did not think of asking the theologians about this.

Second Analysis Error

Let us now simplify the problem and suppose that angels pack onto the pinhead without leaving empty spaces. Now the space occupied by two overlapping angels equals the space each would occupy alone minus the amount by which they overlap or

```
space for two overlapping angels
    = 2 * space occupied by an angel -
       space occupied by an angel * overlap factor
    = 2 * space occupied by an angel * (1.0 - overlap factor / 2)
```

Thus

```
space for one angel with overlap = space occupied by an angel *
    (1.0 - overlap factor / 2)
```

and

```
number of angels on pinhead = area of pinhead / space for one an
    gel with overlap
```

Well, we certainly got that wrong the first time.

Design Error

The radius of the pin is given in millimeters and the space requirements of an angel are given in square micrometers. Our calculations need to take this difference in units into account. We leave the actual correction as an exercise.

Conclusions

There are three lessons to draw from all this. First, the people who write programs usually are not the ones most familiar with the problem domain. Consequently, many programs fail to solve problems correctly either because they completely ignore important factors or because they treat factors incorrectly. Second, careful analysis and design are essential and demand careful thought. As you can see, the errors had nothing to do with programming per se, and they would have occurred even if we were solving the problem with paper and pencil. And by the way, before writing a program to solve a problem, we definitely need to know how to do it correctly by hand. We are not going to make a practice of making analysis and design errors, and we did so just this once in order to make a point. Third, just because computers perform complex calculations at lightning speed does not mean we should have unquestioning confidence in their outputs.

SUMMARY

In this lesson, you learned:

■ Java programs use the int data type for whole numbers (integers) and `double` for floating-point numbers (numbers with decimals).

■ Java variable and method names consist of a letter followed by additional letters or digits. Java keywords cannot be used as names.

■ `final` variables behave as constants; their values cannot change after they are declared.

■ Arithmetic expressions are evaluated according to precedence. Some expressions yield different results for integer and floating-point operands.

■ Strings may be concatenated to form a new string.

■ The compiler catches syntax errors. The JVM catches run-time errors. Logic errors, if they are caught, are detected by the programmer or user of the program at run time.

■ A useful way to find and remove logic errors is to insert debugging output statements to view the values of variables.

VOCABULARY *Review*

Define the following terms:

arithmetic expression	logic error	run-time error
comments	package	semantics
exception	pseudocode	syntax
literal	reserved words	virus

REVIEW *Questions*

WRITTEN QUESTIONS

Write a brief answer to the following questions.

1. Write a pseudocode algorithm that determines the batting average of a baseball player. *Hint:* To compute a batting average, divide number of hits by number of at-bats. Batting averages have three decimal places.

2. Give examples of an integer literal, a floating-point literal, and a string literal.

3. Declare variables to represent a person's name, age, and hourly wage.

4. Why must care be taken to order the operators in an arithmetic expression?

5. Is it possible to assign a value of type `int` to a variable of type `double`? Why or why not?

6. State which of the following are valid Java identifiers. For those that are not valid, explain why.
    A. `length`

B. `import`

C. `6months`

D. `hello-and-goodbye`

E. `HERE_AND_THERE`

FILL IN THE BLANK

Complete the following sentences by writing the correct word or words in the blanks provided.

1. In mixed-mode arithmetic with operand types `int` and `double`, the result type is always _____.

2. A method's name, parameters, and return type are also known as its _____.

3. The operation that joins two strings together is called _____.

4. End-of-line comments begin with the symbol _____.

5. A quotient results when the _____ operator is used with two operands of type _____.

PROJECTS

PROJECT 3-1

The surface area of a cube can be known if we know the length of an edge. Write a program that takes the length of an edge (an integer) as input and prints the cube's surface area as output. (*Remember*: analyze, design, implement, and test.)

PROJECT 3-2

Write a program that takes the radius of a sphere (a double) as input and outputs the sphere's diameter, circumference, surface area, and volume.

PROJECT 3-3

The kinetic energy of a moving object is given by the formula $KE=(1/2)mv^2$, where m is the object's mass and v is its velocity. Modify the program of Lesson 2, Project 2-5 so that it prints the object's kinetic energy as well as its momentum.

PROJECT 3-4

An employee's total weekly pay equals the hourly wage multiplied by the total number of regular hours plus any overtime pay. Overtime pay equals the total overtime hours multiplied by 1.5 times the hourly wage. Write a program that takes as inputs the hourly wage, total regular hours, and total overtime hours and displays an employee's total weekly pay.

PROJECT 3-5

Modify the program of Project 3-4 so that it prompts the user for the regular and overtime hours of each of five working days.

PROJECT 3-6

Use the `TurtleGraphics` package to display the employee's wages in a histogram. A histogram consists of a set of parallel horizontal lines. The length of each line is proportional to the quantity of the corresponding data item. Thus, after taking inputs and computing results, your program should create a pen that displays five horizontal lines of varying length.

CRITICAL *Thinking*

During the summer before the academic year, the registrar's office must enter new data for incoming freshmen. Design and implement a program that prompts the user for the following inputs:

Last name

First name

Class year (an integer)

Campus phone

After all the inputs are taken, the program should echo them as output.

INTRODUCTION TO CONTROL STATEMENTS

OBJECTIVES

Upon completion of this lesson, you should be able to:

- Use the increment and decrement operators.
- Use standard math methods.
- Use `if` and `if-else` statements to make choices.
- Use `while` and `for` loops to repeat a process.
- Construct appropriate conditions for control statements using relational operators.
- Detect and correct common errors involving loops.

Estimated Time: 3.5 hours

VOCABULARY

control statements

counter

count-controlled loop

flowchart

infinite loop

iteration

off-by-one error

overloading

random walk

sentinel

task-controlled loop

All the programs to this point have consisted of short sequences of instructions that are executed one after the other. Such a scheme, even if we allowed the sequence of instructions to become extremely long, would not be very useful. In computer programs, as in real life, instructions must express repetition and selection. Expressing these notions in Java is the major topic of this lesson, but before doing so we present a couple of topics that we will use throughout the rest of the lesson.

4.1 Additional Operators

Strange to say, the operators presented in this section are completely unnecessary, and we could easily manage without them; however, Java programmers use them frequently, and we cannot ignore them. Fortunately, they are convenient and easy to use.

Extended Assignment Operators

The assignment operator can be combined with the arithmetic and concatenation operators to provide extended assignment operators. Following are several examples:

```
int a = 17;
String s = "hi";


a += 3;             // Equivalent to a = a + 3;
```

91

```
a -= 3;             // Equivalent to a = a - 3;
a *= 3;             // Equivalent to a = a * 3;
a /= 3;             // Equivalent to a = a / 3;
a %= 3;             // Equivalent to a = a % 3;
s += " there";      // Equivalent to s = s + " there";
```

All these examples have the format

```
variable op= expression;
```

which is equivalent to

```
variable = variable op expression;
```

Note that there is no space between op and =. The extended assignment operators and the standard assignment operator have the same precedence.

Increment and Decrement

Java includes increment (++) and decrement (--) operators that increase or decrease a variable's value by one:

```
int m = 7;
double x = 6.4;


m++;        // Equivalent to m = m + 1;
x--;        // Equivalent to x = x - 1.0;
```

Here and throughout the book we use these operators only in the manner just illustrated; however, they can also appear in the middle of expressions. The rules for doing so are tricky and involve complexities that lead to programming errors and confusion. We encourage you to restrict yourself to the simplest uses of these operators. The precedence of the increment and decrement operators is the same as unary plus, unary minus, and cast.

Extra for Experts

For more information about these additional operators, see Appendix B.

EXERCISE 4.1

1. Translate the following statements to equivalent statements that use extended assignment operators:
   a. x = x * 2;
   b. y = y % 2;

2. Translate the following statements to equivalent statements that do not use the extended assignment operators:
   a. x += 5;
   b. x *= x;

4.2 Standard Classes and Methods

The standard Java library includes two classes that are frequently useful. These are the `Math` and the `Random` classes. The `Math` class provides a range of common mathematical methods, whereas the `Random` class supports programs that incorporate random numbers.

The `Math` Class

The `Math` class is quite extensive; however, we limit our attention to the methods listed in Table 4-1. Notice that two methods in the table are called `abs`. They are distinguished from each other by the fact that one takes an integer and the other takes a double parameter. Using the same name for two different methods is called *overloading*.

> **Extra for Experts**
>
> Other useful methods, including trigonometric methods, are described in Appendix B.

TABLE 4-1
Seven methods in the Math class

METHOD	WHAT IT DOES
`Static int abs(int x)`	Returns the absolute value of an integer `x`.
`static double abs(double x)`	Returns the absolute value of a double `x`.
`static double pow(double base, double exponent)`	Returns the base raised to the exponent.
`static long round(double x)`	Returns `x` rounded to the nearest whole number. (Note: Returned value must be cast to an `int` before assignment to an `int` variable.)
`static int max(int a, int b)`	Returns the greater of `a` and `b`.
`static int min(int a, int b)`	Returns the lesser of `a` and `b`.
`static double sqrt(double x)`	Returns the square root of `x`.

The `sqrt` Method

The next code segment illustrates the use of the sqrt method:

```
// Given the area of a circle, compute its radius.
// Use the formula a = πr², where a is the area and r is the radius.

double area = 10.0, radius;
radius = Math.sqrt(area / Math.PI);
```

To understand this code we must consider two points. First, messages are usually sent to objects; however, if a method's signature is labeled `static`, the message instead is sent to the method's class. Thus, to invoke the `sqrt` method, we send the `sqrt` message to the `Math` class. Second, in addition to methods, the `Math` class includes good approximations to several important constants. Here we use `Math.PI`, which is an approximation for π accurate to about 17 decimal places.

The Remaining Methods

The remaining methods described in Table 4-1 are illustrated in the following program code:

```
int m;
double x;

m = Math.abs(-7);            // m equals 7
x = Math.abs(-7.5);          // x equals 7.5

x = Math.pow(3.0, 2.0);      // x equals 3.0²·⁰ equals 9.0
x = Math.pow(16.0, 0.25);    // x equals 16.0⁰·²⁵ equals 2.0

m = Math.max(20, 40);        // m equals 40
m = Math.min(20, 40);        // m equals 20
m = (int) Math.round(3.14);  // m equals 3
m = (int) Math.round(3.5);   // m equals 4
```

The methods pow and sqrt both expect parameters of type double. If an int is used instead, it is automatically converted to a double before the message is sent. The methods max and min also have versions that work with doubles.

The Random Class

Programs are often used to simulate random events such as the flips of a coin, the arrival times of customers at a bank, the moment-to-moment fluctuations of the stock market, and so forth. At the heart of all such programs is a mechanism called a *random number generator* that returns numbers chosen at random from a predesignated interval. Java's random number generator is implemented in the Random class and utilizes the methods nextInt and nextDouble as described in Table 4-2.

TABLE 4-2
Methods in the Random class

METHOD	WHAT IT DOES
int nextInt(int n)	Returns an integer chosen at random from among 0, 1, 2, ..., $n - 1$
double nextDouble()	Returns a double chosen at random between 0.0 and 1.0, inclusive.

A program that uses the Random class first must import java.util.Random. Following is a segment of code that illustrates the importing of java.util.Random and the use of the nextInt method:

```
import java.util.Random;
. . .

// Generate 6 integers chosen at random from among 0, 1, 2

Random generator = new Random();
int i;

for (i = 1; i <= 6; i++){
    System.out.print(generator.nextInt(3) + " ");
}
```

The output from this segment of code is different every time it is executed Following are the results from three executions:

```
2 0 0 2 0 2
0 1 2 1 0 0
1 1 2 2 2 1
```

The method `nextDouble` behaves in a similar fashion but returns a `double` between 0.0 and 1.0.

EXERCISE 4.2

1. Assume that `x` has the value 3.6 and `y` has the value 4. State the value of the variable `z` after the following statements:

   a. `z = Math.sqrt(y);`
   b. `z = Math.round(x);`
   c. `z = Math.pow(y, 3);`
   d. `z = Math.round(Math.sqrt(x));`

2. Write code segments to print the following values in a terminal window:
   a. A random integer between 1 and 20, inclusive
   b. A random double between 1 and 10, inclusive.

4.3 A Shortcut for Inputting Data

When a program needs user inputs, it should first notify the user by displaying a prompt. Until now we have handled prompts by using `System.out.print` messages. However, there is a more convenient mechanism. Prompts can be passed as parameters to `read` messages, as shown in the following example:

```
fahrenheit = reader.readDouble("Enter degrees Fahrenheit: ");
```

We will use this approach throughout the rest of the lesson.

4.4 A Visit to the Farm

To introduce the main topic of this lesson, control statements, we begin with a "real world" example. Once upon a time in a faraway land, Jack visited his cousin Jill in the country and offered to milk the cow. Jill gave him a list of instructions:

```
fetch the cow from the field;
tie her in the stall;
milk her into the bucket;
pour the milk into the bottles;
drive her back into the field;
clean the bucket;
```

Although Jack was a little taken aback by Jill's liberal use of semicolons, he had no trouble following the instructions. A year later, Jack visited again. In the meantime, Jill had acquired a herd of cows, some red and some black. This time, when Jack offered to help, Jill gave him a more complex list of instructions:

```
herd the cows from the field into the west paddock;
while (there are any cows left in the west paddock){
   fetch a cow from the west paddock;
   tie her in the stall;
   if (she is red){
      milk her into the red bucket;
      pour the milk into red bottles;
   }else{
      milk her into the black bucket;
      pour the milk into black bottles;
   }
   put her into the east paddock;
}
herd the cows from the east paddock back into the field;
clean the buckets;
```

These instructions threw Jack for a loop (pun intended) until Jill explained

```
while (some condition){
   do stuff;
}
```

means do the stuff repeatedly as long as the condition holds true, and

```
if (some condition){
   do stuff 1;
}else{
   do stuff 2;
}
```

means if some condition is true, do stuff 1, and if it is false, do stuff 2.

"And what about all the semicolons and braces?" asked Jack.

"Those," said Jill, "are just a habit I picked up from programming in Java, where `while` and `if-else` are called *control statements*."

*E*XERCISE 4.4

1. Why does Jill use a while statement in her instructions to Jack?

2. Why does Jill use an `if-else` statement in her instructions to Jack? Write pseudocode control statements that are similar in style to the farm example for the following other situations:
   a. If a checker piece is red, then put it on a red square; otherwise, put it on a black square.
   b. If your shoes are muddy, then take them off and leave them outside the door.
   c. Pick up all the marbles on the floor and put them into a bag.

EXERCISE 4.4 Continued

3. Describe in English what the following code segments do:

a.

```
if (x is larger than y){
   temp = x;
   x = y;
   y = temp;
}else{
   temp = y;
   y = x;
   x = temp;
}
```

b.

```
sum = 0;
count = 1;
read an integer into total;
while (count is less than or equal to total){
   read an integer into x;
   sum = sum + Math.abs(x);
   count++;
}
if (total is greater than 0)
   print (sum / total)
```

4.5 The if and if-else Statements

We now explore in greater detail the if-else statement and the slightly simpler but related if statement. The meanings of if and else in Java sensibly adhere to our everyday usage of these words. Java and other third-generation programming languages achieve their programmer–friendly qualities by combining bits and pieces of English phrasing with some of the notational conventions of elementary algebra.

Principal Forms

To repeat, in Java, the if and if-else statements allow for the conditional execution of statements. For instance

```
if (condition){
   statement;        //Execute these statements if the
   statement;        //condition is true.
}
```

```
if (condition){
    statement;          //Execute these statements if the
    statement;          //condition is true.
}else{
    statement;          //Execute these statements if the
    statement;          //condition is false.
}
```

The indicated semicolons and braces are required; however, the exact format of the text depends on the aesthetic sensibilities of the programmer, who should be guided by a desire to make the program as readable as possible. Notice that braces always occur in pairs and that there is no semicolon immediately following a closing brace.

Additional Forms

The braces can be dropped if only a single statement follows the word `if` or `else`; for instance

```
if (condition)
    statement;
```

```
if (condition)
    statement;
else
    statement;
```

```
if (condition){
    statement;
       ...
    statement;
}else
    statement;
```

```
if (condition)
    statement;
else{
    statement;
       ...
    statement;
}
```

Braces

In general, it is better to overuse braces than to underuse them. Likewise, in expressions, it is better to overuse parentheses. The extra braces or parentheses can never do any harm, and their presence helps to eliminate logic errors.

Boolean Expressions

The condition in an `if` statement must be a **Boolean expression**. This type of expression returns the value `true` or `false`.

Flowchart

Figure 4-1 shows a diagram called a *flowchart* that illustrates the behavior of if and if-else statements. When the statements are executed, either the left or the right branch is executed depending on whether the condition is true or false.

FIGURE 4-1
Flowcharts for the if and if-else statements

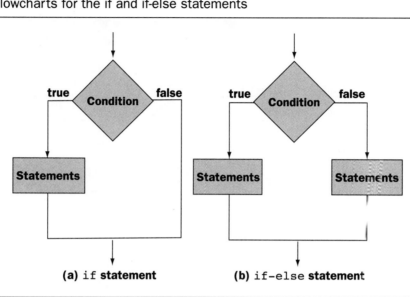

(a) if statement   (b) if-else statement

Examples

Following are some examples of if statements:

```
// Increase a salesman's commission by 10% if his sales are over $5000
if (sales > 5000)
    commission *= 1.1;
```

```
// Pay a worker $14.5 per hour plus time and a half for overtime
pay = hoursWorked * 14.5;
if (hoursWorked > 40){
    overtime = hoursWorked - 40;
    pay += overtime * 7.25;
}
```

```
// Let c equal the larger of a and b
if (a > b)
    c = a;
else
    c = b;
```

Relational Operators

The above previous examples all use the relational operator for greater than (>); however, there are five other relational operators. Table 4-3 shows the complete list of relational operators available for use in Java.

TABLE 4-3
Relational operators

OPERATOR	WHAT IT MEANS
>	greater than
>=	greater than or equal to
<	less than
<=	less than or equal to
==	equal to
!=	not equal to

The notation for the last two relational operators is rather peculiar at first glance, but it is necessary. The double equal signs (==) distinguish the equal to operator from the assignment operator (=). In the not equal to operator, the exclamation mark (!) is read as not. When these expressions are evaluated, their values will be either true or false depending on the values of the operands involved. For example, suppose

```
a = 3           c = 10
b = 7           d = -20
```

then

```
a < b           is true
a <= b          is true
a == b          is false
a != b          is true
a - b > c + d   is true  (the precedence of > is lower than + and -)
a < b < c       is invalid (syntactically incorrect)
a == b == c     is invalid
```

EXERCISE 4.5

1. What type of expression must the condition of an `if` statement contain?

2. Describe the role of the curly braces ({}) in an `if` statement.

3. What is the difference between an `if` statement and an `if-else` statement?

4. Assume that `x` is 5 and `y` is 10. Write the values of the following expressions:

   a. `x <= 10`

   b. `x - 2 != 0`

   c. `x > y`

EXERCISE 4.5 Continued

5. Given the following mini-specifications, write expressions involving relational operators:
   a. Determine if an input value x is greater than 0.
   b. Determine if a given number of seconds equals a minute.
   c. If a, b, and c are the lengths of the sides of a triangle and c is the largest side, determine if the triangle is a right triangle. (*Hint*: Use the Pythagorean equation and round the operand before comparing.)

6. Write the outputs of the following code segments:
   a.

```
int x = 20, y = 15, z;

if (x < y)
    z = 10;
else
    z = 5;
System.out.println(z);
```

   b.

```
int x = 2;

if (Math.round(Math.sqrt(x)) == 1)
    System.out.println("Equal");
else
    System.out.println("Not equal");
```

7. Given the following mini-specifications, write expressions involving `if-else` statements and output statements:
   a. Print the larger of two numbers.
   b. Prompt the user for two whole numbers and input them. Then print the numbers in numeric order.

4.6 The `while` Statement

The `while` statement provides a looping mechanism that executes statements repeatedly for as long as some condition remains true. Following is the `while` statement's format:

```
while (condition)        // loop test
    statement;           // one statement inside the loop body
```

```
while (condition){       // loop test
    statement;           // many statements
    statement;           // inside the
    ...                  // loop body
}
```

If the condition is false from the outset, the statement or statements inside the loop never execute. Figure 4-2 uses a flowchart to illustrate the behavior of a `while` statement.

FIGURE 4-2
Flowchart for a `while` statement

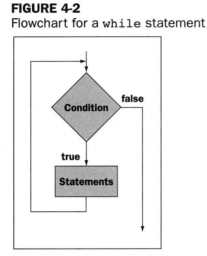

To help you become familiar with `while` statements, several short examples follow.

Compute 1 + 2 + ... + 100

The first example computes and displays the sum of the integers between 1 and 100, inclusive:

```
// Compute 1 + 2 + ... + 100

int sum = 0, cntr = 1;
while (cntr <= 100){
    sum += cntr;      // point p (we refer to this location in Table 4-4)
    cntr++;           // point q (we refer to this location in Table 4-4)
}
System.out.println (sum);
```

The behavior of this portion of code is clear. The variable `cntr` acts as a counter that controls how many times the loop executes. The counter starts at 1. Each time round the loop, it is compared to 100 and incremented by 1. Clearly the code inside the loop is executed exactly 100 times, and each time through the loop, `sum` is incremented by increasing values of `cntr`.

Count-Controlled Loops

This is an example of what is called a ***count-controlled loop***. The variable `cntr` is called the ***counter***.

Tracing the Variables

To understand the loop fully, we must analyze the way in which the variables change on each pass or *iteration* through the loop. Table 4-4 helps in this endeavor. On the 100th iteration, cntr is increased to 101, so there is never a 101st iteration, and we are confident that the sum is computed correctly.

TABLE 4-4
Trace of how variables change on each iteration through a loop

ITERATION NUMBER	VALUE OF CNTR AT POINT P	VALUE OF SUM AT POINT P	VALUE OF CNTR AT POINT Q
1	1	1	2
2	2	1 + 2	3
...	...	...	...
100	100	1 + 2 +...+ 100	101

Adding Flexibility

In the next example, we again add a sequence of integers, but vary the counter's starting value, ending value, and increment:

```
// Display the sum of the integers between a startingValue
// and an endingValue, using a designated increment.

int cntr, sum, startingValue, endingValue, increment;

startingValue = 10;
endingValue = 100;
increment = 7;

sum = 0;
cntr = startingValue;
while (cntr <= endingValue){
    sum += cntr;
    cntr += increment;
}
System.out.println (sum);
```

This portion of code computes the value of 10 + 17 + 24 + ... + 94. For greater flexibility the code could be modified to ask the user for the starting value, the ending value, and the increment.

Counting Backwards

We can also run the counter backward as in the next example, which displays the square roots of the numbers 25, 20, 15, and 10. Here the counter variable is called number:

```
// Display the square roots of 25, 20, 15, and 10

int number = 25;
while (number >= 10){
```

```
      System.out.println ("The square root of " + number +
                          " is " + Math.sqrt (number));
      number -= 5;
   }
```

The output is

```
The square root of 25 is 5.0
The square root of 20 is 4.47213595499958
The square root of 15 is 3.872983346207417
The square root of 10 is 3.1622776601683795
```

Task-Controlled Loop

Sometimes loops are structured so that they continue to execute until some task is accomplished. These are called *task-controlled loops*. To illustrate we write code that finds the first integer for which the sum $1 + 2 + ... + n$ is over a million:

```
// Display the first value n for which 1 + 2 + . . . + n
// is greater than a million

int sum = 0;
int number = 0;
while (sum <= 1000000){
   number++;
   sum += number;            // point p
}
System.out.println (number);
```

To verify that the code works as intended, we can reason as follows:

- The first time we reach point p, number = 1, sum = 1, and sum <= 1,000,000.

- The second time we reach point p, number = 2, sum = 1 + 2, and sum <= 1,000,000.

- Etc. ...

- The last time we reach point p, number = n, sum = 1 + 2 + ... + n and sum > 1,000,000.

- After that we will not enter the loop again, and number contains the first value to force the sum over a million.

Common Structure

All the preceding examples share a common structure:

```
initialize variables                            // initialize
while (condition){                              // test
   perform calculations and                     // loop
   change variables involved in the condition   // body
}
```

In order for the loop to terminate, each iteration through the loop must move the variables involved in the condition significantly closer to satisfying the condition.

EXERCISE 4.6

1. When does a while loop terminate execution?

2. List the four components of a `while` loop.

3. What happens if the condition of a `while` loop is false from the outset?

4. Describe in English what the following code segments do:

   a.

   ```
   int expo = 1, limit = 10;

   while (expo <= limit)
       System.out.println(expo + " " + Math.pow(2, expo));
   }
   ```

   b.

   ```
   KeyboardReader reader = new KeyboardReader();
   int product = 1;
   int x = reader.readInt("Enter a positive number or -999 to halt");

   while (x != -999){
      product *= x;
      x = reader.readInt("Enter a positive number or -999 to halt");
   }
   ```

5. Write code segments to perform the following tasks:
   a. Print the squares and cubes of the first 10 positive integers.
   b. Print 10 random integers between 1 and 10 inclusive.
   c. Input names and ages of people until a person's age is 100.

4.7 The for Statement

Count-controlled loops are used so frequently that many programming languages (including Java) include a special statement to make them easy to write. It is called the `for` statement, and it combines counter initialization, condition test, and update into a single expression. Following is its form:

```
for (initialize counter; test counter; update counter)
   statement;      // one statement inside the loop body
```

```
for (initialize counter; test counter; update counter){
   statement;      // many statements
   statement;      // inside the
   . . .;          // loop body
}
```

When the statement is executed, the counter is initialized. Then, as long as the test yields `true`, the statements in the loop body are executed, and the counter is updated. It is essential to understand that the counter is updated at the bottom of the loop, after the statements in the body have been executed. Even though the update appears at the top of the loop, it is executed at the bottom.

To demonstrate how the `for` statement works, we have rewritten the count-controlled loops presented in the previous sections:

```java
// Compute 1 + 2 + … + 100

int sum = 0, cntr;
for (cntr = 1; cntr <= 100; cntr++)
    sum += cntr;
System.out.println (sum);
```

```java
// Display the sum of the integers between a startingValue
// and an endingValue, using a designated increment.

int cntr, sum, startingValue, endingValue, increment;

startingValue = 10;
endingValue = 100;
increment = 7;

sum = 0;
for (cntr = startingValue; cntr <= endingValue; cntr += increment)
    sum += cntr;
System.out.println (sum);
```

```java
// Display the square roots of 25, 20, 15, and 10

int number;
for (number = 25; number >= 10; number -= 5)
    System.out.println ("The square root of " + number +
                        " is " + Math.sqrt (number));
```

Draw a Spiral

Below is a `for` statement that draws a spiral that wraps three times around the pen's home position at the center of the graphics window (see Figure 4-3):

```
StandardPen pen = new StandardPen();
double stepSize, degreesSoFar;

stepSize = 0;

for (degreesSoFar = 0; degreesSoFar <= 3 * 360; degreesSoFar += 33){
   stepSize++;
   pen.move (stepSize);
   pen.turn (33);
}
```

FIGURE 4-3
A spiral that wraps three times around the home position

Random Walk

If we draw a picture in which every turn of the pen is chosen at random, we are creating what is called a *random walk*. Figure 4-4 shows two random walks of 100 steps with a step size of 5. Every time the following code is executed a different random walk is generated:

```
Random generator = new Random();
StandardPen pen = new StandardPen();
int i, turnAmount;

for (i = 1; i <= 100; i++){
   turnAmount = generator.nextInt(360);
   pen.turn (turnAmount);
   pen.move (5);
}
```

FIGURE 4-4
Two random walks of 100 steps with a step size of 5

Count-Controlled Input

Programs often need to read and process repeating inputs. For instance, consider a program that computes the average of a list of numbers. Here the repeating input is a single number. As each number is read into the program, it is added to a sum. When all the numbers have been read, the program computes and prints the average. For maximum flexibility the program must process a list of any length, but this requirement seemingly creates a dilemma. When we write the program, we have no way of knowing how many numbers there will be in the list. So how can we write the program? There are two approaches. We illustrate one method in this section and the other in Section 4.8.

In the first method, we begin by asking the user for the length of the list and then we read exactly that many additional values:

```
KeyboardReader reader = new KeyboardReader();
double number, sum = 0;
int i, count;

count = reader.readInt("How long is the list? ");
for (i = 1; i <= count; i++){
   number = reader.readDouble("Enter a positive number: ");
   sum += number;
}

if (count == 0)
   System.out.println ("You entered no numbers.");
else
   System.out.println ("The average is " + sum / count);
```

Following is a sample run:

```
How long is the list? 3
Enter a positive number: 1.1
Enter a positive number: 2.2
Enter a positive number: 3.3
The average is 2.1999999999999997
```

Declaring the Loop Control Variable in a `for` Loop

The loop control variables in the examples shown thus far have been declared outside of and above the loop structure. However, the `for` loop allows the programmer to declare the loop control variable inside of the loop header. Following are equivalent loops that show these two alternatives:

```
int i;                          // Declare control variable above loop

for (i = 1; i <= 10; i++)
   System.out.println(i);
```

```
for (int i = 1; i <= 10; i++)    // Declare control variable in loop header
   System.out.println(i);
```

Although both loops are equivalent in function, the second alternative is considered preferable on most occasions for two reasons:

1. The loop control variable is visible only within the body of the loop where it is intended to be used.

2. The same name can be declared again in other for loops in the same program.

We discuss this important property of variable names, called *scope*, in more detail in Lesson 5.

EXERCISE 4.7

1. Describe in English what the following code segments do:
   a.

```
for (int expo = 1; expo <= limit; expo++)
    System.out.println(expo + " " + Math.pow(2, expo));
}
```

   b.

```
int base = 2;

for (int count = expo; count > 1; count--)
    base = base * base;
```

2. Write code segments that use for loops to perform the following tasks:
   a. Print the squares and cubes of the first 10 positive integers.
   b. Build a string consisting of the first 10 positive digits in descending order.

3. Translate the following for loops to equivalent while loops:
   a.

```
Pen StandardPen = new StandardPen();

for (int i = 1; i <= 100; i++){
    pen.turn(3.6);
    pen.move(1.6);
}
```

   b.

```
int base = 2;

for (int count = expo; count > 1; count--)
    base = base * base;
```

4.8 Nested Control Statements and the break Statement

Control statements can be nested inside each other in any combination that proves useful. We now present several illustrative examples and also demonstrate a mechanism for breaking out of a loop early, that is, before the loop condition is false. All the examples use for loops, but similar examples can be constructed using while loops.

Print the Divisors

As a first example, we write a code segment that asks the user for a positive integer n, and then prints all its proper divisors, that is, all divisors except one and the number itself. For instance, the proper divisors of 12 are 2, 3, 4, and 6. A positive integer d is a divisor of n if d is less than n and n % d is zero. Thus, to find n's proper divisors, we must try all values of d between 2 and n / 2. Here is the code:

```
// Display the proper divisors of a number

int n = reader.readInt("Enter a positive integer: ");

int limit = n / 2;

for (int d = 2; d <= limit; d++){
   if (n % d == 0)
      System.out.print (d + " ");
}
```

Is a Number Prime?

A number is prime if it has no proper divisors. We can modify the previous code segment to determine if a number is prime simply by counting its proper divisors. If there are none, the number is prime. Following is code that implements this plan:

```
// Determine if a number is prime

int n = reader.readInt("Enter an integer greater than 2: ");

int count = 0;
int limit = n/2;

for (int d = 2; d <= limit; d++){
   if (n % d == 0)
      count++;
}

if (count != 0)
   System.out.println ("Not prime.");
else
   System.out.println ("Prime.");
```

The break Statement

Most programmers, including the authors of this text, enjoy the challenge of trying to write efficient programs. You can do two things to improve the efficiency of the previous segment of code. First, the limit does not need to be as large as n / 2. If a*b equals n, then either a or b must be less than or equal to the square root of n. Second, as soon as we find the first divisor of n, we know n is not a prime, so there is no point in going around the loop again. To get out of a loop prematurely, that is, before the loop condition is false, we can use a break statement. A loop, either for or while, terminates immediately when a break statement is executed.

In the following segment of code, we check d after the for loop terminates. If n has a divisor, the break statement executes, the loop terminates early, and d is less than or equal to the limit. Following is the code:

```
// Determine if a number is prime

int n = reader.readInt("Enter an integer greater than 2: ");

int limit = (int)Math.sqrt (n);

int d;                                // Declare control variable here

for (d = 2; d <= limit; d++){
   if (n % d == 0)
      break;
}

if (d <= limit)                       // So it's visible here
   System.out.println ("Not prime.");
else
   System.out.println ("Prime.");
```

Note that the loop control variable d must now be declared above the loop so that it will be visible below it.

Sentinel-Controlled Input

In addition to the count-controlled input mentioned in the previous section, there is a second method for handling repeating user inputs. We again use the example of finding the average of a list of numbers. Now we read numbers repeatedly until we encounter a special value called a *sentinel* that marks the end of the list. For instance, if all the numbers in the list are positive, then the sentinel could be –1, as shown in the following code:

```
KeyboardReader reader = new KeyboardReader();
double number, sum = 0;
int count = 0;

while (true){
   number = reader.readDouble("Enter a positive number or -1 to quit: ");
   if (number == -1) break;
   sum += number;
   count++;
}
```

```
if (count == 0)
    System.out.println ("The list is empty.");
else
    System.out.println ("The average is " + sum / count);
```

Following is a sample run:

```
Enter a positive number or -1 to quit: 1.1
Enter a positive number or -1 to quit: 2.2
Enter a positive number or -1 to quit: 3.3
Enter a positive number or -1 to quit: -1
The average is 2.1999999999999997
```

EXERCISE 4.8

1. Describe in English what the following code segments do:

a.

```
for (int i = 1; i <= limit; i++)
    if (i % 2 == 0)
        System.out.println(i);
```

Extra for Experts

Like any other high-level language, Java is rich in control statements. For example, the `switch` statement, the `do-while` statement, and the `continue` statement allow the programmer to express selection and repetition in a different manner than the control statements in this lesson. For details on these statements, see Appendix B.

b.

```
Random gen = new Random();
int myNumber = gen.nextInt(10);
int x = 0;
int yourNumber;

while (x == 0){
    System.out.println("I'm guessing a number between 1 and 10.");
    yourNumber = reader.readInt("Which number is it? ");
    if (myNumber == yourNumber){
        System.out.println("That's it!");
        break;
    }else System.out.println("Sorry, try again");
}
```

2. Write code segments that use loops to perform the following tasks:
  a. Print the squares and cubes of the first 10 positive, odd integers.
  b. Build a string consisting of the first 10 positive, even digits in descending order.

Case Study: The Folly of Gambling

It is said, with some justification, that only the mathematically challenged gamble. Lotteries, slot machines, and gambling games in general are designed to take in more money than they pay out. Even if gamblers get lucky and win a few times, in the long run they lose. For this case study we have invented a game of chance called Lucky Sevens that seems like an attractive proposition, but which is, as usual, a sure loser for the gambler. The rules of the game are simple:

- Roll a pair of dice.

- If the sum of the spots equals 7, the player wins $4; else the player loses $1.

To entice the gullible, the casino tells players that there are lots of ways to win: (1, 6), (2, 5), etc. A little mathematical analysis reveals that there are not enough ways to win to make the game worthwhile; however, many people's eyes glaze over at the first mention of mathematics, so the challenge is to write a program that demonstrates the futility of playing the game.

Request

Write a program that demonstrates the futility of playing Lucky Sevens.

Analysis

We use the random number generator to write a program that simulates the game. The program asks the user how many dollars he has, plays the game repeatedly until the money is gone, and displays the number of rolls taken. The program also displays the maximum amount of money held by the player, thus demonstrating that getting ahead at some point does not avoid the inevitable outcome. Figure 4-5 shows the proposed interface.

FIGURE 4-5
Interface for the Lucky Sevens simulator

```
How many dollars do you have? 100
You are broke after 543 rolls.
You should have quit after 47 rolls when you had $113
```

Design

The design is captured in the following pseudocode:

```
read the initial amount the gambler has to wager
initialize to zero a counter representing the number of rolls

the maximum amount equals the initial amount
the count at the maximum equals zero

while (there is any money left){
   increment the rolls counter
   roll the dice

   if (the dice add to seven)
      add $4 to the gambler's amount
   else
      subtract $1 from the gambler's amount

   if (the amount is now greater than ever before){
      remember this maximum amount
      remember the current value of the rolls counter

}
```

```
        }
        display the rolls counter
        display the maximum amount
        display the count at the maximum amount
```

Implementation

Following is a program based on the pseudocode:

```java
/*LuckySevens.java
Simulate the game of lucky sevens until all funds are depleted.
1) Rules:
        roll two dice
        if the sum equals 7, win $4, else lose $1
2) The inputs are:
        the amount of money the user is prepared to lose
3) Computations:
        use the random number generator to simulate rolling the dice
        loop until the funds are depleted
        count the number of rolls
        keep track of the maximum amount
4) The outputs are:
        the number of rolls it takes to deplete the funds
        the maximum amount
*/

import TerminalIO.KeyboardReader;
import java.util.Random;

public class LuckySevens {
   public static void main (String [] args) {

      KeyboardReader reader = new KeyboardReader();
      Random generator = new Random();

      int die1, die2,         // two dice
          dollars,            // initial number of dollars (input)
          count,              // number of rolls to reach depletion
          maxDollars,         // maximum amount held by the gambler
          countAtMax;         // count when the maximum is achieved

      // Request the input
      dollars = reader.readInt("How many dollars do you have? ");

      // Initialize variables
      maxDollars = dollars;
      countAtMax = 0;
      count = 0;

      // Loop until the money is gone
      while (dollars > 0){
         count++;
```

```
        // Roll the dice.
        die1 = generator.nextInt (6) + 1; // 1-6
        die2 = generator.nextInt (6) + 1; // 1-6

        // Calculate the winnings or loses
        if (die1 + die2 == 7)
           dollars += 4;
        else
           dollars -= 1;

        // If this is a new maximum, remember it
        if (dollars > maxDollars){
           maxDollars = dollars;
           countAtMax = count;
        }
    }


    // Display the results
    System.out.println
        ("You are broke after " + count + " rolls.\n" +
         "You should have quit after " + countAtMax +
         " rolls when you had $" + maxDollars + ".");
    }
}
```

Output

Running this program is just about as exciting (in our opinion) as going to Las Vegas and it's a lot cheaper. (Perhaps we should translate it into a Java applet as shown in a later lesson in this book, make it part of a Web page, and charge people 10 cents each to run it.) Following are the results from several trial runs:

```
How many dollars do you have? 100
You are broke after 255 rolls.
You should have quit after 35 rolls when you had $110.
```

```
How many dollars do you have? 100
You are broke after 500 rolls.
You should have quit after 179 rolls when you had $136.
```

```
How many dollars do you have? 1000000
You are broke after 6029535 rolls.
You should have quit after 97 rolls when you had $1000003.
```

These results show that there is very little money to be gained in this game of chance—regardless of how much you have available to gamble.

4.9 Errors in Loops

We can easily make logic errors when coding loops, but we can avoid many of these errors if we have a proper understanding of a loop's typical structure. A loop usually has four component parts:

1. **Initializing statements.** These statements initialize variables used within the loop.

2. **Terminating condition.** This condition is tested before each pass through the loop to determine if another iteration is needed.

3. **Body statements.** These statements execute on each iteration and implement the calculation in question.

4. **Update statements.** These statements, which usually are executed at the bottom of the loop, change the values of the variables tested in the terminating condition.

A careless programmer can introduce logic errors into any one of these components. To demonstrate, we first present a simple but correct `while` loop and then show several revised versions, each with a different logic error. The correct version is

```
//Compute the product of the odd integers from 1 to 100
//Outcome — product will equal 3*5*...*99
product = 1;
i = 3;
while (i <= 100){
    product = product * i;
    i = i + 2;
}
System.out.println (product);
```

Initialization Error

We first introduce an error into the initializing statements. Because we forget to initialize the variable `product`, it retains its default value of zero.

```
//Error — failure to initialize the variable product
//Outcome — zero is printed
i = 3;
while (i <= 100){
    product = product * i;
    i = i + 2;
}
System.out.println (product);
```

Off-by-One Error

The next error involves the terminating condition:

```
//Error — use of "< 99" rather than "<= 100" in the
//      terminating condition
//Outcome — product will equal 3*5...*97
product = 1;
i = 3;
while (i < 99){
```

```
      product = product * i;
      i = i + 2;
   }
System.out.println (product);
```

This is called an *off-by-one error*, and it occurs whenever a loop goes around one too many or one too few times. This is one of the most common types of looping errors and is often difficult to detect. Do not be fooled by the fact that, in this example, the error is glaringly obvious.

Infinite Loop

Following is another error in the terminating condition:

```
//Error — use of "!= 100" rather than "<= 100" in the terminating condition
//Outcome — the program will never stop
product = 1;
i = 3;
while (i != 100){
   product = product * i;
   i = i + 2;
}
System.out.println (product);
```

The variable i takes on the values 3, 5, ..., 99, 101, ... and never equals 100. This is called an *infinite loop*. Anytime a program responds more slowly than expected, it is reasonable to assume that it is stuck in an infinite loop. Do not pull the plug. Instead, on a PC, select the terminal window and type Ctrl+C; that is, press Control and "C" simultaneously. This will stop the program.

Error in Loop Body

Following is an error in the body of the loop. Again, the error is comically obvious because we are pointing it out, but these kinds of errors often can be difficult to detect—particularly for the person who wrote the program.

> **Hot Tip**
>
> Turn to the supplemental materials for special instructions relating to your development environment and the ways to break out of an infinite loop in your environment.

```
//Error — use of + rather than * when com-
   puting product
//Outcome — product will equal 3+5+...+99
product = 1;
i = 3;
while (i <= 100){
   product = product + i;
   i = i + 2;
}
System.out.println (product);
```

Update Error

If the update statement is in the wrong place, the calculations can be thrown off even if the loop iterates the correct number of times:

```
//Error — placement of the update statement in the wrong place
//Outcome — product will equal 5*7*...*99*101
product = 1;
i = 3;
while (i <= 100){
   i = i + 2;             //this update statement should follow the calculation
   product = product * i;
}
System.out.println (product);
```

Effects of Limited Floating-Point Precision

Numbers that are declared as double have about 18 decimal digits of precision. This is very good, but it is not perfect and can lead to unexpected errors. Consider the following lines of code, which seem to be free of logic errors, yet produce an infinite loop:

```
double x;
for (x = 0.0; x != 1.0; x += 0.1)
   System.out.print (x + " ");
```

When this code runs, the expected output is

```
0.0  0.1  0.2  0.3  0.4  0.5  0.6  0.7  0.8  0.9  1.0
```

However, the actual output is

```
0.0   0.1   0.2   0.30000000000000004   0.4   0.5   0.6   0.7   0.7999999999999999
      0.8999999999999999   0.9999999999999999   1.0999999999999999   1.2   1.3
      1.4000000000000001   1.5000000000000002   ... etc ...
```

To understand what went wrong, consider the decimal representation of $\frac{1}{3}$. It is 0.33333... The 3s go on forever, and consequently no finite representation is exact. The same sort of thing happens when 1/5 is represented in binary as a double. Consequently, in the previous code, x never exactly equals 1.0 and the loop never terminates. To fix the code, we rewrite it as

```
double x, delta;
delta = 0.01;
for (x = 0.0; x <= 1.0 + delta; x += 0.1)
   System.out.print (x + " ");
```

The code now works correctly provided delta is less than the increment 0.1. The new output is

```
0.0  0.1  0.2  0.30000000000000004  0.4  0.5  0.6  0.7  0.7999999999999999
     0.8999999999999999  0.9999999999999999
```

Debugging Loops

If you suspect that you have written a loop that contains a logic error, inspect the code and make sure the following items are true:

- Variables are initialized correctly before entering the loop.

- The terminating condition stops the iterations when the test variables have reached the intended limit.

- The statements in the body are correct.

- The update statements are positioned correctly and modify the test variables in such a manner that they eventually pass the limits tested in the terminating condition.

In addition, when writing terminating conditions, it is usually safer to use one of the operators

```
<       <=      >       >=
```

than either of the operators

```
==      !=
```

as demonstrated earlier.

Also, if you cannot find an error by inspection, then use `System.out.println` statements to "dump" key variables to the terminal window. Good places for these statements are

- Immediately after the initialization statements

- Inside the loop at the top

- Inside the loop at the bottom

You will then discover that some of the variables have values different than expected, and this will provide clues that reveal the exact nature and location of the logic error.

*E*XERCISE 4.9

1. Describe the logic errors in the following loops:

a.

```
// Print the odd numbers between 1 and limit, inclusive
for (int i = 1; i < limit; i++)
   if (i % 2 == 1)
      System.out.println(i);
```

b.

```
// Print the first ten positive odd numbers
int number = 1;
while (number != 10)
   System.out.println(number);
   number += 2;
}
```

Design, Testing, and Debugging Hints

■ Most errors involving selection statements and loops are not syntax errors caught at compile time. Thus, you will detect these errors only after running the program, and perhaps then only with extensive testing.

■ The presence or absence of the `{}` symbols can seriously affect the logic of a selection statement or loop. For example, the following selection statements have a similar look but a very different logic:

```
if (x > 0){
    y = x;
    z = 1 / x;
}


if (x > 0)
    y = x;
    z = 1 / x;
```

The first selection statement guards against division by 0; the second statement only guards against assigning x to y. The next pair of code segments shows a similar problem with a loop:

```
while (x > 0){
    y = x;
    x = x - 1;
}


while (x > 0)
    y = x;
    x = x - 1;
```

The first loop terminates because the value of x decreases within the body of the loop; the second loop is infinite because the value of x decreases below the body of the loop.

■ When testing programs that use `if` or `if-else` statements, be sure to use test data that forces the program to exercise all of the logical branches.

■ Use an `if-else` statement rather than two `if` statements when the alternative courses of action are mutually exclusive.

■ When testing a loop, be sure to use limit values as well as typical values. For example, if a loop should terminate when the control variable equals 0, run it with the values 0, –1, and 1.

■ Be sure to check entry conditions and exit conditions for each loop.

■ For a loop with errors, use debugging output statements to verify the values of the control variable on each pass through the loop. Check this value before the loop is initially entered, after each update, and after the loop is exited.

SUMMARY

In this lesson, you learned:

■ Java has some useful operators for extended assignment, such as +=, and for increment and decrement.

■ The Math class provides several useful methods, such as sqrt and abs.

■ The Random class allows you to generate random integers and floating-point numbers.

■ if and if-else statements are used to make one-way and two-way decisions.

■ The comparison operators, such as ==, <=, and >=, return Boolean values that serve as conditions of control statements.

■ The while loop allows the program to run a set of statements repeatedly until a condition becomes false.

■ The for loop is a more concise version of the while loop.

■ Other control statements, such as an if statement, can be nested within loops. A break statement can be used in conjunction with an if statement to terminate a loop early.

■ There are many kinds of logic errors that can occur in loops. Examples are the off-by-one error and the infinite loop.

VOCABULARY *Review*

Define the following terms:		
control statements	infinite loop	random walk
counter	iteration	sentinel
count-controlled loop	off-by-one error	task-controlled loop
flowchart	overloading	

REVIEW *Questions*

WRITTEN QUESTIONS

Write a brief answer to the following questions.

1. Assume that the variables x and y contain the values 19 and 2, respectively. Indicate if the Boolean expressions below are true, false, or syntactically incorrect.
   A. x <= y

B. x * 2 > y

C. x - 1 == y * 9

D. x < y < 25

E. x * 2 != y

2. For each of the following items, write a valid Java statement.
   A. Display "greater" if the value of variable x is greater than the value of variable y. Otherwise, display "less."

   B. Add 10 to the value of x and display this value if the variable y is negative.

   C. Display the string A if x is greater than 90, B if x is greater than 80 and less than or equal to 90, or C otherwise.

3. Indicate whether or not each of the following loop headings is syntactically correct. If incorrect, explain why.
   A. while (x > 0)

   B. while (y = 10)

   C. while x != 0

4. Write a valid Java statement for each of the following items.
   A. Output the positive numbers from x up to y.

   B. Output the product of the squares of the numbers from x up to y.

   C. Output the numbers from y down to 0.

5. Assume that the variables x and y contain integers. Write code to perform the following tasks.
   A. Output the largest value, using an if statement.

   B. Output the largest value, using the method Math.max.

PROJECTS

PROJECT 4-1

When you first learned to divide, you expressed answers using a quotient and a remainder rather than a fraction or decimal quotient. For example, if you divided 9 by 2, you gave the answer as 4r. 1. Write a program that takes two integers as inputs and displays their quotient and remainder as outputs. Do not assume that the integers are entered in any order, but be sure to divide the larger integer by the smaller integer.

PROJECT 4-2

Write a program that takes the lengths of three sides of a triangle as inputs. The program should display whether or not the triangle is a right triangle.

PROJECT 4-3

A 2-minute telephone call to Lexington, Virginia, costs $1.15. Each additional minute costs $0.50. Write a program that takes the total length of a call in minutes as input and calculates and displays the cost.

PROJECT 4-4

The German mathematician Gottfried Leibniz developed the following method to approximate the value of π:

$\pi/4 = 1 - 1/3 + 1/5 - 1/7 + \ldots$

Write a program that allows the user to specify the number of iterations used in this approximation and displays the resulting value.

PROJECT 4-5

A local biologist needs a program to predict population growth. The inputs would be the initial number of organisms, the rate of growth (a real number greater than 0), the number of hours it takes to achieve this rate, and a number of hours during which the population grows. For example, one might start with a population of 500 organisms, a growth rate of 2, and a growth period to achieve this rate of 6 hours. Assuming that none of the organisms die, this would imply that this population would double in size every 6 hours. Thus, after allowing 6 hours for growth, we would have 1000 organisms, and after 12 hours, we would have 2000 organisms. Write a program that takes these inputs and displays a prediction of the total population.

PROJECT 4-6

Computers use the binary system, which is based on powers of 2. Write a program that displays the positive powers of 2. When the user enters the exponent at a prompt, the program displays 2 to that power. The program halts when the user enters –1.

PROJECT 4-7

Modify the program of Project 4-6 so that the user can specify the base (2 or higher) as well. The first line of the output should display which base was entered.

PROJECT 4-8

Teachers in most school districts are paid on a schedule that provides a salary based on their number of years of teaching experience. For example, a beginning teacher in the Bellingham School District might be paid $20,000 the first year. For each year of experience after this up to 10 years, a 2% increase over the preceding value is received. Write a program that displays a salary schedule for teachers in a school district. The inputs are the starting salary, the percentage increase, and the number of years in the schedule. Each row in the schedule should contain the year number and the salary for that year.

CRITICAL *Thinking*

Do the mathematical analysis needed to show that the Lucky Sevens game is not so lucky for the gambler. (*Hint:* The answer involves comparing the number of possible combinations of all totals and the number of possible combinations of 7.)

GETTING STARTED WITH JAVA

REVIEW *Questions*

TRUE/FALSE

Circle T if the statement is true or F if it is false.

T F 1. The first generation of programming language is assembly language.

T F 2. Java is an example of a high-level language.

T F 3. Mistakes found early in the coding process are much more expensive to fix than mistakes found later in the process.

T F 4. Byte code is a program that behaves like a computer.

T F 5. An arithmetic expression consists of operands and binary operators combined as in algebra.

T F 6. Programs manipulate objects by sending them methods.

T F 7. An integer is a positive or negative whole number.

T F 8. Strings are objects, not primitive data types.

T F 9. A relational operator is used to compare data items.

T F 10. Most, but not all, information in a computer is represented in binary form.

FILL IN THE BLANK

Complete the following sentences by writing the correct word or words in the blanks provided.

1. OOP stands for _____.

2. The software responsible for translating a program in a high-level language to machine code is called a(n) _____.

3. JVM stands for _____.

4. When an object receives a message, the object responds by running a block of code called a(n) _____.

5. Numbers with a fractional part are called _____.

6. When evaluating an expression, Java performs operations of higher _____ first unless overridden by _____.

7. Use the _____ operator to create a new string out of existing strings.

8. The `while` statement implements a _____.

9. A(n) _____ error occurs when a loop goes around one too many or one too few times.

10. A(n) _____ error occurs when a loop never stops.

WRITTEN QUESTIONS

Write a brief answer to the following questions or problems.

1. What is the purpose of a variable in a program?

2. What are the three types of programming errors? Give a brief example of each.

3. Describe the differences between the data types double and int.

4. Assume that the variables x and y contain the values 8 and 4, respectively. What are the values of the expressions listed below?
   A. `x + y * 2`

   B. `(x + y) / 3`

C. x - y * 3

D. x + y * 1.5

5. Write a valid Java statement that adds 5 to the value of variable x if the value of variable y is greater than 10.

6. A program has the following loop heading: `while (3 < x < 10)`. Is the heading syntactically correct? If incorrect, explain why.

7. Write a loop that outputs the first 10 positive powers of 2.

PROJECTS

SCANS **PROJECT U1-1**

Light travels at $3 * 10^8$ meters per second. A light year is the distance a light beam would travel in one year. Write a program that calculates and displays the value of a light year.

SCANS **PROJECT U1-2**

Write a program that expects the length and width of a rectangle as inputs. The program should calculate and display the rectangle's area and perimeter.

SCANS **PROJECT U1-3**

Top pick videos rent for $3.00 a night, whereas oldies rent for $2.00. Write a program that prompts the user for the number of each type of video to rent and outputs the total cost for that night.

SCANS **PROJECT U1-4**

The local bookstore has a markup of 10 percent on each book sold. Write a program that takes the sales price of a book as input and displays the following outputs:

■ The markup amount of the book just sold.

■ The wholesale amount (to go to the publisher) of the book just sold.

■ The total sales prices of all of the books sold thus far.

■ The total markup amount of all of the books sold thus far.

SCANS **CRITICAL**_Thinking_

Modify the program of Project U1-4 so that it continues to prompt the user for the price of books. The prompts should end when the user enters a negative number for the price. The program should then display the total sales price and total markup of the books sold.

THE NEXT STEP WITH JAVA

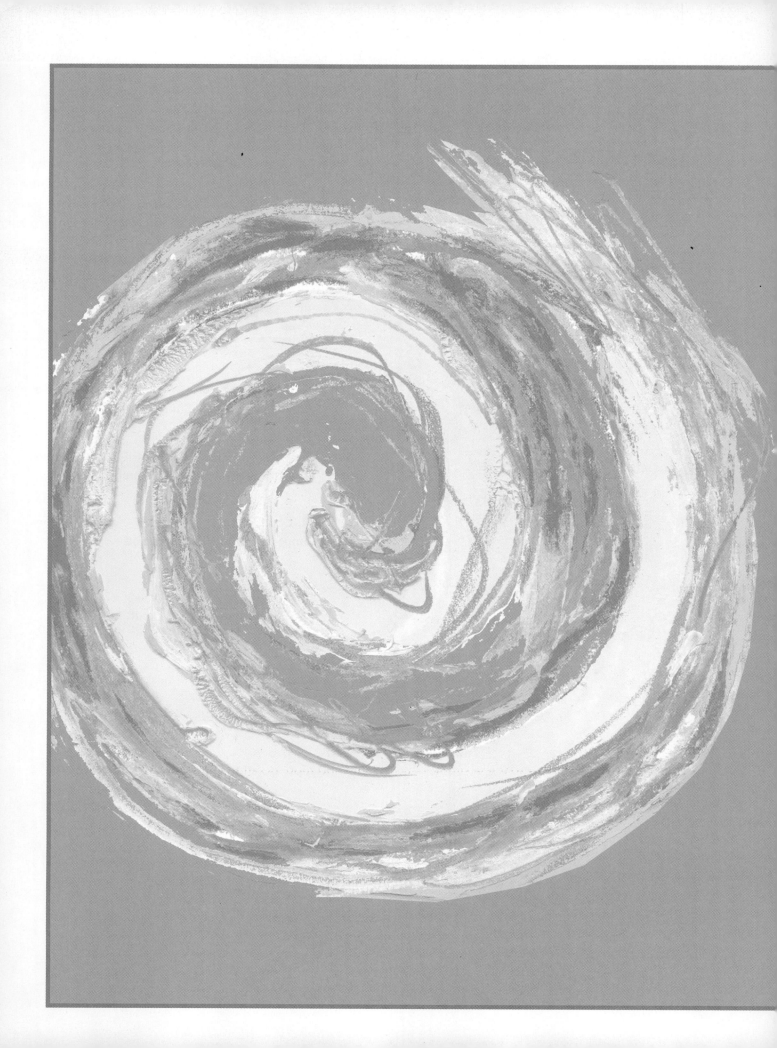

INTRODUCTION TO DEFINING CLASSES

OBJECTIVES

Upon completion of this lesson, you should be able to:

- Design and implement a simple class from user requirements.

- Organize a program in terms of a view class and a model class.

- Use visibility modifiers to make methods visible to clients and restrict access to data within a class.

- Write appropriate mutator methods, accessor methods, and constructors for a class.

- Understand how parameters transmit data to methods.

- Use instance variables, local variables, and parameters appropriately.

- Organize a complex task in terms of helper methods.

Estimated Time: 3.5 hours

VOCABULARY

accessor

actual parameter

behavior

constructor

encapsulation

formal parameter

helper method

identity

instantiation

lifetime

mutator

scope

state

visibility modifier

We introduced basic object-oriented terminology in Lesson 1 and have used it repeatedly since then. Until now, we have focused on choosing among predefined classes to solve problems. We have shown how to declare variables of different classes, assign objects to these variables, and send them messages. In this lesson, we explore the internal workings of objects. We introduce the basic structure of class definitions, so that you will be able to read and modify classes and create classes of your own. We restrict our focus to a few simple concepts and add more detail in later lessons.

5.1 The Internal Structure of Classes and Objects

As we stated in Lesson 1, an object is a run-time entity that contains data and responds to messages. A class is a software package or template that describes the characteristics of similar objects. These characteristics are of two sorts: variable declarations that define an object's data requirements (instance variables) and methods that define its behavior in response to messages. The combining of data and behavior into a single software package is called *encapsulation*. An object is an instance of its class, and the process of creating a new object is called *instantiation*.

Classes, Objects, and Computer Memory

We begin our discussion of classes and objects by considering how the Java virtual machine (JVM) handles them. When a Java program is executing, the computer's memory must hold

- All class templates in their compiled form

- Variables that refer to objects

- Objects as needed

Each method's compiled byte code is stored in memory as part of its class's template. Memory for data, on the other hand, is allocated within objects. Although all class templates are in memory at all times, individual objects come and go. An object first appears and occupies memory when it is instantiated, and it disappears automatically when no longer needed. The JVM knows if an object is in use by keeping track of whether or not there are any variables referencing it. Because unreferenced objects cannot be used, Java assumes that it is okay to delete them from memory. Java does this during a process called *garbage collection*. In contrast, C++ programmers have the onerous responsibility of deleting objects explicitly. Forgetting to delete unneeded objects wastes scarce memory resources, and accidentally deleting an object too soon or more than once can cause programs to crash. In large programs, these mistakes are easy to make and difficult to find. Fortunately, Java programmers do not have to worry about the problem.

Three Characteristics of an Object

Three characteristics of objects must be emphasized. First, an object has *behavior* as defined by the methods of its class. Second, an object has *state*, which is another way of saying that at any particular moment its instance variables have particular values. Typically, the state changes over time in response to messages sent to the object. Third, an object has its own unique *identity*, which distinguishes it from all other objects in the computer's memory, even those that might momentarily have the same state. An object's identity is handled behind the scenes by the Java virtual machine and should not be confused with the variables that might refer to the object. Of the variables, there can be none, one, or several. When there are none, the garbage collector purges the object from memory. Shortly, we will see an example in which two variables refer to the same object.

Clients, Servers, and Interfaces

When messages are sent, two objects are involved—the sender and the receiver, also called the *client* and the *server*, respectively. A client's interactions with a server are limited to sending it messages, so consequently a client needs to know nothing about the internal workings of a server. A client needs to know only a server's *interface*, that is, the list of the methods supported by the server. The server's data requirements and the implementation of its methods are hidden from the client, an approach we referred to as *information hiding* in Lesson 1. Only the person who writes a class needs to understand its internal workings. In fact, a class's implementation details can be changed radically without affecting any of its clients provided its interface remains the same.

EXERCISE 5.1

1. What is the difference between a class and an object?

EXERCISE 5.1 Continued

2. What happens to an object's memory storage when it is no longer referenced by a variable?

3. List the three important characteristics of an object.

4. Describe the client-server relationship.

5. What is the interface of a class?

5.2 A Student Class

The first class we develop in this lesson is called student. We begin by considering the class from a client's perspective. Later we will show its implementation. From a client's perspective, it is enough to know that a student object stores a name and three test scores and responds to the messages shown in Table 5-1.

TABLE 5-1
The interface for the student class

METHODS	DESCRIPTIONS
void setName(aString)	Example: stu.setName ("Bill"); Sets the name of stu to Bill.
String getName()	Example: str = stu.getName(); Returns the name of stu.
void setScore (whichTest, testScore)	Example: stu.setScore (3, 95); Sets the score on test 3 to 95. If whichTest is not 1, 2, or 3, then 3 is substituted automatically.
int getScore(whichTest)	Example: score = stu.getScore (3); Returns the score on test 3. If whichTest is not 1, 2, or 3, then 3 is substituted automatically.
int getAverage()	Example : average = stu.getAverage(); Returns the average of the test scores.
int getHighScore()	Example: highScore = stu.getHighScore(); Returns the highest test score.
String toString()	Example: str = stu.toString(); Returns a string containing the student's name and test scores.

Using Student Objects

Some portions of code illustrate how a client instantiates and manipulates student objects. First, we declare several variables, including two variables of type student.

```
Student s1, s2;        // Declare the variables
String str;
int i;
```

As usual, we do not use variables until we have assigned them initial values. We assign a new student object to s1 using the operator new:

```
s1 = new Student();    // Instantiate a student and associate it with the
                       // variable s1
```

It is important to emphasize that the variable s1 is a reference to a student object and is *not* a student object itself.

A student object keeps track of the name and test scores of an actual student. Thus, for a brand new student object, what are the values of these data attributes? That depends on the class's internal implementation details, but we can find out easily by sending messages to the student object via its associated variable s1:

```
str = s1.getName();
System.out.println (str);    // yields ""
i = s1.getHighScore();
System.out.println (i);      // yields 0
```

Apparently, the name was initialized to an empty string and the test scores to zero. Now we set the object's data attributes by sending it some messages:

```
s1.setName ("Bill");    // Set the student's name to "Bill"
s1.setScore (1,84);     // Set the score on test 1 to 84
s1.setScore (2,86);     //                 on test 2 to 86
s1.setScore (3,88);     //                 on test 3 to 88
```

Messages that change an object's state are called ***mutators***. To see if the mutators worked correctly, we use other messages to access the object's state (called *accessors*):

```
str = s1.getName();       // str equals "Bill"
i = s1.getScore (1);      // i equals 84
i = s1.getHighScore();    // i equals 88
i = s1.getAverage();      // i equals 86
```

The object's string representation is obtained by sending the toString message to the object:

```
str = s1.toString();
  // str  now equals
  // "Name:    Bill\nTest 1:  84\nTest2:  86\nTest3:  88\nAverage: 86"
```

When displayed in a terminal window (Figure 5-1), the string is broken into several lines as determined by the placement of the newline characters (`'\n'`). In addition to the explicit use of the `toString` method, there are other situations in which the method is called automatically. For instance, `toString` is called implicitly when a student object is concatenated with a string or is an argument to the method `println`:

```
str = "The best student is: \n" + s1;
   // Equivalent to: str = "The best student is: \n" + s1.toString();
System.out.println (s1);
   // Equivalent to: System.out.println (s1.toString());
```

FIGURE 5-1

Implicit use of `toString` when a student object is used in a `println` method

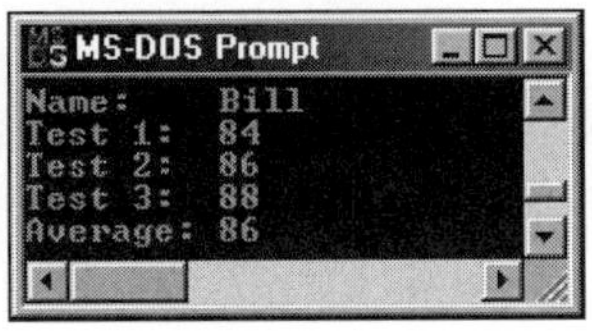

Because of these valuable implicit uses of the `toString` method, we frequently include this method in the classes we write. If we forget, however, Java provides a very simple version of the method through the mechanism of inheritance (mentioned in Lesson 1). The simplified version does little more than return the name of the class to which the object belongs.

Objects, Assignment, and Aliasing

We close this demonstration by associating a student object with the variable s2. Rather than instantiating a new student, we assign s1 to s2:

```
s2 = s1;              // s1 and s2 now refer to the same student
```

The variables s1 and s2 now refer to the *same* student object. This might come as a surprise because we might reasonably expect the assignment statement to create a second student object equal to the first, but that is not how Java works. To demonstrate that s1 and s2 now refer to the same object, we change the student's name using s2 and retrieve the same name using s1:

```
s2.setName ("Ann");   // Set the name
str = s1.getName();   // str equals "Ann". Therefore, s1 and s2 refer
                      // to the same object.
```

Table 5-2 shows code and diagrams that clarify the manner in which variables are affected by assignment statements. At any time, it is possible to break the connection between a variable and the object it references. Simply assign the value `null` to the variable:

```
Student s1;
s1 = new Student();    // s1 references the newly instantiated student
...                    // Do stuff with the student
s1 = null;             // s1 no longer references anything
```

TABLE 5-2
How variables are affected by assignment statements

CODE	DIAGRAM	COMMENTS
`int i, j;`	i ??? j ???	i and j are memory locations that have not yet been initialized, but which will hold integers.
`i = 3;` `j = i;`	i 3 j 3	i holds the integer 3. j holds the integer 3.
`Student s, t;`	s ??? t ???	s and t are memory locations that have not yet been initialized, but which will hold references to student objects.
`s = new Student();` `t = s;`	s t → student object ←	s holds a reference to a student object. t holds a reference to the same student object.

Table 5-2 demonstrates that assignment to variables of numeric types such as `int` produces genuine copies, whereas assignment to variables of object types does not.

Primitive Types, Reference Types, and the `null` Value

We mentioned earlier that two or more variables can refer to the same object. To better understand why this is possible we need to consider how Java classifies types. In Java, all types fall into two fundamental categories:

1. **Primitive types:** `int`, `double`, `boolean`, `char`, and the shorter and longer versions of these

2. **Reference types:** all classes, for instance, `String`, `Student`, `KeyboardReader`, and so on

As we first pointed out in Lesson 2, variables in these two categories are represented differently in memory. A variable of a primitive type is best viewed as a box that contains a value of that primitive type. In contrast, a variable of a reference type is thought of as a box that contains a pointer to an object. Thus, the state of memory after the following code is executed is shown in Figure 5-2.

```
int number = 45;
String word = "Hi";
```

FIGURE 5-2
The difference between primitive and reference variables

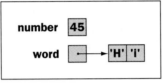

As previously mentioned, reference variables can be assigned the value `null`. If a reference variable previously pointed to an object, and no other variable currently points to that object, the computer reclaims the object's memory during garbage collection. This situation is illustrated in the following code segment and in Figure 5-3:

```
Student student = new Student("Mary", 70, 80, 90);
student = null;
```

FIGURE 5-3
The `Student` variable before and after it has been assigned the value `null`

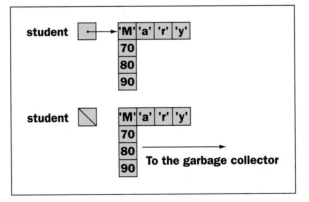

A reference variable can be compared to the `null` value, as follows:

```
if (student == null)
   // Don't try to run a method with that student!
else
   // Process the student

while (student != null){
   // Process the student
   // Obtain the next student from whatever source
}
```

As we already know from Lesson 3, when a program attempts to run a method with an object that is `null`, Java throws a ***null pointer exception***, as in the following example:

```
String str = null;
System.out.println (str.length());  // OOPS! str is null, so Java throws a
                                     // null pointer exception
```

☆ The Structure of a Class Template

Having explored the `student` class from a client's perspective, we now address the question of how to implement it. All classes have a similar structure consisting of four parts:

1. The class's name and some modifying phrases

2. A description of the instance variables

3. One or more methods that indicate how to initialize a new object (called ***constructor*** methods)

4. One or more methods that specify how an object responds to messages

The order of these parts can be varied arbitrarily provided part 1 (the class's name) comes first; however, for the sake of consistency, we will usually adhere to the order listed, which yields the following class template:

```
public class <name of class> extends <some other class>{

   // Declaration of instance variables
   private <type> <name>;
   ...

   // Code for the constructor methods
   public <name of class>() {
      // Initialize the instance variables
      ...
   }
   ...

   // Code for the other methods
   public <return type> <name of method> (<parameter list>){
      ...
   }
   ...
}
```

Some of the phrases used in the template need to be explained:

```
public class
```

Class definitions usually begin with the keyword `public`, indicating that the class is accessible to all potential clients. There are some alternatives to `public` that we ignore for now.

```
<name of class>
```

Class names are user-defined symbols, and thus, they must adhere to the rules for naming variables and methods. It is common to start class names with a capital letter and variable and method names with a lowercase letter. There is one exception. Names of final variables are usually completely capitalized.

```
extends <some other class>
```

Java organizes its classes in a hierarchy (see Lesson 1). At the root, or base, of this hierarchy is a class called `Object`. In the hierarchy, if class A is immediately above another class B, we say that A is the *superclass* or *parent* of B and B is a *subclass* or *child* of A (Figure 5-4). Each class, except `Object`, has exactly one parent and can have any number of children.

FIGURE 5-4
Relationship between superclass and subclass

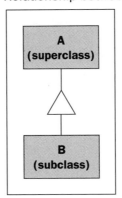

When a new class is created, it is incorporated into the hierarchy by extending an existing class. The new class's exact placement in the hierarchy is important because a new class inherits the characteristics of its superclass through a process called *inheritance* (Lesson 1). The new class then adds to and modifies these inherited characteristics, or in other words, the new class *extends* the superclass. If the clause `extends <some other class>` is omitted from the new class's definition, then by default, the new class is assumed to be a subclass of `Object`.

```
private <type> <name>
```

Instance variables are nearly always declared to be `private`. This prevents clients from referring to the instance variables directly. Making instance variables `private` is an important aspect of information hiding.

```
public <return type> <name of method>
```

Methods are usually declared to be public, which allows clients to refer to them.

The clauses private and public are called *visibility modifiers*. If both private and public are omitted, the consequences vary with the circumstances. Without explaining why, suffice it to say that in most situations, omitting the visibility modifier is equivalent to using public. In most situations, we will use private for instance variables unless there is some compelling reason to declare them public.

To illustrate the difference between private and public, suppose the class Student has a private instance variable name and a public method setName. Then

```
Student s;
s = new Student();
s.name = "Bill";      // Rejected by compiler because name is private
s.setName ("Bill")    // Accepted by compiler because setName is public
```

As a final note concerning our class template, notice that the constructor does not have a return type, that is, the name of the type of the value that it returns. All other methods do.

Implementation of the Student Class

Adhering to the format of our class template, we now implement the Student class. It is important to realize that other implementations are acceptable provided they adhere to the interface standards already established for student classes. Following is the code:

```java
/* Student.java
Manage a student's name and three test scores.
*/
public class Student {

    //Instance variables
    //Each student object has a name and three test scores
    private String name;          //Student name
    private int test1;            //Score on test 1
    private int test2;            //Score on test 2
    private int test3;            //Score on test 3

    //Constructor method

    public Student(){
    //Initialize a new student's name to the empty string and the test
    //scores to zero.
        name = "";
        test1 = 0;
        test2 = 0;
        test3 = 0;
    }

    //Other methods

    public void setName (String nm){
    //Set a student's name
        name = nm;
    }
```

```java
    public String getName (){
    //Get a student's name
        return name;
    }

    public void setScore (int i, int score){
    //Set test i to score
        if       (i == 1) test1 = score;
        else if (i == 2) test2 = score;
        else             test3 = score;
    }

    public int getScore (int i){
    //Retrieve score i
        if       (i == 1) return test1;
        else if (i == 2) return test2;
        else             return test3;
    }

    public int getAverage(){
    //Compute and return the average
        int average;
        average = (int) Math.round((test1 + test2 + test3) / 3.0);
        return average;
    }

    public int getHighScore(){
    //Determine and return the highest score
        int highScore;
        highScore = test1;
        if (test2 > highScore) highScore = test2;
        if (test3 > highScore) highScore = test3;
        return highScore;
    }

    public String toString(){
    //Construct and return a string representation of the student
        String str;
        str = "Name:    " + name  + "\n" +    // "\n" denotes a newline
              "Test 1:  " + test1 + "\n" +
              "Test 2:  " + test2 + "\n" +
              "Test 3:  " + test3 + "\n" +
              "Average: " + getAverage();
        return str;
    }
}
```

We explore the structure and behavior of methods in more detail later in this lesson. For now, the meaning of the code is fairly obvious. All the methods, except the constructor method, have a return type, although the return type may be void, indicating that the method in fact returns nothing. To summarize: When an object receives a message, the object activates the corresponding method. The method then manipulates the object's data as represented by the instance variables.

Constructors

The principal purpose of a constructor is to initialize the instance variables of a newly instantiated object. Constructors are activated when the keyword new is used and at no other time. A constructor is never used to reset instance variables of an existing object.

A class template can include more than one constructor, provided each has a unique parameter list; however, all the constructors must have the same name—that is, the name of the class. The constructors we have seen so far have had empty parameter lists and are called *default constructors*.

If a class template contains no constructors, the Java virtual machine provides a primitive default constructor behind the scenes. This constructor initializes numeric variables to zero and object variables to null, thus indicating that the object variables currently reference no objects. If a class contains even one constructor, however, the Java virtual machine no longer provides a default constructor automatically.

To illustrate these ideas, we add several constructors to the Student class. The following code lists the original default constructor and two additional ones:

```java
// Default constructor -- initialize name to the empty string and
// the test scores to zero.
public Student(){
   name = "";
   test1 = 0;
   test2 = 0;
   test3 = 0;
}

// Additional constructor -- initialize the name and test scores
// to the values provided.
public Student(String nm, int t1, int t2, int t3){
   name = nm;
   test1 = t1;
   test2 = t2;
   test3 = t3;
}

// Additional constructor -- initialize the name and test scores
// to match those in the parameter s.
public Student(Student s){
   name = s.name;
   test1 = s.test1;
   test2 = s.test2;
   test3 = s.test3;
}
```

A class is easier to use when it has a variety of constructors. Following is some code that shows how to use the different Student constructors. In a program, we would use the constructor that best suited our immediate purpose:

```java
Student s1, s2, s3;
s1 = new Student();                        // First student object has
                                           // name "" and scores 0,0,0
```

```
s2 = new Student ("Bill",70,80,90);  // Second student object has
                                     // name "Bill" and scores 70,80,90

s3 = new Student (s2);               // Third student object also has
                                     // name "Bill" and scores 70,80,90

s3.setName ("Ann");                  // Third student object now has
s3.setScore (1,75);                  // name "Ann" and scores 75,80,90
```

There are now three completely separate student objects. For a moment, two of them had the same state—that is, the same values for their instance variables—but that changed in the last two lines of code.

Chaining Constructors

When a class includes several constructors, the code for them can be simplified by *chaining* them. For example, the three constructors in the Student class each do the same thing—initialize the instance variables. We can simplify the code for the first and third constructors by calling the second constructor. To call one constructor from another constructor, we use the notation

```
this(<parameters>);
```

Thus, the code for the constructors shown earlier becomes

```
// Default constructor -- initialize name to the empty string and
// the test scores to zero.
public Student(){
    this("", 0, 0, 0);
}


// Additional constructor -- initialize the name and test scores
// to the values provided.
public Student(String nm, int t1, int t2, int t3){
    name = nm;
    test1 = t1;
    test2 = t2;
    test3 = t3;
}


// Additional constructor -- initialize the name and test scores
// to match those in the parameter s.
public Student(Student s){
    this(s.name, s.test1, s.test2, s.test3);
}
```

*E*XERCISE 5.2

1. What are mutators and accessors? Give examples.

2. List two visibility modifiers and describe when they are used.

EXERCISE 5.2 Continued

3. What is a constructor method?

4. Why do we include a `toString` method with a new user-defined class?

5. How can two variables refer to the same object? Give an example.

6. Explain the difference between a primitive type and a reference type and give an example of each.

7. What is the `null` value?

8. What is a null pointer exception? Give an example.

9. How does a default constructor differ from other constructors?

10. How does Java handle the initialization of instance variables if no constructors are provided?

11. What is the purpose of a constructor that expects another object of the same class?

5.3 Editing, Compiling, and Testing the Student Class

To use the `Student` class, we must save it in a file called **Student.java** and compile it by typing

```
javac Student.java
```

in a terminal window. If there are no compile-time errors, the compiler creates the byte code file **Student.class**. Once the `Student` class is compiled, applications can declare and manipulate student objects provided that

- The code for the application and **Student.class** are in the same directory or

- The **Student.class** is part of a package (see Appendix G)

Following is a small program that uses and tests the `Student` class. Figure 5-5 shows the results of running such a program.

> **Hot Tip**
>
> See the supplemental materials on the book's Web site for instructions specific to your development environment.

```java
public class TestStudent{

    public static void main (String[] args){
        Student s1, s2;
        String str;
        int i;

        s1 = new Student();      // Instantiate a student object
        s1.setName ("Bill");     // Set the student's name to "Bill"
```

```
        s1.setScore (1,84);      // Set the score on test 1 to 84
        s1.setScore (2,86);      //                    on test 2 to 86
        s1.setScore (3,88);      //                    on test 3 to 88
        System.out.println("\nHere is student s1\n" + s1);

        s2 = s1;                 // s1 and s2 now refer to the same object
        s2.setName ("Ann");      // Set the name through s2
        System.out.println ("\nName of s1 is now: " + s1.getName());
    }
}
```

FIGURE 5-5
Output from the TestStudent program

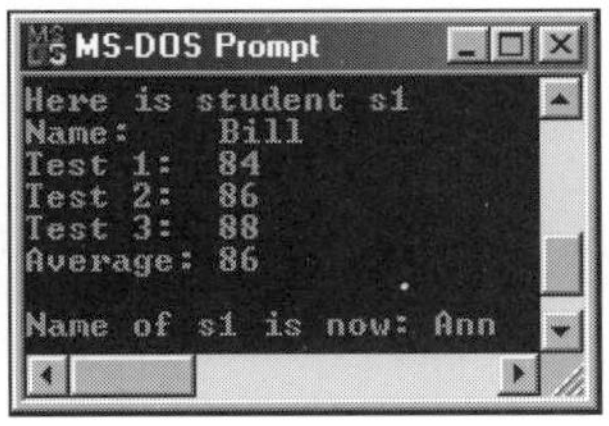

Finding the Location of Run-time Errors

Finding run-time errors in programs is no more difficult when there are several classes instead of just one. To illustrate, we introduce a run-time error into the Student class and then run the TestStudent program again. Following is a listing of the modified and erroneous lines of code. Figure 5-6 shows the error messages generated when the program runs.

```
public int getAverage(){
    int average = 0;
    average = (int) Math.round((test1 + test2 + test3) / average);
    return average;
}
```

FIGURE 5-6
Divide by zero run-time error message

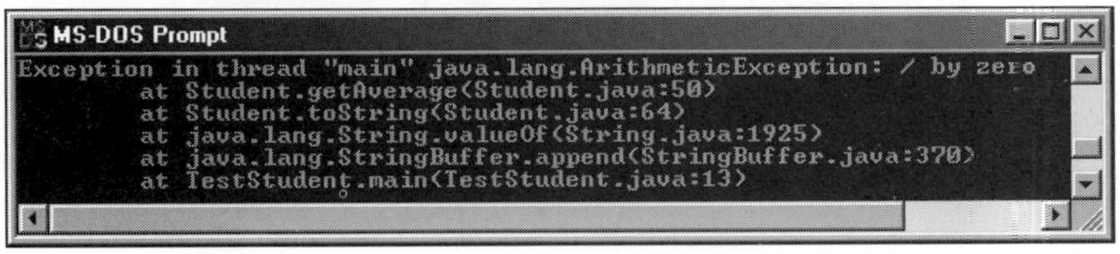

The messages indicate that

■ An attempt was made to divide by zero in the Student class's getAverage method (line 50)

■ Which had been called from the Student class's toString method (line 64)

■ Which had been called by some methods we did not write

■ Which, finally, had been called from the TestStudent class's main method (line 13)

Following are the lines of code mentioned:

```
Student getAverage line 50 :
         average = (int) Math.round ((test1 + test2 + test3) / average);
Student toString line 64   :
         "Average: " + getAverage();
TestStudent main line 13       :
         System.out.println ("\nHere is student s1\n" + s1);
```

We can now unravel the error.

- In line 13 of `main`, the concatenation (+) of `s1` makes an implicit call `s1.toString()`.

- In line 64 of `toString`, the `getAverage` method is called.

- In line 50 of `getAverage`, a division by zero occurs.

Case Study 1: Student Test Scores

Request

Write a program that allows the user to compare test scores of two students. Each student has three scores.

Analysis

A user's interaction with the program is shown in Figure 5-7.

FIGURE 5-7
The interface for the student test scores program

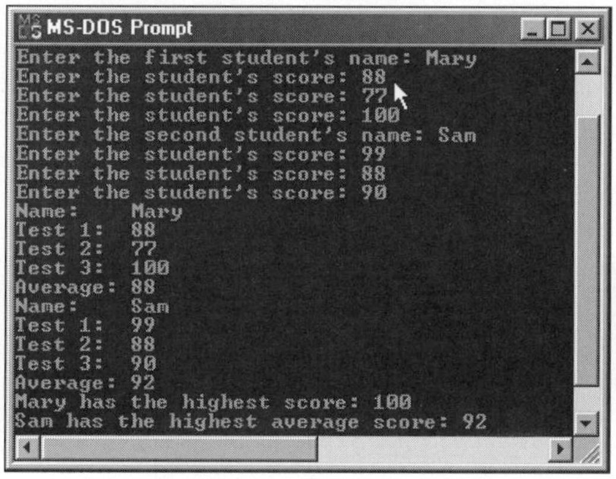

As you can see, the program

1. Prompts the user for the data for the two students.

2. Displays the information for each student, followed by the names of the students with the highest score and the highest average score.

As a standard part of analysis, we determine which classes are needed to support the application, and we delineate each class's overall responsibilities. The nature of the current problem suggests the use of two classes:

1. `Student`: Not surprisingly, the `Student` class presented earlier exactly fits the needs of this program.

2. `StudentInterface`: This class supports the user interface and declares and manipulates two student objects.

In general, it is a good idea to divide the code for most interactive applications into two sets of classes. One set of classes, which we call the **view**, handles the interactions with the human users, such as input and output operations. The other set of classes, called the **model**, represents the data used by the application. One of the benefits of this separation of responsibilities is that one can write different views for the same data model, such as a terminal-based view and a graphical-based view, without changing a line of code in the data model. Alternatively, one can write different representations of the data model without altering a line of code in the views. In most of the case studies that follow, we apply this framework, called the **model/view pattern**, to structure the code.

Design

During analysis, we decided to base the implementation on two classes: `Student` and `StudentInterface`. Now, during design, we specify the characteristics of these classes in detail. This involves determining the data requirements of each class and the methods that will be needed by the clients of the classes. This process is usually straightforward. To illustrate, let us pretend for the moment that we have not already written the `Student` class.

Designing the `Student` Class

We know from the work completed during analysis that a student object must keep track of a name and three test scores. The high score and the average can be calculated when needed. Thus, the data requirements are clear. The `Student` class must declare four instance variables:

```
private String name;
private int test1;
private int test2;
private int test3;
```

To determine the `Student` class's methods, we look at the class from the perspective of the clients who will be sending messages to student objects. In this application, the interface is the only client. There are some clues that help us pick the appropriate methods:

The interface needs to instantiate two student objects. This indicates the need for a constructor method, which we always include anyway.

When the user enters input data, the view needs to tell each student object its name and three test scores. This can be handled by two mutator methods: `setName(theName)` and `setScore(whichTest, testScore)`.

The view needs to ask the student objects for their complete information, the highest score, and the average score. This suggests four accessor methods: `toString()`, `getScore(whichTest)`, `getHighScore()`, and `getAverage()`.

We summarize our findings in a **class summary** box:

```
Class:
    Student
Private Instance Variables:
    String name
    int test1
    int test2
    int test3
Public Methods:
    constructors
    void setName (theName)
    String getName()
    void setScore (whichTest, testScore)
    int getScore (whichTest)
    int getAverage()
    int getHighScore()
    String toString()
```

Normally, we would complete a class's design by writing pseudocode for methods whose implementation is not obvious, so we skip this step here.

Designing the StudentInterface Class

The following is the class summary box for the StudentInterface class:

```
Class:
    StudentInterface
Private Instance Variables:
    Student student1
    Student student2
Public Methods:
    static void main (args)
```

Implementation

The code for the Student class has already been presented. Code for the StudentInterface class follows:

```java
import TerminalIO.KeyboardReader;

public class StudentInterface{

    public static void main (String[] args){
        // Instantiate the students and the keyboard object
        Student student1 = new Student();
        Student student2 = new Student();
        KeyboardReader reader = new KeyboardReader();
```

```
        String name;
        int score;

        // Input the first student's data
        name = reader.readLine("Enter the first student's name: ");
        student1.setName(name);
        for (int i = 1; i <= 3; i++){
           score = reader.readInt("Enter the student's score: ");
           student1.setScore(i, score);
        }

        // Input the second student's data
        name = reader.readLine("Enter the second student's name: ");
        student2.setName(name);
        for (int i = 1; i <= 3; i++){
           score = reader.readInt("Enter the student's score: ");
           student2.setScore(i, score);
        }

        // Output the two students' information
        System.out.println(student1);
        System.out.println(student2);

        // Output the student with the highest score
        if (student1.getHighScore() > student2.getHighScore()){
           name = student1.getName();
           score = student1.getHighScore();
        }else{
           name = student2.getName();
           score = student2.getHighScore();
        }
        System.out.println(name + " has the highest score: " + score);

        // Output the student with the highest average score
        if (student1.getAverage() > student2.getAverage()){
           name = student1.getName();
           score = student1.getAverage();
        }else{
           name = student2.getName();
           score = student2.getAverage();
        }
        System.out.println(name + " has the highest average score: " +
                    score);
   }
}
```

5.4 The Structure and Behavior of Methods

As mentioned in earlier lessons, a method is a description of a task that is performed in response to a message. The purpose of this section is to examine more closely some related concepts such as parameters, return types, and local variables.

The Structure of a Method Definition

Methods generally have the following form:

```
<visibility modifier> <return type> <method name> (<parameter list>){

    <implementing code>
}
```

Note the following points:

- The visibility modifier `public` is used when the method should be available to clients of the defining class. The visibility modifier `private` should be used when the method is merely a "helper" used by other methods within the class. We will say more about helper methods shortly.

- The return type should be `void` when the method returns no value. A `void` method often is a mutator, that is, a method that modifies an object's variables. If not `void`, the return type can be any primitive or reference type. Methods that return a value often are accessors, that is, methods that allow clients to examine the values of instance variables.

- Method names have the same syntax as other Java identifiers. The programmer should be careful to use names that describe the tasks that the methods perform, however; the names of verbs or verb phrases, such as `getName`, are usually appropriate for methods.

- As mentioned earlier in this book, parentheses are required whether or not parameters are present. The parameter list, if present, consists of one or more pairs of type names and parameter names, separated by commas.

A method's implementing code can be omitted. In that case, the method is called a *stub*. Stubs are used to set up skeletal, incomplete, but running programs during program development. For example, here is a class that contains only variable declarations and method stubs:

```
public class SomeClass{

    private int someVariable1, someVariable2;

    public void mutator1(int valueIn){}

    public void mutator2(int valueIn){}

    public int accessor1(){
        return 0;
    }
}
```

Return Statements

If a method has a return type, its implementing code must have at least one `return` statement that returns a value of that type. There can be more than one `return` statement in a method; however, the first one executed ends the method. Following is an example of a method that has two return statements but executes just one of them:

```
boolean odd(int i){
    if (i % 2 == 0)
```

```
        return false;
   else
        return true;
}
```

A `return` statement in a void method quits the method and returns nothing.

Formal and Actual Parameters

Parameters listed in a method's definition are called *formal parameters.* Values passed to a method when it is invoked are called *arguments* or *actual parameters.* As an example, consider the following two code segments:

```
// Client code

Student s = new Student();
KeyboardReader reader = new KeyboardReader();
int testScore = reader.readInt("Enter a test score:");
s.setScore(1, testScore);
```

```
// Server code

public void setScore (int i, int score){
   if        (i == 1) test1 = score;
   else if (i == 2) test2 = score;
   else              test3 = score;
}
```

In our example, the literal 1 and the variable `testScore` are the actual parameters and the names `i` and `score` are the formal parameters. When a method is called, the value of the actual parameter is automatically transferred to the corresponding formal parameter immediately before the method is activated. Thus, the number 1 and value of `testScore` are transferred to `i` and `score` immediately before `setScore` is activated (see Figure 5-8). It is important to understand that the variable `testScore` and the parameter `score` are otherwise completely independent of each other. For instance, changing the value of `score` would have no effect on the value of `testScore`.

FIGURE 5-8
Parameter passing

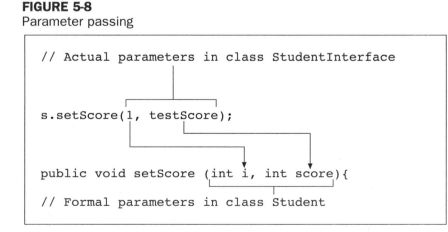

As mentioned in Lesson 3, when a method has multiple parameters, the caller must provide the right number and types of values. That is, the actual parameters must match the formal parameters in position and type. The rules for matching the types of a formal and an actual parameter are similar to those for assignment statements. The actual parameter's type must be either the same as or less inclusive than the type of the corresponding formal parameter. For example, the method `Math.sqrt`, which has a single formal parameter of type `double`, can receive either a `double` or an `int` as an actual parameter from the caller.

Parameters and Instance Variables

The purpose of a parameter is to pass information to a method. The purpose of an instance variable is to maintain information in an object. These roles are clearly shown in the method `setScore`. This method receives the score in the formal parameter `score`. This value is then transferred to one of the instance variables `test1`, `test2`, or `test3`.

Local Variables

Occasionally, it is convenient to have temporary working storage for data in a method. The programmer can declare *local variables* for this purpose. A good example occurs in the method `getAverage`. This method declares a variable `average`, assigns it the result of computing the average of the integer instance variables, and returns its value:

```java
public int getAverage(){
    int average;
    average = (int) Math.round((test1 + test2 + test3) / 3.0);
    return average;
}
```

Note that there is no need for the method to receive data from the client, so we do not use a parameter. Likewise, there is no need for the object to remember the average, so we do not use an instance variable for that.

Helper Methods

Occasionally, a task performed by a method becomes so complex that it helps to break it into subtasks to be solved by several other methods. To accomplish this, a class can define one or more methods to serve as *helper methods*. These methods are usually private, because only methods already defined within the class need to use them. For example, it is helpful to define a `debug` method when testing a class. This method expects a string and a double as parameters and displays these values in the terminal window. Following is the code:

```java
private void debug(String message, double value){
    System.out.println(message + " " + value);
}
```

This method can be called from any other method in the class to display information about the state of an integer or double variable. For example, the `Student` method `getAverage` might use this method as follows:

```java
public int getAverage(){
    int average;
```

```
    average = (int) Math.round((test1 + test2 + test3) / 3.0);
    debug("Average:", average);
    return average;
}
```

The advantage to this approach is that debugging statements throughout the class can be turned on or off by commenting out a single line of code:

```
private void debug(String message, double value){
    //System.out.println(message + " " + value);
}
```

We will see other examples of helper methods in the next case study.

EXERCISE 5.4

1. Explain the difference between formal parameters and actual parameters.

2. How does Java transmit data by means of parameters?

3. Define a method `sum`. This method expects two integers as parameters and returns the sum of the numbers ranging from the first integer to the second one.

4. What is the purpose of local variables?

5.5 Scope and Lifetime of Variables

As we have seen repeatedly, a class definition consists of two principal parts: a list of instance variables and a list of methods. When an object is instantiated, it receives its own complete copy of the instance variables, and when it is sent a message, it activates the corresponding method in its class. Thus, it is the role of objects to contain data and to respond to messages, and it is the role of classes to provide a template for creating objects and to store the code for methods. When a method is executing, it does so on behalf of a particular object, and the method has complete access to the object's instance variables. From the perspective of the methods, the instance variables form a common pool of variables accessible to all the class's methods. For this reason, we sometimes refer to them as *global variables*, in contrast to the variables declared within a method, which we call local variables.

Scope of Variables

The *scope* of a variable is that region of the program within which it can validly appear in lines of code. The scope of a parameter or a local variable is restricted to the body of the method that declares it, whereas the scope of a global or instance variable is all the methods in the defining class. Fortunately, the compiler flags as an error any attempt to use variables outside of their scope. Following is an example that illustrates the difference between local and global scope:

```
public class ScopeDemo {

    private int iAmGlobal;
```

```
public void clientMethod (int parm){

    int iAmLocal;
    ...

private int helperMethod (int parm1, int parm2){

    int iAmLocalToo;
    ...
}
...
```

Table 5-3 shows where each of the variables and parameters can be used (i.e., its scope):

TABLE 5-3
Variables and their scope

VARIABLE	helperMethod	clientMethod
iAmGlobal	Yes	Yes
parm	No	Yes
iAmLocal	No	Yes
parm1 and parm2	Yes	No
iAmLocalToo	Yes	No

Notice that formal parameters are also local in scope; that is, their visibility is limited to the body of the method in which they are declared.

Block Scope

Within the code of a method, there can also be nested scopes. Variables declared within any compound statement enclosed in braces are said to have *block scope*. They are visible only within the code enclosed by braces. For example, consider the following for loop to sum 10 input numbers. The accumulator variable sum is declared above the loop so the program can access it after the loop terminates. The loop declares its control variable i within its header and a local variable number to accept input within its body. The variables i and number thus have block scope, which is appropriate because they are needed only within the loop, and not outside it:

```
int sum = 0;
KeyboardReader reader = new KeyboardReader();
for (int i = 1; i <= 10; i++){
    int number = reader.readInt("Enter a number: ");
    sum += number;
}
System.out.println("The sum is " + sum);
```

Lifetime of Variables

The *lifetime* of a variable is the period during which it can be used. Local variables and formal parameters exist during a single execution of a method. Each time a method is called, it gets a fresh set of formal parameters and local variables, and once the method stops executing, the formal parameters and local variables are no longer accessible. Instance variables, on the other hand, last for the lifetime of an object. When an object is instantiated, it gets a complete set of fresh instance variables. These variables are available every time a message is sent to the object, and they, in some sense, serve as the object's memory. When the object stops existing, the instance variables disappear too.

Duplicating Variable Names

Because the scope of a formal parameter or local variable is restricted to a single method, the same name can be used within several different methods without causing a conflict. Whether or not we use the same name in several different methods is merely a matter of taste. When the programmer reuses the same local name in different methods, the name refers to a different area of storage in each method. In the next example, the names iAmLocal and parm1 are used in two methods in this way:

```java
public class ScopeDemo {

    private int iAmGlobal;

    public void clientMethod (int parm1){

        int iAmLocal;
        ...
    }

    private int helperMethod (int parm1, int parm2){

        int iAmLocal;
        ...
    }
    ...
}
```

A local name and a global variable name can also be the same, as shown in the following code segment:

```java
public class ScopeDemo {

    private int iAmAVariable;

    public void someMethod (int parm){

        int iAmAVariable;
        ...
        iAmAVariable = 3;         //Refers to the local variable
        this.iAmAVariable = 4;    //Refers to the global variable
        ...
```

```
    }

    public void someOtherMethod(int iAmAVariable){
       ...
       this.iAmAVariable = iAmAVariable;  //Assign the value of the
                                          //parameter
       ...                                //to the global variable
    }
    ...
}
```

In this example, the local variable `iAmAVariable` is said to *shadow* the global variable with the same name. Shadowing is considered a dangerous programming practice because it greatly increases the likelihood of making a coding error. When the variable name is used in the method, it refers to the local variable, and the global variable can be referenced only by prefixing "`this.`" to the name. The programmer uses the symbol `this` to refer to the current instance of a class within that class's definition.

When to Use Instance Variables, Parameters, and Local Variables

The only reason to use an instance variable is to remember information within an object. The only reason to use a parameter is to transmit information to a method. The only reason to use a local variable is for temporary working storage within a method. A very common mistake is to misuse one kind of variable for another. Following are the most common examples of these types of mistakes.

MISTAKE 1: GLOBAL VARIABLE USED FOR TEMPORARY WORKING STORAGE

This is perhaps the most common mistake programmers make with variables. As we have seen, a global variable is in fact not temporary, but survives the execution of the method. No harm may be done. If more than one method (or the same method on different calls) uses the same variable for its temporary storage, however, these methods might share information in ways that cause subtle bugs. For instance, suppose we decide to include an instance variable `sum` to compute the average score in the `Student` class. We also decide to compute the sum with a loop that uses the method `getScore` as follows:

```
private int sum;
...

public int getAverage(){
   for (int i = 1; i <= 3; i++)
      sum += getScore(i);
   return (int) Math.round(sum / 3.0);
}
```

The method is quite elegant but contains an awful bug. It runs correctly only the first time. The next time the method is called, it adds scores to the `sum` of the previous call, thus producing a much higher average than expected.

MISTAKE 2: LOCAL VARIABLE USED TO REMEMBER INFORMATION IN AN OBJECT

As we have seen, this intent cannot be realized because a local variable disappears from memory after its method has executed. This mistake can lead to errors in cases in which the programmer uses the same name for a local variable and a global variable and believes that the reference to the local variable is really a reference to the global variable (see our earlier discussion of shadowing). All that is required to cause this error is the use of a type name before the first assignment to the variable when it is used in a method. Following is an example from the Student class:

```
public void setName (String nm){
//Set a student's name
    String name = nm;        //Whoops! we have just declared name local.
}
```

In this case, the variable name has been accidentally "localized" by prefixing it with a type name. Thus, the value of the parameter nm is transferred to the local variable instead of the instance variable, and the Student object does not remember this change.

MISTAKE 3: METHOD ACCESSES DATA BY DIRECTLY REFERENCING GLOBAL VARIABLE WHEN IT COULD USE PARAMETER INSTEAD

Methods can communicate by sharing a common pool of variables or by the more explicit means of parameters and return values. Years of software development experience have convinced computer scientists that the second approach is better even though it seems to require more programming effort. There are three reasons to prefer the use of parameters:

1. Suppose that several methods share a pool of variables and that one method misuses a variable. Then other methods can be affected, and the resulting error can be difficult to find. For example, as the following code segment shows, if method m1 mistakenly sets the variable x to 0 and if method m2 uses x as a divisor, then when the program is run, the computer will signal an error in m2, even though the source of the error is in m1.

```
// Server class
 public class ServerClass{

    private int x;

    public void m1(){

       ...
       x = 0;              // The real source of the error
    }

    public void m2(){
       int y = 10 / x;  // Exact spot of run-time error
    }

    ...
 }
```

```
// Client class

public class ClientClass{
    private s = new ServerClass();
    public void m3(){
        s,m1();         // Misuse of x occurs, but is hidden from client
        s,m2();         // Run-time error occurs
    }
    ...
}
```

2. It is easier to understand methods and the relationships between them when communications are explicitly defined in terms of parameters and return values.

3. Methods that access a pool of shared variables can be used only in their original context, whereas methods that are passed parameters can be reused in many different situations. Reuse of code boosts productivity, so programmers try to create software components (in this case, methods) that are as reusable as possible. The method Math.sqrt is a good example of a context-independent method.

To summarize, it is a good idea to keep the use of global variables to a minimum, using them only when necessary to track the state of objects, and to use local variables and parameters wherever possible.

EXERCISE 5.5

1. What are the lifetimes of an instance variable, a local variable, and a parameter?

2. What is shadowing? Give an example and describe the bad things that shadowing might cause to happen in a program.

3. Consider the following code segment:

```
public class SomeClass{

    private int a, b;

    public void aMutator(int x, y){
        int c, d;
        <lots of code goes here>
    }
}
```

a. List the instance variables, parameters, and local variables in this code.
b. Describe the scope of each variable or parameter.
c. Describe the lifetime of each variable or parameter.

5.6 Turtle Graphics: Colors, Pen Widths, and Movement

Before we turn to our next case study, we need to introduce some other features of turtle graphics.

Color

As you might have noticed, the default color of a pen in turtle graphics is blue. However, you can change the color of a pen by sending it the setColor message. This message expects a parameter of type Color, which is included in the package java.awt. For example, the following code segment draws a vertical red line using the constant Color.red:

```
import java.awt.Color;
...
StandardPen pen = new StandardPen();
pen.setColor(Color.red);
pen.move(50);
```

The Color class includes several other constants to express commonly used colors, as shown in Table 5-4. For now do not worry about the meaning of the phrase "public static final Color" that precedes the name of each color.

TABLE 5-4
Turtle graphics Color constants

COLOR CONSTANT	COLOR
public static final Color red	red
public static final Color yellow	yellow
public static final Color blue	blue
public static final Color orange	orange
public static final Color pink	pink
public static final Color cyan	cyan
public static final Color magenta	magenta
public static final Color black	black
public static final Color white	white
public static final Color gray	gray
public static final Color lightGray	light gray
public static final Color darkGray	dark gray

Pen Width

The default width of a pen is two pixels (picture elements). For a finer or broader stroke, reset this value by sending the message setWidth to a pen. This message requires an integer parameter specifying the number of pixels. For example, the following line of code sets a pen's width to 5 pixels:

```
pen.setWidth(5);
```

A New Way to Move

The move method introduced in Lesson 2 makes the pen move a given number of pixels in its current direction. However, we often want a pen to move to a given position from its current position. To accomplish this task, the TurtleGraphics package includes another version of move that expects the coordinates of the new position as parameters. Thus, for example, the expression move(0,0) does the same thing as home(). The parameters to this method can be any coordinates in the Cartesian system, where the origin (0,0) is the pen's home position at the center of the graphics window.

Note that the method move(aDistance) and move(x, y) have the same name but do different things. This is an example of *overloaded methods*, that is, two or more methods in a class having the same name but differing in either the number or type of their parameters. Table 5-5 provides a complete list of the pen messages.

TABLE 5-5
Pen messages

PEN MESSAGE	DESCRIPTION
void home()	The pen jumps to the center of the graphics window without drawing and points north.
void setDirection(double degrees)	The pen points in the indicated direction. Due east corresponds to 0 degrees, north to 90 degrees, west to 180 degrees, and south to 270 degrees. Because there are 360 degrees in a circle, setting the direction to 400 would be equivalent to 400 – 360 or 40 and setting it to –30 would be equivalent to 360 – 30 or 330.
void turn(double degrees)	The pen adds the indicated degrees to its current direction. Positive degrees correspond to turning counterclockwise. The degrees can be an integer or floating-point number.
void down()	The pen lowers itself to the drawing surface.
void up()	The pen raises itself from the drawing surface.
void move(double distance)	The pen moves the specified distance in the current direction. The distance can be an integer or floating-point number and is measured in pixels. The size of a pixel depends on the monitor's resolution. For instance, when we say that a monitor's resolution is 800 by 600, we mean that the monitor is 800 pixels wide and 600 pixels high.
void move(double x, double y)	Moves the pen to the position (x, y).
void drawstring(String string)	Draws the string at the pen's position.
void setColor(Color color)	Sets the pen's color to the specified color.
void setWidth(int width)	Sets the pen's width to the specified width.

Case Study 2: Smiling Faces

Thus far, we have used a pen in graphics programs to draw shapes. As shapes get more complex, it is helpful to represent them as classes with distinct behavior in their own right. For example, the well-known smiling face icon has a circular head, two circular eyes, and a mouth. In this case study, we show how to turn this description of a common shape into a set of objects that the user can create and manipulate easily without directly asking a pen to do everything.

User Request

Write a program that allows the user to display and move a smiling face.

Analysis

The program prompts the user for the initial position of a smiling face. After the user enters this information, the program displays the face in a sketchpad window and prompts the user for a new position. After the user enters the new position, the program moves the face to it. The user can either continue to move the face in this manner or close the sketchpad window. Figure 5-9 shows a sample interface.

FIGURE 5-9
The interface for the smiling face program

Classes

We define two classes, `TestSmilingFace` and `SmilingFace`. The first class contains the method `main`, which handles the user interaction and creates and sends messages to the smiling face. The second class represents the smiling face, which either draws itself at its current position or erases itself (by first setting the pen color to white and then redrawing itself).

Design of `SmilingFace`

As you can see from the illustration (Figure 5-9), a smiling face consists of three circles and three line segments. To draw these, a pen is needed. In addition, it must know the coordinates of its center. Thus, there are three instance variables, one of type `standardPen` and two of type `double`. The radius of the face's outline, fixed at 50 pixels, is not represented by an instance variable.

The class has two constructors and three public instance methods. The default constructor positions a face of radius 50 at the pen's home position in the window. The other constructor expects the user to provide the coordinates of the face's center point.

The instance method `draw` expects no parameters and draws the face's elements at its current position. The instance method `erase` erases the face at its current position by setting the pen color to white and redrawing the face. The instance method `move` sets the face's center point coordinate to new values.

The private helper method `drawCircle` is used to draw a face's three circles. This method is based on the algorithm for drawing a 100-sided polygon introduced in Lesson 2. We also use a private helper method `drawLine` to draw the face's smile. Both methods use the pen method `move(x, y)` to place the pen at the appropriate locations. Following is the class summary box for `SmilingFace`:

```
Class:
   SmilingFace
Private Instance Variables:
   StandardPen pen
   double xPosition
   double yPosition
Public Methods:
   constructor
   void draw()
   void erase()
   void move(double x, double y)
Private Methods:
   void drawCircle
      (double x, double y, double r)
   void drawLine
      (double x1, double y1,
       double x2, double y2)
```

Implementation of `SmilingFace`

Following is a complete listing of the class `SmilingFace`, followed by some comments:

```java
import TurtleGraphics.*;
import java.awt.Color;

public class SmilingFace {

    private StandardPen pen;
    private double xPosition, yPosition;

    public SmilingFace(){
        xPosition = 0;
        yPosition = 0;
        pen = new StandardPen();
        pen.setColor(Color.red);
    }

    public SmilingFace(double x, double y){
        this();
        xPosition = x;
        yPosition = y;
    }

    public void draw(){
        double radius = 50.0;
```

```java
      // Draw the outline of the face
      drawCircle(xPosition, yPosition, radius);

      // Draw the left, then the right, eye.
      drawCircle(xPosition - radius / 2.5,
      yPosition + radius / 3, radius / 4);
      drawCircle(xPosition + radius / 2.5, yPosition + radius / 3,
            radius / 4);

      // Draw the horizontal part of the mouth
      drawLine(xPosition - radius / 3, yPosition - radius / 2,
            xPosition + radius / 3, yPosition - radius / 2);

      // Draw the left smile line
      drawLine(xPosition - radius / 3    , yPosition - radius / 2,
            xPosition - radius / 3 - 5, yPosition - radius / 2 + 5);

      // Draw the right smile line
      drawLine(xPosition + radius / 3    , yPosition - radius / 2,
            xPosition + radius / 3 + 5, yPosition - radius / 2 + 5);
   }

   public void erase(){
      pen.setColor(Color.white);
      draw();
      pen.setColor(Color.red);
   }


   public void move(double x, double y){
      xPosition = x;
      yPosition = y;
   }

   private void drawCircle(double x, double y, double r){
      double side = 2.0 * Math.PI * r / 120.0;
      pen.up();
      pen.move(x + r, y - side / 2.0);
      pen.setDirection(90);
      pen.down();
      for (int i = 0; i < 120; i++){
         pen.move(side);
         pen.turn(3);
      }
   }

   private void drawLine(double x1, double y1, double x2, double y2){
      // A stub method — exercise!
   }
}
```

Note the use of the helper methods `drawCircle` and `drawLine` in the method `draw`. Each helper method sends a message to the common instance variable pen but has parameters for the rest of the data. These data vary with the call, and thus we need to pass them as parameters. Note also that the method `draw` is called as a helper method within the method `erase`. If we had not structured this code in terms of helper methods, it would have been quite a bit longer, more complex, and unnecessarily repetitive.

Design and implementation of `TestSmilingFace`

The class `TestSmilingFace` contains the `main` method and its design and implementation are straightforward. After setting up the smiling face and the keyboard, the `main` method draws the face and enters a `while (true)` loop to handle the user's inputs. Following is the code:

```
import TurtleGraphics.*;
import TerminalIO.*;

public class TestSmilingFace {

   public static void main (String[] args){
      KeyboardReader reader = new KeyboardReader();
      double x, y, radius;
      x = reader.readDouble("Initial x position: ");
      y = reader.readDouble("Initial y position: ");
      SmilingFace face = new SmilingFace(x, y);
      face.draw ();

      while (true){
         x = reader.readDouble("New x position: ");
         y = reader.readDouble("New y position: ");
         face.erase();
         face.move(x, y);
         face.draw();
      }
   }
}
```

This program allows for many extensions, such as changing a face's radius, color, and mood. Some of these possibilities appear in the programming problems at the end of this lesson.

SUMMARY

In this lesson, you learned:

- Java class definitions consist of instance variables, constructors, and methods.

- Constructors initialize an object's instance variables when the object is created. A default constructor expects no parameters and sets the variables to reasonable default values. Other constructors expect parameters that allow clients to set up objects with specified data.

- Mutator methods modify an object's instance variables, whereas accessor methods merely allow clients to observe the values of these variables.

- The visibility modifier `public` is used to make methods visible to clients, whereas the visibility modifier `private` is used to encapsulate or restrict access to variables and methods.

- Helper methods are methods that are called from other methods in a class definition. They are usually declared to be private.

- Variables within a class definition can be instance variables, local variables, or parameters. Instance variables are used to track the state of an object. Local variables are used for temporary working storage within a method. Parameters are used to transmit data to a method.

- A formal parameter appears in a method's signature and is referenced in its code. An actual parameter is a value passed to a method when it is called. A method's actual parameters must match its formal parameters in number, position, and type.

- The scope of a variable is the area of program text within which it is visible. The scope of an instance variable is the entire class within which it is declared. The scope of a local variable or a parameter is the body of the method within which it is declared.

- The lifetime of a variable is the period of program execution during which its storage can be accessed. The lifetime of an instance variable is the same as the lifetime of a particular object. The lifetime of a local variable and a parameter is the time during which a particular call of a method is active.

VOCABULARY *Review*

Define the following terms:		
accessor	formal parameter	mutator
actual parameter	helper method	scope
behavior	identity	state
constructor	instantiation	visibility modifier
encapsulation	lifetime	

REVIEW *Questions*

WRITTEN QUESTIONS

Write a brief answer to the following questions.

1. Explain the difference between a class and an instance of a class.

2. Explain the difference between the visibility modifiers `public` and `private`.

3. What are accessor and mutator methods?

4. Develop a design for a new class called `BaseballPlayer`. The variables of this class are

    name (a `String`)

    team (a `String`)

    home runs (an `int`)

    batting average (a `double`)

    Express your design in terms of a class summary box. The class should have a constructor and methods for accessing and modifying all of the variables.

5. Explain how a parameter transmits data to a method.

6. What are local variables and how should they be used in a program?

PROJECTS

PROJECT 5-1

Add the extra constructors to the Student class of this lesson's first case study (Student Test Scores), and test these methods thoroughly with a Tester program.

PROJECT 5-2

A student object should validate its own data. The client runs this method, called validateData(), with a student object, as follows:

```
String result = student.validateData();
if (result == null)
   <use the student>
else
   System.out.println(result);
```

If the student's data are valid, the method returns the value null; otherwise, the method returns a string representing an error message that describes the error in the data. The client can then examine this result and take the appropriate action.

A student's name is invalid if it is an empty string. A student's test score is invalid if it lies outside the range from 0 to 100. Thus, sample error messages might be

```
"SORRY: name required"
```

and

```
"SORRY: must have 0 <= test score <= 100".
```

Implement and test this method.

PROJECT 5-3

Modify the smiling faces program of this lesson in the following ways and test each change with the tester application:

A. Complete the method drawLine.

B. Add the instance variable radius and color and the mutators setRadius and setColor.

C. Draw a sad face (angled lines point down).

D. Add the instance variable `smiling`, which is `true` if the face is happy and `false` if the face is sad, and the mutator `setMood(aBoolean)`. The `draw` method should draw either type of face depending on the value of this variable.

PROJECT 5-4

Redo the Lucky Sevens dice-playing program from Lesson 4 so that it uses dice objects. That is, design and implement a `Dice` class. Each instance of this class should contain the die's current side. Instead of using the `Random` class, the method `roll` should generate a new side using the method `Math.random()`. This method returns a `double` number d, where $0 <= d < 1$. To obtain a random number between 1 and 6 inclusive, you must multiply `Math.random()` by 6, cast the result to an `int`, and add 1. There should be an accessor method for a die's current value. The method `roll` is the only mutator method. Be sure to test the `Dice` class in a simple tester program before incorporating it into the application.

PROJECT 5-5

Develop a new class called `Car`. A car displays two wheels, a body (a long rectangle), and a passenger compartment (a shorter rectangle). Be sure to include the appropriate helper methods. Test-drive your new class in an interface similar to that of the smiling faces program.

PROJECT 5-6

Patrons of a library can borrow up to three books. A patron, therefore, has a name and up to three books. A book has an author and a title. Design and implement two classes, `Patron` and `Book`, to represent these objects and the following behavior:

■ The client can instantiate a book with a title and author.

■ The client can examine but not modify a book's title or author.

■ The client can ask a patron whether it has borrowed a given book (identified by title).

■ The client can tell a patron to return a given book (identified by title).

■ The client can tell a patron to borrow a given book.

The `Patron` class should use a separate instance variable for each book (a total of three). Each of these variables is initially `null`. When a book is borrowed, the patron looks for a variable that is not `null`. If no such variable is found, the method returns `false`. If a `null` variable is found, it is reset to the new book and the method returns `true`. Similar considerations apply to the other methods. Use the method `aString.equals(aString)` to compare two strings for equality. Be sure to include appropriate `toString` methods for your classes and test them with a tester program.

CRITICAL *Thinking*

Explain how you could modify the `Dice` class created in Project 5-4 to allow dice to be displayed with turtle graphics.

CONTROL STATEMENTS CONTINUED

OBJECTIVES

Upon completion of this lesson, you should be able to:

- Construct complex Boolean expressions using the logical operators && (AND), || (OR), and ! (NOT).

- Construct truth tables for Boolean expressions.

- Understand the logic of nested `if` statements and extended `if` statements.

- Test `if` statements in a comprehensive manner.

- Construct nested loops.

- Create appropriate test cases for `if` statements and loops.

Estimated Time: 3.5 hours

VOCABULARY

arithmetic overflow

boundary condition

combinatorial explosion

complete code coverage

equivalence class

extended `if` statement

extreme condition

logical operator

nested `if` statement

nested loop

quality assurance

robust

truth table

This lesson explores more advanced aspects of the control statements introduced in Lesson 4. Topics include logical operators, nested `if` statements, and nested loops. The lesson also describes strategies for testing programs that contain control statements. Programmers try to write programs that are free of logic errors, but they seldom succeed. Consequently, they must test their programs thoroughly before releasing them—and even so, errors will still slip through. Notice that we say "will" instead of "might." Software is so incredibly complex that no significant software product has ever been released free of errors; however, the situation would be much worse if we stopped emphasizing the importance of testing.

6.1 Logical Operators

Java includes three *logical operators* equivalent in meaning to the English words AND, OR, and NOT. These operators are used in the Boolean expressions that control the behavior of `if`, `while`, and `for` statements. Before we examine how these operators are used in Java, we review their usage in English. For instance, consider the following sentences:

1. **If** the sun is shining **AND** it is 8 a.m. **then** let's go for a walk **else** let's stay home.

2. **If** the sun is shining **OR** it is 8 A.M. **then** let's go for a walk **else** let's stay home.

3. **If NOT** the sun is shining **then** let's go for a walk **else** let's stay home.

The structure of all three sentences is similar, but their meanings are very different. For clarity we have emphasized key words. In these sentences, the phrases "the sun is shining" and "it is 8 A.M." are operands and the words AND, OR, and NOT are operators. At any particular moment, the value of a condition (true or false) depends on the values of the operands (also true or false) and the operator's meaning. For instance

■ In the first sentence, the operator is AND. Consequently, if both operands are true, the condition as a whole is true. If either or both are false, the condition is false.

■ In the second sentence, which uses OR, the condition is false only if both operands are false; otherwise, it is true.

■ In the third sentence, the operator NOT has been placed before the operand, as it would be in Java. This looks a little strange in English but is still understandable. If the operand is true, then the NOT operator makes the condition as a whole false.

We summarize these observations in the three parts of Table 6-1. Each part is called a *truth table*, and it shows how the value of the overall condition depends on the values of the operands. All combinations of values are considered. When there is one operand, there are two possibilities. For two operands, there are four; and for three operands, there are eight possibilities. In general there are 2^n combinations of true and false for n operands.

TABLE 6-1
Truth tables for three example sentences

THE SUN IS SHINING	IT IS 8 A.M.	THE SUN IS SHINING AND IT IS 8 A.M.	ACTION TAKEN
true	true	true	go for a walk
true	false	false	stay at home
false	true	false	stay at home
false	false	false	stay at home
THE SUN IS SHINING	IT IS 8 A.M.	THE SUN IS SHINING OR IT IS 8 A.M.	ACTION TAKEN
true	true	true	go for a walk
true	false	true	go for a walk
false	true	true	go for a walk
false	false	false	stay at home
THE SUN IS SHINING	NOT THE SUN IS SHINING	ACTION TAKEN	
true	false	stay at home	
false	true	go for a walk	

Dropping the column labeled "action taken," we can combine the information in the three truth tables in Table 6-1 into one table of general rules, as illustrated in Table 6-2. The letters P and Q represent the operands.

TABLE 6-2
General rules for AND, OR, and NOT

P	Q	P AND Q	P OR Q	NOT P
true	true	true	true	false
true	false	false	true	
false	true	false	true	true
false	false	false	false	

Three Operators at Once

Now that we know the rules, it is easy to construct and understand more complex conditions. Consider the following sentences:

A. *If* (the sun is shining **AND** it is 8 a.m.) **OR** (**NOT** your brother is visiting) *then* let's go for a walk *else* let's stay at home.

We have added parentheses to remove ambiguity. As usual, expressions inside parentheses are evaluated before those that are not. So now when do we go for a walk? The answer is at 8 A.M. on sunny days or when your brother does not visit; however, rearranging the parentheses changes the meaning of the sentence:

B. *If* the sun is shining **AND** (it is 8 A.M. **OR** (**NOT** your brother is visiting)) *then* let's go for a walk *else* let's stay at home.

Now before we go for a walk, the sun must be shining. In addition, one of two things must be true. Either it is 8 A.M. or your brother is not visiting. It does get a little confusing. Making truth tables for these sentences would make their meanings completely clear.

Java's Logical Operators and Their Precedence

In Java the operators AND, OR, and NOT are represented by `&&`, `||`, and `!`, respectively. Before writing code that uses these operators, we must consider their precedence as shown in Table 6-3. Observe that NOT (`!`) has the same high precedence as other unary operators, whereas AND (`&&`) and OR (`||`) have low precedence, with OR below AND.

TABLE 6-3
Positions of the logical and relational operators in the precedence scheme

OPERATION	SYMBOL	PRECEDENCE (FROM HIGHEST TO LOWEST)	ASSOCIATION
Grouping	( )	1	Not applicable
Method selector	.	2	Left to right
Unary plus	+	3	Not applicable
Unary minus	–	3	Not applicable
Not	!	3	Not applicable
Multiplication	*	4	Left to right
Division	/	4	Left to right
Remainder or modulus	%	4	Left to right
Addition	+	5	Left to right
Subtraction	–	5	Left to right
Relational operators	< <= > >= == !=	6	Not applicable
And	&&	8	Left to right
Or	||	9	Left to right
Assignment operators	= *= /= %= += –=	10	Right to left

Examples Using Logical Operators

Following are some illustrative examples based on the employment practices at ABC Company. The company screens all new employees by making them take two written tests. A program then analyzes the scores and prints a list of jobs for which the applicant is qualified. Following is the relevant code:

> **Hot Tip**
>
> A complete table of operator precedence can be found in the Appendix C.

```
KeyboardReader reader = new KeyboardReader();
int score1, score2;
score1 = reader.readInt("Enter the first test score: ");
score2 = reader.readInt("Enter the second test score: ");

// Managers must score well (90 or above) on both tests.
```

```
if (score1 >= 90 && score2 >= 90)
    System.out.println("Qualified to be a manager");

// Supervisors must score well (90 or above) on just one test
if (score1 >= 90 || score2 >= 90)
    System.out.println("Qualified to be a supervisor");

// Clerical workers must score moderately well on one test
// (70 or above), but not badly (below 50) on either.
if ((score1 >= 70 || score2 >= 70) &&
    !(score1 < 50 || score2 < 50))
    System.out.println("Qualified to be a clerk");
```

Boolean Variables

The complex Boolean expressions in the preceding examples can be simplified by using Boolean variables. A Boolean variable can be `true` or `false` and is declared to be of type `boolean`. Now we rewrite the previous examples using Boolean variables:

```
KeyboardReader reader = new KeyboardReader();
int score1, score2;
boolean bothHigh, atLeastOneHigh, atLeastOneModerate, noLow;
score1 = reader.readInt("Enter the first test score: ");
score2 = reader.readInt("Enter the second test score: ");
bothHigh            =  (score1 >= 90 && score2 >= 90); // parentheses
atLeastOneHigh      =  (score1 >= 90 || score2 >= 90); // optional
atLeastOneModerate =  (score1 >= 70 || score2 >= 70); // here
noLow               = !(score1 <  50 || score2 <  50);
if (bothHigh)
    System.out.println("Qualified to be a manager");
if (atLeastOneHigh)
    System.out.println("Qualified to be a supervisor");
if (atLeastOneModerate && noLow)
    System.out.println("Qualified to be a clerk");
```

Rewriting Complex Boolean Expressions

A complex `if` statement is sometimes so confusing that it is better rewritten as a series of simpler ones. Here is an example in a mixture of English and Java that we call *javish*:

```
if (the sun shines && (you have the time || it is Sunday))
    let's go for a walk;
else
    let's stay home;
```

In order to rewrite the previous code, we first create a truth table for the complex if statement, as shown in Table 6-4.

TABLE 6-4
Truth table for complex if statement

P: THE SUN SHINES	Q: YOU HAVE TIME	R: IT IS SUNDAY	P && (Q || R)	ACTION TAKEN
true	true	true	true	walk
true	true	false	true	walk
true	false	true	true	walk
true	false	false	false	stay home
false	true	true	false	stay home
false	true	false	false	stay home
false	false	true	false	stay home
false	false	false	false	stay home

Then implement each line of the truth table with a separate if statement involving only && (AND) and ! (NOT). Applying the technique here yields:

```
if ( the sun shines &&  you have time &&  it is Sunday) walk;
if ( the sun shines &&  you have time && !it is Sunday) walk;
if ( the sun shines && !you have time &&  it is Sunday) walk;
if ( the sun shines && !you have time && !it is Sunday) stay home;
if (!the sun shines &&  you have time &&  it is Sunday) stay home;
if (!the sun shines &&  you have time && !it is Sunday) stay home;
if (!the sun shines && !you have time &&  it is Sunday) stay home;
if (!the sun shines && !you have time && !it is Sunday) stay home;
```

In this particular example, the verbosity can be reduced without reintroducing complexity by noticing that the first two if statements are equivalent to

```
if ( the sun shines &&  you have time) walk;
```

and the last four are equivalent to

```
if (!the sun shines) stay home;
```

Putting all this together yields:

```
if ( the sun shines &&  you have time) walk;
if ( the sun shines && !you have time &&  it is Sunday) walk;
if (!the sun shines) stay home;
```

Of course, it is also possible to go in the other direction: that is, combine several if statements into a single more complex one, but no matter how we choose to represent complex conditions, truth tables are an essential tool for verifying the accuracy of the result. We can use them anytime we are uncertain about the meaning of the if statements we write.

Some Useful Boolean Equivalences

There is often more than one way to write a Boolean expression. For instance, the following pairs of Boolean expressions are equivalent, as truth tables readily confirm:

!(p || q)	equivalent to	!p && !q
!(p && q)	equivalent to	!p || !q
p || (q && r)	equivalent to	(p || q) && (p || r)
p && (q || r)	equivalent to	(p && q) || (p && r)

Using these equivalences sometimes enables us to rewrite a condition in a more easily understood form. Following is an example in which we display the word "reject" if x is not in the interval [3, 5], or alternatively, if x is less than 3 or greater than 5:

```
if (!(3 <= x && x <= 5))   System.out.println("reject");
if (!(3 <= x) || !(x <= 5)) System.out.println("reject");
if (x < 3 || x > 5)        System.out.println("reject");
```

Short-circuit Evaluation

The Java virtual machine sometimes knows the value of a Boolean expression before it has evaluated all of its parts. For instance, in the expression (p && q), if p is false, then so is the expression, and there is no need to evaluate q. Likewise, in the expression (p || q), if p is true, then so is the expression, and again there is no need to evaluate q. This approach, in which evaluation stops as soon as possible, is called *short-circuit evaluation*. In contrast, some programming languages use *complete evaluation*, in which all parts of a Boolean expression are always evaluated. These two methods nearly always produce the same results; however, there are times when short-circuit evaluation is advantageous. Consider the following example:

```
KeyboardReader reader = new KeyboardReader();
int count, sum;
count = reader.readInt("Enter the count: ");
sum = reader.readInt("Enter the sum: ");

if (count > 0 && sum / count > 10)
   System.out.println("average > 10");
else
   System.out.println("count = 0 or average <= 10");
```

If the user enters 0 for the count, the condition (count > 0 && sum / count > 10) contains a potential division by zero; however, because of short-circuit evaluation the division by zero is avoided.

EXERCISE 6.1

1. Fill in the truth values in the following truth table:

P	Q	! ((P || Q) && (P && Q))

2. Assume that A is true and B is false. Write the values of the following expressions:
   a. A || B
   b. A && B
   c. A && ! B
   d. ! (A || B)

3. Construct truth tables for the expressions listed in under the heading "Some Useful Boolean Equivalences" in this section to show that they are equivalent.

4. List the logical operators in the order in which each one would be evaluated at run time.

5. Construct a Boolean expression that tests whether the value of variable x is within the range specified by the variables min (the smallest) and max (the largest).

Case Study 1: Compute Weekly Pay

We illustrate the use of logical operators by writing a program to compute weekly pay.

Request

Write a program to compute the weekly pay of hourly employees.

Analysis

Employees are paid at a base rate for the first 40 hours they work each week. Hours over 40 are paid at an overtime rate equal to twice the base rate. An exception is made for part-time employees, who are always paid at the regular rate, no matter how many hours they work. The hourly rate is in the range $6.75 to $30.50 and hours worked in the range 1 to 60. We use a type attribute to distinguish between full-time (type 1) and part-time (type 2) employees. Figure 6-1 shows the user interface.

We would also like the program to be *robust*, that is, to handle invalid inputs without crashing or producing meaningless results. The easiest and best way to achieve this end is to check data values as soon as they are entered and reject those that are invalid. The user is then given another opportunity to enter a correct value, as shown in Figure 6-2.

FIGURE 6-1
Interface for the compute weekly pay program

```
Enter employee data
   Name (or blank to quit): Susan Jones
   Type (1 or 2): 1
   Hourly rate (between 6.75 and 30.50, inclusive): 10.50
   Hours worked (between 1 and 60, inclusive): 50
   The weekly pay for Susan Jones is $630.0
Enter employee data
   Name (or blank to quit): Bill Smith
   Type (1 or 2): 2
   Hourly rate (between 6.75 and 30.50, inclusive): 15.00
   Hours worked (between 1 and 60, inclusive): 60
   The weekly pay for Bill Smith is $900.0
Enter employee data
   Name (or blank to quit):
```

FIGURE 6-2
How the program responds to invalid inputs

```
Enter employee data
   Name (or blank to quit): Patricia Nelson
   Type (1 or 2): 3
   Type (1 or 2): 0
   Type (1 or 2): 1
   Hourly rate (between 6.75 and 30.50, inclusive): 99.00
   Hourly rate (between 6.75 and 30.50, inclusive): 3.75
   Hourly rate (between 6.75 and 30.50, inclusive): 20.89
   Hours worked (between 1 and 60, inclusive): 100
   Hours worked (between 1 and 60, inclusive): 25
   The weekly pay for Patricia Nelson is $522.25
```

Following the approach introduced in Lesson 5, we divide the work of the application into two classes: an interface class (`PayrollSystemInterface`) and an employee class (`Employee`). The `Employee` class has four instance invariables:

- Name

- Type

- Date

- Hours

   and three responsibilities:

- Provide information about data validation rules (`getNameRules`, `getTypeRules`, etc)

- Set instance variables provided the values are valid (return `true` if valid and `false` otherwise)

- Get the name and weekly pay

Figure 6-3 summarizes these points. The interface class has the usual structure and has the single method main, so we omit a class summary.

FIGURE 6-3
Summary of the Employee class

```
Class:
    Employee
Private Instance Variables:
  String name
  int type
  double rate
  int hours
Public Methods:
  constructor
  String getNameRules()
  String getTypeRules()
  String getRateRules()
  String getHoursRules()
  boolean setName(String nm)
  boolean setType(int tp)
  boolean setRate(double rt)
  boolean setHours(int hrs)
  String getName()
  double getPay()
```

Design

Following is the pseudocode for the interface:

```
while (true){
    read name, break if blank else set the employee name
    read type until valid and set the employee type
    read rate until valid and set the employee rate
    read hours until valid and set the employee hours
    ask the employee for name and pay and print these
}
```

An employee object computes pay as follows:

```
if (hours <= 40 || type == 2)
    pay = rate * hours;
else
    pay = rate * 40 +  rate * 2 * (hours - 40);
```

Implementation

The implementation uses two new String methods, trim and equals. When a trim() message is sent to a string, a new string that contains no leading or trailing spaces is returned:

```
String inputName, trimmedName;
inputName = reader.readLine("Enter the name: ");
trimmedName = inputName.trim();
```

The `equals` method is used to determine if two string objects contain equal strings. This is in contrast to the `==` operator, which determines if two string variables refer to the same object. Following is an illustration:

```
String a, b;
a = "cat";
b = reader.readLine("What do you call a small domestic feline? ");

if (a == b)
   System.out.println("a and b reference the same object.");
else
   System.out.println("a and b reference different objects.');

if (a.equals(b))
   System.out.println
   ("a and b reference objects that contain equal strings.");
else
   System.out.println
   ("a and b reference objects that contain unequal strings");
```

If the user enters "cat" when this code is run, the output is

```
a and b reference different objects.
a and b reference objects that contain equal strings.
```

We now return to the case study program and present the implementation, which is complicated by all the error checking we have decided to do. The interface class restricts itself to interacting with the user, and the `Employee` class controls data validation and computation of pay:

```
/* PayrollSystemInterface.java
1. Request employee name, type, pay rate, and hours.
2. Print employee name and pay.
3. Repeat until the name is blank.*/

import TerminalIO.KeyboardReader;

public class PayrollSystemInterface {

    public static void main (String [] args) {
        KeyboardReader reader = new KeyboardReader();
        Employee emp;      // employee
        String name;       //    name
        int    type;       //    type
        double rate;       //    hourly pay rate
        int    hours;      //    hours worked
        String prompt;     // user prompt;

        while (true){

            // Get the name and break if blank
            System.out.println("Enter employee data");
            name = reader.readLine("  Name (or blank to quit): ");
```

```
      name = name.trim(); // Trim off leading and trailing spaces
      if (name.length() == 0) break;
      emp = new Employee();
      emp.setName(name);

      // Get the type until valid
      while (true){
         prompt = "  Type (" + emp.getTypeRules() + "): ";
         type = reader.readInt(prompt);
         if (emp.setType(type)) break;
      }

      // Get the hourly pay rate until valid
      while (true){
         prompt = "  Hourly rate (" + emp.getRateRules() + "): ";
         rate = reader.readDouble(prompt);
         if (emp.setRate(rate)) break;
      }

      // Get the hours worked until valid
      //   To illustrate the possibilities we compress this code
      //   into a single hard-to-read statement.
      while (!emp.setHours(reader.readInt
            ("  Hours worked (" + emp.getHoursRules() + "): ")));

      // Print the name and pay
      System.out.println("  The weekly pay for " + emp.getName() +
                         " is $" + emp.getPay());
      }
   }
}
```

```
/*  Employee.java
1. Instance variables: name, type, rate, hours
2. Methods to
   get data validation rules
   set instance variables if data is valid
   get name and pay */

public class Employee {

   // Private Instance Variables:
   private String name;
   private int type;
   private double rate;
   private int hours;

   // Public Methods:
   public Employee(){
      name = "";
      type = 0;
```

```
        rate = 0;
        hours = 0;
   }

   public String getNameRules(){
      return "nonblank";
   }

   public String getTypeRules(){
      return "1 or 2";
   }

   public String getRateRules(){
      return "between 6.75 and 30.50, inclusive";
   }

   public String getHoursRules(){
      return "between 1 and 60, inclusive";
   }

   public boolean setName(String nm){
      if (nm.equals(""))
         return false;
      else{
         name = nm;
         return true;
      }
   }

   public boolean setType(int tp){
      if (tp != 1 && tp != 2)
         return false;
      else{
         type = tp;
         return true;
      }
   }

   public boolean setRate(double rt){
      if (!(6.75 <= rt && rt <= 30.50))
         return false;
      else{
         rate = rt;
         return true;
      }
   }

   public boolean setHours(int hrs){
      if (!(1 <= hrs && hrs <= 60))
         return false;
      else{
         hours = hrs;
         return true;
      }
```

```
    }

    public String getName(){
        return name;
    }

    public double getPay(){
        double pay;
        if (hours <= 40 || type == 2)
            pay = rate * hours;
        else
            pay = rate * 40 +  rate * 2 * (hours - 40);
        return pay;
    }
}
```

6.2 Testing if Statements

Quality assurance is the ongoing process of making sure that a software product is developed to the highest standards possible subject to the ever-present constraints of time and money. As we learned in Lesson 1, faults are fixed most inexpensively early in the development life cycle; however, no matter how much care is taken at every stage during a program's development, eventually the program must be run against well-designed test data. Such data should exercise a program as thoroughly as possible. At a minimum, the test data should try to achieve **complete code coverage**, which means that every line in a program is executed at least once. Unfortunately, this is not the same thing as testing all possible logical paths through a program, which would provide a more thorough test, but also might require considerably more test data.

We now design test data for the preceding case study. Because the program is so simple, the test data will provide complete code coverage and test all possible logical paths through the program. Varying the hourly rate has no particular significance in this problem, so we use an hourly rate of $10 for all the tests.

First, we test with an employee type of 1 and hours worked equal to 30 and 50 hours. Because we must compare the program's output with the expected results, we have chosen numbers for which it is easy to perform the calculations by hand. Having tested the program for the input 30 hours, we feel no need to test it for 29 or 31 hours, because we realize that exactly the same code is executed in all three cases. Likewise, we do not feel compelled to test the program for 49 and 51 hours. All the sets of test data that exercise a program in the same manner are said to belong to the same **equivalence class**, which means they are equivalent from the perspective of testing the same paths through the program. When the employee type is 1, test data for the payroll program fall into just two equivalence classes: hours between 0 and 40 and hours greater than 40.

The test data should also include cases that assess a program's behavior under **boundary conditions**—that is, on or near the boundaries between equivalence classes. It is common for programs to fail at these points. For the payroll program, this requirement means testing with hours equal to 39, 40, and 41.

We should test under **extreme conditions**—that is, with data at the limits of validity. For this we choose hours worked equal to 0 and 168 hours.

Testing with an employee type of 2 is much simpler, because the number of hours does not matter, but just to be on the safe side, we test with the hours equal to 30 and 50.

Finally, we must test the data validation rules. We need to enter values that are valid and invalid, and we must test the boundary values between the two. This suggests that we test using

- Type equal to 0, 1, 2, and 3

- Hourly rate equal to 6.49, 6.50, 10, 30.50, and 30.51

- Hours worked equal to 0, 1, 30, 60, and 61

Table 6-5 summarizes our planned tests. If from this discussion you draw the conclusion that testing is a lot of work, you are correct. Many software companies spend as much money on testing as they do on analysis, design, and implementation combined. The programs in this book, however, are fairly short and simple, and testing takes only a moderate amount of time.

> **Extra for Experts**
>
> For a discussion of an approach that puts testing at the center of software development, see Kent Beck, *Extreme Programming Explained: Embrace Change* (Boston: Addison-Wesley 2000).

TABLE 6-5
Test data for the payroll program

TYPE OF TEST	DATA USED
Code coverage	employee type: 1 hourly rate: 10 hours worked: 30 and 50
Boundary conditions	employee type: 1 hourly rate: 10 hours worked: 39, 40, and 41
Extreme conditions	employee type: 1 hourly rate: 10 hours worked: 0 and 168
Tests when the employee type is 2	employee type: 2 hourly rate: 10 hours worked: 30 and 50
Data validation rules	type: 0, 1, 2, and 3 hourly rate: 6.49, 6.50, 10, 30.50, and 30.51 hours worked: 0, 1, 30, 60, and 61

EXERCISE 6.2

1. Describe appropriate test data for the following code segments:

a.

```
if (number > 0)
    <action 1>
else
    <action 2>
```

EXERCISE 6.2 Continued

b.

```
if (0 < number && 100 > number)
    <action 1>
else
    <action 2>
```

2. What happens when we provide complete code coverage of a program?

3. What is an equivalence class? Give an example.

4. What are boundary conditions? Give an example.

5. What are extreme conditions? Give an example.

6. Suppose a teacher uses grades from 0 to 100 and wants to discount all grades below 60 in her records. Discuss the equivalence classes, boundary conditions, and extreme conditions used to test a program that processes this information.

Technology Careers

ARTIFICIAL INTELLIGENCE, ROBOTS, AND SOFTBOTS

You have seen in this lesson that a computer not only calculates results but also responds to conditions in its environment and takes the appropriate actions. This additional capability forms the basis of a branch of computer science known as *artificial intelligence*, or AI. AI programmers attempt to construct computational models of intelligent human behavior. These tasks involve, among many others, interacting in English or other natural languages, recognizing objects in the environment, reasoning, creating and carrying out plans of action, and pruning irrelevant information from a sea of detail.

There are many ways to construct AI models. One way is to view intelligent behavior as patterns of *production rules*. Each rule contains a set of conditions and a set of actions. In this model, an intelligent agent, either a computer or a human being, compares conditions in its environment to the conditions of all of its rules. Those rules with matching conditions are scheduled to fire—meaning that their actions are triggered—according to a higher-level scheme of rules. The set of rules is either hand-coded by the AI programmer or "learned" by using a special program known as a *neural net*.

Among other things, AI systems have been used to control *robots*. Although not quite up to the performance of Data in the TV series *Star Trek: The Next Generation*, these robots do perform mundane tasks such as assembling cars.

AI systems also are embedded in software agents known as *softbots*. For example, softbots exist to filter information from electronic mail systems, to schedule appointments, and to search the World Wide Web for information.

For a detailed discussion of robots and softbots, see Rodney Brooks, "Intelligence Without Representation," in *Mind Design II*, ed. John Haugeland (Cambridge, MA: MIT Press, 1997), and Patti Maes, "Agents That Reduce Work and Information Overload," *Communications of the ACM*, Volume 37, No. 7 (July 1994): 30–40.

6.3 *Nested* `if` *Statements*

A program's logic is often complex. Logical operators (`&&`, `||`, and `!`) provide one mechanism for dealing with this complexity. *Nested* `if` *statements* offer an alternative. Following is an everyday example of nested `if`s written in Javish:

```
if (the time is after 7 PM){
    if (you have a book)
        read the book;
    else
        watch TV;
}else
    go for a walk;
```

Although this code is not complicated, it is a little difficult to determine exactly what it means without the aid of the truth table illustrated in Table 6-6.

TABLE 6-6
Truth table for reading a book, watching TV, or going for a walk

AFTER 7 P.M.	HAVE A BOOK	ACTION TAKEN
true	true	read book
true	false	watch TV
false	true	walk
false	false	walk

Having made the table, we are certain that we understand the code correctly. Of course, it is better to make the table first and then write code to match. As a substitute for a truth table, we can draw a flowchart as shown in Figure 6-4. Again, it is better to draw the flowchart before writing the code. Truth tables and flowcharts are useful design tools whenever we must deal with complex logic.

FIGURE 6-4
Flowchart for reading a book, watching TV, or going for a walk

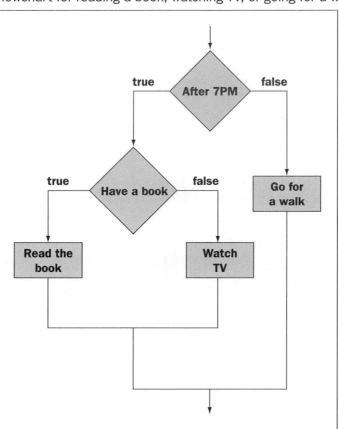

Determine a Student's Grade

Following is a second example of nested `if` statements. The code determines a student's grade based on his test average:

```
testAverage = reader.readInt("Enter the test average: ");
if (testAverage >= 90)
   System.out.println("grade is A");
else{
   if (testAverage >= 80)
      System.out.println("grade is B");
   else{
      if (testAverage >= 70)
         System.out.println("grade is C");
      else{
         if (testAverage >= 60)
            System.out.println("grade is D");
         else{
            System.out.println("grade is F");
```

```
            }
        }
    }
}
```

Because in the absence of braces an else is associated with the immediately preceding if, we can drop the braces and rewrite the code as follows:

```
testAverage = reader.readInt("Enter the test average: ");
if (testAverage >= 90)
    System.out.println("grade is A");
else
    if (testAverage >= 80)
        System.out.println("grade is B");
    else
        if (testAverage >= 70)
            System.out.println("grade is C");
        else
            if (testAverage >= 60)
                System.out.println("grade is D");
            else
                System.out.println("grade is F");
```

or after changing the indentation slightly as follows:

```
testAverage = reader.readInt("Enter the test average: ");
if (testAverage >= 90)
    System.out.println("grade is A");
else if (testAverage >= 80)
    System.out.println("grade is B");
else if (testAverage >= 70)
    System.out.println("grade is C");
else if (testAverage >= 60)
    System.out.println("grade is D");
else
    System.out.println("grade is F");
```

This last format is very common and is used whenever a variable is compared to a sequence of threshold values. This form of the if statement is sometimes called an *extended if statement* or a *multiway if statement*, as compared to the two-way and one-way if statements we have seen earlier.

Did You Know?

In Java, the switch statement provides an alternative to the extended if statement. See Appendix B for details.

EXERCISE 6.3

1. Construct a truth table that shows all the possible paths through the following nested if statement:

```
if (the time is before noon)
    if (the day is Monday)
        take the computer science quiz
    else
        go to gym class
else
    throw a Frisbee in the quad
```

2. What is the difference between a nested `if` statement and a multiway `if` statement?

6.4 Logical Errors in Nested `ifs`

It is easy to make logical errors when writing nested `if` statements. In this section we illustrate several fairly typical mistakes.

Misplaced Braces

One of the most common mistakes involves misplaced braces. Consider how repositioning a brace affects the following code:

```
// Version 1
if (the weather is wet){
  if (you have an umbrella)
     walk;
  else
     run;
}

// Version 2
if (the weather is wet){
  if (you have an umbrella)
     walk;
}else
   run;
```

To demonstrate the differences between the two versions, we construct a truth table—as shown in Table 6-7.

TABLE 6-7
Truth table for version 1 and version 2

THE WEATHER IS WET	YOU HAVE AN UMBRELLA	VERSION 1 OUTCOME	VERSION 2 OUTCOME
true	true	walk	walk
true	false	run	none
false	true	none	run
false	false	none	run

The truth table shows exactly how different the two versions are.

Removing the Braces

This example raises an interesting question. What happens if the braces are removed? In such situations, Java pairs the else with the closest preceding if. Thus

```
if (the weather is wet)
    if (you have an umbrella)
        walk;
    else
        run;
```

Remember that indentation is just a stylistic convention intended to improve the readability of code and means nothing to the computer. Consequently, reformatting the above code as follows does not change its meaning, but will almost certainly mislead the unwary programmer.

```
if (the weather is wet)
    if (you have an umbrella)
        walk;
else
    run;
```

Introducing a Syntax Error

Now we consider a final variation:

```
if (the weather is wet)
    if (you have an umbrella)
        open umbrella;
        walk;
    else
        run;
```

Oops, this contains a compile-time error. Can you spot it? The second if is followed by more than one statement, so braces are required:

```
if (the weather is wet)
   if (you have an umbrella){
      open umbrella;
      walk;
   }else
      run;
```

Remembering that it is better to overuse than to underuse braces, we could rewrite the code as follows:

```
if (the weather is wet){
   if (you have an umbrella){
      open umbrella;
      walk;
   }else{
      run;
   }
}
```

Computation of Sales Commissions

We now attempt to compute a salesperson's commission and introduce a logical error in the process. Commissions are supposed to be computed as follows:

- 10% if sales are greater than or equal to $5,000

- 20% if sales are greater than or equal to $10,000

Following is our first attempt at writing the corresponding code:

```
if (sales >= 5000)
   commission = sales * 1.1;      // line a
else if (sales >= 10000)
   commission = sales * 1.2;      // line b
```

To determine if the code works correctly, we check it against representative values for the sales, namely, sales that are: less than $5,000, equal to $5,000, between $5,000 and $10,000, equal to $10,000, and greater than $10,000. As we can see from Table 6-8, the code is not working correctly.

TABLE 6-8
Calculation of commissions for various sales levels

VALUE OF SALES	LINES EXECUTED	VALIDITY
1,000	neither line a nor line b	correct
5,000	line a	correct
7,000	line a	correct
10,000	line a	incorrect
12,000	line a	incorrect

Corrected Computation of Sales Commissions

After a little reflection, we realize that the conditions are in the wrong order. Here is the corrected code:

```
if (sales >= 10000)
    commission = sales * 1.2;        // line b
else if (sales >= 5000)
    commission = sales * 1.1;        // line a
```

Table 6-9 confirms that the code now works correctly.

TABLE 6-9
Corrected calculation of commissions for various sales levels

VALUE OF SALES	LINES EXECUTED	VALIDITY
1,000	neither line a nor line b	correct
5,000	line a	correct
7,000	line a	correct
10,000	line b	correct
12,000	line b	correct

Avoiding Nested `ifs`

Sometimes getting rid of nested `ifs` is the best way to avoid logical errors. This is easily done by rewriting nested `ifs` as a sequence of independent `if` statements. For example consider the following code for computing sales commissions:

```
if (5000 <= sales && sales < 10000)
    commission = sales * 1.1;
if (10000 <= sales)
    commission = sales * 1.2;
```

And here is another example involving the calculation of student grades:

```
if (90 <= average            ) grade is A;
if (80 <= average && average < 90) grade is B;
if (70 <= average && average < 80) grade is C;
if (60 <= average && average < 70) grade is D;
if (            average < 60) grade is F;
```

The first question people usually ask when confronted with these alternatives is which is faster, by which they mean which will execute most rapidly? In nearly all situations the difference in speed is negligible, so a much better question is which is easier to write and maintain correctly? There is no hard and fast answer to this question, but you should always consider it when writing complex code.

EXERCISE 6.4

1. A tax table provides rates for computing tax based on incomes up to and including a given amount. For example, income above $20,000 up to and including $50,000 is taxed at 18%. Find the logic errors in the following code that determines the tax rate for a given income:

```
if (income > 10000)
    rate = 0.10;
else if (income > 20000)
    rate = 0.18;
else if (income > 50000)
    rate = 0.40;
else
    rate = 0.0;
```

2. Write a correct code segment for the problem in Question 1.

6.5 Nested Loops

There are many programming situations in which loops are nested within loops—these are called *nested loops*. The first case study in this lesson provided an example of this. We now consider another. In Lesson 4, we showed how to determine if a number is prime. The code involved a `for` loop, and by nesting this `for` loop inside another, we can compute all the primes between two limits. The outside loop feeds a sequence of numbers to the inside loop. Following is the code:

```
lower = reader.readInt("Enter the lower limit: ");
upper = reader.readInt("Enter the upper limit: ");
for (n = lower; n <= upper; n++){
    innerLimit = (int)Math.sqrt (n);
    for (d = 2; d <= innerLimit; d++){
        if (n % d == 0)
            break;
    }
    if (d > limit)
        System.out.println (n + " is prime");
}
```

Following is the output when the user enters 55 and 75:

```
59 is prime
61 is prime
67 is prime
71 is prime
73 is prime
```

If the user wants to enter repeated pairs of limits, we enclose the code in yet another loop:

```
lower = reader.readInt("Enter the lower limit or -1 to quit: ");
while (lower != -1){
```

```
    upper = reader.readInt("Enter the upper limit: ");
    for (n = lower; n <= upper; n++){
        innerLimit = (int)Math.sqrt (n);
        for (d = 2; d <= innerLimit; d++){
            if (n % d == 0)
                break;
        }
        if (d > innerLimit)
            System.out.println (n + " is prime");
    }
    lower = reader.readInt("Enter the lower limit or -1 to quit: ");
}
```

EXERCISE 6.5

1. Write the outputs of the following code segments:

a.

```
for (int i = 1; i <= 3; i++)
    for (int j = 1; j <= 3)
        System.out.print(j + " ");
```

b.

```
for (int i = 1; i <= 3; i++){
    for (int j = 1; j <= 3)
        System.out.print(j + " ");
    System.out.println("");
}
```

2. Write code segments that solve the following problems:

a. Output the numbers 1 to 25 in consecutive order, using 5 rows of 5 numbers each.

b. Output 5 rows of five numbers. Each number is the sum of its row position and column position. The position of the first number is (1, 1).

6.6 Testing Loops

The presence of looping statements in a program increases the challenge of designing good test data. Frequently, loops do not iterate some fixed number of times, but instead iterate zero, one, or more than one time depending on a program's inputs. When designing test data, we want to cover all three possibilities. To illustrate, we develop test data for the print divisors program presented in Lesson 4. First, let's look at the code again:

```
// Display the proper divisors of a number
n = reader.readInt("Enter a positive integer: ");
limit = n / 2;
for (d = 2; d <= limit; d++){
    if (n % d == 0)
        System.out.print (d + " ");
}
```

By analyzing the code, we conclude that if n equals 0, 1, 2, or 3, the limit is less than 2, and the loop is never entered. If n equals 4 or 5, the loop is entered once. If n is greater than 5, the loop is entered multiple times. All this suggests the test data shown in Table 6-10. After testing the program with this data, we feel reasonably confident that it works correctly.

TABLE 6-10
Test data for the count divisors program

TYPE OF TEST	DATA USED
No iterations	0, 1, 2, and 3
One iteration	4 and 5
Multiple iterations for a number with divisors	24
Multiple iterations for a number without divisors	29

Combinatorial Explosion

The surprisingly large amount of testing needed to validate even a small program suggests an interesting question. Suppose a program is composed of three parts and that it takes five tests to verify each part independently. Then how many tests does it take to verify the program as a whole? In the unlikely event that the three parts are independent of each other and utilize the same five sets of test data, then five tests suffice. However, it is far more likely that the behavior of each part affects the other two and also that the parts have differing test requirements. Then all possible combinations of tests should be tried, that is 5*5*5 or 125. We call this multiplicative growth in test cases a *combinatorial explosion*, and it pretty much guarantees the impossibility of exhaustively testing large complex programs; however, programmers still must do their best to test their programs intelligently and well.

Robust Programs

So far, we have focused on showing that a program that uses loops produces correct results when provided with valid inputs but, surprisingly, that is not good enough. As we learned when we were testing programs with if statements earlier in this lesson, we also should consider how a program behaves when confronted with invalid data. After all, users frequently make mistakes or do not fully understand a program's data entry requirements. As we have learned, a program that tolerates errors in user inputs and recovers gracefully is *robust*. The best and easiest way to write robust programs is to check user inputs immediately on entry and reject those that are invalid. We illustrate this technique in the next case study. At this stage, there are limits to how thoroughly we can check inputs, so in the case study, we merely make sure that inputs fall in the range specified by the prompt.

*E*XERCISE 6.6

1. Describe appropriate test data for the following code segments:

a.

```
while (number > 0)
    <action>
```

EXERCISE 6.6 Continued

b.

```
while (0 < number && 100 > number)
    <action>
```

2. Design test data for Project 4-6 (in Lesson 4).

3. What would be reasonable test data for a loop that does not execute a fixed number of times?

4. What is a robust program? Give an example.

Case Study 2: Fibonacci Numbers

There is a famous sequence of numbers that occurs frequently in nature. In 1202, the Italian mathematician Leonardo Fibonacci presented the following problem concerning the breeding of rabbits. He assumed somewhat unrealistically that:

1. Each pair of rabbits in a population produces a new pair of rabbits each month.

2. Rabbits become fertile one month after birth.

3. Rabbits do not die.

He then considered how rapidly the rabbit population would grow on a monthly basis when starting with a single pair of newborn rabbits.

To answer the question, we proceed one month at a time:

■ At the beginning of month 1, there is one pair of rabbits. (total = 1 pair)

■ At the beginning of month 2, our initial pair of rabbits, A, will have just reached sexual maturity, so there will be no offspring. (total = 1 pair)

■ At the beginning of month 3, pair A will have given birth to pair B. (total = 2 pair)

■ At the beginning of month 4, pair A will have given birth to pair C and pair B will be sexually mature. (total = 3 pair)

■ At the beginning of month 5, pairs A and B will have given birth to pairs D and E, while pair C will have reached sexual maturity. (total = 5 pair)

■ And so on.

If we continue in this way, we obtain the following sequence of numbers
1 1 2 3 5 8 13 21 34 55 89 144 233 ...

called the **Fibonacci numbers**. Notice that each number, after the first two, is the sum of its two predecessors. Referring back to the rabbits, see if you can demonstrate why this should be the case. Although the sequence of numbers is easy to construct, there is no known formula for calculating the nth Fibonacci number, which gives rise to the following program request.

Request

Write a program that can compute the nth Fibonacci number on demand, where n is a positive integer.

Analysis, Design, and Implementation

The user input should be a positive integer or –1 to quit. Other inputs are rejected. The proposed interface is shown in Figure 6-5.

FIGURE 6-5
Interface for the Fibonacci program

```
Enter a positive integer or -1 to quit: 8
Fibonacci of 8 is 21
```

Following is the code:

```java
import TerminalIO.KeyboardReader;

public class Fibonacci {

    public static void main (String [] args) {
        KeyboardReader reader = new KeyboardReader();
        int n;              //The number entered by the user
        int fib;            //The nth Fibonacci number
        int a,b,count;      //Variables that facilitate the computation

        while (true){

            // Ask the user for the next input
            n = reader.readInt("Enter a positive integer or -1 to quit: ");
            if (n == -1) break;
            while (n <= 0)
                n = reader.readInt(
                    "Enter a positive integer or -1 to quit: ");

            //Calculate the nth Fibonacci number
            fib = 1;                    //Takes care of case n = 1 or 2
            a = 1;
            b = 1;
            count = 3;
            while (count <= n){  //Takes care of case n >= 3
                fib = a + b;        //Point p. Referred to later.
                a = b;
                b = fib;
                count = count + 1;
            }

            //Print the nth Fibonacci number
            System.out.println ("Fibonacci of " + n + " is " + fib);
        }
    }
}
```

Loop Analysis

The loop in the Fibonacci program is not obvious at first glance, so to clarify what is happening, we construct Table 6-11. This table traces the changes to key variables on each pass through the loop.

TABLE 6-11
Changes to Key Variables on Each Pass Through the Loop

COUNT AT POINT P	A AT POINT P	B AT POINT P	FIBONACCI NUMBER AT POINT P
3	1	1	2
4	1	2	3
5	2	3	5
6	3	5	8
...	...	...	...
n	$(n-2)$th Fibonacci number	$(n-1)$th Fibonacci number	nth Fibonacci number

Test Data

We complete the case study by developing suitable test data:

■ To make sure the program is robust, we try the following sequence of inputs for n: –3, 0, 1, 2, –1.

■ To make sure the computation is correct when the second inner loop is not entered, we try n equal to 1 and 2.

■ To make sure the computation is correct when the second inner loop is entered one or more times, we let n equal 3 and 6.

As all these tests were successful, we can hardly be blamed for thinking that our program works perfectly; however, it contains a completely unexpected problem. When n equals 80, the program returns the value –285,007,387. The problem is due to **arithmetic overflow**. In Java and most programming languages, integers have a limited range (see Lesson 3) and exceeding that range leads to strange results. Adding one to the most positive integer in the range yields the most negative integer, whereas subtracting one from the most negative yields the most positive. Welcome to the strange world of computer arithmetic, where bizarre behavior is always lurking to trip the unwary. To detect the problem automatically, we could include extra lines of code that test for an unexpected switch to a negative value. A somewhat similar problem cost the French space program half a billion dollars and a great deal of embarrassment when a computer guided rocket and its payload exploded shortly after takeoff.

Design, Testing, and Debugging Hints

■ Most errors involving selection statements and loops are not syntax errors caught at compile time. Thus, you will detect these errors only after running the program, and perhaps then only with extensive testing.

■ The presence or absence of braces can seriously affect the logic of a selection statement or loop. For example, the following selection statements have a similar look but a very different logic:

```
if (x > 0){
    y = x;
    z = 1 / x;
}

if (x > 0)
    y = x;
    z = 1 / x;
```

■ The first selection statement guards against division by 0; the second statement only guards against assigning x to y. The next pair of code segments shows a similar problem with a loop:

```
while (x > 0){
    y = x;
    x = x - 1;
}

while (x > 0)
    y = x;
    x = x - 1;
```

■ The first loop terminates because the value of x decreases within the body of the loop; the second loop is infinite because the value of x decreases below the body of the loop.

■ When testing programs that use `if` or `if-else` statements, be sure to use test data that force the program to exercise all of the logical branches.

■ When testing a program that uses `if` statements, it helps to formulate equivalence classes, boundary conditions, and extreme conditions.

■ Use an `if-else` statement rather than two `if` statements when the alternative courses of action are mutually exclusive.

■ When testing a loop, be sure to use limit values as well as typical values. For example, if a loop should terminate when the control variable equals 0, run it with the values 0, –1, and 1.

■ Be sure to check entry conditions and exit conditions for each loop.

■ For a loop with errors, use debugging output statements to verify the values of the control variable on each pass through the loop. Check this value before the loop is initially entered, after each update, and after the loop is exited.

SUMMARY

In this lesson, you learned:

■ A complex Boolean expression contains one or more Boolean expressions and the logical operators `&&` (AND), `||` (OR), and `!` (NOT).

- A truth table can determine the value of any complex Boolean expression.

- Java uses short-circuit evaluation of complex Boolean expressions. The evaluation of the operands of || stops at the first true value, whereas the evaluation of the operands of && stops at the first false value.

- Nested if statements are another way of expressing complex conditions. A nested if statement can be translated to an equivalent if statement that uses logical operators.

- An extended or multiway if statement expresses a choice among several mutually exclusive alternatives.

- Loops can be nested in other loops.

- Equivalence classes, boundary conditions, and extreme conditions are important features used in tests of control structures involving complex conditions.

VOCABULARY *Review*

Define the following terms:

arithmetic overflow	extended if statement	nested loop
boundary condition	extreme condition	quality assurance
combinatorial explosion	logical operator	robust
complete code coverage	nested if statement	truth table
equivalence class		

REVIEW *Questions*

WRITTEN QUESTIONS

Write your answers to the following questions.

1. List the three logical operators.

2. Construct a truth table for the expression P OR NOT Q.

3. Suppose P is true and Q is false. What is the value of the expression P AND NOT Q?

4. Write an `if` statement that displays whether or not a given number is between a lower bound min and an upper bound max, inclusive. Use a logical operator in the condition.

5. Rewrite the `if` statement in Question 4 to use a nested `if` statement.

6. Write a nested loop that displays a 10 by 10 square of asterisks.

PROJECTS

In keeping with the spirit of this lesson, each program should be robust and should validate the input data. You should try also to formulate the appropriate equivalence classes, boundary conditions, and extreme conditions and use them in testing the programs.

PROJECT 6-1

In a game of guessing numbers, one person says, "I'm thinking of a number between 1 and 100." The other person guesses "50." The first person replies, "No, the number is less." The second person then guesses "25," and so on, until she guesses correctly. Write a program that plays this game. The computer knows the number (a random number between 1 and 100) and the user is the guesser. At the end of the game, the computer displays the number of guesses required by the user to guess the number correctly.

PROJECT 6-2

Rewrite the program of Project 6-1 so that the user knows the number and the computer must guess it.

PROJECT 6-3

Write a program that expects a numeric grade as input and outputs the corresponding letter grade. The program uses the following grading scale:

NUMERIC RANGE	LETTER GRADE
96–100	A+
92–95	A
90–91	A–
86–89	B+
82–85	B
80–81	B–
76–79	C+
72–75	C
70–71	C–
66–69	D+
62–65	D
60–61	D–
0–59	F

PROJECT 6-4

Write a Java method `getLetterGrade` that is based on the grading scale of Project 6-3. This method expects the numeric grade as a parameter and returns a string representing the letter grade. The method header should have the prefix `static` so it can be called from `main`. Use this method in a program that inputs a list of grades (ending with –1) and outputs the class average, the class minimum, and the class maximum as letter grades.

PROJECT 6-5

The Euclidean algorithm can be used to find the greatest common divisor (gcd) of two positive integers (n_1, n_2). You can use this algorithm in the following manner:
  A. Compute the remainder of dividing the larger number by the smaller number.
  B. Replace the larger number with the smaller number and the smaller number with the remainder.
  C. Repeat this process until the smaller number is zero:

The larger number at this point is the gcd of n_1 and n_2.

Write a program that lets the user enter two integers and then prints each step in the process of using the Euclidean algorithm to find their gcd.

PROJECT 6-6

Review the case study in Lesson 4 in which the Lucky Sevens gambling game program was created. Remove the code that deals with the maximum amount held. Then modify the program so that it runs the simulation 100 times and prints the average number of rolls. (*Hint*: Put the `while` loop inside a `for` statement that loops 100 times. Accumulate the total count and at the end divide by 100.)

PROJECT 6-7

Write a program to print the perimeter and area of rectangles using all combinations of heights and widths running from 1 foot to 10 feet in increments of 1 foot. Print the output in headed columns.

PROJECT 6-8

Write a turtle graphics program that allows the user to select a function for plotting a curve and displaying it as a graphical image. The curves should correspond to the following equations:

$y = x$

$y = x^2$

$y = x^n$

$y = 1.5^x$

The user should input the starting value of x and the ending value of x for each function chosen.

CRITICAL *Thinking*

✦ Read the sections of the ACM Code of Ethics that deal with designing and testing reliable computer systems. Prepare a written report to present to your class on the way in which the ACM Code deals with this issue.

IMPROVING THE USER INTERFACE

We do not judge a book by its cover because we are interested in its contents, not its appearance. However, we do judge a software product by its interface because we have no other way to access its functionality. In this lesson, we explore several ways to improve a program's interface. First, we present some standard techniques for enhancing terminal-based interfaces, and then we show how to develop graphical user interfaces (GUIs). The transition to GUIs involves making two adjustments to our thinking. First, the structure of a GUI program differs significantly from that of a terminal-based program. Second, a GUI program is event driven, meaning that it is inactive until the user clicks a button or selects a menu option. In contrast, a terminal-based program maintains constant control over the interactions with the user. Put differently, a terminal-based program prompts the user for inputs, whereas a GUI program waits for user commands. This distinction will become clearer as you read this lesson. This lesson also introduces the data type char and shows how to print output as columns of strings and numbers.

7.1 A Thermometer Class

The demonstrations in this lesson all involve converting temperatures between Fahrenheit and Celsius. To support these conversions we first introduce a Thermometer class. This class stores the temperature internal in Celsius; however, the temperature can be set and retrieved in either Fahrenheit or Celsius. Following is a listing:

```java
public class Thermometer {

    private double degreesCelsius;

    public void setCelsius(double degrees){
        degreesCelsius = degrees;
    }

    public void setFahrenheit(double degrees){
        degreesCelsius = (degrees - 32.0) * 5.0 / 9.0;
    }

    public double getCelsius(){
        return degreesCelsius;
    }

    public double getFahrenheit(){
        return degreesCelsius * 9.0 / 5.0 + 32.0;
    }
}
```

7.2 Repeating Sets of Inputs and Type char

In Lesson 4, we introduced two techniques for handling repeating sets of inputs. We called these count-controlled and sentinel-controlled input. We now present a third technique that we call *query-controlled input*. Before each set of inputs after the first, the program asks the user if there are more inputs. Figure 7-1 shows an example of query-controlled input.

FIGURE 7-1
Interface for a query-controlled temperature conversion program

```
Enter degrees Fahrenheit: 32
The equivalent in Celsius is 0.0


Do it again (y/n)? y


Enter degrees Fahrenheit: 212
The equivalent in Celsius is 100.0


Do it again (y/n)?
```

The program is implemented by means of two classes—a class to handle the user interface and the `Thermometer` class. Following is pseudocode for the interface class:

```
instantiate a thermometer
char doItAgain = 'y'
while (doItAgain equals 'y' or 'Y'){
    read degrees Fahrenheit and set the thermometer
    ask the thermometer for the degrees in Celsius and display
    read doItAgain                        //The user responds with 'y' or 'n'
}
```

The key to this pseudocode is the character variable doItAgain. This variable controls how many times the loop repeats. Initially, the variable equals 'y'. As soon as the user enters a character other than 'y' or 'Y', the program terminates. Following is a complete listing of the interface class:

```
/* ConvertWithQuery.java
Repeatedly convert from Fahrenheit to Celsius until the user
signals the end.
*/

import TerminalIO.*;

public class ConvertWithQuery {
    public static void main (String [] args) {
        KeyboardReader reader = new KeyboardReader();
        Thermometer thermo = new Thermometer();
        char doItAgain = 'y';

        while (doItAgain == 'y' || doItAgain == 'Y'){
            thermo.setFahrenheit
                (reader.readDouble("\nEnter degrees Fahrenheit: "));
            System.out.println
                ("The equivalent in Celsius is " + thermo.getCelsius());

            doItAgain = reader.readChar("\nDo it again (y/n)? ");
        }
    }
}
```

In this code, observe that a character literal is enclosed within single quotation marks. A character variable holds a single character and is declared using the keyword char. The readChar method reads the first character entered on a line. And finally, 'Y' and 'y' are not the same character.

EXERCISE 7.2

1. Describe the structure of a query-controlled loop that processes repeated sets of inputs.

2. What is a character literal?

3. What is the difference between 'y', 'Y', "y", and "Y"?

7.3 A Menu-Driven Conversion Program

Menu-driven programs begin by displaying a list of options from which the user selects one. The program then prompts for additional inputs related to that option and performs the needed computations, after which it displays the menu again. Figure 7-2 shows how this idea can be used to extend the temperature conversion program.

FIGURE 7-2
Interface for a menu-driven version of the temperature conversion program

```
1) Convert from Fahrenheit to Celsius
2) Convert from Celsius to Fahrenheit
3) Quit
Enter your option: 1

Enter degrees Fahrenheit: 212
The equivalent in Celsius is 100

1) Convert from Fahrenheit to Celsius
2) Convert from Celsius to Fahrenheit
3) Quit
Enter your option: 2

Enter degrees Celsius: 0
The equivalent in Fahrenheit is 32

1) Convert from Fahrenheit to Celsius
2) Convert from Celsius to Fahrenheit
3) Quit
Enter your option: 3
```

Following is the corresponding pseudocode followed by the program:

```
instantiate a thermometer
menuOption = 4
while (menuOption != 3){
    print menu
    read menuOption
    if (menuOption == 1){
        read fahrenheit and set the thermometer.
        ask the thermometer to convert and print the results
    }else if (menuOption == 2){
        read celsius and set the thermometer
        ask the thermometer to convert and print the results
    }else if (menuOption != 3)
        print "Invalid option"
}
```

```
/* TempConversion.java
A menu-driven temperature conversion program that converts from
Fahrenheit to Celsius and vice versa.
```

```java
*/

import TerminalIO.*;

public class ConvertWithMenu {
    public static void main (String [] args) {
        KeyboardReader reader = new KeyboardReader();
        Thermometer thermo = new Thermometer();
        String menu;                //The multiline menu
        int menuOption;             //The user's menu selection

        //Build the menu string
        menu = "\n1) Convert from Fahrenheit to Celsius"
             + "\n2) Convert from Celsius to Fahrenheit"
             + "\n3) Quit"
             + "\nEnter your option: ";

        //Set up the menu loop
        menuOption = 4;
        while (menuOption != 3){

            //Display the menu and get the user's option
            menuOption = reader.readInt(menu);
            System.out.println ("");

            //Determine which menu option has been selected

            if (menuOption == 1){

                //Convert from Fahrenheit to Celsius
                thermo.setFahrenheit
                    (reader.readDouble("Enter degrees Fahrenheit: "));
                System.out.println
                    ("The equivalent in Celsius is " + thermo.getCelsius());

            }else if (menuOption == 2){

                //Convert from Celsius to Fahrenheit
                thermo.setCelsius
                    (reader.readDouble("Enter degrees Celsius: "));
                System.out.println
                    ("The equivalent in Fahrenheit is " +
                     thermo.getFahrenheit());

            }else if (menuOption != 3){

                //Invalid option
                System.out.println ("Invalid option");
            }
        }
    }
}
```

7.5 The GUI Program Explained

The execution sequence in the program proceeds as follows:

1. Program execution begins as usual in method `main`. The `theGUI` object is instantiated and sent the `setSize` and `setVisible` messages. The `setSize` message indicates the size of the window as measured in pixels. The first parameter indicates the width and the second the height. A window is invisible until it receives a `setVisible(true)` message. Once the window is visible, there are no more statements to execute in `main`, and execution in `main` terminates; however, the program does not end. Instead it becomes inactive until the user clicks a command button or the GUI's close icon.

2. As soon as `theGUI` object is instantiated, the constructor executes and the window objects are instantiated and added to the window. These **window objects** represent the labels, data entry fields, and command buttons that comprise the constituent components of the window.

3. Every time the user clicks a command button, the JVM sends the `buttonClicked` message to the `theGUI` object. Execution then begins anew in the `theGUI` object's `buttonClicked` method, proceeds through the method until the last line has been executed, and terminates. The program then becomes inactive again.

4. When the user clicks the GUI's close icon, the program ends.

Line by Line Explanation

Following is a line-by-line explanation of the code.

Importing Packages

```
import javax.swing.*;
import BreezySwing.*;
```

GUI programs must import the two packages `javax.swing` and `BreezySwing`. These packages contain classes that support the overall behavior of a GUI-based program and its window objects. Rather than list all the individual classes involved by name, we use a star (*), thus indicating that we want to import all needed classes from these packages.

GBFrame

```
public class ConvertWithGUI extends GBFrame{
```

A GUI program must be a subclass of `GBFrame`.

Declare Window Object Variable

```
    // Declare variables for the window objects.
    private JLabel       fahrenheitLabel;
    private JLabel       celsiusLabel;
    private DoubleField  fahrenheitField;
    private DoubleField  celsiusField;
    private JButton      fahrenheitButton;
    private JButton      celsiusButton;
```

Here we declare the variables that are associated with the window objects.

The Add Method

```
// Constructor
public ConvertWithGUI(){
   // Instantiate and add window objects to the window.
   fahrenheitLabel  = addLabel       ("Fahrenheit" ,1,1,1,1);
   celsiusLabel     = addLabel       ("Celsius"    ,1,2,1,1);
   fahrenheitField  = addDoubleField (32.0         ,2,1,1,1);
   celsiusField     = addDoubleField (0.0          ,2,2,1,1);
   fahrenheitButton = addButton      (">>>>>>"     ,3,1,1,1);
   celsiusButton    = addButton      ("<<<<<<"     ,3,2,1,1);
}
```

The `add` methods instantiate, initialize, and position the window objects. Each type of window object has a different purpose:

- A *label object* displays text in the window. This text normally is used to label some other window object, such as a data entry or data display field.

- A *double field object* can accept user input and/or display program output.

- A *button object* activates the `buttonClicked` method when clicked by the user.

Window objects are positioned in an imaginary grid (see Figure 7-4), and the grid automatically adjusts itself to the needed number of rows and columns.

FIGURE 7-4
An imaginary grid superimposed on the program's interface

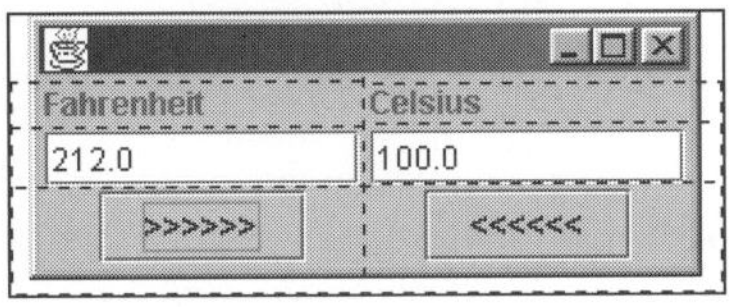

The syntax for adding a window object indicates its position and size in this grid:

```
<name of object> = add<type>
   (<initial value>,   //An object's initial value varies depending on type.
    <row #>,           //Row position in grid. Our example has 3 rows.
    <column #>,        //Column position in grid. Our example has 2 columns.
    <width>,           //Width of object, usually 1 grid cell.
    <height>);         //Height of object, usually 1 grid cell.
```

Button Click Events

```
// Respond to button click events
public void buttonClicked (JButton buttonObj){
```

When the user clicks a command button, the JVM sends the `buttonClicked` message to the `theGUI` object. These lines begin the method's definition. Notice that the method has one parameter, a button object. When the method is called, this parameter corresponds to the button clicked by the user.

Declare Local Variables

```
// Local variables
Thermometer thermo = new Thermometer();
```

Here we declare variables that are local to the `buttonClicked` method.

Determine Button Clicked

```
// Determine which button was clicked.
if (buttonObj == fahrenheitButton){
```

Here we determine if the button clicked by the user equals the `fahrenheitButton`. In general, there can be any number of command buttons in a window.

read and Write Numbers

```
//Convert from Fahrenheit to Celsius
thermo.setFahrenheit(fahrenheitField.getNumber());
celsiusField.setNumber (thermo.getCelsius());
```

The `getNumber` and `setNumber` methods read and write numbers from and to numeric fields, respectively.

The rest of the program now should be fairly self-explanatory.

EXERCISE 7.5

1. Draw a picture of the window that results from running each of the following code segments:

a.

```
label1 = addLabel("Annual Income", 1,1,1,1);
field1 = addDoubleField(0,          1,2,1,1);
label2 = addLabel("Tax Rate",       2,1,1,1);
field2 = addDoubleField(0.15,       2,2,1,1);
label3 = addLabel("Tax",            3,1,1,1);
field3 = addDoubleField(0,          3,2,1,1);
btn = addButton("Compute Tax",      4,1,2,1);
```

b.

```
btn1 = addButton("1", 1,1,1,1);
btn2 = addButton("2", 1,2,1,1);
btn3 = addButton("3", 2,1,1,1);
btn4 = addButton("4", 2,2,1,1);
```

EXERCISE 7.5 Continued

2. Write code segments that would produce each of the following windows:

a.

b.

3. Write the dimensions of the window that results from the following message:

```
setSize(300, 250);
```

4. Write the structure of the buttonClicked method for a window that has three command buttons.

7.6 Other Window Objects and Methods

In our sample program, we encountered three types of window objects and several of the messages that they recognize. We now build on that foundation and introduce some additional window objects with their methods.

Before looking at the details, it is helpful to make a distinction between those classes and methods that are part of Java Swing and those that are unique to BreezySwing. All the methods for adding window objects to the user interface and for responding to user events are part of BreezySwing. The window objects themselves are either part of Swing or are derived from objects in Swing. For instance, labels and command buttons are part of Swing, whereas double fields are derived from Swing's standard text fields. Appendix H makes the distinctions clear. Programs that use Swing must import javax.swing.* and those that use BreezySwing must in addition import BreezySwing.*.

> **Extra for Experts**
>
> For a complete list of window objects and their methods, see Appendix H.

Integer Field Objects

An object of class IntegerField is called an *integer field object*, and as the name suggests, it can be used to enter or display an integer value. An integer field should always be initialized to an integer and never to a floating-point value. The principal methods for manipulating integer fields are as follow:

int getNumber()	which reads an integer from an input field
void setNumber(anInteger)	which prints a number in an output field

The same method names are used for manipulating double fields. As we learned in Lesson 1, using the same message or method name with different classes is called *polymorphism*.

Text Field Objects

An object of class `JTextField` is called a *text field object* and can hold one line of string data. A text field is useful for entering or displaying such things as names and descriptions. It must be initialized to a string. The principal methods for manipulating text fields are as follow:

`String getText()`   which reads a string from an input field

`void setText(aString)`   which prints a one-line string in an output field

Text Area Objects

An object of class `JTextArea` is called a *text area object* and is similar to a text field object except that it can handle several lines of text at a time. A text area can be used for entering or displaying a person's address or any other multiline descriptive information. Whereas a text field typically has a width and height of one grid cell, a text area is usually several cells wide and high. The principal methods for manipulating a text area are as follow:

`String getText()`   which reads a multiline string from an input field

`void setText(aString)`   which prints a multiline string in an output field

`void append(aString)`   which appends a multiline string to the end of the text already present in the output field

Summary of Methods

Table 7-1 contains a summary of the methods discussed so far together with several new methods.

TABLE 7-1
Summary of window object methods

TYPE OF OBJECT	SIGNATURE OF METHOD	DESCRIPTION
IntegerField	`void setNumber(anInteger)` `double getNumber()`	Displays `anInteger` on the screen. If the number on the screen is a valid integer, then reads the number and returns it. If the number is not a valid integer, then sets it to 0 and returns 0.
	`boolean isValid()`	Determines if the number entered on the screen is a valid integer.
DoubleField	`void setNumber(aDouble)` `double getNumber()`	Displays `aDouble` on the screen. If the number on the screen is a valid double, then reads the number and returns it. If the number is not a valid double, then sets it to 0 and returns 0.
	`boolean isValid()`	Determines if the number entered on the screen is a valid double.
	`void setPrecision(anInteger)`	Sets the field's precision to the specified number. When a double is displayed in the field, the number of digits after the decimal point is equal to the precision.

TABLE 7-1 (Continued)
Summary of window object methods

TYPE OF OBJECT	SIGNATURE OF METHOD	DESCRIPTION
	`int getPrecision()`	If the precision is never set or if it is set to −1, then the format of the number on the screen varies and depends on the size of the number; however, at most six digits are displayed. Returns the value of the precision.
JTextField	`String getText()` `void setText(aString)`	Returns the text entered in the field. Sets the text of the field to the specified string.

JTextArea	`String getText()`
	`void setText(aString)`
	
	`void append(aString)`
		Returns the text entered in the field.
		Sets the text of the field to the specified string.
		Appends the specified string to the text area.

JLabel	`String getText()` `void setText(aString)`	Returns the text of the label. Sets the text of the label to the specified string.

JButton	`void setLabel(aString)`
	
	`String getLabel()`
		Sets the text written on the button to the specified string.
		Returns the text written on the button.

All Window Controls	`void setVisible(true/false)`	If `false`, then hides the control so that the user can no longer see it on the screen. If `true`, then makes the control visible again.
	`void setEnabled (true/false)`	If `false`, then disable the control for user input. If `true`, then enable the control for user input. Default is enabled.
	`void requestFocus()`	Moves the focus to the control.

Declaring Window Objects

Following is a list that shows how to instantiate the window objects discussed so far:

```
aLabel      = addLabel         ("..."    ,r,c,w,h);
anInteger   = addIntegerField (<integer>,r,c,w,h);
aDouble     = addDoubleField  (<double> ,r,c,w,h);
aJTextField = addTextField     ("..."    ,r,c,w,h);
aJTextArea  = addTextArea      ("..."    ,r,c,w,h);
aJButton    = addButton        ("..."    ,r,c,w,h);
```

The `messageBox` Method

A *message box* is a convenient device for popping up messages outside an application's main window. For instance, we might want to tell the user of our temperature conversion program that she must not enter a temperature greater than 10,000 (see Figure 7-5 for an example).

FIGURE 7-5
A pop-up message box for the temperature conversion program

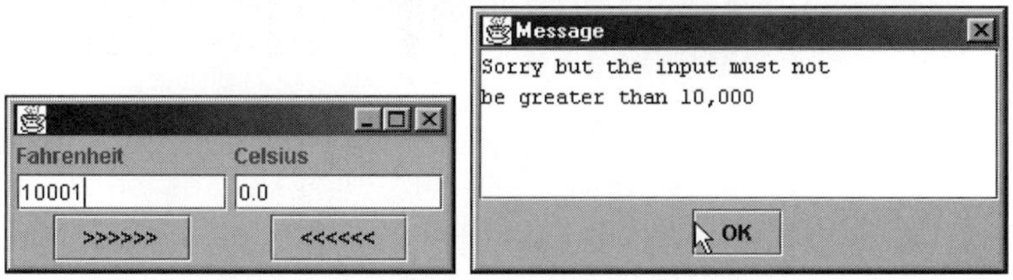

(a) Main window   (b) Message box

The code for activating a message box always appears inside a GUI class, which in our example is the `ConvertWithGUI` class. The key piece of code consists of sending the message `messageBox` to the object `this`:

```
this.messageBox ("Sorry but the input must not \nbe greater than 10,000");
```

In the line of code, the word `this` refers to the `theGUI` object itself. For the convenience of programmers, Java allows the word `this` to be omitted, so the code can be written as:

```
messageBox ("Sorry but the input must not \nbe greater than 10,000");
```

Another version of `messageBox` allows the programmer to specify the box's height and width in pixels. The following code displays the message "Hello world!" in a box that is 300 pixels wide and 100 pixels high:

```
messageBox ("Hello world!", 300, 100);
```

Setting the Look and Feel

Each GUI-based operating system, such as Windows, MacOS, and Motif (for UNIX), has its own look and feel. Java's Swing toolkit provides a default look and feel called *Metal* that is system independent and is used in most GUIs in this book. However, Swing allows the programmer to set the look and feel of a window as well as any of its subcomponents. To accomplish this with `BreezySwing`, we call the method `setLookAndFeel` with the `String` parameter "METAL," "MOTIF," or "OTHER." On a Windows system, "OTHER" changes the look and feel to Windows. Method `main` is a convenient place to call the `setLookAndFeel` method. The following code segment shows how to do this in the temperature conversion program:

```
public static void main (String[] args){
    ConvertWithGUI theGUI = new ConvertWithGUI();
    theGUI.setLookAndFeel("MOTIF");
    theGUI.setSize (250, 100);    //Set the window's size in pixels
    theGUI.setVisible (true);     //Make the window visible
}
```

Figure 7-6 compares the Metal look and the Motif look.

FIGURE 7-6
The Metal look and feel versus the Motif look and feel

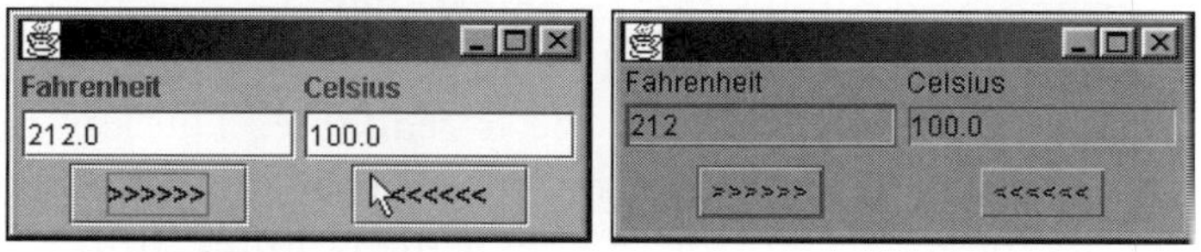

(a) Metal   (b) Motif

EXERCISE 7.6

1. What is the difference between a text field and a text area?

2. Write a code segment that displays an exit message in a message box.

3. Describe the role of the method `isValid()` for double fields and integer fields.

> **Hot Tip**
>
> For complete documentation on BreezySwing, including a tutorial and downloadable source code and byte code, consult this book's Web site at http://www.wlu.edu/~lambertK/hsjava

4. What is the effect of the `doubleField` method `setPrecision(anInteger)`?

5. Write statements that perform the following tasks:
   a. Add a double field to row 1, column 2, with a width and height of 1, and an initial value of 0, and assign the field to the variable `field`.
   b. Set the field's precision to 3 decimal places.
   c. Retrieve a number from the field and store it in the variable `number`.
   d. Output the value 3.14 to the field.

7.7 Formatted Output

Occasionally, programs must display tables that contain columns of words and numbers. Unless these tables are formatted carefully, they are unreadable. To illustrate, Figure 7-7 shows a table of names, sales, and commissions, with and without formatting. Although both tables contain exactly the same data, only the formatted one is readable. The key feature of a formatted table is that each column has a designated width, and all the values in a column are justified in the same manner—either to the left, right, or center of the column. In the sales table, the names in the first column are left justified, and the numbers in the other two columns are right justified.

FIGURE 7-7
A table of sales figures shown with and without formatting

```
            NAME SALES COMMISSION
            Catherine 23415 2341.5
            Ken 321.5 32.15
            Martin 4384.75 438.48
            Tess 3595.74 359.57


        Version 1: Unreadable without formatting

     NAME                 SALES      COMMISSION
     Catherine         23415.00         2341.50
     Ken                 321.50           32.15
     Martin             4384.75          438.48
     Tess               3595.74          359.57


        Version 2: Readable with formatting
```

Format, a class in BreezySwing, contains a method called justify that supports the process of positioning values in fields. The justify method can position a value left, right, or center within a field of some designated width. Table 7-2 shows words and numbers justified in fields of width 10.

TABLE 7-2
Words and numbers justified in fields of width 10

LEFT	RIGHT	CENTERED
0123456789	0123456789	0123456789
cat	cat	cat
dog	dog	dog
elephant	elephant	elephant
123	123	123
45678	45678	45678
3.14	3.14	3.14
155.76	155.76	155.76

Here is a code segment that embeds the word "cat" left justified in a string of length 8 together with several other examples:

```
import BreezySwing.Format;
. . .
Format.justify ('l', "cat", 8);        // "cat" left justified in a string of
                                        // length 8 yields the string
                                        // "cat     "

Format.justify ('r', 45678, 7);        // 45678 right justified in a string of
                                        // length 7 yields the string
                                        // "  45678"

Format.justify ('c', "dog", 11);       // "dog" centered in a string of
                                        // length 11 yields the string
                                        // "    dog    "

Format.justify ('r', 2.534, 10, 2);    // 2.534 right justified in a string of
                                        // length 10 with a precision of 2 yields
                                        // "      2.53"
```

In the code, the `justify` message is sent, not to an object, but to the class `Format`. This is not the first time we have seen messages sent to a class. When using the `justify` method, we need to be aware that it comes in four slightly different flavors, as described in Table 7-3.

TABLE 7-3
The four versions of the `Format.justify` method

METHOD	WHAT IT DOES
`String justify (char alignment, String aString, int length)`	Returns a string of the indicated `length` with `aString` embedded and aligned to the left ('l'), center ('c'), or right ('r').
`String justify (char alignment, char aCharacter, int length)`	Returns a string of the indicated `length` with `aCharacter` embedded and aligned to the left ('l'), center ('c'), or right ('r').
`String justify (char alignment, long aLongInteger, int length)`	Returns a string of the indicated `length` with `aLongInteger`embedded and aligned to the left ('l'), center ('c'), or right ('r').
`String justify (char alignment, double aDouble, int length, int precision)`	Returns a string of the indicated `length` with `aDouble` embedded and aligned to the left ('l'), center ('c'), or right ('r'). The `precision` specifies the number of digits displayed to the right of the decimal point.

To better illustrate the use of precision, Figure 7-8 shows the effect of printing the number 1.23456 in a field of width 10 with precisions that range from 0 to 9. Notice that the number is rounded up or extra zeros are added as appropriate. The field is filled with stars (*) if the width is insufficient to display the number with the requested precision.

> **Did You Know?**
>
> We have not discussed long integers, but suffice it to say that an integer can be used anytime a long integer is specified as a parameter. See Appendix B for a further description of long integers.

FIGURE 7-8
1.23456 displayed with precisions ranging from 0 to 9

```
The number with precision 0:          1
The number with precision 1:        1.2
The number with precision 2:       1.23
The number with precision 3:      1.235
The number with precision 4:     1.2346
The number with precision 5:    1.23456
The number with precision 6:   1.234560
The number with precision 7:  1.2345600
The number with precision 8: 1.23456000
The number with precision 9:***********
```

Following is the code that was used to create the demonstration:

```
i = 0;
while (i <= 9){
    str = "The number with precision " + i + ":"
        + Format.justify ('r', number, 10, i);
    System.out.println (str);
    i = i + 1;
}
```

EXERCISE 7.7

1. Write code segments to produce the following formatted strings:
   a. " One space "
   b. " Two spaces"
   c. "Three spaces   "
   d. The value of `int` variable `i`, right-justified in a field of six columns.
   e. The value of `double` variable `d`, centered in a field of ten columns with a precision of 2.

2. Write the values returned by the following expressions (include spaces within the strings where relevant):
   a. Format.justify('r', 33, 5)
   b. Format.justify('c', "Hello", 7)
   c. Format.justify('l', 3.145, 5, 2)

Case Study: A Sales Table

We now write a program to capture sales data and display it in a formatted table. The program also illustrates the use of graphical user interfaces and private helper methods.

Request

Write a program that allows the user to enter the names and annual sa es figures for any number of salespeople. The program should display a formatted table of the names, sales, and commissions (at 10 percent of the sales amount) followed by the total of all sales and commissions.

Analysis

Figure 7-9 shows the proposed interface for the program. The user repeatedly

■ Inputs a salesperson's name (no more than ten characters) in a text fie d

■ Inputs the salesperson's annual sales amount (a floating-point number) in a double field

■ Then clicks on the **Enter** button

Each time the user clicks on the **Enter** button, a new line of information is appended to a text area that contains the sales table. Finally, the user clicks on the **Display Totals** button, at which point the totals are displayed and both buttons are disabled, thereby preventing further user inputs or commands.

FIGURE 7-9
Proposed interface for the sales table program

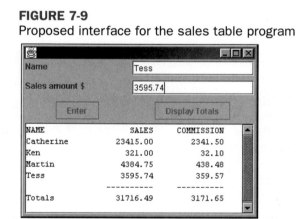

Design

The data in the sales table are formatted as follows:

■ Names are left justified in a field of width 12.

■ Sales, commissions, and totals are right justified in fields of width 15 with a precision of 2.

Following is pseudocode for the `buttonClicked` method:

```
if (the Enter button is pressed) {
    read the salesperson's name and the sales amount
    calculate the commission
    format and display the name, sales amount, and commission
    increment the totals
}else{
    format and display the totals
    disable the command buttons
}
```

The `buttonClicked` method has rather a lot to do, so we assign some of the work to helper methods. Taking the helper methods into account yields the following pseudocode:

```
void buttonClicked(JButton buttonObj){
   if (the Enter button is pressed) {
      processInputs()
   }else{
      displayDashes()
      displayNumbers ("Totals", totalSales, totalCommissions)
   }
}

void processInputs(){
   read the salesperson's name and sales amount
   calculate the commission
   displayNumbers (name, sales, commission)
   increment the totals
}

void displayNumbers (String str, double num1, double num2){
   format and display str, num1, and num2
}

void displayDashes(){
   format and display dashes above the totals
}
```

Figure 7-10 contains a diagram called a ***structure chart*** that shows the relationship between `buttonClicked` and its helpers.

FIGURE 7-10
A structure chart for `buttonClicked` and its helpers

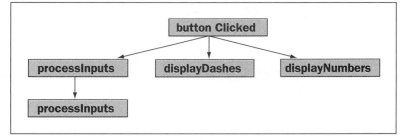

Implementation

Following is the complete code for the program. Notice the technique used for disabling and for setting the focus to a window object.

```
/* SalesTable.java
Display a table of names, sales, and commissions with totals.
1. The user enters each person's name and sales and clicks on the Enter
   button.
2. The program then computes the commission as 10 percent of sales and
   appends this person's data to the table.
```

```
3. When the user clicks on the Display Totals button, the program
   displays the total sales and total commissions and blocks further user
   actions other than closing the window.
*/

import javax.swing.*;
import BreezySwing.*;

public class SalesTable extends GBFrame {


    // Declare variables for the window objects
    private JLabel        nameLabel;
    private JLabel        salesLabel;
    private JTextField    nameField;
    private DoubleField   salesField;
    private JButton       enterButton;
    private JButton       totalsButton;
    private JTextArea     output;


    // Define the other instance variables
    private double  totalSales;         //The total of all sales
    private double  totalCommissions;   //The total of all sales commissions

    // Constructor
    public SalesTable(){
       // Define the table's header line
       String header = Format.justify('l', "NAME", 12) +
                       Format.justify('r', "SALES", 15) +
                       Format.justify('r', "COMMISSION", 15) + "\n";

       // Instantiate the window objects
       nameLabel    = addLabel        ("Name"              ,1,1,1,1);
       salesLabel   = addLabel        ("Sales amount $"    ,2,1,1,1);
       nameField    = addTextField    (""                  ,1,2,1,1);
       salesField   = addDoubleField  (0                   ,2,2,1,1);
       enterButton  = addButton       ("Enter"             ,3,1,1,1);
       totalsButton = addButton       ("Display Totals" ,  3,2,1,1);
       output       = addTextArea     (header              ,4,1,3,4);

       // Disable the text area because we don't want the user to change it
       // Set the focus to name field in preparation for the user's first
       // input
       output.setEnabled(false);
       nameField.requestFocus();

       // Initialize the totals to 0.
       totalSales = 0;
       totalCommissions = 0;
    }

    // Respond to the command buttons
```

```java
public void buttonClicked (JButton buttonObj){
   if (buttonObj == enterButton){
      processInputs();
      nameField.requestFocus();    //Move the cursor to the name field
   }else{
      enterButton.setEnabled(false);      //Prevent further user action
      totalsButton.setEnabled(false);     //by disabling the command
                                          //buttons

      displayDashes();
      displayNumbers ("Totals", totalSales, totalCommissions);
   }
}


// Read the inputs, compute the commissions, format and display the
// name, sale, and commission
private void processInputs(){
   // Declare the local variables
   String name;                     //The salesperson's name
   double sales;                    //                       sales
   double commission;               //                       commission

   // Read the user input
   name = nameField.getText();
   sales = salesField.getNumber();

   // Calculate the commission
   commission = sales * 0.10;

   // Display the name, sales, and commission
   displayNumbers (name, sales, commission);

   // Increment the totals
   totalSales += sales;
   totalCommissions += commission;
}


// Format another line and append to the text area
private void displayNumbers (String str, double num1, double num2){
   String numberLine = Format.justify ('l', str, 12) +
                       Format.justify ('r', num1, 15, 2) +
                       Format.justify ('r', num2, 15, 2);
   output.append (numberLine + "\n");
}


// Display dashes between the sales figures and the totals
private void displayDashes(){
   String dashLine = Format.justify ('l', " ", 12) +
                     Format.justify ('r', "----------", 15) +
                     Format.justify ('r', "----------", 15);
   output.append (dashLine + "\n");
}
```

```
public static void main (String[] args){
    SalesTable theGUI = new SalesTable();
    theGUI.setSize (350, 225);
    theGUI.setVisible (true);
}
}
```

7.8 GUIs and Applets

As mentioned in Lesson 2, an applet is a Java program that runs in a Web browser. Instead of running in a terminal window, an applet has a graphical user interface that appears embedded in the Web page. Now that you have completed this lesson, you can convert many Java applications to applets. The techniques for doing so are described in the lesson on HTML and applets. If you wish, you can skip to that lesson now.

SUMMARY

In this lesson, you learned:

- A terminal I/O interface can be extended to handle repeated sets of inputs, by using either a query-based pattern or a menu-driven pattern.

- A graphical user interface (GUI) allows the user to interact with a program by displaying window objects and handling mouse events.

- In a terminal-based program, the program controls most of the interaction with the user, whereas GUI-based programs are driven by user events.

- The two primary tasks of a GUI-based program are to arrange the window objects in a window and handle interactions with the user.

- GUI-based programs are more complex than terminal-based programs. Much of this complexity involves learning to use Java's Swing toolkit. The use of additional toolkits such as `BreezySwing` eases the development of GUI-based programs and facilitates that transition to competence with Swing, however.

VOCABULARY *Review*

Define the following terms:

button object	message box	text area object
double field object	Metal	text field object
integer field object	query-controlled input	window object
label object	structure chart	

REVIEW *Questions*

FILL IN THE BLANK

Complete each of the following statements by writing your answer in the blank provided.

1. In contrast to terminal I/O programs, GUI programs are _____ driven.

2. A button allows the user to select a(n) _____.

3. Two types of window objects that support numeric input and output are a(n) _____ and a(n) _____.

4. A window object that supports the input and output of a single line of text is a(n) _____.

5. A separate window that pops up with information is a(n) _____.

PROJECTS

When developing a program that uses a GUI, much of the analysis phase is occupied with sketching layouts of the user interface. These drawings help the programmer to determine which window objects are needed and to determine their arrangement, position, and extent in the window. Moreover, the design of the computation can be postponed until the user interface part is coded and tested. When the look of the interface matches the sketches resulting from analysis, the remaining parts of the program, which handle button clicks and so forth, can be designed, coded, and tested. We recommend that you follow this incremental development strategy in the projects and activities that follow. Because many solutions recast ones already done in earlier lessons, you can borrow code from the previous versions.

PROJECT 7-1

Redo Project 4-4 from Lesson 4 (computing the value of π) with a GUI.

PROJECT 7-2

Redo Project 4-5 from Lesson 4 (predicting population growth) with a GUI.

PROJECT 7-3

Newton's method for computing the square root of a number consists of approximating the actual square root by means of a set of transformations. Each transformation starts with a guess at the square root. A better approximation is then (guess + number / guess) / 2. This result becomes the guess for the next approximation. The initial guess is 1. Write a GUI program that allows the user to enter a number and the number of approximations to compute its square root.

PROJECT 7-4

Modify the program of Project 7-3 so that the user can view the successive approximations in a text area. (*Hint*: Build a formatted string of the approximations during the computation.)

PROJECT 7-5

John has $500 to invest. Sue knows of a mutual fund plan that pays 10 percent interest, compounded quarterly (that is, every 3 months, the principal is multiplied by the 2.5 percent and the result is added to the principal; more generally, the amount of gain each quarter is equal to current balance * (1 + interest rate / 500)). Write a program that will tell John how much money will be in the fund after 20 years. Make the program general; that is, it should take as inputs the interest rate, the initial principal, and the number of years to stay in the fund. The output should be a table whose columns are the year number, the principal at the beginning of the year, the interest earned, and the principal at the end of the year.

PROJECT 7-6

The TidBit Computer Store has a credit plan for computer purchases. There is a 10 percent down payment and an annual interest rate of 12 percent. Monthly payments are 5 percent of the listed purchase price minus the down payment. Write a program that takes the purchase price as input. The program should display a table, with appropriate headers, of a payment schedule for the lifetime of the loan. Each row of the table should contain the following items:

■ The month number (beginning with 1)

■ The current total balance owed

■ The interest owed for that month

■ The amount of principal owed for that month

■ The payment for that month

■ The balance remaining after payment

The amount of interest for a month is equal to balance * rate / 12. The amount of principal for a month is equal to the monthly payment minus the interest owed.

CRITICAL *Thinking*

A company approaches you about the need for a program and wonders whether to ask for a terminal-based user interface or a graphical user interface. Discuss the issues involved in choosing between these two interfaces from a client's perspective.

THE NEXT STEP WITH JAVA

REVIEW *Questions*

TRUE/FALSE

Circle T if the statement is true or F if it is false.

T   F   1.   A mutator method is used to ask an object for the values of its data attributes.

T   F   2.   The purpose of a constructor is to change the data type of an object.

T   F   3.   Two variables can refer to the same object.

T   F   4.   `private` variables are visible within their class and to all clients of that class.

T   F   5.   Each method can declare its own private variables, called local variables.

T   F   6.   The lifetime of a variable is the region on the program within which it can be used.

T   F   7.   An extended `if` statement allows a program to choose among mutually exclusive alternatives.

T   F   8.   The logical operator OR is indicated by !.

T   F   9.   A `boolean` variable is used to manipulate characters and strings.

T   F   10.   It is possible to test all programs to show that they are completely correct.

FILL IN THE BLANK

Complete the following sentences by writing the correct word or words in the blanks provided.

1. The process of creating a new object is called _____.

2. The process of deleting unreferenced objects from memory is called _____.

3. If a variable is declared outside all methods, it is said to be _____.

4. The access modifier that makes methods visible to all clients is _____.

5. Two methods in a program that have the same name but not the same number and types of parameters are said to be _____.

6. When a variable of a reference type is declared but not given a value, its default value is _____.

7. The easiest way to increase numbers by one in a program is to use the _____ operator.

8. The logical operators are _____, _____, and _____.

9. The _____ statement provides a simple way to get out of a loop before all of the statements in the loop process.

10. To determine all the possible values of a Boolean expression, one can use a(n) _____ table.

WRITTEN QUESTIONS

Write your answers to the following questions or problems.

1. Explain the difference between a global variable and a local variable and give an example of each.

2. Assume that x, y, and z are boolean variables. Draw truth tables for the following expressions.
   A. x && y || z

   B. !(x || y || z)

   C. x && (y || z)

3. Define a class called counter. A counter contains an integer which initially is 0 but which can be incremented, decremented, or reset to 0. Counter objects should respond to the mutators increment(), decrement(), and reset(), and to the accessor getValue().

4.   What is data encapsulation? Why is it important?

5.   Describe what a class constructor does.

PROJECTS

SCANS **PROJECT U2-1**

Write a program that takes as inputs the lengths of three sides of a triangle and displays in a message box whether the triangle is scalene, isosceles, or equilateral. Useful facts:

■   In a triangle, the longest side must be less than the sum of the other two sides.

■   A scalene triangle has all sides unequal.

■   An isosceles triangle has two sides equal.

■   An equilateral triangle has all sides equal.

SCANS **PROJECT U2-2**

In the game of craps, a player provides an initial bankroll and bets from this amount on each roll of the dice. On each roll, the sum of the faces is taken. The outcomes are as follow:

■   If 7 or 11 is rolled, the player wins.

■   If 2, 3, or 12 is rolled, the player loses.

■   Otherwise, the number rolled becomes the player's point. The player rolls the dice repeatedly until the player wins by making point (getting the same number as on the first roll) or loses by crapping out (getting a 7).

Design and implement a craps machine that allows the user to play craps. This machine should be defined as a new class. The interface accepts an amount of money representing an initial bankroll. Before each roll of the dice, the user must make a bet. The interface should control the user's options by enabling and disabling the appropriate command buttons. At the end of the game, program should display the amount of the user's current bankroll (after adding the gains and deducting the losses).

PROJECT U2-3

A perfect number is a positive integer such that the sum of the divisors equals the number. Thus, 28 = 1 + 2 + 4 + 7 + 14 is a perfect number. If the sum of the divisors is less than the number, it is deficient. If the sum exceeds the number, it is abundant. Write a program that takes a positive integer as input and displays a message box that indicates whether the number entered is perfect, deficient, or abundant. Your program should define the following two methods:

```
boolean isDivisor (int number, int divisor)
int divisorSum (int number)
```

The method `isDivisor` returns `true` if the `divisor` parameter is a divisor of the `number` parameter, and `false` otherwise. The `divisorSum` method uses `isDivisor` to accumulate and return the sum of the proper divisors of the `number` parameter. Be sure to design and test the program incrementally; that is, verify that `isDivisor` works correctly before using it in `divisorSum`.

PROJECT U2-4

A standard physics experiment is to drop a ball to see how high it bounces. Once the "bounciness" of the ball is determined, the ratio gives a bounciness index. For example, if a ball dropped from a height of 10 feet bounces 6 feet high, the index is 0.6 and the total distance traveled by the ball is 16 feet after one bounce. If the ball continues bouncing, the distance after two bounces would be 10 + 6 + 3.6 = 25.6 ft. Note that the distance traveled for each bounce is the distance to the floor plus 0.6 of that distance as the ball comes back up.

Write a program that takes as inputs the initial height of the ball (in feet), the index of the ball's bounciness, and the number of times the ball is allowed to continue bouncing. The program should output the total distance traveled by the ball. At some point in the process, the distance traveled by the ball after a bounce might become negligible, for example, less than 0.00001 inches. If that stage is reached, terminate the process and output the total distance.

CRITICAL *Thinking*

A number is prime if it has no divisors (other than 1) that are less than or equal to its square root. The number 1 is not prime. Design and implement a method, `isPrime`, that returns `true` if its parameter is a prime number and `false` otherwise. You should use the `isDivisor` method developed in Project U2-3 in the implementation of `isPrime`. Then use these methods in a program that takes as input a number N and displays as output a list of the first N prime numbers.

ARRAYS, RECURSION, AND COMPLEXITY

Unit 3

🕐 **Estimated Time for Unit: 14 hrs.**

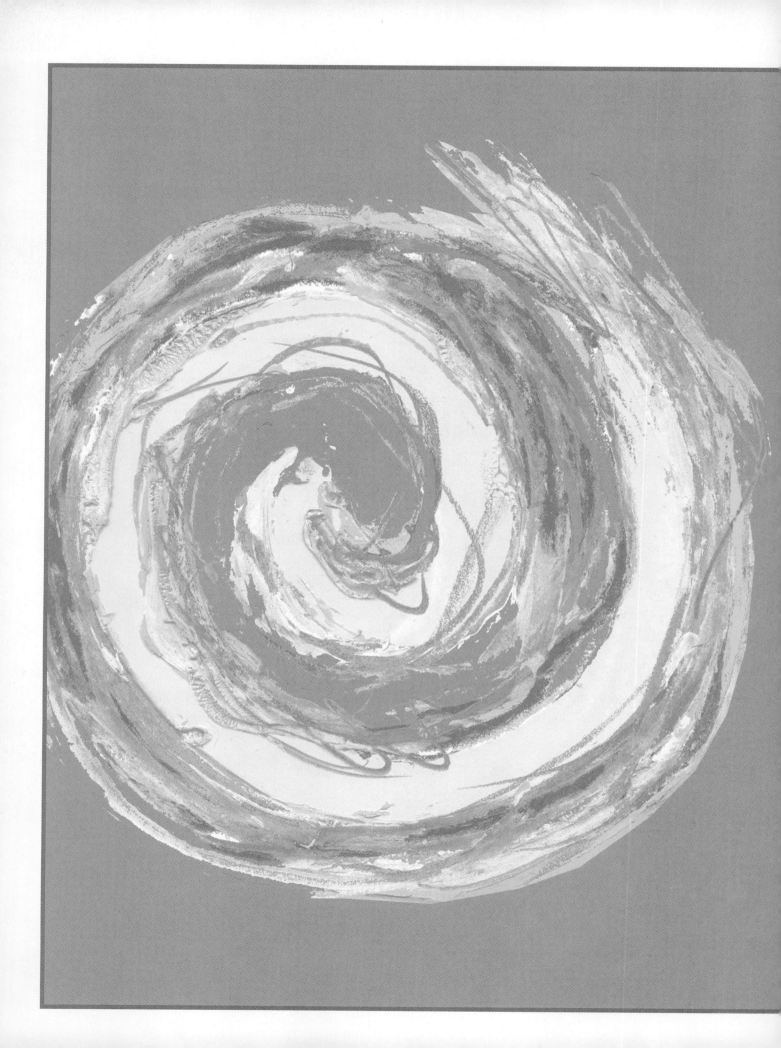

INTRODUCTION TO ARRAYS

OBJECTIVES

Upon completion of this lesson, you should be able to:

- Write programs that handle collections of similar items.

- Declare array variables and instantiate array objects.

- Manipulate arrays with loops.

- Write methods to manipulate arrays.

- Create parallel arrays and two-dimensional arrays.

Estimated Time: 3.5 hours

VOCABULARY

array

element

index

initializer list

logical size

multidimensional array

one-dimensional array

parallel arrays

physical size

ragged array

range bound error

subscript

two-dimensional array

There are situations in which programs need to manipulate many similar items, a task that would be extremely awkward using the language features encountered so far. Earlier we developed a Student class with a name and three test scores. Each test score required a separate instance variable. Imagine how tedious and lengthy the code would have become if a student had 20 scores. Fortunately, there is a way to handle this dilemma. Most programming languages, including Java, provide a data structure called an *array*, which consists of an ordered collection of similar items. An array, as a whole, has a single name, and the items in an array are referred to in terms of their position within the array. This lesson explains the mechanics of declaring arrays and several basic algorithms for manipulating them. Using an array, it is as easy to manipulate a million test scores as it is three.

8.1 Conceptual Overview

To demonstrate the need for arrays, let us consider the data for a Student class if there are no arrays, but there are 20 rather than 3 test scores. The declarations for the instance variables look like this:

```
private String name;
private int test1,  test2,  test3,  test4,  test5,
            test6,  test7,  test8,  test9,  test10,
            test11, test12, test13, test14, test15,
            test16, test17, test18, test19, test20;
```

and the computation of the average score looks like this:

```
// Compute and return a student's average
public int getAverage(){
    int average;
    average = (test1 + test2  + test3  + test4  + test5 +
            test6  + test7  + test8  + test9  + test10 +
            test11 + test12 + test13 + test14 + test15 +
            test16 + test17 + test18 + test19 + test20) / 20;
    return average;
}
```

Other methods are affected in a similar manner; however, arrays restore sanity to the situation. The items in an array are called *elements*, and for any particular array, all the elements must all be of the same type. The type can be any primitive or reference type. For instance, we can have an array of test scores, an array of names, or even an array of student objects. Figure 8-1 illustrates these ideas. In the figure, each array contains five elements, or has a *length* of five. The first element in the array test is referred to as test[0], the second as test[1], and so on. Here we encounter Java's convention of numbering from 0 rather than from 1, a convention that is guaranteed to cause us grief whenever we accidentally revert to our lifelong habit of counting from 1. Thus, the elements in an array of length 100 are numbered from 0 to 99. An item's position within an array is called its *index* or *subscript*. In Figure 8-1, the array indexes appear within square brackets ([ ]).

FIGURE 8-1
Three arrays, each containing five elements

	Array of five integers called **test**		Array of five strings called **name**		Array of five characters called **grade**	
1st	85	test[0]	"Bill"	name[0]	'B'	grade[0]
2nd	100	test[1]	"Sue"	name[1]	'C'	grade[1]
3rd	75	test[2]	"Grace"	name[2]	'B'	grade[2]
4th	87	test[3]	"Tom"	name[3]	'A'	grade[3]
5th	68	test[4]	"John"	name[4]	'C'	grade[4]

*E*XERCISE 8.1

1. A program needs many variables to store and process data. How does an array solve this problem?

2. How does the programmer access an item in an array?

3. Mary is using an array of doubles to store an employee's wage amounts for each day of the week (Monday through Friday). Draw a picture of this array with sample items and references to each one.

8.2 Simple Array Manipulations

The mechanics of manipulating arrays are fairly straightforward, as illustrated in the following segments of code. First, we declare and instantiate an array of 500 integer values. (Section 8.4 discusses array declarations in greater detail.) By default, all of the values are initialized to 0:

```
int[] abc = new int[500];
```

Next, we declare some other variables:

```
int i = 3;
int temp;
double avFirstFive;
```

The basic syntax for referring to an array element has the form

```
<array name>[<index>]
```

where <index> must be between 0 and the array's length less 1. The subscript operator ([ ]) has the same precedence as the method selector (.). To illustrate, we assign values to the first five elements:

```
abc[0] = 78;                 //1st element 78
abc[1] = 66;                 //2nd element 66
abc[2] = (abc[0] + abc[1]) / 2; //3rd element average of first two
abc[i] = 82;                 //4th element 82 because i is 3
abc[i + 1] = 94;             //5th element 94 because i + 1 is 4
```

When assigning a value to the 500th element, we must remember that its index is 499, not 500:

```
abc[499] = 76;               //500th element 76
```

Fortunately, the JVM checks the values of subscripts before using them and throws an `ArrayIndexOutOfBoundsException` if they are out of bounds (less than 0 or greater than the array length less 1). The detection of a *range bound error* is similar to the JVM's behavior when a program attempts to divide by zero.

In our present example, subscripts must be between 0 and 499. Later in the lesson, we show how to work with arrays of any size and how to write loops that are not tied to a literal value (in this case, 500).

```
abc[-1] = 74;                //NO! NO! NO! Out of bounds
abc[500] = 88;               //NO! NO! NO! Out of bounds
```

To compute the average of the first five elements, we could write

```
avFirstFive = (abc[0] + abc[1] + abc[2] + abc[3] + abc[4])/5;
```

It often happens that we need to interchange elements in an array. To demonstrate, following is code that interchanges any two adjacent elements:

```
// Initializations
. . .
abc[3] = 82;
abc[4] = 95;
i = 3;
. . .


// Interchange adjacent elements
temp = abc[i];            // temp      now equals 82
abc[i] = abc[i + 1];      // abc[i]    now equals 95
abc[i + 1] = temp;        // abc[i + 1] now equals 82
```

We frequently need to know an array's length, but we do not have to remember it. The array itself makes this information available by means of a public instance variable called `length`:

```
System.out.println ("The size of abc is: " + abc.length);
```

EXERCISE 8.2

1. Assume that the array a contains the five integers 34, 23, 67, 89, and 12. Write the values of the following expressions:
   a. a[1]
   b. a[a.length − 1]
   c. a[2] + a[3]

2. What happens when a program attempts to access an item at an index that is less than zero or greater than or equal to the array's length?

8.3 Looping Through Arrays

There are many situations in which it is necessary to write a loop that iterates through an array one element at a time. Following are some examples based on the array abc of 500 integers. Later in this section, we will show how to work with arrays of any size and how to write loops that are not tied to a literal value (in this case, 500).

Sum the Elements

The following is code that sums the numbers in the array abc. Each time through the loop we add a different element to the sum. On the first iteration we add abc[0] and on the last abc[499].

```
int sum;
sum = 0;
for (int i = 0; i < 500; i++)
    sum += abc[i];
```

Count the Occurrences

We can determine how many times a number x occurs in the array by comparing x to each element and incrementing count every time there is a match:

```java
int x;
int count;
x = ...;                          //Assign some value to x
count = 0;
for (int i = 0; i < 500; i++){
   if (abc[i] == x)
      count++;                    //Found another element equal to x
}
```

Determine Presence or Absence

To determine if a particular number is present in the array, we could count the occurrences, but alternatively, we could save time by breaking out of the loop as soon as the first match is found. The following is code based on this idea. The Boolean variable found indicates the outcome of the search:

```java
int x;
boolean found;
x = ...;
found = false;                  // Initially assume x is not present
for (int i = 0; i < 500; i++){
   if (abc[i] == x){
      found = true;
      break;                     // No point in continuing once x is found
   }                             // so break out of the loop
}
if (found)
   System.out.println("Found");
else
   System.out.println("Not Found");
```

Determine First Location

As a variation on the preceding example, we show how to find the first location of x in the array. The variable loc initially equals −1, meaning that we have not found x yet. We then iterate through the array, comparing each element to x. As soon as we find a match, we set loc to the location and break out of the loop. If x is not found, loc remains equal to −1.

```java
int x;
int loc;
x = ...;
loc = -1;
for (int i = 0; i < 500; i++){
   if (abc[i] == x){
      loc = i;
      break;
   }
```

```
   }
   if (loc == -1)
      System.out.println("Not Found");
   else
      System.out.println("Found at index " + loc);
   }
```

Working with Arrays of Any Size

The examples in this section have assumed that the array contains 500 elements. It is possible and also desirable to write similar code that works with arrays of any size, however. We simply replace the literal 500 with a reference to the array's instance variable `length` in each of the loops. For example, this code would sum the integers in an array of any size:

```
int sum;
sum = 0;
for (int i = 0; i < abc.length; i++)
   sum += abc[i];
```

*E*XERCISE 8.3

1. Write a loop that prints all of the items in an array a to the terminal screen.

2. Repeat Question 1 but print the items in reverse order.

3. Write a loop that locates the first occurrence of a negative integer in an array a. When the loop is finished, the variable `index` should contain the index of the negative number or the length of the array if there were no negative numbers in the array.

4. Describe what the following code segments do:
   a.

```
for (int i = 0; i < a.length; i++)
   a[i] = Math.abs(a[i]);
```

   b.

```
String str = "";
for (int i = 0; i < a.length; i++)
   str += a[i];
```

5. What is the advantage of using the instance variable `length` in a loop with an array?

8.4 Declaring Arrays

Earlier, we declared an array of 500 integers as follows:

```
int[] abc = new int[500];
```

In doing so, we combined two separate statements:

```
int[] abc;               // Declare abc to be a variable that can
                         // reference an array of integers.
abc = new int[500];      // Instantiate an array of 500 integers for abc to
                         // reference.
```

Arrays are objects and must be instantiated before being used. Several array variables can be declared in a single statement like this:

```
int[] abc, xyz;
abc = new int[500];
xyz = new int[10];
```

or like this:

```
int[] abc = new int[500], xyz = new int[10];
```

Array variables are null before they are assigned array objects. Failure to assign an array object can result in a null pointer exception, as shown in the next code segment:

```
int[] abc;
abc[1] = 10;     // runtime error: null pointer exception
```

Because arrays are objects, two variables can refer to the same array, as indicated in Figure 8-2 and the next segment of code:

```
int[] abc, xyz;
abc = new int[5];            // Instantiate an array of five
                             integers
xyz = abc;                   // xyz and abc refer to the same array
xyz[3] = 100;                // Changing xyz changes abc as well.
System.out.println (abc[3]); // 100 is displayed.
```

FIGURE 8-2
Two variables can refer to the same array object

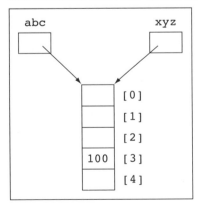

If we want abc and xyz to refer to two separate arrays that happen to contain the same values, we could copy all of the elements from one array to the other, as follows:

```
int[] abc, xyz;          // Declare two array variables
int i;
abc = new int[10];       // Instantiate an array of size 10
for (i = 0; i < 10; i++) // Initialize the array
    abc[i] = i*i;        //    a[0]=0 and a[1]=1 and a[2]=4, etc.

xyz = new int[10];       // Instantiate another array of size 10
for (i = 0; i < 10; i++) // Initialize the second array
    xyz[i] = abc[i];
```

Also, because arrays are objects, Java's garbage collector sweeps them away when they are no longer referenced:

```
int[] abc, xyz;
abc = new int[10];   // Instantiate an array of ten integers.
xyz = new int[5];    // Instantiate an array of five integers.
xyz = null;          // The array of five integers is no longer referenced
                     // so the garbage collector will sweep it away.
```

Arrays can be declared, instantiated, and initialized in one step. The list of numbers between the braces is called an *initializer list*.

```
int[] abc = {1,2,3,4,5} // abc now references an array of five integers.
```

As mentioned at the outset, arrays can be formed from any collection of similar items. Following then are arrays of doubles, characters, Booleans, strings, and students:

```
double[]    ddd = new double[10];
char[]      ccc = new char[10];
boolean[]   bbb = new boolean[10];
String[]    ggg = new String[10];
Student[]   sss = new Student[10];
String      str;

ddd[5] = 3.14;
ccc[5] = 'Z';
bbb[5] = true;
ggg[5] = "The cat sat on the mat.";
sss[5] = new Student();

sss[5].setName ("Bill");
str = sss[5].getName() + ggg[5].substring(7);
    // str now equals "Bill sat on the mat."
```

There is one more way to declare array variables, but its use can be confusing. Here it is:

```
int aaa[];               // aaa is an array variable.
```

That does not look confusing, but what about this?

```
int aaa[], bbb, ccc[];    // aaa and ccc are array variables.
                          // bbb is not. This fact might go unnoticed.
```

Instead, it might be better to write:

```
int[] aaa, ccc;           // aaa and ccc are array variables
int bbb;                  // bbb is not. This fact is obvious.
```

EXERCISE 8.4

1. Declare and instantiate array variables for the following data:

   a. An array of 15 doubles

   b. An array of 20 strings

2. What is an initializer list?

3. Use an initializer list to create the following arrays:

   a. 5 test scores of 100, 90, 75, 60, and 88

   b. 3 interest rates of 0.12, 0.05, and 0.15

   c. 2 strings, your first name and last name

4. Why is it better to use the form `<type>[] <variable>` instead of `<type> <variable>[]` when declaring an array variable?

> **Warning**
>
> Once an array is instantiated, its size cannot be changed, so make sure the array is large enough from the outset.

8.5 *Working with Arrays That Are Not Full*

When an array is instantiated, the computer automatically fills its cells with default values. For example, each cell in an array of `int` initially contains the value 0. The application then replaces these values with new ones as needed. An application might not use all the cells available in an array, however. For example, one might create an array of 20 `int`s but receive only 5 `int`s from interactive input. This array has a *physical size* of 20 cells but a *logical size* of 5 cells currently used by the application. From the application's perspective, the remaining 15 cells contain garbage. Clearly, the application should only access the first 5 cells when asked to display the data, so using the array's physical size as an upper bound on a loop will not do. We solve this problem by tracking the array's logical size with a separate integer variable. The following code segment shows the initial state of an array and its logical size:

```
int[] abc = new int[50];
int size = 0;
```

Note that `abc.length` (the physical size) is 50, whereas `size` (the logical size) is 0.

Processing Elements in an Array That Is Not Full

In Section 8.3, we showed how to generalize a loop to process all the data in an array of any size. The loop accesses each cell from position 0 to position `length − 1`, where `length` is the array's instance variable. When the array is not full, one must replace the array's length with its logical size in the loop. Following is the code for computing the sum of the integers currently available in the array `abc`:

```
int[] abc[50];
int size = 0;

... code that puts values into some initial portion of the array and sets
    the value of size ...

int sum = 0;
for (int i = 0; i < size; i++)
   sum += abc[i];
```

Adding Elements to an Array

The simplest way to add a data element to an array is to place it after the last available item. One must first check to see if there is a cell available and then remember to increment the array's logical size. The following code shows how to add an integer to the end of array `abc`:

```
if (size < abc.length){
   abc[size] = anInt;
   size++;
}
```

When `size` equals `abc.length`, the array is full. The `if` statement prevents a range error from occurring. Remember that Java arrays are of fixed size when they are instantiated, so eventually they become full. We will examine a way of skirting this limitation of arrays in Lesson 10.

We can also insert an element at an earlier position in the array. This process requires a shifting of other elements and is also presented in Lesson 10.

Removing Elements from an Array

Removing a data element from the end of an array requires no change to the array itself. We simply decrement the logical size, thus preventing the application from accessing the garbage elements beyond that point. (Removing a data element from an arbitrary position is discussed in Lesson 10.)

*E*XERCISE 8.5

1. What happens when the programmer tries to access an array cell whose index is greater than or equal to its logical size?

2. Describe an application that uses an array that might not be full.

8.6 Parallel Arrays

There are situations in which it is convenient to declare what are called *parallel arrays*. Suppose we want to keep a list of people's names and ages. This can be achieved by using two arrays in which corresponding elements are related. For instance

```
String[] name = {"Bill", "Sue", "Shawn", "Mary", "Ann"};
int[]    age  = {20    , 21   , 19      , 24    , 20};
```

Thus, Bill's age is 20 and Mary's is 24. Note that related items have the same index. There are many other uses for parallel arrays, but continuing on with our present example, the following is a segment of code that finds the age of a particular person:

```
String searchName;
int correspondingAge = -1;
int i;

searchName = ...;                       // Set this to the desired name
for (i = 0; i < name.length; i++){      // name.length is the array's size
   if (searchName.equals (name[i]){
      correspondingAge = age[i];
      break;
   }
}

if (correspondingAge == -1)
   System.out.println(searchName + " not found.");
else
   System.out.println("The age is " + correspondingAge);
```

In this example, the parallel arrays are both full and the loops use the instance variable `length`. When the arrays are not full, the code will need an extra variable to track their logical sizes, as discussed earlier.

EXERCISE 8.6

1. What are parallel arrays?

2. Describe an application in which parallel arrays might be used.

3. Declare and instantiate the variables for parallel arrays to track the names, ages, and Social Security numbers of 50 employees.

4. Assume that the array `names` contains the names of people in a phone book and the parallel array `numbers` contains their phone numbers. Write a code segment that displays each name and number in formatted columns (using the method `Format.justify` introduced in Lesson 7). Names should be left justified in a width of 20 columns. You may assume that each number is the same length.

5. Write a code segment that creates parallel arrays containing the first 10 nonnegative powers of 2. One array should contain the exponent and the other array should contain 2 raised to that power.

8.7 Two-Dimensional Arrays

The arrays we have been studying so far can represent only simple lists of items and are called *one-dimensional arrays*. For many applications, *multidimensional arrays* are more useful. A table of numbers, for instance, can be implemented as a *two-dimensional array*. Figure 8-3 shows a two-dimensional array with four rows and five columns.

FIGURE 8-3

A two-dimensional array with four rows and five columns

	col 0	col 1	col 2	col 3	col 4
row 0	00	01	02	03	04
row 1	10	11	12	13	14
row 2	20	21	22	23	24
row 3	30	31	32	33	34

Suppose we call the array `table`; then to indicate an element in `table`, we specify its row and column position, remembering that indexes start at 0:

```
x = table[2][3];   // Set x to 23, the value in (row 2, column 3)
```

Sum the Elements

The techniques for manipulating one-dimensional arrays are easily extended to two-dimensional arrays. For instance, the following is code that sums all the numbers in `table`. The outer loop iterates four times and moves down the rows. Each time through the outer loop, the inner loop iterates five times and moves across a different row.

```
int i, j;
int sum = 0;
for (i = 0; i < 4; i++){     // There are four rows: i = 0,1,2,3
   for (j = 0; j < 5; j++){ // There are five columns: j = 0,1,2,3,4
      sum += table[i][j];
   }
}
```

This segment of code can be rewritten without using the numbers 4 and 5. The value `table.length` equals the number of rows, and `table[i].length` is the number of columns in row `i`.

```
int i, j;
int sum = 0;
for (i = 0; i < table.length; i++){
   for (j = 0; j < table[i].length; j++){
      sum += table[i][j];
   }
}
```

Sum the Rows

Rather than accumulate all the numbers into a single sum, we now compute the sum of each row separately and place the results in a one-dimensional array called rowSum. This array has four elements, one for each row of the table. The elements in rowSum are initialized to 0 automatically by virtue of the declaration.

```
int i, j;
int[] rowSum = new int[4];
for (i = 0; i < table.length; i++){
   for (j = 0; j < table[i].length; j++){
      rowSum[i] += table[i][j];
   }
}
```

Declare and Instantiate

Declaring and instantiating two-dimensional arrays is accomplished by extending the processes used for one-dimensional arrays:

```
int[][] table;              // The variable table can reference a
                            // two-dimensional array of integers.
table = new int[4][5];      // Instantiate table as an array of size 4,
                            // each of whose elements will reference an array
                            // of 5 integers.
```

Figure 8-4 shows another diagram of table that illustrates the perspective revealed in the previous piece of code. The variable table references an array of four elements. Each of these elements in turn references an array of five integers. Although the diagram is complex, specifying an element in the resulting two-dimensional array is the same as before, for instance, table[2][3].

FIGURE 8-4
Another way of visualizing a two-dimensional array

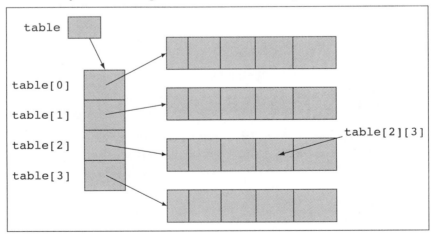

Initializer lists can be used with two-dimensional arrays. This requires a list of lists. The number of inner lists determines the number of rows, and the size of each inner list determines the size of the corresponding row. The rows do not have to be the same size, but they are in this example:

```
int[][] table = {{ 0, 1, 2, 3, 4},      // row 0
                 {10,11,12,13,14},      // row 1
                 {20,21,22,23,24},      // row 2
                 {30,31,32,33,34}};     // row 3
```

Variable Length Rows

Occasionally, the rows of a two-dimensional array are not all the same length. We call these *ragged arrays*, and we just mention them in passing. Consider the following improbable declaration:

```
int[][] table;
table     = new int[4][];   // table has 4 rows
table[0] = new int[6];      // row 0 has 6     elements
table[1] = new int[10];     // row 1 has 10    elements
table[2] = new int[100];    // row 2 has 100 elements
table[3] = new int[1];      // row 3 has 1     element
```

Finally, remember that all the elements of a two-dimensional array must be of the same type, whether they are integers, doubles, strings, or whatever.

EXERCISE 8.7

1. What are two-dimensional arrays?

2. Describe an application in which a two-dimensional array might be used.

3. Write a code segment that searches a two-dimensional array for a negative integer. The loop should terminate at the first instance of a negative integer in the array, and the variables `row` and `col` should be set to its position. Otherwise, the variables `row` and `col` should equal the number of rows and columns in the array (we assume that each row has the same number of columns).

4. Describe the contents of the array after the following code segment is run:

```
int [][] matrix = new int[5][5];

for (int row = 0; row < matrix.length; row++)
   for (int col = 0; col < matrix[row].length; col++)
      matrix[row][col] = row * col;
```

8.8 Arrays and Methods

When any object is used as a parameter to a method, what actually gets passed is a reference to the object and not the object itself, as illustrated in Figure 8-5. In other words, the actual and formal parameters refer to the same object, and changes the method makes to the object's state are still in effect after the method terminates. In the figure, the method changes the student's name to Bill, and after the method finishes executing the name is still Bill.

FIGURE 8-5
Passing a reference to an object as a parameter

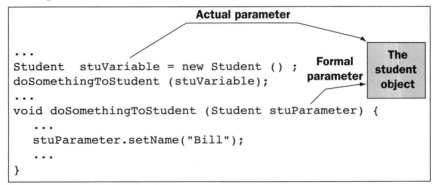

Arrays are objects, so the same rules apply. When an array is passed as a parameter to a method, the method manipulates the array itself and not a copy. Changes made to the array in the method are still in effect after the method has completed its execution. Consequently, passing an array to a method leads to trouble if the method accidentally mishandles the array. A method can also instantiate a new object or a new array and return it using the `return` statement. Following are some illustrations based on examples presented earlier.

Sum the Elements

First, we look at a method that computes the sum of the numbers in an integer array. When the method is written, there is no need to know the array's size. The method works equally well with integer arrays of all sizes, as long as those arrays are full; however, the method cannot be used with arrays of other types, for instance, doubles. Notice that the method makes no changes to the array and therefore is "safe."

```
int sum (int[] a){
   int i, result = 0;
   for (i = 0; i < a.length; i++)
      result += a[i];
   return result;
}
```

Using the method is straightforward:

```
int[] array1 = {10, 24, 16, 78, -55, 89, 65};
int[] array2 = {4334, 22928, 33291};
...
if (sum(array1) > sum(array2)) ...
```

Search for a Value

The code to search an array for a value is used so frequently in programs that it is worth placing in a method. Following is a method to search an array of integers. The method returns the location of the first array element equal to the search value or –1 if the value is absent:

```
int search (int[] a, int searchValue){
    int location, i;
    location = -1;
    for (i = 0; i < a.length; i++){
        if (a[i] == searchValue){
            location = i;
            break;
        }
    }
    return location;
}
```

Sum the Rows

Following is a method that instantiates a new array and returns it. The method computes the sum of each row in a two-dimensional array and returns a one-dimensional array of row sums. The method works even if the rows are not all the same size. We also rely on the fact that Java provides a default value of 0 at each position in the new array.

```
int[] sumRows (int[][] a){
    int i, j;
    int[] rowSum = new int[a.length];
    for (i = 0; i < a.length; i++){
        for (j = 0; j < a[i].length; j++){
            rowSum[i] += a[i][j];
        }
    }
    return rowSum;
}
```

Following is code that uses the method. Notice that we do not have to instantiate the array oneD because that task is done in the method sumRows.

```
int[][] twoD = {{1,2,3,4}, {5,6}, {7,8,9}};
int[] oneD;

oneD = sumRows (twoD); // oneD now references the array created and returned
                       // by the method sumRows. It equals {10, 11, 24}
```

Copy an Array

Earlier, we saw that copying an array must be done with care. Assigning one array variable to another does not do the job. It merely yields two variables referencing the same array. We examine a method that attempts to solve the problem. The first parameter represents the original array, and the second is the copy. The original is instantiated before the method is called, and the copy is instantiated in the method.

```
void copyOne(int[] original, int[] copy){
   copy = new int[original.length];
   for (int i = 0; i < original.length; i++){
      copy[i] = original[i];
   }
}
```

We now run this method in the following code segment:

```
int[] orig = {1,2,3,4,5};
int[] cp;
...
copyOne (orig, cp);
```

When copyOne terminates, we would like the variable cp to refer to copy. However, that does not happen. Even though the method creates a copy of the original array and assigns it to the array parameter (copy = new int[original.length];), the original variable cp is not changed and does not refer to the array created in the method. We can achieve our goal more successfully by writing a method that returns a copy. We then call the method and assign the returned copy to cp. Following is the code:

```
// First the method
int[] copyTwo (int[] original){
   int[] copy = new int[original.length];
   for (int i = 0; i < original.length; i++){
      copy[i] = original[i];
   }
   return copy;
}

// And here is how we call it.
int[] orig = {1,2,3,4,5};
int[] cp;
...
cp = copyTwo (orig);
```

EXERCISE 8.8

1. What happens when one uses the assignment operator (=) with two array variables?

2. Discuss the issues involved with copying an array.

3. Write a method that returns the average of the numbers in an array of `double`.

EXERCISE 8.8 Continued

4. Write a method `subArray` that expects an array of `int` and two `ints` as parameters. The integers represent the starting position and the ending position of a subarray within the parameter array. The method should return a new array that contains the elements from the starting position to the ending position.

5. Write a method that searches a two-dimensional array for a given integer. This method should return an object of class `Point`, which contains a row and a column. The constructor for `Point` is `Point(anInteger, anInteger)`.

8.9 Arrays of Objects

We examined the use of an array of strings earlier in this lesson. Arrays can hold objects of any type, or more accurately, references to objects. For example, one can declare, instantiate, and fill an array of students (see Lesson 5) as follows:

```
// Declare and reserve 10 cells for student objects
Student[] studentArray = new Student[10];

// Fill array with students
for (int i = 0; i < studentArray.length; i++)
    studentArray[i] = new Student("Student " + i, 70+i, 80+i, 90+i);
```

When an array of objects is instantiated, each cell is `null` by default until reset to a new object. The next code segment prints the average of all students in the `studentArray`. Pay special attention to the technique used to send a message to objects in an array:

```
// Print the average of all students in the array.

int sum = 0;
for (int i = 0; i < studentArray.length; i++)
    sum += studentArray[i].getAverage();   // Send message to object in array
System.out.println("The class average is " + sum / accountArray.length);
```

EXERCISE 8.9

1. Write a method `getHighStudent` that expects an array of students as a parameter. The method returns the `Student` object that contains the highest score. You may assume that the `Student` class has a method `getHighScore()`. (*Hint*: The method should declare a local variable of type `Student` to track the student with the highest score. The initial value of this variable should be `null`.)

EXERCISE 8.9 Continued

2. What happens when the following code segment is executed?

```
// Declare and reserve 10 cells for student objects
Student[] studentArray = new Student[10];

// Add 5 students to the array
for (int i = 0; i < 5; i++)
    studentArray[i] = new Student("Student " + i, 70+i, 8C+i, 90+i);

// Print the names of the students
for (int i = 0; i < studentArray.length; i++)
    System.out.println(studentArray[i].getName());
```

CASE STUDY: Student Test Scores Again

In Lesson 5 we developed a program for keeping track of student test scores. We now build on that program in two ways:

1. We extend the program so that it allows the user to maintain an array of students.

2. We modify the student class so that the three grades are stored in an array rather than in three separate instance variables.

Both changes illustrate the use of arrays to maintain lists of data.

Request

Modify the student test scores program from Lesson 5 so that it allows the user to maintain an array of students.

Analysis

Now that we know how to create GUIs, we provide an interface (see Figure 8-6) that allows us to view the current student in an array of students. The interface has buttons that support navigation through this array by moving to the first (<<), last (>>), next (>), or previous (<) student in the array. The interface also has buttons that allow the user to add a new student to the end of the array or modify an existing student. The interface displays the index of the current student (Current Index) and the current length of the array (Count). Table 8-1 explains each of these features in more detail.

FIGURE 8-6
Interface for the student test scores program

TABLE 8-1
Description of buttons

BUTTON	WHAT IT DOES
Add	Creates a new student object with the data displayed and inserts it at the end of the array. The new student becomes the current student. Error checking makes sure that the array of students in not yet full and that the student data is valid.
Modify	Replaces the current student's data with the data displayed, provided it is valid.
<<	Moves to the first student in the array and displays its data.
<	Moves to the previous student in the array and displays its data.
>	Moves to the next student in the array and displays its data.
>>	Moves to the last student in the array and displays its data.

Design

We break the design into two parts, one for each class used in the program.

The `StudentTestScores` Class: This is the interface class, and it contains three private instance variables for the data:

■ An array of `student` objects

■ The selected index (an `int`)

■ The current number of students (an `int`).

The `buttonClicked` method calls one of several private methods depending on which button is clicked. These methods either move through the array of students or update its contents in some way. We provide implementations of several of these methods and leave the others as exercises. There is also a method to validate the student's data before entering a new student in the array or modifying an existing student.

The Student Class: For this program we make two major changes to the `student` class described in Lesson 5:

1. The three test scores are stored in an array. This provides more flexibility than did the use of a separate instance variable for each test, and in the future it will be easy to modify the class to deal with a larger number of tests.

2. The `student` class provides a `validateData` method. Now any application that needs to validate student data can do so easily. For variety, the approach taken to data validation is somewhat different than that used in the `Employee` class of Lesson 6. If the validation code is placed in the user interface class, it would need to be repeated in every user interface that works with student objects, an approach that is wasteful, tedious, and difficult to maintain.

Implementation

Following is the code for the two classes. To save space we have kept comments to a minimum; however, we have used descriptive names for variables and methods and hope you will find the code fairly self-documenting.

```java
import javax.swing.*;
import BreezySwing.*;

public class StudentTestScores extends GBFrame{

    // Declare window objects --------------------------------------

    private JButton addButton, modifyButton, firstButton,
                previousButton, nextButton, lastButton;

    private JLabel blankLine1, nameLabel, test1Label, test2Label,
                test3Label, averageLabel, blankLine2, countLabel,
                indexLabel;

    private JTextField nameField;

    private IntegerField test1Field, test2Field, test3Field,
                averageField, countField, indexField;

    // Other instance variables ------------------------------

    private Student[] students;              // Array of students
    private int indexSelectedStudent;    // Position of current student
    private int studentCount;             // Current number of students

    // Constructor------------------------------------------------

    public StudentTestScores(){

        // Initialize the data
        indexSelectedStudent = -1;
        studentCount = 0;
        students = new Student[10];

        // Instantiate window objects
        addButton    = addButton ("Add"   ,2,4,1,1);
        modifyButton = addButton ("Modify",3,4,1,1);

        blankLine1      = addLabel (""   , 6,1,1,1);
        firstButton     = addButton ("<<", 7,1,1,1);
        previousButton  = addButton ("<",  7,2,1,1);
        nextButton      = addButton (">",  7,3,1,1);
        lastButton      = addButton (">>", 7,4,1,1);

        nameLabel       = addLabel ("Name"   ,1,1,1,1);
        test1Label      = addLabel ("Test 1" ,2,1,1,1);
        test2Label      = addLabel ("Test 2" ,3,1,1,1);
        test3Label      = addLabel ("Test 3" ,4,1,1,1);
```

```
      averageLabel  = addLabel ("Average"  ,5,1,1,1);
      nameField  = addTextField         ("",1,2,2,1);
      test1Field = addIntegerField    (0 ,2,2,1,1);
      test2Field = addIntegerField    (0 ,3,2,1,1);
      test3Field = addIntegerField    (0 ,4,2,1,1);
      averageField = addIntegerField (0 ,5,2,1,1);
      blankLine2  = addLabel          (""              ,8,1,1,1);
      countLabel  = addLabel          ("Count"         ,9,1,1,1);
      countField  = addIntegerField (0                ,9,2,1,1);
      indexLabel  = addLabel          ("Current Index" ,9,3,1,1);
      indexField  = addIntegerField (-1                ,9,4,1,1);

      // These fields are read-only
      averageField.setEditable (false);
      countField.setEditable (false);
      indexField.setEditable (false);

      displayCurrentStudent();
   }

// buttonClicked method--------------------------------------

public void buttonClicked (JButton buttonObj){
   if      (buttonObj == addButton)       add();
   else if (buttonObj == modifyButton)    modify();
   else if (buttonObj == firstButton)     displayFirst();
   else if (buttonObj == previousButton) displayPrevious();
   else if (buttonObj == nextButton)      displayNext();
   else if (buttonObj == lastButton)      displayLast();
}

// Private methods--------------------------------------------

private void add(){
   if (studentCount == students.length){
      messageBox ("SORRY: student array is full");
      return;
   }

   Student stu = getDataOnScreen();
   String str = stu.validateData();

   if (str != null){        // If the data is invalid,
      messageBox (str);      // then exit the method without
      return;                // adding the student
   }

   students[studentCount] = stu;
   indexSelectedStudent = studentCount;
   studentCount++;

   displayCurrentStudent();
}
```

```java
private Student getDataOnScreen(){
    String nm = nameField.getText().trim();

    int[] tests = new int[3];
    tests[0] = test1Field.getNumber();
    tests[1] = test2Field.getNumber();
    tests[2] = test3Field.getNumber();

    Student stu = new Student (nm, tests);
    return stu;
}

private void modify(){
  // Completion of this method is left as an exercise
}

private void displayFirst(){
    if (studentCount == 0)
       indexSelectedStudent = -1;
    else
       indexSelectedStudent = 0;
    displayCurrentStudent();
}

 private void displayPrevious(){
   // Completion of this method is left as an exercise
}

private void displayNext(){
    if (studentCount == 0)
       indexSelectedStudent = -1;
    else
       indexSelectedStudent
           = Math.min (studentCount - 1, indexSelectedStudent + 1);
    displayCurrentStudent();
}

private void displayLast(){
  // Completion of this method is left as an exercise
}

private void displayCurrentStudent(){
    if (indexSelectedStudent == -1){
       nameField.setText ("");
       test1Field.setNumber (0);
       test2Field.setNumber (0);
       test3Field.setNumber (0);
       averageField.setNumber (0);
    }else{
       Student stu = students[indexSelectedStudent];
       nameField.setText (stu.getName());
       test1Field.setNumber (stu.getScore(1));
```

```
            test2Field.setNumber (stu.getScore(2));
            test3Field.setNumber (stu.getScore(3));
            averageField.setNumber (stu.getAverage());
        }
        countField.setNumber (studentCount);
        indexField.setNumber (indexSelectedStudent);
    }

    // main-------------------------------------------------------

    public static void main (String[] args){
        StudentTestScores theGUI = new StudentTestScores();
        theGUI.setSize (400, 250);
        theGUI.setVisible(true);
    }
}
```

```
public class Student {

    private String name;
    private int[] tests = new int[3];

    public Student(){
        name = "";
        for (int i = 0; i < 3; i++)
            tests[i] = 0;
    }

    public Student(String nm, int[] t){
        name = nm;
        for (int i = 0; i < 3; i++)
            tests[i] = t[i];
    }

    public Student(Student s){
        name = s.name;
        for (int i = 0; i < 3; i++)
            tests[i] = s.tests[i];
    }

    public void setName (String nm){
        name = nm;
    }

    public String getName (){
        return name;
    }

    public void setScore (int i, int score){
        tests[i - 1] = score;
```

```java
    }

    public int getScore (int i){
        return tests[i - 1];
    }

    public int getAverage(){
        int sum = 0;
        for (int i = 0; i < 3; i++)
            sum += tests[i];
        return sum / 3;
    }

    public int getHighScore(){
        int highScore;
        highScore = tests[0];
        for (int i = 1; i < 3; i++){
            highScore = Math.max (highScore, tests[i]);
        }
        return highScore;
    }

    public String toString(){
        String str;
        str = "Name:    " + name  + "\n";
        for (int i = 0; i < 3; i++){
            str += "test " + i + ":   " + tests[i] + "\n";
        }
        str += "Average: " + getAverage();
        return str;
    }

    public String validateData(){
    //Returns null if there are no errors else returns
    //an appropriate error message.
        if (name.equals ("")) return "SORRY: name required";
        for (int i = 0; i < 3; i++){
            if (tests[i] < 0 || tests[i] > 100){
                String str = "SORRY: must have "+ 0
                        + " <= test score <= " + 100;
                return str;
            }
        }
        return null;
    }
}
```

8.10 *Applying the Model/View Pattern to the Case Study*

In the preceding case study, we failed to take full advantage of the model/view pattern (see Lesson 5 if you need to review this topic). A large complex task is best accomplished by dividing it into simpler, cooperating subtasks. In the case study, we mixed code for controlling the interface with code for managing the application's underlying data. The StudentTestScores class manages a complex interface and at the same time performs basic manipulations on the array of students. We should have divided the StudentTestScores class in two. The first class, StudentTestScoresView, manages the interface, and the second class, StudentTestScoresModel, supports all manipulations of the student array and communicates with student objects.

To illustrate, we take a segment of code from the StudentTestScores class and split it between the classes StudentTestScoresView and StudentTestScoresModel. The code deals with the task of adding a new student to the array of students. First, here is the code as it appears in the StudentTestScores class:

```
public void buttonClicked (Button buttonObj){
   if (buttonObj == addButton) add();
   ...
}


private void add(){
   if (studentCount == students.length){
      messageBox ("SORRY: student array is full");
      return;
   }

   Student stu = getDataOnScreen();
   String str = stu.validateData();

   if (str != null){          // If the data is invalid,
      messageBox (str);       // then exit the method without
      return;                 // adding the student
   }

   students[studentCount] = stu;
   indexSelectedStudent = studentCount;
   studentCount++;

   displayCurrentStudent();
}
```

In this segment, the code is split fairly equally between managing the interface (getting data from the screen and displaying error messages) and manipulating the array (including worrying about whether or not the array is full and updating the student count and the index of the selected student).

The corresponding code in the StudentTestScoresView class follows. The code deals primarily with the interface and calls a method in the model to manipulate the data.

```
public void buttonClicked (Button buttonObj){
   if (buttonObj == addButton){

      // Get the data from the screen
      Student stu = getDataOnScreen();

      // Ask the model to add the student to the array.
      // If model encounters any problems, it returns an error message
      // else it returns null.
      String str = model.add (stu);
      if (str != null)
         messageBox (str);
      else
         displayCurrentStudent();
   }
   ...
}
```

Following is the code in the model. It is completely independent of the view. The code checks the length of the array and makes sure the data are valid before adding the student to the array. The model keeps track of the student count and the index of the selected student.

```
public String add (Student stu){
   if (studentCount == students.length)
      return "SORRY: student array is full";

   String str = stu.validateData();
   if (str != null)
      return str;

   students[studentCount] = stu;
   indexSelectedStudent = studentCount;
   studentCount++;

   return null;
}
```

Design, Testing, and Debugging Hints

■ Three things should be done to set up an array:

1. Declare an array variable.

2. Instantiate an array object and assign it to the array variable.

3. Initialize the cells in the array with data, as appropriate.

■ When creating a new array object, try to come up with an accurate estimate of the number of cells for the data. If you underestimate, some data will be lost; if you overestimate, some memory will be wasted.

■ Remember that array variables are null until they are assigned array objects.

- To avoid index out-of-bounds errors, remember that the index of an array cell ranges from 0 (the first position) to the length of the array minus 1.

- To access the last cell in an array, use the expression `<array>.length - 1`.

- As a rule of thumb, it is best to avoid having more than one array variable refer to the same array object. When you want to copy the contents of one array to another, do not use the assignment `A = B`; instead, write a copy method and use the assignment `A = arrayCopy(B)`.

- When an array is not full, take care to track the current number of elements and do not attempt to access a cell that is beyond the last element.

SUMMARY

In this lesson, you learned:

- Arrays are collections of similar items or elements. The items in arrays are ordered by position. Arrays are useful when a program needs to manipulate many similar items, such as a group of students or a number of test scores.

- Arrays are objects. Thus, they must be instantiated and they can be referred to by more than one variable.

- An array can be passed to a method as a parameter and returned as a value.

- Parallel arrays are useful for organizing information with corresponding elements.

- Two-dimensional arrays store values in a row-and-column arrangement similar to a table.

VOCABULARY *Review*

Define the following terms:		
array	multidimensional array	ragged array
element	one-dimensional array	range bound error
index	parallel arrays	subscript
initializer list	physical size	two-dimensional array
logical size		

REVIEW *Questions*

WRITTEN QUESTIONS

Write a brief answer to the following questions.

1. Assume the following declarations are made and indicate which items below are valid subscripted variables.

    ```
    int a[] = new int[10];
    char b[] = new char[6];
    int x = 7, y = 2;
    double z = 0.0;
    ```

    A. `a[0]`

    B. `b[0]`

    C. `c[1.0]`

    D. `b['a']`

    E. `b[a]`

    F. `a[x + y]`

    G. `a[x % y]`

    H. `a[10]`

    I. `c[-1]`

    J. `a[a[4]]`

2. Assume that the array a defined in Question 1 contains the following values.

    ```
    1   4   6   8   9   3   7   10   2   9
    ```

    Indicate if the following are valid subscripts of a and, if so, state the value of the subscript. If invalid, explain why.

    A. `a[2]`

B. `a[5]`

C. `a[a[2]]`

D. `a[4 + 7]`

E. `a[a[5] + a[2]]`

F. `a[Math.sqrt(2)]`

3. List the errors in the following array declarations.
   A. `int intArray[] = new double[10];`

   B. `int intArray[] = new int[1.5];`

   C. `double[] doubleArray = new double[-10]`

D. `int intMatrix[] [] = new int[10];`

4. Write a method `selectRandom` that expects an array of integers as a parameter. The method should return the value of an array element at a randomly selected position.

5. Write code to declare and instantiate a two-dimensional array of integers with five rows and four columns.

6. Write code to initialize the array of Question 5 with randomly generated integers between 1 and 20.

PROJECTS

In some of the following projects, you are asked to write helper methods to process arrays. If you are calling these methods from the **main** method, be sure to begin the helper method's header with the reserved word **static**.

PROJECT 8-1

Write a program that takes 10 integers as input. The program places the even integers into an array called `evenList`, the odd integers into an array called `oddList`, and the negative integers into an array called `negativeList`. The program displays the contents of the three arrays after all of the integers have been entered.

PROJECT 8-2

Write a program that takes 10 floating-point numbers as inputs. The program displays the average of the numbers followed by all of the numbers that are greater than the average. As part of your design, write a method that takes an array of doubles as a parameter and returns the average of the data in the array.

PROJECT 8-3

The mode of a list of numbers is the number listed most often. Write a program that takes 10 numbers as input and displays the mode of these numbers. Your program should use parallel arrays and a method that takes an array of numbers as a parameter and returns the maximum value in the array.

PROJECT 8-4

The median of a list of numbers is the value in the middle of the list if the list is arranged in order. Add to the program of Project 8-3 the capability of displaying the median of the list of numbers.

PROJECT 8-5

Modify the program of Project 8-4 so that it displays not only the median and mode of the list of numbers but also a table of the numbers and their associated frequencies.

PROJECT 8-6

Complete the student test scores application from this lesson's case study and test it thoroughly. Then make the following modifications:

■ Add a field to the user interface that displays the class average (the average of the averages). When there are no students, display 0 in this field.

■ Add buttons and methods that support displaying

■ The student with the highest test score (if there are more than one, display the first)

■ The student with the highest average (if there are more than one, display the first)

PROJECT 8-7

A magic square is a two-dimensional array of positive integers such that the sum of each row, column, and diagonal is the same constant. The following example is a magic square whose constant is 34:

16	3	2	13
5	10	11	8
9	6	7	12
4	15	14	1

Write a program that takes 16 integers as inputs. The program should determine whether or not the square is a magic square and display the result in a text area.

PROJECT 8-8

Pascal's triangle can be used to recognize coefficients of a quantity raised to a power. The rules for forming this triangle of integers are such that each row must start and end with a 1, and each entry in a row is the sum of the two values diagonally above the new entry. Thus, four rows of Pascal's triangle are

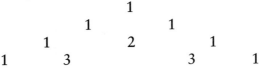

This triangle can be used as a convenient way to get the coefficients of a quantity of two terms raised to a power (binomial coefficients). For example

$(a+b)^3 = 1 \times a^3 + 3a^2b + 3ab^2 + 1 \times b^3$

where the coefficients 1, 3, 3, and 1 come from the fourth row of Pascal's triangle.

Write a program that takes the number of rows (up to, say, 10) as input and displays Pascal's triangle for those rows.

PROJECT 8-9

In the game of Penny Pitch, a two-dimensional board of numbers is laid out as follows:

```
1  1  1  1  1

1  2  2  2  1

1  2  3  2  1

1  2  2  2  1

1  1  1  1  1
```

A player tosses several pennies on the board, aiming for the number with the highest value. At the end of the game, the sum total of the tosses is returned. Develop a program that plays this game. The program should perform the following steps each time the user selects the **Toss** button:

■ Generate two random numbers for the row and column of the toss.

■ Add the number at this position to a running total.

■ Display the board, replacing the numbers with Ps where the pennies land.

(*Hint*: You should use a two-dimensional array of square objects for this problem. Each square contains a number like those shown and a Boolean flag that indicates whether or not a penny has landed on that square.)

CRITICAL *Thinking*

You have been using a method for searching for data in arrays like the one described in this lesson, when your friend tells you that it's a poor way to do searching. She says that you're examining every element in the array to discover that the target element is not there. A better way, she says, is to assume that the elements in the array are in alphabetical order. Then, examine the element at the middle position in the array first. If that element matches the target element, you're done. Otherwise, if that element is less than the target element, continue the same kind of search in just the portion of the array to the left of the element just examined. Otherwise, continue the same kind of search in just the portion of the array to the right of the element just examined.

Write an algorithm for this search process, and explain why it is better than the search algorithm discussed in this lesson.

CLASSES CONTINUED

Lesson 5 presented an overview of classes that allowed you to learn to read, modify, and define them. The examples of classes discussed there are simplified versions of what real programmers would see, however. Defining classes is only one aspect of object-oriented programming. The real power of object-oriented programming comes from its capacity to reduce code and to distribute responsibilities for such things as error handling in a software system. This capability can be exploited only when you have an understanding of some related concepts. Following is a brief summary of some of these concepts, which we explore in detail in this lesson:

Static Variables and Methods. When information needs to be shared among all instances of a class, that information can be represented in terms of static variables and it can be accessed by means of static methods.

Interfaces. A Java interface specifies the set of methods available to clients of a class. An interface provides a way of requiring a class to implement a set of methods and a way of informing clients about services regardless of implementation detail. Interfaces thus provide the glue that holds a set of cooperating classes together.

Inheritance. Java organizes classes in a hierarchy. Classes inherit the instance variables and methods of the classes above them in the hierarchy. A class can extend its inherited characteristics by adding instance variables and methods and by overriding inherited methods. Thus, *inheritance* provides a mechanism for reusing code and can greatly reduce the effort required to implement a new class.

Abstract Classes. Some classes in a hierarchy must never be instantiated. They are called *abstract classes.* Their sole purpose is to define features and behavior common to their subclasses.

Polymorphism. Methods in different classes with a similar function are usually given the same name. This is called *polymorphism.* Polymorphism makes classes easier to use because programmers need to memorize fewer method names. In a well-designed class hierarchy, polymorphism is employed as much as possible. A good example of a polymorphic message is `toString`. Every object, no matter which class it belongs to, understands the `toString` message and responds by returning a string that describes the object.

Preconditions and Postconditions. Clients need to know how to use a method correctly and what results to expect if it is so used. Preconditions specify the correct use of a method and postconditions describe what will result if the preconditions are satisfied.

Exceptions for Error Handling. When a method's preconditions are violated, a foolproof way to catch the errors is to throw exceptions, thereby halting program execution at the point of the errors.

Reference Types. The identity of an object and the fact that there can be multiple references to the same object are issues that arise when comparing two objects for equality and when copying an object. There are also subtle rules to master when manipulating objects of different but related types in a hierarchy.

9.1 *Class* (`static`) *Variables and Methods*

The variables and methods discussed thus far in the book have been instance variables and methods. An instance variable belongs to an object and is allocated storage when the object is created. Each object has its own set of instance variables. An instance method is activated when a message is sent to the object. Java also supports the use of class variables and methods. A *class variable* belongs to a class. Its storage is allocated at program start-up and is independent of the number of instances created. A *class method* is activated when a message is sent to the class rather than to an object. The modifier `static` is used to designate class variables and methods. To illustrate, we make some modifications to the `Student` class of Lesson 5.

Counting the Number of Students Instantiated

Suppose we want to count all the student objects instantiated during the execution of an application. To do so, we introduce a variable, which we call `studentCount`. This variable is incremented in the constructor every time a student object is instantiated. Because the variable is independent of any particular student object, it must be a class variable. In addition, we need two methods to manipulate the `studentCount` variable: one to initialize the variable to 0 at the beginning of the application and the other to return the variable's value on demand. These methods are called `setStudentCount` and `getStudentCount`, respectively. Because these methods do not manipulate any particular student object, they must be class methods.

Modifying the Student Class

Following are the modifications needed to add the class variable and the two class methods in the Student class. We are adding the class variable and methods to the end of the class template. There is no rule that says they must be placed there, but it is as good a location as any other and is the one usually used in this book.

```
public class Student {

    private String name;
    ... rest of the instance variables go here ...

    public Student(){
        studentCount++;      // Increment the count when a student is
                             // instantiated

        name = "";
        test1 = 0;
        test2 = 0;
        test3 = 0;
    }

    public void setName (String nm){
        name = nm;
    }

    ... rest of the methods without change go here ...

    //--------------- class variables and methods ----------------

    static private int studentCount;

    static public void setStudentCount(int count){
        studentCount = count;
    }

    static public int getStudentCount(){
        return studentCount;
    }
}
```

Following is some code that illustrates the new capabilities of the Student class:

```
...
Student.setStudentCount (0);          // Initialize count to 0
s1 = new Student();                   // Instantiate a student object
...
s2 = new Student();                   // Instantiate a student object
...
s3 = new Student();                   // Instantiate a student object
messageBox (Student.getStudentCount()); // Displays 3
```

Notice that class messages are sent to a class and not to an object. Also, notice that we do not attempt to manipulate the studentCount variable directly because, in accordance with the good programming practice of information hiding, we declared the variable to be private.

In general, we use a `static` variable in any situation in which all instances share a common data value. We then use `static` methods to provide public access to these data.

Class Constants

By using the modifier `final` in conjunction with `static`, we create a *class constant*. The value of a class constant is assigned when the variable is declared, and it cannot be changed later. To illustrate the use of class constants, we modify the `Student` class again by adding two class constants: `MIN_SCORE` and `MAX_SCORE`. We use these constants in the method `setScore` to hold the score between `MIN_SCORE` and `MAX_SCORE`. It is customary to capitalize the names of class constants. Following are the relevant modifications to the `Student` class:

```java
public class Student {

    private String name;
    ... rest of the instance variables go here ...

    ... no changes in the methods up to this point ...

    public void setScore (int i, int score){
        // Limit the score to the interval [MIN_SCORE, MAX_SCORE]
        score = Math.max (MIN_SCORE, score);
        score = Math.min (MAX_SCORE, score);

        if      (i == 1) test1 = score;
        else if (i == 2) test2 = score;
        else             test3 = score;
    }

    ... no changes in the methods here ...

    //--------------- static variables and methods ----------------

    static final public int MIN_SCORE = 0;
    static final public int MAX_SCORE = 100;

    ... no changes in the rest of the static stuff ...
}
```

The method `max` in class `Math` returns the maximum of its two parameters and `min` returns their minimum. We declare the two class constants as public because clients might like to access them. Following is a segment of code that illustrates the `Student` class's new features:

```java
s = new Student();
s.setScore(1, -20);                    // Too small, will be set to MIN_SCORE
s.setScore(2, 150);                    // Too large, will be set to MAX_SCORE
s.setScore(3, 55);                     // Value is acceptable
System.out.println (s);                // Displays scores of 0, 100, and 55
System.out.println (Student.MIN_SCORE);     // Displays 0
System.out.println (Student.MAX_SCORE);     // Displays 100
```

Rules for Using `static` Variables

There are two simple rules to remember when using `static` variables:

1. Class methods can reference only the `static` variables, and never the instance variables.

2. Instance methods can reference `static` and instance variables.

The `Math` Class Revisited

By now you may have guessed that all the methods and variables in the `Math` class are static. `Math.PI` refers to a static constant, while `Math.max(MIN_SCORE, score)` activates a static method.

The `Static` Method `Main`

All the interface classes presented so far, terminal based or GUI, have included the `static` method `main`. Now we can understand more about how `main` works. Consider the following example:

```
import ...;
import ...;

public class MyApp ...{
   ...
   public static void main (String[] args){
      ...
   }
}
```

When the user runs this program by typing

```
java MyApp
```

the Java interpreter sends the message `main` to the class `MyApp`.

Static Helper Methods

We previously presented programs in which instance methods called helper methods that also were instance methods. We now apply the same technique to static methods. As a trivial demonstration, we write a simple temperature conversion program in which `static` `main` calls several other `static` methods:

```
import TerminalIO.*;

public class Convert {

   private static KeyboardReader reader = new KeyboardReader();

   public static void main (String [] args) {
      while (true)
         printCelsius (convertToCelsius (readFahrenheit()));
   }

   private static double readFahrenheit(){
```

```
        return reader.readDouble(("Enter degrees Fahrenheit: "));
   }

   private static double convertToCelsius (double fahrenheit){
        return (fahrenheit - 32.0) * 5.0 / 9.0;
   }

   private static void printCelsius (double celsius){
        System.out.println ("The equivalent in Celsius is " + celsius);
   }
}
```

We use this technique as little as possible because it makes for awkward and difficult-to-maintain programs. Rather than decompose a problem into a system of cooperating `static` methods, it is much better to decompose it into a system of cooperating classes. With the latter approach, `static main` usually is limited to the small but essential role of starting everything off.

EXERCISE 9.1

1. Describe the manner in which Java allocates memory for instance variables and static variables.

2. List three possible situations in which static methods might be included in classes.

3. What error occurs in the following code?

```
public class SomeClass{

   private int instVar = 0;

   static public void someMethod(int x){
      classVar = instVar + classVar + x;
   }

   static private int classVar = 0;

   ...

}
```

4. Why is it a good idea to define all constants as `public` and `static`?

9.2 Java Interfaces—The Client Perspective

The term *interface* is used in two different ways. On the one hand, an interface is the part of a software system that interacts with human users. On the other, it is a list of a class's public methods. Throughout this lesson we will use the term in its latter sense. A class's interface provides the information needed to use a class without revealing anything about its implementation.

When related classes have the same interface, they can be used interchangeably in a program. House painting provides an everyday example. Small delicate brushes are used to paint around windows and doors and large coarse brushes to paint expanses of wall. Yet the different types of brushes are used in the same manner. They are all dipped in paint and wiggled backward and forward on the painting surface. They have, in other words, the same interface Instructions for how to use one apply to all. Likewise, in a program, code for manipulating a class applies equally to all classes that share the same interface.

We can illustrate these ideas in Java using turtle graphics. The StandardPen used in earlier lessons is just one of five classes that conform to the same interface. Two others are WigglePen and RainbowPen. A WigglePen draws wiggly lines, and a RainbowPen draws randomly colored lines. We can think of these as special effects pens; but as pens, they all have the same general behavior and respond to the same messages.

The Pen Interface

In Lesson 5, we described the interface for a standard pen by listing its methods in a table; however, Java provides a more formal mechanism called, not surprisingly, an interface. Following is the code for the Pen interface:

```
// Pen.java

import java.awt.Color;

public interface Pen {
    public void    down();
    public void    drawString (String text);
    public void    home();
    public void    move (double distance);
    public void    move (double x, double y);
    public void    setColor (Color color);
    public void    setDirection (double direction);
    public void    setWidth (int width);
    public String  toString();
    public void    turn (double degrees);
    public void    up();
}
```

Note that this code is quite simple. It consists of the signatures of the methods followed by semicolons. The interface provides programmers with the information needed to use pens of any type correctly. It is important to realize that an interface is not a class; however, when a class is defined, there is a mechanism, which we will see shortly, to specify that the class conforms to the interface.

Drawing with Different Types of Pens

As a short example, we write code to draw a square with three different types of pens:

```
import TurtleGraphics.*;
import java.awt.Color;

public class TestPens {
    public static void main (String[] args){
        // Declare three variables of the interface type called Pen.
        Pen p1, p2, p3;
```

```
// Instantiate three different types of pens and
// associate them with the Pen variables.
p1 = new StandardPen();
p2 = new WigglePen();
p3 = new RainbowPen();

// Draw a square with the standard pen.
for (int i = 1; i <= 4; i++){
   p1.move(50);
   p1.turn(90);
}

// Draw a square with the wiggle pen.
for (int i = 1; i <= 4; i++){
   p2.move(50);
   p2.turn(90);
}

// Draw a square with the rainbow pen.
for (int i = 1; i <= 4; i++){
   p3.move(50);
   p3.turn(90);
}
   }
}
```

The three pen variables (p1, p2, and p3) are declared as Pen, which is the name of the interface. Then the variables are associated with different types of pen objects. Each object responds to exactly the same messages, those listed in the Pen interface, but with slightly different behaviors. This is an example of polymorphism, which was first mentioned in Lesson 1.

The output from the program is shown in Figure 9-1. Because this book is not printed in full color, some of the detail is lost. The first square is in blue and has straight sides. The second square, also in blue, has wiggly sides. The third square has straight sides, and each side is in a different randomly chosen color.

FIGURE 9-1
A square drawn with three types of pens

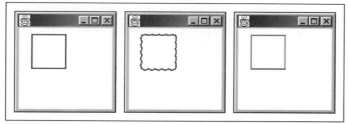

EXERCISE 9.2

1. State the purpose of a Java interface.

2. Why don't all classes have interfaces?

9.3 Java Interfaces—The Implementation Perspective

We now show the role interfaces play in the implementation of classes. For example, suppose we need to perform some basic manipulations on circles and rectangles. These manipulations include positioning, moving, and stretching these basic geometric shapes. In addition, we want shapes to implement methods that compute their area, draw themselves with a pen, and return descriptions of themselves. Without any concern for implementation details, we can now describe the interface shared by circles and rectangles, as shown in the following code:

```java
import TurtleGraphics.Pen;

public interface Shape {
   public double area();
   public void    draw (Pen p);
   public double getXPos();
   public double getYPos();
   public void    move (double xLoc, double yLoc);
   public void    stretchBy (double factor);
   public String toString();
}
```

Classes `Circle` and `Rect`

We implement circles and rectangles in classes we call `Circle` and `Rect`, respectively. We do not use the more obvious name `Rectangle` because Java already includes a class with that name. Working with two classes that have the same name is not impossible, but it does involve complexities we are not ready to discuss. The outline for both implementations looks like this:

```java
public class Circle implements Shape{
   ...
}
public class Rect implements Shape{
   ...
}
```

The key feature is the phrase `implements Shape`. The presence of this phrase implies that

- Both classes implement all the methods listed in the `Shape` interface.
- A variable declared as `Shape` can be associated with an object of either class.

Following is a complete implementation of both classes:

```
import TurtleGraphics.Pen;

public class Circle implements Shape {

   private double xPos, yPos;
   private double radius;

   public Circle() {
      xPos = 0;
      yPos = 0;
      radius = 1;
   }

   public Circle (double xLoc, double yLoc, double r) {
      xPos = xLoc;
      yPos = yLoc;
      radius = r;
   }

   public double area() {
      return Math.PI * radius * radius;
   }

   public void draw (Pen p) {
      double side = 2.0 * Math.PI * radius / 120.0;
      p.up();
      p.move (xPos + radius, yPos - side / 2.0);
      p.setDirection (90);
      p.down();
      for (int i = 0; i < 120; i++){
         p.move (side);
         p.turn (3);
      }
   }

   public double getXPos() {
      return xPos;
   }

   public double getYPos() {
      return yPos;
   }

   public void move (double xLoc, double yLoc) {
      xPos = xLoc;
      yPos = yLoc;
   }

   public void stretchBy (double factor) {
      radius *= factor;
   }
```

```
    public String toString() {
        String str = "CIRCLE\n"
                   + "Radius: " + radius + "\n"
                   + "(X,Y) Position: (" + xPos + "," + yPos + ")\n"
                   + "Area: " + area();
        return str;
    }
}
```

```
import TurtleGraphics.Pen;

public class Rect implements Shape {

    private double xPos, yPos;
    private double height, width;

    public Rect() {
        xPos = 0;
        yPos = 0;
        height = 1;
        width = 1;
    }

    public Rect (double xLoc, double yLoc, double h, double w) {
        xPos = xLoc;
        yPos = yLoc;
        height = h;
        width = w;
    }

    public double area() {
        return height * width;
    }

    public void draw (Pen p) {
        p.up();
        p.move (xPos, yPos);
        p.down();
        p.setDirection (0); p.move (width);
        p.turn (-90); p.move (height);
        p.turn (-90); p.move (width);
        p.turn (-90); p.move (height);
    }

    public double getXPos() {
        return xPos;
    }
```

```
        public double getYPos() {
           return yPos;
        }

        public void move (double xLoc, double yLoc) {
           xPos = xLoc;
           yPos = yLoc;
        }

        public void stretchBy (double factor) {
           height *= factor;
           width *= factor;
        }

        public String toString() {
           String str = "RECTANGLE\n"
                      + "Width & Height: " + width + " & " + height +"\n"
                      + "(X,Y) Position: (" + xPos + "," + yPos + ")\n"
                      + "Area: " + area();
           return str;
        }
     }
```

Testing the Classes

The code for both classes is easy to understand, so we now write a small test program that instantiates a circle and a rectangle and subjects them to a few basic manipulations. Embedded comments explain what is happening, and Figure 9-2 shows the output:

```
import TurtleGraphics.*;
import java.awt.Color;
import TerminalIO.KeyboardReader;

public class TestShapes {
   public static void main (String[] args) {

      // Declare and instantiate a pen, a circle and a rectangle
      Pen p = new StandardPen();
      Shape s1 = new Circle (20, 20, 20);
      Shape s2 = new Rect (-20, -20, 10, 20);

      // Draw the circle and rectangle
      s1.draw (p);
      s2.draw (p);

      // Display a description of the circle and rectangle
      System.out.println (s1);  // toString method called implicitly
      System.out.println (s2);  // toString method called implicitly

      // Pause until the user is ready to continue
      KeyboardReader reader = new KeyboardReader();
      reader.pause();
```

```
        // Erase the circle and rectangle
        p.setColor (Color.white);
        s1.draw (p);
        s2.draw (p);
        p.setColor (Color.red);

        // Move the circle and rectangle, change their size, and redraw
        s1.move (30, 30);              s2.move (-30, -30);
        s1.stretchBy (2);             s2.stretchBy (2);
        s1.draw (p);                   s2.draw (p);
    }
}
```

FIGURE 9-2
Output from the TestShapes program

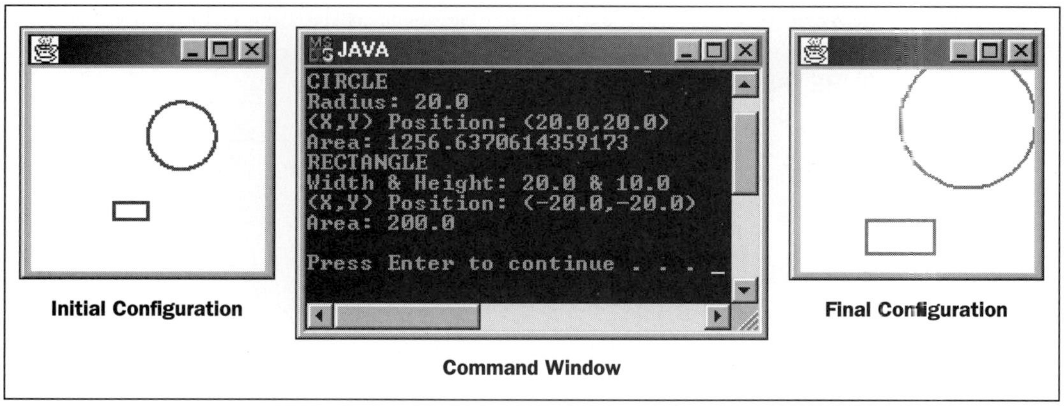

Initial Configuration

Command Window

Final Configuration

Final Observations

Before closing this section, we must mention several points:

- An interface contains only methods, never variables.

- The methods in an interface are usually public.

- If more than one class implements an interface, its methods are polymorphic.

- A class can implement methods in addition to those listed in the interface, as we will illustrate soon.

- A class can implement more than one interface, a feature that we are not going to explore.

- Interfaces can be organized in an inheritance hierarchy, another feature we are not going to explore.

EXERCISE 9.3

1. Write an interface for the student class from Lesson 5.

2. When the programmer uses the expression implements <an interface> in a class definition, how does the compiler react?

9.4 Code Reuse Through Inheritance

In Java, all classes are part of an immense hierarchy, with the class Object at the root. Each class inherits the characteristics (variables and methods) of the classes above it in the hierarchy. A class can add new variables to these inherited characteristics as needed. It also can add new methods and/or modifies inherited methods.

Review of Terminology

To make it easier to talk about inheritance, we begin by reviewing the needed terminology. Figure 9-3 shows part of a class hierarchy, with Object as always at the *root* (the top position in an upside down tree). Below Object are its subclasses, but we show only one, which we call AAA. Because AAA is immediately below Object, we say that it extends Object. Similarly, BBB and CCC extend AAA. The class immediately above another is called its superclass, so AAA is the superclass of BBB and CCC. A class can have many subclasses, and all classes, except Object, have exactly one superclass. The *descendants* of a class consist of its subclasses, plus their subclasses, and so on.

FIGURE 9-3
Part of a class hierarchy

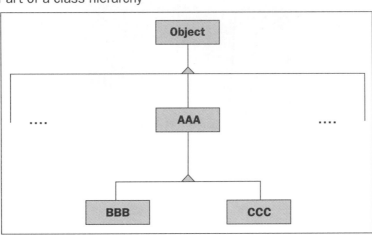

Wheel as a Subclass of Circle

As our first illustration of inheritance, we implement the class Wheel as a subclass of Circle. A wheel is just a circle with spokes, so much of the code needed to implement Wheel is already in Circle. We first present the code and a brief test. Comments in the code should make it fairly self-explanatory, but a more detailed explanation follows:

```
import TurtleGraphics.Pen;

public class Wheel extends Circle {

    private int spokes;       // The number of spokes in the wheel
                              // xPos, yPos, and radius are inherited
                              // from Circle

    public Wheel() {
```

```
        super();             // Activate the constructor Circle() to
                             // initialize xPos, yPos, and radius.
        spokes = 0;          // Now initialize spokes.
    }

    public Wheel (double xLoc, double yLoc, double r, int s) {
        super (xLoc, yLoc, r);  // Activate the constructor
                                // Circle (double xLoc, double yLoc, double r
    )
                                // to initialize xPos, yPos, and radius.
        spokes = s;             // Now initialize spokes.
    }

    public void draw (Pen p) {
        // Draw the wheel's rim by calling the draw method in the superclass.
        super.draw (p);

        // Draw the spokes
        for (int i = 1; i <= spokes; i++){
            p.up();
            p.move (xPos, yPos);
            p.setDirection (i * 360.0 / spokes);
            p.down();
            p.move (radius);
        }
    }

    public void setSpokes (int s) {
        spokes = s;
    }

    public String toString() {
        String str = "WHEEL\n"
                    + "Radius: " + radius + "\n"
                    + "Spokes: " + spokes + "\n"
                    + "(X,Y) Position: (" + xPos + "," + yPos + ")\n"
                    + "Area: " + area();
        return str;
    }
}
```

Testing the Wheel Class

Following is a test program that draws a circle and a wheel:

```
// Declare and instantiate a pen, a circle and a wheel
Pen p = new StandardPen();
Shape s1 = new Circle (20, 20, 20);
Shape s2 = new Wheel (-20, -20, 20, 6);

// Draw the circle and wheel
s1.draw (p);
s2.draw (p);
```

Figure 9-4 shows the results of this program.

FIGURE 9-4
A circle and a wheel with the same radius but different positions

Detailed Explanation

We now explain the implementation of Wheel in detail.

Class Header

In the class header, we see that Wheel extends Circle, thereby indicating that it is a subclass of Circle and inherits all of Circle's variables and methods. The clause "implements Shape" is omitted from the header because Wheel inherits this property from Circle automatically.

Variables

The variable spokes, indicating the number of spokes in a wheel, is the only variable declared in the class. The other variables (xPos, yPos, and radius) are inherited from Circle; however, in order to reference these variables in Wheel methods, Circle must be modified slightly. In Circle, these variables must be declared protected instead of private. This designation indicates that Circle's descendants can access the variables while still hiding them from all other classes. The change in Circle looks like this:

```
protected double xPos, yPos;
protected double radius;
```

Protected Methods

Methods can be designated as protected also; however, we will not have any reason to use protected methods in this lesson. As with protected variables, a protected method is accessible to a class's descendants, but not to any other classes in the hierarchy.

Constructors and super

Constructors in class Wheel explicitly initialize the variable spokes; however, constructors in the superclass Circle initialize the remaining variables (xPos, yPos, and radius). The keyword super is used to activate the desired constructor in Circle, and the parameter list used with super determines which constructor in Circle is called. When used in this way, super must be the first statement in Wheel's constructors.

Other Methods and super

The keyword super also can be used in methods other than constructors, but in a slightly different way. First, it can appear in any place within a method. Second, it takes the form:

```
super.<method name> (<parameter list>);
```

Such code activates the named method in the superclass (note that the two methods are polymorphic). In comparison, the code

```
this.<method name> (<parameter list>);    // Long form
                                          //     or
<method name> (<parameter list>);         // Short form
```

activates the named method in the current class. We see an example in the `Wheel` class's `draw` method:

```
// Draw the wheel's rim
super.draw (p);
```

Why Some Methods Are Missing

Not all the `Shape` methods are implemented in `Wheel`. Instead they are inherited unchanged from `Circle`. For instance, if the `move` message is sent to a wheel object, the `move` method in `Circle` is activated.

Why Some Methods are Modified

Whenever a wheel object must respond differently to a message than a circle object, the corresponding method must be redefined in class `Wheel`. The methods `draw` and `toString` are examples. When convenient, the redefined method can use `super` to activate a method in the superclass.

Why There Are Extra Methods

A subclass often has methods that do not appear in its superclass. The method `setSpokes` is an example. This method provides a more specific piece of behavior than you would find in circles.

What Messages Can Be Sent to a Wheel

Because `Wheel` is a subclass of `Circle`, it automatically implements `Shape`. Therefore, a variable of type `Shape` can be instantiated as a `new Wheel` and can receive all `Shape` messages:

```
Shape someShape = new Wheel();
someShape.<any Shape message>;
```

The variable `someShape` cannot be sent the message `setSpokes`, however, even though it is actually a wheel. From the compiler's perspective, `someShape` is limited to receiving messages in the `Shape` interface. There are two ways to circumvent this limitation. The variable `someShape` is either declared as type `Wheel` in the first place, or it is cast to class `Wheel` when it is sent a message unique to class `Wheel`. Following is an example:

```
Wheel v1 = new Wheel();
Shape v2 = new Wheel();

v1.setSpokes (6);           // v1 can be sent all Wheel messages
((Wheel)v2).setSpokes (6);  // v2 must first be cast to class Wheel before
                            // being sent this message
```

Of course, it is a mistake to cast a variable to a type that conflicts with its true identity. Doing so results in a run-time error. For instance:

```
Shape s = new Circle();      // s is a circle

((Wheel)s).setSpokes (6);    // s cannot be cast to class Wheel
```

We cover more examples of casting objects in Lesson 10.

EXERCISE 9.4

1. What is a class hierarchy? Give an example.

2. What syntax is used to get one class to inherit data and behavior from another class?

3. How does the keyword `super` work with constructors?

4. How does the keyword `super` work with methods other than constructors?

5. What is the role of the visibility modifier `protected` in a class hierarchy?

6. Find the error in the following code and suggest a remedy for the problem:

```
Shape s = new Wheel();
s.setSpokes (5);
```

9.5 Inheritance and Abstract Classes

When we examine the `Circle` and `Rect` classes, we see duplication of code. Inheritance provides a mechanism for reducing this duplication. To illustrate, we define a new class that is a superclass of `Circle` and `Rect` and contains all the variables and methods common to both. We will never have any reason to instantiate this class, so we will make it an *abstract class*, that is, a class that cannot be instantiated. The classes that extend this class and that are instantiated are called *concrete classes*.

It would be nice to call the new class `Shape`; however, `Shape` is already the name of our interface. Instead we will call the class `AbstractShape`. It is convenient, though not necessary, to have this new class implement the `Shape` interface. Then, the subclasses `Circle` and `Rect` no longer need to implement `Shape` explicitly.

Because `AbstractShape` is going to implement `Shape`, it must include all the `Shape` methods, even those such as `area` that are completely different in the subclasses and share no code. Methods in `AbstractShape` such as `area` for which we cannot write any code are called *abstract methods*, and we indicate that fact by including the word `abstract` in their headers.

Our extended hierarchy of classes is shown in Figure 9-5.

FIGURE 9-5
The shapes hierarchy

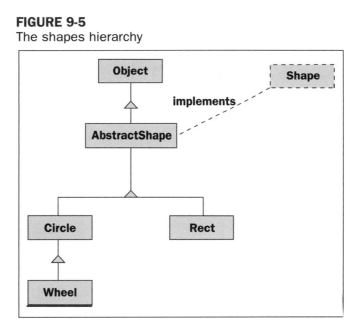

It takes rather a lot of code to implement all these classes; however, the code is straightforward, and the embedded comments explain the tricky parts. Pay particular attention to the attribute `final`, which is used for the first time in class `AbstractShape`. A *final method* is a method that cannot be overridden by a subclass.

```
import TurtleGraphics.Pen;

// Notice the use of the word "abstract" in the class header.
// This class implements the Shape interface.
// We don't need to say that the class extends Object as that is the
// default.

abstract public class AbstractShape implements Shape {

    // Here we declare variables common to all subclasses.

    protected double xPos;
    protected double yPos;


    // Even though this class is never instantiated, it needs constructors
    // to initialize its variables.

    public AbstractShape (){
        xPos = 0;
        yPos = 0;
    }

    public AbstractShape (double xLoc, double yLoc){
        xPos = xLoc;
```

```
        yPos = yLoc;
    }


    // There is no code for the next two methods; therefore, they are
    abstract
    // and terminate with a semicolon. All subclasses must define these
    methods.

    abstract public double area();

    abstract public void draw (Pen p);

    // These next three methods will never be changed in a subclass;
    therefore,
    // they are declared final, meaning they cannot be overridden.

    public final double getXPos(){
        return xPos;
    }

    public final double getYPos(){
        return yPos;
    }

    public final void move (double xLoc, double yLoc){
        xPos = xLoc;
        yPos = yLoc;
    }


    // Another abstract method to be defined in subclasses.

    abstract public void stretchBy (double factor);

    // Subclasses will override this method.
    // Notice that the method calls area(). More will be said about
    // this later.

    public String toString(){
        String str = "(X,Y) Position: (" + xPos + "," + yPos + ")\n"
                   + "Area: " + area();
        return str;
    }

}
```

```
import TurtleGraphics.Pen;

// This class extends AbstractShape and in the process implements
```

```
// the Shape interface.

public class Circle extends AbstractShape {

    protected double radius;

    public Circle() {
        super();                // Activate a constructor in AbstractShape.
        radius = 1;             // Then initialize radius.
    }

    public Circle (double xLoc, double yLoc, double r) {
        super (xLoc, yLoc);    // Activate a constructor in AbstractShape.
        radius = r;             // Then initialize radius.
    }

    // The next three methods were abstract in the superclass.
    // Now we define them.

    public double area() {
        return Math.PI * radius * radius;
    }

    public void draw (Pen p) {
        double side = 2.0 * Math.PI * radius / 120.0;
        p.up();
        p.move (xPos + radius, yPos - side / 2.0);
        p.setDirection (90);
        p.down();
        for (int i = 0; i < 120; i++){
            p.move (side);
            p.turn (3);
        }
    }

    public void stretchBy (double factor) {
        radius *= factor;
    }

    // Notice that the toString method calls the corresponding method in the
    // superclass in order to accomplish its task.

    // In the superclass, the toString method calls area, which will
    // activate the area
    // method in this class and not the area method in the superclass.

    public String toString() {
        String str = "CIRCLE\n"
                   + "Radius: " + radius + "\n"
                   + super.toString();
```

290 Unit 3 Arrays, Recursion, and Complexity

```
         return str;
      }
   }
```

```
   // We have already explained most of the major points in this class.

   import TurtleGraphics.Pen;

   public class Wheel extends Circle {

      private int spokes;

      public Wheel() {
         super();
         spokes = 0;
      }

      public Wheel (double xLoc, double yLoc, double r, int s) {
         super (xLoc, yLoc, r);
         spokes = s;
      }

      public void draw (Pen p) {
         // Draw the wheel's rim
         super.draw (p);

         // Draw the spokes
         for (int i = 1; i <= spokes; i++){
            p.up();
            p.move (xPos, yPos);
            p.setDirection (i * 360.0 / spokes);
            p.down();
            p.move (radius);
         }
      }

      public void setSpokes (int s) {
         spokes = s;
      }

      // We could not call super.area() in this toString method, because
      // doing so would have activated the method in Circle rather than the
      // method we wanted in AbstractShape.

      public String toString() {
         String str = "WHEEL\n"
                   + "Radius: " + radius + "\n"
                   + "Spokes: " + spokes + "\n"
                   + "(X,Y) Position: (" + xPos + "," + yPos + ")\n"
                   + "Area: " + area();
```

```
        return str;
    }
}
```

```
// No additional comments are needed in this class. All the important
// points have already been made.

import TurtleGraphics.Pen;

public class Rect extends AbstractShape {

    private double height, width;

    public Rect() {
        super();
        height = 1;
        width = 1;
    }

    public Rect (double xLoc, double yLoc, double h, double w) {
        super (xLoc, yLoc);
        height = h;
        width = w;
    }

    public double area() {
        return height * width;
    }

    public void draw (Pen p) {
        p.up();
        p.move (xPos, yPos);
        p.down();
        p.setDirection (0); p.move (width);
        p.turn (-90); p.move (height);
        p.turn (-90); p.move (width);
        p.turn (-90); p.move (height);
    }

    public void stretchBy (double factor) {
        height *= factor;
        width *= factor;
    }

    public String toString() {
        String str = "RECTANGLE\n"
                    + "Width & Height: " + width + " & " + height +"\n"
                    + super.toString();
        return str;
    }
}
```

EXERCISE 9.5

1. What is an abstract class? Give an example.

2. Why do we declare abstract methods?

3. What is a final method? Give an example.

4. Consult the documentation for the `TurtleGraphics` package and draw a class hierarchy diagram of the pen classes.

9.6 Some Observations About Interfaces and Inheritance

We now quickly review some major features of interfaces and inheritance and make a few additional observations.

- A Java interface has a name and consists of a list of method headers.

- One or more classes can implement the same interface.

- If a variable is declared to be of an interface type, then it can be associated with an object from any class that implements the interface.

- If a class implements an interface, then all its subclasses do so implicitly.

- A subclass inherits all the characteristics of its superclass. To this basis, the subclass can add new variables and methods or modify inherited methods.

- Characteristics common to several classes can be collected in a common abstract superclass that is never instantiated.

- An abstract class can contain headers for abstract methods that are implemented in the subclasses.

- A class's constructors and methods can utilize constructors and methods in the superclass.

- Inheritance reduces repetition and promotes the reuse of code.

- Interfaces and inheritance promote the use of polymorphism.

Now let us consider additional observations.

Finding the Right Method

When a message is sent to an object, Java looks for a matching method. The search starts in the object's class and if necessary continues up the class hierarchy.

- Consequently, in the preceding program, when the `move` message is sent to a circle or a rectangle, the `move` method in the `AbstractShape` class is activated. There is no `move` method in either the `Circle` or `Rect` classes.

- On the other hand, when the `stretchBy` message is sent to a circle, Java uses the corresponding method in the `Circle` class.

■ When the `toString` message is sent to a circle, execution begins in the `Circle` class, temporarily transfers to the superclass, and finishes up in the `Circle` class.

```
public String toString() {
   String str = "CIRCLE\n"
              + "Radius: " + radius + "\n"
              + super.toString();              // Transfer to superclass
   return str;
}
```

In the superclass `AbstractShape`, however, something tricky happens:

```
public String toString(){
   String str = "(X,Y) Position: (" + xPos + "," + yPos + ")\n"
              + "Area: " + area();          // Something tricky here
   return str;
}
```

Which `area` method is being called, the one in `AbstractShape` or the one in `Circle`? Actually, this question is not so hard to answer. We must stop to consider which object is involved in all of this. It is a circle object; therefore, the `area` method in the `Circle` class is activated. Nonetheless, it does seem strange that the `toString` method in the superclass activates the `area` method in the subclass.

To be fair, we (the authors) must admit that the last example was specially contrived to be tricky. You may work with Java for a year or more before encountering anything similar.

Implementation, Extension, Overriding, and Finality

You may have noticed that there are four ways in which methods in a subclass can be related to methods in a superclass:

1. **Implementation of an abstract method:** As we have seen, each subclass is forced to implement the abstract methods specified in its superclass. Abstract methods are thus a means of requiring certain behavior in all subclasses.

2. **Extension:** There are two kinds of extension:
   a. The subclass method does not exist in the superclass.
   b. The subclass method invokes the same method in the superclass and also extends the superclass's behavior with its own operations.

3. **Overriding:** In the case of *overriding*, the subclass method does not invoke the superclass method. Instead, the subclass method is intended as a complete replacement of the superclass method.

4. **Finality:** The method in the superclass is complete and cannot be modified by the subclasses. We declare such a method to be `final`.

Working Without Interfaces

Interfaces are a useful and powerful mechanism for organizing code; however, they are not necessary. We discussed classes in Lesson 5 without needing them, and we could have managed without them in this lesson, too. Without the `Shape` interface, the implementation of `AbstractShape` remains the same except for the header:

```
abstract public class AbstractShape {
```

And defining a variable as `AbstractShape` allows the variable to associate with objects from any shape class:

```
AbstractShape s1, s2, s3;
s1 = new Circle();
s2 = new Rect();
s3 = new Wheel();


s2.<any message in AbstractShape>;
```

Because the `AbstractShape` class contains a list of all the shape methods, we can send any of the shape messages to the variables `s1`, `s2`, and `s3`. Of course, we still cannot send the `setSpokes` message to `s3` without first casting `s3` to the `Wheel` class.

So should you or shouldn't you use interfaces? This is not really a question of vital importance in an introductory programming class where all the programs are relatively short and simple; however, the prevailing wisdom suggests that we use hierarchies of interfaces to organize behavior and hierarchies of classes to maximize code reuse. Justifying this advice is beyond this book's scope.

*E*XERCISE 9.6

1. Describe the process by which the JVM locates the right method to execute at run time in the following example:

```
// In the server's code

private int myData;

public String someMethod(int x){
   return myData + super.someMethod(x);
}

// In the client's code

System.out.println(someObject.someMethod(10));
```

CASE STUDY: Compute Weekly Pay Revisited

We illustrate most of the concepts presented so far in this lesson by redoing the payroll case study from Lesson 6. To refresh your memory, Figure 9-6 shows a slightly modified version of the interface. The change involves displaying the total payroll after the last name is entered.

FIGURE 9-6
Interface for the compute weekly pay program

```
Enter employee data
   Name (or blank to quit): Susan Jones
   Type (1 or 2): 1
   Hourly rate (between 6.75 and 30.50, inclusive): 10.50
   Hours worked (between 1 and 60, inclusive): 50
   The weekly pay for Susan Jones is $630.0
Enter employee data
   Name (or blank to quit): Bill Smith
   Type (1 or 2): 2
   Hourly rate (between 6.75 and 30.50, inclusive): 15.00
   Hours worked (between 1 and 60, inclusive): 60
   The weekly pay for Bill Smith is $900.0
Enter employee data
   Name (or blank to quit):

Total pay: $1530.0
```

Request

This is exactly the same as in Lesson 6, that is, write a program to compute the weekly pay of hourly employees.

Analysis

Most aspects of the analysis are unchanged from Lesson 6, except for how we plan to decompose the program into classes. Before presenting the details, we would like to point out that our approach is overly elaborate for such a simple problem; however, if we are to master this lesson's concepts, we had best begin in a simple context. The approach presented here scales up well to larger, complex programs.

The interface is essentially the same as in Lesson 6 and is implemented in the class `PayrollSystemInterface`.

An employee hierarchy (see Figure 9-7) replaces the single Employee class used in Lesson 6. In this hierarchy, Employee is an abstract class and contains most of the code. The two concrete classes implement a getPay method using a different algorithm for full-time and part-time employees. In Lesson 6, the two algorithms are combined into a single getPay method. When the rules for performing an operation differ depending on type, it is considered best to create separate classes for each type. We saw an example of this rule in the shapes hierarchy. Each type of shape is drawn in a different manner, so rather than write a single complex draw method that draws all shapes, we give each shape its own class and its own simpler draw method. For the sake of variety, we are not using a Java interface.

FIGURE 9-7
An employee hierarchy

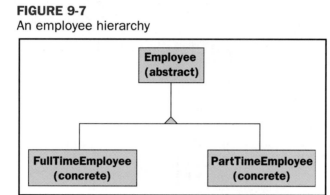

Design

The design of the interface class is unchanged from Lesson 6. The Employee class contains all the instance variables and methods. The type variable used in Lesson 6 is no longer needed. All the instance methods are complete, except for getPay, which is abstract. In addition, the Employee class contains static variables and methods. Static constants indicate the range of valid values for hours and pay rate. Static methods return strings that describe the range of valid input values. In addition, a static variable keeps track of the total pay, and a static method returns its value. The classes FullTimeEmployee and PartTimeEmployee merely implement a constructor and the getPay method. Figure 9-8 summarizes the classes.

FIGURE 9-8
Summary of the classes in the employee hierarchy

```
Abstract Class:
   Employee
Protected Instance Variables:
   String name
   double rate
   int hours
Public Instance Methods:
   boolean setName(String nm)
   boolean setRate(double rt)
   boolean setHours(int hrs)
   String getName()
   abstract double getPay()
Public Static Variables:
   double LOW_RATE = 6.75
   double HIGH_RATE = 30.50
   double LOW_HOURS = 1
   double HIGH_HOURS = 60
Protected Static Variables:
   double totalPay = 0
Public Static Methods:
   String getNameRules()
   String getTypeRules()
   String getRateRules()
   String getHoursRules()
   boolean typeOK(int type)
   double getTotalPay()
```

```
Concrete Class:
   FullTimeEmployee
Public Instance Methods:
   double getPay()
```

```
Concrete Class:
   PartTimeEmployee
Public Instance Methods:
   double getPay()
```

Implementation

The code follows:

```
/* PayrollSystemInterface.java
1. Request employee name, type, pay rate, and hours.
2. Print employee name and pay.
3. Repeat until the name is blank.
4. Print the total pay. */

import TerminalIO.KeyboardReader;

public class PayrollSystemInterface {

    public static void main (String [] args) {

        KeyboardReader reader = new KeyboardReader();
```

```
      Employee emp;      // employee
      String name;       //   name
      int    type;       //   type
      double rate;       //   hourly pay rate
      int    hours;      //   hours worked
      String prompt;     // user prompt;

      while (true){

          // Get the name and break if blank
          System.out.println("Enter employee data");
          name = reader.readLine("  Name (or blank to quit): ");
          name = name.trim(); // Trim off leading and trailing spaces
          if (name.length() == 0) break;

          // Get the type until valid
          while (true){
              prompt = "  Type (" + Employee.getTypeRules() + "): ";
              type = reader.readInt(prompt);
              if (Employee.typeOK(type)) break;
          }

          // Instantiate an employee of the correct type and set the name
          if (type == 1)
              emp = new FullTimeEmployee();
          else
              emp = new PartTimeEmployee();
          emp.setName(name);

          // Get the hourly pay rate until valid
          while (true){
              prompt = "  Hourly rate (" + Employee.getRateRules() + "): ";
              rate = reader.readDouble(prompt);
              if (emp.setRate(rate)) break;
          }

          // Get the hours worked until valid
          //    To illustrate the possibilities we compress this code
          //    into a single unreadable statement.
          while (!emp.setHours(reader.readInt
                  ("  Hours worked (" + Employee.getHoursRules() + "): ")));

          // Print the name and pay
          System.out.println
              ("  The weekly pay for " + emp.getName() +
               " is $" + emp.getPay());
      }

      // Print the total pay
      System.out.println  ("\nTotal pay: " + Employee.getTotalPay());
   }
 }
```

```java
abstract public class Employee {

// Protected Instance Variables:
   protected String name;
   protected double rate;
   protected int hours;

// Public Methods:
   public Employee(){
      name = "";
      rate = 0;
      hours = 0;
   }

   public boolean setName(String nm){
      if (nm.equals(""))
         return false;
      else{
         name = nm;
         return true;
      }
   }

   public boolean setRate(double rt){
      if (!(LOW_RATE <= rt && rt <= HIGH_RATE))
         return false;
      else{
         rate = rt;
         return true;
      }
   }

   public boolean setHours(int hrs){
      if (!(LOW_HOURS <= hrs && hrs <= HIGH_HOURS))
         return false;
      else{
         hours = hrs;
         return true;
      }
   }

   public String getName(){
      return name;
   }

   abstract public double getPay();

   //----------------------------------------

   public static double LOW_RATE = 6.75;
   public static double HIGH_RATE = 30.50;
```

```java
    public static double LOW_HOURS = 1;
    public static double HIGH_HOURS = 60;

    protected static double totalPay = 0;

    public static String getNameRules() {
        return "nonblank";
    }

    public static String getTypeRules() {
        return "1 or 2";
    }

    public static String getRateRules() {
        return getRule (LOW_RATE, HIGH_RATE);
    }

    public static String getHoursRules() {
        return getRule (LOW_HOURS, HIGH_HOURS);
    }

    public static boolean typeOK (int type) {
        return type == 1 || type == 2;
    }

    public static double getTotalPay() {
        return totalPay;
    }

    private static String getRule (double low, double high) {
            return "between " + low + " and " + high + ", inclusive";
    }
}
```

```java
public class FullTimeEmployee extends Employee {

    public FullTimeEmployee(){
        super();
    }

    public double getPay() {
        double pay;
        if (hours <= 40)
            pay = rate * hours;
        else
            pay = rate * 40 +  rate * 2 * (hours - 40);
        totalPay += pay;
        return pay;
    }
}
```

```
public class PartTimeEmployee extends Employee {

   public PartTimeEmployee() {
      super();
   }

   public double getPay() {
      double pay;
      pay = rate * hours;
      totalPay += pay;
      return pay;
   }
}
```

9.7 Acceptable Classes for Parameters and Return Values

The rules of Java, as enforced by the compiler, state that in any situation in which an object of class BBB is expected, it is always acceptable to substitute an object of a subclass but never of a superclass. The reason is simple. A subclass of BBB inherits all of BBB's methods, whereas no guarantees can be made about the methods in the superclass. The following code segment illustrates these points (the results would be the same if we substituted Shape for AbstractShape in the first line):

```
AbstractShape s;
Circle c;
Wheel w;

s = new Circle();    // Accepted by the compiler
c = new Circle();    // Accepted by the compiler
w = new Circle();    // Rejected by the compiler
c = new Wheel();     // Accepted by the compiler
```

In the rest of this section, we will apply these principles to method parameters and return values. We already know that objects can be passed to and returned from methods. Actually, to speak more precisely, we should say references to objects can be passed to and returned from methods. It is obvious that an object must exist before it is passed to a method, but it is easy to forget that changes made to the object in the method persist after the method stops executing. On the other hand, an object returned by a method is usually created in the method, and it continues to exist after the method stops executing.

Rectangle In, Circle Out

For our first example we write a method that takes a rectangle as an input parameter and returns a circle. The circle has the same area and position as the rectangle. The method makes no changes to the rectangle, and it has to instantiate the circle:

```
static private Circle makeCircleFromRectangle (Rect rectangle){
   double area = rectangle.area();
   double radius = Math.sqrt (area / Math.PI);
   Circle circle = new Circle (rectangle.getXPos(),
                               rectangle.getYPos(),
                               radius);
   return circle;
}
```

Any Shape In, Circle Out

We now modify the previous method so that it accepts any shape as an input parameter—circle, rectangle, or wheel. The fact that all shapes understand the area method makes the task easy:

```
static private Circle makeCircleFromAnyShape (Shape shape){
   double area = shape.area();
   double radius = Math.sqrt (area / Math.PI);
   Circle circle = new Circle (shape.getXPos(),
                               shape.getYPos(),
                               radius);
   return circle;
}
```

Any Shape In, Any Shape Out

It is also possible for a method to return an arbitrary rather than a specific shape. The next method has two input parameters. The first parameter is a shape, and the second indicates the type of shape to return:

```
static private Shape makeOneShapeFromAnother (Shape inShape, String type){
   Shape outShape;                                    // declare outShape
   double area, radius, width, height;
   double x = inShape.getXPos();
   double y = inShape.getYPos();

   area = inShape.area();
   if (type.equals ("circle")){
      radius = Math.sqrt (area / Math.PI);
      outShape = new Circle (x, y, radius);           // assign a circle
   }
   else if (type.equals ("rectangle")){
      width = height = Math.sqrt (area);
      outShape = new Rect (x, y, width, height);      // assign a rectangle
   }
   else{ // it is a wheel
      radius = Math.sqrt (area / Math.PI);
```

```
            outShape = new Wheel (x, y, radius, 6);        // assign a wheel
        }
        return outShape;
    }
```

The following code is a test of the previous method with the program's output shown in Figure 9-9.

```
public class TestShapes {

    public static void main (String[] args){
        Rect rect;
        Shape shape1, shape2, shape3;

        rect = new Rect (1,1,4,6);
        shape1 = makeOneShapeFromAnother (rect, "circle");
        shape2 = makeOneShapeFromAnother (rect, "rectangle");
        shape3 = makeOneShapeFromAnother (rect, "wheel");

        System.out.println ("\nRectangle Area: " + rect.area() +
                            "\nCircle    Area: " + shape1.area() +
                            "\nRectangle Area: " + shape2.area() +
                            "\nWheel     Area: " + shape3.area());

    }

    static private Shape makeOneShapeFromAnother (Shape inShape,
                                                  String type){

    ... code as shown above ...
    }
}
```

FIGURE 9-9
Areas of various shapes made from a rectangle

```
Rectangle Area: 24.0
Circle    Area: 24.000000000000004
Rectangle Area: 23.999999999999996
Wheel     Area: 24.000000000000004
```

EXERCISE 9.7

1. State the rules for passing a parameter of one class to a method that expects a parameter of another class.

9.8 Error Handling with Classes

In Lesson 6, we introduced a means of handling possible error conditions in a system that uses classes and objects. In this approach, a class's mutator method returns a `boolean` value to indicate whether the operation has been successful or an error has occurred and the operation has failed. In addition, the class provides a method that returns a string that states a rule describing the valid use of the mutator method. For example, following is the code for these two methods in an `Employee` object, followed by its use in some client code:

```
// In the Employee class
public String getHoursRules(){
    return "between 1 and 60, inclusive";
}

public boolean setHours(int hrs){
    if (!(1 <= hrs && hrs <= 60))
        return false;
    else{
        hours = hrs;
        return true;
    }
}
// In the client that uses an Employee object
// Input the hours worked until valid
while (!emp.setHours(reader.readInt("Hours worked(" + emp.getHoursRules()
                                    + "): ")));
```

Clearly, this kind of error checking improves upon the situation in Lesson 5, where our classes simply let errors go undetected. In this section, we introduce a more formal way of describing error conditions in code and another way of detecting and responding to errors.

Preconditions and Postconditions

Before we can implement code for error handing, we must determine what the error conditions for a class are. A systematic way to do this is to state these conditions in the class's interface as *preconditions* and *postconditions*. We can think of preconditions and postconditions as the subject of a conversation between the user and implementer of a method. Following is the general form of the conversation:

Implementer: "Here are the things that you must guarantee to be true before my method is invoked. They are its preconditions."

User: "Fine. And what do you guarantee will be the case if I do that?"

Implementer: "Here are the things that I guarantee to be true when my method finishes execution. They are its postconditions."

A method's preconditions describe what should be true before it is called, and its postconditions describe what will be true after it has finished executing. The preconditions describe the expected values of parameters and instance variables that the method is about to use. Postconditions describe the return value and any changes made to instance variables. Of course, if the caller does not meet the preconditions, then the method probably will not meet the postconditions.

In most programming languages, preconditions and postconditions are conveniently written as comments placed directly above a method's header. Let us add such documentation to a method header for the `Student` method `setScore` from Lesson 5. There are preconditions on each of the method's parameters:

1. The parameter `i`, which represents the position of the score, must be greater than or equal to 1 and less than or equal to 3.

2. The parameter `score` must be greater than or equal to 0 and less than or equal to 100.

The method's postcondition states that the test score at position `i` has been set to `score`. We now return the `boolean` value `true` if the preconditions have been satisfied or `false` otherwise. Following is the code:

```
/*
 * Precondition: 1 <= i <= 3
 * Precondition: 0 <= score <= 100
 * Postcondition: test score at position i is set to score
 * Returns: true if the preconditions are satisfied or false otherwise
 */
public boolean setScore(int i, int score){
   if (i < 1 || i > 3 || score < 0 || score > 100)
      return false;
   if       (i == 1) test1 = score;
   else if (i == 2) test2 = score;
   else                 test3 = score;
   return true;
}
```

Not all methods have pre- and postconditions. For example, the `Student` method `getName` simply returns the student's name, so its documentation mentions just the return value.

The writing of pre- and postconditions for each method might seem like a tedious task; however, that's how the developers of Java have done it, as an inspection of Sun's Java documentation reveals. And remember that, like the people at Sun, you are writing code primarily for other people to read.

*E*XERCISE 9.8

1. Write preconditions and postconditions for the methods of the `Student` class from Lesson 5. If you answered Question 1 in Exercise 9.3, put these comments in the interface; otherwise, put them in the class.

9.9 Exceptions

As you have seen in earlier lessons, Java throws an exception to signal a run-time error. There are occasions when you can throw your own exceptions in the classes you write. We now give an overview of how to do this.

Examples of Exceptions

Java provides a hierarchy of exception classes that represent the most commonly occurring exceptions. Following is a list of some of the commonly used exception classes in the package `java.lang`:

```
Exception
    RuntimeException
        ArithmeticException
        IllegalArgumentException
        IllegalStateException
        IndexOutOfBoundsException
            StringIndexOutOfBoundsException
            ArrayIndexOutOfBoundsException
        NullPointerException
        UnsupportedOperationException
```

Java throws an arithmetic exception when a program attempts to divide by 0 and a `null` pointer exception when a program attempts to send a message to a variable that does not reference an object. An array index out-of-bounds exception is thrown when the integer in an array subscript operator is less than 0 or greater than or equal to the array's length. Other types of exceptions, such as illegal state exceptions and illegal argument exceptions, can be used to enforce preconditions on methods. Other packages such as `java.util` define still more types of exceptions. In general, you determine which preconditions you want to enforce and then choose the appropriate type of exception to throw from Java's repertoire.

The syntax of the statement to throw an exception is

```
throw new <exception class>(<a string>);
```

where `<a string>` is the message to be displayed. When you are in doubt about which type of exception to throw, you can fall back on a `RuntimeException`. Following is an example:

```
if (number < 0)
    throw new RuntimeException("Number should be nonnegative");
```

How Exceptions Work

At run time, the computer keeps track of the dynamic context of a program. This context includes a chain of method calls, beginning with the method `main` in the main application class and ending with the currently executing method. When a piece of code in this method throws an exception, the computer examines the code immediately surrounding it for a `try-catch` statement (more on this statement later). If no such statement is found in this context, control returns immediately to the caller of the method. Once again, if no `try-catch` statement is found in that method, control moves up to its caller, and so on, until method `main` is reached. If no `try-catch` statement has been located at any point in this process, the computer halts the program with a trace of the method calls, the type of exception, and its error message, examples of which you have seen in earlier lessons.

Throwing Exceptions to Enforce Preconditions

A more hard-nosed approach to error handling is to have a class throw exceptions to enforce all of its methods' preconditions. Let's adopt that approach for the `Student` method `setScore` discussed earlier. We know the preconditions, so we begin by choosing the appropriate exception classes and describing these in the documentation. We will throw an `IllegalArgumentException` if either parameter violates the preconditions. Because the method either succeeds in setting a score or throws an exception, it returns `void` instead of a `boolean` value. The method header summarizes our error handling:

```
/*
 * Precondition: 1 <= i <= 3
 * Precondition: 0 <= score <= 100
 * Postcondition: test score at position i is set to score
 * throws IllegalArgumentException if i < 1 or i > 3
 * throws IllegalArgumentException if score < 0 or score > 100
 */
public void setScore(int i, int score){
   if (i < 1 || i > 3)
      throw new IllegalArgumentException("i must be >= 1 and <= 3");
   if (score < 0 || score > 100)
      throw new IllegalArgumentException("score must be >= 0 and <= 100");
   if       (i == 1) test1 = score;
   else if (i == 2) test2 = score;
   else             test3 = score;
}
```

Catching an Exception

As you can see, the use of exceptions can make a server's code pretty foolproof. However, clients must still check the preconditions of such methods if they do not want these exceptions to halt their programs with run-time errors. There are two ways to do this:

1. Use a simple `if-else` statement to ask the right questions about the parameters before calling a method.

2. Embed the call to the method within a `try-catch` statement.

   The `try-catch` statement allows a client to

■ Attempt the call of a method whose preconditions might be violated.

■ Catch any exceptions that the method might throw and respond to them gracefully.

For example, following is some code that displays the exception's error message in the terminal window instead of halting the program with the same message and a call trace:

```
Student s = new Student("Bill", 100, 80, 75);
try{
   s.setScore(4, 85);
}catch(IllegalStateException e){
   System.out.println(e);
}
```

When the `setScore` method throws the `IllegalArgumentException`, the computer passes it as a parameter to the `catch` clause, which assumes immediate control and continues execution.

This code catches and handles an exception only of the specified type. Suppose a method can throw two different types of exceptions, such as `IllegalArgumentException` and `IllegalStateException`. To catch either one of these, one can include two catch clauses:

```
try{
    someObject.someMethod(param1, param2);
}catch(IllegalStateException e){
    System.out.println(e);
}catch(IllegalArgumentException e){
    System.out.println(e);
}
```

The computer runs down the list of `catch` clauses until the exception's type matches that of a parameter or no match is found. If no match is found, the exception is passed up the call chain as described earlier.

To guarantee that any exception is caught, you can use the generic `Exception` class, which matches any exception type:

```
try{
    s.setScore(4, 200);
}catch(Exception e){
    System.out.println(e);
}
```

*E*XERCISE 9.9

1. Locate all of the methods in the `student` class from Lesson 5 in which exceptions could be thrown and include the exceptions in these methods.

9.10 Reference Types, Equality, and Object Identity

In Lessons 2, 5, and 6, we made a distinction between variables of primitive types—which contain numbers, characters, Booleans—and variables of reference types—which contain references or pointers to objects, but never the objects themselves. Thus, it is possible for more than one variable to point to the same object, a situation known as *aliasing*. This occurs when the programmer assigns one object variable to another. It is also possible, of course, for two object variables to refer to distinct objects of the same type.

Comparing Objects for Equality

The possibility of aliasing can lead to unintended results when comparing two object variables for equality. There are two ways to compare objects for equality:

1. Use the equality operator ==.

2. Use the instance method `equals`. This method is defined in the `Object` class and uses the `==` operator by default. This method is similar to the method `toString`, which was discussed earlier in this book and which, by default, returns the name of the object's class for any object that does not override it. All classes, which are subclasses of `Object`, inherit the method `equals` and use it when it is not overridden in the receiver object's class.

Consider the following code segment, which reads a string from the keyboard, uses both methods to compare this string to a string literal, and outputs the results:

```
String str = reader.readString();        // Read string from keyboard.

System.out.println (str == "Java");       // Displays false no matter what
                                          // string was entered.
System.out.println (str.equals ("Java")); // Displays true if the string
                                          // entered was "Java", and false
                                          // otherwise.
```

Following is the explanation:

■ The objects referenced by the variable `str` and the literal "`Java`" are two different string objects in memory, even though the characters they contain might be the same. The first string object was created in the keyboard reader during user input; the second string object was created internally within the program.

■ The operator `==` compares the references to the objects, not the contents of the objects. Thus, if the two references do not point to the same object in memory, `==` returns `false`. Because the two strings in our example are not the same object in memory, `==` returns `false`.

■ The method `equals` returns `true`, even when two strings are not the same object in memory, if their characters happen to be the same. If at least one pair of characters fails to match, the method `equals` returns `false`.

■ A corollary of these facts is that the operator `!=` can return `true` for two strings, even though the method `equals` also returns `true`.

■ To summarize, `==` tests for object identity, whereas `equals` tests for structural similarity as defined by the implementing class.

The operator `==` also can be used with other objects, such as buttons and menu items. In these cases, too, the operator tests for object identity: a reference to the same object in memory. With window objects, the use of `==` is appropriate, because most of the time we want to compare references. For other objects, however, such as the student objects discussed in Lesson 5, the use of `==` should be avoided. To test two student objects for equality, we implement the method `equals` in the `Student` class. We will consider two students equal if

■ They are identical.

or

■ They are instances of `Student` and their names are equal.

Following is the code for the method:

```
// Compare two students for equality
   public boolean equals (Object other){
      if (this == other)                   // Test for identity
         return true;
```

```
        if (! other instanceof Student)        // Test for a Student
            return false;
        Student s = (Student)other;             // Cast to a Student
        return name.equals (s.getName());       // Compare the names
    }
```

Note that the method expects an Object as a parameter. This means that the user can pass an object of any class when the method is called. The method should first compare the receiver object (indicated by the word this) to the parameter object for identity using ==. If the two objects are not identical, the method examines their contents only if the parameter object is in fact an instance of the Student class. Therefore, the method must next do one of two things:

1. Return false if the parameter object is not an instance of Student. The operator instanceof is used to determine the class or interface of an object.

2. If the parameter object is an instance of class Student, cast its class down from Object to Student before accessing the data within it.

Copying Objects

As mentioned in Lesson 5, the attempt to copy an object with a simple assignment statement can cause a problem. The following code creates two references to one student object when the intent is to copy the contents of one student object to another:

```
Student s1, s2;
s1 = new Student ("Mary", 100, 80, 75);
s2 = s1;                                    // s1 and s2 refer to the same
                                            object
```

When clients of a class might copy objects, there is a standard way of providing a method that does so. The class implements the Java interface Cloneable. This interface authorizes the method clone, which is defined in the Object class, to construct a field-wise copy of the object. We now can rewrite the foregoing code so that it creates a copy of a student object:

```
Student s1, s2;
s1 = new Student ("Mary", 100, 80, 75);
s2 = s1.clone();                    // s1 and s2 refer to different objects
```

Note that == returns false and equals returns true for an object and its clone.

The implementation of the clone method returns a new instance of Student with the values of the instance variables from the receiver student. Following is the code for method clone:

```
// Clone a new student
public Object clone(){
    return new Student (name, test1, test2, test3);
}
```

Many of Java's standard classes, such as String, already implement the Cloneable interface, so they include a clone method. When instance variables of a class are themselves objects that are cloneable, it is a good idea to send them the clone message to obtain copies when implementing the clone method for that class. This process is called *deep copying* and can help minimize program errors.

Because tests for equality and cloning are fairly standard operations in all implementations, the methods `equals` and `clone` should be added to the Java interface for your classes, if there is one.

EXERCISE 9.10

1. Why should a programmer use the method `equals` instead of the operator `==` to compare two objects for equality?

2. What are the outputs when the following code segment is run?

```
Student s1 = new Student("Bill", 100, 85, 60);
Student s2 = new Student("Bill", 100, 85, 60);
String name = "Bill";

System.out.println(s1.equals(s2));
System.out.println(s1 == s2);
System.out.println(s1.equals(name));
```

3. What happens when an object is assigned to a variable?

4. How can you obtain a true copy of an object?

SUMMARY

In this lesson, you learned:

- Class (static) variables provide storage for data that all instances of a class can access but do not have to own separately. Class (static) methods are written primarily for class variables.

- An interface specifies a set of methods that implementing classes must include. An interface gives clients enough information to use a class.

- Polymorphism and inheritance provide a means of reducing the amount of code that must be written by servers and learned by clients in a system with a large number of cooperating classes. Classes that extend other classes inherit their data and methods. Methods in different classes that have the same name are polymorphic. Abstract classes, which are not instantiated, exist for the sole purpose of organizing related subclasses and containing their common data and methods.

- Error handling can be distributed among methods and classes by using preconditions, postconditions, and exceptions.

- Because of the possibility of aliasing, the programmer should provide an `equals` method for comparing two objects for equality and a `clone` method for creating a copy of an object.

VOCABULARY *Review*

Define the following terms:

abstract class	concrete class	overriding
abstract method	final method	postcondition
class (static) method	inheritance	precondition
class (static) variable	interface	

REVIEW *Questions*

FILL IN THE BLANK

Complete the following sentences by writing the correct word or words in the blanks provided.

1. Methods and variables that belong to a class rather than an instance are called _____ or _____ variables and methods.

2. The keyword used to invoke a constructor or method in a superclass is called _____.

3. The visibility modifier _____ makes a method or variable visible to subclasses but not to other clients.

4. A(n) _____ class contains common behavior and data for a set of subclasses but is not instantiated.

5. A(n) _____ method consists of just a head and forces all subclasses to implement it.

6. _____ and _____ state the assumptions that are true before a method executes correctly and after it executes correctly.

7. The method _____ is the conventional Java method for comparing two objects for equality, whereas the method _____ is the conventional Java method for copying an object.

PROJECTS

PROJECT 9-1

Design a hierarchy of classes that models the classification of your favorite region of the animal kingdom. Your hierarchy should be at most three classes deep and should employ abstract classes on the first two levels.

PROJECT 9-2

Design a hierarchy of classes that represents the classification of artifacts, such as vehicles.

PROJECT 9-3

Add a method `perimeter` to the `Shape` hierarchy from this lesson. This method should return the circumference of a circle and a wheel and the perimeter of a rectangle.

PROJECT 9-4

Add a `Triangle` class to the `Shape` hierarchy from this lesson. Note the following points:

- A triangle is specified by three vertices or pairs of coordinates. The first pair is the position (xPos, yPos).

- The `move` method for a triangle, which adds the *x* and *y* distances to each of the vertices, must override the `move` method in the abstract class; therefore, the `move` method in the abstract class cannot be final.

- The distance between two points (x1,y1) and (x2,y2) is equal to the square root of ((x1 − x2) * (x1 − x2) + (y1 − y2) * (y1 − y2)).

- The area of a triangle can be computed from its vertices using the formula ½ * the absolute value of (x1 * y2 − x2 * y1 + x2 * y3 − x3 * y2 + x3 * y1 − x1 * y3).

- A triangle is stretched away from its position at (xPos,yPos). Thus, the other two vertices are incremented by multiplying their distance from (xPos,yPos) by the factors. For example, the new value of x2 is equal to xPos + (x2 − xPos) * factor.

PROJECT 9-5

Modify the payroll system of the case study so that taxes are deducted from gross pay. The tax rate is a flat 10 percent.

PROJECT 9-6

Browse Java's class hierarchy on Sun's Web site (see Appendix A). Write an essay that describes the design ideas underlying a class hierarchy that you find interesting among Java's classes.

CRITICAL *Thinking*

Jack has written software that uses many similar classes and has written interfaces for them. However, he never writes abstract classes, which he considers too much work. Jill tells him that he needs to use abstract classes where they would be helpful. What can you say to support Jill's advice? Use an example from this lesson.

ARRAYS CONTINUED

OBJECTIVES

Upon completion of this lesson, you should be able to:

- Use string methods appropriately.

- Write a method for searching an array.

- Understand why a sorted array can be searched more efficiently than an unsorted array.

- Write a method to sort an array.

- Write methods to perform insertions and removals at given positions in an array.

- Understand the issues involved when working with arrays of objects.

- Perform simple operations with Java's `ArrayList` class.

Estimated Time: 3.5 hours

VOCABULARY

binary search

bubble sort

immutable object

insertion sort

linear search

modal

selection sort

substring

wrapper class

In Lesson 8, we examined how to declare array variables, instantiate array objects, and manipulate arrays using the subscript operator, loops, and methods. The current lesson covers more complex operations on arrays, such as searching, sorting, insertions, and removals. Along the way, we examine issues that arise in the use of arrays of objects and we introduce Java's `ArrayList` class. As a prelude to these topics, we begin with a look at some advanced string methods.

10.1 Advanced Operations on Strings

Thus far in this text, we have used strings without manipulating their contents very much. However, most text processing applications spend time examining the characters in strings, taking them apart, and building new strings. For example, consider the problem of extracting words from a line of text. To obtain the first word, we could copy the string's characters to a new string until we reach the first space character in the string (assuming the delimiter between words is the space) or we reach the length of the string. Following is a code segment that uses this strategy:

```
// Create a sample string
String original = "Hi there!";

// Variable to hold the first word, set to empty string
String word = "";

// Visit all the characters in the string
for (int i = 0; i < original.length(); i++){

    // Or stop when a space is found
    if (original.charAt(i) == ' ')
        break;

    // Add the non-space character to the word
    word += original.charAt(i);
}
```

As you can see, this code combines the tasks of finding the first space character and building a *substring* of the original string. The problem is solved much more easily by using two separate string methods that are designed for these tasks. The first method, indexOf, expects the target character as a parameter and returns the position of the first instance of that character or –1 if the character is not in the string. The second method, substring, expects two integer parameters indicating the starting and ending positions of the substring. This method returns the substring that runs from the starting position up to but not including the ending position. Following is code that uses these methods:

```
String original = "Hi there!";

// Search for the position of the first space
int endPosition = original.indexOf(' ');

// If there is no space, use the whole string
if (endPosition == -1)
    endPosition = original.length();

// Extract the first word
String word = original.substring(0, endPosition);
```

Table 10-1 describes some commonly used `string` methods.

TABLE 10-1
Some commonly used string methods

METHOD	DESCRIPTION
charAt (anIndex) returns char	Ex: chr = myStr.charAt(4); Returns the character at the position anIndex. Remember that the first character is at position 0. An exception is thrown (i.e., an error is generated) if anIndex is out of range (i.e., does not indicate a valid position within myStr).
compareTo (aString) returns int	Ex: i = myStr.compareTo("abc"); Compares two strings alphabetically. Returns 0 if myStr equals aString, a value less than 0 if myStr string is alphabetically less than aString, and a value greater than 0 if myStr string is alphabetically greater than aString.
equals (aString) returns boolean equalsIgnoreCase (aString) returns boolean	Ex: boolean = myStr.equals("abc"); Returns true if myStr equals aString; else returns false. Because of implementation peculiarities in Java, never test for equality like this: myStr == aString Similar to equals but ignores case during the comparison.
indexOf (aCharacter) returns int	Ex: i = myStr.indexOf('z') Returns the index within myStr of the first occurrence of aCharacter or –1 if aCharacter is absent.
indexOf (aCharacter, beginIndex) returns int	Ex: i = myStr.indexOf('z', 6); Similar to the preceding method except the search starts at position beginIndex rather than at the beginning of myStr. An exception is thrown (i.e., an error is generated) if beginIndex is out of range (i.e., does not indicate a valid position within myStr).
indexOf (aSubstring) returns int	Ex: i = myStr.indexOf("abc") Returns the index within myStr of the first occurrence of aSubstring or –1 if aSubstring is absent.
indexOf (aSubstring, beginIndex) returns int	Ex: i = myStr.indexOf("abc", 6) Similar to the preceding method except the search starts at position beginIndex rather than at the beginning of myStr. An exception is thrown (i.e., an error is generated) if beginIndex is out of range (i.e., does not indicate a valid position within myStr).
length() returns int	Ex: i = myStr.length(); Returns the length of myStr.
replace (oldChar, newChar) returns String	Ex: str = myStr.replace('z', 'Z'); Returns a new string resulting from replacing a l occurrences of oldChar in myStr with newChar. **myStr is not changed**.
substring (beginIndex) returns String	Ex: str = myStr.substring(6); Returns a new string that is a substring of myStr. The substring begins at location beginIndex and extends to the end of myStr. An exception is thrown (i.e., an error is generated) if beginIndex is out of range (i.e., does not indicate a valid position within myStr).

TABLE 10-1 (Continued)
Some commonly used string methods

METHOD	DESCRIPTION
substring (beginIndex, endIndex) returns String	Ex: str = myStr.substring(4, 8); Similar to the preceding method except the substring extends to location endIndex − 1 rather than to the end of myStr.
toLowerCase() returns String	Ex: str = myStr.toLowerCase(); str is the same as myStr except that all letters have been converted to lowercase. **myStr is not changed**.
toUpperCase() returns String	Ex: str = myStr.toUpperCase(); str is the same as myStr except that all letters have been converted to uppercase. **myStr is not changed**.
trim() returns String	Ex: str = myStr.trim(); str is the same as myStr except that leading and trailing spaces, if any, are absent. **myStr is not changed**.

Note that there are no mutator methods for strings. The reason for this is that strings are *immutable objects*. Once a string is created, its length cannot change and one cannot modify any of its characters.

EXERCISE 10.1

1. Indicate the outputs of the following code segments:

a.

```
String str = "The rain in Spain falls mainly on the plain";
System.out.println(str.indexOf(' '));
```

b.

```
String str = "The rain in Spain falls mainly on the plain";
System.out.println(str.indexOf(' ', 4));
```

c.

```
String str = "The rain in Spain falls mainly on the plain";
System.out.println(str.substring(4));
```

d.

```
String str = "The rain in Spain falls mainly on the plain";
System.out.println(str.substring(4, 8));
```

EXERCISE 10.1 Continued

e.

```
String str = "The rain in Spain falls mainly on the plain";
int begin = 0;
while (begin < str.length()){
    int end = str.indexOf(' ', begin);
    if (end == -1)
        end = str.length();
    String word = str.substring(begin, end);
    System.out.println(word);
    begin = end + 1;
}
```

2. Write code segments that perform the following tasks:
   a. Replace every blank space character in the string `str` with a newline character (`'\n'`).
   b. Find the index of the first instance of the substring `"the"` in the string `str`.
   c. Find the index of the first instance of the substring `"the"` after the midpoint of the string `str`.
   d. Count the number of instances of the whole word `"the"` in the string `str`.

10.2 Searching

Searching collections of elements for a given target element is a very common operation in software systems. Some examples are the `indexOf` methods for strings discussed earlier. In this section, we examine two typical methods for searching an array of elements—a linear search and a binary search.

Linear Search

In Lesson 8, we developed the code for a method that searches an array of `int` for a given target value. The method returns the index of the first matching value or –1 if the value is not in the array. Following is the code:

```
int search (int[] a, int searchValue){
    for (int i = 0; i < a.length; i++)
        if (a[i] == searchValue)
            return i;
    return -1;
}
```

The method examines each element in sequence, starting with the first one, to determine if a target element is present. The loop breaks if the target is found. The method must examine every element to determine the absence of a target. This method of searching is usually called *linear search*.

Searching an Array of Objects

Suppose we have an array of names that we want to search for a given name. A name is a `String`. We cannot use the search method developed already. But we can use a similar loop in the code for a different search method that expects an array of `String` and a target `String` as parameters. The only change in the loop is that two string elements must be compared with the method `equals` instead of the operator `==`. Following is the code:

```
int search (String[] a, String searchValue){
   for (i = 0; i < a.length; i++)
      if (a[i].equals(searchValue))
         return i;
   return -1;
}
```

This method can be generalized to work with any objects, not just strings. We simply substitute `Object` for `String` in the formal parameter list. The method still works for strings, and we can also use it to search an array of `Student` objects for a target student, assuming that the `Student` class includes an appropriate `equals` method. Following is a code segment that uses this single method to search arrays of two different types:

```
String[]  stringArray = {"Hi", "there", "Martin"};
Student[] studentArray = new Student[5];
Student   stu = new Student("Student 1", 100, 100, 100);

for (int i = 0; i < studentArray.length; i++)
   studentArray[i] = new Student("Student " + (i + 1), 100, 100, 100);

int stringPos = search(stringArray, "Martin");      // Returns 2
int studentPos = search(studentArray, stu);         // Returns 0
```

Binary Search

The method of linear search works well for arrays that are fairly small (a few hundred elements). As the array gets very large (thousands or millions of elements), however, the behavior of the search degrades (more on this in Lesson 11). When we have an array of elements that are in ascending order, such as a list of numbers or names, there is a much better way to proceed. For example, in ordinary life, we do not use a linear search to find a name in a phone book. If we are looking for "Lambert," we open the book at our estimate of the middle page. If we're not on the "La" page, we look before or after, depending on whether we have opened the book at the "M" page or the "K" page. For computation, we can formalize this kind of search technique in an algorithm known as *binary search*. This method is much faster than linear search for very large arrays.

The basic idea of binary search is to examine the element at the array's midpoint on each pass through the search loop. If the current element matches the target, we return its position. If the current element is less than the target, then we search the part of the array to the right of the midpoint (containing the positions of the greater items). Otherwise, we search the part of the array to the left of the midpoint (containing the positions of the lesser items). On each pass through the loop, the current leftmost position or the current rightmost position is adjusted to track the portion of the array being searched. Following is a Java method that performs a binary search on an array of integers:

```
int search (int[] a, int searchValue){
    int left = 0;                          // Establish the initial
    int right = a.length - 1;              // endpoints of the array
    while (left <= right){                 // Loop until the endpoints cross
        int midpoint = (left + right) / 2; // Compute the current midpoint
        if (a[midpoint] == searchValue)    // Target found; return its index
            return midpoint;
        else if (a[midpoint] < searchValue) // Target to right of midpoint
            left = midpoint + 1;
        else                               // Target to left of midpoint
            right = midpoint - 1;
    }
    return -1;                             // Target not found
}
```

Figure 10-1 shows a trace of a binary search for the target value 5 in the array 1 3 5 7 9 11 13 15 17. Note that on each pass through the loop, the number of elements yet to be examined is reduced by half. As we shall see in Lesson 11, herein lies the advantage of binary search over linear search for very large arrays.

FIGURE 10-1
A trace of a binary search of an array

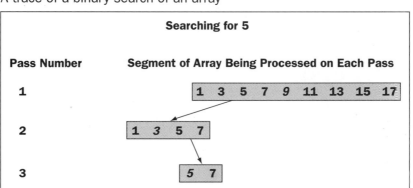

Comparing Objects and the `Comparable` Interface

When using binary search with an array of objects, we must compare two objects. But objects do not understand the < and > operators, and we have seen that == is not a wise choice for comparing two objects for equality. However, classes that implement the `Comparable` interface include the method `compareTo`, which performs the three different comparisons. Here is the signature of `compareTo`:

```
public int compareTo(Object other)
```

The behavior of compareTo is summarized in Table 10-2.

TABLE 10-2
The behavior of method compareTo

USAGE OF compareTo	VALUE RETURNED
obj1.compareTo(obj2)	0 if obj1 is equal to obj2, using equals
obj1.compareTo(obj2)	A negative integer, if obj1 is less than obj2
obj1.compareTo(obj2)	A positive integer, if obj1 is greater than obj2

For example, the String class implements the Comparable interface; thus, the second output of the following code segment is 0:

```
String str = "Mary";
System.out.println(str.compareTo("Suzanne"));    // Outputs -6
System.out.println(str.compareTo("Mary"));       // Outputs 0
System.out.println(str.compareTo("Bob"));        // Outputs 11
```

The other output integers are system dependent, but the first should be negative, whereas the third should be positive (in the example given, they are –6 and 11, respectively).

Before sending the compareTo message to an arbitrary object, that object must be cast to Comparable, because Object does not implement the Comparable interface or include a compareTo method. Following is the code for the binary search of an array of objects:

```
int search (Object[] a, Object searchValue){
    int left = 0;
    int right = a.length — 1;
    while (left <= right){
        int midpoint = (left + right) / 2;
        int result = ((Comparable)a[midpoint]).compareTo(searchValue);
        if (result == 0)
            return midpoint;
        else if (result < 0)
            left = midpoint + 1;
        else
            right = midpoint — 1;
    }
    return -1;
}
```

Implementing the Method compareTo

As mentioned earlier, objects that are ordered by the relations less than, greater than, or equal to must understand the compareTo message. Their class must implement the Comparable interface and their interface, if there is one, should also include the method compareTo. Suppose, for example, that the Student class of Lesson 5, which has no interface, is modified to support comparisons of students' names. Following are the required changes to the code:

```
public class Student implements Comparable{

    <data declarations>

    public int compareTo(Object other){

        // The parameter must be an instance of Student
        if (! (other instanceof Student))
            throw new IllegalArgumentException("Parameter must be a Student");

        // Obtain the student's name after casting the parameter
        String otherName = ((Student)other).getName();

        // Return the result of comparing the two students' names
        return name.compareTo(otherName);
    }

    <other methods>
}
```

EXERCISE 10.2

1. Why is a linear search called "linear"?

2. Write a linear search method that searches an array of objects for a target object.

3. Which elements are examined during a binary search of the array 34 56 78 85 99 for the target element 100?

4. Jack advises Jill of a modification to linear search that improves its performance when the array is sorted: If the target element is less than the current element, the target cannot be in the array. Modify the linear search method for integers to accomplish this.

5. Describe what the following code segment does:

```
boolean inOrder = true;
for (int i = 0; i < a.length - 1; i++)
    if (a[i] > a[i + 1]){
        inOrder = false;
        break;
    }
```

10.3 Sorting

We have seen that if the elements in an array are in ascending order, we can write some efficient methods for searching the array. However, when the elements are in random order, we need to rearrange them before we can take advantage of any ordering. This process is called *sorting*. Suppose we have an array a of five integers that we want to sort from smallest to largest. In Figure 10-2, the values currently in a are as depicted on the left; we want to end with values as they appear on the right.

FIGURE 10-2
An array before and after sorting

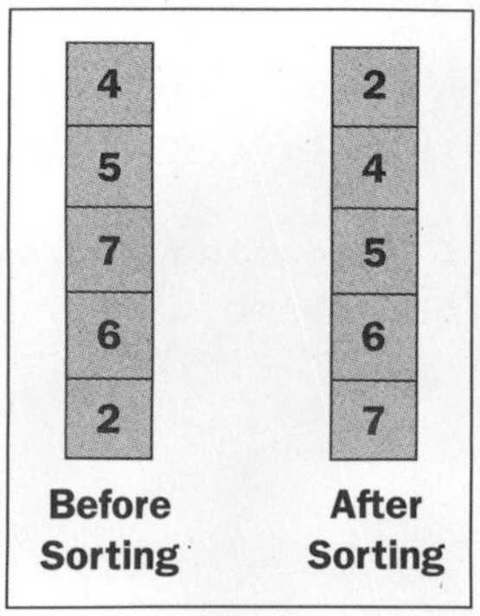

Before Sorting	After Sorting
4	2
5	4
7	5
6	6
2	7

Many sort algorithms have been developed, and in this section we cover a few that are easy to write but not very efficient to run. More sophisticated and more efficient sort algorithms are discussed in Lesson 11.

Selection Sort

The basic idea of a *selection sort* is

```
For each index position i
    Find the smallest data value in the array from positions i
    through length - 1, where length is the number of data values stored.

    Exchange the smallest value with the value at position i.
```

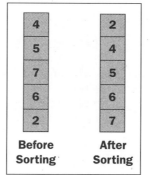

Table 10-3 shows a trace of the elements of an array after each exchange of elements is made. The items just swapped are marked with asterisks, and the sorted portion is shaded. Notice that in the second and fourth passes, since the current smallest numbers are already in place, we need not exchange anything. Also, after the last exchange, the number at the end of the array is automatically in its proper place.

TABLE 10-3
A trace of the data during a selection sort

UNSORTED ARRAY	AFTER 1ST PASS	AFTER 2ND PASS	AFTER 3RD PASS	AFTER 4TH PASS
4	1*	1	1	1
2	2	2*	2	2
5	5	5	3*	3
1	4*	4	4	4*
3	3	3	5*	5

Before writing the algorithm for this sorting method, note the following:

- If the array is of length n, we need $n - 1$ steps.
- We must be able to find the smallest number.
- We need to exchange appropriate array items.

When the code is written for this sort, note that strict inequality ($<$) rather than weak inequality ($<=$) is used when looking for the smallest remaining value. The algorithm to sort by selection is

```
For each i from 0 to n - 1 do
   Find the smallest value among a[i], a[i + 1], . . . a[n - 1]
   and store the index of the smallest value in minIndex
   Exchange the values of a[i] and a[index], if necessary
```

In Lesson 8, we saw a segment of the code we need to find the smallest value of array a. With suitable changes, we will incorporate this segment of code in a method, findMinimum, for the selection sort. We also will use a method swap to exchange two elements in an array.

Using these two methods, the implementation of a selection sort method is

```
public static void selectionSort(int[] a){
   for (int i = 0; i < a.length - 1; i++){
      int minIndex = findMinimum(a, i);
      if (minIndex != i)
         swap(a, i, minIndex);
   }
}
```

The method for finding the minimum value in an array takes two parameters, the array and the position to start the search. The method returns the index position of the minimum element in the array. Its implementation uses a `for` loop:

```
public static int findMinimum(int[] a, int first){
   int minIndex = first;

   for (int i = first + 1; i < a.length; i++)
      if (a[i] < a[minIndex])
         minIndex = i;

   return minIndex;
}
```

The `swap` method exchanges the values of two array cells:

```
public static void swap(int[] a, int x, int y){
   int temp = a[x];
   a[x] = a[y];
   a[y] = temp;
}
```

Bubble Sort

Given a list of items stored in an array, a *bubble sort* causes a pass through the array to compare adjacent pairs of items. Whenever two items are out of order with respect to each other, they are swapped. The effect of such a pass through an array of items is traced in Table 10-4. The items just swapped are marked with asterisks, and the sorted portion is shaded. Notice that after such a pass, we are assured that the array will have the item that comes last in order in the final array position. That is, the last item will "sink" to the bottom of the array, and preceding items will gradually "percolate" to the top.

TABLE 10-4
A trace of the data during one pass of a bubble sort

UNSORTED ARRAY	AFTER 1ST PASS	AFTER 2ND PASS	AFTER 3RD PASS	AFTER 4TH PASS
5	4*	4	4	4
4	5*	2*	2	2
2	2	5*	1*	1
1	1	1	5*	3*
3	3	3	3	5*

The bubble sort algorithm involves a nested loop structure. The outer loop controls the number of (successively smaller) passes through the array. The inner loop controls the pairs of adjacent items being compared. If we ever make a complete pass through the inner loop without having to make an interchange, we can declare the array sorted and avoid all future passes through the array. A pseudocode algorithm for bubble sort is

```
Initialize counter k to zero
Initialize boolean exchangeMade to true
While (k < n - 1) and exchangeMade
   Set exchangeMade to false
   Increment counter k
   For each j from 0 to n - k
      If item in jth position > item in (j + 1)st position
         Swap these items
         Set exchangeMade to true
```

A complete Java method to implement a bubble sort for an array of integers is shown in the following code:

```java
public static void bubbleSort(int[] a){
   int k = 0;
   boolean exchangeMade = true;

   // Make up to n - 1 passes through array, exit early if no exchanges
   // are made on previous pass

   while ((k < a.length - 1) && exchangeMade){
      exchangeMade = false;
      k++;
      for (int j = 0; j < a.length - k; j++)
         if (a[j] > a[j + 1]){
            swap(a, j, j + 1);
            exchangeMade = true;
         }
   }
}
```

Insertion Sort

Although it reduces the number of data interchanges, the selection sort apparently will not allow an effective—and automatic—loop exit if the array becomes ordered during an early pass. In this regard, bubble sort is more efficient than selection sort for an array that is nearly ordered from the beginning. Even with just one item out of order, however, bubble sort's early loop exit can fail to reduce the number of comparisons that are made.

The *insertion sort* attempts to take greater advantage of an array's partial ordering. The goal is that on the kth pass through, the kth item among

```
a[0], a[1], ..., a[k]
```

should be inserted into its rightful place among the first k items in the array. Thus, after the kth pass (k starting at 1), the first k items of the array should be in sorted order. This is analogous to the fashion in which many people pick up playing cards and order them in their hands. Holding the first $(k - 1)$ cards in order, a person will pick up the kth card and compare it with cards already held until its appropriate spot is found. The following steps will achieve this logic:

```
For each k from 1 to n - 1 (k is the index of array element to insert)
   Set itemToInsert to a[k]
   Set j to k - 1
   (j starts at k - 1 and is decremented until insertion position is found)
   While (insertion position not found) and (not beginning of array)
      If itemToInsert < a[j]
         Move a[j] to index position j + 1
         Decrement j by 1
      Else
         The insertion position has been found
         itemToInsert should be positioned at index j + 1
```

In effect, for each pass, the index j begins at the $(k - 1)$st item and moves that item to position $j + 1$ until we find the insertion point for what was originally the kth item.

An insertion sort for each value of k is traced in Table 10-5. In each column of this table, the data items are sorted in order relative to each other above the item with the asterisk; below this item, the data are not affected.

TABLE 10-5
A trace of the data during an insertion sort

UNSORTED ARRAY	AFTER 1ST PASS	AFTER 2ND PASS	AFTER 3RD PASS	AFTER 4TH PASS
2	2	1*	1	1
5 ←	5 (no insertion)	2	2	2
1	1 ←	5	4*	3*
4	4	4 ←	5	4
3	3	3	3 ←	5

To implement the insertion sort algorithm in Java, we use the following code:

```java
public static void insertionSort(int[] a){
   int itemToInsert, j;
   boolean stillLooking;

   // On the kth pass, insert item k into its correct position among
   // the first k entries in array.

   for (int k = 1; k < a.length; k++){
         // Walk backwards through list, looking for slot to insert a[k]
      itemToInsert = a[k];
      j = k - 1;
      stillLooking = true;
```

```
        while ((j >= 0) && stillLooking )
           if (itemToInsert  < a[j]) {
               a[j + 1] = a[j];
                j--;
           }else
               stillLooking = false;
           // Upon leaving loop, j + 1 is the index
           // where itemToInsert  belongs
           a[j + 1] = itemToInsert;
    }
}
```

Sorting Arrays of Objects

Any of the sort methods can be modified to sort arrays of objects. We assume that the objects implement the `Comparable` interface and support the method `compareTo`. Then, we simply replace the type of all array parameters with `Object` and make the appropriate use of `compareTo` in which the comparison operators are used. For example, here is the relevant change for the selection sort in the method `findMinimum`:

```
public static int findMinimum(Object[] a, int first){
   int minIndex = first;

   for (int i = first + 1; i < a.length(); i++)
      if (((Comparable)a[i]).compareTo(a[minIndex]) < 0)
         minIndex = i;

   return minIndex;
}
```

Testing Sort Algorithms

The sort algorithms developed thus far should be tested. The skeleton of a short tester program follows. The program loads an array with 20 random integers between 0 and 99, displays the array's contents, runs a sort method, and displays the array's contents again.

> **Note** ☑
>
> You also should test the methods with an array that is already sorted.

```
public class TestSortAlgorithms{

   public static void main(String[] args){

      int[] a = new int[20];

      //Initialize the array to random numbers between 0 and 99
      for (int i = 0; i < a.length; i++)
         a[i] = (int)(Math.random() * 100);

      printArray(a);
      selectionSort(a);              // Pick one of three to test
      //bubbleSort(a);
```

```
        //insertionSort(a);
        printArray(a);
    }

    static public void printArray(int[] a){
        for (int i = 0; i < a.length; i++)
            System.out.print(a[i] + " ");
        System.out.println("");
    }


    // static sort methods and their helpers go here
}
```

EXERCISE 10.3

1. Draw a diagram that shows the contents of the array 8 7 6 5 4 after each number is moved in a selection sort.

2. Draw a diagram that shows the contents of the array 8 7 6 5 4 after each number is moved in a bubble sort, until the 8 arrives at the end of the array.

3. Describe the behavior of the selection sort, bubble sort, and insertion sort with an array that is already sorted. How many exchanges are made in each sort for an array of size *n*?

4. Modify the bubble sort method so that it sorts an array of objects.

10.4 Insertions and Removals

In Lesson 8, we discussed how to add or remove an element at the end of an array that is not full. In this section, we show how to perform these operations at arbitrary positions within an array. For simplicity, we make four assumptions:

1. Arrays are of fixed size; thus, when an array becomes full, insertions are not performed.

2. We are working with an array of objects, although we can modify the code to cover arrays of integers, employees, or whatever element type is desired.

3. For successful insertions, 0 <= target index <= logical size. The new element is inserted before the element currently at the target index, or after the last element if the target index equals the logical size.

4. For successful removals, 0 <= target index < logical size.

When an assumption is not satisfied, the operation is not performed and we return `false`; otherwise, the operation is performed and we return `true`.

In the examples that follow, we use the following data declarations:

```
final int DEFAULT_CAPACITY = 5;
int logicalSize = 0;
Object[] array = new Object[DEFAULT_CAPACITY];
```

As you can see, the array has an initial logical size of 0 and a default physical capacity of 5. For each operation that uses this array, we provide a description of the implementation strategy and an annotated Java code segment. At the end of this section, we ask you to develop some static methods to perform these operations on arrays.

Inserting an Item into an Array at an Arbitrary Position

Inserting an item into an array differs from replacing an item in an array. In the case of a replacement, an item already exists at the given index position and a simple assignment suffices. Moreover, the logical size of the array does not change. In the case of an insertion, we must do six things:

1. Check for available space before attempting an insertion; if there is no space, return `false`.

2. Check the validity of the target index and return `false` if it is not >= 0 and <= logical size.

3. Shift the items from the logical end of the array to the target index down by one position.

4. Assign the new item to the cell at the target index.

5. Increment the logical size by one.

6. Return `true`.

Figure 10-3 shows these steps for the insertion of an item at position 1 in an array of four items.

FIGURE 10-3
Inserting an item into an array

Shift down item at n - 1		Shift down item at n - 2		Shift down item at i		Now safe to replace item at position 1		Array after insertion is finished	
0	D1	0	D1	0	D1	0	D1	0	D1
1	D2	1	D2	1	D2	1	D2	1	D5
2	D3	2	D3	2	D3	2	D2	2	D2
3	D4	3	D4	3	D3	3	D3	3	D3
4		4	D4	4	D4	4	D4	4	D4

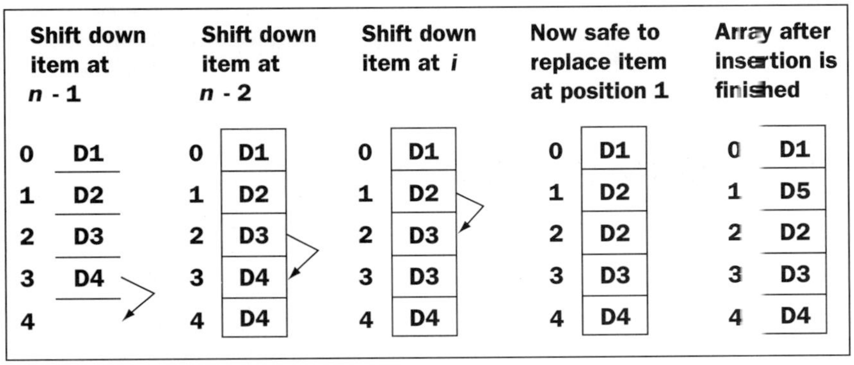

As you can see, the order in which the items are shifted is critical. If we had started at the target index and copied down from there, we would have lost two items. Thus, we must start at the logical end of the array and work back up to the target index, copying each item to the cell of its successor. Following is the Java code for the insertion operation:

```
// Check for a full array and return false if full
if (logicalSize == array.length)
    return false;

// Check for valid target index and return false if not valid
if (targetIndex < 0 || targetIndex > logicalSize)
    return false;
```

```
// Shift items down by one position
for (int i = logicalSize; i > targetIndex; i--)
    array[i] = array[i - 1];

// Add new item, increment logical size, and return true

array[targetIndex] = newItem;
logicalSize++;
return true;
```

Removing an Item from an Array

Removing an item from an array involves the inverse process of inserting an item into the array. Following are the steps in this process:

1. Check the validity of the target index and return `false` if it is not >= 0 and < logical size.

2. Shift the items from the target index to the logical end of the array up by one position.

3. Decrement the logical size by one.

4. Return `true`.

Figure 10-4 shows these steps for the removal of an item at position 1 in an array of five items.

FIGURE 10-4
Removing an item from an array

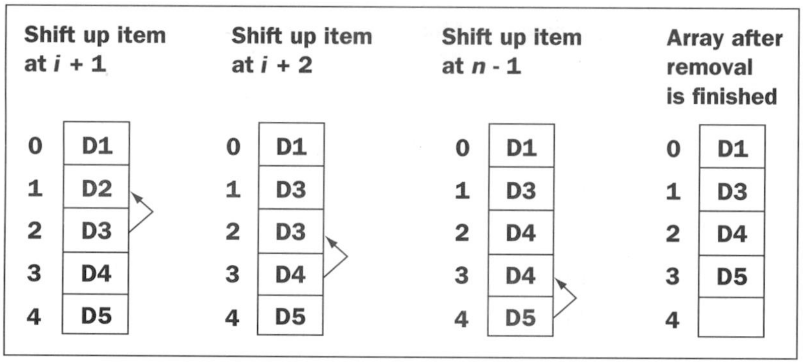

As with insertions, the order in which we shift items is critical. For a removal, we begin at the item following the target position and move toward the logical end of the array, copying each item to the cell of its predecessor. Following is the Java code for the removal operation:

```
// Check for valid target index and return false if not valid
if (targetIndex < 0 || targetIndex >= logicalSize)
    return false;

// Shift items up by one position
for (int i = targetIndex; i < logicalSize - 1; i++)
    array[i] = array[i + 1];

// Decrement logical size and return true
logicalSize--;
return true;
```

Of course, there are other ways to handle potential errors in these operations, as discussed in earlier lessons. Instead of returning a Boolean value, one can return a string indicating the type of error or `null` indicating success. Alternatively, one can throw an exception for each error and return `void`.

A Tester Program for Array Methods

The operations just discussed are so frequently used that it is a good idea to provide methods for them. Ideally, one implements them as `static` methods in a class that serves a utility function similar to Java's `Math` class. In the following code, we specify two of these methods in the context of a tester program. We leave their complete development for you to try in Exercise 10.4, Question 2.

A method to insert a new item at a given index position, `insertItem`, expects the array, its logical size, the target index, and the new item as parameters. `insertItem` returns `true` if the operation is successful and `false` otherwise. This method does not increment the logical size; that responsibility is left to the client, who must check the Boolean value returned to take the appropriate action. A similar method named `removeItem` can be developed for removals.

Following is a short tester program that uses the method described previously:

```
public class Tester{
   public static void main(String[] args){

      // Create an initial array with 3 strings.
      Object[] array = {"hi", "there", "Mary"};
      int logicalSize = 3;
      boolean successful = false;

      // Insert strings at positions 0 and 1.
      successful = insertItem(array, logicalSize, 0, "Jack");
      if (successful)
         logicalSize++;
      successful = insertItem(array, logicalSize, 1, "says");
      if (successful)
         logicalSize++;

      // Display new physical size and contents.
      System.out.println(array.length);
      for (int i = 0; i < logicalSize; i++)
         System.out.print(array[i] + " ");
   }

   // Definitions of array methods go here
   static public boolean insertItem(Object[] array, int logicalSize,
                                    int targetIndex, Object newItem){
      // Exercise
   }

   static public boolean removeItem(Object[] array, int logicalSize,
                                    int targetIndex){
      // Exercise
   }

}
```

Although our methods allow clients to perform insertions and removals, clients must still track the logical size of an array and update it. In addition, there is an upper bound on the number of items a client can insert into an array. We learn how to overcome these limitations of arrays shortly. But first, we must consider some unfinished business with the use of objects in arrays.

EXERCISE 10.4

1. Describe the design strategy for inserting an element at an arbitrary position in an array.

2. Complete the two static methods for insertion and removal of an element at an arbitrary position in an array.

3. Describe what the following code segments do:

a.

```
if (logicalSize == a.length){
    int[] temp = new int[a.length * 2];
    for (int i = 0; i < a.length; i++)
        temp[i] = a[i];
    a = temp;
}
```

b.

```
if (a.length >= logicalSize * 4){
    int[] temp = new int[a.length * 2];
    for (int i = 0; i < a.length; i++)
        temp[i] = a[i];
    a = temp;
}
```

10.5 Working with Arrays of Objects

The element type of an array can be a primitive type, a reference type (either an abstract or a concrete class), or an interface. The processing of an array of a primitive type, such as array of `int`, is straightforward. Likewise, working with an array of a concrete class, such as `Student`, poses no particular problems. The reason for this is that all of the elements in these arrays, whether integers or students, are of exactly the same type and respond to the same set of operators or messages. When the element type of an array is an interface, an abstract class, or a superclass of one or more other classes, however, the array can actually contain objects of different types, so they might not all respond to a common set of messages. In this section, we deal with the problems that arise with arrays of objects of different types.

Polymorphism, Casting, and `instanceof`

It is quite common to declare and instantiate an array of some interface type, such as the `Shape` interface in Lesson 9. For instance, following is code that reserves 10 cells for shapes:

```
Shape[] shapes = new Shape[10];
```

Now we can store in this array instances of any class that implements Shape, such as Rect, Circle, or Wheel, as follows:

```
shapes[0] = new Rect(20, 20, 40, 40);      // Cell 0 refers to a Rect
shapes[1] = new Circle(100, 100, 20);      // Cell 1 refers to a Circle
shapes[2] = new Wheel(200, 200, 20, 6);    // Cell 2 refers to a Wheel
```

As long as we send Shape messages to the elements of this array, we can ignore the fact that they are of different concrete classes (that's what polymorphism is all about). For instance, let us now draw all the shapes in the array:

```
Pen pen = new StandardPen();
for (int i = 0; i < 3; i++)
    shapes[i].draw(pen);
```

We can also move all the shapes, stretch them, change their colors, or do whatever else is specified in the Shape interface quite easily. As soon as we want to do something more specific to a shape, however, such as setting the number of spokes in a wheel, we must resort to some of the tricks mentioned in Lesson 9. Let us assume that we know the position of the wheel object in the array (in our example, it's at position 2). Then, to set its spokes to 5, we perform the following steps:

1. Access the array element with the subscript.

2. Cast the element, which is masquerading as a Shape, to a Wheel.

3. Send the setSpokes(5) message to the result.

   Following is the code:

```
((Wheel) shapes[2]).setSpokes(5);
```

Note the use of parentheses to override the precedence of the method selector, which would otherwise be run before the cast operation. Failure to cast in this code causes a compile-time error.

Now suppose we don't know the position of a wheel in the array of shapes, but we want to set the spokes of each wheel to 5. A loop is a logical choice for this task, but we cannot simply cast each element to a Wheel and send it the setSpokes message, because not all elements are wheels. If we attempt to cast an object to a type that is not its actual type, a ClassCastException is thrown. Clearly, in this case, we must first determine that a shape is a wheel before casting, and Java's instanceof operator comes to our rescue. Following is a loop that solves the problem:

```
for (int i = 0; i < shapes.length; i++)
    if (shapes[i] instanceof Wheel)
        ((Wheel) shapes[i]).setSpokes(5);
```

Although we have been examining an array of an interface type in this example, the same considerations apply to arrays of abstract classes or of superclasses of one or more other classes. Let us now summarize the use of objects in an array by making two fundamental points:

1. When the element type of an array is a reference type or interface, objects of those types or any subtype (subclass or implementing class) can be directly inserted into the array.

2. After accessing an object in an array, care must be taken to send it the appropriate messages or to cast it down to a type that can receive the appropriate messages.

Arrays of `Object`

The most general type of array is of course an array whose element type is `Object`. This array is the most flexible of any we have seen thus far. Not only can we insert any object into an array of `Object`, but we also can replace any array of `Object` with another array of any reference type (that is, pass one as a parameter or return it as a value of a method). We have already seen examples of general searching and sorting methods that rely on this feature of an array of `Object`. From the implementer's perspective, in the case of a linear search, there is no need to worry about the actual type of the array elements, because all objects understand the `equals` message and that is the only message sent to the array elements. In the case of the binary search and the sorting methods, the elements each must be sent the `compareTo` message. Before doing that, the method must cast them to `Comparable` after retrieving them from the array. Therefore, the client must take care to pass an array of comparable objects as a parameter to these methods.

Generally, you should exercise caution after an object is accessed in an array of `Object`. More often than not, casting must occur, because `Object` includes so few of the methods that the array element actually supports.

EXERCISE 10.5

1. Assume that the `student` class used here is as defined in Lesson 8. Describe the errors in the following code segments, or state that they are correct:

a.

```
Object[] a = new Object[10];
a[0] = new Student();
a[1] = "Hi there";
System.out.println(a[1].indexOf("there"));
```

b.

```
Object[] a = new Object[10];
a[0] = new Student();
a[1] = "Hi there";
System.out.println((String)a[1].indexOf("there"));
```

c.

```
Object[] a = new Object[10];
a[0] = new Student();
a[1] = "Hi there";
System.out.println((String[1]).indexOf("there"));
```

d.

```
Object[] a = new Object[10];
a[0] = new Student();
a[1] = "Hi there";
System.out.println((String[0]).indexOf("there"));
```

10.6 BreezySwing: *Menus, Scrolling List Boxes, and Dialogs*

In preparation for the next case study, we add drop-down menus, scrolling lists, and dialogs to our growing repertoire of GUI features. Drop-down menus provide an alternative to a confused jumble of command buttons. A scrolling list is basically a mechanism that allows users to view and interact with an underlying list of strings. We already have encountered an example of dialogs, namely a message box, but in this section, we show how to construct customized dialogs.

Menus

Menus provide a convenient mechanism for entering commands into a program. A menu system consists of a menu bar, a number of menus, and for each menu, several selections. It is also possible to have submenus, but we ignore these for now. It is easy to add a menu system to an application. We simply declare a menu item object for each menu selection. For instance, suppose we want to move the editing commands for the student test scores program to a menu. In addition, we would like a menu of commands to sort the students by name, by high score, and by average. The following code adds the two menus to the application's interface:

```
// Declare menu item variables
JMenuItem addMI, modifyMI, deleteMI,
          sortByNameMI, sortByHighScoreMI, sortByAverageScoreMI;

public SomeApplication(){

   // Instantiate menu items
   addMI    = addMenuItem ("Edit", "Add");
   modifyMI = addMenuItem ("Edit", "Modify");
   deleteMI = addMenuItem ("Edit", "Delete");

   sortByNameMI         = addMenuItem ("Sort", "By Name");
   sortByHighScoreMI    = addMenuItem ("Sort", "By High Score");
   sortByAverageScoreMI = addMenuItem ("Sort", "By Average Score ");
}
```

The first menu is called **Edit** and has three items, and the second, called **Sort**, also has three items. When the user selects a menu item, the JVM sends a menuItemSelected message to the application, so we need to write the corresponding method. Following is an illustrative segment of code from this method:

```
public void menuItemSelected (JMenuItem menuItemObj){
   if (menuItemObj == addMI)
      add();
   else if (menuItemObj == modifyMI){
      modify();
   . . .
   etc.
}
```

Scrolling Lists

Figure 10-5 illustrates the use of a *scrolling list*. Scrolling lists are instances of the class JList as defined in the package javax.swing. When the user clicks on an entry in a scrolling list, the entry is automatically highlighted, thus giving the user visual feedback. At the same time, the program is notified of a single-click event. When the user double-clicks on an entry, again it is highlighted, but the program is notified of two events—a single-click event followed by a double-click event.

FIGURE 10-5
An interface containing a scrolling list

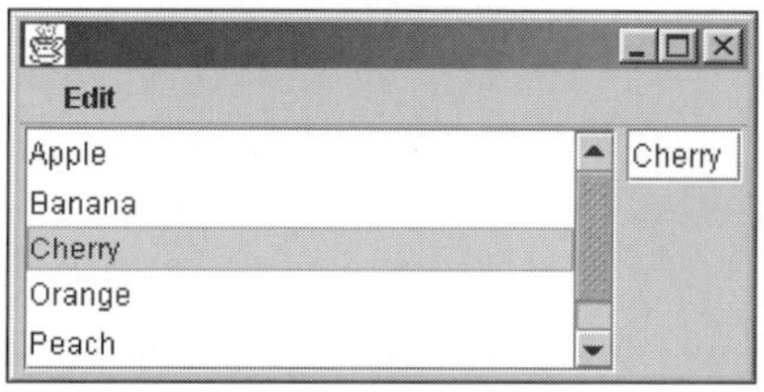

Java sets up a scrolling list according to the model/view pattern introduced in Lesson 8. Associated with a scrolling list window object is a *list model,* which contains the data displayed in the scrolling list. When the programmer adds a scrolling list to an interface with the method addList, BreezySwing automatically creates an instance of the class DefaultListModel and associates it with the scrolling list. The programmer can then send messages to either the scrolling list or its model to accomplish such tasks as asking which item, if any, has been selected or selecting an item. In addition, a program can add entries to and remove entries from a scrolling list. Table 10-6 describes many of the most useful methods for manipulating a scrolling list and Table 10-7 describes useful methods for its model. Table 10-8 describes the methods, included in the classes GBFrame, GBDialog, and GBApplet, for responding to single- and double-click events.

TABLE 10-6
The most useful methods for scrolling lists

JList METHOD	WHAT IT DOES
ListModel getModel()	Returns the model for the list. You should cast the result to a DefaultListModel.
int getSelectedIndex()	Returns the position of the selected item.
Object getSelectedValue()	Returns the selected item. You should cast the result to a String when using strings.
void setSelectedIndex(int index)	Selects the item at the given index.
void setSelectedValue(Object obj, boolean shouldScroll)	Selects the given item.

TABLE 10-7
The most useful methods for scrolling lists' models

DefaultListModel METHOD	WHAT IT DOES
add(int index, Object obj)	Inserts an item at the given position.
addElement(Object obj)	Adds an item to the end of the list.
void clear()	Makes the list empty.
Object get(int index)	Returns the item at the given position.
Object remove(int index)	Removes the item at the given position.
boolean removeElement(Object obj)	Removes the first instance of the given item.
Object set(index i, Object obj)	Replaces the item at the given position with the given item.
int size()	Returns the number of items in the list.
Object[] toArray()	Returns an array of the items.

TABLE 10-8
Two BreezySwing methods for responding to list events

NAME OF THE METHOD	WHAT IT DOES
ListItemSelected (JList listObj) returns void	The framework invokes this method when the user selects a list item with a single click or a double click. Applications are not required to include this method, but if they do not, the single-click event is ignored. The parameter is the list containing the selected entry.
listDoubleClicked (JList listObj, String itemClicked) returns void	The framework invokes this method when a list item is double-clicked. Applications are required to include this method but may leave it blank if no programmatic response is required. The parameters are the list and the list item where the event occurred. (*Note*: This method is invoked after the method listItemSelected.)

A Sample Program

The next program illustrates the use of drop-down menus and scrolling lists. Its interface was shown in Figure 10-5. At start-up, the program displays a scrolling list of fruits with the first fruit selected. When the user selects a fruit, its name appears in a text field. When the user selects the menu option **Edit/Delete**, the program removes the selected item from the list and selects the first item. When the user selects the menu option **Edit/Add**, the program adds the text in the field to the end of the scrolling list and selects it. An appropriate test is performed to ensure that the program does not attempt to delete from or select an item in an empty list. The code's comments explain the use of the relevant methods:

```java
import javax.swing.*;
import BreezySwing.*;

public class TuityFruity extends GBFrame{

    JList list;                        // The scrolling list
    JTextField field;
    JMenuItem addMI, deleteMI;

    DefaultListModel listModel;   // The scrolling list's model

    public TuityFruity(){

        // Instantiate window objects
        list  = addList(          1,1,1,1);
        field = addTextField("", 1,2,1,1);
        addMI    = addMenuItem("Edit", "Add");
        deleteMI = addMenuItem("Edit", "Delete");

        // Save a reference to the list's model for later use
        listModel = (DefaultListModel)list.getModel();

        // Add initial fruits to the list
        listModel.add(0, "Apple");
        listModel.add(1, "Banana");
        listModel.add(2, "Cherry");
        listModel.add(3, "Orange");
        listModel.add(4, "Peach");
        listModel.add(5, "Pear");

        // Select the first fruit in the list
        list.setSelectedIndex(0);
    }

    public void listItemSelected(JList listObj){

        // Transfer the selected item to the field
        String str = (String)list.getSelectedValue();
        field.setText(str);
    }

    public void menuItemSelected(JMenuItem mi){
        if (mi == addMI){

            // Add the field's text to the end of the list,
            // select it, and scroll to it if necessary
            String str = field.getText();
            listModel.addElement(str);
            list.setSelectedValue(str, true);
```

```
        }else if (listModel.size() != 0){

            // Delete the selected item and select the first
            // item if the list is not empty
            listModel.removeElementAt(list.getSelectedIndex());
            if (listModel.size() != 0)
                list.setSelectedIndex(0);
        }
    }

    static public void main(String[] args){
        TuityFruity theGUI = new TuityFruity();
        theGUI.setSize(300, 150);
        theGUI.setVisible(true);
    }
}
```

Dialogs

Usually, a dialog is *modal*, meaning that the rest of the application is inaccessible as long as the dialog is active. Users quit most dialogs by clicking an **OK** or a **Cancel** button. The **OK** button closes a dialog and transmits data entered by the user back to the rest of the application, whereas the **Cancel** button closes a dialog and discards the data.

Dialogs are implemented in much the same way as application windows, but by extending the class GBDialog rather than GBFrame. We illustrate the implementation and use of dialogs by borrowing some code from the next case study. Figure 10-6 shows the application's main window and accompanying dialog. The dialog is activated when the user selects menu option **Edit/Add**

> **Note** ☑️
>
> In the last lesson of this book, we show how to create dialogs using the standard Java classes.

or **Edit/Modify**, at which point the dialog is activated and passed a student object. The dialog then retains control of the application until the user clicks the dialog's **OK** or **Cancel** button. If the user clicks **OK**, the student object is updated with the data on the screen, but if the user clicks **Cancel**, no changes are made to the student object. In either event, the dialog then closes and control returns to the main window.

FIGURE 10-6
A program with a modal dialog

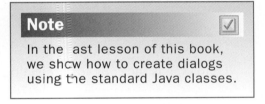

Main Window

Student Dialog

First, we show the code for instantiating and opening the dialog. This code is located in the class for the main window. The comments explain the details:

```java
. . .
public class StudentTestScoresView extends GBFrame{
. . .

   //Instantiate the dialog passing it
   // this      -- a reference to the application object itself
   // tempStu  -- a reference to a student object
   StudentDialog studentDialog
                = new StudentDialog (this, tempStu);

   //Tell the dialog to show itself, thereby giving it control until
   //the user clicks either the OK or Cancel button.
   studentDialog.show();

   //As soon as the dialog closes, control returns to this point.
   //We now ask the dialog whether the user clicked the OK or the
   //Cancel button.
   if (studentDialog.getDlgCloseIndicator().equals ("OK")){
      . . . the user clicked the OK button . . .
   }else{
      . . . the user clicked the Cancel button . . .
   }

. . .
```

Following is the code for the dialog. Again, comments explain the details:

```java
/*  StudentDialog.java

1.) This is the dialog for the student test scores program.
2) It displays the student passed to it.
3) The user can then change the data in the dialog's window.
4) If the user clicks the OK button, the student is updated with
   the data in the window.
5) If the user clicks the Cancel button, the dialog closes and returns
   without modifying the student.
*/

import javax.swing.*;
import BreezySwing.*;

public class StudentDialog extends GBDialog{

   //Window objects
   private JLabel nameLabel, test1Label, test2Label, test3Label;

   private JTextField nameField;
   private IntegerField test1Field, test2Field, test3Field;
```

```
      private JButton btnOK, btnCancel;

      //Instance variables
      private Student student;         //The student being modified

      public StudentDialog (JFrame f, Student stu){
      //Constructor
      //  Preconditions  -- the input parameters are not null
      //  Postconditions -- the dialog's window is initialized
      //                 -- the student variable is set
      //                 -- the student's data are displayed in the
      //                    dialog's window

         //Housekeeping required in every dialog
         super (f);

         //Set the dialog's size and title
         setSize (250,150);
         setTitle ("Student Dialog");

         //Set the dialog's default value for the close indicator to Cancel.
         //If the user closes the dialog without clicking either the OK or
         //Cancel button, the default takes effect.
         setDlgCloseIndicator ("Cancel");

         //Save the student reference and display the student data in the
         //dialog's window.
         student = stu;

         // Instantiate the window objects
         nameLabel     = addLabel ("Name"     ,1,1,1,1);
         test1Label    = addLabel ("Test 1"   ,2,1,1,1);
         test2Label    = addLabel ("Test 2"   ,3,1,1,1);
         test3Label    = addLabel ("Test 3"   ,4,1,1,1);

         nameField    = addTextField    ("",1,2,2,1);
         test1Field = addIntegerField (0 ,2,2,1,1);
         test2Field = addIntegerField (0 ,3,2,1,1);
         test3Field = addIntegerField (0 ,4,2,1,1);

         btnOK     = addButton ("OK"    ,5,1,1,1);
         btnCancel = addButton ("Cancel",5,2,1,1);

         // Display the student's information
         nameField.setText        (student.getName());
         test1Field.setNumber     (student.getScore(1));
         test2Field.setNumber     (student.getScore(2));
         test3Field.setNumber     (student.getScore(3));
      }

      public void buttonClicked (JButton buttonObj){
      //Responds to the OK and Cancel buttons.
```

```
// Preconditions  -- one of the two buttons has been clicked
// Postconditions -- if the Cancel button then
//                       the student is not modified
//                       the close indicator equals Cancel
//                       the dialog is closed
//                       control returns to the caller
//                  -- if the OK button then
//                       the student is modified
//                       the close indicator equals OK
//                       the dialog is closed
//                       control returns to the caller

   //Get the data from the screen
   String name = nameField.getText();
   int score1 = test1Field.getNumber();
   int score2 = test2Field.getNumber();
   int score3 = test3Field.getNumber();
   String   validationErrors;

   if (buttonObj == btnCancel)                  //Cancel button

      //Close the dialog and return to the caller
      dispose();

   else{                                        //OK button

         //Update the student with the screen data
         student.setName(name);
         student.setScore(1, score1);
         student.setScore(2, score2);
         student.setScore(3, score3);

         //Set the close indicator to OK, close the dialog, and
         //return to the caller.
         setDlgCloseIndicator ("OK");
         dispose();
   }
}
}
```

CASE STUDY: Student Test Scores Yet Again

In this case study, we show how to organize a program in terms of several user interface and data model classes. We essentially provide a different view with extra functions for the student test scores program of Lesson 8.

Request

Modify the student test scores program of Lesson 8 so that it allows the user to sort the students.

Analysis

We provide three ways to sort the students: by name, by highest score, and by highest average score. To simplify the interface, we make two changes:

1. The editing and sorting commands are hidden in two drop-down menus.

2. The main window contains a scrolling list and a text area. The user navigates to a student by selecting a name in the scrolling list. When a name is selected, that student's detailed information is displayed in a text area. A dialog pops up for editing a student's information when the user selects the menu options Edit/Add or Edit/Modify. The same dialog pops up to modify a student when the user double-clicks on a name. Modifications and deletions occur with respect to the currently selected student. If there are names in the list, one is always selected.

The interface for the program was shown in Figure 10-6, which showed the main window and the dialog. Table 10-9 describes the menu options and Table 10-10 describes the actions taken when a user manipulates the scrolling list.

TABLE 10-9
The menu options for the student test scores program

MENU OPTION	WHAT IT DOES
Edit/Add	Pops up a dialog to allow the user to enter information for a new student. If the user selects OK, attempts to add the student to the model. If the addition is successful, the view is updated by selecting the new student's name and displaying its detailed information.
Edit/Modify	If the scrolling list is not empty, pops up a dialog to allow the user to modify information for the selected student. If the user selects OK, the view is updated with the new information.
Edit/Delete	If the scrolling list is not empty, removes the selected student from the model and updates the view by selecting the first student, if there is one.
Sort/By Name	Sorts the students in the model by name and updates the view, selecting the current student.
Sort/By Highest Score	Sorts the students in the model by highest score and updates the view, selecting the current student.
Sort/By Highest Average	Sorts the students in the model by highest average and updates the view, selecting the current student.

TABLE 10-10
The responses of the student test scores program to list manipulations

USER MANIPULATION OF THE LIST	ACTION TAKEN BY THE PROGRAM
Single-click on an item	The selected student's detailed information appears in the text area.
Double-click on an item	The selected student's detailed information appears in the text area and a dialog pops up to allow the user to modify the student's information.

Classes

This application has two view classes, StudentTestScoresView and StudentDialog, and two model classes, Student and StudentTestScoresModel. We already have discussed the Student class in Lessons 5 and 8 and the StudentDialog class earlier in this lesson.

The responsibilities of StudentTestScoresView are similar to those mentioned in the case study of Lesson 8:

■ Set up the interface, which now includes a scrolling list, a text area, and two menus.

■ Respond to menu selections and list box selections by popping up a dialog and sending the appropriate messages to the model.

■ Refresh the list box and text area with information from the model when necessary.

The responsibilities of StudentTestScoresModel are also similar to those mentioned in the case study of Lesson 8:

■ Add students to and remove them from a list of students.

■ Track the currently selected student.

■ Sort the students according to the desired category.

■ Provide information to the view for display.

By far the most important aspect of this application is the interface or set of public messages for StudentTestScoresModel. These are the messages that the view sends to the model to get much of the work done. Table 10-11 describes this interface.

TABLE 10-11
The interface for the `StudentTestScoresModel` class

`StudentTestScoresModel` METHOD	WHAT IT DOES
`String add(Student newStudent)`	If there is room in the model's list and the new student's name is not already in use, adds the new student at the end of the model's list and returns null. Otherwise, returns an error message.
`void modify(Student newStudent)`	*Precondition*: There is at least one student in the model's list. *Postcondition*: The currently selected student is replaced with `newStudent` and this becomes the current student.
`void delete()`	*Precondition*: There is at least one student in the model's list. *Postcondition*: The currently selected student is removed from the model's list and the first student in the list, if there is one, becomes the current student.
`Student getCurrentStudent()`	If the model's list has at least one student, returns the currently selected student. Otherwise, returns null.
`String[] getNames()`	Returns an array of the names of the students in the model's list.
`void setCurrentStudent(String name)`	*Precondition*: There is one and only one student with this name in the model's list. *Postcondition*: The model's current student becomes the student with this name.
`void sortByName()`	Sorts the model's list of students by name.
`void sortByHighScore()`	Sorts the model's list of students by highest score.
`void sortByAverage()`	Sorts the model's list of students by highest average.

Design and Implementation of StudentTestScoresView

The main window class delegates to a dialog the responsibility for editing a student object. The model tracks the current student and maintains the list of students. Thus, we must develop only the logic for responding to user commands and updating the window objects with information. Most of this activity involves sending messages to other objects. For example, when a list item is selected, the view

■ Extracts the selected name from the scrolling list

■ Sends the name with the `setCurrentStudent` message to the model

■ Sends a message to itself to update the window objects with information from the model

Practically every user interaction causes an update of the information in the view. To simplify this task, we package it in a single method, `displayCurrentStudent`, which refreshes both the list box and the text area. Following is the pseudocode for this method:

```
Get the current student from the model
If the student is null
    Clear the scrolling list
    Set the text area to ""
Else
    Get the names from the model
    Clear the scrolling list
    Transfer the names to the scrolling list
    If the scrolling list is not empty
        Select the current student's name
    Set the text area to the current student's information
```

Following is a listing of the implementation:

```
/* StudentTestScoresView.java

1) This program maintains a list of students and displays their names
   in a scrolling list control.
2) Single-clicking on a name displays the student's information.
3) Double-clicking on a name allows the student's information to be
   changed.
4) Other operations are supported by means of an Edit menu with the
   options:
   Add     -- adds a new student to the end of the list and selects the
              name in the scrolling list
   Modify -- modifies the selected student
   Delete -- deletes the selected student
5) The selected student is the one corresponding to the highlighted
   name in the scrolling list control.

*/

import javax.swing.*;
import BreezySwing.*;

public class StudentTestScoresView extends GBFrame{

    //Window objects
    private JLabel namesLB, detailedInfoLB;
    private JList nameList;
    private JTextArea detailedInfoField;
    private JMenuItem addMI, modifyMI, deleteMI,
            sortByNameMI, sortByHighScoreMI, sortByAverageScoreMI;

    // Other instance variables --------------------------------
```

```
        private StudentTestScoresModel model;

        // Constructor--------------------------------------------------

        public StudentTestScoresView(){
           setTitle("Student Test Scores");
           model = new StudentTestScoresModel();

           // Instantiate window objects
           namesLB           = addLabel    ("Names"                  ,1,1,1,1);
           detailedInfoLB    = addLabel    ("Detailed Information",1,2,1,1);

           nameList          = addList     (                         2,1,1,5);
           detailedInfoField = addTextArea (""                       ,2,2,1,5);


           addMI    = addMenuItem ("Edit", "Add");
           modifyMI = addMenuItem ("Edit", "Modify");
           deleteMI = addMenuItem ("Edit", "Delete");
           sortByNameMI         = addMenuItem ("Sort", "By Name");
           sortByHighScoreMI    = addMenuItem ("Sort", "By High Score");
           sortByAverageScoreMI = addMenuItem ("Sort", "By Average Score ");
           displayCurrentStudent();
        }

        public void listItemSelected (JList listObj){
        //Displays the information for the student whose name is selected.
        //  Preconditions  -- a name in the name list is single-clicked
        //  Postconditions -- the student corresponding to the name
        //                     is selected and her info is displayed

           String name = (String)nameList.getSelectedValue();
           model.setCurrentStudent(name);
           displayCurrentStudent();
        }

        public void listDoubleClicked (JList listObj, String itemClicked){
        //Opens a modify dialog on the student whose name is selected.
        //Note: Double-clicking on a name automatically triggers the single-
        //  click event first.
        //  Preconditions  -- a name in the list is double-clicked
        //  Postconditions -- see the modifySelectedStudent method

           modify();
        }

        public void menuItemSelected (JMenuItem mi){
        //Responds to a menu selection
        //  Preconditions  -- none
        //  Postconditions -- see the methods corresponding to the menu items
```

```
      if       (mi == addMI)     add();
   else if (mi == modifyMI) modify();
   else if (mi == deleteMI) delete();
   // Handling sort options is an exercise
}

// Private methods------------------------------------------

private void add(){
//Adds a new student.
//   Preconditions   -- none
//   Postconditions -- if the user cancels the dialog, then no change
//                  -- else the new student is selected
//                        she is added to the end of the student list
//                        her name is added to the end of the name list
//                        her info is displayed
//                        she becomes the selected item in both lists

   Student tempStu = new Student();
   StudentDialog studentDialog
               = new StudentDialog (this, tempStu);
   studentDialog.show();
   if (studentDialog.getDlgCloseIndicator().equals ("OK")){
      String message = model.add (tempStu);
      if (message != null){
         messageBox(message);
         return;
      }
      model.setCurrentStudent(tempStu.getName());
      displayCurrentStudent();
   }
}

private void modify(){
  // Completion of this method is left as an exercise
}

private void delete(){
  // Completion of this method is left as an exercise
}

private void displayCurrentStudent(){
   Student stu = model.getCurrentStudent();
   DefaultListModel listModel = (DefaultListModel) nameList.getModel();
   if (stu == null){
      listModel.clear();
      detailedInfoField.setText("");
   }else{
      String[] names = model.getNames();
      listModel.clear();
      for (int i = 0; i < names.length; i++)
         listModel.add(i, names[i]);
```

```
         nameList.setSelectedValue(stu.getName(), true);
         detailedInfoField.setText(stu.toString());
      }
   }


   // main-------------------------------------------------------

   public static void main (String[] args){
      StudentTestScoresView theGUI = new StudentTestScoresView();
      theGUI.setSize (300, 300);
      theGUI.setVisible(true);
   }
}
```

Design and Implementation of StudentTestScoresModel

The development of this class follows from the interface described earlier. The model tracks the current student with a separate instance variable, which initially is `null` and becomes `null` when the model's list becomes empty. This variable is reset when a new student is added, when a student is deleted, and when a student is selected. The method `getNames` provides the view with an array of names that reflects the corresponding positions in the model's list. The private method `findStudent` performs a linear search to locate a student with a given name. The three sort methods and the delete method are left as exercises. Following is the code:

```
public class StudentTestScoresModel{

   private Student[] students;        // The list of students
   private int studentCount;          // The logical size
   private Student currentStudent;    // The currently selected student

   public StudentTestScoresModel(){
      students = new Student[15];
      studentCount = 0;
      currentStudent = null;
   }

   public Student getCurrentStudent(){
      return currentStudent;
   }

   public String[] getNames(){
      String[] names = new String[studentCount];
      for (int i = 0; i < studentCount; i++)
         names[i] = students[i].getName();
      return names;
   }

   public void setCurrentStudent(String name){
      currentStudent = findStudent(name);
   }
```

```java
public String add(Student newStudent){
    String message = newStudent.validateData();
    if (message != null)
        return message;
    if (studentCount == students.length)
        return "SORRY: student array is full";
    Student stu = findStudent(newStudent.getName());
    if (stu != null)
        return "SORRY: that student's name is already in use";
    students[studentCount] = newStudent;
    currentStudent = newStudent;
    studentCount++;
    return null;
}

public void modify(Student newStudent){
    // Exercise
}

public void delete(){
    // Exercise
}

// Three sort methods are exercises

private Student findStudent(String name){
    for (int i = 0; i < studentCount; i++)
        if (name.equals(students[i].getName()))
            return students[i];
    return null;
}
}
```

10.7 The Class `java.util.ArrayList`

As we have seen, the array is a powerful data structure that has many uses. In earlier sections of this lesson, we developed many complex but useful methods for manipulating arrays. However, arrays are easiest to use when

- We know how many data elements will be added to them, so we don't run out of cells or waste any cells

- We know they are full

    When these conditions do not hold, clients must

- Find a way to increase the length of the array when it becomes full or shrink it when many cells become unoccupied

- Track the array's logical size with a separate variable

    If necessary, we could develop methods that would increase or decrease the length of an array, but they would add complexity to our code and still not relieve clients of the need to maintain a distinct logical size for each array. Fortunately, clients have a better option in these cases.

Like most object-oriented languages, Java provides a wide range of classes for maintaining collections of objects. The collection class most like an array is called `ArrayList` and is included in the package `java.util`. In this section, we give an overview of some simple operations on array lists.

Declaring and Instantiating an Array List

An array list is an object, so it is instantiated like any other object, as in the following example:

```
import java.util.ArrayList;

ArrayList list = new ArrayList();
```

Note that the programmer specifies no initial length, as is done with arrays. An array list has a default length, but the programmer has no need to know what it is. An array list tracks its own physical size and logical size, which initially is 0. When a client inserts objects into an array list, the list automatically updates its logical size and adds cells to accommodate new objects if necessary.

Using `ArrayList` Methods

The programmer manipulates an array list by sending it messages. There are methods for examining an array list's logical size, testing it for emptiness (it's never full, at least in theory), insertions, removals, examining or replacing elements at given positions, and searching for a given element. Table 10-12 contains descriptions of these commonly used methods.

TABLE 10-12
Some commonly used `ArrayList` methods

`ArrayList` METHOD	WHAT IT DOES
`boolean isEmpty()`	Returns `true` if the list contains no elements and `false` otherwise.
`int size()`	Returns the number of elements currently in the list.
`Object get(int index)`	Returns the element at `index`.
`Object set(int index, Object obj)`	Replaces the element at `index` with `obj` and returns the old element.
`void add(int index, Object obj)`	Inserts `obj` before the element at `index` or after the last element if `index` equals the size of the list.
`Object remove(int index)`	Removes and returns the element at `index`.
`int indexOf(Object obj)`	Returns the index of the first instance of `obj` in the list or −1 if `obj` is not in the list.

Let us extend the earlier code segment by loading the array list with several strings and then displaying them in the terminal window:

```
import java.util.ArrayList;

ArrayList list = new ArrayList();

for (int i = 0; i < 5; i++)            // List contains
```

```
        list.add(i, "Item" + (i + 1));        // Item1 Item2 Item3 Item4 Item5


  for (int i = 0; i < list.size(); i++) // Display
     System.out.println(list.get(i));        // Item1
                                             // Item2
                                             // Item3
                                             // Item4
                                             // Item5
```

The next code segment performs some example searches:

```
System.out.println(list.indexOf("Item3"));        // Displays 2
System.out.println(list.indexOf("Martin"));        // Displays -1
```

Our final code segment removes the first element from the list and displays that element and the list's size after each removal, until the list becomes empty:

```
while (! list.isEmpty()){
   Object obj = list.remove(0);
   System.out.println(obj);
   System.out.println("Size: " + list.size());
}
```

Array Lists and Objects

The array list is a powerful data structure. There are some restrictions on their use, however. First, unlike an array, an array list can contain only objects, not primitive types. We explore a way of working around this restriction in the next subsection. Second, although it's easy to insert any object into an array list, care must be taken when manipulating objects extracted from an array list. Remember that the elements come out as objects, which must be cast down to the appropriate classes before they are sent messages.

Extra for Experts

The methods discussed here represent only a small subset of the methods supported by array lists. For details on the other methods, see Appendix B or consult Sun's documentation.

Primitive Types and Wrapper Classes

As mentioned earlier, Java distinguishes between primitive data types (numbers, characters, Booleans) and objects (instances of `String`, `Employee`, `Student`, etc.). Variables and arrays can refer either to primitive data types or to objects, as in

```
int x;                    // An integer variable
int nums[];               // An array of integers
Student student;          // A Student variable
Student students[];       // An array of Students
```

However, the items in an array list must all be objects. Thus

```
ArrayList list = new ArrayList();
list.add (3.14);              // Invalid (compile-time error), 3.14 is not
                              // an object
list.add (new Student());     // Valid
```

Furthermore, there are occasions when we desire to store primitive data types in lists, which we can do if we first convert them to objects. Java provides *wrapper classes* for this purpose. Following is an example that illustrates how to convert an integer to and from its wrapper class `Integer`:

```
Integer intObject;            // Variable for wrapper object
int i, j;
i = 3;
intObject = new Integer (i); // Wrap 3 in an Integer wrapper object
j = intObject.intValue();     // Unwrap 3 from the Integer wrapper object
```

As you can see from this code, the wrapper object `intObject` serves as a container in which the integer value 3 is stored or wrapped. The `intValue` method retrieves or unwraps the value in `intObject`. All wrapper objects understand the `equals` and `compareTo` messages, so they can be included in arrays that are searched and sorted. However, they cannot be used directly as operands in standard arithmetic expressions. Usually, casting as well as unwrapping is necessary. For example, the next code segment shows how to compute the sum of the first two integers in an array list:

```
ArrayList list = new ArrayList();

// Wrap ints before insertion
list.add(0, new Integer(55));
list.add(1, new Integer(66));

// They come out as Objects, so cast down before unwrapping
int sum = ((Integer)list.get(0)).intValue() +
          ((Integer)list.get(1)).intValue();
```

Like strings, wrapper objects are immutable; once they have been instantiated, the primitive values they contain cannot be changed. The wrapper classes for all the primitive data types are listed in Table 10-13.

TABLE 10-13
Primitive data types and their corresponding wrapper classes

PRIMITIVE DATA TYPE	WRAPPER CLASS	METHOD FOR UNWRAPPING
boolean	Boolean	boolean booleanValue()
char	Character	char charValue()
byte	Byte	byte byteValue()
short	Short	short shortValue()
int	Integer	int intValue()
long	Long	long longValue()
float	Float	float floatValue()
double	Double	double doubleValue()

EXERCISE 10.7

1. Write a method `sum` that expects an `ArrayList` as a parameter. The method returns an `int` representing the sum of the integers in the array list. The method should assume that the list contains only `Integer` objects.

2. Do the sort methods developed earlier for arrays of objects work for arrays of `Integer` objects without modification? Justify your answer.

Extra for Experts

Most of the wrapper classes also include useful static methods for such tasks as converting digits to integers and so forth. See Sun's Java documentation for details.

SUMMARY

In this lesson, you learned:

■ A linear search is a simple search method that works well for small and medium-sized arrays.

■ A binary search is a clever search method that works well for large arrays but assumes that the elements are sorted.

■ Comparisons of objects are accomplished by implementing the `Comparable` interface, which requires the `compareTo` method.

■ Selection sort, bubble sort, and insertion sort are simple sort methods that work well for small and medium-sized arrays.

■ Insertions and removals of elements at arbitrary positions are complex operations that require careful design and implementation.

- One can insert objects of any class into an array of Object. When they are retrieved from the array, however, objects must be cast down to their classes before sending them most messages.

- The limitation of a fixed size array can be overcome by using Java's ArrayList class. An array list tracks and updates its logical size and provides many useful methods to clients.

- A wrapper class, such as Integer, provides a way of packaging a value of a primitive type, such as int, in an object so that it can be stored in an array of Object or an array list.

VOCABULARY *Review*

Define the following terms:

binary search	insertion sort	selection sort
bubble sort	linear search	substring
immutable object	modal	wrapper class

REVIEW *Questions*

FILL IN THE BLANK

Complete the following sentences by writing the correct word or words in the blanks provided.

1. A search algorithm that examines each element, starting with the first one, is called a(n) _____ search.

2. A search algorithm that examines the element at the list's midpoint on each pass through the loop is called a(n) _____ search.

3. A sort algorithm that exchanges the smallest element with the first one is called a(n) _____ sort.

4. A sort algorithm that percolates the largest element to the end of a list is called a(n) _____ sort.

5. The method _____, which is required by the _____ interface, is used to compare two objects.

6. After retrieving an object from an array of Object, one must be careful to use the _____ operator before sending messages to that object.

7. Java's _____ class supports an array object that tracks its own logical size.

8. Java's _____ classes allow values of primitive types to masquerade as objects.

PROJECTS

PROJECT 10-1

Write a program that inputs 10 integers into an array, sorts the array with a selection sort, and displays its contents before and after the sort.

PROJECT 10-2

Write a GUI program that allows the user to input integers into an array and search it for a given value. The interface has three integer input fields and three command buttons. The roles of the fields are as follow:

■ The field labeled "Array Length" allows the user to specify the length of the array of integers used by the program.

■ The field labeled "Data Entry" allows the user to enter an integer into the array.

■ The field labeled "Target Value" allows the user to enter a number for searching the array.

The functions of the buttons are as follow:

■ The button labeled "Set Length" resets the program's array to a new array of the specified length and resets its logical size to 0.

■ The button labeled "Insert Data" allows the user to insert an integer into the array or displays a message box if the array is full.

■ The button labeled "Search" allows the user to search the array for the given target value. The results of this search, including the position if the value is found, are displayed in a message box.

PROJECT 10-3

Modify the program in Project 10-2 so that it sorts the array after each data entry and then uses a binary search for each search.

PROJECT 10-4

Complete the program from the case study and test it.

PROJECT 10-5

Jill points out that the program in the case study has a major flaw. When a student is added or modified, the changes might alter the ordering of the students in the list. For example, if the list is already sorted by name, a new student should not be placed at the end of the list, but instead at its alphabetically ordered position. Jill suggests a way of solving this problem that you should now implement. The model will track the ordering of the students with an instance variable named sortCategory, whose values are "name", "high score", and "average score". The default value is "name". Each time a sort method is called, the sortCategory variable is set to the corresponding value. Each time a student is added or modified, the model examines the sortCategory variable and sorts its list according to the current category.

PROJECT 10-6

After working on Project 10-5, Jack notices that when the list of students is sorted by name, you can use a binary search to locate a given student. Modify the program so that the model can decide which search method to use.

PROJECT 10-7

Modify the model in the case study so that it uses an array list instead of an array.

PROJECT 10-8

Write a GUI program that has two text areas and two command buttons: **Analyze** and **Clear**. One text area is for user input and the other is for program output. When the user clicks the **Analyze** button, the program displays the number of words entered in the input text area, the longest word, and the longest word's length. When the user clicks the **Clear** button, the program clears the input text area.

PROJECT 10-9

Modify the program in Project 10-8 so that it displays a list of the words in the text area and their associated frequencies. A word's frequency is the number of times it appears in the text. You should use an array of `String` for the words and a parallel array of `int` for the frequencies. The program should sort the list of words before output. If the number of unique words exceeds 50, stop the processing of input and display a message in a message box.

CRITICAL *Thinking*

Jack is trying to decide whether to use an array or an instance of Java's `ArrayList` class in an application. Explain to him the costs and benefits of using the one data structure or the other.

RECURSION, COMPLEXITY, AND SEARCHING AND SORTING

OBJECTIVES

Upon completion of this lesson, you should be able to:

■ Design and implement a recursive method to solve a problem.

■ Understand the similarities and differences between recursive and iterative solutions of a problem.

■ Check and test a recursive method for correctness.

■ Understand how a computer executes a recursive method.

■ Perform a simple complexity analysis of an algorithm using big-O notation.

■ Recognize some typical orders of complexity.

■ Understand the behavior of a complex sort algorithm such as the quicksort.

Estimated Time: 3.5 hours

VOCABULARY

activation record

big-O notation

binary search algorithm

call stack

complexity analysis

infinite recursion

iterative process

quicksort

recursive method

recursive step

stack

stack overflow error

stopping state

tail-recursive

In this lesson, we continue our discussion of sorting and searching and introduce two new topics, recursion and complexity analysis. These topics are intertwined because searching and sorting can involve recursion and complexity analysis. A recursive algorithm is one that refers to itself by name in a manner that appears to be circular. Everyday algorithms, such as a recipe to bake cake or instructions to change car oil, are not expressed recursively, but recursive algorithms are common in computer science. Complexity analysis is concerned with determining an algorithm's efficiency—that is, how its run time varies as a function of the quantity of data processed. Consider the searching and sorting algorithms presented in Lesson 10. When we test these algorithms on arrays of 10 to 20 elements, they are blindingly fast, but how fast can we expect them to be when the arrays are 100 times larger? Since painting two houses generally takes twice as long as painting one, we might guess that the same linear relationship between size and speed applies equally to sorting algorithms. We would be quite wrong, however, and in this lesson, we will learn techniques for analyzing algorithms more accurately. In later computer science courses, you will study this lesson's topics in greater depth.

11.1 Recursion

When asked to add the integers from 1 to n, we usually think of the process iteratively. We start with 0, add 1, then 2, then 3, and so forth until we reach n, or expressed differently

```
sum(n) = 1 + 2 + 3 + ... + n, where n >= 1
```

Java's looping constructs make implementing the process easy. There is, however, a completely different way to look at the problem, which at first seems very strange:

```
sum(1) = 1
sum(n) = n + sum(n - 1) if n > 1
```

At first glance, expressing `sum(n)` in terms of `sum(n - 1)` seems to yield a circular definition, but closer examination shows that it does not. Consider, for example, what happens when the definition is applied to the problem of calculating `sum(4)`:

```
sum(4) = 4 + sum(3)
       = 4 + 3 + sum(2)
       = 4 + 3 + 2 + sum(1)
       = 4 + 3 + 2 + 1
```

The fact that `sum(1)` is defined to be 1 without making reference to further invocations of sum saves the process from going on forever and the definition from being circular. Functions that are defined in terms of themselves in this way are called *recursive*. The following, for example, are two ways to express the definition of factorial, the first iterative and the second recursive:

1. factorial(n) = 1 * 2 * 3 * ... * n, where n >= 1

2. factorial(1) = 1

    factorial(n) = n * factorial(n - 1) if n > 1

In this case, no doubt, the iterative definition is more familiar and thus easier to understand than the recursive one; however, such is not always the case. Consider the definition of Fibonacci numbers first encountered in Lesson 6. The first and second numbers in the Fibonacci sequence are 1. Thereafter, each number is the sum of its two immediate predecessors, as follows:

```
1  1  2  3  5  8  13  21  34  55  89  144  233 ...
```

or

```
fibonacci(1) = 1
fibonacci(2) = 1
fibonacci(n) = fibonacci(n - 1) + fibonacci(n - 2) if n > 2
```

This is a recursive definition, and it is hard to imagine how one could express it nonrecursively.

From these examples, we can see that recursion involves two factors. First, some function `f(n)` is expressed in terms of `f(n - 1)` and perhaps `f(n - 2)` and so on. Second, to prevent the definition from being circular, `f(1)` and perhaps `f(2)` and so on are defined explicitly.

Implementing Recursion

Given a recursive definition of some process, it is usually easy to write a *recursive method* that implements it. A method is said to be recursive if it calls itself. Let us start with a method that computes factorials:

```
int factorial (int n){
//Precondition n >= 1
   if (n == 1)
      return 1;
   else
      return n * factorial (n - 1);
}
```

For comparison, the following is an iterative version of the method. As you can see, it is slightly longer and no easier to understand.

```
int factorial (int n){
   int product = 1;
   for (int i = 2; i <= n; i++)
      product = product * i;
   return product;
}
```

As a second example of recursion, following is a method that calculates Fibonacci numbers:

```
int fibonacci (int n){
   if (n <= 2)
      return 1;
   else
      return fibonacci (n - 1) + fibonacci (n - 2);
}
```

Tracing Recursive Calls

We can better understand recursion if we trace the sequence of recursive calls and returns that occur in a typical situation. Suppose we want to compute the factorial of 4. We call `factorial(4)`, which in turn calls `factorial(3)`, which in turn calls `factorial(2)`, which in turn calls `factorial(1)`, which returns 1 to `factorial(2)`, which returns 2 to `factorial(3)`, which returns 6 to `factorial(4)`, which returns 24, as shown in the following diagram:

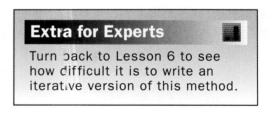

Extra for Experts

Turn back to Lesson 6 to see how difficult it is to write an iterative version of this method.

```
factorial(4)
          calls factorial(3)
                        calls factorial(2)
                                      calls factorial(1)
                                      which returns 1
                        which returns 2 * 1 or 2
          which returns 3 * 2 or 6
which returns 4 * 6 or 24
```

At first, it seems strange to have all these invocations of the `factorial` method, each in a state of suspended animation, waiting for the completion of the ones further down the line. When the last invocation completes its work, it returns to its predecessor, which completes its work, and so forth up the line, until eventually the original invocation reactivates and finishes the job. Fortunately, we do not have to repeat this dizzying mental exercise every time we use recursion.

Guidelines for Writing Recursive Methods

Just as we must guard against writing infinite loops, so too we must avoid recursions that never come to an end. First, a recursive method must have a well-defined termination or *stopping state*. For the factorial method, this was expressed in the lines

```
if (n == 1)
   return 1;
```

Second, the *recursive step*, in which the method calls itself, must eventually lead to the stopping state. For the factorial method, the recursive step was expressed in the lines

```
else
   return n * factorial(n - 1);
```

Because each invocation of the factorial method is passed a smaller value, eventually the stopping state must be reached. Had we accidentally written

```
else
   return n * factorial(n + 1);
```

the method would describe an *infinite recursion*. Eventually, the user would notice and terminate the program, or else the Java interpreter would run out of memory, at which point the program would terminate with a *stack overflow error*.

Following is a subtler example of a malformed recursive method:

```
int badMethod (int n){
   if (n == 1)
      return 1;
   else
      return n * badMethod(n - 2);
}
```

This method works fine if n is odd, but when n is even, the method passes through the stopping state and keeps on going. For instance

```
badMethod(4)
  calls badMethod(2)
    calls badMethod(0)
      calls badMethod(-2)
        calls badMethod(-4)
          calls... badMethod(-6)
             . . .
```

Run-time Support for Recursive Methods

Computers provide the following support at run time for method calls:

- A large storage area known as a **call stack** is created at program start-up.
- When a method is called, an **activation record** is added to the top of the call stack.
- The activation record contains, among other things, space for the parameters passed to the method, the method's local variables, and the value returned by the method.
- When a method returns, its activation record is removed from the top of the stack.

To understand how a recursive method uses the call stack, we ignore, for the sake of simplicity, all parts of the activation record except for the parameters and the return value. The method factorial has one of each:

```
int factorial (int n){
   if (n <= 1)
      return 1;
   else
      return n * factorial (n - 1);
}
```

Thus, an activation record for this method requires cells for the following items:

- The value of the parameter n
- The return value of factorial

Suppose we call factorial(4). A trace of the state of the call stack during calls to factorial down to factorial(1) is shown in Figure 11-1.

FIGURE 11-1
Activation records on the call stack during recursive calls to factorial

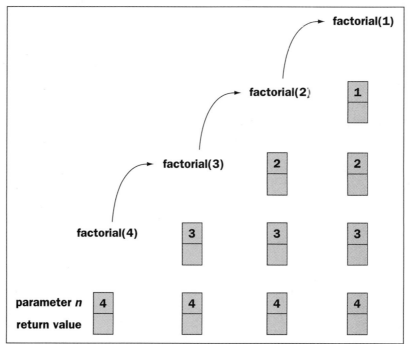

When the recursion unwinds, the return value from each call is multiplied by the parameter n in the record below it, and the top record is removed, as shown in the trace in Figure 11-2.

FIGURE 11-2
Activation records on the call stack during returns from recursive calls to `factorial`

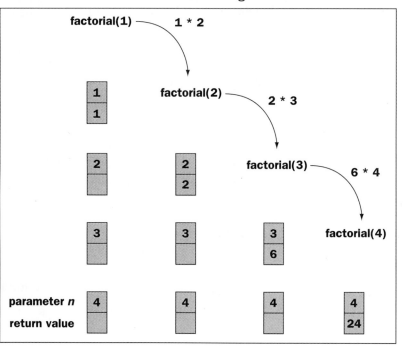

When to Use Recursion

Recursion can always be used in place of iteration, and vice versa. Ignoring the fact that arbitrarily substituting one for the other is pointless and sometimes difficult, the question of which is better to use remains. Recursion involves a method repeatedly calling itself. Executing a method call and the corresponding `return` statement usually takes longer than incrementing and testing a loop control variable. In addition, a method call ties up some memory that is not freed until the method completes its task. Naïve programmers often state these facts as an argument against ever using recursion. However, there are many situations in which recursion provides the clearest, shortest, and most elegant solution to a programming task—as we shall soon see. As a beginning programmer, you should not be overly concerned about squeezing the last drop of efficiency out of a computer. Instead, you need to master useful programming techniques, and recursion ranks among the best.

We close this section by presenting two well known and aesthetically pleasing applications of recursion: the Towers of Hanoi and the Eight Queens problem.

Towers of Hanoi

Many centuries ago in the city of Hanoi, the monks in a certain monastery were continually engaged in what now seems a peculiar enterprise. Sixty-four rings of increasing size had been placed on a vertical wooden peg (Figure 11-3). Beside it were two other pegs, and the monks were attempting to move all the rings from the first to the third peg—subject to two constraints:

■ Only one ring could be moved at a time.

■ A ring could be moved to any peg, provided it was not placed on top of a smaller ring.

FIGURE 11-3
The Towers of Hanoi

The monks believed that the world would end and humankind would be freed from suffering when the task was finally completed. The fact that the world is still here today and you are enduring the frustrations of writing computer programs seems to indicate the monks were interrupted in their work. They were, but even if they had stuck with it, they would not finish anytime soon. A little experimentation should convince you that for n rings, $2^n - 1$ separate moves are required. At the rate of one move per second, $2^{64} - 1$ moves take about 600 billion years.

It might be more practical to harness the incredible processing power of modern computers to move virtual rings between virtual pegs. We are willing to start you on your way by presenting a recursive algorithm for printing the required moves. In the spirit of moderation, we suggest

> **Warning** ⚠️
>
> Although you should try this program with different numbers, you should stick with smaller numbers (i.e., under 10). Large values of n, even with modern processing speeds, can still take a long time to run and could tie up your computer for some time. Do not attempt to run this program with 64 rings.

that you begin by running the program for small values of *n*. Figure 11-4 shows the result of running the program with three rings. In the output, the rings are numbered from smallest (1) to largest (3). You might try running the program with different numbers of rings to satisfy yourself that the printed output is correct. The number of lines of output corresponds to the formula given earlier.

FIGURE 11-4
Running the TowersOfHanoi program with three rings

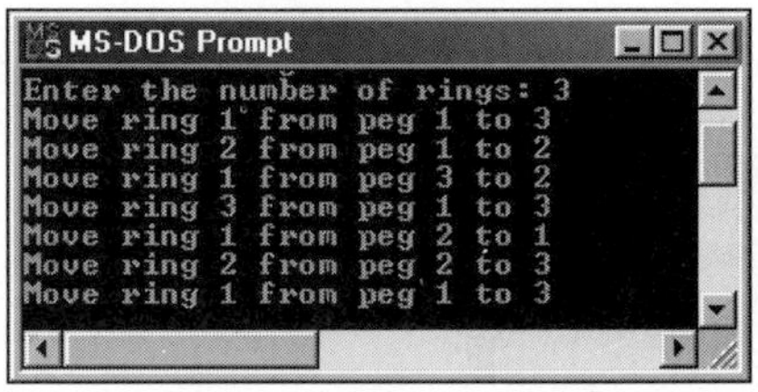

The program uses a recursive method called move. The first time this method is called, it is asked to move all *n* rings from peg 1 to peg 3. The method then proceeds by calling itself to move the top *n* − 1 rings to peg 2, prints a message to move the largest ring from peg 1 to peg 3, and finally calls itself again to move the *n* − 1 rings from peg 2 to peg 3. Following is the code:

```
/* TowersOfHanoi.java
Print the moves required to move the rings in the Towers of Hanoi problem.
1) Enter the number of rings as input.
2) WARNING: Do not run this program with 64 rings.
*/

import TerminalIO.KeyboardReader;

public class TowersOfHanoi {

    public static void main (String [] args) {
    //Obtain the number of rings from the user.
    //Call the recursive move method to move the rings from peg 1 to peg 3
    //with peg 2 available for intermediate usage.
    //   Preconditions  -- number of rings != 64
    //   Postconditions -- the moves are printed in the terminal window

        KeyboardReader reader = new KeyboardReader();
        int numberOfRings = reader.readInt("Enter the number of rings: ");
        move (numberOfRings, 1, 3, 2);
    }

    static void move (int n, int i, int j, int k){
    //Print the moves for n rings going from peg i to peg j
    //   Preconditions  -- none
    //   Postconditions -- the moves have been printed

        if (n > 0){                     //Stopping state is n == 0

            //Move the n-1 smaller rings from peg i to peg k
            move (n - 1, i, k, j);

            //Move the largest ring from peg i to peg j
```

```
        System.out.println("Move ring " + n + " from peg " + i + " to "
                  + j);

        //Move the n-1 smaller rings from peg k to peg j
        move (n - 1, k, j, i);

        //n rings have now been moved from peg i to peg j.
      }
    }
  }
```

Eight Queens Problem

The Eight Queens problem consists of placing eight queens on a chessboard in such a manner that the queens do not threaten each other. A queen can attack any other piece in the same row, column, or diagonal, so there can be at most one queen in each row, column, and diagonal of the board. It is not obvious that there is a solution, but Figure 11-5 shows one.

FIGURE 11-5
A solution of the Eight Queens problem

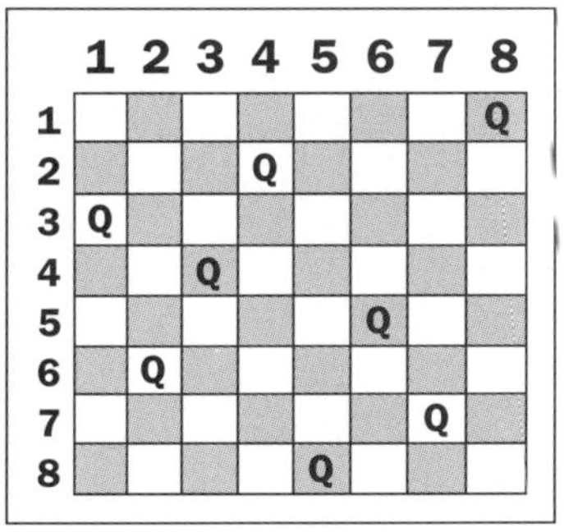

We now present a program that attempts to solve this problem and others of a similar nature. We call it the ManyQueens program, and it attempts to place n queens safely on an $n \times n$ board. The program either prints a solution or a message saying that there is none (Figure 11-6).

FIGURE 11-6
Output of the ManyQueens program for boards of size 2, 4, and 8

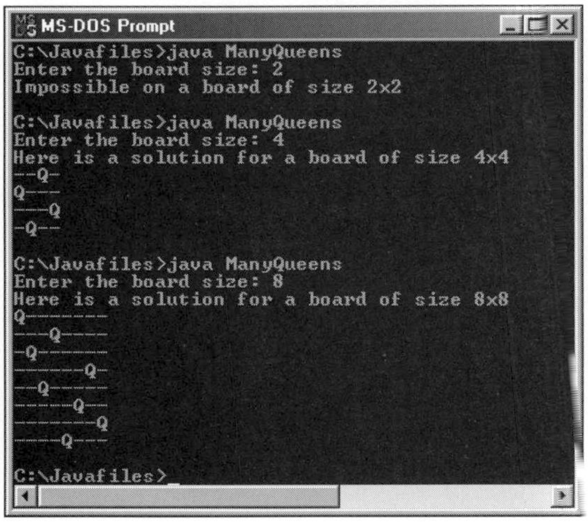

At the heart of the program is a recursive method called `canPlaceQueen`. Initially, the board is empty, and the first time the method is called, it places a queen at the top of column 1. It then calls itself to place a queen in the first safe square of column 2 and then again to place a queen in the first safe square of column 3 and so forth, until finally it calls itself to place a queen in the first safe square of the last column. If at some step (say, for column 5) the method fails, then it returns and processing resumes in the previous column by looking for the next safe square. If there is one, then the process moves onward to column 5 again or else back to column 3. And so it goes. Either a solution is found or all possibilities are exhausted. The program includes a second method called `attacked`. It determines if a queen placed in row r, column c is threatened by any queens already present in columns 1 to $c - 1$. Following is the code:

```
/* ManyQueens.java
Determine the solution to the Many Queens problem for a chessboard
of any size.
1) There is a single input indicating the size of the board.
2) If there is a solution display it, else indicate that there is none.
*/

import TerminalIO.KeyboardReader;

public class ManyQueens {

    public static void main (String [] args) {
    // Process the user's input. Call a recursive function
    //to determine if there is a solution. Print the results.
    //   Preconditions  -- the command line parameter is an integer greater
    //                      than or equal to 1
    //   Postconditions -- display a solution or a message stating that there
    //                      is none

        int i, j;          //Indices indicating board positions
        int boardSize;     //The size of the board, for instance, 8 would
                           //indicate an 8x8 board
        boolean[][] board; //A two-dimensional array representing the board
                           //An entry of false indicates that a square is
                           //unoccupied

        //Initialize the variables
        KeyboardReader reader = new KeyboardReader();
        boardSize = reader.readInt("Enter the board size: ");
        board = new boolean[boardSize][boardSize];
        for (i = 0; i < boardSize; i++)
           for (j = 0; j < boardSize; j++)
              board[i][j] = false;

        //Determine if there is a solution
        if (! canPlaceQueen (0, board))

           //There is no solution
           System.out.println ("Impossible on a board of size " +
                            boardSize + "x" + boardSize);
```

```
      else{

          //There is a solution, so print it
          System.out.println ("Here is a solution for a board of size " +
                              boardSize + "x" + boardSize);
          for (i = 0; i < boardSize; i++){
             for (j = 0; j < boardSize; j++){
                if (board[i][j])
                   System.out.print ("Q");
                else
                   System.out.print ("-");
             }
             System.out.println();
          }


      }
}

static boolean canPlaceQueen (int col, boolean[][] board){
//Mark as true the first unattacked location in column col that
//permits a solution across the remaining columns.
//  Preconditions  -- 0 <= col < board.length
//  Postconditions -- if an entry in col gets marked true
//                     return true else return false

   int i;
   for (i = 0; i < board.length; i++){ //Iterate down the column
      if (! attacked (i, col, board)){ //if square is not under attack
         if (col == board.length -1){  //if this is the last column
            board[i][col] = true;       //end recursion, set square true
            return true;                //recursive ascent true
         }else{                         //else
            board[i][col] = true;       //trial solution, set square true
                                        //if recursive descent succeeds
            if (canPlaceQueen (col + 1, board))
               return true;             //recursive ascent true
            else                        //else
               board[i][col] = false;   //trial solution didn't work
         }                              //end if
      }                                 //end if
   }
   return false;                        //recursive ascent false
}

static boolean attacked (int row, int col, boolean[][] board){
//Determine if the square at location (row, col) is under attack.
//from any queen in columns 0 to col - 1
//  Preconditions  -- 0 <= row, col < board.length
//  Postconditions -- returns true if square under attack else false
```

```
//Look for horizontal attack
int i, j, k;
for (j = 0; j < col; j++){
   if (board[row][j])
      return true;
}


//Look for attack from a descending diagonal
i = row - 1;
j = col - 1;
for (k = 0; k <= Math.min(i, j); k++){
   if (board[i][j])
      return true;
   else{
      i--;
      j--;
   }
}

//Look for attack from an ascending diagonal
i = row + 1;
j = col - 1;
for (k = 0; k <= Math.min(board.length - i - 1, j); k++){
   if (board[i][j])
      return true;
   else{
      i++;
      j--;
   }
}

   return false;
   }
}
```

EXERCISE 11.1

1. What keeps a recursive definition from being circular?

2. What are the two parts of any recursive method?

3. Why is recursion more expensive than iteration?

4. What are the benefits of using recursion?

EXERCISE 11.1 Continued

5. Consider the following definition of the method `raise`, which raises a given number to a given exponent:

```
int raise(int base, int expo){
    if (expo == 0)
        return 1;
    else
        return base * raise(base, expo - 1);
}
```

Draw a trace of the complete execution of `raise(2, 5)`.

6. Consider the following method:

```
int whatAMethod(int n){
    if (n == 0)
        return 1;
    else
        return whatAMethod(n);
}
```

What happens during the execution of `whatAMethod(3)`?

11.2 Complexity Analysis

There is an important question we should ask about every method we write. What is the effect on the method of increasing the quantity of data processed? Does doubling the data double the method's execution time, triple it, quadruple it, or have no effect? This type of examination is called *complexity analysis*. Let us consider some examples.

Sum Methods

First, consider the sum method presented in Lesson 8. This method processes an array whose size can be varied. To determine the method's execution time, beside each statement we place a symbol ($t1$, $t2$, etc.) that indicates the time needed to execute the statement. Because we have no way of knowing what these times really are, we can do no better.

```
int sum (int[] a){
    int i, result;
    result = 0;                        // Assignment: time = t1
    for (i = 0; i < a.length; i++){    // Overhead for going once around the
                                       // loop: time = t2
        result += a[i];                // Assignment: time = t3
    }
    return result;                     // Return: time = t4
}
```

PROGRAMMING SKILLS: RECURSION NEED NOT BE EXPENSIVE

We have seen that the use of recursion has two costs: Extra time and extra memory are required to manage recursive function calls. These costs have led some to argue that recursion should never be used in programs. However, as Guy Steele has shown (in "Debunking the 'Expensive Procedure Call' Myth," *Proceedings of the National Conference of the ACM*, 1977), some systems can run recursive algorithms as if they were iterative ones, with no additional overhead. The key condition is to write a special kind of recursive algorithm called a ***tail-recursive*** algorithm. An algorithm is tail-recursive if no work is done in the algorithm after a recursive call. For example, according to this criterion, the factorial method that we presented earlier is not tail-recursive because a multiplication is performed after each recursive call. We can convert this version of the factorial method to a tail-recursive version by performing the multiplication before each recursive call. To do this, we will need an additional parameter that passes the accumulated value of the factorial down on each recursive call. In the last call of the method, this value is returned as the result:

```
int tailRecursiveFactorial (int n, int result){
   if (n == 1)
      return result;
   else
      return tailRecursiveFactorial (n - 1, n * result);
}
```

Note that the multiplication is performed before the recursive call of the method—that is, when the parameters are evaluated. On the initial call to the method, the value of `result` should be 1:

```
int factorial (int n){
   return tailRecursiveFactorial (n, 1);
}
```

Steele showed that a smart compiler could translate tail-recursive code in a high-level language to a loop in machine language. The machine code treats the method's parameters as variables associated with a loop and generates an ***iterative process*** rather than a recursive one. Thus, there is no linear growth of method calls, and extra stack memory is not required to run tail-recursive methods on these systems.

The catch is that a programmer must be able to convert a recursive method to a tail-recursive method and find a compiler that generates iterative machine code from tail-recursive methods. Unfortunately, some methods are difficult or impossible to convert to tail-recursive versions, and the needed optimizations are not part of most standard compilers. If you find that your Java compiler supports this optimization, you should try converting some methods to tail-recursive versions and see if they run faster than the original versions.

Adding these times together and remembering that the method goes around the loop n times, where n represents the array's size, yields

```
executionTime
    = t1 + n * (t2 + t3) + t4
    = k1 + n * k2           where k1 and k2 are method-dependent constants
    ≈ n * k2                for large values of n
```

Thus, the execution time is linearly dependent on the array's length, and as the array's length increases, the contribution of $k1$ becomes negligible. Consequently, we can say with reasonable accuracy that doubling the length of the array doubles the execution time of the method. Computer scientists express this linear relationship between the array's length and execution time using *big-O notation*:

```
executionTime = O(n).
```

Or phrased slightly differently, the execution time is of order n. Observe that from the perspective of big-O notation, we make no distinction between a method whose execution time is

```
1000000 + 1000000*n
```

and one whose execution time is

```
n / 1000000
```

although from a practical perspective the difference is enormous.

Complexity analysis can also be applied to recursive methods. Following is a recursive version of the sum method. It too is $O(n)$.

```
int sum (int[] a, int i){
    if (i >= a.length)              // Comparison: t1
        return 0;                   // Return: t2
    else
        return a[i] + sum (a, i + 1);  // Call and return: t3
}
```

The method is called initially with i = 0. A single activation of the method takes time

```
t1 + t2      if  i >= a.length
```

and

```
t1 + t3      if  i < a.length.
```

The first case occurs once and the second case occurs the `a.length` times that the method calls itself recursively. Thus, if n equals `a.length`, then

```
executionTime
    = t1 + t2 + n * (t1 + t3)
    = k1 + n * k2          where k1 and k2 are method-dependent constants
    = O(n)
```

Other O(*n*) Methods

Several of the array processing methods presented in Lessons 8 and 10 are O(*n*). Following is a linear search method from Lesson 10:

```
int search (int[] a, int searchValue){
   for (i = 0; i < a.length; i++)     // Loop overhead: t1
      if (a[i] == searchValue)        // Comparison: t2
         return i;                    // Return point 1: t3
   return location;                   // Return point 2: t4
}
```

The analysis of the linear search method is slightly more complex than that of the `sum` method. Each time through the loop, a comparison is made. If and when a match is found, the method returns from the loop with the search value's index. If we assume that the search is usually made for values present in the array, then on average, we can expect that half the elements in the array be examined before a match is found. Putting all of this together yields

```
executionTime
   = (n / 2) * (t1 + t2) + t3
   = n * k1 + k2                 where k1 and k2 are method-dependent constants.
   = O(n)
```

Now let us look at a method that processes a two-dimensional array:

```
int[] sumRows (int[][] a){
   int i, j;
   int[] rowSum = new int[a.length];        // Instantiation: t1
   for (i = 0; i < a.length; i++){          // Loop overhead: t2
      for (j = 0; j < a[i].length; j++){ // Loop overhead: t3
         rowSum[i] += a[i][j];               // Assignment: t4
      }
   }
   return rowSum;                            // Return: t5
}
```

Let n represent the total number of elements in the array and r the number of rows. For the sake of simplicity, we assume that each row has the same number of elements, say, c. The execution time can be written as

```
executionTime
   = t1 + r * (t2 + c * (t3 + t4)) + t5
   = (k1 + n * k2) + (n/c) * t2 + n * (t3 + t4) + t5   where r = n/c
   = (k1 + n * k2) + n * (t2 / c + t3 + t4) + t5
   = k2 + n * k3                            where k1, k2, k3, and k4 are constants
   = O(n)
```

Notice that we have replaced `t1` by `(k1 + n * k2)`. This is based on the perhaps unreasonable assumption that the JVM can allocate a block of memory for the array `rowSum` in constant time (`k1`) followed by the time needed to initialize all entries to zero (`n * k2`).

An O(n^2) Method

Not all array processing methods are O(n), as an examination of the bubbleSort method reveals. Let us first analyze a "dumber" version of this method than the one presented in Lesson 10. This one does not track whether or not an exchange was made in the nested loop, so there is no early exit.

```
void bubbleSort(int[] a){
   int k = 0;

   // Make n - 1 passes through array

   while (k < a.length() - 1){              // Loop overhead: t1
      k++;
      for (int j = 0; j < a.length() - k; j++)   // Loop overhead: t2
         if (a[j] > a[j + 1])                // Comparison: t3
            swap(a, j, j + 1);               // Assignments: t4

   }
}
```

The outer loop of the sort method executes $n - 1$ times, where n is the length of the array. Each time the inner loop is activated, it iterates a different number of times. On the first activation it iterates $n - 1$ times, on the second $n - 2$, and so on, until on the last activation it iterates once. Thus, the average number of iterations is $n / 2$. On some iterations, elements a[i] and a[j] are interchanged in time t4, and on other iterations, they are not. So on the average iteration, let's say time t5 is spent doing an interchange. The execution time of the method can now be expressed as:

```
executionTime
   = t1 + (n - 1) * (t1 + (n / 2) * (t2 + t3 - t5))
   = t1 + n * t1 - t1 + (n * n / 2) * (t2 + t3 + t4) -
                  (n / 2) * (t2 + t3 + t4)
   = k1 + n * k2 + n * n * k3
   ≈ n * n * k3                    for large values of n
   = O(n²)
```

As mentioned in Lesson 10, we can alter this method to track whether or not an exchange was made within the nested loop. If no exchange was made, then the array must be sorted and we can exit the method early. However, because we usually make an exchange on each pass on the average, this trick does not improve the bubble sort's complexity on the average. Nevertheless, it can improve the method's behavior to linear in the best case (a case in which the array is already sorted).

Common Big-O Values

We have already seen several methods that are O(n) and one that is O(n^2). These are just two of the most frequently encountered big-O values. Table 11-1 lists some other common big-O values together with their names.

TABLE 11-1
Names of some common big-O values

BIG-O VALUE	NAME
O(1)	Constant
O(log n)	Logarithmic
O(n)	Linear
O(n log n)	n log n
O(n^2)	Quadratic
O(n^3)	Cubic
O(2^n)	Exponential

As an example of O(1), consider a method that returns the sum of the first and last numbers in an array. This method's execution time is independent of the array's length. In other words, it takes constant time. Later in the lesson, we will see examples of methods that are logarithmic and n log n.

The values in Table 11-1 are listed from "best" to "worst." For example, given two methods that perform the same task, but in different ways, we tend to prefer the one that is O(n) over the one that is O(n^2). This statement requires some elaboration. For instance, suppose that the exact run time of two methods is

```
10,000 + 400n          // method 1
```

and

```
10,000 + n²            // method 2
```

For small values of n, method 2 is faster than method 1; however, and this is the important point, for all values of n larger than a certain threshold, method 1 is faster. The threshold in this example is 400. So if you know ahead of time that n will always be less than 400, you are advised to use method 2, but if n will have a large range of values, method 1 is superior.

To get a feeling for how the common big-O values vary with *n*, consider Table 11-2. We use base 10 logarithms. This table vividly demonstrates that a method might be useful for small values of *n*, but totally worthless for large values. Clearly, methods that take exponential time have limited value, even if it were possible to run them on the world's most powerful computer for billions of years. Unfortunately, there are many important problems for which even the best algorithms take exponential time. You can achieve lasting fame by being the first person to replace one of these exponential time algorithms with one that takes less than exponential time.

TABLE 11-2
How big-O values vary depending on *n*

n	1	LOG *n*	*n*	*n* LOG *n*	n^2	n^3	2^n
10	1	1	10	10	100	1,000	1,024
100	1	2	100	200	10,000	1,000,000	≈ 1.3 e30
1,000	1	3	1,000	3,000	1,000,000	1,000,000,000	≈ 1.1 e301

An O(r^n) Method

We have seen two algorithms for computing Fibonacci numbers, one iterative and the other recursive. The iterative algorithm presented in Lesson 6 is O(*n*). However, the much simpler recursive algorithm presented earlier in this lesson is O(r^n), where $r \approx 1.62$. While O(r^n) is better than O(2^n), it is still exponential. It is beyond the book's scope to prove that the recursive algorithm is O(r^n). Nonetheless, it is easy to demonstrate that the number of recursive calls increases rapidly with *n*. For instance, Figure 11-7 shows the calls involved when we use the recursive method to compute the sixth Fibonacci number. To keep the diagram reasonably compact, we write (6) instead of fibonacci(6).

> **Did You Know?**
>
> By the way, from the perspective of complexity analysis, we do not need to distinguish between base 2 and base 10 logarithms because they differ only by a constant factor:
>
> $\log^2 n = \log^{10} n * \log^2 10$

FIGURE 11-7
Calls needed to compute the sixth Fibonacci number recursively

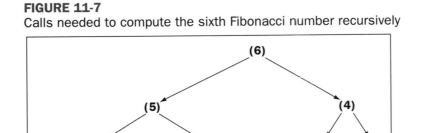

Table 11-3 shows the number of calls as a function of n.

TABLE 11-3
Calls needed to compute the nth Fibonacci number recursively

n	CALLS NEEDED TO COMPUTE *n*TH FIBONACCI NUMBER
2	1
4	5
8	41
16	1973
32	4356617

The values in Table 11-3 were obtained by running the following program:

```java
public class Tester{

    private static int count;

    public static void main (String[] args){
        for (int i = 1; i <= 5; i++){
            count = 0;
            int n = (int)Math.pow(2,i);
            int fibn = fibonacci(n);
            System.out.println ("" + n + ":" + count);
        }
    }

    public static int fibonacci (int n){
        count++;
        if (n <= 2)
            return 1;
        else
            return fibonacci(n - 1) + fibonacci(n - 2);
    }
}
```

Programs such as this are frequently useful for gaining an empirical sense of an algorithm's efficiency.

EXERCISE 11.2

1. Using big-O notation, state the time complexity of the following recursive methods:
   a. `factorial`
   b. `raise` (see Exercise 11.1, Question 5)

2. Recursive methods use stack space. Using big-O notation, state the space complexity of the following recursive methods:
   a. `factorial`
   b. `fibonacci`

3. State the time complexity of the following sort method:

```
void sort(int[] a){
    for (int j = 0; j < a.length - 1; j++){
        int minIndex = j;
        for (int k = j + 1; k < a.length; k++)
            if (a[k] < a[minIndex])
                minIndex = k;
        if (minIndex != j){
            int temp = a[j];
            a[j] = a[minIndex];
            a[minIndex] = temp;
        }
    }
}
```

11.3 Binary Search

Searching is such a common activity that it is important to do it quickly. As mentioned earlier, a linear search starts at the beginning of an array and looks at consecutive elements until either the search value is located or the array's end is encountered. Imagine using this technique to find a number by hand in a list of 10 million entries. It would take an intolerably long time, especially if the elements are strings (recall that all characters in two strings must be compared to ensure equality).

Alternatively, as mentioned in Lesson 10, if we know in advance that the list is in ascending order, we can quickly zero in on the search value or determine that it is absent using the *binary search algorithm*. We shall show that this algorithm is O(log *n*).

We start by looking at the middle of the list. We might be lucky and find the search value immediately. If not, we know whether to continue the search in the first or the second half of the list. Now we reapply the technique repeatedly. At each step, we reduce the search region by a factor of 2. Soon we either must find the search value or narrow the search down to a single element. A list of one million entries involves at most 20 steps.

Figure 11-8 is an illustration of the binary search algorithm. We are looking for the number 320. At each step, we highlight the sublist that might still contain 320. Also at each step, all the numbers are invisible except the one in the middle of the sublist, which is the one that we are comparing to 320.

FIGURE 11-8
Binary search algorithm

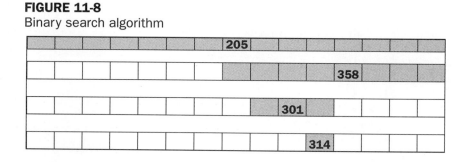

After only four steps, we have determined that 320 is not in the list. Had the search value been 205, 358, 301, or 314, we would have located it in four or fewer steps. The binary search algorithm is guaranteed to search a list of 15 sorted elements in a maximum of four steps. Incidentally, the list with all the numbers visible looks like Figure 11-9.

FIGURE 11-9
The list for the binary search algorithm with all numbers visible

15	36	87	95	100	110	194	205	297	301	314	358	451	467	486

Table 11-4 shows the relationship between a list's length and the maximum number of steps needed to search the list. To obtain the numbers in the second column, add 1 to the larger numbers in the first column and take the logarithm base 2. Hence, a method that implements a binary search is $O(\log n)$.

TABLE 11-4
Maximum number of steps needed to binary search lists of various sizes

LENGTH OF LIST	MAXIMUM NUMBER OF STEPS NEEDED
1	1
2 to 3	2
4 to 7	3
8 to 15	4
16 to 31	5
32 to 63	6
64 to 127	7
128 to 255	8
256 to 511	9
512 to 1023	10
1024 to 2047	11
2^n to $2^{n+1} - 1$	$n + 1$

We now present two versions of the binary search algorithm, one iterative and one recursive, and both $O(\log n)$. We will forgo a formal analysis of the complexity. First, the iterative version, as introduced in Lesson 10:

```
// Iterative binary search of an ascending array
int search (int[] a, int searchValue){
    int left = 0;                          // Establish the initial
    int right = a.length - 1;              // endpoints of the array
    while (left <= right){                 // Loop until the endpoints cross
        int midpoint = (left + right) / 2; // Compute the current midpoint
        if (a[midpoint] == searchValue)    // Target found; return its index
            return midpoint;
        else if (a[midpoint] < searchValue)  // Target to right of midpoint
            left = midpoint + 1;
        else                               // Target to left of midpoint
            right = midpoint - 1;
    }
    return -1;                             // Target not found
}
```

Figure 11-10 illustrates an iterative search for 320 in the list of 15 elements. L, M, and R are abbreviations for `left`, `midpoint`, and `right`. At each step, the figure shows how these variables change. Because 320 is absent from the list, eventually (`left > right`) and the method returns –1.

FIGURE 11-10
Steps in an iterative binary search for the number 320

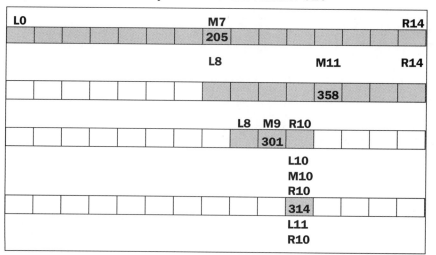

Now for the recursive version of the algorithm:

```
// Recursive binary search of an ascending array
int search (int[] a, int searchValue, int left, int right){
   if (left > right)
      return —1;
   else{
      int midpoint = (left + right) / 2;
      if (a[midpoint] == searchValue)
        return midpoint;
      else if (a[midpoint] < searchValue)
        return search (a, searchValue, midpoint + 1, right);
      else
        return search (a, searchValue, left, midpoint - 1);
   }
}
```

At heart, the two versions are similar, and they use the variables `left`, `midpoint`, and `right` in the same way. Of course, they differ in that one uses a loop and the other uses recursion. We conclude the discussion by showing how the two methods are called:

```
int[] a = {15,36,87,95,100,110,194,205,297,301,314,358,451,467,486};
int x = 320;
int location;

location = search (a, x);                  // Iterative version
location = search (a, x, 0, a.length - 1); // Recursive version
```

EXERCISE 11.3

1. The efficiency of the method `raise` in Exercise 11.1, Question 5 can be improved by the following changes: If the exponent is even, then raise the base to the exponent divided by 2 and return the square of this number. Otherwise, the exponent is odd, so `raise` the number as before. Rewrite the method `raise` using this strategy.

2. Draw a trace of the complete execution of `raise(2, 10)` as defined in Question 1 in this exercise.

3. What is the time complexity of `raise` in Question 1?

11.4 Quicksort

The sort algorithms presented in Lesson 10 are $O(n^2)$. There are a number of variations on the algorithms, some of which are marginally faster, but they too are $O(n^2)$. In contrast, there are also several much better algorithms that are $O(n \log n)$. *Quicksort* is one of the simplest of these. The general idea behind quicksort is this: Break an array into two parts and then move elements around so that all the larger values are in one end and all the smaller values are in the other. Each of the two parts is then subdivided in the same manner, and so on until the subparts contain only a single value, at which point the array is sorted. To illustrate the process, suppose an unsorted array, called a, looks like Figure 11-11.

FIGURE 11-11
Unsorted array

5	12	3	11	2	7	20	10	8	4	9

Phase 1

1. If the length of the array is less than 2, then done.

2. Locate the value in the middle of the array and call it the *pivot*. The pivot is 7 in this example (Figure 11-12).

FIGURE 11-12
Step 2 of quicksort

5	12	3	11	2	*7*	20	10	8	4	9

3. Tag the elements at the left and right ends of the array as i and j, respectively (Figure 11-13).

FIGURE 11-13
Step 3 of quicksort

5	12	3	11	2	*7*	20	10	8	4	9
i										j

4. While a[i] < pivot value, increment i.
   While a[j] >= pivot value, decrement j (Figure 11-14).

FIGURE 11-14
Step 4 of quicksort

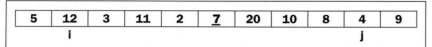

5	12	3	11	2	<u>7</u>	20	10	8	4	9
	i								j	

5. If i > j then
       end the phase
   else
       interchange a[i] and a[j] (Figure 11-15).

FIGURE 11-15
Step 5 of quicksort

5	4	3	11	2	<u>7</u>	20	10	8	12	9
	i								j	

6. Increment i and decrement j.
   If i > j then end the phase (Figure 11-16).

FIGURE 11-16
Step 6 of quicksort

5	4	3	11	2	<u>7</u>	20	10	8	12	9
		i					j			

7. Repeat Step 4, that is,
       While a[i] < pivot value, increment i
       While a[j] >= pivot value, decrement j (Figure 11-17).

FIGURE 11-17
Step 7 of quicksort

5	4	3	11	2	<u>7</u>	20	10	8	12	9
			i		j					

8. Repeat Step 5, that is,
       If i > j then
           end the phase
       else
           interchange a[i] and a[j] (Figure 11-18).

FIGURE 11-18
Step 8 of quicksort

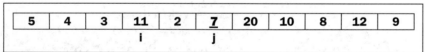

5	4	3	<u>7</u>	2	11	20	10	8	12	9
			i		j					

9. Repeat Step 6, that is,
   Increment i and decrement j.
   If i < j then end the phase (Figure 11-19).

FIGURE 11-19
Step 9 of quicksort

5	4	3	7	2	11	20	10	8	12	9
				ij						

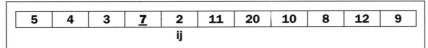

10. Repeat Step 4, that is,
    While `a[i]` < pivot value, increment `i`
    While `a[j]` >= pivot value, decrement `j` (Figure 11-20)

FIGURE 11-20
Step 10 of quicksort

5	4	3	7	2	11	20	10	8	12	9
				j	i					

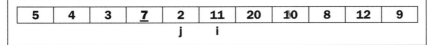

11. Repeat Step 5, that is,
    If `i > j` then
      end the phase
    else
      interchange `a[i]` and `a[j]`.

12. This ends the phase. Split the array into the two subarrays `a[0..j]` and `a[i..10]`. For clarity, the left subarray is shaded (Figure 11-21). Notice that all the elements in the left subarray are less than or equal to the pivot, and those in the right are greater than or equal to the pivot.

FIGURE 11-21
Step 12 of quicksort

5	4	3	7	2	11	20	10	8	12	9

Phase 2 and Onward

Reapply the process to the left and right subarrays and then divide each subarray in two and so on until the subarrays have lengths of at most one.

Complexity Analysis

We now present an informal analysis of the quicksort's complexity. During Phase 1, `i` and `j` moved toward each other. At each move, either an array element is compared to the pivot or an interchange takes place. As soon as `i` and `j` pass each other, the process stops. Thus, the amount of work during phase 1 is proportional to n, the array's length.

The amount of work in Phase 2 is proportional to the left subarray's length plus the right subarray's length, which together yield n. And when these subarrays are divided, there are four pieces whose combined length is n, so the combined work is proportional to n yet again. At successive phases, the array is divided into more pieces, but the total work remains proportional to n.

To complete the analysis, we need to determine how many times the arrays are subdivided. We will make the optimistic assumption that each time the dividing line turns out to be as close to the center as possible. In practice, this is not usually the case. We already know from our discussion of the binary search algorithm that when we divide an array in half repeatedly, we arrive at a single element in about $\log_2 n$ steps. Thus the algorithm is $O(n \log n)$ in the best case. In the worst case, the algorithm is $O(n^2)$.

Implementation

The quicksort algorithm can be coded using either an iterative or a recursive approach. The iterative approach also requires a data structure called a *stack*. Because we have described it recursively, we might as well implement it that way too.

```
void quickSort (int[] a, int left, int right){

   if (left >= right) return;

   int i = left;
   int j = right;
   int pivotValue = a[(left + right) / 2];
   while (i < j){
      while (a[i] < pivotValue) i++;
      while (pivotValue < a[j]) j--;
      if (i <= j){
         int temp = a[i];
         a[i] = a[j];
         a[j] = temp;
         i++;
         j--;
      }
   }
   quickSort (a, left, j);
   quickSort (a, i, right);
}
```

EXERCISE 11.4

1. Describe the strategy of quicksort and explain why it can reduce the time complexity of sorting from $O(n^2)$ to $O(n \log n)$.

2. Why is quicksort not $O(n \log n)$ in all cases? Describe the worst-case situation for quicksort.

3. Describe three strategies for selecting a pivot value in quicksort.

4. Jack has a bright idea: When the length of a subarray in quicksort is less than a certain number, say, 50 elements, run an insertion sort to process that subarray. Explain why this is a bright idea.

Case Study: Comparing Sort Algorithms

For the benefit of those who are unconvinced by mathematical analysis, we now develop a program that compares the speed of our two sort algorithms.

Request

Write a program that allows the user to compare sort algorithms.

Analysis

The program compares bubble sort and quicksort. Because quicksort runs so much more quickly than bubble sort, we do not run both sorts on the same array. Instead, we run quicksort on an array that is 100 times longer than the array used with bubble sort. Also, because we have already compared these algorithms by counting their operations, we record run times and compare these instead. The proposed interface is shown in Figure 11-22.

FIGURE 11-22
How run time varies with array length for bubble sort
on the left and quicksort on the right

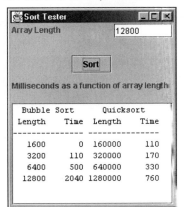

The user enters the size of the array of integers and clicks the **Sort** button. The program then performs these actions:

1. Loads two arrays with randomly generated integers ranging from 0 to 100,000. One array is of the size specified by the user, and the other array is 100 times that size.

2. Runs the bubble sort algorithm on the smaller array and the quicksort algorithm on the larger array, and records the running times of each sort in milliseconds.

3. Displays the array sizes and run times for each sort in labeled columns.

Design

The bubble sort and quicksort algorithms have already been presented in this text. There are two other primary tasks to consider:

1. Load an array with randomly generated numbers.

2. Obtain the run time of a sort.

We accomplish the first task by using the expression `(int)(Math.random() * (100000))` to generate the integer assigned to each cell in an array.

We accomplish the second task by using Java's `Date` class, as defined in the package `java.util`. When the program creates a new instance of `Date`, this object contains the current date down to the nearest millisecond, on the computer's clock. Thus, one can record the date at the beginning and end of any process, by creating two `Date` objects, as follows:

```
Date d1 = new Date();    // Record the date at the start of a process.
<run any process>
Date d2 = new Date();    // Record the date at the end of a process.
```

To obtain the elapsed time between these two dates, one can use the `Date` instance method `getTime()`. This method returns the number of milliseconds from January 1, 1970, 00:00:00 GMT until the given date. Thus, the elapsed time in milliseconds for the example process can be computed as follows:

```
long elapsedTime = d2.getTime() — d1.getTime();
```

Implementation

To obtain the neatly formatted output shown in Figure 11-22, it is necessary to use the `Format` class as explained in Lesson 7. Following is the code:

```
import javax.swing.*;
import java.util.*;
import BreezySwing.*;

public class ComparingSortAlgorithms extends GBFrame{

    private JLabel arrayLengthLabel, resultsLabel;
    private IntegerField arrayLengthField;
    private JButton sortButton;
    private JTextArea resultsTextArea;

    public ComparingSortAlgorithms(){
       setTitle ("Sort Tester");

       // Instantiate window objects
       arrayLengthLabel = addLabel ("Array Length",1,1,1,1);
       arrayLengthField = addIntegerField (0,1,2,1,1);
       sortButton = addButton("Sort",2,1,3,1);
       resultsLabel = addLabel ("Milliseconds as a function of array length",
                          3,1,3,1);
       resultsTextArea = addTextArea ("Area",4,1,3,4);

       //Set the text to column headers
       String str = Format.justify ('L', "  Bubble Sort", 15)
                + Format.justify ('L', "    Quicksort", 16) + "\n"
                + Format.justify ('R', "Length", 7)
                + Format.justify ('R', "Time", 8)
                + Format.justify ('R', "Length", 8)
```

```
                    + Format.justify ('R', "Time", 8) + "\n"
                    + Format.justify ('R', "---------------", 15)
                    + Format.justify ('R', "----------------", 16) + "\n";
    resultsTextArea.setText (str);
}


public void buttonClicked (JButton buttonObj){

    //Get the array length and instantiate two arrays,
    //one of this length and the other a 100 times longer.
    int arrayLength = arrayLengthField.getNumber();
    int[] a1 = new int[arrayLength];
    int[] a2 = new int[arrayLength*100];

    //Initialize the first array
    for (int i = 0; i < a1.length; i++)
       a1[i] = (int)(Math.random() * (100000));
          // Random numbers between 0 and 100,000

    //Initialize the second array
    for (int i = 0; i < a2.length; i++){
       a2[i] = (int)(Math.random() * (100000));
    }

    //Declare timers
    Date d1, d2;
    long elapsedTime1, elapsedTime2;

    //Time bubble sort
    d1 = new Date();
    bubbleSort (a1);
    d2 = new Date();
    elapsedTime1 = d2.getTime() - d1.getTime();

    //Time quicksort
    d1 = new Date();
    quickSort (a2, 0, a2.length - 1);
    d2 = new Date();
    elapsedTime2 = (d2.getTime() - d1.getTime());

    //Display results in text area
    resultsTextArea.append
       ( Format.justify ('R', "" + arrayLength, 7)
       + Format.justify ('R', "" + elapsedTime1, 8)
       + Format.justify ('R', "" + arrayLength*100, 8)
       + Format.justify ('R', "" + elapsedTime2, 8) + "\n");
}

private void bubbleSort (int[] a){
//Bubble sort
    for (int i = 0; i < a.length - 1; i++){
       for (int j = i + 1; j < a.length; j++){
```

```
            if (a[i] > a[j]){
                int temp = a[i];
                a[i] = a[j];
                a[j] = temp;
            }
        }
    }
}

private void quickSort (int[] a, int left, int right){
//Quicksort

    if (left >= right) return;

    int i = left;
    int j = right;
    int pivotValue = a[(left + right)/2];
    while (i < j){
        while (a[i] < pivotValue) i++;
        while (pivotValue < a[j]) j--;
        if (i <= j){
            int temp = a[i];
            a[i] = a[j];
            a[j] = temp;
            i++;
            j--;
        }
    }
    quickSort (a, left, j);
    quickSort (a, i, right);
    return;
}

public static void main (String[] args){
    ComparingSortAlgorithms theGUI = new ComparingSortAlgorithms();
    theGUI.setSize (250, 300);
    theGUI.setVisible(true);
}
}
```

Design, Testing, and Debugging Hints

- When designing a recursive method, be sure that
  1. The method has a well-defined stopping state.
  2. The method has a recursive step that changes the size of the data, so that the stopping state will eventually be reached.

- Recursive methods can be easier to write correctly than the equivalent iterative methods.

- More efficient code is usually more complex than less efficient code. Thus, it may be harder to write more efficient code correctly than less efficient code. Before trying to make your code more efficient, you should demonstrate through analysis that the proposed improvement is really significant (for example, you will get $O(n \log n)$ behavior rather than $O(n^2)$ behavior).

SUMMARY

In this lesson, you learned:

- A recursive method is a method that calls itself to solve a problem.

- Recursive solutions have one or more base cases or termination conditions that return a simple value or void. They also have one or more recursive steps that receive a smaller instance of the problem as a parameter.

- Some recursive methods also combine the results of earlier calls to produce a complete solution.

- The run-time behavior of an algorithm can be expressed in terms of big-O notation. This notation shows approximately how the work of the algorithm grows as a function of its problem size.

- There are different orders of complexity, such as constant, linear, quadratic, and exponential.

- Through complexity analysis and clever design, the order of complexity of an algorithm can be reduced to produce a much more efficient algorithm.

- The quicksort is a sort algorithm that uses recursion and can perform much more efficiently than selection sort, bubble sort, or insertion sort.

VOCABULARY *Review*

Define the following terms:

activation record	infinite recursion	stack
big-O notation	iterative process	stack overflow error
binary search algorithm	quicksort	stopping state
call stack	recursive method	tail-recursive
complexity analysis	recursive step	

REVIEW *Questions*

FILL IN THE BLANK

Complete the following sentences by writing the correct word or words in the blanks provided.

1. The _____ of a recursive algorithm is the part in which a problem is solved directly, without further recursion.

2. The _____ of a recursive algorithm is the part in which the problem is reduced in size.

3. The memory of a computer is formatted into a large _____ to support recursive method calls.

4. The memory for each recursive method call is organized in a group of cells called a(n) _____.

5. The type of error in a recursive algorithm that causes it to run forever is called a(n) _____.

6. When a recursive method does not stop, a(n) _____ error occurs at run time.

7. The linear, quadratic, and logarithmic orders of complexity are expressed as _____, _____, and _____ using big-O notation.

8. The bubble sort algorithm has a run-time complexity of _____ in the best case and _____ in the worst case.

9. The quicksort algorithm has a run-time complexity of _____ in the best case and _____ in the worst case.

PROJECTS

PROJECT 11-1

Use a `Tester` program to implement and test a recursive method to compute the greatest common divisor (gcd) of two integers. The recursive definition of gcd is

```
gcd(a, b) = b, when a = 0
gcd(a, b) = gcd(b, a % b), when a > 0
```

Note ☑

Some of the projects in this lesson ask you to implement a method and test it in a `Tester` program. Be sure that the method is defined as a `static` method; otherwise, you will get a syntax error.

PROJECT 11-2

Write a recursive method that returns a string with the characters in reverse order and test the method with a `Tester` program. The string and the index position should be parameters. If the position is less than the string's length, recurse with the rest of the string after this position and return the result of appending the character at this position to the result. Otherwise, return the empty string.

PROJECT 11-3

Design, implement, and test a recursive method that expects a positive integer parameter and returns a string representing that integer with commas in the appropriate places. The method might be called as follows:

```
String formattedInt = insertCommas(1000000);  // Returns "1,000,000"
```

(*Hint*: Recurse by repeated division and build the string by concatenating after each recursive call.)

PROJECT 11-4

The phrase "*n* choose *k*" is used to refer to the number of ways in which we can choose *k* objects from a set of *n* objects, where $n >= k >= 0$. For example, 52 choose 13 would express the number of possible hands that could be dealt in the game of bridge. Write a program that takes the values of *n* and *k* as inputs and displays as output the value *n* choose *k*. Your program

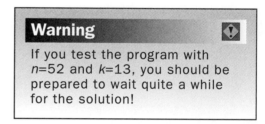

Warning

If you test the program with *n*=52 and *k*=13, you should be prepared to wait quite a while for the solution!

should define a recursive method, `nChooseK(n, k)`, that calculates and returns the result. (*Hint*: We can partition the selections of *k* objects from *n* objects as the groups of *k* objects that come from *n* − 1 objects and the groups of *k* objects that include the *n*th object in addition to the groups of *k* − 1 objects chosen from among *n* − 1 objects.)

PROJECT 11-5

Modify the case study of this lesson so that it counts comparison and exchange operations in both sort algorithms and displays these statistics as well. Run the program with two array sizes and make a prediction on the number of comparisons, exchanges, and run times for a third size.

PROJECT 11-6

Write a tester program to help assess the efficiency of the Towers of Hanoi program. This program should be similar to the one developed for the Fibonacci method.

PROJECT 11-7

Write a tester program to help assess the efficiency of the Many Queens program. This program should be similar to the one developed for the Fibonacci method.

CRITICAL *Thinking*

Jill is trying to decide whether to use a recursive algorithm or an iterative algorithm to solve a problem. Explain to her the costs and benefits of using one method or the other.

ARRAYS, RECURSION, AND COMPLEXITY

TRUE/FALSE

Circle T if the statement is true or F if it is false.

T F   1. In Java, an array is an ordered collection of methods.

T F   2. Because arrays are objects, two variables can refer to the same array.

T F   3. The length of a Java array is fixed at compile time.

T F   4. One responsibility of the view portion of a program is to instantiate and arrange window objects.

T F   5. Static variables are associated with a class, not with its instances.

T F   6. Subclasses can see both public and private names declared in their parent classes.

T F   7. If you need to use the cast operator, remember that you never cast down, only cast up.

T F   8. A linear search runs more efficiently than a binary search.

T F   9. Sorting methods generally cannot perform in better than $O(n^2)$ run time.

T F 10. Loops are always preferable to recursive methods for solving problems.

FILL IN THE BLANK

Complete the following sentences by writing the correct word or words in the blanks provided.

1. A(n) _____ is a collection of similar items or elements that are ordered by position.

2. An item's position within an array is called its _____ or _____.

3. Two arrays in which the corresponding elements are related are called _____ arrays.

4. The number of elements currently stored and used within an array is called its _____ size.

5. Classes that are never instantiated are called _____ .

6. Java organizes classes in a(n) _____ .

7. The toString message, which is understood by every object, no matter which class it belongs to, is a good example of _____.

8. A search method that repeatedly visits the midpoint of an array is called a(n) _____ search.

9. A sorting method that repeatedly moves elements around a pivot element is called a(n) _____.

10. Recursive methods have two parts, the _____ and the _____.

WRITTEN QUESTIONS

Write a brief answer to the following questions.

1. Write statements for the following items that declare array variables and assign the appropriate array objects to them.
   A. intNumbers, an array of 5 integers.

   B. realNumbers, an array of 100 real numbers.

   C. bools, an array of 10 Booleans.

   D. words, an array of 20 strings.

2. Write a `for` loop that initializes an array of 10 integers to the first 10 positive integers.

3. Repeat Question 2, but use an initializer list.

4. There are several ways in which methods in a subclass can be related to methods in its superclass. Describe at least two of these.

5. Explain why one would use `static` variables and `static` methods.

PROJECTS

PROJECT U3-1

Write a program that takes 10 floating-point numbers as inputs. The program displays the average of the numbers followed by all of the numbers that are greater than the average. As part of your design, write a method that takes an array of doubles as a parameter and returns the average of the data in the array.

PROJECT U3-2

Write a program to keep statistics for a basketball team consisting of 12 players. Statistics for each player should include shots attempted, shots made, and shooting percentage; free throws attempted, free throws made, and free throw percentage; offensive rebounds and defensive rebounds; assists; turnovers; and total points. Place these data in parallel arrays. Appropriate team totals should be listed as part of the output.

SCANS PROJECT U3-3

Modify the program of Project U3-2 so that it uses a two-dimensional array instead of the parallel arrays for the statistics.

SCANS PROJECT U3-4

A summation method returns the sum of the numbers from a lower bound to an upper bound. Write a static recursive method for summations and run it with a `tester` program that displays the values of the parameters on each call and the returned value on each call.

SCANS PROJECT U3-5

Write a `static` method that builds a sorted array list from a randomly ordered array list. The method should throw an exception if the parameter's elements are not `Comparable` objects. Test the method in a `tester` program.

SCANS CRITICAL *Thinking*

A bank provides several kinds of accounts, among them checking accounts and saving accounts. Design a simple banking system data model that represents these accounts. Be sure to make use of abstract classes, inheritance, polymorphism, and encapsulation. The result of your work should be a set of class summary boxes for the data model of the banking system.

USING ABSTRACT DATA TYPES

Unit 4

⊗ **Estimated Time for Unit: 14 hrs.**

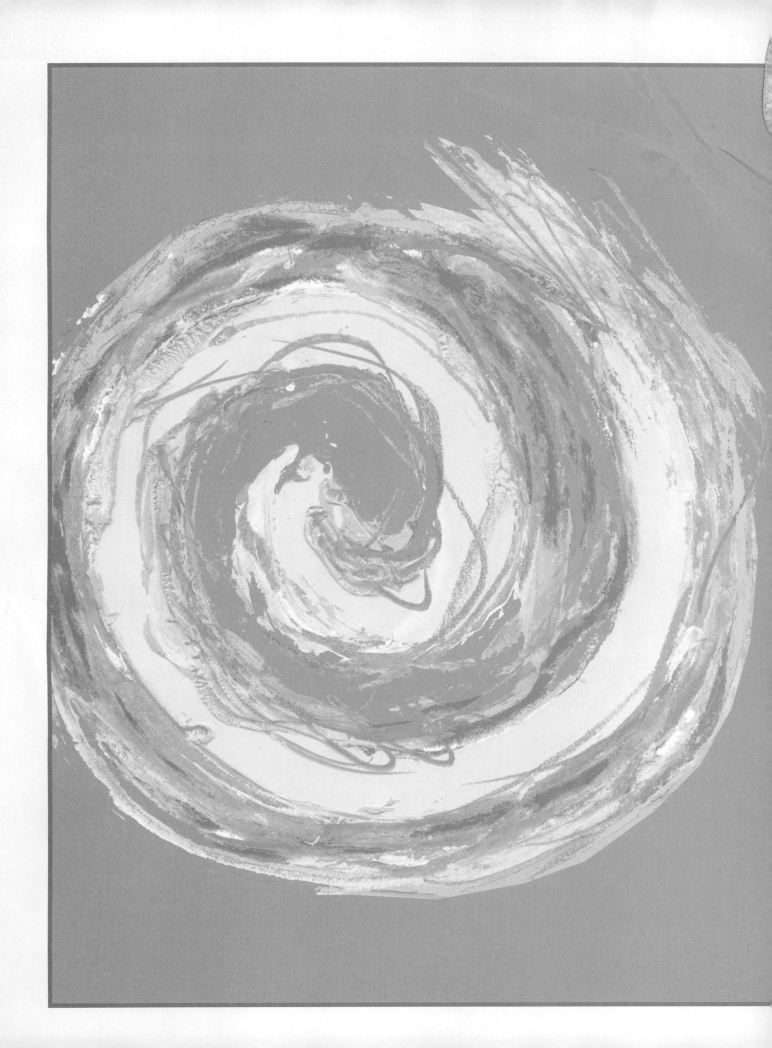

OBJECT-ORIENTED ANALYSIS AND DESIGN

In preceding lessons, we have learned Java's fundamental mechanisms for working with classes. We have written many programs that use classes, and we have seen how classes are combined to solve problems. We have not, however, addressed the larger question of how to take a significant problem and come up with a system of interacting classes that implement a solution. We now show you how this is done. We do not expect you to become proficient users of the processes described. Proficiency will come in later courses devoted to software development techniques and not in this course, which emphasizes fundamental programming concepts and Java's core syntax. As you read the lesson, you will see how an experienced programmer chooses classes, develops class hierarchies, and determines the relationships and interactions between classes. Try not to get lost in the details. By the end of the lesson you will have a deeper understanding of how developers think in an object-oriented way about problem solving.

Much of the lesson is organized around a case study based on a computerized adventure game. Case studies throughout this book have presented programming in terms of a software development process consisting of request, analysis, design, and implementation. In this lesson, we explore analysis and design in more detail. There are many methodologies for doing object-oriented analysis and design. These methodologies have two components—a step-by-step process that you follow from request through implementation and various graphical schemes for representing analysis and design decisions. The dominant graphical scheme at this time, and the one we will utilize, is called the **Unified Modeling Language (UML)**. Using UML, we show how to think in an object-oriented way about problem solving without becoming enmeshed in too many technical details. Throughout, our emphasis is on building an intuitive understanding of how objects work together to accomplish a task rather than on mastering all the details of the software development process or the formalities of UML.

Extra for Experts

For an excellent introduction to the Unified Modeling Language see *UML Distilled*, by Martin Fowler.

12.1 Introduction

To put the lesson in perspective, we begin with a little of the history of analysis and design. In the late 1960s and in the 1970s, the ever-increasing size and complexity of software systems led to what was then a revolution in software development techniques. The first structured programming languages were introduced, previously unstructured languages were enhanced to make them structured, and structured methodologies of analysis and design were discovered and popularized. Industry adopted these techniques as the only rational way to develop systems that were becoming larger and more complex every day. Since then a second revolution has taken place. In the mid-1990s companies began using object-oriented languages and tools to develop most of their new applications. In addition, we have seen the introduction of object-oriented operating systems and object-oriented database systems. Overall, many of the software products and practices of the preceding 40 years have been replaced by a new generation of object-oriented ones.

From a student's perspective, object-oriented methodologies are appealing because they provide a single consistent model and methodology for dealing with the three major phases of software development—analysis, design, and implementation. The models used to illustrate small object-oriented programs are exactly the same as the one used to describe the decomposition of large problems. With object-oriented methodologies, there is no artificial break between programming-in-the-large and programming-in-the-small. The ideas of abstraction, encapsulation, and inheritance that are encountered when first learning an object-oriented language are used again when analyzing and designing large systems.

Analysis and design are at the heart of the software development process, and numerous techniques have been devised for assisting in the task of doing object-oriented analysis and design (OOA&D). These techniques have been grouped in various combinations to form the methodologies that are proclaimed in books and implemented in CASE (computer-aided software engineering) tools. At the moment, the leading graphical notation used in these methodologies is UML. Although the various methodologies have their proponents and detractors, they all share a common goal—to assist in creating and communicating the models that are the major products of analysis and design. Any methodology used iteratively, with intelligence and imagination, leads to ever-increasing insight into what a system ought to do and how it might do it. Thus we attempt to give you an overall feeling for how to decompose a system into classes without becoming overly concerned with the technical details of the particular methodology.

To experience the power and effectiveness of object-oriented analysis and design, we must tackle problems of considerable size and complexity. Unfortunately, most large problems that we could potentially use as examples suffer from one or more of the following defects:

1. We must acquire considerable domain expertise before understanding the problems. *Domain expertise* means knowledge of the field in which the problem occurs. For example, problems in the field of banking require knowledge of accounting and finance, among other fields.

2. The problems involve too many uninteresting and burdensome details.

3. Some dimensions of the problems are too easy, whereas others are too hard.

The first difficulty mentioned is particularly distressing because, without domain expertise, we cannot fully understand proposed solutions and cannot suggest alternatives. To overcome this problem, simplified versions of real problems are sometimes presented in textbooks such as this. In the authors' experience, however, this process of simplification results in problems that are unconvincing because they are overly artificial. Surprisingly, we have found that completely artificial problems—namely games—can be designed that are free of all of the drawbacks mentioned. In this lesson we will use a game of adventure, which we have created as our example.

12.2 *Overview of Analysis and Design*

The goal of analysis is to model what a system does. The goal of design is to model how it might do it. During analysis fundamental classes, interrelationships, and behavior are determined, and these are added to and refined during design as implementation decisions are made; however, we do not draw a clear line of demarcation between the two phases. Together we treat them as a continuum of activity that moves from the general to the specific, finishing with a description of a system that can be passed to programmers for coding.

Determining the major classes needed in a system is fairly straightforward. The nouns in the description of a problem point the way to an initial list of candidate classes and their attributes. Although classes are eventually organized into hierarchies, it is best not to do this too soon, but to wait until more insight is gained into the workings of a system.

Determining methods is more difficult. Verbs, to some extent, map into methods, but not with the same reliability as nouns into classes and attributes. A better approach to discovering methods is to examine the activities encompassed by a system. Some of these activities are immediately obvious from the description of the problem, and others become apparent when attempts are made at designing the user interface. Examining activities leads to an understanding of the patterns of communications that exist between the classes and thus to knowledge of each class's responsibilities and collaborators. Role-playing and a blackboard are useful props during this process, and the results are recorded using the diagramming conventions of UML. Describing the function and signature of each method completes analysis and design. The process is iterative and implementing prototypes can be very helpful. At any time during the process there can be new insights that lead to changes in work already completed.

Two subtleties of this process must be understood. First and foremost, there is no single correct realization of a system. There are many different combinations of classes, responsibilities, and collaborations that work well together and many more that work badly. Good combinations involve simpler patterns of communications than bad combinations, because they are modified more easily, and responsibilities are distributed more evenly. An analogy helps us to understand this. Consider a corporation. In one style of management, a company's president looks over every employee's shoulder, telling him what to do and when to do it. But a company operates much more effectively if the employees understand the objectives of the company and their roles in achieving them and are then allowed to make their own decisions, communicating with each other as necessary. Too often beginners tended to create systems that mirror the first style of management.

A second subtlety, and one that is more difficult to grasp, is the difference between the intrinsic attributes of a class and those that are added in order to support a particular pattern of communications. For instance, in a library system, we might discover during analysis that

- Author and title are intrinsic attributes of books.

- It is essential to keep track of which books are checked out to which patrons.

During design, after considering the various activities that involve books and patrons, we must decide how to implement the second requirement. One possibility is to add the non-intrinsic attribute *patron* to *book*, but there are others. The final choice depends on implementation considerations and not on any intrinsic characteristics of books or patrons.

12.3 Request

We are now ready to consider the lesson's extended case study. We begin as usual with a request from a hypothetical customer. We are asked to implement an adventure game whose broad outline is described as follows:

Imagine a world of many places connected to each other by paths (Figure 12-1 shows a corner of such a world). Through this world a heroine wanders collecting treasures and weapons. Dragons, giants, and other monsters guard the items, so the heroine must defeat these foes in battle before picking up the items. A battle's outcome depends on luck, the relative strength of the contestants, and the power of their weapons. Upon death an entity drops all its items, and the heroine can then pick up these items. As she moves from place to place, the heroine constructs a map of the portion of the world she has seen so far. She also keeps a diary in which she records the actions she performs during the game (moving, picking things up, fighting battles).

FIGURE 12-1
A corner of an adventure world near the entrance to a giant's castle

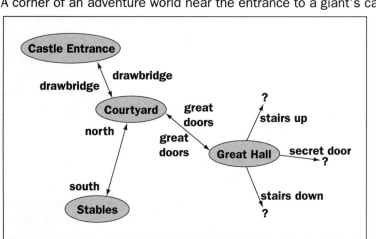

As Figure 12-1 shows, the heroine can pass between the Great Hall and the Courtyard by going through the great doors. From the Courtyard, going south leads to the Stables, and from the Stables going north returns to the Courtyard. The heroine has not finished exploring the paths from the Great Hall. Stairs lead up and down, and there is a secret door behind a tapestry, but the destination of these paths is currently unknown.

An obvious advantage of this problem is that we are all domain experts from the outset. The world of the game is imaginary and is easy to understand. The game deals with familiar situations and has simple rules. Moving, picking things up, and dropping them are everyday activities. Battles with giants and ogres are less common, fortunately, but easy to picture. Another advantage is that the game is free of the numerous tedious details that dominate real-world problems of similar complexity.

The game can be expanded in many ways, both minor and major. Limiting the heroine's carrying capacity is an example of a minor modification. Adding a store where the heroine can buy and sell weapons and treasures is slightly more difficult. Allowing several users, each controlling a separate heroine, to enter the game world simultaneously leads to a networked-based design and extensive modifications suited to a more advanced computer science course.

12.4 Analysis

Although the description of the game is simple, it involves a surprising number of elements, and the subsequent system is fairly complex. A smaller example would not allow us to illustrate important features of object-oriented systems development; however, the complexity has been carefully chosen to yield an interesting hierarchy of classes. There are numerous associations between the classes, and many of the activities involve several classes simultaneously. Working with this problem, we will see that objects are of many different sorts—people, places, things, events, and abstractions in the problem domain. In addition, objects manage computer resources and interfaces. Some objects, such as treasures, are little more than repositories for data and consist of only a few attributes and the methods needed to access them. Other objects, such as the entities, are complex. They implement methods that support the activities of the game (moving from place to place, fighting battles, picking up items), and their internal states are constantly changing.

The initial portion of the analysis is not object-oriented and is the same regardless of the language or methodology used to implement the system. It consists of clarifying the customer's request and designing the interfaces. Once that has been done, we can undertake the object-oriented aspect of the process and determine an appropriate decomposition of the software into a system of cooperating classes.

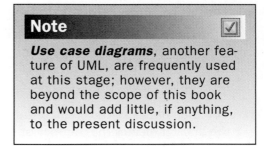

Note ☑

Use case diagrams, another feature of UML, are frequently used at this stage; however, they are beyond the scope of this book and would add little, if anything, to the present discussion.

Additional Facts Concerning the Game

During our interviews with the customer who requested the software, we learn the following additional details of the game:

- The object of the game is for the heroine, under the user's control, to collect 100 units of treasure as quickly as possible and return to the entrance without losing all of her nine lives.

- Each treasure is worth some number of units.

■ At the start of the game, the user does not know how many treasures there are in the world.

■ There are many places, but no unreachable ones. There may be places from which there is no return, however, such as the bottom of a deep well.

■ Each path connects two places, but some paths are one-way only, such as a wild raft ride down dangerous rapids.

■ The heroine passes instantly from place to place by following the paths, and no game actions occur on the paths.

■ Every place, path, entity, weapon, and treasure has a name and description.

■ Until the heroine follows a path, she does not know where it leads, and once she does know, she adds the destination to her map. Figure 12-1 shows the heroine's map after she has explored just a portion of a giant's castle. In this illustration, the entrance to the world is assumed to start at the entrance to the castle.

■ The structure of an adventure world is stored in a text file, and at the beginning of a game, the user selects one of these files. At any time during a game, the user can save the current state of the game and exit.

■ At any given moment, an item (treasure or weapon) is either carried by an entity or is lying around in some place. Items are never located on paths.

■ The rules of battle are slightly convoluted. When the user enters a place guarded by one or more monsters, she can avoid a battle simply by leaving the place. If the user decides to fight, she/he selects a foe. At that point, the numerical strength of the heroine is multiplied by one plus the numerical force of all her weapons (strength * (1 + force of all weapons)). The resulting number is multiplied by a random number between one and ten, representing luck, to give what we call the **battle number**. The same thing is done for the foe with whom she is fighting. The winner is whoever has the larger battle number. If the heroine loses, she forfeits one of her nine lives, and her strength is decremented by one. If she loses her ninth life, the game is over. If there is a draw, there are no changes. If the monster loses, it drops all of its items (weapons and treasures) and dies, and the heroine's strength is incremented by one. The user is able to view all relevant information about the heroine's and monster's states before choosing to fight a battle.

■ The entries in the heroine's diary vary depending on the type of event recorded:

  ■ **Move** – Time, place, path, destination

  ■ **Pickup** – Time, place, item

  ■ **Battle** – Time, place, monster, heroine's battle number, monster's battle number

■ The time indicates the elapsed time in seconds since the beginning of the game. In addition, the diary indicates the number of lives the heroine has remaining, her strength, and the total force of all her weapons.

Graphical User Interface

The overall requirement is to design an interactive program that allows a user to enter the world we have described and to control the actions of the heroine. The interface must display names and descriptions of all things in the game, as well as the heroine's map and diary. Games of this sort usually involve animated graphics, but clearly these are beyond our current capabilities, so we settle for an interface based on the window controls encountered so far. This interface is shown in Figure 12-2.

FIGURE 12-2
Proposed interface for the game

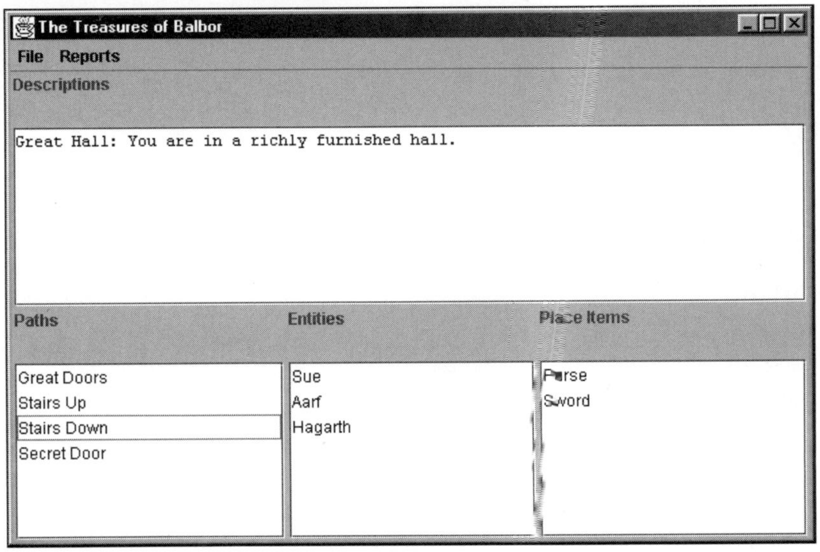

In the following paragraphs, we explain the workings of the interface.

Overview

There are two menus. The first (**File**) allows us to open and save the game. The second (**Reports**) displays the heroine's map and diary and redisplays the current place's description. The window's three lists and single text area display relevant information about the state of the game. When the heroine moves to a new location, the text area displays a description of the place. The text area is also used to display descriptions of other things in the game. We now explain these features in more detail.

Paths list

This is a list of all the paths leading from the current location. Clicking on a path's name causes the path's description to display in the text area. The description says nothing about the path's destination, which is discovered by following the path. The following statement is the description of the secret door:

This door looks little used.

Double-clicking on a path causes the heroine to move along the path to its destination.

Entities List

This is a list of all the entities located in the current place. It includes the heroine and her foes. Clicking on an entity displays its description in the text area. For instance, Hagarth is described as:

Hagarth: A very giant of a giant

Strength: 10

Force of weapons: 20

Value of treasures: 10

Weapon Club: Shaped from a tree trunk Force: 10

Treasure Belt: Gold belt with diamond buckle Value: 10

Weapon Dagger: As large as a small sword Force: 10

Double-clicking on a foe initiates a battle between the heroine and the foe. Double-clicking on the heroine has no effect.

Place Items list

This is a list of all the items located in the current place. Click on an item to see its description. Double-clicking on an item causes the heroine to pick up the item.

File/Open menu item

This command opens a file dialog that is used to select a game file.

File/Save menu item

This command opens a file dialog that is used to save the current state of the game.

Reports/Map menu item

This command displays a map of the portion of the world explored so far (Figure 12-3)

FIGURE 12-3

The map and diary after the heroine has explored a portion of the world near the entrance

Map	Diary	
Map of the world seen so far:	Diary of events.	
Castle Entrance	TIME	EVENT
Drawbridge to Courtyard	3 sec	In Castle Entrance PICKUP
Courtyard		the Ring.
Drawbridge to ?	7 sec	MOVE from Castle Entrance
South to ?		and follow Drawbridge to
Great Doors to Great Hall		Courtyard.
Great Hall	16 sec	MOVE from Courtyard and
Great Doors to ?		follow Great Doors to
Stairs Up to Turret		Great Hall.
Stairs Down to ?	18 sec	In Great Hall BATTLE
Secret Door to ?		against Aarf with battle
Turret		numbers of 1100 to 110.
Stairs Down to Great Hall	57 sec	MOVE from Great Hall and
		follow Stairs Up to Turret.
	67 sec	MOVE from Turret and follow
		Stairs Down to Great Hall.

Reports/Diary menu item

This command displays a list of all the actions the heroine has performed to date (Figure 12-3).

Report/Current Location menu item

This command displays the name and description of the current place.

Format of the Game's Text Files

We now specify the structure of the text file that describes the adventure world. The structure of the file is the same for a new game and for one saved during play. The fact that we have not yet learned how to process a text file in Java is not an impediment. Just as there are many ways to structure the graphical user interface, so too there are many ways to structure the text file. We divide the file into labeled sections, and each section contains multiple lines. Figure 12-4 shows the structure. Clearly, a game file can be created or read using any standard text editor.

FIGURE 12-4
Structure of a game file

```
Time
  elapsedTime
Places
  name, "description"
  etc...
Paths
  name, "description", fromPlaceName  toPlaceName
  etc...
Hero
  name, strength, lives, placeName, "description"
Foes
  name, strength, placeName, "description"
  etc...
Treasures
  name, value, name of place or entity, "description"
  etc...
Weapons
  name, force, name of place or entity, "description"
  etc...
```

In the figure:

■ Elapsed time indicates how long the game was in progress when saved. The elapsed time for a new game is zero. When a game is reloaded, time starts at the indicated elapsed time.

■ Names of places, entities, and items are assumed to be unique. Names of paths are unique within a place.

■ Because descriptions contain punctuation marks, they are enclosed in quotes.

■ All paths are treated as if they are one-way only. Thus a two-way path is represented by a matching pair of one-way paths.

■ The location of the heroine and foes is indicated by a place name.

■ Treasures and weapons are located in a place or are carried by an entity. The name indicates which place an item can be found or which entity is carrying an item.

In Figure 12-4, we do not deal with the problem of how to represent the map and diary, but leave this as an exercise to be attempted in a later lesson (Lesson 20) after you have learned more about files.

Finding the Classes

Developing an accurate description of the problem and designing the interface and file structure is time consuming and difficult, but there is no point in going further until this work is finished. If we make any mistakes, then all our subsequent work is affected adversely, and the longer mistakes go undetected, the more expensive they are to correct.

Assuming that we now understand the user requirements of the game, we are ready to take a first pass at decomposing the system into classes. In general, insights gained later in the process might lead to some changes in this decomposition, but that will not happen here. Our first step is to reread the extended description of the problem and extract the nouns. Some of these nouns represent classes and others represent attributes. We ignore synonyms, that is, different nouns that name the same thing. As mentioned earlier, classes are of many different types—people, places, events, things, and abstractions, plus interface and resource managers. Table 12-1 shows our initial list of classes.

TABLE 12-1
Initial list of classes

CLASS	DESCRIPTION
People	Heroine, Foe
Places	GameWorld, Place, Path
Things	Treasure, Weapon
Abstractions	Map, Diary
Events	MoveEvent, BattleEvent, PickupEvent
Interface Management	GameView and various window controls (labels, lists, menu items, etc.)
Resource Management	GameFile

We consider Map and Diary to be abstractions because we are interested in their content rather than their physical manifestation. The entries in the diary record events. The GameFile class will handle all the details of moving information in and out of the game file. The fact that we do not yet know how to implement this class does not prevent us from specifying its behavior and role in the system.

The problem description also contains many nouns that describe attributes. Examples include names of people, places, and things, strength of people, force of weapons, etc. We will return to these attributes in more detail later.

Representing Relationships Between Classes

Having identified the major classes, we now consider their interrelationships. Relationships between classes are usually divided into three categories: inheritance, aggregation, and other association. These are described in the following paragraphs.

Inheritance

This is the relationship between a class and its subclasses. It is also called the *is-a relationship*, as in "a circle *is-a* shape."

Aggregation

This is the relationship between a class and its constituent parts, if they also happen to be classes. It is also called the *has-a relationship*, as in "a boat *has-a* rudder."

Other Association

This category encompasses all other relationships and is called the *knows-a relationship*. In a problem description, these relationships might be recognized by verbs such as carries, eats, and rides and phrases such as "is next to."

Figure 12-5 shows how each of these relationships is represented in UML using what are called *class diagrams*.

FIGURE 12-5
How relationships are represented in UML

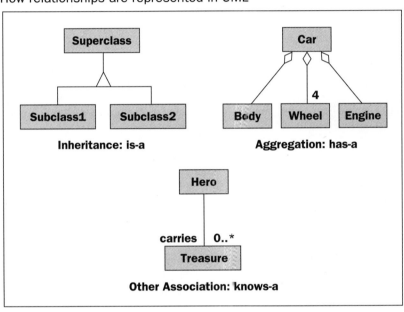

Knows-a associations are sometimes labeled with a word or phrase that describes the relationship. In has-a and knows-a relationships, the association between classes is assumed to be one-to-one. That is, one object of the first class is associated with one of the second, but UML includes special multiplicity indicators that can be used when this is not the case. These indicators are placed on the line joining two classes. The indicator pertains to the class to which it is closest. Table 12-2 shows a list of the possible indicators (*M* and *N* represent positive integers with $M < N$).

TABLE 12-2
UML multiplicity indicators

MULTIPLICITY INDICATOR	DESCRIPTION
M	Indicates exactly *M*
M..N	Indicates from *M* to *N*
M..*	Indicates *M* or more

Relationships Between the Classes in the Game

We now have the tools to represent the relationships between the classes in the game. There are too many classes and relationships to include in a single diagram. We start with Figure 12-6. In this figure, we use the generic word `Entity` to represent the heroine and foes and `Item` to represent food and weapons.

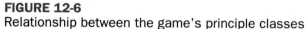

FIGURE 12-6
Relationship between the game's principle classes

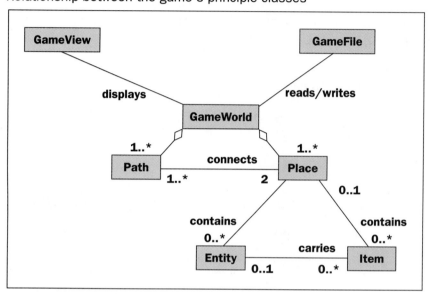

To paraphrase, the diagram says that

The `GameView` displays the `GameWorld`. The `GameFile` transfers the `GameWorld` to and from disk. The `GameWorld` is an aggregate of one or more (1..*) places and paths. Each path connects two places, and each place is connected to at least one other. An entity is located in a place, and an item is either located in a place or carried by an entity. A place contains zero or more (0..*) entities and items, and an entity carries zero or more items.

The introduction of `Entity` and `Item` in Figure 12-6 suggests that we add these classes to our system as abstract superclasses, with `Heroine` and `Foe` as subclasses of `Entity` and `Treasure` and `Weapon` as subclasses of `Item`. But we need not stop there. Many things in the game have a name and description, which suggests introducing the abstract superclass `NamedThing`. Figure 12-7 summarizes these observations. The classes `Map` and `Diary` are not part of the hierarchy, but are included in Figure 12-7 because the heroine carries them.

FIGURE 12-7
The `NamedThing`, `Entity`, and `Item` hierarchies

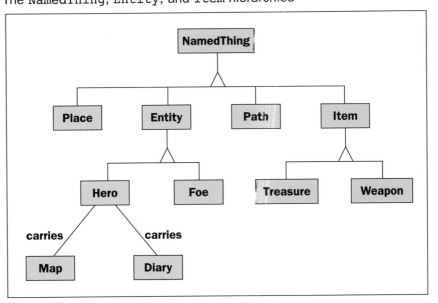

The principal advantage of creating class hierarchies is code sharing. The class `NamedThing` will include instance variables for name and description and instance methods for accessing them. These variables and methods are then accessible to all the subclasses of `NamedThings`. However, class hierarchies also have a disadvantage. Classes in a hierarchy become interdependent, and code changes higher up in a hierarchy can adversely affect classes lower in the hierarchy. If the logical relationship between the classes in a hierarchy is weak, these adverse effects are more likely to occur. In the present situation it seems reasonable to think of `Heroine` and `Foe` as types of `Entity`, so we do not expect unfavorable consequences later.

We can develop additional hierarchal relationships between the classes if we are willing to ignore our own advice about there being a logical relationship between the classes. For instance, in Figure 12-6, we see that `Entity` and `Place` are both associated with many instances of `Item`, and in the final implementation of the system both are likely to contain a list of items. Consequently, we could introduce an abstract superclass of `Entity` and `Place` called `ThingWithItems`, but doing so feels like a distortion of the game's inherent structure that would outweigh any benefit from code sharing.

We close this section by examining the relationship between the diary and the events it records. All the events have time and place in common, which suggest an `Event` class. In addition, each type of event (move, pickup, and battle) has its own unique data requirements, thus yielding the hierarchy shown in Figure 12-8.

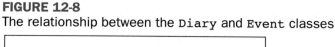

FIGURE 12-8
The relationship between the `Diary` and `Event` classes

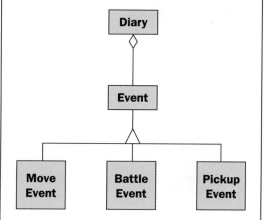

Assigning Responsibilities

Eventually, we must decide all the details concerning how classes interact. We will need to determine completely and exactly who sends what messages to whom. As a first step in this process, we assign a set of responsibilities to each class.

We begin by rereading the problem description, looking for any hints indicating the responsibilities of the objects. In general terms, an object is responsible for remembering its internal state (instance variables) and for responding to messages sent to it by other objects (methods). Unfortunately, there are usually numerous different ways of partitioning the responsibilities among objects. But some ways will seem more natural and lead to simpler code than others. As nouns help identify classes and their attributes, so verbs in a problem's description frequently indicate the methods that classes must implement. Sometimes it takes several iterations to assign responsibilities in what seems like a reasonable manner. Following the advice we gave earlier about distributing responsibilities among the classes rather than allowing any single class to assume a disproportionate role, we arrive at the distribution illustrated in Table 12-3.

TABLE 12-3
Distribution of class responsibilities

CLASS	RESPONSIBILITIES
GameView	Provides the graphical user interface to the game. Communicates user-initiated commands to the GameWorld. Obtains file names from the user. Tells the GameFile to perform input and output operations.
GameWorld	Knows the state of the game and makes this information available to the interface. Responds to user-initiated commands. Responds to messages from the GameFile during the process of transferring a game to and from a file.
GameFile	Knows the structure of the text file used to store a game. On input, it reads a file and communicates the content to the GameWorld. On output, it asks the GameWorld for its contents and stores these contents in a file.
NamedThing	Knows its name and description.
Item	Same as NamedThing and can be associated with places and entities.
Treasure	Same as Item and has a value.
Weapon	Same as Item and has a force.
Place	Same as NamedThing and can be associated with paths.
Path	Same as NamedThing and can be associated with places.
Entity	Same as NamedThing and can compute its battle number. Knows its strength, the force of its weapons, and the value of its treasures.
Heroine	Same as Entity and can move, pick up items, and initiate a battle against a foe. Knows how many lives remain. Updates her Map and Diary.
Foe	Same as Entity, can respond to a blow from the heroine and can drop items when defeated.
Map	Knows where the heroine has been and can display this information in a readable form.
Diary	Knows the events initiated by the heroine and can display this information in a readable form.
Event	There are three types of events. Each entity knows how to record a particular type of event.

That concludes our analysis. We now understand the problem thoroughly. We have designed an interface and a suitable file structure for the game. We know the classes, their relationships, and their major responsibilities.

EXERCISE 12.4

1. Does UML provide any support for describing user requirements? If so, what form does this support take?

2. How do we recognize classes and attributes from an informal description of user requirements?

EXERCISE 12.4 Continued

3. Describe in English the meaning of the expression 0..1 from a UML class diagram.

4. Describe in English the meaning of the expression 0..* from a UML class diagram.

5. Explain the difference between aggregation (the has-a relationship) and inheritance (the is-a relationship) and give one example of each.

6. Give an informal description in English of the relationships expressed by the following class diagram:

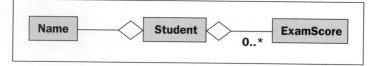

7. Draw a class diagram that illustrates the relationships among the classes in the following informal description: A library has many books and patrons and a patron can borrow up to three books.

8. Draw a class diagram that illustrates the relationships among the classes in the following informal description: A bank has many accounts. Accounts can be checking accounts, savings accounts, or credit accounts.

12.5 Design

Design is more exacting and technically difficult than analysis. It consists of devising the patterns of communication needed to support the game. In UML, this is done using *collaboration diagrams*. We proceed by identifying the game's principal activities and developing a pattern of communication to support each. In the present situation, activities are initiated at the user interface and correspond to selecting menu options and clicking and double-clicking on list items. In what follows, we investigate some typical activities in detail. Other activities are left as exercises for the interested reader.

Activity: Select a Path

We begin with one of the simplest activities. The user clicks on a path. The interface responds by displaying a description of the path. The description does not include information about where the path goes. That can be discovered only by commanding the heroine to move along the path. We present our implementation strategy in three forms. First, we write a narrative that describes the sequences of messages sent. Second, we summarize the narrative in a collaboration diagram. And third, we write pseudocode for the methods revealed in the previous two steps.

The Narrative

Before beginning, we must point out that narratives are often the result of experimentation. When the best solution is not obvious, the designer tries several different patterns of communication and picks the one that is simplest. Following then, is our narrative for the activity of selecting a path:

■ When the user clicks on a path name, the Java virtual machine calls the method listItemSelected in the GameView. This method determines which list the user clicked and calls a helper method.

■ The helper method, displaySelectedPath, asks the GameWorld to get the path's name and description by sending it the message getPathString(pathName).

■ The method getPathString in GameWorld asks the heroine for the current place by sending her the message getPlace. We assume that the GameWorld knows the heroine and the heroine always knows where she is located.

■ Once the GameWorld knows the current place, it asks the place to get the path with the indicated name by sending the message getPath(pathName) to the place. We assume that a place has a list of all the paths leading from that place.

■ The GameWorld now asks the path retrieved in the previous step for its name description by sending it the message toString. This description is then returned to the helper method in the GameView, where it is displayed in the text area.

The Collaboration Diagram

The collaboration diagram in Figure 12-9 shows a graphical representation of the narrative. The diagram is not able to capture all the nuances of the narrative, but it does provide an excellent overview. In the figure, rectangles represent objects of the indicated classes. The colons (:) are required. Arrows are labeled with the names of methods, and numbers indicate the sequence in which the methods are activated.

FIGURE 12-9
Collaboration diagram for the activity of selecting a path

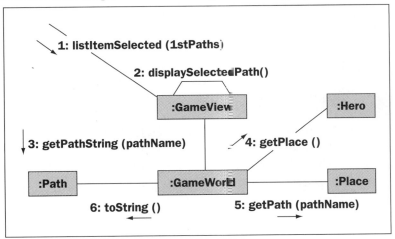

The Pseudocode

The narrative and the collaboration diagram provide an excellent basis for writing pseudocode (shown following) that further clarifies our intentions. As part of the pseudocode, we also list needed instance variables.

```
GameView    private GameWorld gameWorld;
            private JList lstPaths;      // The list of path names

            public void listItemSelected(JList listObj){
                ...
                else if (listObj == lstPaths) displaySelectedPath();
                ...
            }

            private void displaySelectedPath(){
                String pathName = selected path name;
                String str = gameWorld.getPathString(pathName);
                display str in the text area;
            }

GameWorld   private Heroine heroine;

            public String getPathString(String pathName){
                Place heroineLocation = heroine.getPlace();
                Path selectedPath = heroineLocation.getPath(pathName);
                return selectedPath.toString();

Heroine     private Place place;           // the heroine's location

            public Place getPlace(){
                return place;
            }

Place       private List paths;            // list of paths leading from place

            public Path getPath(String pathName){
                Path namedPath = search the list of paths for the named path;
                return namedPath;
            }

Path        public String toString(){
                return name + ": " + description;
            }
```

Before we consider the next activity, let us note some important points about the activity just discussed:

■ **Changes During Implementation**—It is inevitable that the code written during implementation will vary slightly from the plans made during design. In particular, some of a class's internal helper methods may not show up when we are writing the collaboration diagrams and pseudocode. This tends to make the diagrams and pseudocode incomplete rather than incorrect. However, it is always a good idea to update the collaboration diagrams as changes occur. On the other hand, once the system has been implemented, the pseudocode has served its purpose and can be thrown away.

■ **The Role of the GameWorld**—Notice the intermediary role the GameWorld plays in the previous scheme. The interface, GameView, always communicates with the GameWorld rather than directly with the various elements within the world. This level of indirection seems awkward, but it isolates the view from changes in the model and vice versa.

■ **Class Summary Diagrams**—The additional information gained during the previous process can be added to class summary diagrams. We illustrate with just two (shown following), but in practice we would do the same thing for all the classes.

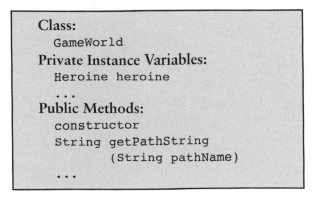

```
Class:
    GameWorld
Private Instance Variables:
    Heroine heroine

    ...
Public Methods:
    constructor
    String getPathString
            (String pathName)

    ...
```

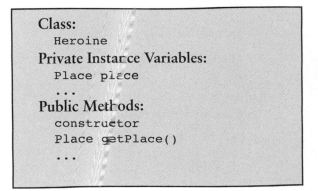

```
Class:
    Heroine
Private Instance Variables:
    Place place

    ...
Public Methods:
    constructor
    Place getPlace()

    ...
```

Activity: Pick Up an Item

Picking up an item involves a fairly complex pattern of communications. This time we skip the narrative and present just a collaboration diagram (Figure 12-10) and associated pseudocode. Before presenting either, however, we must have a clear statement of the expected behavior. We assume that the user double-clicks an item in the **Place Items** list. If there are any foes in the place or if the heroine has no lives left, then the action fails and a message is displayed in the text area; otherwise, the selected item is moved from the place's list to the heroine's list and the interface is updated.

FIGURE 12-10

Collaboration diagram for the activity of picking up an item

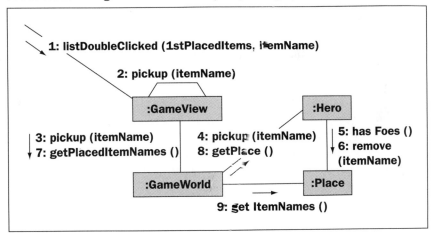

In Figure 12-10, messages 1 through 6 cover removing the item from the place and adding it to the heroine. Messages 7 through 9 update the **Place Items** list in the user interface. For the sake of simplicity, we have omitted from the collaboration diagram and the pseudocode the details of updating the heroine's diary.

```
GameView      private GameWorld gameWorld;
              private JList lstPlaceItems; // The list of place item names

              public void listDoubleClicked (JList listObj, String
              itemClicked){
                  ...
                  else if (listObj == lstPlaceItems) pickup(itemClicked);
                  ...
              }

              private void pickup(String itemName){
                  String errorMessage = gameWorld.pickup(itemName);
                  if (errorMessage.equals(""){
                      String[] names = gameWorld.getPlaceItemNames();
                      update lstPlaceItems with the names;
                  }else{
                      display errorMessage in the text area;
                  }
              }

GameWorld     private Heroine heroine;

              public String pickup(String itemName){
                  return heroine.pickup(itemName);
              }

              public String[] getPlaceItemNames(){
                  return heroine.getPlace().getItemNames();
              }

Heroine       private Place place;        // the heroine's location
              private List items;         // located in class Entity
              private int lives;          // number of lives remaining

              public String pickup(String itemName){
                  if (lives == 0)
                      return "The heroine is out of lives and cannot pick up.";
                  else if (place.hasFoes())
                      return "Cannot pick up. There are foes present.";
                  else{
                      Item item = place.removeItem(itemName);
                      items.add(item);
                      return "";          // No error message.
                  }
              }

              // getPlace already presented
```

```
Place        private List items;
             private List foes;

             public boolean hasFoes(){
                 return false if the foes list is empty else true;
             }

             public Item remove(String itemName){
                 remove the named item from the list;
                 return the item;
             }
```

Activity: Move

The move activity is initiated when the user double-clicks a name in the **Paths** list. If the heroine has no lives left, she is not able to move. After the move is completed, several aspects of the interface are updated. These updated items are detailed in Table 12-4.

TABLE 12-4
Updated aspects of the interface

INTERFACE ELEMENT	CHANGE MADE
Paths list	The list shows the names of all paths leading from the place to which the heroine has moved. We will call this "the new place" for convenience.
Entity list	The list shows the names of all entities located in the new place.
Place Items list	The list shows the names of all items located in the new place.
Descriptions text area	The text area displays the name and description of the new place.

In the collaboration diagram (Figure 12-11) and pseudocode (shown following), we update only the Paths list and ignore the process of updating the Entities list, the Place Items list, and the description in the text area. We also omit the messages and classes needed to update the heroine's diary.

FIGURE 12-11
Collaboration diagram for the activity of moving

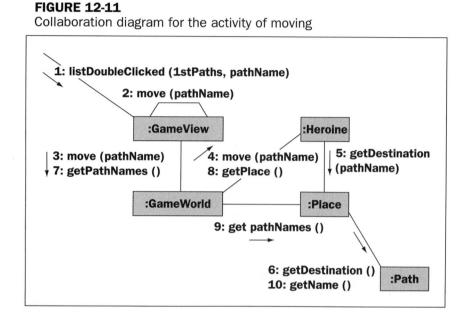

```
GameView    private GameWorld gameWorld;
            private JList lstPaths;        // List of path names

            public void listDoubleClicked(JList listObj, String
            itemClicked){
               ...
               else if (listObj == lstPaths) move(itemClicked);
               ...
            }

            private void move(String pathName){
                String errorMessage = gameWorld.move(pathName);
                if (errorMessage.equals("")){
                    String[] pathNames = gameWorld.getPathNames();
                    display pathNames;
                    other updates to the interface go here ...
                }else
                    display errorMessage in text area;
            }

GameWorld   private Heroine heroine;

            public String move(String pathName){
                return heroine.move(pathName);
            }

            public String[] getPathNames(){
```

```
                                return heroine.getPlace().getPathNames();
                            }

Heroine         private Place place;

                public String move(String pathName){
                    if (lives == 0)
                        return "The heroine is out of lives and cannot move.";
                    else{
                        place = place.getDestination(pathName);
                        return "";
                    }
                }

                // getPlace() presented in a previous subsection

Place           private List paths;            // list of paths leading from place

                public Place getDestination(String pathName){
                    Path namedPath = search the list of paths for the named path;
                    Place destination = namedPath.getDestination();
                    return destination;
                }

                public String[] getPathNames(){
                    traverse the list of paths;
                    ask each path for its name (path.getName());
                    build an array of the path names;
                    return the array of path names;
                }

Path            private Place destination;
                private String name;                    // located in class NamedThing

                public Place getDestination(){
                    return destination;
                }

                public String getName(){                // located in class NamedThing
                    return name;
                }
```

These examples demonstrate the overall approach taken during design. By the time we have repeated the process for all the game's activities, we should know exactly how to implement the system.

EXERCISE 12.5

1. Why are analysis and design separate steps in the software development process?

2. Explain how activities are used in the design process.

3. Explain how narratives are used in the design process.

4. Explain how collaboration diagrams are used in the design process.

5. Explain how you write pseudocode using collaboration diagrams.

6. What information goes into a class summary diagram?

12.6 Implementation

It seems strange to start discussing the implementation while the design is incomplete; however, doing so makes a great deal of sense. If we are somehow on the wrong track and our planned design contains unanticipated flaws, we would like to know about the problems sooner rather than later. Therefore, we now propose implementing the system in stages, one activity at a time. If there are flaws, we can correct them before going too far in the wrong direction.

Loading the game from a text file is the first activity we must implement, but unfortunately, it is the most complex and involves techniques that are not discussed until later in the book (Lesson 20, which is about files). To circumvent this problem (commonly referred to as a "workaround" in programming jargon), we instead write a method that creates a hard-coded game world. The method, `createHardCodedWorld`, resides in the `GameWorld` class and is called when the user selects menu option File/Open. With the hard-coded game world as a basis, we implement the activities of selecting a path and moving. All other aspects of the game are omitted. A listing of this limited code follows, and we encourage you to compare the code carefully with the diagrams presented during analysis and design. Code for the complete system is available from your instructor, and end-of-lesson projects lead you through the design and implementation of the other activities.

```java
abstract public class NamedThing{
    protected String name;
    protected String description;

    public NamedThing(String n, String d){
        name = n;
        description = d;
    }

    public String getName(){
        return name;
    }

    public String toString(){
        return name + ": " + description;
    }
}
```

```java
import java.util.*;

abstract public class Entity extends NamedThing{
   protected int strength;
   protected List items;

   public Entity(String nm, String desc, int strngth){
      super(nm, desc);
      strength = strngth;
      items = new ArrayList();
   }
}
```

```java
public class Heroine extends Entity{
   private Place place;
   private int lives;

   public Heroine(String nm, String desc, int strngth){
      super(nm, desc, strngth);
      lives = 9;
   }

   public Place getPlace(){
      return place;
   }

   public String move(String pathName){
      if (lives == 0)
         return "The heroine is out of lives and cannot move.";
      else{
         Place newPlace = place.getDestination(pathName);
         place = newPlace;
         return "";
      }
   }

   public void startAt(Place plc){
      place = plc;
   }
}
```

```java
public class Path extends NamedThing{
   private Place destination;

   public Path(String nm, String desc, Place dest){
      super(nm, desc);
      destination = dest;
   }
```

```java
    public Place getDestination(){
        return destination;
    }
}
```

```java
import java.util.*;

public class Place extends NamedThing{
    private List paths;
    private List items;
    private List foes;

    public Place(String n, String d){
        super(n, d);
        paths = new ArrayList();
        items = new ArrayList();
        foes = new ArrayList();
    }

    public void addPath(Path path){
        paths.add(path);
    }

    public Place getDestination(String pathName){
        Path namedPath = getPath(pathName);
        return namedPath.getDestination();
    }

    public Path getPath(String pathName){
        Path namedPath = null;
        for (int i = 0; i < paths.size(); i++){
            namedPath = (Path)paths.get(i);
            if (namedPath.name.equals(pathName)) break;
        }
        return namedPath;
    }

    public String[] getPathNames(){
        String[] pathNames = new String[paths.size()];
        for (int i = 0; i < paths.size(); i++)
            pathNames[i] = ((Path)paths.get(i)).getName();
        return pathNames;

    }
}
```

```
public class GameWorld{
    private Heroine heroine;

    public void createHardCodedWorld(){
        Place entrance
          = new Place("Castle Entrance",
          "You are standing in front of a drawbridge.");
        Place courtyard
          = new Place("Courtyard",
          "Horses' hooves ring against rough cobbles.");
        Place stables
          = new Place("Stables",
          "Twenty horse stalls line the walls.");
        Place greatHall
          = new Place("Great Hall",
          "You are in a richly furnished hall.");
        Place dungeon
          = new Place("Dungeon",
          "Groans of the oppressed fill the air.");
        Place turret
          = new Place("Turret",
          "You are looking out over the castle's lands.");
        Place well
          = new Place("Well",
          "You have fallen into a deep, slippery well. \nThere is no way
          out.");

        heroine
          = new Heroine("Sue",
          "Our strong and worthy heroine, who never says no" +
          "\nto a rousing adventure.", 10);
        heroine.startAt(entrance);

        entrance.addPath
          (new Path("Drawbridge",
          "Rotting planks and rusting chains do not a good bridge make.",
          courtyard));
        courtyard.addPath
          (new Path("Drawbridge",
          "Rotting planks and rusting chains do rot a good bridge make.",
          entrance));

        courtyard.addPath
          (new Path("South",
          "Careful where you step.",
          stables));
        stables.addPath
          (new Path("North",
          "Careful where you step.",
          courtyard));
```

```
     courtyard.addPath
        (new Path("Great Doors",
        "Push hard. The doors are immense.",
        greatHall));
     greatHall.addPath
        (new Path("Great Doors",
        "Pull hard. The doors are immense.",
        courtyard));

     greatHall.addPath
        (new Path("Stairs Up",
        "A winding staircase leads up into the darkness.",
         turret));
     turret.addPath
        (new Path("Stairs Down",
        "A winding staircase leads down into the darkness.",
        greatHall));

     greatHall.addPath
        (new Path("Stairs Down",
        "A winding staircase leads down into the darkness.",
        dungeon));
     dungeon.addPath
        (new Path("Stairs Up",
        "A winding staircase leads up into the darkness.",
        greatHall));

     greatHall.addPath
        (new Path("Secret Door",
        "This door looks little used.",
        well));
  }

public String[] getPathNames(){
   return heroine.getPlace().getPathNames();
}

public String getPathString(String pathName){
   return heroine.getPlace().getPath(pathName).toString();
}

public String getPlaceString(){
   if (heroine == null)
      return "You must open a game file first.";
   else
      return heroine.getPlace().toString();
}

public String move(String pathName){
   return heroine.move(pathName);
}
}
```

```java
import javax.swing.*;
import BreezySwing.*;

public class GameView extends GBFrame {

    // Menu items
    private JMenuItem miOpen;

    // Labels
    private JLabel lbPaths;
    private JLabel lbEntities;
    private JLabel lbPlaceItems;
    private JLabel lbDescriptions;

    // Lists
    private JList lstPaths;
    private JList lstEntities;
    private JList lstPlacesItems;

    // Text area
    private JTextArea taDescription;

    // Other instance variables
    private GameWorld gameWorld;

//---------------------- Constructor

    public GameView(){

        // Set the window's title
        setTitle("The Treasures of Balbor");

        // Add menu items
        miOpen      = addMenuItem("File"   , "Open");

        // Add labels
        lbDescriptions = addLabel("Descriptions  " , 1,1,1,1);
        lbPaths        = addLabel("Paths         " , 8,1,1,1);
        lbEntities     = addLabel("Entities      " , 8,2,1,1);
        lbPlaceItems   = addLabel("Place Items   " , 8,3,1,1);

        // Add text area
        taDescription = addTextArea("" ,2,1,3,5);

        // Add lists
        lstPaths       = addList(9,1,1,6);
        lstEntities    = addList(9,2,1,6);
        lstPlacesItems = addList(9,3,1,6);

        // Instantiate the game world.
        gameWorld = new GameWorld();
    }
```

```java
//--------------------- Public Methods

    public void listDoubleClicked(JList listObj, String itemClicked){
       if (listObj == lstPaths)
          move(itemClicked);
    }

    public void listItemSelected(JList listObj){
       if (listObj == lstPaths)
          displaySelectedPath();
    }

    public void menuItemSelected(JMenuItem menuItemObj){
       if (menuItemObj == miOpen)
          open();
    }

//--------------------- public static void main

    public static void main(String[] args){
       GameView theGUI = new GameView();
       theGUI.setSize (600, 400);
       theGUI.setVisible (true);
    }

//--------------------- Private Methods

    private void displaySelectedPath(){
       String pathName = (String)(lstPaths.getSelectedValue());
       String str = gameWorld.getPathString(pathName);
       taDescription.setText(str);
    }

    private void move(String pathName){
       String errorMessage = gameWorld.move(pathName);
       if (! errorMessage.equals(""))
          taDescription.setText(errorMessage);
       else
          updateAllControls();
    }

    private void open(){
       gameWorld.createHardCodedWorld();
       updateAllControls();
    }

    private void updateAllControls(){
       // Update place description
       String str = gameWorld.getPlaceString();
       taDescription.setText(str);
```

```
        // Update lists
        updateList(lstPaths, gameWorld.getPathNames());
    }

    private void updateList(JList list, String[] names){
        DefaultListModel listModel = (DefaultListModel)list.getModel();
        listModel.clear();
        for (int i = 0; i < names.length; i++)
            listModel.addElement(names[i]);
    }
}
```

*E*XERCISE 12.6

1. Why bother implementing the code for a software system when its design is incomplete?

SUMMARY

In this lesson, you learned:

■ The Unified Modeling Language (UML) provides a graphical notation for depicting the relationships among classes and the manner in which objects communicate.

■ A class diagram can be constructed from an informal description of user requirements. The three major types of relationships among classes are the is-a relationship (inheritance), the has-a relationship (aggregation), and the knows-a relationship (any other).

■ Classes and their attributes are derived from the nouns in a problem description.

■ A narrative of the communication among objects can be derived from a description of activities in a software system. This communication can then be depicted in collaboration diagrams, from which pseudocode can be derived.

VOCABULARY *Review*

Define the following terms:		
class diagram	is-a relationship	Unified Modeling Language
collaboration diagram	knows-a relationship	(UML)
has-a relationship		

REVIEW *Questions*

FILL IN THE BLANK

Complete the following sentences by writing the correct word or words in the blanks provided.

1. The leading graphical notation used in the analysis and design of software is called _____.

2. The _____ provides a graphical description of the relationships among classes.

3. _____ is a relationship in which one class contains one or more other classes.

4. _____ is a relationship in which one class is a parent of one or more other classes.

5. The notation for expressing one or more instances of something is _____.

6. The _____ provides a graphical description of the way in which objects communicate.

7. During design, activity can be expressed informally in a(n) _____.

8. You can pick out the classes and attributes of a software system by looking at the _____ in a problem description.

9. The last step in a design is to express the methods of the software system using _____.

10. The user requirements of a software system can be described with _____.

PROJECTS

What follows are implementation and design projects based on the adventure game. For all of them you should at least develop collaboration diagrams and pseudocode; however, to obtain greater satisfaction, you will probably want to write implementing code. As a starting point for your implementations, you could use the code presented in Section 12.6; however, this code builds a rather incomplete adventure world. So we have provided additional code to build an almost entire world; only maps, diaries, and events are missing. This additional code includes all needed constructors and other supporting methods. Your instructor can provide this code in a machine-readable format. You should read and run this code before proceeding. With the new code, as you move from place to place, all the interface lists are updated. If you do all the projects, you will have implemented the complete game. We recommend that you do the projects in the order listed. Except when explicitly requested, ignore maps, diaries, and events. A complete executable version of the game, without source code, is available from your instructor.

PROJECT 12-1

Incorporate into the game the activity of clicking on an entity's name. Repeat for the activity of clicking on an item's name.

PROJECT 12-2

Incorporate the menu option **Reports/Current Location.**

PROJECT 12-3

Implement the activity of picking up an item. Remember the heroine cannot pick up an item if a live foe is present.

PROJECT 12-4

Draw collaboration diagrams, write pseudocode, and implement the activity of fighting a battle.

PROJECT 12-5

Incorporate a map into the game. This depends on a new class called Map. The map itself is stored as a string in the Map class. You will find the String methods indexOf and substring useful in this endeavor. Before adding a new place name to the map, use indexOf to determine if the name is already present. When you travel along a path, you will learn its destination. If you have not been along this path before, then on the map the destination shows as a question mark, which should be replaced by the destination name.

PROJECT 12-6

Incorporate the diary and events into the game. Show all times in the diary as zero.

PROJECT 12-7

Incorporate into the game the ElapsedTimer class shown in the following code:

```
import java.util.*;

public class ElapsedTimer {
   private int startTime;
   private long clockStart;

   public ElapsedTimer(int startTm) {
      startTime = startTm;
      clockStart = (new Date()).getTime();
   }

   public int getTime(){
      long clockNow = (new Date()).getTime();
      return startTime + (int)((clockNow - clockStart) / 1000);
   }
}
```

CRITICAL *Thinking*

Jill is trying to decide whether to use UML to describe the analysis and design of a software system. Explain to her the costs and benefits of using this notation.

LINEAR COLLECTIONS: LISTS

OBJECTIVES

Upon completion of this lesson, you should be able to:

- Distinguish fundamental categories of collections, such as linear, hierarchical, graph, and unordered.

- Understand the basic features of lists and their applications.

- Use the list interface and the major list implementation classes.

- Recognize the difference between index-based operations and content-based operations on lists.

- Use an iterator to perform position-based operations on a list.

- Understand the difference between an iterator and a list iterator.

- Describe the restrictions on the use of list operations and iterator operations.

Estimated Time: 3.5 hours

VOCABULARY

abstract data type (ADT)

abstraction

backing store

children

collection

content-based operation

free list

graph collection

head

hierarchical collection

index-based operation

iterator

linear collection

list iterator

object heap

parent

position-based operation

tail

unordered collection

During the first half of this book, we introduced you to the basic elements of programming and then showed you how to organize a software system in terms of cooperating methods, objects, and classes. In this and the next few lessons, we explore several frequently used classes called *collections*. Although they differ in structure and use, collections all have the same fundamental purpose—they help programmers organize data in programs effectively. In this lesson and the next two lessons, we examine the use of several different types of collections from a client's perspective. Lessons 16 through 18 consider the issues in implementing them. This lesson begins with an overview of collections and then explores the most widely used type, the list.

13.1 Overview of Collections

A collection, as the name implies, is a group of items that we want to treat as a conceptual unit. Nearly every nontrivial piece of software involves the use of collections, and although much of what you learn in computer science comes and goes with changes in technology, the basic principles of organizing collections endure. The arrays discussed in Lessons 8 and 10 are the most common and fundamental type of collection. Other important types of collections include strings, stacks, lists, queues, binary search trees, heaps, graphs, maps, sets, and bags. Collections can be homogeneous, meaning that all items in the collection must be of the same type, or heterogeneous, meaning the items can be of different types. In most languages, arrays are homogeneous, although as we saw in Lesson 10, an array of objects can contain different types of objects. In some collections, the items are restricted to being objects. In other collections, items are restricted to one type only, such as characters within a string. In still others, the items can be objects or primitive data types such as `double` or `int`. An important distinguishing characteristic of collections is the manner in which they are organized. We now give a survey of four main categories of collections: linear collections, hierarchical collections, graph collections, and unordered collections.

Linear Collections

The items in a *linear collection* are, like people in a line, ordered by position. Each item except the first has a unique predecessor, and each item except the last has a unique successor. As shown in Figure 13-1, D2's predecessor is D1, and its successor is D3.

FIGURE 13-1
A linear collection

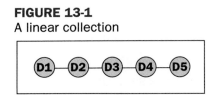

Everyday examples of linear collections are grocery lists, stacks of dinner plates, and a line of customers waiting at a bank.

Hierarchical Collections

Data items in *hierarchical collections* are ordered in a structure reminiscent of an upside down tree. Each data item except the one at the top has just one predecessor, its *parent*, but potentially many successors, called its *children*. As shown in Figure 13-2, D3's predecessor (parent) is D1, and its successors (children) are D4, D5, and D6.

FIGURE 13-2
A hierarchical collection

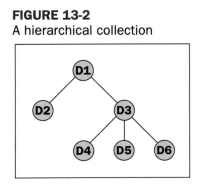

A company's organization tree and a book's table of contents are examples of hierarchical collections.

Graph Collections

A *graph collection*, also called a *graph*, is a collection in which each data item can have many predecessors and many successors. As shown in Figure 13-3, all elements connected to D3 are considered to be both its predecessors and successors.

FIGURE 13-3
A graph collection

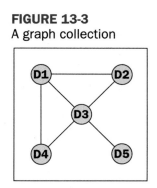

Examples of graphs are maps of airline routes between cities and electrical wiring diagrams for buildings. We do not explore graphs further in this book.

Unordered Collections

As the name implies, items in an ***unordered collection*** are not in any particular order, and one cannot meaningfully speak of an item's predecessor or successor. Figure 13-4 shows such a structure.

FIGURE 13-4
An unordered collection

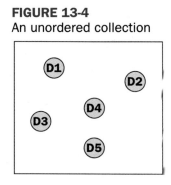

A bag of marbles is an example of an unordered collection. Although one can put marbles into and take marbles out of a bag, once in the bag, the marbles are in no particular order.

Operations on Collections

Collections are typically dynamic rather than static, meaning they can grow or shrink with the needs of a problem. Also, their contents change throughout the course of a program. The actual manipulations that can be performed on a collection vary with the type of collection being used, but generally, the operations fall into several broad categories that are outlined in Table 13-1.

TABLE 13-1
Categories of operations on collections

CATEGORY	DESCRIPTION
Search and retrieval	These operations search a collection for a given target item or for an item at a given position. If the item is found, either it or its position is returned. If the item is not found, a distinguishing value such as `null` or −1 is returned.
Removal	This operation deletes a given item or the item at a given position.
Insertion	This operation adds an item to a collection and usually at a particular position within the collection.
Replacement	Replacement combines removal and insertion into a single operation.
Traversal	This operation visits each item in a collection. Depending on the type of collection, the order in which the items are visited can vary. During a traversal, items can be accessed or modified. Some traversals also permit the insertion or removal of items from the underlying collection.
Test for equality	If items can be tested for equality, then the collections containing them can also be tested for equality. To be equal, two collections must contain equal items at corresponding positions. For unordered collections, of course, the requirement of corresponding positions can be ignored. Some collections, such as strings, also can be tested for their position in a natural ordering using the comparisons less than and greater than.
Determination of size	Every collection contains a finite number of items. This number is the collection's size. Some collections also have a maximum capacity, or number of places available for storing items. An egg carton is a familiar example of a container with a maximum capacity.
Cloning	This operation creates a copy of an existing collection. The copy usually shares the same items as the original, a feat that is impossible in the real world. In the real world, a copy of a bag of marbles could not contain the same marbles as the original bag, given a marble's inability to be in two places at once. The rules of cyberspace are more flexible, however, and there are many situations in which we make these strange copies of collections. What we are copying is the structure of the collection, not the elements it contains. It is possible, however, and sometimes useful to produce a deep copy of a collection in which both the structure and the items are copied.

Abstract Data Types

From the foregoing discussion, we see that a collection consists of data organized in a particular manner together with methods for manipulating the data. Those who use collections in their programs have a rather different perspective on collections than those who are responsible for implementing them in the first place, however.

Users of collections need to know how to declare and use each type of collection. From their perspective, a collection is seen as a means for storing and accessing data in some predetermined manner, without concern for the details of the collection's implementation. From the users' perspective a collection is an *abstraction*, and for this reason, in computer science collections are called *abstract data types* (ADTs).

Developers of collections, on the other hand, are concerned with implementing a collection's behavior in the most efficient manner possible, with the goal of providing the best performance to users of the collections. For each category of collections (linear, hierarchical, etc.), we examine one or more abstract data types and one or more implementations of that type.

The idea of abstraction is not unique to a discussion of collections. It is an important principle in many endeavors both in and out of computer science. For example, when studying the effect of gravity on a falling object, we try to create an experimental situation in which we can ignore incidental details such as the color and taste of the object (what sort of apple was it that hit Newton on the head?). When studying mathematics, we do not concern ourselves with what the numbers might be used to count, fishhooks or arrowheads, but try to discover abstract and enduring principles of numbers. A house plan is an abstraction of the physical house, and it allows us to focus on structural elements without being overwhelmed by incidental details such as the color of the kitchen cabinets, which is important to the eventual house but not to the house's structural relationships. In computer science, we also use abstraction as a technique for ignoring or hiding details that are, for the moment, inessential, and we often build up a software system layer by layer, each layer being treated as an abstraction by the layers above that utilize it. Without abstraction, we would need to consider all aspects of a software system simultaneously, an impossible task. Of course, the details must be considered eventually, but in a small and manageable context.

In Java, methods are the smallest unit of abstraction, classes and their interfaces are the next in size, and packages are the largest. In this text, we will implement abstract data types as classes and their interfaces.

Multiple Implementations

A major concern of the computer scientist is how best to implement different types of collections. There are usually numerous possibilities; however, many of these take so much space or run so slowly that they can be dismissed as pointless. Those that remain tend to be based on four underlying approaches to organizing and accessing memory:

1. Arrays

2. Linear linked structures

3. Other linked structures

4. Hashing into an array

We discuss the first two approaches in Lesson 16, and we encounter the other two later in the book when we study the implementation of hierarchical and unordered collections.

We close this section with a mundane detail. When there is more than one way to implement a collection, programmers define a variable of an interface type and assign to it an object that uses the desired implementation. For instance, `java.util` includes three classes that implement the `List` interface. These classes are `LinkedList`, `ArrayList`, and `Vector`. In the following code snippet, the programmer has chosen the `LinkedList` implementation:

```
List lst = new LinkedList();
```

To select a different implementation, the programmer just substitutes `ArrayList()` or `Vector()` for `LinkedList()` in this code.

Collections and Casting

With the exception of arrays, strings, string buffers, and bit sets, Java collections can contain any kind of object and nothing but objects. As we first saw in Lesson 10, these constraints have several consequences:

1. Primitive types, such as `int`, must be placed in a wrapper before being added to a collection.

2. It is impossible to declare a collection that is restricted to just one type of object.

> **Hot Tip** ◎
>
> For examples of casting as used with a collection, you should review the last section of Lesson 10.

3. Items coming out of a collection are, from the compiler's perspective, instances of `Object`, and they cannot be sent type-specific messages until they have been cast.

EXERCISE 13.1

1. Give one example from everyday life of a linear collection, a hierarchical collection, a graph collection, and an unordered collection.

2. For each of the following objects, give the type of collection (linear, hierarchical, graph, or unordered) that would best fit its representation in software:
   a. A recipe
   b. A box of cereal
   c. An outline of a book
   d. A map of the Interstate Highway System

3. What is abstraction? Give an example.

4. An abstract data type consists of an interface and one or more implementing classes. Explain.

5. Why is casting needed when using collections?

13.2 Lists

Overview

A list supports manipulation of items at any point within a linear collection. Some common examples of lists include:

- A *recipe*, which is a list of instructions.
- A *string*, which is a list of characters.
- A *document*, which is a list of words.
- A *file*, which is a list of data blocks on disk.

In all these examples, order is critically important, and shuffling the items renders the collections meaningless; however, the items in a list are not necessarily sorted. Words in a dictionary and names in a phone book are examples of sorted lists, but the words in this paragraph equally form a list and are unsorted. Although the items in a list are always logically contiguous, they need not be physically contiguous. Array implementations of lists use physical position to represent logical order, but linked implementations do not.

The first item in a list is at its **head**, whereas the last item in a list is at its **tail**. In a list, items retain position relative to each other over time, and additions and deletions affect predecessor/successor relationships only at the point of modification. Figure 13-5 shows how a list changes in response to a succession of operations. The operations are described in Table 13-2.

FIGURE 13-5
The states in the lifetime of a list

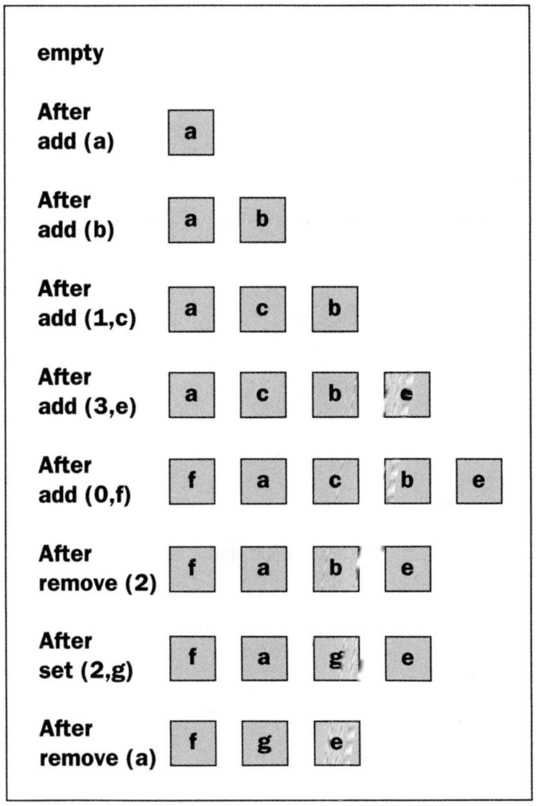

empty	
After add (a)	a
After add (b)	a b
After add (1,c)	a c b
After add (3,e)	a c b e
After add (0,f)	f a c b e
After remove (2)	f a b e
After set (2,g)	f a g e
After remove (a)	f g e

TABLE 13-2
List operations

OPERATION	WHAT IT DOES
add(o)	Adds object o to a list's tail.
add(i, o)	Inserts object o at the ith index in a list, where the first item is at index 0.
remove(o)	Removes the first instance of object o from a list.
remove(i)	Removes the object at the ith index in a list.
set(i, o)	Replaces the object at the ith index with object o.

Categories of List Operations

Except for the basic operations for determining size, equality of two lists, and cloning, there are no standard operations for lists. For instance, the operation of putting a new item in a list is sometimes called "add" and sometimes "insert." If we look at most textbooks on data structures and at the ADT list provided in Java, however, we can discern several broad categories of operations, which we call index-based operations, content-based operations, and position-based operations.

Index-based operations manipulate items at designated positions within a list. Suppose a list contains n items. Because a list is linearly ordered, we can unambiguously refer to an item in a list via its relative position from the head of the list using an index that runs from 0 to $n - 1$. Thus, the head is at index 0 and the tail is at index $n - 1$. Table 13-3 shows some fundamental index-based operations.

TABLE 13-3
Index-based operations

INDEX-BASED OPERATION	WHAT IT DOES
add(i, o)	Opens up a slot in the list at index i and inserts object o in this slot.
get(i)	Returns the object at index i.
remove(i)	Removes and returns the object at index i.
set(i, o)	Replaces the object at index i with the object o and returns the original object.

When viewed from this perspective, lists are sometimes called *vectors* or *sequences*, and in their use of indexes, they are reminiscent of arrays. However, an array is a concrete data type with a specific and unvarying implementation based on a single block of physical memory, whereas a list is an abstract data type that can be represented in a variety of different ways, among which are array implementations. In addition, a list has a much larger repertoire of basic operations than an array, even though all list operations can be mimicked by suitable sequences of array operations.

Like the array subscript operation, each index-based list operation throws an exception if the specified index is out of range. In the case of Java's list classes, this exception is an IndexOutOfBoundsException.

Content-based operations are based not on an index but on the content of a list. Most of these operations search for an object equal to a given object before taking further action. Table 13-4 outlines some basic content-based operations.

TABLE 13-4
Content-based operations

CONTENT-BASED OPERATION	WHAT IT DOES
add(o)	Adds object o at a list's tail.
contains(o)	Returns true if a list contains an object equal to object o.
indexOf(o)	Returns the index of the first instance of object o in a list.
remove(o)	Removes the first instance of object o from a list and returns true if o is removed, else returns false.

Position-based operations are performed relative to a currently established position within a list, and in `java.util`, they are provided via an *iterator*. An iterator is an object that allows a client to navigate through a list and perform various operations at the current position. We examine iterators later in this lesson.

The List Interface

Table 13-5 lists the methods in the interface `java.util.List`. The classes `ArrayList` and `LinkedList` both implement this interface. Note that the `List` interface is quite lengthy. The interface includes both the methods discussed thus far and also the methods in the `Collection` interface, which specifies more general methods supported by lists and other collections. We discuss the `Collection` interface in Lesson 15.

TABLE 13-5
The `List` interface

METHOD	DESCRIPTION
`void add(int index, Object element)`	Inserts the specified element at the specified position in this list.
`boolean add(Object o)`	Appends the specified element to the end of this list.
`boolean contains(Object o)`	Returns true if this list contains the specified element.
`Object get(int index)`	Returns the element at the specified position in this list.
`int indexOf(Object o)`	Returns the index in this list of the first occurrence of the specified element or –1 if this list does not contain this element.
`int lastIndexOf(Object o)`	Returns the index in this list of the last occurrence of the specified element or –1 if this list does not contain this element.
`Object remove(int index)`	Removes the element at the specified position in this list.
`boolean remove(Object o)`	Removes the first occurrence in this list of the specified element.
`Object set(int index, Object element)`	Replaces the element at the specified position in this list with the specified element and returns the old element.
`boolean isEmpty()`	Returns true if this list contains no elements.
`int size()`	Returns the number of elements in this list.
`boolean addAll(Collection c)`	Appends all of the elements in the specified collection to the end of this list, in the order that they are returned by the specified collection's iterator.
`boolean addAll(int index, Collection c)`	Inserts all of the elements in the specified collection into this list at the specified position.

TABLE 13-5 Continued
The List interface

METHOD	DESCRIPTION
void clear()	Removes all of the elements from this list.
Object clone()	Not officially listed here because it is inherited from Object.
boolean containsAll(Collection c)	Returns true if this list contains all of the elements of the specified collection.
boolean equals(Object o)	Compares the specified object with this list for equality.
int hashCode()	Returns the hash code value for this list. (Please ignore this method for now. We will discuss hashing in Lesson 17.)
Iterator iterator()	Returns an iterator over the elements in this list in proper sequence.
ListIterator listIterator()	Returns a list iterator of the elements in this list in proper sequence.
ListIterator listIterator(int index)	Returns a list iterator of the elements in this list in proper sequence, starting at the specified position in this list.
boolean removeAll(Collection c)	Removes from this list all of the elements that are contained in the specified collection.
boolean retainAll(Collection c)	Retains only the elements in this list that are contained in the specified collection.
List subList(int fromIndex, int toIndex)	Returns a view of the portion of this list between the specified fromIndex, inclusive, and toIndex, exclusive.
Object[] toArray()	Returns an array containing all of the elements in this list in proper sequence.
Object[] toArray(Object[] a)	Returns an array containing all of the elements in this list in proper sequence; the run-time type of the returned array is that of the specified array.
String toString()	Not officially listed here because it is inherited from Object.

To make certain that there are no ambiguities in the meaning of the operations shown in Table 13-5, we now present an example that shows a sequence of these operations in action. This sequence is listed in Table 13-6.

TABLE 13-6
The effects of some list operations

LIST OPERATION	STATE OF THE LIST AFTER THE OPERATION	VALUE RETURNED	COMMENT
			Initially, the list is empty.
add(0,a)	a		The list contains the single item a.
add(1,b)	a b		a is the head, b is the tail.
add(1,c)	a c b		c is at index 1.
isEmpty()	a c b	false	The list is not empty.
size()	a c b	3	The list contains three items.
indexOf(b)	a c b	2	The index of b is 2.
indexOf(q)	a c b	-1	q is not in the list.
contains(c)	a c b	true	c is in list.
get(1)	a c b	c	Return c, which is at index 1.
get(3)	a c b	exception	The index is out of range, so throw an exception.
set(2,e)	a c e	b	Replace b at index 2 with e and return b.
remove(0)	c e	a	Remove a at position 0 and return it. c is now at the head of the list.
remove(2)	c e	exception	The index is out of range, so throw an exception.
remove(1)	c	e	Remove and return e.
remove(0)		c	Remove and return c.
isEmpty()		true	The list is empty.
remove(0)		exception	The index is out of range, so throw an exception.
set(0,a)		exception	The index is out of range, so throw an exception.

Applications of Lists

Heap Storage Management

When you studied recursion, you learned one aspect of Java memory management, the call stack. Now we complete that discussion by showing how free space in the *object heap* can be managed using a linked list. Heap management schemes can have a significant impact on an application's overall performance, especially if the application creates and abandons many objects during the course of its execution. Implementers of Java virtual machines are therefore willing to spend a great deal of effort to organize the heap in the most efficient manner possible. Their elaborate solutions are beyond this book's scope, so we present a simplified scheme here.

In our scheme, contiguous blocks of free space on the heap are linked together in a *free list*. When an application instantiates a new object, the JVM searches the free list for the first block large enough to hold the object and returns any excess space to the free list. When the object is no longer needed, the garbage collector returns the object's space to the free list. The scheme, as stated, has two defects. Over time, large blocks on the free list become fragmented into many smaller blocks, and searching the free list for blocks of sufficient size can take $O(n)$ running time, where n is the number of blocks in the list. To counteract fragmentation, the garbage collector periodically reorganizes the free list by recombining physically adjacent blocks. To reduce search time, multiple free lists can be used. For instance, if an object reference requires 4 bytes, then list 1 could consist of blocks of size 4; list 2, blocks of size 8; list 3, blocks of size 16; list 4, blocks of size 32; and so on. The last list would contain all blocks over some designated size. In this scheme, space is always allocated in units of 4 bytes, and space for a new object is taken from the head of the first nonempty list containing blocks of sufficient size. Allocating space for a new object now takes $O(1)$ time unless the object requires more space than is available in the first block of the last list. At that point, the last list must be searched, giving the operation a maximum running time of $O(n)$, where n is the size of the last list.

In this discussion, we have completely ignored two difficult problems. The first problem has to do with deciding when to run the garbage collector. Running the garbage collector takes time away from the application, but not running it means the free lists are never replenished. The second problem concerns how the garbage collector identifies objects that are no longer referenced and, consequently, no longer needed. (This problem is not within the scope of this text.)

Organization of Files on a Disk

A computer's file system has three major components—a directory of files, the files themselves, and free space. To understand how these work together to create a file system, we first consider a disk's physical format. Figure 13-6 shows the standard arrangement. The disk's surface is divided into concentric *tracks*, and each track is further subdivided into *sectors*. The numbers of these vary depending on the disk's capacity and physical size; however, all tracks contain the same number of sectors and all sectors contain the same number of bytes. For the sake of this discussion, let us suppose that a sector contains 8 Kbytes of data plus a few additional bytes reserved for a pointer. A sector is the smallest unit of information transferred to and from the disk, regardless of its actual size, and a pair of numbers (t, s) specifies a sector's location on the disk, where t is the track number and s the sector number. Figure 13-6 shows a disk with n tracks. The k sectors in track 0 are labeled from 0 to $k - 1$.

FIGURE 13-6
Tracks and sectors on the surface of a disk

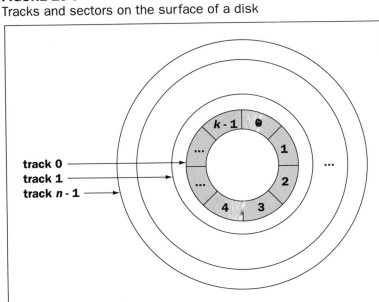

A file system's directory is organized as a hierarchical collection. The directory's internal structure is not a suitable topic for this lesson. However, let us suppose that it occupies the first few tracks on the disk and contains an entry for each file. This entry holds the file's name, creation date, size, and so forth. In addition, it holds the address of the sector containing the first bytes in the file. Depending on its size, a file might be completely contained within a single sector or it might span several sectors. Usually, the last sector is only partially full, and no attempt is made to recover the unused space. The sectors that make up a file do not need to be physically adjacent because each sector except the last one ends with a pointer to the sector containing the next portion of the file. Finally, sectors that are not in use are linked together in a free list. When new files are created, they are allocated space from this list, and when old files are deleted, their space is returned to the list.

Because all sectors are the same size and because space is allocated in sectors, a file system does not experience the same fragmentation problem encountered in Java's object heap. Nonetheless, there is still a difficulty. To transfer data to or from the disk, read/write heads must first be positioned to the correct track, the disk must rotate until the desired sector is under the heads, and then the transfer of data takes place. Of these three steps, the transfer of data takes the least time. Fortunately, data can be transferred to or from several adjacent sectors during a single rotation without the need to reposition the heads. Thus, a disk system's performance is optimized when multisector files are not scattered across the disk. Over time, however, as files of varying sizes are created and destroyed, this sort of scattering becomes frequent, and the file system's performance degrades. As a countermeasure, file systems include a utility, run either automatically or at the explicit request of the user, which reorganizes the file system so that the sectors in each file are contiguous and have the same physical and logical order.

Implementation of Other ADTs

Lists are frequently used to implement other ADTs, such as stacks and queues. There are two ways to do this:

1. Extend the list class, making the new class a subclass of the list class.

2. Use an instance of the list class within the new class and let the list contain the data items.

For example, `java.util` implements a `Stack` class by extending a list class called `Vector`. Extension is not a wise choice in this case, however, because this version of `Stack` inherits the methods from `Vector` that allow users to access items at positions other than the top, thus violating the spirit of the stack ADT. In the case of stacks and queues, a better design decision is to contain a list within the stack or queue. In that case, all of the list operations are available to the implementer, but only the essential stack or queue operations are available to the user. On the other hand, suppose we wanted to implement a sorted list, which is not part of `java.util`. A sorted list has 90 percent of the behavior of a list, including most of the indexed-based, object-based, and positional operations. The only methods that differ are `add`, which inserts an item in its proper place rather than at the end of the list, and mutators for other insertions or replacements, which are disallowed because they might violate the natural ordering of the objects in the list. Clearly in this case, sorted lists should extend the behavior of lists rather than contain them.

ADTs that use lists inherit their performance characteristics. For example, a stack that uses an array-based list has the performance characteristics of an array-based stack, whereas a stack that uses a link-based list has characteristics of a link-based stack.

The primary advantage of using a list ADT to implement another ADT is that coding becomes easier. Instead of operating on a concrete array or linked structure, the implementer of a stack need only call the appropriate list methods.

In Lesson 15 (Unordered Collections: Sets and Maps) and Lesson 18 (Implementing Trees and Priority Queues) we will see other situations in which lists can be used in the implementation of ADTs although, in the interest of optimizing performance, we do not always do so.

*E*XERCISE 13.2

1. Describe the difference between index-based and content-based operations on lists.

2. Assume that the list variable `list` has been assigned a new list object. Draw pictures of the state of the list after each of the following operations:

   a. `for (int i = 1; i <= 4; i++) list.add("" + i);`

   b. `list.remove(2);`

   c. `list.add(1, "5");`

   d. `list.remove("4");`

   e. `list.set(0, "8");`

EXERCISE 13.2 Continued

3. Write code segments to perform the following tasks with the list object named `list`:
   a. Remove all the objects from the list.
   b. Add the strings "1", "2", and "3" to positions 0, 1, and 2.
   c. Add the string "4" to the end of the list.
   d. Replace the object at position 1 with the string "6".
   e. Insert the string "7" at position 2.
   f. Display the size of the list and all its contents in the terminal window.

4. What is the object heap? Describe how the computer uses a list to manage the object heap.

5. Jill wants to represent a deck of cards for a game-playing program. Is a list a wise choice for this problem? Justify your answer.

Case Study: Maintain a List of Tasks (A To-Do List)

This case study consists of a program that maintains a to-do list. We are going to present a partial solution and leave its completion and extension for the end-of-lesson projects. The case study is divided into a view and model. Within the model, the to-do list itself is implemented as `List`.

Request

Write a program that allows the user to maintain a list of tasks, commonly known as a to-do list.

Analysis

Each task in the list consists of a name and a description. The name is a single line of text. The description consists of a multiline chunk of text. Thus, the interface should display separate areas for entering or displaying the two parts of a task. We use a text field for the name and a text area for the task. Figure 13-7 shows a task displayed in the proposed interface.

FIGURE 13-7
Interface for a to-do list application

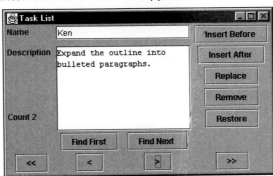

The interface provides a window on the currently selected task in the list. The user navigates the list of tasks by selecting one of the movement buttons in the bottom row. The user enters, removes, or replaces a task by selecting a button from the column at the right of the interface.

Classes

The implementation is based on the three classes `TaskListView`, `TaskListModel`, and `Task`, whose responsibilities are shown in Table 13-7.

TABLE 13-7
Classes and responsibilities

CLASS	RESPONSIBILITY
`TaskListView`	Responds to user requests and interacts with the model.
`TaskListModel`	Maintains the to-do list in response to requests from the view and keeps track of the current task.
`Task`	Stores the name and description of one task and provides these on demand.

Design

The design of the `TaskListView` class is straightforward, and we let the code (shown in the Implementation section that follows) speak for itself. The `Task` class is trivial, and we leave both its design and implementation as an end-of-lesson project (Project 13-1). That leaves only the `TaskListModel` class to consider. This class has two instance variables. One is the to-do list and the other is an indicator of which task is current. Table 13-8 summarizes the methods. There is a close correspondence between methods in this class and the command buttons in the interface.

TABLE 13-8
The `TaskList` methods

METHOD	WHAT IT DOES
`boolean hasCurrentPosition()`	Returns `true` if the model has a current position; otherwise, returns `false`.
`Task get()`	Returns the current task or `null` if there is none.
`int size()`	Returns the number of tasks in the to-do list.
`String insertBefore(Task task)`	Inserts the new task before the current task. The new task becomes current. Returns an error message if the new task does not have a name or if there was no current task in a nonempty list; otherwise, returns `null`.

TABLE 13-8
The `TaskList` methods (Continued)

METHOD	WHAT IT DOES
`String insertAfter(Task task)`	Inserts the new task after the current task. The new task becomes current. Returns an error message if the new task does not have a name or if there was no current task in a nonempty list; otherwise, returns `null`.
`String replace(Task task)`	Replaces the current task with `task`. The new task becomes current. Returns an error message if the new task does not have a name or if there was no current task; otherwise, returns `null`.
`String remove()`	Removes the current task. If the list becomes empty or the deleted task was the last task, no task is current; otherwise, the next task becomes the current task. Returns an error message if there was no current task; otherwise, returns `null`.
`String getFirst()`	Makes the first task current if there is one. Always returns `null`.
`String getPrevious()`	Makes the previous task current if there is one, else no change. Always returns `null`.
`String getNext()`	Makes the next task current if there is one, else no change. Always returns `null`.
`String getLast()`	Makes the last task current if there is one. Always returns `null`.
`String findFirst(Task task)`	Starting at the beginning of the list, searches for a task whose name is the same as the one in the specified task. Makes current the first instance of a task with this name or leaves no task current if the search fails. Returns an error message if the specified task has no name; otherwise, returns `null`.
`String findNext(Task task)`	Starting at the current task, searches for a task whose name is the same as the one in the specified task. Makes current the first instance of a task with this name or leaves no task current if the search fails. Returns an error message if the specified task has no name; otherwise, returns `null`.

Implementation

Following is the code of the class `TaskListView`:

```
import javax.swing.*;
import BreezySwing.*;

public class TaskListView extends GBFrame{

    // Window objects ------------------------------------

    private JButton findFirstButton, findNextButton, insertBeforeButton,
                    insertAfterButton, replaceButton, removeButton,
                    restoreButton, firstButton, previousButton, nextButton,
                    lastButton;

    private JLabel nameLabel, descriptionLabel, countLabel;

    private JTextField nameField;
    private JTextArea  descriptionField;

    // Other instance variables --------------------------------

    private TaskListModel model;
    private String oldName, oldDescription;

    // Constructor----------------------------------------------

    public TaskListView(){

        // Instantiate window objects
        setTitle ("Task List");
        findFirstButton     = addButton ("Find First"    ,6,2,1,1);
        findNextButton      = addButton ("Find Next "    ,6,3,1,1);
        insertBeforeButton  = addButton ("Insert Before" ,1,4,1,1);
        insertAfterButton   = addButton ("Insert After"  ,2,4,1,1);
        replaceButton       = addButton ("Replace"       ,3,4,1,1);
        removeButton        = addButton ("Remove"        ,4,4,1,1);
        restoreButton       = addButton ("Restore"       ,5,4,1,1);

        firstButton    = addButton ("<<", 7,1,1,1);
        previousButton = addButton ("<",  7,2,1,1);
        nextButton     = addButton (">",  7,3,1,1);
        lastButton     = addButton (">>", 7,4,1,1);

        nameLabel        = addLabel    ("Name"        ,1,1,1,1);
        descriptionLabel = addLabel    ("Description" ,2,1,1,1);
        countLabel       = addLabel    ("Count 0"     ,5,1,1,1);

        nameField        = addTextField ("" ,1,2,2,1);
        descriptionField = addTextArea  (""  ,2,2,2,4);
```

```
        model = new TaskListModel();
        oldName = oldDescription = "";
}


// buttonClicked method---------------------------------------

public void buttonClicked (JButton buttonObj){
    if (buttonObj == insertBeforeButton)
        displayResultsOf (model.insertBefore (getDataOnScreen()));

    else if (buttonObj == insertAfterButton)
        displayResultsOf (model.insertAfter (getDataOnScreen()));

    else if (buttonObj == replaceButton)
        displayResultsOf (model.replace (getDataOnScreen()));

    else if (buttonObj == removeButton){
        if (unprocessedDataOnScreen()) return;
        displayResultsOf (model.remove());

    }else if (buttonObj == restoreButton){
        nameField.setText (oldName);
        descriptionField.setText (oldDescription);

    }else if (buttonObj == firstButton){
        if (unprocessedDataOnScreen()) return;
        displayResultsOf (model.getFirst());

    }else if (buttonObj == previousButton){
        if (unprocessedDataOnScreen()) return;
        displayResultsOf (model.getPrevious());

    }else if (buttonObj == nextButton){
        if (unprocessedDataOnScreen()) return;
        displayResultsOf (model.getNext());

    }else if (buttonObj == lastButton){
        if (unprocessedDataOnScreen()) return;
        displayResultsOf (model.getLast());

    }else if (buttonObj == findFirstButton){
        if (unprocessedDescriptionOnScreen()) return;
        displayResultsOf (model.findFirst (getDataOnScreen()));

    }else if (buttonObj == findNextButton){
        if (unprocessedDescriptionOnScreen()) return;
        displayResultsOf (model.findNext (getDataOnScreen()));
    }
}

// Private methods---------------------------------------------
```

```java
   private Task getDataOnScreen(){
      String oldName = nameField.getText().trim();
      String oldDescription = descriptionField.getText();

      Task task = new Task (oldName, oldDescription);
      return task;
   }

   private boolean unprocessedDataOnScreen(){
      if (oldName.equals (nameField.getText().trim()) &&
          oldDescription.equals (descriptionField.getText()))
        return false;
      else{
        messageBox ("Unprocessed data on screen!");
        return true;
      }
   }

   private boolean unprocessedDescriptionOnScreen(){
      if (oldDescription.equals (descriptionField.getText()))
        return false;
      else{
        messageBox ("Unprocessed description on screen!");
        return true;
      }
   }

   private void displayResultsOf (String str){
      if (str != null)
        messageBox (str);
      else{
        if (!model.hasCurrentPosition()){
           nameField.setText ("");
           descriptionField.setText ("");
        }else{
           Task task = model.get();
           nameField.setText (task.getName());
           descriptionField.setText (task.getDescription());
        }
        oldName = nameField.getText();
        oldDescription = descriptionField.getText();
        countLabel.setText ("Count " + model.size() + "     ");
      }
   }

   public static void main (String[] args){
      TaskListView theGUI = new TaskListView();
      theGUI.setSize (400, 250);
      theGUI.setVisible(true);
   }
}
```

The implementation of `TaskListModel` uses a `List` class and is left as a project at the end of this lesson (Project 13-1).

13.3 Iterators

As mentioned earlier, an iterator supports position-based operations on a list. An iterator uses the underlying list as a *backing collection*, and the iterator's current position is always in one of three places:

1. Just before the first item

2. Between two adjacent items

3. Just after the last item

Initially, when an iterator is first instantiated, the position is immediately before the first item. From this position the user can either navigate to another position or modify the list in some way. For lists, `java.util` provides two types of iterators, a simple iterator and a list iterator. We now examine both types of iterators.

The Simple Iterator

In Java, a simple iterator is an object that responds to messages specified in the interface `java.util.Iterator`, as summarized in Table 13-9.

TABLE 13-9
The `Iterator` interface

ITERATOR METHOD	WHAT IT DOES
`boolean hasNext()`	Returns `true` if there are any items following the current position.
`Object next()`	*Precondition*: `hasNext` returns true. Throws a `NoSuchElementException` if `hasNext` returns `false`. Returns the next item and advances the position.
`void remove()`	*Precondition*: `next` has recently been called. Throws an `IllegalStateException` if the `next` method has not yet been called or if the `remove` method has already been called after the last call to the `next` method. Removes the item returned by the most recent call of `next`.

You create an iterator object by sending the message `iterator` to a list, as shown in the following code segment:

```
Iterator iter = someList.iterator();
```

The list serves as a ***backing store*** for the iterator. A backing store is a storage area, usually a collection, where the data elements are maintained. The relationship between these two objects is depicted in Figure 13-8.

FIGURE 13-8
Attaching an iterator to a list object

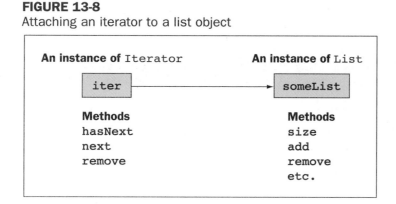

The methods `hasNext` and `next` are for navigating, whereas the method `remove` mutates the underlying list. Note that simple iterators are not restricted to lists but can be used with any other Java collections, although the method `remove` might not be supported by some implementations.

The next code segment demonstrates a traversal of a list to display its contents using an iterator:

```
while (iter.hasNext())
    System.out.println(iter.next());
```

Note that you should avoid doing the following things:

■ Sending a mutator message, such as `add`, to the backing list when an iterator is active.

■ Sending the message `remove` to an iterator when another iterator is open on the same backing list.

The List Iterator

A ***list iterator*** responds to messages specified in the interface `java.util.ListIterator`. This interface extends the `Iterator` interface with several methods for navigation and modifying the backing list. Table 13-10 shows the additional navigational methods.

TABLE 13-10
Additional navigation methods

NAVIGATION	ACTION
`hasPrevious()`	Returns `true` if there are any items preceding the current position.
`previous()`	Returns the previous item and moves the position backward.
`nextIndex()`	Returns the index of the next item or –1 if none.
`previousIndex()`	Returns the index of the previous item or –1 if none.

Conspicuously absent from this roster of operations are ones for moving directly to either the beginning or end of a list. The authors of `java.util` omitted these operations for reasons best known to themselves. The lack of an operation for returning to the head of a list is not critical because instantiating a new list iterator has the same effect; however, a succession of next operations is the only way to move to a list's tail.

The additional mutator operations work at the currently established position in the list (see Table 13-11).

TABLE 13-11
Additional mutator operations

MUTATOR OPERATION	DESCRIPTION
add(o)	Inserts object o at the current position (list iterator only).
set(o)	Replaces the last item returned by next or previous (list iterator only).

Using a List Iterator

In Table 13-12, we present a sequence of list iterator operations and indicate the state of the underlying list after each operation. Remember that a list iterator's current position is located before the first item, after the last item, or between two items. In the table, the current position is indicated by a comma and by an integer variable called current position. Suppose the list contains n items. Then

■ current position = i if it is located before the item at index i, where $i = 0, 1, 2, \ldots, n - 1$

■ current position = n if it is located after the last item

Notice in Table 13-12 that there is always a current position. From the specification for the ListIterator interface, we know that remove and set operate on the last item returned by a successful next or previous operation, provided there have been no intervening add or remove operations. In the table, we highlight this last item returned in boldface. If no item is highlighted, then remove and set are invalid. The highlighted item, when present, can be on either side of the current position indicator—on the left after a next operation or on the right after a previous operation.

TABLE 13-12
The effects of iterator operations on a list

LIST ITERATOR OPERATION	CURRENT POSITION AFTER THE OPERATION	STATE OF THE LIST AFTER THE OPERATION	VALUE RETURNED	COMMENT
instantiate a new list iterator over a list that contains the items a b c	0	,a b c	a list iterator object	Initially, the list contains a, b, and c, and the current position equals 0. The following operations use this iterator object, and some change the state of the underlying list.
hasNext()	0	,a b c	true	There are items following the current position.

("," indicates the current position and boldface indicates the last item returned)

TABLE 13-12 Continued
The effects of iterator operations on a list

LIST ITERATOR OPERATION	CURRENT POSITION AFTER THE OPERATION	STATE OF THE LIST AFTER THE OPERATION	VALUE RETURNED	COMMENT
next()	1	a, b c	a	Return a and advance the current position.
next()	2	a b,c	b	Return b and advance the current position.
remove()	1	a,c	void	Remove b, the last item returned by previous or next. Note the location of the current position.
add(b)	2	a b,c	void	Insert b immediately to the left of the current position indicator.
next()	3	a b c,	c	Return c and advance the current position.
next()	3	a b c,	exception	The current position is at the end of the list; therefore, it is impossible to retrieve a next item.
hasNext()	3	a b c,	false	The current position is at the end of the list; therefore, there is no next item.
hasPrevious()	3	a b c,	true	There are items preceding the current position.
previous()	2	a b,**c**	c	Return c and move the current position backward.

("," indicates the current position and boldface indicates the last item returned)

TABLE 13-12 Continued
The effects of iterator operations on a list

LIST ITERATOR OPERATION	CURRENT POSITION AFTER THE OPERATION	STATE OF THE LIST AFTER THE OPERATION	VALUE RETURNED	COMMENT
remove()	2	a b,	void	Remove c, the last item returned by previous or next. Note the location of the current position.
previous()	1	a,**b**	b	Return b and move the current position backward.
set(e)	1	a,**e**	void	Replace b, the last item returned by previous or next. The item e is now considered the last item returned.
add(b)	2	a b,e	void	Insert b immediately to the left of the current position indicator.
add(c)	3	a b c,e	void	Insert c immediately to the left of the current position indicator.
remove()	3	a b c,e	exception	add has occurred since the last next or previous.
previous()	2	a b,**c** e	c	Return c and move the current position backward.
previous()	1	a,**b** c e	b	Return b and move the current position backward.

("," indicates the current position and boldface indicates the last item returned)

EXERCISE 13.3

1. Assume the iterator `iter` has been opened on a list containing the strings "1", "2", and "3". Describe the effects of the following code segments as they are run in sequence:
   a. `Object obj = iter.next();`
   b. `iter.remove();`
   c. `obj = iter.next();`
   d. `boolean state = iter.hasNext();`
   e. `for (int i = 1; i <= 3; i++) iter.next();`

2. Write code segments to accomplish the following tasks with the list iterator `iter`. You may assume that they are performed in sequence:
   a. Move to the last item and display it.
   b. Move to the first item and display it.
   c. Remove the item at the middle position.
   d. Replace the last item with the string "last".
   e. Insert the string "middle" at the middle position.

3. Describe the position of the object in a list that is accessed by the methods `set` and `remove` of a list iterator.

4. Suppose Jack is running an iterator on a list and he also mutates the list with a list method. Describe the reaction of the computer.

5. Suppose Jill opens two iterators on the same list. Describe what happens when one iterator attempts to remove an item from the list.

SUMMARY

In this lesson, you learned:

- There are several fundamental categories of collections, among which are linear collections, hierarchical collections, graph collections, and unordered collections.

- A list is a linear collection in which elements can be accessed at any position.

- A complete set of list operations includes position-based operations, content-based operations, and index-based operations.

- There is one list interface and several implementations, such as `ArrayList` and `LinkedList`.

- An iterator and a list iterator are two objects that allow clients to perform position-based operations on a list.

VOCABULARY *Review*

Define the following terms:

abstract data type (ADT)	graph collection	list iterator
abstraction	head	object heap
backing store	hierarchical collection	parent
children	index-based operation	position-based operation
collection	iterator	tail
content-based operation	linear collection	unordered collection
free list		

REVIEW *Questions*

FILL IN THE BLANK

Complete the following sentences by writing the correct word or words in the blanks provided.

1. A(n) _____ collection contains elements that are ordered by position and have unique successors and predecessors.

2. A(n) _____ collection contains elements that are in no particular order.

3. A(n) _____ collection contains elements that have at most one predecessor and zero or more successors.

4. _____ collections are useful for representing airline routes and circuit diagrams.

5. A(n) _____ -based operation uses an integer value to locate an element in a list.

6. A(n) _____ -based operation expects an element as a parameter and accesses this element in a list.

7. The classes _____, _____, and _____ implement the `List` interface in Java.

8. A(n) _____ tracks the current position in a list and allows clients to advance to the next position or remove the element at the current position.

9. A(n) _____ tracks the current position in a list and allows clients to move to the previous position and insert, remove, or replace an element at the current position.

10. The positions of elements in a list are numbered from _____ to the _____.

PROJECTS

PROJECT 13-1

Complete the case study program from this lesson by adding the classes `Task` and `TaskListModel` and then test the program.

PROJECT 13-2

Modify the case study program from this lesson so that it allows the user to scroll through all the tasks in a message box. When the user selects a new button named **View All**, the `TaskListView` responds by sending the message `toString` to the `TaskListModel`, which returns a string consisting of all the tasks. This string is then displayed in a message box.

PROJECT 13-3

Write a GUI-based program that allows the user to perform the following tasks:

■ Add a noun to a list of nouns.

■ Add a verb to a list of verbs.

■ Generate a random sentence from the two lists.

Sentences should be of the form "the <noun> <verb> the <noun> with a <noun>." For example, if the list of nouns contains "girl," "ball," and "bat" and the list of verbs contains "hit," a random sentence is "the girl hit the ball with a bat" Note that some sentences might appear nonsensical although they are grammatically correct.

PROJECT 13-4

Modify the program from Project13-3 to maintain a history list of the sentences that have been generated. Add a button to display all the sentences in a message box.

PROJECT 13-5

Modify the program from Project 13-4 to generate only sentences that have not been seen before. The program should generate a candidate sentence and examine its history list for a matching sentence. If a match is not found, this sentence is displayed as usual and added to the history list. If a match is found, the program repeats this process until no match is found or five attempts have been made. After the fifth unsuccessful attempt to generate a unique sentence, the program should ask the user to enter more nouns and/or verbs.

PROJECT 13-6

Modify the program from Project 13-5 so that it allows the user to reject nonsensical sentences. When the user selects the **Reject Sentence** button, the program searches the history list for a sentence that matches the one just generated. If a match is found, the program removes this sentence from the list.

CRITICAL *Thinking*

Jack has just completed programming Projects 13-1 and 13-2 of this lesson and Jill examines his code. She tells him that the task list can be modeled more naturally with a list iterator. Jack replies, "No way! My code will be horrendous!" Discuss the advantages and disadvantages of this alternative.

LINEAR COLLECTIONS: STACKS AND QUEUES

The list collections discussed in Lesson 13 are the most widely used linear collections. There are many applications that call for linear collections with a more restricted set of operations, however. In this lesson, we explore three such restricted linear collections, the *stack*, the *queue*, and a special type of queue called the *priority queue*. We take a client's perspective on these collections and defer a close examination of implementations until Lessons 16 and 18.

14.1 Stacks

Stacks are linear collections in which access is completely restricted to just one end, called the *top*. The classical example is the stack of clean trays found in every cafeteria. Whenever a tray is needed, it is removed from the top of the stack, and whenever clean ones come back from the scullery, they are again placed on the top. No one ever takes some particularly fine tray from the middle of the stack, and it is even possible that trays near the bottom are never used. Stacks are said to adhere to a last-in first-out protocol (LIFO). The last tray brought back from the scullery is the first one taken by a customer.

The operations for putting items on and removing items from a stack are called *push* and *pop* respectively. Figure 14-1 shows a stack as it might appear at various stages.

FIGURE 14-1
Some states in the lifetime of a stack

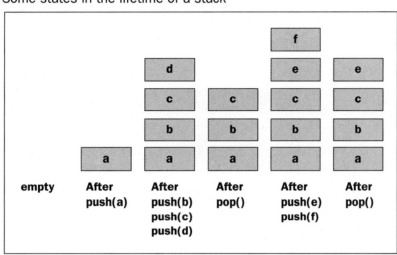

empty   **After push(a)**   **After push(b) push(c) push(d)**   **After pop()**   **After push(e) push(f)**   **After pop()**

Initially, the stack is empty, and then an item called *a* is pushed. Next, three more items called *b*, *c*, and *d* are pushed, after which the stack is popped, and so forth.

Other everyday examples of stacks include plates and bowls in our kitchen cupboards and PEZ® dispensers. Although we continually add more papers to the top of the piles on our desks, these piles do not quite qualify because we often need to remove a long-lost paper from the middle. With a genuine stack, the item we get next is always the one added most recently.

The Stack Interface

The `java.util` package includes a `Stack` class that is a subclass of `Vector`. This is a poor choice of implementation for a stack, because clients can treat stacks as vectors, thus violating the spirit of a stack. Therefore, we provide our own `Stack` interface with the implementing classes `ArrayStack` and `LinkedStack`, along the lines of Java's `List` collections. Our `Stack` interface, as shown in Table 14-1, is fairly simple.

TABLE 14-1
The `Stack` interface

METHOD	DESCRIPTION
`Object peekTop()`	*Precondition*: The stack is not empty. *Throws*: An `IllegalStateException` if the stack is empty. Returns the object at the top of the stack.
`Object pop()`	*Precondition*: The stack is not empty. *Throws*: An `IllegalStateException` if the stack is empty. Removes and returns the object at the top of the stack.
`void push(Object obj)`	Adds `obj` to the top of the stack.
`int size()`	Returns the number of objects in the stack.

A simple example illustrates the use of the `Stack` interface and the class `ArrayStack`. In this example, the items in a list are transferred to the stack and then displayed. Their display order is the reverse of their order in the list:

```
List lst = new ArrayList();        // Create list and add objects
.. put some objects into the list

Stack stk = new ArrayStack();      // Create stack and transfer objects
for (int i = 0; i < lst.size(); i++)
   stk.push(lst.get(i));

while (stk.size() > 0)             // Display objects from stack
   System.out.println(stk.pop());
```

Applications of Stacks

Applications of stacks in computer science are numerous. Following are just a few examples:

- Parsing expressions in context-free programming languages—a problem in compiler design.

- Translating infix expressions to postfix form and evaluating postfix expressions—discussed later in this lesson.

- Backtracking algorithms—discussed later in this lesson and occurring in problems such as automated theorem proving and game playing.

- Managing computer memory in support of method calls—discussed later in this lesson.

- Supporting the "undo" feature in text editors, word processors, spreadsheet programs, drawing programs, and similar applications.

- Maintaining a history of the links visited by a Web browser.

We will now discuss three applications of stacks. First, we present algorithms for evaluating arithmetic expressions. These algorithms apply to problems in compiler design, and we will use them in one of the lesson's case studies and in one of the projects at the end of this lesson. Second, we describe a general technique for using stacks to solve backtracking problems. The end-of-lesson projects explore applications of the technique. Third, we examine the role of stacks in computer memory management. Not only is this topic interesting in its own right, but it also provides, as we saw in Lesson 11, a foundation for understanding recursion.

Evaluating Arithmetic Expressions

We are so accustomed to evaluating simple arithmetic expressions that we give little conscious thought to the rules involved, and we are surprised by the difficulty of writing an algorithm to do the same thing. It turns out that an indirect approach to the problem works best. First, we transform an expression from its familiar *infix form* to a *postfix form*, and then we evaluate the postfix form. In the infix form, each operator is located between its operands, whereas in the postfix form, an operator immediately follows its operands. Table 14-2 gives several simple examples.

TABLE 14-2
Some infix and postfix expressions

INFIX FORM	POSTFIX FORM	VALUE
34	34	34
34 + 22	34 22 +	56
34 + 22 * 2	34 22 2 * +	78
34 * 22 + 2	34 22 * 2 +	750
(34 + 22) * 2	34 22 + 2 *	112

There are similarities and differences between the two forms. In both, operands appear in the same order; however, the operators do not. The infix form sometimes requires parentheses; the postfix form never does. Infix evaluation involves rules of precedence; postfix evaluation applies operators as soon as they are encountered. For instance, consider the steps in evaluating the infix expression 34 + 22 * 2 and the equivalent postfix expression 34 22 2 * +.

Infix evaluation: 34 + 22 * 2 → 34 + 44 → 78

Postfix evaluation: 34 22 2 * + → 34 44 + → 78

We now present stack-based algorithms for transforming infix expressions to postfix and for evaluating the resulting postfix expressions. In combination, these algorithms allow us to evaluate an infix expression. In presenting the algorithms, we ignore the effects of syntax errors, but return to the issue in the case study.

Evaluating Postfix Expressions

Evaluation is the simpler process and consists of three steps:

1. Scan across the expression from left to right.

2. On encountering an operator, apply it to the two preceding operands and replace all three by the result.

3. Continue scanning until reaching the expression's end, at which point only the expression's value remains.

To express this procedure as a computer algorithm, we use a stack of operands. In the algorithm, the term *token* refers to either an operand or an operator:

```
create a new stack
while there are more tokens in the expression
   get the next token
   if the token is an operand
      push the operand onto the stack
   else if the token is an operator
      pop the top two operands from the stack
      use the operator to evaluate the two operands just popped
      push the resulting operand onto the stack
   end if
end while
return the value at the top of the stack
```

The time complexity of the algorithm is O(n), where n is the number of tokens in the expression. Table 14-3 shows a trace of the algorithm as it is applied to the expression 4 5 6 * + 3 −.

TABLE 14-3
Tracing the evaluation of a postfix expression

POSTFIX EXPRESSION: 4 5 6 * + 3 −   **RESULTING VALUE:** 31

PORTION OF POSTFIX EXPRESSION SCANNED SO FAR	OPERAND STACK	COMMENT
		No tokens have been seen yet. The stack is empty.
4	4	Push the operand 4.
4 5	4 5	Push the operand 5.
4 5 6	4 5 6	Push the operand 6.
4 5 6 *	4 30	Replace the top two operands by their product.
4 5 6 * +	34	Replace the top two operands by their sum.
4 5 6 * + 3	34 3	Push the operand 3.
4 5 6 * + 3 −	31	Replace the top two operands by their difference. Pop the final value.

Transforming Infix to Postfix

We now show how to translate expressions from infix to postfix. For the sake of simplicity, we restrict our attention to expressions involving the operators *, /, +, and −. (Project 14-1 at the end of this lesson adds the exponentiation operator to the set of operators.) As usual, multiplication and division have higher precedence than addition and subtraction, except when parentheses override the default order of evaluation.

In broad terms, the algorithm scans, from left to right, a string containing an infix expression and simultaneously builds a string containing the equivalent postfix expression. Operands are copied from the infix string to the postfix string as soon as they are encountered. Operators must be held back on a stack until operators of greater precedence have been copied to the postfix string ahead of them, however. Following is a more detailed statement of the process:

1. Start with an empty postfix expression and an empty stack, which will hold operators and left parentheses.

2. Scan across the infix expression from left to right.

3. On encountering an operand, append it to the postfix expression.

4. On encountering an operator, pop off the stack all operators that have equal or higher precedence and append them to the postfix expression. Then push the scanned operator onto the stack.

5. On encountering a left parenthesis, push it onto the stack.

6. On encountering a right parenthesis, shift operators from the stack to the postfix expression until meeting the matching left parenthesis, which is discarded.

7. On encountering the end of the infix expression, transfer the remaining operators from the stack to the postfix expression.

Examples in Tables 14-4 and 14-5 illustrate the procedure.

TABLE 14-4
Tracing the conversion of an infix expression to a postfix expression

INFIX EXPRESSION: 4 + 5 * 6 − 3   **EQUIVALENT POSTFIX EXPRESSION**: 4 5 6 * + 3 −

PORTION OF INFIX EXPRESSION SCANNED SO FAR	OPERATOR STACK	POSTFIX EXPRESSION	COMMENT
			No characters have been seen yet. The stack and PE are empty.
4		4	Append 4 to the PE.
4 +	+	4	Push + onto the stack.
4 + 5	+	4 5	Append 5 to the PE.
4 + 5 *	+ *	4 5	Push * onto the stack.
4 + 5 * 6	+ *	4 5 6	Append 6 to the PE.
4 + 5 * 6 −	−	4 5 6 * +	Pop * and +, append them to the PE, and push −.
4 + 5 * 6 − 3	−	4 5 6 * + 3	Append 3 to the PE.
		4 5 6 * + 3 −	Pop the remaining operators off the stack and append them to the PE.

TABLE 14-5
Tracing the conversion of an infix expression with parentheses to a postfix expression

INFIX EXPRESSION: (4 + 5) * (6 − 3) **EQUIVALENT POSTFIX EXPRESSION**: 4 5 + 6 3 − *

PORTION OF INFIX EXPRESSION SCANNED SO FAR	OPERATOR STACK	POSTFIX EXPRESSION	COMMENT
			No characters have been seen yet. The stack and PE are empty.
(	(		Push (onto the stack.
(4	(	4	Append 4 to the PE.
(4 +	(+	4	Push + onto the stack .
(4 + 5	(+	4 5	Append 5 to the PE.
(4 + 5)	(+	4 5 +	Pop the stack until (is encountered and append operators to the PE.
(4 + 5) *	*	4 5 +	Push * onto the stack.
(4 + 5) * (	* (	4 5 +	Push (onto the stack.
(4 + 5) * (6	* (	4 5 + 6	Append 6 to the PE.
(4 + 5) * (6 −	* (−	4 5 + 6	Push − onto the stack.
(4 + 5) * (6 − 3	* (−	4 5 + 6 3	Append 3 to the PE.
(4 + 5) * (6 − 3)	*	4 5 + 6 3−	Pop stack until (is encountered and append items to the PE.
		4 5 + 6 3 − *	Pop the remaining operators off the stack and append them to the PE.

Backtracking

There are two principal techniques for implementing backtracking algorithms: one uses stacks and the other recursion. Recursion was considered in Lesson 11. We explore the use of stacks for backtracking algorithms in this section. A backtracking algorithm begins in a predefined starting state and then moves from state to state in search of a desired ending state. At any point along the way, when there is a choice between several alternative states, the algorithm picks one, possibly at random, and continues. If the algorithm reaches a state representing an undesirable outcome, it backs up to the last point at which there was an unexplored alternative and tries it. In this way, the algorithm either exhaustively searches all states, or it reaches the desired ending state.

The role of a stack in the process is to remember the alternative states that occur at each juncture. To be more precise:

```
create an empty stack
push the starting state onto the stack
while the stack is not empty
   pop the stack and examine the state
   if the state represents an ending state
      return SUCCESSFUL CONCLUSION
   else if the state has not been visited previously
      mark the state as visited
      push onto the stack all unvisited adjacent states
   end if
end while
return UNSUCCESSFUL CONCLUSION
```

Although short, the algorithm is subtle, and an illustration is needed to elucidate its workings.

Suppose there are just five states, as shown in Figure 14-2, with states 1 and 5 representing the start and end, respectively. Lines between states indicate adjacency. Starting in state 1, the algorithm proceeds to state 4 and then to 3. In state 3, the algorithm recognizes that all adjacent states have been visited and resumes the search in state 2, which leads directly to state 5 and the end. Table 14-6 contains a detailed trace of the algorithm.

FIGURE 14-2
States of the backtracking algorithm

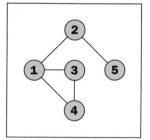

TABLE 14-6
Trace of the backtracking algorithm

NEXT STEP IN ALGORITHM	STACK	CURRENT STATE	VISITED STATES
Push 1.		1	none yet
Pop the stack and note the state.		1	
Mark the state as visited.		1	1
Push unvisited adjacent states.	2 3 4	1	1
Pop stack and note the state.	2 3	4	1
Mark the state as visited.	2 3	4	1 4
Push unvisited adjacent states.	2 3	4	1 4
Pop the stack and note the state.	2 3	3	1 4
Mark the state as visited.	2 3	3	1 4 3
All adjacent states already visited.	2 3	3	1 4 3
Pop the stack and note the state.	2	3	1 4 3
Do nothing, location already visited.	2	3	1 4 3
Pop the stack and note the state.		2	1 4 3
Mark the state as visited.		2	1 4 3 2
Push unvisited adjacent states.	5	2	1 4 3 2
Pop the stack and note the state.		5	1 4 3 2
SUCCESS: this is the ending state.		5	1 4 3 2

Notice in the trace that the algorithm goes directly from state 3 to state 2 without having to back up through states 4 and 1 first. This is a beneficial side effect of using a stack.

It would be interesting to calculate the time complexity of the foregoing algorithm. However, two crucial pieces of information are missing:

1. The complexity of deciding if a state has been visited.

2. The complexity of listing states adjacent to a given state.

If, for the sake of argument, we assume that both of these processes are $O(1)$, then the algorithm as a whole is $O(n)$, where n represents the total number of states.

This discussion has been a little abstract, but at the end of the lesson, Project 14-3 applies backtracking to a maze problem.

Memory Management

During a program's execution, both its code and data occupy computer memory. Although the exact manner in which a computer manages memory depends on the programming language and operating system involved, we can present the following simplified yet reasonably realistic overview. The emphasis must be on the word "simplified" because a detailed discussion is beyond this book's scope.

As you may recall from our earlier discussion, a Java compiler translates a Java program into byte codes. A complex program called the Java virtual machine (JVM) then executes these. The memory, or run-time environment, controlled by the JVM is divided into six regions, as shown on the left side of Figure 14-3.

FIGURE 14-3
The architecture of a run-time environment

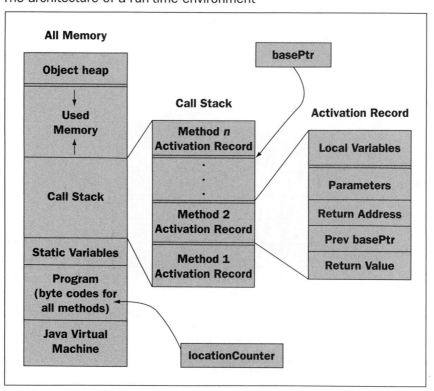

Working up from the bottom, these regions contain

- The Java virtual machine, which executes a Java program. Internal to the JVM are two variables, which we call `locationCounter` and `basePtr`. The `locationCounter` points at the instruction the JVM will execute next. The `basePtr` points at the top activation record's base. More is said about these variables soon.

- Byte codes for all the methods of our program.

- The program's static variables.

- The **call stack**. Every time a method is called, an **activation record** is created and pushed onto the call stack. When a method finishes execution and returns control to the method that called it, the activation record is popped off the stack. The total number of activation records on the stack equals the number of method calls currently in various stages of execution. At the bottom of the stack is the activation record for the method `main`. Above it is the activation record for the method currently called by `main`, and so forth. More will be said about activation records in a moment.

- Unused memory. This region's size grows and shrinks in response to the demands of the call stack and the object heap.

■ The object heap. In Java, all objects exist in a region of memory called the *heap*. When an object is instantiated, the JVM must find space for the object on the heap, and when the object is no longer needed, the JVM's garbage collector recovers the space for future use. When low on space, the heap extends further into the region marked *Unused Memory*.

The activation records shown on the right side of the figure contain two types of information. The regions labeled *Local Variables* and *Parameters* hold data needed by the executing method. The remaining regions hold data that allow the JVM to pass control backward from the currently executing method to the method that called it.

When a method is called, the JVM

1. Creates the method's activation record and pushes it onto the call stack (the activation record's bottom three regions are fixed in size, and the top two vary depending on the number of parameters and local variables used by the method).

2. Saves the `basePtr`'s current value in the region labeled `Prev basePtr` and sets the `basePtr` to the new activation record's base.

3. Saves the `locationCounter`'s current value in the region labeled *Return Address* and sets the `locationCounter` to the first instruction of the called method.

4. Copies the calling parameters into the region labeled *Parameters*.

5. Initializes local variables as required.

6. Starts executing the called method at the location indicated by the `locationCounter`.

While a method is executing, local variables and parameters in the activation record are referenced by adding an offset to the `basePtr`. Thus, no matter where an activation record is located in memory, the local variables and parameters can be accessed correctly provided the `basePtr` has been initialized properly.

Just before returning, a method stores its return value in the location labeled *Return Value*. The value can be a reference to an object, or it can be a primitive data type such as an integer or character. Because the return value always resides at the bottom of the activation record, the calling method knows exactly where to find it.

When a method has finished executing, the JVM

1. Reestablishes the settings needed by the calling method by restoring the values of the `locationCounter` and the `basePtr` from values stored in the activation record.

2. Pops the activation record from the call stack.

3. Resumes execution of the calling method at the location indicated by the `locationCounter`.

Implementing the Stack Classes

Stacks are linear collections, so the natural choices for implementations are based on arrays and linked structures. Instead of using these structures directly, we use the `ArrayList` and `LinkedList` classes mentioned in Lesson 13. Following is the code for the class `ArrayStack`, which uses an `ArrayList`:

```
import java.util.ArrayList;

public class ArrayStack implements Stack{

    private ArrayList list;
```

```
public ArrayStack(){
    list = new ArrayList();
}

public Object peekTop(){
    if (list.isEmpty())
        throw new IllegalStateException("Stack is empty");
    return list.get(list.size() - 1);
}

public Object pop(){
    if (list.isEmpty())
        throw new IllegalStateException("Stack is empty");
    return list.remove(list.size() - 1);
}

public void push(Object obj){
    list.add(obj);
}

public int size(){
    return list.size();
}
}
```

*E*XERCISE 14.1

1. Assume that a stack s has been created. Draw a picture of the state of the stack after each of the following sequences of operations. You should assume that each sequence follows the previous one from a to c:

a.

```
for (int i = 1; i <= 5; i++)
    s.push("" + i);
```

b.

```
s.pop();
s.pop();
```

c.

```
s.push("5");
s.push("6");
```

2. Write code segments that accomplish the following tasks with the stack s:

a. Push the strings "hello" and "there" onto the stack.

b. Make the stack be empty.

c. Print the contents of the stack in the terminal window without removing them permanently. (*Hint:* You can use a temporary data structure to accomplish this.)

EXERCISE 14.1 Continued

3. What information is stored in an activation record and how is it used?

4. Why is a stack such a handy data structure when used to evaluate postfix expressions?

5. Explain what happens when a stack overflow error occurs.

14.2 The StringTokenizer Class

Before we turn to our first case study, we examine a class that is useful in text analysis applications. Sentences are composed of individual words, or tokens. When you read, you automatically break a sentence into its individual tokens, usually using white-space characters such as blanks, tabs, and newline characters as delimiters. Java provides a StringTokenizer class (from the java.util package) that allows you to break a string into individual tokens using either the default delimiters (space, newline, tab, and carriage return) or a programmer-specified delimiter. The process of obtaining tokens from a string tokenizer is called *scanning*. Table 14-7 shows several StringTokenizer methods.

TABLE 14-7
Some commonly used StringTokenizer methods

METHOD	WHAT IT DOES
int countTokens()	Returns the number of tokens in the string tokenizer.
boolean hasMoreTokens()	Returns true if there is still an unscanned token in the string tokenizer.
String nextToken()	Scans through the string tokenizer, returning the next available token.

For example, the following code displays each word of a sentence on a separate line in the terminal output stream:

```
String sentence = "Four score and seven years ago, our fathers set " +
                  "forth on this continent a new nation.";

StringTokenizer tokens = new StringTokenizer(sentence);

while (tokens.hasMoreTokens())
   writer.println (tokens.nextToken());
```

The preceding code produces a surprising result. The list of words displayed by println includes

```
    ago,
    nation.
```
rather than
```
    ago
    nation
```

The reason is simple. The delimiters are space, new-line, tab, and carriage return. Punctuation marks are treated no differently than letters. To add punctuation marks to the list of delimiters, replace the second line of the preceding code with the following two lines:

Note ☑

Remember to import
`java.util.StringTokenizer`.

```
String listOfDelimiters = ".,;?! \t\n\r";
StringTokenizer tokens = new StringTokenizer (sentence, listOfDelimiters);
```

EXERCISE 14.2

1. Assume that the `string` variable `str` refers to a string. Write the code to create a string tokenizer that recognizes decimal digits in `str` as delimiter characters.

2. Assume that the `string` variable `str` refers to a string. Write a code segment that uses a string tokenizer to remove the white-space characters in `str`.

3. Generalize the method used in your answer to Question 2 to remove all the instances of any character from a string.

Case Study 1: A Postfix Expression Evaluator

Earlier in this lesson, we developed an algorithm that uses a stack to evaluate postfix expressions. We now place this algorithm in the context of a program.

Request

Write a program that evaluates postfix expressions.

Analysis

The program expects a string as input. If the string represents a syntactically correct postfix expression, the program displays its value. If the string has a syntax error or semantic error, the program outputs an error message. A sample interface is shown in Figure 14-4.

FIGURE 14-4
The interface for the postfix expression evaluation program

Postfix Evaluator

Expression	Value
4 5 6 + *	44

Evaluate

A syntactically correct postfix expression consists of the operators +, −, *, and / and numbers, which are strings of digits. All operators and operands must be separated by at least one blank space character, tab character, or newline character. Table 14-8 lists some syntactically correct and incorrect expressions.

TABLE 14-8
Some syntactically correct and incorrect expressions

CORRECT SYNTAX	INCORRECT SYNTAX
88 77 +	88 77+
88 77 99 + *	88 + 77
22 77 + 99 −	22 77 $ 99 −

An example semantic error is an attempt to divide by 0, as in the expression 77 0 /.

Classes

The program consists of two classes, `EvaluatorView` and `Evaluator`. `EvaluatorView` simply handles the input and output. `Evaluator` implements the algorithm discussed earlier in this lesson.

Design

The view receives a string from the user, sends it to the evaluator for processing, and receives back a string that is either a number or an error message. The evaluator uses a string tokenizer to extract the operators and operands from the input string. These in turn are fed into the algorithm, which is refined to handle malformed expressions appropriately.

The algorithm makes use of the private helper methods `isOperator`, `isOperand`, and `computeValue`. `isOperator` expects a string as a parameter and compares this string to the strings "+", "−", "*", and "/". If a match occurs, the method returns `true`, and if not, the method returns `false`. `isOperand` determines whether its string parameter represents an integer by testing each character with the method `Character.isDigit`. `computeValue` expects the operator and two operand strings as parameters and returns a string representing the result of computing the expression's value. This method returns `null` if the operator is / and the second operand is 0.

Implementation

Creating the code for the view class is part of the assignment in Project 14-1. A listing of the `Evaluator` class follows:

```
import java.util.StringTokenizer;

public class Evaluator{

    public String run(String input){
        Stack stack = new ArrayStack();
        StringTokenizer tokens = new StringTokenizer(input);
        String operand1 = null, operand2 = null;
```

```
            String error = null;
            while (tokens.hasMoreTokens() && error == null){
                String token = tokens.nextToken();
                if (isOperand(token))
                    stack.push(token);
                else if (isOperator(token)){
                    if (stack.size() != 0){
                        operand2 = (String)stack.pop();
                        if (stack.size() != 0){
                            operand1 = (String)stack.pop();
                            String result = computeValue(operand1, token, operand2);
                            if (result != null)
                                stack.push(result);
                            else
                                error = "Attempt to divide by 0";
                        }else
                            error = "Malformed expression";
                    }else
                        error = "Malformed expression";
                }else
                    error = "Malformed expression";
            }
            if (stack.size() != 1)
                error = "Malformed expression";
            if (error != null)
                return error;
            else
                return (String) stack.pop();
        }

        private boolean isOperand(String s){
            for (int i = 0; i < s.length(); i++)
                if (! Character.isDigit(s.charAt(i)))
                    return false;
            return true;
        }

        private boolean isOperator(String s){
            return s.equals("+") ||
                   s.equals("-") ||
                   s.equals("*") ||
                   s.equals("/");
        }

        private String computeValue(String op1, String op, String op2){
            int result = 0;
            int intOp1 = Integer.valueOf(op1).intValue();
            int intOp2 = Integer.valueOf(op2).intValue();
            if (op.equals("+"))
                result = intOp1 + intOp2;
            else if (op.equals("-"))
                result = intOp1 - intOp2;
```

```
      else if (op.equals("*"))
         result = intOp1 * intOp2;
      else if (op.equals("/"))
         if (intOp2 == 0)
            return null;
         else
            result = intOp1 / intOp2;
      return "" + result;
   }
}
```

14.3 Queues and Priority Queues

Like stacks, queues are linear collections. However, insertions in a queue are restricted to one end, called the *rear*, and removals are restricted to the other end, called the *front*. A queue thus supports a first-in first-out protocol (FIFO). Queues are omnipresent in everyday life and occur in any situation where people or things are lined up for processing on a first-come, first-served basis. Checkout lines in stores, highway tollbooth lines, and airport baggage check-in lines are familiar examples of queues.

Queues have two fundamental operations: *enqueue*, which adds an item to the rear of a queue, and *dequeue*, which removes an item from the front. Figure 14-5 shows a queue as it might appear at various stages in its lifetime. In the figure, the queue's front is on the left and its rear is on the right.

FIGURE 14-5
The states in the lifetime of a queue

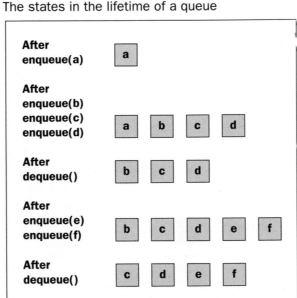

Initially, the queue is empty. Then an item called *a* is enqueued. Next three more items called *b*, *c*, and *d* are enqueued, after which an item is dequeued, and so forth.

Related to queues is an ADT called a *priority queue*. In a queue, the item dequeued or served next is always the item that has been waiting the longest. But in some circumstances, this restriction is too rigid, and we would like to combine the idea of waiting with a notion of priority. The result is a priority queue, in which higher priority items are dequeued before those of lower priority, and items of equal priority are dequeued in FIFO order. Consider, for example, the manner in which passengers board an aircraft. The first-class passengers line up and board first, and the lower priority coach-class passengers line up and board second. This is not a true priority queue, however, because once the first-class queue has emptied and the coach-class queue starts boarding, late arriving first-class passengers usually go to the end of the second queue. In a true priority queue, they would immediately jump ahead of all the coach-class passengers.

Most examples of queues in computer science involve scheduling access to shared resources, for instance

- CPU access – Processes are queued for access to a shared CPU.

- Disk access – Processes are queued for access to a shared secondary storage device.

- Printer access – Print jobs are queued for access to a shared printer.

Process scheduling can use either simple queues or priority queues. For example, processes involving keyboard input and screen output are often given higher priority access to the CPU than those that are computationally intensive. The result is that users, who tend to judge a computer's speed by its response time, are given the impression that the computer is fast.

Processes waiting for a shared resource also can be prioritized by their expected duration, with short processes given higher priority than longer ones, again with the intent of improving the apparent response time of a system. Imagine 20 print jobs queued up for access to a printer. If 19 jobs are one page long and one job is 200 pages long, more users will be happy if the short jobs are given higher priority and are printed first.

The Queue Interface

The `java.util` package does not include classes for queues. Therefore, we provide our own `Queue` interface with the implementing classes `ArrayQueue` and `LinkedQueue`. The `Queue` interface is shown in Table 14-9.

TABLE 14-9
The `Queue` interface

METHOD	DESCRIPTION
`Object dequeue()`	*Precondition*: The queue is not empty. *Throws*: An `IllegalStateException` if the queue is empty. Removes and returns the object at the front of the queue.
`void enqueue(Object obj)`	Adds `obj` to the rear of the queue.
`Object peekFront()`	*Precondition*: The queue is not empty. *Throws*: An `IllegalStateException` if the queue is empty. Returns the object at the front of the queue.
`int size()`	Returns the number of objects in the queue.

Table 14-10 gives a short illustration of queue operations in action.

TABLE 14-10
A trace of some Queue operations

OPERATION	STATE OF THE QUEUE AFTER THE OPERATION	VALUE RETURNED	COMMENT
			Initially, the queue is empty.
enqueue(a)	a		The queue contains the single item a.
enqueue(b)	a b		a is at the front of the queue and b is at the rear.
enqueue(c)	a b c		c is added at the rear.
size()	a b c	3	The queue contains three items.
peekFront()	a b c	a	Return the front item on the queue without removing it.
dequeue()	b c	a	Remove the front item from the queue and return it. b is now the front item.
dequeue()	c	b	Remove and return b.
dequeue()		c	Remove and return c.
size()		0	The queue contains no items.
peekFront()		exception	Peeking at an empty queue throws an exception.
dequeue()		exception	Trying to dequeue an empty queue throws an exception.
enqueue(d)	d		d is the front item.

Applications of Queues

We now look briefly at two applications of queues: one involving computer simulations and the other using round-robin CPU scheduling.

Simulations

Computer simulations are used to study the behavior of real-world systems, especially when it is impractical or dangerous to experiment with these systems directly. For example, a computer simulation could mimic traffic flows on a busy highway. Urban planners could then experiment with factors affecting traffic flows, such as the number and types of vehicles on the highway, the speed limits for different types of vehicles, the number of lanes in the highway, the frequency of tollbooths, and so on. Outputs from such a simulation might include the total number of vehicles able to move between designated points in a designated period and the average duration of a trip. By running the simulation with many combinations of inputs, the planners could determine how best to upgrade sections of the highway subject to the ever-present constraints of time, space, and money.

As a second example, consider the problem faced by the manager of a supermarket when trying to determine the number of checkout clerks to schedule at various times of the day. Some important factors in this situation are

■ The frequency with which new customers arrive

■ The number of checkout clerks available

■ The number of items in a customer's shopping cart

■ The period of time considered

These factors could be inputs to a simulation program, which would then determine the total number of customers processed, the average time each customer waits for service, and the number of customers left standing in line at the end of the simulated time period. By varying the inputs, particularly the frequency of customer arrivals and the number of available checkout clerks, a simulation program could help the manager make effective staffing decisions for busy and slow times of the day. By adding an input that quantifies the efficiency of different checkout equipment, the manager can even decide whether it is cheaper to add more clerks or buy better equipment.

A common characteristic of both examples, and of simulation problems in general, is the moment-by-moment variability of essential factors. Consider the frequency of customer arrivals at checkout stations. If customers arrived at precise intervals, each with exactly the same number of items, it would be easy to determine how many clerks to have on duty. Such regularity does not reflect the reality of a supermarket, however. Sometimes several customers show up at practically the same instant, and at other times no new customers arrive for several minutes. In addition, the number of items varies from customer to customer, and therefore, so does the amount of service required by each customer. All this variability makes it impossible to devise formulas to answer simple questions about the system, such as how customer-waiting time varies with the number of clerks on duty. A simulation program, on the other hand, avoids the need for formulas by imitating the actual situation and collecting pertinent statistics.

Simulation programs use a simple technique to mimic variability. For instance, suppose new customers are expected to arrive on average once every 4 minutes. Then during each minute of simulated time, a program can generate a random number between 0 and 1. If the number is less than 1/4, the program adds a new customer to a checkout line; otherwise, it does not. More sophisticated schemes based on probability distribution functions produce even more realistic results. Obviously, each time the program runs, the results change slightly, but this only adds to the realism of the simulation.

Now let us discuss the common role played by queues in these examples. Both examples involve service providers and service consumers. In the first example, service providers include tollbooths and traffic lanes, and service consumers are the vehicles waiting at the tollbooths and driving in the traffic lanes. In the second example, clerks provide a service that is consumed by waiting customers. To emulate these conditions in a program, we associate each service provider with a queue of service consumers.

Simulations operate by manipulating these queues. At each tick of an imaginary clock, a simulation adds varying numbers of consumers to the queues and gives consumers at the head of each queue another unit of service. Once a consumer has received the needed quantity of service, it leaves the queue and the next consumer steps forward. During the simulation, the program accumulates statistics such as how many ticks each consumer waited in a queue and the percentage of time each provider is busy. The duration of a tick is chosen to match the problem being simulated. It could represent a millisecond, a minute, or a decade. In the program itself, a tick probably corresponds to one pass through the program's major processing loop.

Object-oriented languages are well-suited to implementing simulation programs. For instance, in a supermarket simulation, each customer is an instance of a Customer class. A customer object keeps track of when the customer starts standing in line, when service is first received, and how much service is required. Likewise, a clerk is an instance of a Clerk class, and each clerk object contains a queue of customer objects. A Simulator class coordinates the activities of the customers and clerks. At each clock tick, the simulation object

■ Generates new customer objects as appropriate

■ Assigns customers to cashiers

■ Tells each cashier to provide one unit of service to the customer at the head of the queue

Round-Robin CPU Scheduling

Most modern computers allow multiple processes to share a single CPU. There are various techniques for scheduling these processes. The most common, called *round robin scheduling*, adds new processes to the end of a *ready queue*, which consists of processes waiting to use the CPU. Each process on the ready queue is dequeued in turn and given a slice of CPU time. When the time slice runs out, the process is returned to the rear of the queue, as shown in Figure 14-6.

FIGURE 14-6
Scheduling processes for a CPU

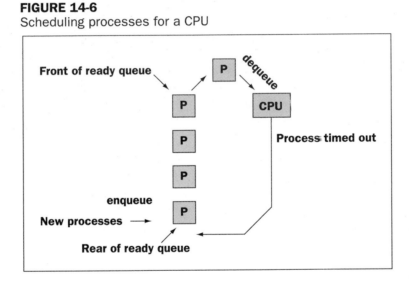

Generally, not all processes need the CPU with equal urgency. For instance, user satisfaction with a computer is greatly influenced by the computer's response time to keyboard and mouse inputs; thus, it makes sense to give precedence to processes handling these inputs. Round-robin scheduling adapts to this requirement by using a priority queue and assigning each process an appropriate priority. As a follow-up to this discussion, the chapter's second case study shows how a priority queue can be used to schedule patients in an emergency room.

Implementing the Queue Classes

The implementation of the queue classes is similar to that of the stack classes. Following is the code for the class `LinkedQueue`, which uses a `LinkedList`:

```java
import java.util.LinkedList;

public class LinkedQueue implements Queue{

    private LinkedList list;

    public LinkedQueue(){
        list = new LinkedList();
    }

    public Object peekFront(){
        if (list.isEmpty())
            throw new IllegalStateException("Queue is empty");
        return list.get(0);
    }

    public Object dequeue(){
        if (list.isEmpty())
            throw new IllegalStateException("Queue is empty");
        return list.remove(0);
    }
    public void enqueue(Object obj){
        list.add(obj);
    }
    public int size(){
        return list.size();
    }
}
```

The Priority Queue Interface

As mentioned earlier, the queue ADT can be extended to the notion of a priority queue. When items are added to a priority queue, they are assigned a rank order. When they are dequeued, items of higher priority are removed before those of lower priority. Items of equal priority are dequeued in the usual FIFO order. The `PriorityQueue` interface extends the `Queue` interface through the addition of a single method

```java
void enqueue(Object item, int priority)
```

where `priority` is a positive integer representing the priority of the item being enqueued. Items can still be enqueued using the method

```java
void enqueue(Object item)
```

and they are assigned a default priority of 1.

The syntax for extending an interface is similar to the syntax for extending a class:

```
public <SomeInterface> extends <SomeOtherInterface> {

    // Methods specific to SomeInterface go here

}
```

However, as we shall see, the classes that implement the new interface need not extend the classes that implement the interface being extended.

In this book, we show two implementations of PriorityQueue. These are called HeapPriorityQueue and LinkedPriorityQueue. The first is discussed in Lesson 18, and the second is examined next. The constructor for LinkedPriorityQueue has the form

```
LinkedPriorityQueue(int maxPriority)
```

where maxPriority is a positive integer indicating the highest priority to be used with this priority queue.

The following code segment shows how to declare and use a priority queue:

```
// Create a new priority queue to hold items with priorities 1 and 2
PriorityQueue q = new LinkedPriorityQueue (2);

// Add the integers 1,2,3 to the queue with a priority of 1
for (int i = 1; i <= 3; i++)
    q.enqueue(new Integer(i), 1);

// Add the integers 10,11,12 to the queue with a priority of 2
for (i = 10; i <= 12; i++)
    q.enqueue(new Integer(i), 2);

// Dequeue and display all integers in the queue
while (! q.isEmpty())
    System.out.println(((Integer)q.dequeue()).intValue());
```

In this example, integers go onto the priority queue in the order 1, 2, 3, 10, 11, 12, but leave in the order 10, 11, 12, 1, 2, 3, thus demonstrating the role played by priorities.

Implementation of a Linked Priority Queue

The linked implementation is based on an array of subqueues, and an item with priority *n* goes on the queue at index position *n* − 1. Figure 14-7 shows a priority queue with four priorities.

FIGURE 14-7
A linked priority queue with four priorities

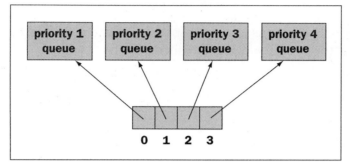

We call this a linked implementation because each array element contains a reference to a queue. The completion of the linked implementation of priority queues is left as a project at the end of the lesson.

EXERCISE 14.3

1. Assume that a queue q has been created. Draw a picture of the state of the queue after each of the following sequences of operations. You should assume that each sequence follows the other from a to c:

a.

```
for (int i = 1; i <= 5; i++)
    q.enqueue("" + i);
```

b.

```
q.dequeue();
q.dequeue();
```

c.

```
q.enqueue("5");
q.enqueue("6");
```

2. Write code segments that accomplish the following tasks with the queue q:
   a. Enqueue the strings "hello" and "there" onto the queue.
   b. Make the queue be empty.
   c. Print the contents of the queue in the terminal window without removing them permanently. (*Hint*: You can use a temporary data structure to accomplish this.)

3. Name three processes in the real world that can be simulated using queues.

EXERCISE 14.3 Continued

4. Assume that a priority queue q has been created with three priorities. Draw a picture of the state of the queue after each of the following sequences of operations. You should assume that each sequence follows the other from a to c:

a.

```
for (int i = 1; i <= 3; i++)
    q.enqueue("" + i, i);
```

b.

```
q.dequeue();
q.dequeue();
```

c.

```
q.enqueue("5", 2);
q.enqueue("6", 3);
```

5. Write code segments that accomplish the following tasks with the priority queue q:
   a. Enqueue the strings "hello" and "there" onto the queue with priority 1.
   b. Make the queue be empty.

6. Jack says he can't print the items in a priority queue without permanently removing them. Jill says he can. Who is right and why?

7. For each of the following applications, state which data structure would be appropriate—stack, queue, or priority queue.
   a. Tracking a line of customers at a supermarket.
   b. Tracking the information for a series of method calls on a computer.
   c. Scheduling patients in a hospital emergency room.

14.4 BreezySwing: Check Boxes and Radio Buttons

To our growing list of window objects we now add check boxes and radio button groups. Before diving into the details, we present a simple demonstration interface. Figure 14-8 shows a user interface from a demo program and contains, among other window objects, the following features:

■ Two check boxes labeled *Driver* and *Passenger* that are currently checked.

■ A radio button group containing buttons labeled *Married*, *Single*, and *Divorced* with the option *Single* selected.

FIGURE 14-8
Some sample check boxes and radio buttons

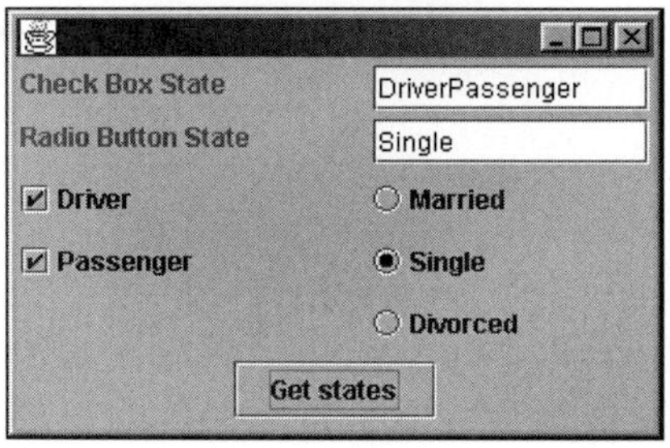

Following is a listing of the demo program, which we discuss in the next two subsections:

```
import javax.swing.*;
import BreezySwing.*;

public class CheckBoxTester extends GBFrame{

    private JLabel checkLabel, radioLabel;
    private JTextField checkField, radioField;

    private JCheckBox cbDriver, cbPassenger;

    private JRadioButton rbMarried, rbSingle, rbDivorced;

    private JButton getStateBTN;

    public CheckBoxTester(){

        // Add fields to display states of boxes and buttons
        checkLabel = addLabel("Check Box State",    1,1,1,1);
        radioLabel = addLabel("Radio Button State", 2,1,1,1);
        checkField = addTextField("", 1,2,2,1);
        radioField = addTextField("", 2,2,2,1);

        // Add check boxes
        cbDriver    = addCheckBox("Driver",    3,1,1,1);
        cbPassenger = addCheckBox("Passenger", 4,1,1,1);

        // Add radio buttons
```

```
      rbMarried  = addRadioButton("Married",  3,3,1,1);
      rbSingle   = addRadioButton("Single",   4,3,1,1);
      rbDivorced = addRadioButton("Divorced", 5,3,1,1);

      getStateBTN = addButton("Get states", 6,1,3,1);

      // Mark the default check box and radio button
      cbDriver.setSelected (true);
      rbSingle.setSelected (true);

      // Add the radio buttons to a button group
      ButtonGroup bgMaritalStatus = new ButtonGroup();
      bgMaritalStatus.add(rbMarried);
      bgMaritalStatus.add(rbSingle);
      bgMaritalStatus.add(rbDivorced);
   }

   public void buttonClicked(JButton buttonObj){
      String cbStr = "", rbStr = "";
      if (cbDriver.isSelected())
         cbStr = "Driver";
      if (cbPassenger.isSelected())
         cbStr = cbStr + "Passenger";
      checkField.setText(cbStr);
      if (rbMarried.isSelected())
         rbStr = "Married";
      else if (rbDivorced.isSelected())
         rbStr = "Divorced";
      else if (rbSingle.isSelected())
         rbStr = "Single";
      radioField.setText(rbStr);
   }

   public static void main(String[] args){
      CheckBoxTester tpo = new CheckBoxTester();
      tpo.setSize (300, 200);
      tpo.setVisible (true);
   }
}
```

Check Boxes

Check boxes are instantiated in a now familiar manner. For instance

```
cbDriver = addCheckBox ("Driver", 3,1,1,1);
```

Table 14-11 shows two frequently used methods: `setSelected` and `isSelected`.

TABLE 14-11
Two methods for check box instantiation

NAME OF METHOD	WHAT IT DOES
`setSelected (aBoolean)`	If aBoolean is true, then mark the check box or radio button; else clear the check box or radio button.
`isSelected()returns boolean`	Return `true` if marked; else return `false`.

Unlike radio buttons, more than one check box can be selected simultaneously, so the `isSelected` method can return `true` for more than one check box at any given time. The code for `buttonClicked` in the demo program illustrates the different logic for testing the states of check boxes and radio buttons:

```
public void buttonClicked(JButton buttonObj){
    String cbStr = "", rbStr = "";
    if (cbDriver.isSelected())
        cbStr = "Driver";
    if (cbPassenger.isSelected())
        cbStr = cbStr + "Passenger";
    checkField.setText(cbStr);
    if (rbMarried.isSelected())
        rbStr = "Married";
    else if (rbDivorced.isSelected())
        rbStr = "Divorced";
    else if (rbSingle.isSelected())
        rbStr = "Single";
    radioField.setText(rStr);
}
```

Radio Buttons

Radio buttons behave as a group, insofar as selecting one automatically deselects the others. To use radio buttons, one must instantiate a `ButtonGroup` and several radio buttons and then add each radio button to the group. In the demo program, radio buttons are instantiated as follows:

```
rbMarried  = addRadioButton("Married",  3,3,1,1);
rbSingle   = addRadioButton("Single",   4,3,1,1);
rbDivorced = addRadioButton("Divorced", 5,3,1,1);
```

The code to select a default radio button and to associate the radio buttons in a button group goes in the constructor method:

```
// Mark the default check box and radio button
cbDriver.setSelected (true);
rbSingle.setSelected (true);

// Add the radio buttons to a button group
ButtonGroup bgMaritalStatus = new ButtonGroup();
```

```
bgMaritalStatus.add(rbMarried);
bgMaritalStatus.add(rbSingle);
bgMaritalStatus.add(rbDivorced);
```

Later, when the program needs to know which radio button has been selected, it sends the isSelected() message to each radio button until one of them returns true.

Case Study 2: An Emergency Room Scheduler

Request

Write a program that allows a supervisor to schedule treatments for patients coming into a hospital's emergency room. Because some patients are in more critical condition than others, they are not treated on a strictly first-come, first-served basis, but are assigned a priority when admitted. Patients with a high priority receive attention before those with a lower priority.

Analysis

Patients come into the emergency room in one of three conditions, which in ascending order of priority are

1. Fair

2. Critical

3. Serious

The program allows the user to enter a patient's name and condition. When the user selects the **Schedule** button, the patient is placed in line for treatment according to the severity of his condition. When the user selects the **Treat Next Patient** button, the program removes and displays the patient first in line with the most serious condition. When the user selects the **Treat All Patients** button, the program removes and displays all patients in order from patient to serve first to patient to serve last.

Each command button produces an appropriate message in the output area. Table 14-12 lists the interface's responses to the commands.

TABLE 14-12
The commands of the emergency room program

COMMAND	RESPONSE
Schedule	<patient name> is added to the <condition> list
Treat Next Patient	<patient name> is being treated
Treat All Patients	<patient name> is being treated
	...
	<patient name> is being treated

Proposed Interface

We now propose the interface in Figure 14-9 for the system.

FIGURE 14-9
The user interface for the emergency room program

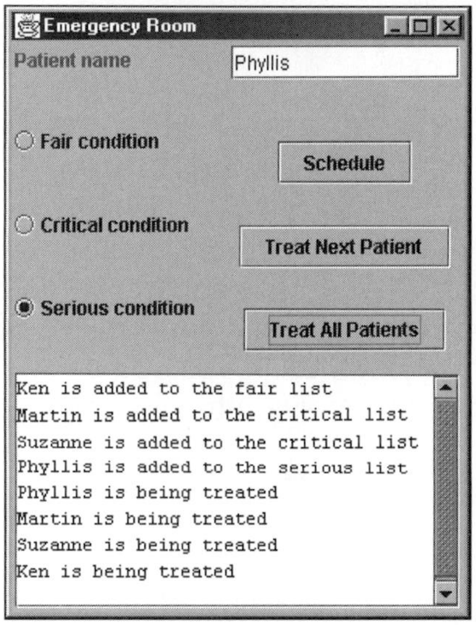

The application is divided into a view class, called ERView, and a model class, called ERModel. As usual, the view interacts with the user and sends messages to the model. The model maintains a priority queue of patients. The design and implementation of the system is left as a programming project.

SUMMARY

In this lesson, you learned:

- A stack is a linear collection that enforces a last-in, first-out order of elements.

- Operations on stacks are pushed for insertion and popped for removal of elements. Elements are accessed at just one end of a stack called the top.

- A queue is a linear collection that enforces a first-in, first-out order of elements.

- Operations on queues are *enqueue* for insertion and *dequeue* for removal of elements. Elements are enqueued at one end of the queue called the rear and dequeued at the other end called the front.

- A priority queue is a linear collection that enforces a first-in, first-out order of elements when they have equal priority and orders them by priority otherwise.

VOCABULARY*Review*

Define the following terms:		
front	priority queue	round-robin scheduling
infix form	push	token
pop	queue	top
postfix form	rear	

REVIEW*Questions*

FILL IN THE BLANK

Complete the following sentences by writing the correct word or words in the blanks provided.

1. The order in which elements are accessed in a stack is called _____ order.

2. The order in which elements are accessed in a queue is called _____ order.

3. The operation to insert an element into a stack is called _____.

4. The operation to remove an element from a stack is called _____.

5. Elements are inserted into a queue at one end called the _____.

6. Elements are removed from a queue at one end called the _____.

7. The process of returning to a previous state in a computation or a search is called _____.

8. The modeling of a process that uses a queue to schedule events is called _____.

9. A(n) _____ orders elements according to a ranking scheme.

10. A recursive process is supported using a(n) _____.

PROJECTS

PROJECT 14-1

Complete the first case study program and test it. Then add the operator ^ to the language of postfix expressions. This operator represents exponentiation. Thus, for example, the expression 2 3 ^ should evaluate to 8. Test your program with this new operator.

PROJECT 14-2

A palindrome is a sentence that reads the same forward and backward. For example, "ABLE WAS I ERE I SAW ELBA" is a palindrome attributed to Napoleon. Write a program that tests its inputs for palindromes. (*Hint*: Use a string tokenizer and a stack.)

PROJECT 14-3

Write a program that solves a maze problem. In this particular version of the problem, a hiker must find a path to the top of a mountain. Assume that the hiker leaves a parking lot, marked P, and explores the maze until she reaches the top of a mountain, marked T. Figure 14-10 shows what this particular maze looks like.

FIGURE 14-10
A maze problem

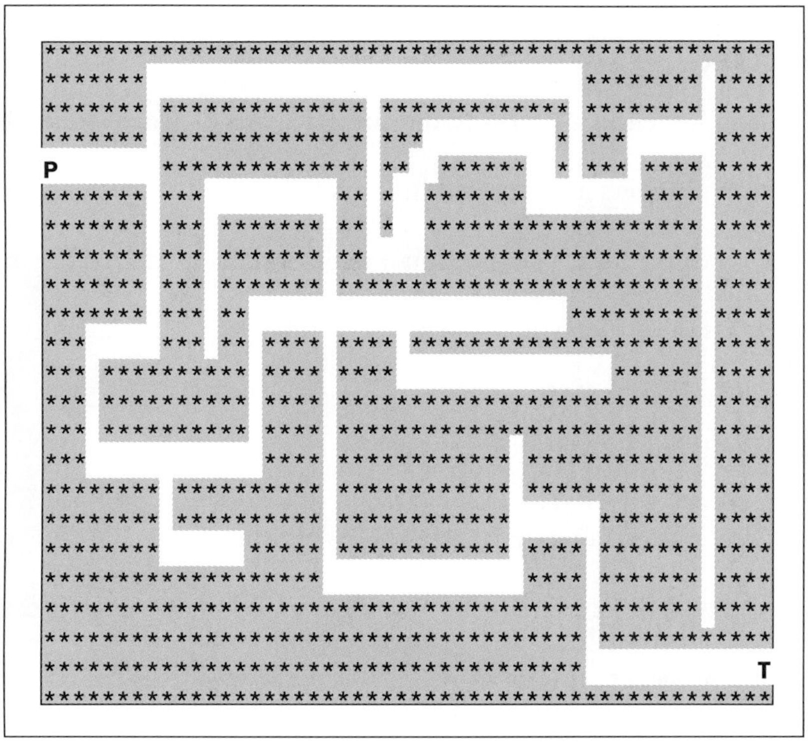

Java source code for the program's interface can be found on the data CD together with executable code for the program as a whole. You should run the program a few times before writing your own solution. The interface allows the user to enter a picture of the maze as a grid of characters. The character * marks a barrier, and P and T mark the parking lot and mountain top, respectively. A blank space marks a step along a path. The interface includes a **Set maze** button, and when the user selects it, the view should send a message to the model with the contents of the grid as a string parameter. When the user then selects the **Solve** button, the model attempts to find a path through the maze and returns "solved" or "unsolved" to the view depending on the outcome. In the model, begin by representing the maze as a matrix of characters (P, T, *, or space) and during the search mark each visited cell with a dot. Redisplay the grid at the end with the dots included. The following is the backtracking algorithm that is at the core of the solution:

```
Instantiate a stack
Locate the character 'P' in the matrix and replace it with a ' '
Push its location onto the stack
While the stack is not empty
   Pop a location, loc, off the stack

   Store a dot in the matrix at position loc
   For each cell of the matrix adjacent to loc
      If the cell contains a 'T'
         Return true
      If the cell contains a ' '
         Push its location onto the stack

   EndFor
Endwhile
Return false
Return false
```

PROJECT 14-4

Complete the implementation of the linked priority queue.

PROJECT 14-5

Complete the case study involving the emergency room scheduler.

PROJECT 14-6

Write a program that maintains a wait list of students for admission to a college course. Seniors are given first priority, followed by juniors, sophomores, and freshmen. The program should allow the user to perform the following tasks:

■ Enter a student's name and class, adding that student to the wait list

■ Remove the next student from the wait list

■ Clear the wait list

When any of these operations is performed, a display is updated with the appropriate information. The structure and user interface of this program can be similar to that of the emergency room scheduler.

CRITICAL *Thinking*

Jack complains to Jill, the designer of the priority queue ADT, that there is no way of knowing what the priority of a given item is after it has been entered into the queue. Discuss the alternative responses that Jill could give to Jack.

UNORDERED COLLECTIONS: SETS AND MAPS

The collection ADTs we have covered thus far are all ordered. That is, each item in an ordered collection has a position at which the client can locate it. Another category contains the unordered collections. From the client's perspective, the items in an unordered collection are in no particular positions. Thus, none of the operations on an unordered collection are position-based. Clients can insert, retrieve, or remove objects from unordered collections, but they cannot access the ith item, the next item, or the previous item. Some examples of unordered collections are sets and maps. This lesson gives a client's view of these collections. Implementation strategies are examined in Lesson 17.

15.1 Sets

The concept of a set should be familiar from mathematics. A *set* is a collection of items that from the client's perspective are unique. That is, there are no duplicate items in a set. There are many operations on sets in mathematics. Some of the most typical are

- Test for the empty set.

- Return the number of items in the set.

- Add an item to the set.

- Remove an item from the set.

- Test for set membership (whether or not a given item is in the set).

- Return the *union* of two sets. The union of two sets A and B is a set that contains all of the items in A and all of the items in B.

- Return the *intersection* of two sets. The intersection of two sets A and B is the set of items in A that are also items in B.

- Return the *difference* of two sets. The difference of two sets A and B is the set of items in A that are not also items in B.

- Test a set to determine whether or not another set is its *subset*. The set B is a subset of set A if and only if B is an empty set or all of the items in B are also in A.

To describe the contents of a set, we use the notation {<item1> . . . <item-n>} and assume that the items are in no particular order. Table 15-1 shows the results of some operations on example sets.

TABLE 15-1
Results of some typical set operations

SETS A AND B	A.UNION(B)	A.INTERSECTION(B)	A.DIFFERENCE(B)	A.SUBSET(B)
{12 5 17 6} {42 17 6}	(12 5 42 17 6}	{17 6}	{12 5}	false
{21 76 10 3 9} {}	{21 76 10 3 9}	{}	{21 76 10 3 9}	true
{87} {22 87 23}	{22 87 23}	{87}	{}	false
{22 87 23} {87}	{22 87 23}	{87}	{22 23}	true

The `java.util.Set` Interface

The most commonly used methods in the `Set` interface are listed in Table 15-2.

TABLE 15-2
Commonly used methods in the `Set` interface

METHOD	WHAT IT DOES
`boolean add(Object obj)`	If the object is not already in the set, then adds the object to the set, increasing the set's size by one, and returns `true`; otherwise, returns `false`.
`boolean contains(Object obj)`	Returns `true` if the object is in the set, else `false`.
`boolean isEmpty()`	Returns `true` if the set contains no objects, else `false`.
`Iterator iterator()`	Returns an iterator on the set.
`boolean remove(Object obj)`	If the object is in the set, removes it and returns `true`; otherwise, returns `false`.
`int size()`	Returns the number of objects currently in the set.

Note that sets support an `iterator` method. You might have been wondering how you can examine all the items in a set after they have been added, in view of the fact that there is no index-based access as with lists. You use an iterator, which supports the visiting of items in an unspecified order.

Applications of Sets

Aside from their role in mathematics, sets have many applications in the area of data processing. For example, in the field of database management, the answer to a query that contains the conjunction of two keys could be constructed from the intersection of the sets of items containing these keys.

Implementing Class

The implementing class for sets in `java.util` is called `HashSet`. The name derives from the technique by which items are accessed, called *hashing*. We examine this concept in detail in Lesson 17. The following is a trivial illustration of the use of a `HashSet`:

```
Set s = new HashSet();

s.add("Bill");
s.add("Mary");
s.add("Jose");
s.add("Bill");                          // Duplicate element

System.out.println(s.size());               // Prints 3
System.out.println(s.contains("Jose"));         // Prints true
```

Now suppose we want to print the names in this set. By creating an iterator on the set, we can retrieve the names one by one and print them:

```
Iterator iter = s.iterator();

while (iter.hasNext()){
   String name = (String)iter.next();
   System.out.println (name);
}
```

As a third example, let us define a method that uses an iterator to create the intersection of two sets. The intersection of two sets is a new set containing only the items the two sets have in common. Following is the code:

```
Set intersection(Set a, Set b){

   Set result = new HashSet();
   Iterator iter = a.iterator();

   while (iter.hasNext()){
      Object obj = iter.next();
      if (b.contains(obj))
         result.add(obj);
   }

   return result;
}
```

EXERCISE 15.1

1. In what way does a set differ from a list?

2. Assume that the set s contains the string "3". Describe the sequence of sets resulting from the following operations:
   a. s.add("4");
   b. s.add("4");
   c. s.add("5");
   d. s.remove("3");

3. How do you visit all the items in a set?

4. Write a method for the set difference operation.

5. Write a method for the subset operation.

6. Write a method that returns an array of the objects in a set.

7. Suppose you want to work with a set of integers. How will you go about adding integers to the set and accessing them in the set?

15.2 Sorted Sets

Sets are unordered collections; however, there is sufficient need for a sorted version that Java includes the interface SortedSet and the implementation TreeSet. The iterator on this type of set accesses the items in a sorted order, but there is a catch. All the items must be ***mutually comparable***, which is to say, for any two items in the set, e1.compareTo(e2) returns a negative integer, zero, or a positive integer depending on whether e1 is less than, equal to, or greater than e2. The String class and the wrapper classes for the primitive types satisfy this requirement, as does any class that implements the Comparable interface.

Consider, for example, the problem of sorting a list of unique items. We could use one of the sort methods from Lesson 10 or Lesson 11, rewritten, of course, to manipulate a list. But another way to proceed is to transfer the items from the list to a *sorted set* and then transfer the items back to the list. A precondition is that the list contains unique, comparable items. Following is the code:

```
// Sort a list of unique items

List list = new ArrayList();

. . . add unique items to the list . . .

SortedSet set = new TreeSet();

for (int i = 0; i < list.size(); i++) // Copy the items to the sorted set
    set.add(list.get(i));

Iterator iter = set.iterator();    // Copy the items back to the list
list.clear();
while (iter.hasNext())
    list.add(iter.next());
```

The `java.util.SortedSet` Interface

The `SortedSet` interface extends the `Set` interface with the methods listed in Table 15-3.

TABLE 15-3
The `SortedSet` interface

METHOD	WHAT IT DOES
`Comparator comparator()`	Returns the comparator associated with this sorted set, or `null` if it uses its elements' natural ordering.
`Object first()`	Returns the first (lowest) element currently in this sorted set.
`SortedSet headSet(Object toElement)`	Returns a view of the portion of this sorted set whose elements are strictly less than toElement.
`Object last()`	Returns the last (highest) element currently in this sorted set.
`SortedSet subSet(Object fromElement, Object toElement)`	Returns a view of the portion of this sorted set whose elements range from `fromElement`, inclusive, to `toElement`, exclusive.
`SortedSet tailSet(Object fromElement)`	Returns a view of the portion of this sorted set whose elements are greater than or equal to fromElement.

The following code segment uses a sorted set and a pair of iterators to display the contents of a set of strings in alphabetical order:

```
// Create a set of strings and add some to it

Set set1 = new HashSet();

. . . add strings to the set . . .

Set set2 = new TreeSet();              // Copy the strings to a sorted set
Iterator iter1 = set1.iterator();
while (iter1.hasNext())
   set2.add(iter.next());

Iterator iter2 = set2.iterator(); // Print the strings in the sorted set
while (iter2.hasNext())
   System.out.println(iter2.next());
```

*E*XERCISE 15.2

1. Why must the items added to a sorted set be comparable?

2. Explain the restrictions on the use of a sorted set to sort a list.

15.3 Example Application: Word Frequencies

Assume that someone wants to display a table of the frequencies of the words in a segment of text. The table should have two columns. The first column is a sorted list of the unique words. The second column is a list containing the corresponding frequencies of the words in the first column. Figure 15-1 shows a sample output for a string that contains the following text: "This file contains several words and three words in this file appear twice."

FIGURE 15-1
The output of a word frequency program

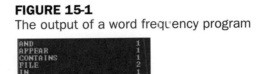

One could implement an algorithm to solve this problem using arrays or lists. But such an algorithm is very complicated. A simpler algorithm uses a list and a sorted set as follows:

1. Transfer all of the words from the text to the list.

2. Create a sorted set of words from this list.

3. Print the words in the sorted set and use these words to look up the associated frequencies in the list and print these frequencies.

Following is the pseudocode:

```
Create a list called wordList

While there are more words in the file
    Read the next word and convert it to uppercase
    Add the word to wordList

Create a sorted set called wordSet from wordList

For each word in wordSet
    Print the word
    Print the number of occurrences of that word in wordList
    Print a newline
```

Following is a further refinement of our algorithm that is closer to Java code:

```
List wordList = new ArrayList();

While there are more words in the file
    String word = read the next word
    wordList.add(word.toUppercase());

SortedSet wordSet = new TreeSet();
for (int i = 0; i < wordList.size())
    wordSet.add(wordlist.get(i));
```

```
Iterator iter = wordSet.iterator();
while (iter.hasNext()){
    String word = (String)iter.next();
    int frequency = occurrencesOf(wordlist, word);
    System.out.println(Format.justify('l', word, 20) +
                       Format.justify('r', frequency, 5));
}
```

This code relies on the helper method `occurrencesOf`, which returns the number of occurrences of a given object in a list. This method's implementation is left as the exercise for this section.

EXERCISE 15.3

1. Write the method `occurrencesOf` for lists.

15.4 Maps

A *map*, sometimes also referred to as a *table*, is a collection in which each item, or *value*, is associated with a unique *key*. Users add, remove, and retrieve items from a map by specifying their keys. One occasionally sees a map referred to as a *keyed list, dictionary*, or an *association list*. The package `java.util` defines several classes, `Dictionary`, `Hashtable`, and `Map`, which all represent maps. Another way to think of a map is as a collection of unique items called *entries* or *associations*. Each entry contains a key and a value (the item).

Table 15-4 shows the data in two maps. The first map is keyed by strings, and the second map is keyed by integers.

TABLE 15-4
A map keyed by strings and a map keyed by integers

MAP 1		MAP 2	
KEY	VALUE	KEY	VALUE
"occupation"	"teacher"	80	"Mary"
"hair color"	"brown"	39	"Joe"
"height"	72	21	"Sam"
"age"	72	95	"Renee"
"name"	"Bill"	40	"Lily"

Note the following points about the two example maps:

- The keys are in no particular order.
- The keys are unique. That is, the keys for a given map form a set.
- The values need not be unique. That is, the same value can be associated with more than one key.

There are many operations that one could perform on maps. At a bare minimum, a client should be able to

- Test a map for emptiness.
- Determine a map's size.
- Insert a value at a given key.
- Remove a given key (also removing the associated value).
- Retrieve a value at a given key.
- Determine whether or not a map contains a key.
- Determine whether or not a map contains a value.
- Examine all of the keys.
- Examine all of the values.

Maps have a wide range of applications. For example, interpreters and compilers of programming languages make use of symbol tables. Each key in a symbol table corresponds to an identifier in a program. The value associated with a key contains the attributes of the identifier—a name, a data type, and other information. Perhaps the most prevalent application of maps is in database management.

The `java.util.Map` Interface

Table 15-5 lists and describes the most frequently used `Map` methods. In this table, the object associated with a key is called its *value*.

TABLE 15-5
The most frequently used `Map` methods

METHOD	WHAT IT DOES
`boolean containsKey(Object key)`	Returns `true` if the map contains the indicated key or `false` otherwise.
`boolean containsValue (Object value)`	Returns `true` if the map contains at least one instance of the indicated value or `false` otherwise.
`Object get(Object key)`	Returns the value associated with the indicated key if the key is in the map or `null` otherwise.
`boolean isEmpty()`	Returns `true` if the map is empty or `false` otherwise.
`Set keySet()`	Returns a set view of the keys in the map.
`Object put(Object key, Object value)`	If the key is already in the map, replaces the previous value with the new value and returns the previous value; otherwise, adds the key and the associated value to the map and returns `null`.
`Object remove(Object key)`	If the key is in the map, removes the key value pair from the map and returns the value; otherwise, returns `null`.
`int size()`	Returns the number of key value pairs currently in the map.
`Collection values()`	Returns a collection view of the values in the map.

Note that the methods `keySet` and `values` allow the client to examine all of a map's keys and values, respectively. We discuss the `Collection` type and the idea of a collection view later in this lesson. For now, suffice it to say that one can open an iterator on a collection view. The following code segment shows how easy it is to visit all the keys and values in a map with the appropriate iterators:

```
Map map = new HashMap();

. . . add a bunch of keys and values to the map

// Obtain the views of the map's keys and values.
Set s = map.keySet();
Collection c = map.values();

// Open iterators on these views and display their contents
Iterator keys = s.iterator();
while (keys.hasNext())
   System.out.println(keys.next());

Iterator values = c.iterator();
while (values.hasNext())
   System.out.println(values.next());
```

Implementing Class

`java.util` provides one implementation of the `Map` interface called `HashMap`. In the following example code segment, we initialize a map with student data:

```
Map studentMap = new HashMap();       //Declare and instantiate a map
int i;
Student stu;

for (i = 1; i <= 4; i++){
   stu = new Student();                //Instantiate a new student
   stu.setId ("s" + i);                //Set the student's attributes
   stu.setName . . .                   //. . .
   stu.setScore . . .                  //. . .
   studentMap.put ("s" + i, stu);      //Add the student to the map using
                                       //the student's id as the key
}
```

Notice the following points about this code:

- We have added an attribute called ID to the `Student` class. Unlike a name, which might be duplicated, an ID is unique.

- A student's ID, being a string, is in fact an object.

- A student ID is both one of its attributes and its key. It is common practice to choose an object's key from among its attributes.

An object is retrieved from a map using the `get` method, as illustrated in this statement that retrieves and displays the student whose key is `s1`:

```
System.out.println (studentMap.get ("s1"));
```

EXERCISE 15.4

1. How do maps differ from sets?

2. What happens when a key is used for inserting a value in a map and that key is already present?

3. State two applications in which a map would be an appropriate data structure.

15.5 Sorted Maps

Sorted maps are to maps as sorted sets are to sets. That is, a sorted map has all the features of a map but in addition allows the client to visit the keys in sorted order. The method `keySet` now returns a sorted set, which can return an iterator that supports a traversal of the map's keys in sorted order. Needless to say, the keys of a sorted map must be comparable.

The `java.util.SortedMap` Interface

The interface for `SortedMap` is similar to the interface for `SortedSet`. It extends the `Map` interface with the methods listed in Table 15-6.

TABLE 15-6
The `SortedMap` interface

METHOD	DESCRIPTION
`Comparator comparator()`	Returns the comparator associated with this sorted map, or `null` if it uses its keys' natural ordering.
`Object firstKey()`	Returns the first (lowest) key currently in this sorted map.
`SortedSet headMap(Object toKey)`	Returns a view of the portion of this sorted map whose keys are strictly less than `toKey`.
`Object lastKey()`	Returns the last (highest) element currently in this sorted map.
`SortedSet subMap(Object fromKey, Object toKey)`	Returns a view of the portion of this sorted map whose keys range from `fromKey`, inclusive, to `toKey`, exclusive.
`SortedSet tailMap(Object fromKey)`	Returns a view of the portion of this sorted map whose keys are greater than or equal to `fromKey`.

Implementing Class and Application

`java.util` includes the class `TreeMap` to implement a sorted map. An excellent application for a sorted map is any database application in which the records are accessed by content (such as a name) and must be maintained in sorted order. For example, the student list of Lessons 8 and 10 could be represented as a sorted map if the student objects must be ordered by ID number.

*E*XERCISE 15.5

1. Write a code segment that displays the keys and values of a sorted map in two columns.

Case Study: The Therapist

To illustrate the use of maps, we offer an amusing program that will allow you to earn a fortune as a nondirective psychotherapist.

Request

Write a program that emulates a nondirective psychotherapist. The practitioner of this kind of therapy is essentially a good listener who responds to a patient's statements by rephrasing them or indirectly asking for more information.

Analysis

Figure 15-2 shows the system's interface as it changes throughout a sequence of exchanges with the user. When the user enters a statement, the program responds in one of two ways:

1. With a randomly chosen hedge, such as "Please tell me more."

2. By changing some key words in the user's input string and appending this string to a randomly chosen qualifier. Thus, to "My teacher always plays favorites," the program might reply with "Why do you say that your teacher always plays favorites?"

FIGURE 15-2
A sequence of interactions between a user and the therapist program

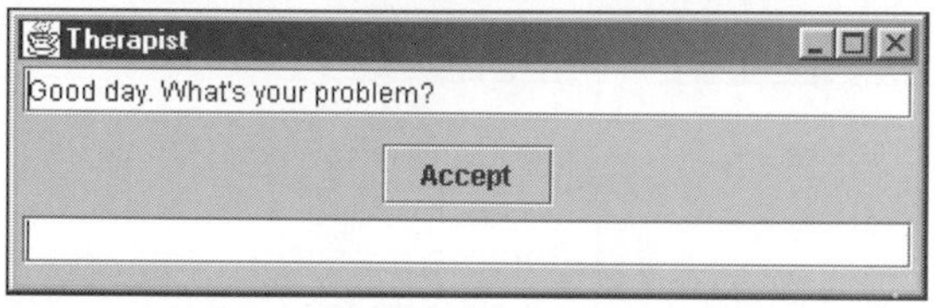

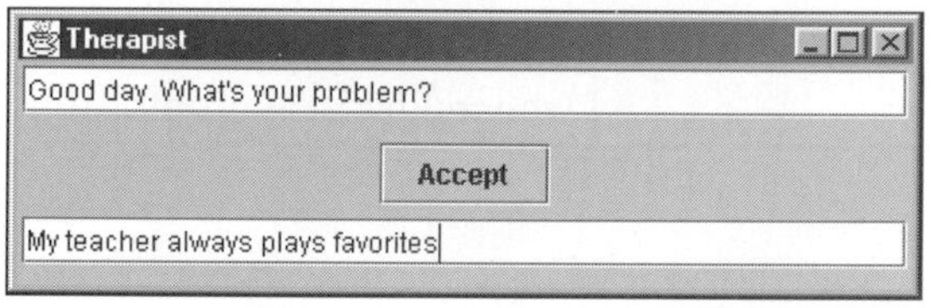

FIGURE 15-2 Continued

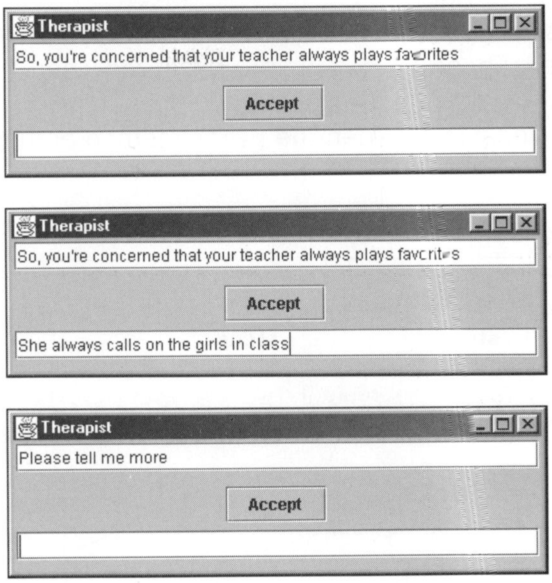

The program consists of two classes: `TherapistInterface` and `Therapist`. A `TherapistInterface` object controls the GUI, passes user inputs to a `Therapist` object, and displays that object's reply. A `Therapist` object does the actual work of constructing a reply from the user's statement.

Design of the TherapistInterface Class

The `TherapistInterface` class creates a new `Therapist` object at program start-up, displays a prompt, and waits for user input. The following is pseudocode for the `buttonClicked` method:

```
void buttonClicked(JButton buttonObj){
    get the string from the patient field
    ask the therapist object for its reply to this string
    clear the patient field
    display the therapist's reply in the therapist field
}
```

Design of the Therapist Class

The Therapist class stores hedges and qualifiers in two sets and stores keywords and their replacements in a map. These collections are initialized when a therapist object is instantiated. The principal method in the Therapist class is called reply. The structure chart in Figure 15-3 shows the relationship between the reply method and its subordinate methods.

FIGURE 15-3
Structure chart for the reply method

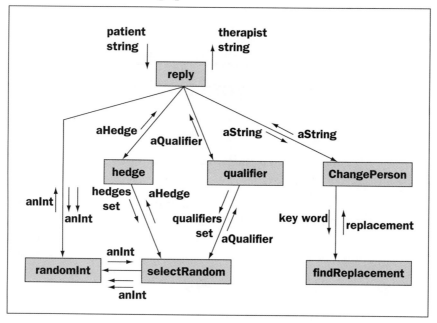

Following is pseudocode for the methods in the structure chart:

```
String reply(String patientString){
    pick a random number between 1 and 3
    if the number is 1
        call the hedge method to return a randomly chosen hedge
    else{
        call the qualifier method to randomly choose a qualifying phrase
        call the changePerson method to change persons in the patient's
        string
        return the concatenation of these two strings
    }
}

String hedge(Set set){
    randomly select a number between 0 and the size of the hedges set - 1
    use that number to return the string from the hedges set
}

String qualifier(Set set){
    randomly select a number between 0 and the size of the qualifiers
    set - 1
    use that number to return the string from the qualifiers set
```

```
    }

    String changePerson(String patientString){
        open a string tokenizer on the patientString (see Lesson 14)
        create an empty result string
        while the tokenizer has more tokens
        get the next token
        find the replacement word for that token
        append the replacement word to the result string
        }
        return the result string
    }

    String findReplacement(String word){
        if the word is a key in the replacements map
        return the value stored at that key
        else
            return the word
    }

    String selectRandom(Set set){
        generate a random number between 0 and one less than the set's size
        use this number to locate a string in the set
        return the string
    }

    int randomInt(int low, int high){
        use Math.random to generate a random double 0 <= x < 1
        map x to an integer low <= i <= high
        return i
    }
```

We are now ready to present the Java code for the classes.

Implementation of the `TherapistInterface` Class

```java
/* TherapistInterface.java
1) This class provides the interface to the therapist system.
2) The user makes a statement and presses the Accept button.
3) The system displays the therapist's response.
*/

import javax.swing.*;
import BreezySwing.*;

public class TherapistInterface extends GBFrame{

    //Window objects
    JTextField therapistField =
            addTextField("Good day. What's your problem?", 1, 1, 1, 1);
    JButton acceptButton    = addButton("Accept"    , 2, 1, 1, 1);
    JTextField patientField  = addTextField(""       , 3, 1, 1, 1);
```

```
        //Instance variable
        private Therapist therapist;        //The therapist object

        public TherapistInterface(){
        //Constructor
        //  Preconditions  -- none
        //  Postconditions -- the window's title is set
        //               -- a therapist object is instantiated

           setTitle("Therapist");
           therapist = new Therapist();
        }

        public void buttonClicked (JButton buttonObj){
        //Responds to the Accept button
        //  Preconditions  -- the Accept button is clicked
        //  Postconditions -- the therapist's response is displayed
        //               -- the patientField is cleared
        //               -- focus is set to the patientField

           String patientString = patientField.getText();
           String therapistString = therapist.reply(patientString);
           therapistField.setText(therapistString);
           patientField.setText("");
           patientField.requestFocus();
        }

        public static void main (String[] args){
        //Instantiates, sizes, and displays the application's main window

           TherapistInterface tpo = new TherapistInterface();
           tpo.setSize (400, 125);
           tpo.setVisible(true);
           ((TherapistInterface)tpo).patientField.requestFocus();
        }
    }
```

Implementation of the `Therapist` **Class**

```
    /* Therapist.java
    1) This class emulates a nondirective psychotherapist.
    2) The major method, reply, accepts user statements and generates
       a nondirective reply.
    */

    import java.util.*;

    public class Therapist extends Object{

       private Set hedgeSet;            //The set of hedges
       private Set qualifierSet;        //The set of qualifiers
```

```java
    private Map  replacementMap;          //The map of replacement words

public Therapist(){
//Constructor
//  Preconditions  -- none
//  Postconditions -- the two sets and the map are instantiated
//                    and initialized

   hedgeSet = new HashSet();
   hedgeSet.add("Please tell me more");
   hedgeSet.add("Many of my patients tell me the same thing");
   hedgeSet.add("It's getting late, maybe we had better quit");

   qualifierSet = new HashSet();
   qualifierSet.add("Why do you say that ");
   qualifierSet.add("You seem to think that ");
   qualifierSet.add("So, you're concerned that ");

   replacementMap = new HashMap();
   replacementMap.put("i", "you");
   replacementMap.put("me", "you");
   replacementMap.put("my", "your");
   replacementMap.put("am", "are");
}

public String reply(String patientString){
//Replies to the patient's statement with either a hedge or
//a string consisting of a qualifier concatenated to
//a transformed version of the patient's statement.
//  Preconditions  -- none
//  Postconditions -- returns a reply

   String reply = "";               //The therapist's reply
   int choice = randomInt(1, 3); //Generate a random number between 1
   and 3

   //If the patient says nothing, then encourage him
   if (patientString.trim().equals(""))
      return "Take your time. Some things are difficult to talk about.";


   //Else reply with a hedge or a qualified response
   if(choice == 1)
      reply = hedge(hedgeSet);                          //Hedge 1/3 of the time
   else if (choice == 2 || choice == 3)
      reply = qualifier(qualifierSet) +                 //Build a qualified
      response
             changePerson(patientString);     //2/3 of the time
   return reply;
}

private String hedge(Set hedgeSet){
//Selects a hedge at random
```

```
//   Preconditions  -- the hedge set has been initialized
//   Postconditions -- returns a randomly selected hedge

    return (String) selectRandom(hedgeSet);
}

private String qualifier(Set qualifierSet){
//Selects a qualifier at random
//   Preconditions  -- the qualifier set has been initialized
//   Postconditions -- returns a randomly selected qualifier

    return (String) selectRandom(qualifierSet);
}

private String changePerson(String str){
//Returns a string created by swapping i, me, etc. for you, your, etc.
//in the string str
//   Preconditions  -- none
//   Postconditions -- returns the created string

    //Tokenize str
    StringTokenizer tokens = new StringTokenizer(str, " \n.,!;?");
    String result = "";                        //Create a response
                                               string

    //Build the response from replacements of the tokens
    while (tokens.hasMoreTokens()){
       String keyWord = tokens.nextToken();
       String replacement = findReplacement(keyWord);
       result = result + replacement + " ";
    }
    return result;
}

private String findReplacement(String keyWord){
//Returns the value associated with the keyword or the keyword itself
//if the keyword is not in the map.
//   Preconditions  -- the replacement map has been initialized
//   Postconditions -- returns the replacement

    keyWord = keyWord.toLowerCase();
    if (replacementMap.containsKey(keyWord))
       return (String) replacementMap.get(keyWord);
    else
       return keyWord;
}

private Object selectRandom(Set set){
//Selects an entry at random from the set
//   Preconditions  -- the set is not empty
//   Postconditions -- returns the random entry
```

```
        int index = randomInt(0, set.size() - 1);
        Iterator iter = set.iterator();
        for (int i = 0; i < index; i++)
            iter.next();
        return iter.next();
    }


    private int randomInt(int low, int high){
    //Generate a random number between low and high
    //  Preconditions  -- low <= high
    //  Postconditions -- returns the random number

        return (int) (low + Math.random() * (high - low  + 1));
    }
}
```

15.6 The Glue That Holds Collections Together

Thus far in this book, we have considered the ways in which different categories of collections vary. Now it is time to ask about the ways in which they are similar. All collections contain objects, have a definite size at any given time, and can grow or shrink in size. Are there any operations that all collections have in common? These operations, if they exist, would serve as a kind of glue that holds collections together, allowing them to interact in very powerful ways.

Addition, Removal, and Membership

Each type of collection we have examined thus far supports some form of addition and removal of elements. Some collections have more than one way to do this; for example, lists have index-based and object-based versions of additions and removals, and a position-based version via a list iterator. It seems that every collection allows at least object-based additions and removals. Indeed, the object-based methods add and remove for lists and sets have the same signature. These collections also support a method to test an object for membership in the collection, namely, contains. Maps include variants of these operations for keys and values, whereas stacks and queues support only additions and removals with more specific names such as pop and dequeue. Clearly any list of general collection operations will have some of these basic operations among them or will use them to implement others.

Iterators

Items can be transferred from a set to a list by using an iterator. An iterator also can be used to transfer items in the other direction, from a list to a set, although other list operations exist to accomplish this as well. The Map method keySet, which returns a set of a map's keys, allows one to open an iterator on a map. It is a critical fact that iterators work the same way, whether they are used with lists, sets, or maps. Indeed, as we shall see in Lesson 16, we can provide iterators for any collections that work in the same manner. Thus, iterators belong in the list of common collection operations.

Other Operations

One common operation on any collection removes all its elements, thus producing an empty collection. The implementation code for this method, called `clear()`, can be the same for any collection if we use an iterator that supports the method `remove`. We simply iterate through the elements and use the `Iterator` method `remove` all the way. This method is in fact implemented in this manner for lists and sets.

Programmers often must construct operations that involve more than one collection. We saw examples earlier in this lesson of the set operations union, intersection, and difference, which the `Set` collection does not include but which we can implement quite easily. Other, more general tasks that apply to any pair of collections cry out for standard methods. Consider the following four:

■ Add all the elements of one collection to another collection.

■ Remove all the elements of one collection from another collection.

■ Retain only the elements of one collection in another collection.

■ Determine whether or not one collection contains all the elements in another collection.

It would be quite simple to implement all of these operations for any pair of collections, including two collections of different types, with just an iterator and the methods `add`, `remove`, and `contains`.

The `java.util.Collection` Interface

Several of the common collection operations discussed thus far are included in the `java.util.Collection` interface. Both the `List` and the `Set` interfaces extend this interface, so these operations are available to lists and sets. Figure 15-4 shows the relationships among the collection interfaces in `java.util`. Note that the `Map` interface does not extend `Collection`. Table 15-7 describes the `Collection` methods.

FIGURE 15-4
The interface hierarchies of the collections in `java.util`

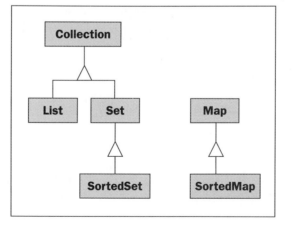

TABLE 15-7
The Collection interface

COLLECTION METHOD	DESCRIPTION
boolean add(Object o)	Ensures that this collection contains the specified element (optional operation).
boolean addAll(Collection c)	Adds all of the elements in the specified collection to this collection (optional operation).
void clear()	Removes all of the elements from this collection (optional operation).
boolean contains(Object o)	Returns true if this collection contains the specified element.
boolean containsAll(Collection c)	Returns true if this collection contains all of the elements in the specified collection.
boolean isEmpty()	Returns true if this collection contains no elements.
Iterator iterator()	Returns an iterator over the elements in this collection.
boolean remove(Object o)	Removes a single instance of the specified element from this collection, if it is present (optional operation).
boolean removeAll(Collection c)	Removes all this collection's elements that are also contained in the specified collection (optional operation).
boolean retainAll(Collection c)	Retains only the elements in this collection that are contained in the specified collection (optional operation).
int size()	Returns the number of elements in this collection.
Object[] toArray()	Returns an array containing all of the elements in this collection.
Object[] toArray(Object[] a)	Returns an array containing all of the elements in this collection whose run-time type is that of the specified array.

Some of the operations in Table 15-7, such as removeAll, are listed as optional. This means that the implementing classes must include these methods but need not support them. In practical terms, if a given method is not supported, the calls to this method in a client's code will compile but these calls will throw an UnsupportedOperationException at run time.

Several operations expect a parameter of type Collection. This means that one can pass for this parameter an object of any class that implements the Collection interface. That would be all of the list and set classes in java.util.

Finally, the list and set classes include constructors that expect a parameter of type Collection. These constructors provide a simple way of converting one type of collection to another.

Some Examples of the Use of General Collection Operations

The following code segments show some examples of the power of the collection methods.

Set union

```
Set unionSet = new HashSet(set1).addAll(set2);
```

Set intersection

```
Set intersectionSet = new HashSet(set1).retainAll(set2);
```

Set difference

```
Set differenceSet = new HashSet(set1).removeAll(set2);
```

Sort a list, removing duplicates

```
List sortedList = new ArrayList(new SortedSet(unsortedList));
```

The `Collections` Class

Given the wide array of operations on collections, the programmer can write new methods for almost any occasion. For example, as we saw in Lesson 10, you can write methods for searching and sorting lists using several different algorithms. Other useful methods, such as searching for a minimum or maximum value, also can be written easily. Several of these operations are so common that `java.util` implements them in a set of static methods, primarily for use with lists. These methods are included in the `Collections` class.

For example, you can sort and search a list of strings as follows:

```
Collections.sort(list);                    // Assume list contains only strings
Collections.binarySearch(list, "Mary");    // See if "Mary" is in list
```

Table 15-8 describes some commonly used `Collections` methods.

TABLE 15-8
Some `Collections` methods

COLLECTIONS **METHOD**	**DESCRIPTION**
`static int binarySearch(List list, Object key)`	Searches the specified list for the specified object using the binary search algorithm.
`static Object max(Collection coll)`	Returns the maximum element of the given collection, according to the natural ordering of its elements.
`static Object min(Collection coll)`	Returns the minimum element of the given collection, according to the natural ordering of its elements.
`static void reverse(List list)`	Reverses the order of the elements in the specified list. This method runs in linear time.
`static void shuffle(List list)`	Randomly permutes the specified list using a default source of randomness.
`static void sort(List list)`	Sorts the specified list into ascending order, according to the natural ordering of its elements.

EXERCISE 15.6

1. State three properties that all collections have.

SUMMARY

In this lesson, you learned:

- A set is an unordered collection of unique objects.

- The objects in a sorted set can be visited in a natural order by using an iterator.

- A map associates a set of keys with values; the values can be accessed, inserted, or removed by using their keys.

- The keys in a sorted map can be visited in their natural order by using the methods `keySet` and `iterator`.

- Java organizes sets and lists in a hierarchy of collections. Both types of collections implement the `Collection` interface, which includes general methods for operating on collections. Java provides an extra set of static methods for manipulating collections in the `Collections` class. Among these are methods for a binary search, a sort, and a shuffle.

VOCABULARY *Review*

Define the following terms:		
association	key	set
association list	keyed list	sorted map
dictionary	map	sorted set
hashing	mutually comparable	value

REVIEW *Questions*

FILL IN THE BLANK

Complete the following sentences by writing the correct word or words in the blanks provided.

1. The items in an unordered collection have no particular _____.

2. The set of items that two other sets have in common is called their _____.

3. The set of items that two other sets have altogether is called their _____.

4. The set of items in the first set that are not present in the second set is called their _____.

5. You visit all the items in a set using a(n) _____.

6. A map contains associations of _____ and _____.

7. To insert, remove, or access a value in a map, one uses the value's _____.

8. A(n) _____ map is a type of map in which you can visit items in sorted order.

9. The _____ methods work with either lists or sets.

10. The _____ class provides a set of static methods for tasks such as sorting and searching lists.

PROJECTS

PROJECT 15-1

Define and test a `Sets` class. This class should include static methods for common operations on sets, such as union, intersection, difference, and subset.

PROJECT 15-2

Write a complete GUI-based program that computes the frequencies of words in a segment of text. The input is entered in a text area. The output is a sorted list of unique words and their associated frequencies in the input text. Use parallel lists and a sorted set in your program.

PROJECT 15-3

Redo the program in Project 15-2 using a sorted map instead of parallel lists.

PROJECT 15-4

A phone book application allows a user to add entries, remove them, and view them. An entry consists of a name and a phone number. The interface should be similar to the Student Test Scores case study in Lesson 10, with the names in a scrolling list and the entry for a selected name in a text area. A dialog allows the user to add a new entry. The model class should use a sorted map to store the entries, keyed by name. Write a program that implements this application.

PROJECT 15-5

Add a history set to the case study in this lesson. The history set keeps track of the user's unique inputs. At regular intervals, the therapist should reply to a randomly chosen item from the history set, using the prefix "Earlier you said that."

PROJECT 15-6

Add a map of key words and their associated responses to the case study of this lesson. Each key word should have more than one possible response. For example, the set of responses for the key word "mother" might be "Your mother keeps coming up in our conversation" and "Tell me more about your parents." At regular intervals, the program should examine the user's input for one of these key words. If a match is found, the program replies with one of the associated responses chosen at random.

CRITICAL *Thinking*

`java.util` does not include the `Map` classes in its hierarchy of collections. Discuss the advantages and disadvantages of this design decision. Propose a way of including maps in the collections hierarchy.

USING ABSTRACT DATA TYPES

REVIEW *Questions*

TRUE/FALSE

Circle T if the statement is true or F if the statement is false.

T   F   1. UML provides graphical notation for describing the results of analysis and design but not user requirements.

T   F   2. Collaboration diagrams belong to the design phase of the software development process.

T   F   3. The elements in a linear collection are ordered by position.

T   F   4. Unordered collections are useful for representing sequences of elements.

T   F   5. A stack is a first-in, first-out collection.

T   F   6. A queue is useful for scheduling resources on a first-come, first-served basis.

T   F   7. The values in a map are accessed by content rather than position.

T   F   8. All iterators support the methods `next`, `hasNext`, and `remove`.

T   F   9. The values in a sorted map cannot be visited in any particular order.

T   F   10. The different categories of collection have almost nothing in common.

FILL IN THE BLANK

Complete the following sentences by writing the correct word or words in the blanks provided.

1. Lists, stack, and queues are examples of _____ collections.

2. Sets and maps are examples of _____ collections.

3. An object that is capable of visiting all the items in a collection is called a(n) _____.

4. A class diagram is the UML notation used during the _____ phase of the software development process.

5. In UML, the symbols 0..* and 1..* mean _____ and _____, respectively.

6. The keys in a map form a(n) _____.

7. The set of elements that two sets have in common is called their _____.

8. The elements in a stack are accessed in _____ order.

9. The collection that allows the client to attach priorities to elements is called the _____.

10. All collections support the method _____, which returns the number of elements.

WRITTEN QUESTIONS

Write a brief answer to the following questions or problems.

1. Write the code that transfers the elements from the list list1 to the list list2. The elements in list2 should be in the reverse order from their original positions in list1.

2. Write the code that transfers the elements from a stack s to a queue q.

3. Write the code that displays all of the elements in a set s in the terminal window.

4. Jack has chosen to use a list to represent a line of customers waiting at a bank teller's window. Discuss the wisdom of this choice and propose and justify a better one.

5. Jill is working on a library application in which each book has a unique ISBN or ID number. Suggest and justify your choice of an appropriate collection for storing books.

PROJECTS

 PROJECT U4-1

Write a program that inputs an unknown number of names into a list. The user terminates the inputs by entering an empty string (by pressing Enter). The program should sort the list alphabetically and output its contents to the terminal window.

 PROJECT U4-2

Add to the program in Project U4-1 the capability of deleting duplicate names from the list. Use a set to accomplish this task.

PROJECT U4-3

Modify the program in Project U4-2 so that it allows the user to enter a password associated with each name. These pairs of data should be stored in a map and the output should be in two columns—one for the names and the other for the passwords.

PROJECT U4-4

Develop and test a method for sorting an arbitrary collection. The method expects a parameter of type `Collection` and returns a value of type `Collection`. If the parameter happens to be a list, the method returns a new list of the elements in sorted order. If the parameter happens to be a set, the method returns a new sorted set of the elements.

CRITICAL *Thinking Activity*

A bag is like a set except that duplicate elements are allowed. Describe the interface for this new collection. Include any methods that seem appropriate.

IMPLEMENTING ABSTRACT DATA TYPES

Unit 5

🕐 **Estimated Time for Unit: 10.5 hrs.**

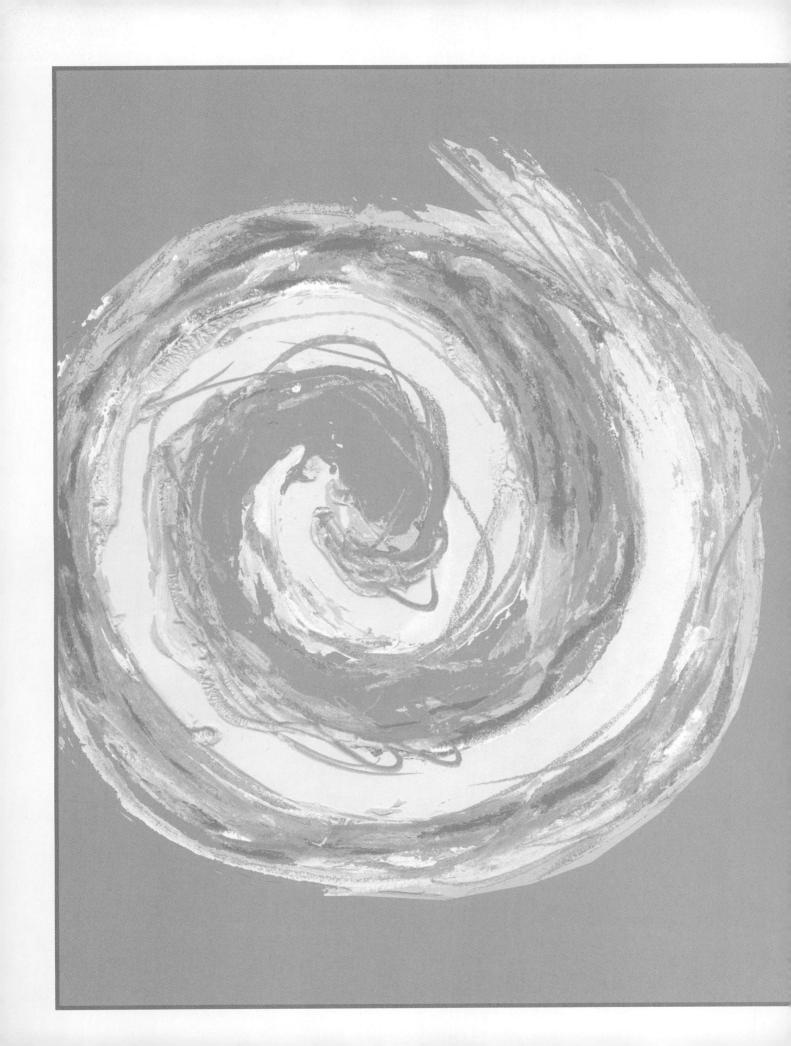

IMPLEMENTING LISTS, STACKS, AND QUEUES

This lesson presents several different implementations of lists and compares their performance characteristics. These implementations fall into two categories: array-based structures and link-based structures. The link-based implementations are in turn of two types: *singly linked structures* and *doubly linked structures*. A variety of other linked structures are used in the implementation of collection classes, and the study of singly and doubly linked structures provides a good foundation for their study. We close the lesson with a brief discussion of the implementation of iterators, stacks, and queues.

16.1 Interfaces, Multiple Implementations, and Prototypes

A class has two aspects: its interface as seen by clients and its internal implementation. The interface is defined by the class's public methods. The internal implementation depends on the class's choice of instance variables and the coding details of its methods. From a client's perspective, it is important that a class's interface provide useful services in a clear, concise, and stable manner. The third characteristic, stability, is critical because changing a class's interface necessitates recoding its clients. On the other hand, changing a class's internal implementation does not disturb the class's clients and may in fact be highly beneficial if it results in greater computing efficiency.

Before the first object-oriented language appeared, computer scientists realized the advantages of separating a resource's interface from its underlying implementation. They called this concept an abstract data type (ADT). Early programming languages lacked mechanisms to support the easy development of ADTs, so they were used only with difficulty and less frequently than warranted. Now, however, with the widespread acceptance of object-oriented languages, the use of ADTs has become pervasive and automatic.

The `List` interface introduced in Lesson 13 is a good example of an ADT. Although we did not examine list implementations in Lesson 13, we did mention that Java provides two—namely `ArrayList` and `LinkedList`. In this lesson, we develop some simplified versions of list implementations and in the process clarify the distinction between interfaces and implementations.

As we saw in Lesson 13, a list ADT is a linear collection of objects ordered by position. At any given moment, each object in a list except the first has a unique predecessor, and each object except the last has a unique successor. Java's list classes provide three types of access to the items they contain:

1. **Indexed-based access.** Methods such as `get`, `set`, `add`, and `remove` expect an integer index as a parameter. This value specifies the position, counting from 0, at which the access, replacement, insertion, or removal occurs.

2. **Object-based access.** Methods such as `contains`, `indexOf`, and `remove` expect an object as a parameter and search the list for the given object. Actually, there are two versions of `remove`, one that is index based and the other object based.

3. **Position-based access.** Through the use of a list iterator, position-based methods support moving to the first, last, next, or previous item in a list. Each of these methods establishes a current position in the list, and we can then access, replace, insert, or remove the item at this current position.

Java's `List` interface includes the index-based and object-based operations, and Java's `ListIterator` interface supports the position-based operations.

Before writing large complex systems, computer scientists sometimes implement a *prototype*. A prototype is a simplified version of a system that includes only the most essential features of the real thing. By experimenting with a prototype, computer scientists are able to explore a system's core issues in a simplified context, free from distracting details. With that idea in mind, in the rest of this lesson, we are going to define and implement several

Extra for Experts

Those who are interested in the full implementations of prototypes for lists can read Sun's downloadable Java source code.

prototypes for lists. The prototypes will be sufficiently complex to allow us to explore the trade-offs between different implementations, yet simple enough to keep the classes small. We will define all our prototypes in terms of interfaces, and we will then implement these interfaces in several different ways. Table 16-1 gives an overview.

TABLE 16-1
An overview of this lesson's interfaces and implementations

INTERFACE	IMPLEMENTATION	DESCRIPTION
IndexedList	FSAIndexedList	Fixed-size array indexed list
	SLIndexedList	Singly linked indexed list
PositionalList	FSAPositionalList	Fixed-size array positional list
	DLPositionalList	Doubly linked positional list

EXERCISE 16.1

1. What is an abstract data type? Give two examples.

2. Describe the difference between index-based access and position-based access to items in a list.

3. What is a prototype?

16.2 The IndexedList *Interface*

Our first prototype consists of a subset of the index-based methods in Java's List interface plus a few others that are described in Table 16-2. If a method's preconditions are not satisfied, it throws an exception.

TABLE 16-2
Public methods in the IndexedList interface

METHOD	PRECONDITIONS	POSTCONDITIONS
void add(int index, Object obj)	The list is not full and 0 <= index <= size	Inserts obj at position index and increases the size by one.
Object get(int index)	0 <= index < size	Returns the object at position index.
boolean isEmpty()	None	Returns true if the list is empty and false otherwise.
boolean isFull()	None	Returns true if the list is full and false otherwise.
Object remove(int index)	0 <= index < size	Removes and returns that object at position index.
void set(int index, Object obj)	0 <= index < size	Replaces the object at position index with obj.
int size()	None	Returns the number of objects in the list.
String toString()	None	Returns the concatenation of the string representations of the items in the list.

As mentioned in earlier lessons, an interface contains method headers, and each implementation is obliged to define all the corresponding methods. An interface can also include comments that state the preconditions and postconditions for each method. Following is the code for the `IndexedList` interface:

```
// File: IndexedList.java
// Interface for the indexed list prototype

public interface IndexedList {

    public void add(int index, Object obj);
    // Preconditions:  The list is not full and
    //                 0 <= index <= size
    // Postconditions: Inserts obj at position index and
    //                 increases the size by one.

    public Object get(int index);
    // Preconditions:  0 <= index < size
    // Postconditions: Returns the object at position index.

    public boolean isEmpty();
    // Postconditions: Returns true if the list is empty or false otherwise.

    public boolean isFull();
    // Postconditions: Returns true if the list is full or false otherwise.

    public Object remove(int index);
    // Preconditions:  0 <= index < size
    // Postconditions: Removes and returns the object at position index.

    public void set(int index, Object obj);
    // Preconditions:  0 <= index < size
    // Postconditions: Replaces the object at position index with obj.

    public int size();
    // Postconditions: Returns the number of objects in the list

    public String toString();
    // Postconditions: Returns the concatenation of the string
    //                 representations of the items in the list.
}
```

EXERCISE 16.2

1. What is the purpose of an interface?

2. What are the preconditions of an index-based operation?

16.3 The Fixed-Size Array Implementation of Indexed Lists

It is easy to implement an indexed list using an array. Figure 16-1 shows an array implementation of the list (D1, D2, D3). The array contains three data items and has two cells unoccupied. In an array implementation of a list, it is crucial to keep track of both the list's size (three in this case) and the array's length (five in this case). We track the list's size in an integer variable that is initially set to 0. Once the list's size equals the array's length, the list is full and no more items can be added. Consequently, clients should always check to see if a list is full before adding items to a fixed-size array-based implementation. Alternatively, it is possible to move a list into a larger array once the existing array becomes full. When a list is instantiated, it must in turn instantiate its underlying array using some predefined length, such as 10.

FIGURE 16-1
An array implementation of a list

The next code segment shows part of our FSAIndexedList class. We have completed only the constructor. Completion of the other methods is left as Project 16-1. All the needed techniques were presented in Lesson 10.

```java
// File: FSAIndexedList.java

import java.io.*;                    // Needed for serialization

public class FSAIndexedList implements IndexedList, Serializable{

    private static int DEFAULT_CAPACITY = 10;   // Array's length

    private Object[] items;                      // The array of objects
    private int listSize;                        // The list size

    public FSAIndexedList(){
        items = new Object[DEFAULT_CAPACITY];
        listSize = 0;
    }

    public void add(int index, Object obj){
        if (isFull())
            throw new RuntimeException("The list is full");
        if (index < 0 || index > listSize)
            throw new RuntimeException
```

```
                ("Index = " + index + " is out of list bounds");
            // Project 16-1
    }

    public boolean isEmpty(){. . .}

    public boolean isFull(){. . .}

    public Object get(int index){. . .}

    public Object remove(int index){. . .}

    public void set(int index, Object obj){. . .}

    public int size(){. . .}

    public String toString(){. . .}
}
```

Note that the class `FSAIndexedList` implements two interfaces: `IndexedList` and `Serializable`. The latter interface is required so that lists can be stored easily on disk (see Lesson 20). Note also that the `add` method contains code to test for its preconditions. When a precondition is violated, the implementation throws an exception (see Lesson 9 for details on exceptions).

*E*XERCISE 16.3

1. The size of a list might not be the same as the length of the array that implements it. Describe the problems that this fact poses for the users and implementers of a list.

2. Why does a list class implement the `Serializable` interface?

3. Describe the use of exceptions in a list implementation.

4. Complete the code for the `FSAIndexedList` method `get`.

16.4 The Singly Linked Implementation of Indexed Lists

Linked structures provide a frequently used mechanism for implementing lists. As the name implies, a linked structure consists of objects linked to other objects. The fundamental building block of such a structure is called a *node*. A node has two parts: an object and references, or *pointers*, to other nodes. Of the many different linking schemes, the singly linked structure (or singly linked list) is the simplest. In a singly linked structure, each node contains an object and a pointer to a successor node. The structure as a whole is accessed via a variable called `head` that points to the first node. Figure 16-2 shows a singly linked structure containing the objects D1, D2, and D3. The last node in a singly linked structure has no successor, which is indicated by a back-slash or *null pointer*.

FIGURE 16-2
A singly linked structure

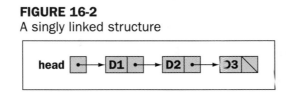

Coding with Nodes

In Java, the nodes in a singly linked structure are instances of a Node class, which we define as follows:

```
public class Node {

    public Object value;    //Object stored in this node
    public Node    next;    //Reference to the next node

    public Node(){
        value = null;
        next = null;
    }

    public Node(Object value, Node next){
        this.value = value;
        this.next = next;
    }
}
```

To keep the discussion that follows as simple as possible, we declare the attributes as public. Later, we will change them to private. We now present some code segments that illustrate how to use the Node class in a singly linked structure.

Building a Linked Structure

First, we build a singly linked structure containing the three strings:

```
Throw
the
ball
```

```
// Build a singly linked representation of the list
// ("Throw", "the", "ball")

// Declare some Node variables
Node head, node0, node1, node2;    //We count from 0 as usual

// Instantiate the nodes
node0 = new Node();
node1 = new Node();
```

```
node2 = new Node();

// Put an object in each node and link the nodes together
head = node0;

node0.value = "Throw";
node0.next  = node1;

node1.value = "the";
node1.next  = node2;

node2.value = "ball";
```

Figure 16-3 shows the result of this effort.

FIGURE 16-3
Singly linked representation of the list ("Throw", "the", "ball")

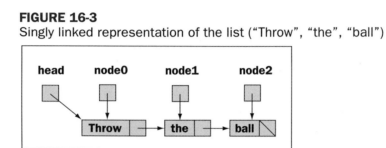

Building the Linked List Again

We can achieve the same result more concisely as illustrated in this next code segment:

```
// More concise code for building the list
// ("Throw", "the", "ball")

// Declare some Node variables
Node head, node0, node1, node2;

// Initialize and link the nodes
node2 = new Node ("ball" , null);        //Warning: a node must be created
node1 = new Node ("the"  , node2);       //before it is used in a link.
node0 = new Node ("Throw", node1);
head  = node0;
```

Building the Linked List for the Last Time

We can even build the list without declaring the variables node0, node1, and node2:

```
// Most concise code for building the list
// ("Throw", "the", "ball")

// Declare the head variable
Node head;
```

```
// Initialize and link the nodes
head = new Node ("ball" , null);
head = new Node ("the"  , head);
head = new Node ("Throw", head);
```

Traversing a Linked List

Now suppose that we know only the head of the list and are asked to print the third word. To do this, we have to traverse the list and follow the pointers as we go.

```
// Print the string in node 2

Node pointer;

pointer = head;              //Now pointing at node 0
pointer = pointer.next;      //Now pointing at node 1
pointer = pointer.next;      //Now pointing at node 2

System.out.println (pointer.value);   //Print the string in node 2
```

To generalize the preceding code, we print the string in node *i*:

```
// Print the string node i, i = 0, 1, 2, . . .

int  index, i = 2;

pointer = head;                       //Start at the beginning of the list
for (index = 0; index < i; index++)   //Traverse the list
      pointer = pointer.next;

System.out.println (pointer.value);   //Print the string in node i
```

Searching a Linked List

We illustrate the basic technique for searching a linked list by looking for the word "cat" and printing "found" or "not found" depending on the outcome:

```
// Search a list for the word "cat" and print "found" or "not found"
// depending on the outcome.

Node pointer;
String str;

for (pointer = head; pointer != null; pointer = pointer.next){
   str = (String)(pointer.value);
   if (str.equals("cat"))
      break;
}
if (pointer == null)
   System.out.println ("not found");
else
   System.out.println ("found");
```

Null Pointer Exceptions

A common error occurs when writing code to manipulate linked structures. It is the null pointer exception, first introduced in Lesson 5. This exception occurs when the code treats null as if it were an object. For instance, consider the following code fragment:

```
Node node0;
. . .
node0.value = "Throw";   //This will generate a null pointer exception if
                         //node0 does not refer to an object.
```

If node0 is used with the dot operator before it has been associated with an object, then a null pointer exception is thrown. There are three ways to deal with this situation. First, we can use the try-catch mechanism to handle the exception immediately or at a higher level:

```
//Handling the exception immediately.
Node node0;
. . .
try{
   node0.value = "Throw";
}catch (NullPointerException e){
   . . . some corrective action goes here . . .
}
```

```
//Handling the exception at a higher level
. . .
try{
   . . . call a method that works with nodes and that might throw
        a null pointer exception . . .
}catch (NullPointerException e){
   . . . some corrective action goes here . . .
}
```

Second, we can detect the problem before it occurs:

```
Node node0;
. . .
if (node0 != null){
   node0.value = "Throw";
}else{
   . . . some corrective action goes here . . .
}
```

Third, we can ignore the exception, in which case the JVM prints an error message in the terminal window.

The SLIndexedList Class

We now have sufficient background to understand the singly linked implementation of the IndexedList prototype. Following is an outline of the class. For now most of the methods are empty, but in the subsections that follow, we will fill them in. Notice that the Node class is defined inside the SLIndexedList class. Thus, it is called a *private inner class*. There are several advantages to using a private inner class. First, it is accessible only to code within the enclosing class. Second, even though its attributes and methods are private, they are visible to the enclosing class. Third, if two classes give their inner class the same name, there is no naming conflict.

```java
// File: SLIndexedList.java

import java.io.*;                        // Needed for serialization

public class SLIndexedList implements IndexedList, Serializable{

    private Node head;                // Pointer to first node
    private int listSize;             // The list size
    private Node nodeAtIndex;         // The node at index position or null if
                                      // past the end of the list.
    private Node nodeBefore;          // The node before index position or null
                                      // if before the beginning of the list.

    public SLIndexedList(){
        head = null;
        listSize = 0;
    }

    public void add(int index, Object obj){}

    public boolean isEmpty(){
        return listSize == 0;
    }

    public boolean isFull(){
        return true;
    }

    public Object get(int index){. . .}

    public Object remove(int index){. . .}

    public void set(int index, Object obj){. . .}

    public int size(){
        return listSize;
    }

    public String toString(){
        String str = "";
        for (Node node = head; node != null; node = node.next)
            str += node.value + " ";
        return str;
    }
```

```
private void locateNode(int index){. . .}

// ---------------- Private inner class for Node -----------------

private class Node {

    private Object value;      //Object stored in this node
    private Node    next;      //Reference to the next node

    private Node(){
       value = null;
       next = null;
    }

    private Node(Object value, Node next){
       this.value = value;
       this.next = next;
    }
  }
}
```

The `locateNode` Method

To locate node i ($i = 0, 1, 2, ...$) in a linked list, we must start at the head node and visit each successive node until we reach node i. This traversal process is used in the methods `get`, `set`, `add`, and `remove`, so to save time, we write a private helper method, `locateNode`, to implement the process. This helper method takes an index i as a parameter and sets the variable `nodeAtIndex` to node i. In addition, it also sets the variable `nodeBefore` to node $i - 1$. The latter variable is used by the methods `add` and `remove`. Figure 16-4 shows the outcome of calling `locateNode(2)`. If the index equals the list size, the method sets `nodeBefore` to the last node and `nodeAtIndex` to null.

FIGURE 16-4

The outcome of calling `locateNode(2)`

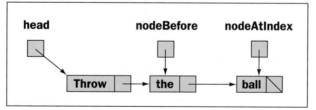

Following is the code for `locateNode`:

```
private void locateNode(int index){
//Obtain pointers to the node at index and its predecessor
//Preconditions    0 <= index <= listSize
//Postconditions   nodeAtIndex points to the node at position index
//                 or null if there is none
//                 nodeBefore points at the predecessor or null
//                 if there is none
   nodeBefore = null;
```

```
        nodeAtIndex = head;
        for (int i = 1; i < listSize && i <= index; i++){
            nodeBefore = nodeAtIndex;
            nodeAtIndex = nodeAtIndex.next;
        }
        if (index == listSize){
            nodeBefore = nodeAtIndex;
            nodeAtIndex = null;
        }
    }
```

The get and set Methods

The methods get and set use locateNode to access the node at a given index position. The get method then retrieves the value in the node, whereas the set method changes the value. Following is the code for get. The set method is left as part of Project 16-2.

```
    public Object get(int index){
        if (index < 0 || index >= listSize)
            throw new RuntimeException
            ("Index = " + index + " is out of list bounds");

        locateNode(index);
        return nodeAtIndex.value;
    }
```

The remove Method

The remove method locates an indicated node, deletes it from the linked list, and returns the value stored in the node. A node is deleted by adjusting pointers. There are two cases to consider.

1. To delete the first node, set the head pointer to the first node's next pointer (Figure 16-5).

FIGURE 16-5
Removing the first node from a linked list

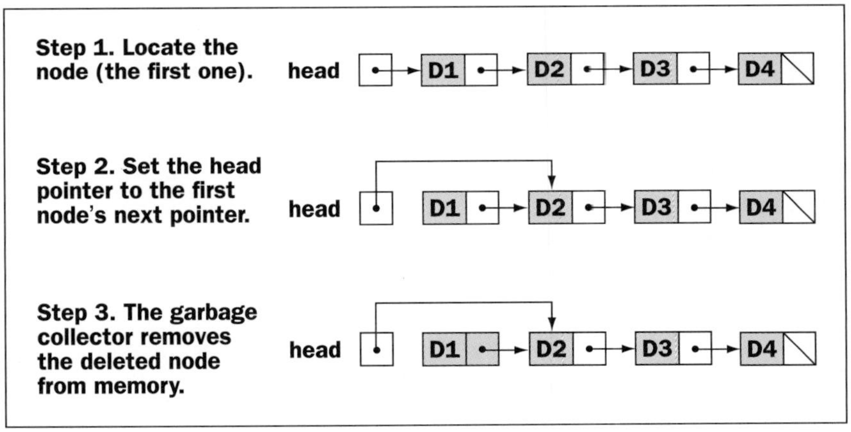

2. To delete any other node, locate it. Then set the predecessor's next pointer to the deleted node's next pointer. (Figure 16-6).

FIGURE 16-6
Removing any node other than the first from a linked list

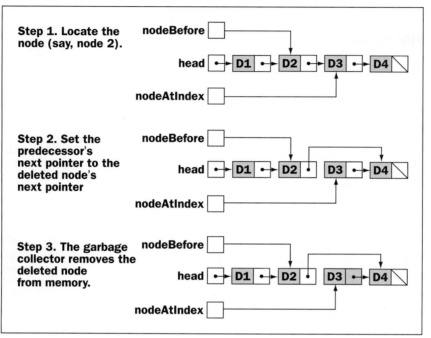

In the second case, if the deleted node is the last one, then the predecessor's next pointer is set to null. Following is the code for the remove method:

```
public Object remove(int index){
    if (index < 0 || index >= listSize)          // Check precondition
        throw new RuntimeException
        ("Index = " + index + " is out of list bounds");

    Object removedObj = null;

    if (index == 0){                        // Case 1: item is first one
        removedObj = head.value;
        head = head.next;
    }else{
        locateNode(index);
        nodeBefore.next = nodeAtIndex.next;
        removedObj = nodeAtIndex.value;
    }

    listSize--;
    return removedObj;
}
```

The add Method

The add method must deal with the following situations:

Case 1: If the index is 0, the new node becomes the first node in the list. To accomplish this, the new node's next pointer is set to the old head pointer, and the head pointer is then set to the new node. Figure 16-7 shows a node with the object D2 being inserted at the beginning of a list.

FIGURE 16-7
Adding a new node at the beginning of a linked list

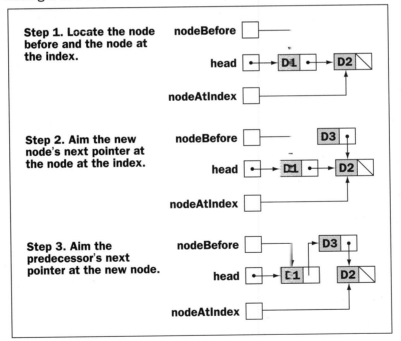

Case 2: If the index is greater than 0, the new node is inserted between the node at position index – 1 and the node at position index or after the last node if the index equals the list size. To accomplish this, we locate the node at position index. We then aim the new node's next pointer at the node at position index and the predecessor's next pointer at the new node. Figure 16-8 shows a node containing the object D3 being inserted at position 1 in a list.

FIGURE 16-8
Adding a new node to a linked list at position 1

Following is the code for the add method:

```
public void add(int index, Object obj){
    if (index < 0 || index > listSize)        // Check precondition
        throw new RuntimeException
            ("Index = " + index + " is out of list bounds");
```

```
        if (index == 0)                          // Case 1: Head of list
            head = new Node(obj, head);
        else{                                     // Case 2: Other positions
            locateNode(index);
            nodeBefore.next = new Node(obj, nodeAtIndex);
        }
        listSize++;
    }
```

EXERCISE 16.4

1. What is a node?

2. What is the null pointer exception?

3. Draw a diagram of the linked structure that is formed by running the following code, which uses the Node class defined in this section:

```
Node node = null;
for (int i = 1; i <= 5; i++)
    node = new Node("" + i, node);
```

16.5 Complexity Analysis of Indexed List Implementations

Users of indexed lists face a dilemma. Which of the two implementations should they use? An understanding of the memory usage and run-time efficiency of the implementations provides an answer. We begin with an analysis of the memory usage.

Memory Usage

Java maintains a region of memory called *dynamic memory* from which it allocates space for objects. Memory for an object is not allocated until the object is instantiated, and when the object is no longer referenced, the memory is reclaimed by garbage collection.

When an FSAIndexedList is instantiated, a single block of *contiguous memory* is allocated for the list's underlying array. If the array is too small, then it fills up, and if it is too large, there is much unused space. In the first instance, an application may fail because at some point it can no longer add items to a list, and in the second instance, it may hog so much memory that the computer's overall performance is degraded. The space occupied by the array depends on two factors: the array's length and the size of each entry. As the array contains references to objects and not the actual objects themselves, each entry is exactly the same size, or 4 bytes on most computers. The total space occupied by a list equals the space needed by the objects plus $4n$ bytes, where n represents the array's length.

With an SLIndexedList, memory is allocated one node at a time and is recovered each time a node is removed. Each node contains two references: one to an object in the list and the other to the next node in the linked structure. Consequently, the total space occupied by a list equals the space needed by the objects plus $8m$ bytes, where m represents the list's length.

We can now compare the memory usage of the two implementations. When the underlying array is less than half full, the array implementation occupies more memory than the corresponding linked implementation. Beyond the halfway point, the array implementation holds the advantage. Consequently, if we can accurately predict the maximum size of our list and if we do not expect the list's size to vary greatly, then an array implementation makes better use of memory. At other times, the linked implementation has the advantage.

Run-Time Efficiency

There are several factors that affect the run-time efficiency of the two implementations. First, consider the problem of accessing an item at a particular position within a list. The entries in an array are in adjacent memory locations, which make it possible to access an entry in constant time. Figure 16-9 shows an array in which each entry is 4 bytes long. The array's *base address* (i.e., the address of the array's first byte) is at location 100, and each successive entry starts 4 bytes past the beginning of the previous one. When we write code that refers to array element a[i], the following computation is performed:

```
Address of array entry i = base address + 4 * i
```

The quantity 4 * i is called the *offset* and equals the difference between the base address and the location of the desired entry. Once the computation has been completed, the array element is immediately accessible. Because the address computation is performed in constant time, accessing array elements is an $O(1)$ operation.

FIGURE 16-9
Memory map for an array with base address 100 and entry size of 4 bytes

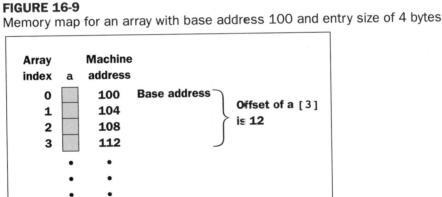

In contrast, the nodes in a linked structure are not necessarily in physically adjacent memory locations. This implies that a node cannot be accessed by adding an offset to a base address; instead, it is located by following a trail of pointers, beginning at the first node. Thus, the time taken to access a node is linearly dependent on its position within the linked structure or $O(n)$. From this discussion we conclude that the get and set methods are $O(1)$ for an array implementation and $O(n)$ for a linked implementation.

Next consider the problem of adding an item to a list. In an array implementation, insertion is preceded by shifting all the array entries at and below the insertion point down one slot. This is an $O(n)$ operation and is followed by the $O(1)$ operation of storing a new reference in the array at the insertion point. Thus, the operation is $O(n)$ overall. For a linked list, locating the insertion point requires a traversal and is an $O(n)$ operation. This is followed by instantiating a new node and tying it into the linked structure, which is an $O(1)$ operation. Thus, the operation is $O(n)$ overall.

A similar analysis shows that removing an item from a list is O(*n*) for both implementations. The `toString` method involves traversing the list from beginning to end and is an O(*n*) operation for both implementations, whereas the remaining operations (`isEmpty`, `isFull`, and `size`) are obviously O(1). Table 16-3 summarizes these findings.

TABLE 16-3
The running times of the indexed list implementations

METHOD	COMPLEXITY FIXED-SIZE ARRAY	SINGLY LINKED LIST
	(FSAIndexedList)	(SLIndexedList)
boolean isEmpty()	O(1)	O(1)
boolean isFull()	O(1)	O(1)
int size()	O(1)	O(1)
void add(int i, Object o)	O(*n*)	O(*n*)
Object get(int i)	O(1)	O(*n*)
Object remove(int i)	O(*n*)	O(*n*)
Object set(int i, Object o)	O(1)	O(*n*)
String toString()	O(*n*)	O(n)

In conclusion, we see that the fixed-size array implementation provides better run-time performance than the singly linked implementation; however, in situations in which we cannot predict a list's maximum size, the array implementation incurs the risk of either running out of space or wasting it. This drawback is overcome by using dynamic rather than fixed-size arrays. When a dynamic array fills, it is replaced by a larger array, and when it shrinks beyond a certain point, it is replaced by a smaller array. Each time this happens, the entries are copied from the old to the new array. Although this approach solves the memory problem, it reintroduces a performance problem. Copying entries between arrays is an O(*n*) operation, but it is experienced only occasionally. In fact, we can show that, on average, this operation can remain O(1), provided dynamic arrays grow and shrink by a factor of 2.

EXERCISE 16.5

1. How are arrays represented in memory, and what effect does this representation have on the performance of array processing?

2. How are linked structures represented in memory, and what effect does this representation have on the performance of linked structure processing?

16.6 Positional Lists

A *positional list* has a more complex interface than an indexed list, and in contrast to an indexed list, it does not provide direct access to an item based on an index. Instead, a client moves a pointer called the ***current position indicator*** forward or backward through the list until

---

a desired position is reached. Other operations can then replace, insert, or remove an item relative to the current position. Table 16-4 gives an overview of the methods organized by category. In the rest of this section, we explain these methods and their use more fully. We call our interface `PositionalList`, and it is similar to Java's standard `ListIterator` interface.

TABLE 16-4
Overview of the `PositionalList` interface

METHOD CATEGORIES	METHOD NAMES
Move	`moveToHead, moveToTail, next, previous`
Check position	`hasNext, hasPrevious`
Modify content	`add, remove, set`
Other	`isEmpty, isFull, size, toString`

Navigating

The current position indicator is part of the state of a positional list, and provided the list is not empty, it always has a value. To navigate in a positional list, a client

- Moves to the head or the tail of the list using the methods `moveToHead` and `moveToTail`
- Determines if either end of the list has been reached using the methods `hasNext` and `hasPrevious`
- Moves to the next or previous item in the list using the methods `next` and `previous`

To illustrate, consider Table 16-5, which shows the effect of navigating in a list of three items. In the table, an arrow represents the current position indicator.

TABLE 16-5
Navigation in a list of three items

ACTION	hasNext	hasPrevious	EFFECT
`moveToHead`	true	false	D1 D2 D3 (indicator before D1)
`next`	true	true	D1 D2 D3 (indicator before D2)
`next`	true	true	D1 D2 D3 (indicator before D3)
`next`	false	true	D1 D2 D3 (indicator after D3)

The following is a code segment that traverses a positional list from beginning to end:

```
list.moveToHead();
while (list.hasNext()){
   Object item = list.next();
```

```
// Methods that modify the list's contents

public void add(Object obj){
   // Exercise
}

public Object remove(){
   // Exercise
}

public void set(Object obj){
   if (lastItemPos == -1)
      throw new RuntimeException (
               "There is no established item to set.");

   items[lastItemPos] = obj;
}

//Method that returns a string representation of the list.

public String toString(){
   String str = "";
   for (int i = 0; i < listSize; i++)
      str += items[i] + " ";
   return str;
}
}
```

*E*XERCISE 16.7

1. Write the code segment for the `FSAPositionalList` constructor method that expects an `IndexedList` as a parameter.

16.8 Doubly Linked Implementation of Positional Lists

W e never use a singly linked structure to implement a positional list because it provides no convenient mechanism for moving one node to the left—that is, to a node's predecessor. In a singly linked list, moving left requires repositioning to the head of the list and then traversing right. The cost of doing this is O(*n*). In a doubly linked list, it is equally easy to move left and right. Both are O(1) operations. Figure 16-10 shows a doubly linked structure with three nodes.

FIGURE 16-10
A doubly linked structure with three nodes

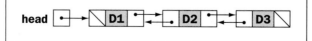

It turns out that the code needed to manipulate a doubly linked list is simplified if one extra node is added at the head of the list. This node is called a *sentinel node,* and it points forward to what was the first node and backward to what was the last node. The head pointer now points to the sentinel node. The resulting structure is called a *circular linked list.* The sentinel node does not contain a list item, and when the list is empty, the sentinel remains. Figure 16-11 shows an empty circular linked list and a circular linked list containing three items.

FIGURE 16-11
Two circular doubly linked lists with sentinel nodes

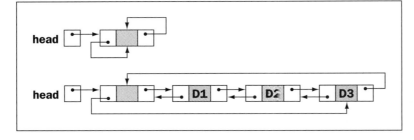

The basic building block of a doubly linked list is a node with two pointers: next, which points right and previous, which points left. We define the node in a private inner class called Node. As in the array implementation, we rely heavily on the variables curPos and lastItemPos; however, they now represent two-way nodes rather than integers. The following is a code segment of the class DLPositionalList. The missing parts are left as Project 16-4.

```
import java.io.*;                  // Needed for serialization

public class DLPositionalList implements PositionalList,
                                          Serializable{

    private Node head;
        //Sentinel head node

    private Node curPos;
        //Current position indicator
        //Points at the node which would be returned by next
        //The current position is considered to be immediately
        //before this node
        //If curPos == head then at end of list
        //If curPos.previous == head then at beginning of list

    private Node lastItemPos;
        //Points at the last item returned by next or previous
        //Equals null initially and after add, remove, moveToHead,
        //moveToTail, and toString

    private int listSize;
        //The number of items in the list

    //Constructor
```

```java
public DLPositionalList(){
   head = new Node(null, null, null);
   head.next = head;
   head.previous = head;
   curPos = head.next;
   lastItemPos = null;
   listSize = 0;
}

public DLPositionalList (IndexedList list){
   // Project 16-4
}

// Methods that indicate the state of the list

public boolean isEmpty(){
   return listSize == 0;
}

public boolean isFull(){
   return false;
}

public boolean hasNext(){
   return curPos != head;
}

public boolean hasPrevious(){
   return curPos.previous != head;
}

public int size(){
   return listSize;
}


// Methods that move the current position indicator

public void moveToHead(){
   curPos = head.next;
   lastItemPos = null;        //Block remove and set until after a
                              //successful next or previous
}

public void  moveToTail(){
   curPos = head;
   lastItemPos = null;        //Block remove and set until after a
                              //successful next or previous
}
```

```
// Methods that retrieve items

public Object next(){                              //Returns the next item
   if (!hasNext())
      throw new RuntimeException
      ("There are no more elements in the list");

   lastItemPos = curPos; //Remember the index of the last item returned
   curPos = curPos.next;                    //Advance the current position
   return lastItemPos.value;
}

public Object previous(){                   //Returns the previous item
   if (!hasPrevious())
      throw new RuntimeException
      ("There are no more elements in the list");

   lastItemPos = curPos.previous; //Remember the index of the last item
                                                      //returned
   curPos = curPos.previous;       //Move the current position backward
   return lastItemPos.value;
}


// Methods that modify the list's contents

public void add(Object obj){
   // To be discussed
}

public Object remove(){
   // Project 16-4
}

public void set(Object obj){
   if (lastItemPos == null)
      throw new RuntimeException (
            "There is no established item to set.");

   lastItemPos.value = obj;
}


//Method that returns a string representation of the list.

public String toString(){
   String str = "";
   for (Node node = head.next; node != head; node = node.next)
      str += node.value + " ";
   return str;
}
```

```java
// ----------------- Private inner class for Node -----------------

private class Node implements Serializable {
    private Object value;        //Value stored in this node
    private Node   next;         //Reference to next node
    private Node   previous;     //Reference to previous node

    private Node(){
        value = null;
        previous = null;
        next = null;
    }

    private Node(Object value){
        this.value = value;
        previous = null;
        next = null;
    }

    private Node(Object value, Node previous, Node next){
        this.value = value;
        this.previous = previous;
        this.next = next;
    }
  }
}
```

The add Method

Figure 16-12 shows the steps required to insert a node into a doubly linked list. The new node is inserted immediately before the one pointed to by curPos.

FIGURE 16-12
Steps required to insert a node into a doubly linked list

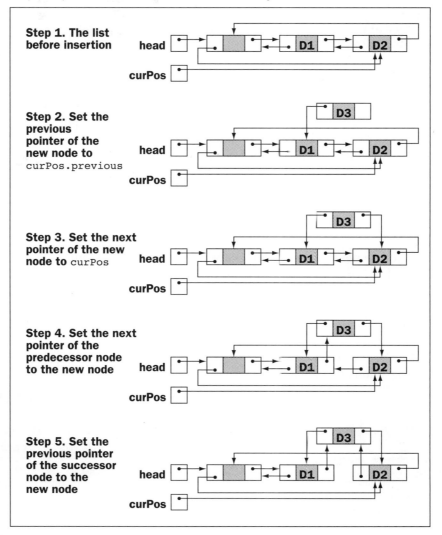

The same steps are required even when there are no data nodes already in the list. In that case, the header node is both the successor and the predecessor of the new node. Following is the code for the add method:

```
public void add(Object obj){
   //Create new node for object obj (steps 2 and 3 in Figure 16-12)
   Node newNode = new Node(obj, curPos.previous, curPos);

   //Link the new node into the list (steps 4 and 5 in Figure 16-12)
   curPos.previous.next = newNode;
   curPos.previous = newNode;
```

```
        //curPos does not change

        listSize++;
        lastItemPos = null;  //Block remove and set until after a successful
                                         //next or previous
    }
```

The add method is remarkably simple; however, without a sentinel node, the code would be considerably more complex.

EXERCISE 16.8

1. What advantages does a doubly linked list have over a singly linked list?

2. What advantages does a circular linked list with a sentinel node have over a plain linked list?

16.9 Complexity Analysis of Positional Lists

The memory requirements of positional and indexed lists are similar. The only difference is that the nodes in doubly linked lists utilize two pointers rather than one. Table 16-7 summarizes the run times of the positional list implementations. The unfilled slots are left to be completed in Exercise 16.9. Because an item is added, removed, or replaced at the current position indicator, no search is required to locate the position.

TABLE 16-7
The run times of the positional list implementations

METHOD	COMPLEXITY FIXED-SIZE ARRAY	DOUBLY LINKED LIST
	(FSAPositionalList)	(DLPositionalList)
boolean isEmpty()	O(1)	O(1)
boolean isFull()	O(1)	O(1)
int size()	O(1)	O(1)
boolean hasNext()	O(1)	O(1)
boolean hasPrevious()	O(1)	O(1)
void moveToHead()	O(1)	O(1)
void moveToTail()	O(1)	
Object next()	O(1)	O(1)
Object previous()	O(1)	O(1)
void add(Object o)		
void remove(Object o)		
void set(Object o)		

EXERCISE 16.9

1. Complete the analysis in Table 16-7 by filling in the correct value in the blank cells.

16.10 Iterators

To a certain extent, the behavior of an iterator is similar to that of a positional list. All iterators maintain a current position pointer to an element in the backing collection. Simple iterators allow the client to move this pointer to the next element and to ask whether there are more elements after the pointer. These iterators may also allow the client to remove the item just visited. List iterators extend this behavior by allowing movement to previous elements and by allowing insertions and replacements of elements as well.

The implementation of an iterator is complicated by two factors:

1. Messages can also be sent to the backing collection. If a mutator message such as add or remove is sent, the state of the backing collection can become inconsistent with the position of the iterator. Thus, an iterator must have a way of tracking mutations to the backing collection and throwing exceptions after they have occurred.

2. More than one iterator can be open on the same backing collection. If an iterator supports mutations to the backing collection, the collection's state can become inconsistent with the positions of the other iterators. Thus, an iterator must also have a way of tracking the mutations that other iterators make and disallowing these as well.

In general, it is most convenient to implement an iterator as a private inner class within the collection class. In the case of a simple iterator, this class implements the Iterator interface, whereas a list iterator implements the ListIterator interface. To track and validate mutations to the backing collection, a private integer instance variable called modCount is declared in the enclosing collection class and is incremented each time a mutator message is sent to the collection. When an iterator is instantiated, it records this count in its own instance variable called expectedModCount. Whenever the iterator receives a message, it compares these two values and throws an exception if they are not equal (meaning that someone sent a mutator message to the backing collection before the current message was sent to the iterator). Whenever the iterator performs a mutation on the backing collection, the two values are incremented to keep them consistent for that iterator. Other iterators, which have their own expectedModCount, can then also detect any inconsistency. The implementation of a simple iterator is left as the task of Project 16-5.

16.11 Implementation of Stacks and Queues

We have already discussed the interfaces and some list-based implementations of stacks and queues in Lesson 13. These implementations have the virtue of simply sending messages to objects to accomplish their tasks. Other implementations exist that resort to direct manipulations of arrays and linked structures, however. We leave these to be completed in Project 16-6.

SUMMARY

In this lesson, you learned:

- Implementations of linear collections can be achieved by using arrays or linked structures.

- There are two types of linked structures used to implement linear collections, singly linked structures and doubly linked structures. A singly linked structure allows clients to move in one direction only, whereas a doubly linked structure allows clients to move in both directions.

- There are various trade-offs between arrays and linked structures. Index-based access is faster with arrays than with linked structures. Linked structures can provide a more economical use of memory than arrays.

- The run-time and memory aspects of arrays and linked structures depend on their underlying representation in computer memory. Arrays are represented with blocks of adjacent memory cells, whereas linked structures contain references to potentially nonadjacent chunks of memory.

VOCABULARY *Review*

Define the following terms:

base address	linked structure	positional list
circular linked list	node	private inner class
contiguous memory	null pointer	prototype
current position indicator	offset	sentinel node
doubly linked structure	pointer	singly linked structure
dynamic memory		

REVIEW *Questions*

FILL IN THE BLANK

Complete the following sentences by writing the correct word or words in the blanks provided.

1. The array implementation of an indexed-based list provides access to an element at a specified position in _____ time.

2. The linked implementation of an indexed-based list provides access to an element at a specified position in _____ time.

3. A singly linked structure contains a sequence of _____, each of which contains a data element and a link to the next _____.

4. The end of a singly linked structure is detected by testing for _____.

5. A linked implementation of a positional list uses a(n) _____ linked structure.

6. The operations of an iterator most closely resemble those of a(n) _____ list.

7. An iterator should disallow _____ messages to be sent to its backing collection.

8. A(n) _____ linked structure would be a wise choice for a stack implementation.

9. A(n) _____ linked structure would be a wise choice for a queue implementation.

10. Iterators are implemented using a(n) _____ class.

PROJECTS

PROJECT 16-1

Complete the class FSAIndexedList and test it with an appropriate tester program.

PROJECT 16-2

Complete the class SLIndexedList and test it with the tester program from Project 16-1.

PROJECT 16-3

Complete the class FSAPositionalList and test it with an appropriate tester program.

PROJECT 16-4

Complete the class DLPositionalList and test it with an appropriate tester program.

PROJECT 16-5

Add an iterator method to the interface IndexedList. Then implement this method in the class FSAIndexedList using the techniques described in this lesson. Test your iterator with an appropriate tester program.

PROJECT 16-6

Do one of the following and test it with an appropriate tester program. You should use an array or a linked structure, not a List class.
   A. An array implementation of a stack
   B. An array implementation of a queue
   C. A linked implementation of a queue
   D. An linked implementation of a stack

CRITICAL *Thinking*

Jack decides to implement an iterator for stacks. Jill uses his code and complains that his iterator should not support a remove method. Discuss the issues involved in this disagreement.

IMPLEMENTING SETS AND MAPS

Most clients who use sets and maps want to build higher-level, more application-specific operations with the primitives provided. These operations likely employ many insertions and retrievals. Thus, the paramount consideration from the implementer's perspective is the speed of insertion and retrieval in sets and maps.

Unordered collections can be implemented using several of the collections already presented. For example, one might use a list to implement a set. This is not a wise choice, however, because a list supports only linear searches and insertions.

Another consideration is that we want sets and maps to contain any objects, not just comparable objects. This implies that we cannot use sorted collections, whose items must be comparables, to implement general unordered collections. It seems that this restriction does not bode well for the implementation of more efficient (better than linear) searches and insertions, which, so far as we have seen, require a special ordering of the data. However, we can overcome this restriction and obtain optimal performance by using a new access technique called *hashing*. Hashing can potentially achieve O(1) efficiency for insertion and retrieval operations. In this lesson, we examine both implementation strategies.

17.1 The Set and Map Prototypes

As we did for linear collections in Lesson 16, here we work with prototypes of sets and maps rather than full versions, so we can examine the essential features of the different implementations. The set prototype's interface is called `SetPT` and its methods appear in Table 17-1.

TABLE 17-1
The `SetPT` interface

METHOD	WHAT IT DOES
`boolean add(Object obj)`	If the object is not already in the set, then adds the object to the set, increasing the set's size by one, and returns `true`; otherwise, returns `false`.
`boolean contains(Object obj)`	Returns `true` if the object is in the set, else `false`.
`boolean isEmpty()`	Returns `true` if the set contains no objects, else `false`.
`Iterator iterator()`	Returns an iterator on the set.
`boolean remove(Object obj)`	If the object is in the set, removes it and returns `true`; otherwise, returns `false`.
`int size()`	Returns the number of objects currently in the set.

The map prototype's interface is called `MapPT` and its methods appear in Table 17-2. The implementations of sets are `ListSetPT` and `HashSetPT`, whereas the implementations of maps are `ListMapPT` and `HashMapPT`.

TABLE 17-2
The `MapPT` interface

METHOD	WHAT IT DOES
`boolean containsKey(Object key)`	Returns `true` if the map contains the indicated key or `false` otherwise.
`boolean containsValue(Object value)`	Returns true if the map contains at least one instance of the indicated value or false otherwise.
`Object get(Object key)`	Returns the value associated with the indicated key if the key is in the map or null otherwise.
`boolean isEmpty()`	Returns true if the map is empty or false otherwise.
`SetPT keySet()`	Returns a set view of the keys in the map.
`Object put(Object key, Object value)`	If the key is already in the map, replaces the previous value with the new value and returns the previous value; otherwise, adds the key and the associated value to the map and returns null.
`Object remove(Object key)`	If the key is in the map, removes the key value pair from the map and returns the value; otherwise, returns null.
`int size()`	Returns the number of key value pairs currently in the map.
`Collection values()`	Returns a collection view of the values in the map.

17.2 List Implementations of Sets and Maps

Sets

The list implementation of sets is fairly simple. A set contains a list. Because we do not have to worry about ordering the elements, they can be added at the head of the list, which is an O(1) operation with a linked list. Thus, we choose an instance of class `LinkedList` to contain the set's elements. Most of the `ListSetPT` methods simply call the corresponding `List` methods to accomplish their tasks. The only exception is the `ListSetPT` method `add`, which must prevent a duplicate object from being inserted into the set. Following is the code for the method `add`:

```
// In the class ListSetPT

public boolean add(Object obj){
   if (list.contains(obj))
      return false;
   else{
      list.add(0, obj);
      return true;
   }
}
```

Maps

Unlike set elements, the entries in a map consist of two parts: a key and a value. Because insertions, accesses, and removals are based on a key rather than an entire entry, the methods in a list implementation of maps cannot simply consist of calls to the corresponding list methods. The `ListMapPT` class deals with this problem by maintaining parallel lists of keys and values. The methods `get`, `put`, and `remove` all rely on a single pattern involving these lists:

```
Find the index of the key in the list of keys
If the index is -1
   Do what is needed when the key does not exist
Else
   Manipulate the element at the index in the list of values
```

If we use instances of `ArrayList` for the lists, then accessing a value in the list of values, once we have located the key in the list of keys, is O(1). The following code employs this pattern in the `ListMapPT` method `get`:

```
public Object get(Object key){
   int index = keysList.indexOf(key);
   if (index == -1)
      return null;
   else
      return valuesList.get(i);
}
```

Complexity Analysis of the List Implementations of Sets and Maps

The list implementation of sets requires very little programmer effort but unfortunately does not perform well. A quick inspection of the major accessing methods shows that almost every one of them is linear. The only exception is the `ListSetPT` method `add`, which has constant-time behavior for insertions at the head of a `LinkedList`.

The list implementation of maps does not behave any better than that of sets. All of the methods that must access a key in the list of keys are linear. Clearly, we should hope for faster implementations. They will come, as we shall see in the next section, with hashing.

EXERCISE 17.2

1. Why is a list a poor choice for implementing an unordered collection?

17.3 Overview of Hashing

Hash Functions

Hashing is a technique of storing and retrieving data in which each item is associated with a *hash code*. This code is based on some property of the item and can be computed in constant time by a function known as a *hash function*. The same hash function is run when an item is inserted, retrieved, or removed, so these operations are potentially O(1). How can this be? Suppose we use the item's hash code to locate the item's index in an array. The expression for this is

```
hashCode % array.length;
```

and it runs in constant time.

There are various ways to generate hash codes, but Java already includes a method, `hashCode()`, for any object. This method returns a large number that may be negative, so the expression for locating an item's index in an array becomes

```
Math.abs(item.hashCode() % array.length)
```

The following short tester program allows the user to input the array's length and the number of items to store and displays the items, their hash codes, and their array index positions:

```
import TerminalIO.KeyboardReader;

public class TestCodes {
   public static void main(String [] args) {
      KeyboardReader reader = new KeyboardReader();
      int arrayLength = reader.readInt("Enter the size of the array: ");
      int numberOfItems = reader.readInt("Enter the number of items: ");

      System.out.println(" Item    hash code  array index");
```

```
      for (int i = 0; i < numberOfItems; i ++){
         String str = "Item " + i;
         int code = str.hashCode();
         int index = Math.abs(code % arrayLength);
         System.out.println(str + " " + code + " " + index);
      }
   }
}
```

Figure 17-1 shows the results of two runs of this program. The first run locates distinct index positions for 10 items in an array of length 20. The second run increases the number of items to 15. In this case, distinct positions are found for each item except items 9 and 10, which share position 8. Clearly, this situation, which is called a *collision*, is not a good thing.

FIGURE 17-1
Computing hash codes and indexes

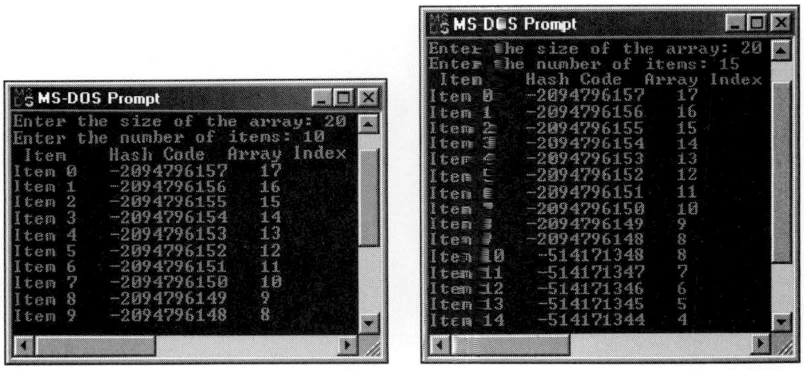

Unfortunately, the collision does not go away when we increase the size of the array. Also, there will be more collisions as the number of items approaches the array's length. In the following section, we examine several methods for resolving collisions.

Linear Collision Processing

For insertions, the simplest way to resolve a collision is to search the array, starting from the collision spot, for the first available empty position—referred to as *linear collision processing*. When a search reaches the last position of the array, the search wraps around to continue from the first position. If we assume the array does not become full and that an array cell is null when unoccupied, the code for insertions is as follows:

```
// Get an initial hash code
int index = item.hashCode() % array.length;

// Stop searching when an empty cell is encountered
while (array[index] != null)

   // Increment the index and wrap around to first position if necessary
   index = (index + 1) % array.length;

// An empty cell is found, so store the item
array[index] = item;
```

Retrievals and removals work in a similar manner, except that we search for an item that matches the target item.

Linear collision processing is prone to a problem known as *clustering*. This situation occurs when the items that cause a collision are relocated to the same region (a cluster) within the array. This placement usually leads to other collisions with other relocated items. During the course of an application, several clusters may develop and coalesce into larger clusters, making the problem worse.

Quadratic Collision Processing

One way to avoid the clustering associated with linear collision processing is to advance the search for an empty position a considerable distance from the collision point. *Quadratic collision processing* accomplishes this by incrementing the current index by the square of a constant on each attempt. If the attempt fails, we increment the constant and try again. Put another way, if we begin with an initial hash code k and a constant c, the formula used on each pass is $k + c^2$.

Following is the code for insertions, updated to use quadratic collision processing:

```
// Set the initial hash code, index, and constant
int hashCode = item.hashCode() % array.length;
int constant = 2;
int index = hashCode % array.length;

// Stop searching when an empty cell is encountered
while (array[index] != null){

    // Increment the index and wrap around to first position if necessary
    index = (hashCode + constant * constant) % array.length;
    constant++;
}

// An empty cell is found, so store the item
array[index] = item;
```

Chaining

In a collision processing strategy known as *chaining*, the items are stored in an array of linked lists, or *chains*. Each item's hash code locates the *bucket*, or index, of the chain in which the item already resides or is to be inserted. The retrieval and removal operations each perform the following steps:

1. Compute the item's hash code or index in the array.

2. Search the linked list at that index for the item.

If the item is found, it can be returned or removed. Figure 17-2 shows an array of linked lists with five buckets and eight items.

FIGURE 17-2
Hashing with five buckets

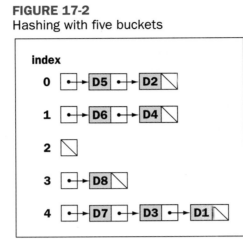

The hash code of each item is the index of its linked list in the array. For example, the items D7, D3, and D1 have the hash code 4.

To insert an item into this structure, we perform the following steps:

1. Compute the item's hash code or index in the array.

2. If the array cell is empty, create a node with the item and assign the node to the cell.

3. Otherwise, a collision occurs. The existing item is the head of a linked list or chain of items at that position. Insert the new item at the head of this list.

Borrowing the Node class discussed in Lesson 16, following is the code for inserting an item using chaining:

```
// Get the hash code
int index = item.hashCode() % array.length;

// Access a bucket and store the item at the head of its linked list
array[index] = new Node(item, array[index]);
```

Load Factors

To understand the complexity analysis of the various hashing methods, you need to become acquainted with the concept of a *load factor* or *density ratio*. An array's load factor is the result of dividing the number of items by the array's capacity. For example, let E be 30 items and let A be 100 array cells. Then the load fac-

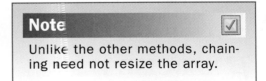

Note ☑

Unlike the other methods, chaining need not resize the array.

tor of the structure, E/A, is 30/100 or 0.3. Without realizing it, we first encountered load factors in our comparison of array and linked-based implementations of lists (Lesson 16), where we claimed that arrays less than half full waste more memory than the corresponding linked structures. In the context of hashing, as the load factor increases, so does the likelihood of collisions.

Complexity Analysis

Linear Collision Processing

As we have seen, the complexity of linear collision processing depends on the load factor as well as the tendency of relocated items to cluster. In the worst case, when the method must traverse the entire array before locating an item's position, the behavior is linear. One study of the linear method (Donald E. Knuth, *The Art of Computer Programming*, Volume 3, *Searching and Sorting*, Menlo Park, CA: Addison-Wesley, 1973) showed that its average behavior in searching for an item that cannot be found is

$$(1/2) \, [1 + 1/(1 - D)^2]$$

where D is the density ratio or load factor.

Quadratic Collision Processing

Because the quadratic method tends to mitigate clustering, we can expect its average performance to be better than that of the linear method. According to Knuth (cited earlier), the average search complexity for the quadratic method is

$$1 - \log_e(1 - D) - (D / 2)$$

for the successful case and

$$1 / (1 - D) - D - \log_e(1 - D)$$

for the unsuccessful case.

Chaining

Analysis shows that the process of locating an item using this strategy consists of two parts:

1. Computing the index

2. Searching a linked list when collisions occur

The first part has constant time behavior. The second part has linear behavior. The amount of work is $O(n)$ in the worst case. In this case, all of the items are in one chain, which is a linked list. However, if the lists are evenly distributed throughout the array and the array is fairly large, the second part can be close to constant as well. In the best case, each array cell is occupied by a chain of length 1, so the performance is exactly $O(1)$. Random insertion of items tends to result in an even distribution. As the load factor increases past 1, however, the lengths of the chains also increase, resulting in degraded performance.

Other trade-offs and optimizations of various hashing strategies are the subject of later courses in computer science.

*E*XERCISE 17.3

1. Explain how hashing can provide constant-time access to a data structure.

2. What causes collisions?

3. How does the linear method of resolving collisions work?

4. What causes clustering?

<u>**EXERCISE 17.3 Continued**</u>

5. How does the quadratic method of resolving collisions work, and how does it mitigate clustering?

6. Compute the load factors for the following situations:
   a. An array of length 30 with 10 items.
   b. An array of length 30 with 30 items.
   c. An array of length 30 with 100 items.

7. Explain how chaining works.

17.4 Hashing Implementation of Maps

Our prototype map class uses the bucket/chaining method described earlier. Thus, the implementation must maintain an array and represent entries in such a manner as to allow chaining. To manage the array, we declare three instance variables table (the array), size (the number of entries in the map), and capacity (the number of cells in the array). To represent an entry, we define the private inner class Entry. The attributes of an entry are similar to those of the node classes of earlier chapters: a key, a value, and a pointer to the next entry in a chain. The value of capacity is by default a constant, which we define as 3 to ensure frequent collisions.

Because the same technique is used to locate the position of an entry for insertions, retrievals, and removals, we implement it in one method, containsKey. From the client's perspective, this method just searches for a given key and returns true or false. From the implementer's perspective, this method also sets the values of some instance variables to information that can be used during insertions, retrievals, and removals. Table 17-3 gives the variables and their roles in the implementation.

TABLE 17-3
The variables used for accessing entries in the class HashMapPT

TEMPORARY INSTANCE VARIABLE	PURPOSE
Entry foundEntry	Contains the entry just located or is undefined otherwise.
Entry priorEntry	Contains the entry prior to the one just located or is undefined otherwise.
int index	Contains the index of the chain in which the entry was just located or is undefined otherwise.

We now examine how containsKey locates an entry's position and sets these variables. Following is the pseudocode for this process:

```
containsKey(key)
Set index to the hash code of the key (using the method described earlier)
Set priorEntry to null
Set foundEntry to table[index]
while (foundEntry != null)
```

```
      if (foundEntry.key equals key)
         return true
      else
         Set priorEntry to foundEntry
         Set foundEntry to foundEntry.next
   return false;
```

As you can see, the algorithm uses `index`, `foundEntry`, and `priorEntry` during the search. If the algorithm hashes to an empty array cell, then no entry was found, but `index` contains the bucket for a subsequent insertion of its first entry. If the algorithm hashes to a nonempty array cell, then the algorithm loops down the chain of entries until it finds a matching entry or runs off the chain. In either case, the algorithm leaves `foundEntry` and `priorEntry` set to the appropriate values for a subsequent retrieval, insertion, or removal of the entry.

The method `get` just calls `containsKey` and returns the value contained in `foundEntry` if the key was found or returns `null` otherwise:

```
get(key)
if containsKey(key)
   return foundEntry.value
else
   return null
```

The method `put` calls `containsKey` to determine whether or not an entry exists at the target key's position. If the entry is found, `put` replaces its value with the new value and returns the old value. Otherwise, `put`

1. Creates a new entry whose next pointer is the entry at the head of the chain.

2. Sets the head of the chain to the new entry.

3. Increments the size.

4. Returns `null`.

Following is the pseudocode for `put`:

```
put(key, value)
if (!containsKey (key))
   Entry newEntry = new Entry (key, value, table[index])
   table[index] = newEntry
   size++
   return null
else
   Object returnValue = foundEntry.value
   foundEntry.value = value
   return returnValue
```

The strategy of the method remove is similar, although remove uses the variable priorEntry when the entry to be removed comes after the head of the chain. Following is the partially completed code of the class HashMapPT:

```java
// HashMapPT

import java.util.Collection;

public class HashMapPT {

    private static final int DEFAULT_CAPACITY = 3;
                                    // Purposely set to a small value in order
                                    // to ensure collisions

    // Temporary variables
    private Entry foundEntry;   // entry just located
                                // undefined if not found
    private Entry priorEntry;   // entry prior to one just located
                                // undefined if not found
    private int   index;        // index of chain in which entry located
                                // undefined if not found


    // Instance variables
    private int   capacity;     // size of table[]
    private Entry table[];      // the table of collision lists
    private int   size;         // number of entries in the map

    public HashMapPT(){
       capacity = DEFAULT_CAPACITY;
       clear();
    }

    public void clear(){
       size = 0;
       table = new Entry[capacity];
    }

    public boolean containsKey (Object key){
       index = Math.abs(key.hashCode()) % capacity;
       priorEntry = null;
       foundEntry = table[index];
       while (foundEntry != null){
          if (foundEntry.key.equals (key))
             return true;
          else{
             priorEntry = foundEntry;
             foundEntry = foundEntry.next;
          }
       }
       return false;
    }

    public boolean containsValue (Object value){
```

```java
        for (int i = 0; i < table.length; i++){
          for (Entry entry = table[i]; entry != null; entry = entry.next)
             if (entry.value.equals (value))
                return true;
        }
     return false;
  }

  public Object get(Object key){
     if (containsKey (key))
        return foundEntry.value;
     else
        return null;
  }

  public boolean isEmpty(){
    return size == 0;
  }

  public SetPT keySet(){
     // Exercise 17.4, Question 1
  }

  public Object put(Object key, Object value){
     if (!containsKey (key)){
        Entry newEntry = new Entry (key, value, table[index]);
        table[index] = newEntry;
        size++;
        return null;
     }else{
        Object returnValue = foundEntry.value;
        foundEntry.value = value;
        return returnValue;
     }
  }

  public Object remove(Object key){
     if (!containsKey (key))
        return null;
     else{
        if (priorEntry == null)
           table[index] = foundEntry.next;
        else
           priorEntry.next = foundEntry.next;
         size--;
         return foundEntry.value;
     }
  }

  public int size(){
     return size;
  }
```

```
public String toString(){
   String rowStr;
   String str = "HashMapPT: capacity = " +  capacity
               + " load factor = " + ((double)size() / capacity);
   for (int i = 0; i < table.length; i++){
      rowStr = "";
      for (Entry entry = table[i]; entry != null; entry = entry.next)
         rowStr += entry + " ";
      if (rowStr != "")
         str += "\nRow " + i + ": " + rowStr;
   }
   return str;
}

public Collection values(){
   // Exercise 17.4, Question 2
}

private class Entry {

   private Object key;       //Key for this entry
   private Object value;     //Value for this entry
   private Entry  next;      //Reference to next entry

   private Entry(){
      key = null;
      value = null;
      next = null;
   }

   private Entry(Object key, Object value, Entry next){
      this.key = key;
      this.value = value;
      this.next = next;
   }

   public String toString(){
      return "(" + key + ", " + value + ")";
   }
}
}
```

Note that the method toString returns not only the string representations of each key/value pair but also the current capacity and load factor of the map. This information allows the client to examine the complexity of the map at run time.

EXERCISE 17.4

1. Add the method `keySet` to the class `HashMapPT`. This method should create and return an instance of class `HashSetPT` that contains the keys in the map (you won't be able to compile or run this code until you implement `HashSetPT`—see the next section).

2. Add the method `values` to the class `HashMapPT`. This method should create and return an object of class `LinkedList` that contains the values in the map.

3. The `put` method can be modified to take advantage of the map's knowledge of the current load factor. Describe a strategy for implementing this change in `put`.

4. Implement a `HashMapPT` constructor that allows the client to specify the capacity of the array.

17.5 Hashing Implementation of Sets

The design of the class `HashSetPT` is quite similar to the design of the class `HashMapPT`. Because we use the same hashing strategy, the instance variables are the same. Each object of class `Entry` now consists of just an item and a pointer to the next entry in the chain, however.

The design of the methods for `HashSetPT` is also virtually the same as the corresponding methods in `HashMapPT`. Following are the differences:

1. The method `contains` searches for an item in an entry instead of a key.

2. The method `add` inserts an item only if it is not already present in the set.

3. The methods `add` and `remove` return a boolean value to indicate the success or failure of an addition or removal.

4. There is a single `iterator` method instead of two methods that return keys and values.

Following is a partial implementation of the class `HashSetPT`, omitting the iterator and the code that is the same as in `HashMapPT`:

```
// HashSetPT

public class HashSetPT {

    // Same data as in HashMapPT

    public HashSetPT(){
        capacity = DEFAULT_CAPACITY;
        clear();
    }

    public boolean add(Object item){
        if (!contains (item)){
            Entry newEntry = new Entry (item, table[index]);
            table[index] = newEntry;
            size++;
            return true;
```

```java
    }else
       return false;
}

public boolean contains (Object item){
    index = Math.abs(item.hashCode()) % capacity;
    priorEntry = null;
    foundEntry = table[index];
    while (foundEntry != null){
       if (foundEntry.item.equals (item))
          return true;
       else{
          priorEntry = foundEntry;
          foundEntry = foundEntry.next;
       }
    }
    return false;
}

public Iterator iterator(){
    // Project 17-6 — must create an inner class as well
}

public boolean remove(Object item){
    if (!contains (item))
       return false;
    else{
       if (priorEntry == null)
          table[index] = foundEntry.next;
       else
          priorEntry.next = foundEntry.next;
       size--;
       return true;
    }
}

public String toString(){
    String rowStr;
    String str = "HashSetPT: capacity = " +  capacity
              + " load factor = " + ((double)size() / capacity);
    for (int i = 0; i < table.length; i++){
       rowStr = "";
       for (Entry entry = table[i]; entry != null; entry = entry.next)
          rowStr += entry + " ";
       if (rowStr != "")
          str += "\nRow " + i + ": " + rowStr;
    }
    return str;
}


private class Entry {
```

```
         private Object item;       //Item for this entry
         private Entry  next;       //Reference to next entry

         private Entry(){
            item = null;
            next = null;
         }

         private Entry(Object item, Entry next){
            this.item = item;
            this.next = next;
         }

         public String toString(){
            return "" + item;
         }
      }
   }
```

EXERCISE 17.5

1. How does the implementation of `HashSetPT` differ from the implementation of `HashMapPT`?

2. Describe a design strategy for the iterator for the class `HashSetPT`. You can assume that the `Iterator` method `remove` is not supported.

3. Write a constructor method for `HashSetPT` that expects a `Collection` as a parameter. The constructor should transfer the items from the collection to the new set.

SUMMARY

In this lesson, you learned:

- The implementations of maps and sets, which use a list, are easy to write but provide inefficient (linear) access to items.

- Hashing can provide constant-time access to items in sets and maps. A hashing strategy uses a hash function to locate the index position of an item in an array.

- When using hashing, the position of a new item can collide with the position of an item already in an array. Several techniques exist to resolve collisions. Among these are linear collision processing, quadratic collision processing, and chaining.

- Chaining employs an array of buckets, which are linked structures that contain the items.

- The run-time and memory aspects of hashing methods involve the load factor of the array. When the load factor (physical size / logical size) approaches 1, the likelihood of collisions, and thus of extra processing, increases.

VOCABULARY *Review*

Define the following terms:

bucket	collision	linear collision processing
chaining	density ratio	load factor
chains	hash code	quadratic collision processing
clustering	hash function	

REVIEW *Questions*

FILL IN THE BLANK

Complete the following sentences by writing the correct word or words in the blanks provided.

1. The list-based implementations of sets and maps access items in _____ time.

2. The hashing implementations of sets and maps can access items in _____ time.

3. The code used to locate an item's position in a hashing technique is called a(n) _____, whereas the function that generates this code is called a(n) _____.

4. A(n) _____ occurs when two items hash to the same index position.

5. The linear method of resolving collisions can produce an undesirable effect known as _____.

6. The _____ method of resolving collisions increments the item's code by the square of an increasing constant.

7. The _____ represents the ratio of the capacity of the array to the number of items.

8. The behavior of hashing strategies can be _____ in the worst case.

9. The chaining strategy of removing collisions uses structures called _____.

10. The `HashMapPT` method `keySet` returns an object of type _____.

PROJECTS

PROJECT 17-1

Convert the program for generating hash codes and index positions (TestCodes in Section 17.3) to a GUI-based program. This version of the program should allow the user to enter the number of items and the load factor in numeric fields. A text area should display the output in formatted columns when the **Run** button is clicked.

PROJECT 17-2

Modify the program from Project 17-1 to count and display the number and positions of the collisions that occur on each run. Use an array of integers to track this information. The data will hash to positions in this array. At the beginning of each run, instantiate the array and set each cell to 0. Each time a position is hit, increment the integer stored there by 1. Display just the indexes and contents of the array and the total number of collisions at the end of each run. Use this version of the program to experiment with various load factors, say, .33, .5, .75, and 1.

PROJECT 17-3

Modify the program from Project 17-2 to implement the linear method of resolving collisions. The code for this method should be packaged in a private Java helper method. Use an array of sufficient capacity to observe any clusters that develop. Track and display the number of comparisons required to resolve collisions as well. Test this method with load factors of .33, .5, .75, and 1 and compare the results to those of Project 17-2.

PROJECT 17-4

Modify the program from Project 17-3 to use the quadratic method of resolving collisions. Use the same test data as in Project 17-3.

PROJECT 17-5

Add a new method of computing the hash code to the program from Project 17-4. This method returns a random integer between 0 and the largest integer allowed by Java. Accumulate results for this method using the same test runs as in earlier projects and compare them with the results using Java's hashCode method.

PROJECT 17-6

Complete the implementation of the iterator for the class HashSetPT. This iterator does not have to support the method remove.

CRITICAL *Thinking*

Another method of resolving collisions is known as *rehashing*. That is, when a collision occurs using one hash function, code can be written to try to find an empty position using a different hash function. Discuss the costs and benefits of this method.

IMPLEMENTING TREES AND PRIORITY QUEUES

A third major category of collections, which we called "hierarchical" in Lesson 13, consists of various types of tree structures. As with lists, these collections have no standard set of operations and most programming languages do not include them as standard classes. Their primary use is in implementing other collections, such as sorted sets and sorted maps in Java and similar types of collections that require efficient searching and that, like priority queues, must impose some priority order on their elements. In this lesson we examine the basic properties of trees that make them useful data structures and explore their role in implementing several types of collections.

18.1 An Overview of Trees

Trees are characterized by the fact that each item can have multiple successors and all items, except a privileged item called the *root*, have exactly one predecessor.

For example, consider Figure 18-1, which is the *parse tree* for the following sentence: "The girl hit the ball with a bat." A parse tree describes the syntactic structure of a sentence in terms of its component parts, such as noun phrases and verb phrases. In this and in all diagrams of trees, the items are called *nodes*. Trees are drawn with the root at the top. Immediately below a node and connected to it by lines are its successors, or *children*. A node without children (in italics in the figure) is called a *leaf*. Immediately above a node is its predecessor, or *parent*. Thus, the root node "Sentence" has two children but no parent. In contrast, the leaf node "ball" has a parent but no children. Any node, such as "Noun phrase," that has children is called an *interior node*.

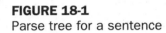

FIGURE 18-1
Parse tree for a sentence

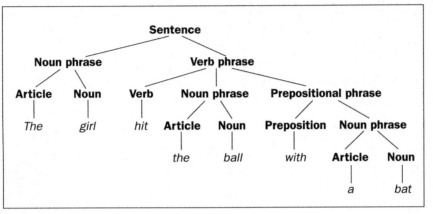

A book's table of contents is another familiar example of a hierarchical collection or tree. In addition, trees are used to organize a computer's file system, as we are reminded every time we view the files on our hard drive.

Talking About Trees

We have already introduced some terminology associated with trees, but there is more. The terminology is a peculiar mix of biological, genealogical, and geometric terms. Table 18-1 provides a quick summary of these terms.

TABLE 18-1
A summary of terms used to describe trees

TERM	DEFINITION
Node	An item stored in a tree.
Root	The topmost node in a tree. It is the only node without a predecessor or parent.
Child	A successor of a node. A node can have more than one child, and its children are viewed as organized in left to right order. The leftmost child is called the first child, and the rightmost is the last child.
Parent	The predecessor of a node. A node can have only one parent.
Siblings	The children of a common parent.
Edge/Branch	The line that connects a parent to its child.
Descendant	A node's descendants include its children, its children's children, and so on, down to the leaves.
Ancestor	A node's ancestors include its parent, its parent's parent, and so on, up to the root.
Path	The sequence of edges that connect a node and one of its descendants.
Path length	The number of edges in a path.
Leaf	A node that has no children.
Interior node	A node that has at least one child.
Depth or level	The depth or level of a node equals the length of the path connecting it to the root. Thus, the root depth or level of the root is 0. Its children are at level 1, and so on.
Height	The height of a tree equals the length of the longest path in the tree, or put differently, the maximum level number among leaves in the tree.
Subtree	The tree formed by considering a node and all its descendants. We exclude the root when forming subtrees.

Figure 18-2 shows a tree and some of its properties.

FIGURE 18-2
A tree and some of its properties

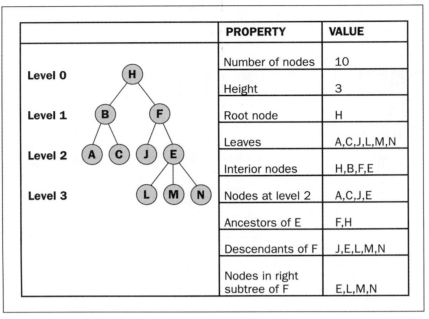

PROPERTY	VALUE
Number of nodes	10
Height	3
Root node	H
Leaves	A,C,J,L,M,N
Interior nodes	H,B,F,E
Nodes at level 2	A,C,J,E
Ancestors of E	F,H
Descendants of F	J,E,L,M,N
Nodes in right subtree of F	E,L,M,N

General Trees and Binary Trees

The trees we have been discussing are sometimes called *general trees* to distinguish them from a special category called *binary trees*. In a binary tree, each node has at most two children, referred to as the *left child* and the *right child*. In a binary tree, when a node has only one child, we distinguish it as being a left child or a right child. Thus, the two trees shown in Figure 18-3 are not the same when considered as binary trees, although they are the same when considered as general trees.

FIGURE 18-3
Two unequal binary trees that have equal sets of nodes

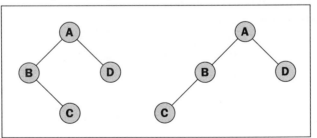

Recursive Definitions of Trees

Although at this point you probably have a clear understanding of what a tree is, we now give a more formal definition. As is often the case, one cannot understand the formal definition without an intuitive grasp of the concept being defined; the formal definition is important, however, because it provides an unambiguous and precise basis for further discussion. Furthermore, because recursive processing of trees is common, we offer recursive definitions of them.

Recursive Definition of a General Tree

A general tree is either empty or consists of a finite set of nodes T. One node r is distinguished from all others and is called the *root*. In addition, the set $T - \{r\}$ is partitioned into disjoint subsets, each of which is a general tree.

Recursive Definition of a Binary Tree

A binary tree is either empty or consists of a root plus a *left subtree* and a *right subtree*, each of which are binary trees.

From now on in this lesson, we restrict our attention to various types of binary trees.

Complete Binary Trees

Trees in nature come in various shapes and sizes, and so do trees as data structures. Some trees are thin, almost linear, whereas others are bushy. The notion of a *complete binary tree* gives a formal cast to the "bushiness" of binary trees. A binary tree is complete if each level except the last has a complete complement of nodes and if the nodes on the last level are filled in from the left (see Figure 18-4). Complete or nearly complete binary trees are considered desirable because they support efficient searching, insertions, and removals.

FIGURE 18-4
Different types of binary trees

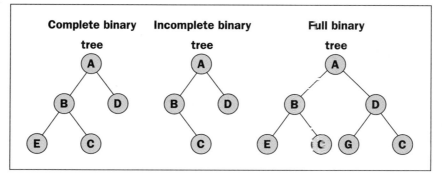

Full Binary Trees

A *full binary tree* contains the maximum number of nodes for its height. Each node in a full binary tree is either an interior node with two nonempty children or a leaf. The number of leaves in a full binary tree is one greater than the number of interior nodes. A full binary tree has the minimum height necessary to accommodate a given number of nodes. Such a tree is *fully balanced*. A fully balanced tree of height d can accommodate up to $2^d - 1$ nodes. In a fully balanced binary tree, there can be up to $2n$ nodes in level n. The height of a fully balanced tree of n nodes is $\log_2 n$. Figure 18-4 shows some examples of trees that have the various properties mentioned. The examples are a complete but not full binary tree, a binary tree that is not complete, and a full binary tree.

Heaps

A *heap* is a binary tree in which the item in each node is greater than or equal to the items in both of its children. This constraint on the order of the nodes is called the *heap property*. You should not confuse this kind of heap with the heap that a computer uses to manage dynamic memory. Figure 18-5 shows two examples of heaps.

FIGURE 18-5
Examples of heaps

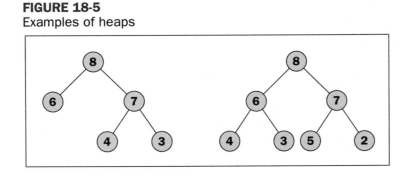

As the figure shows, the largest item is in the root node, and the smallest items are in the leaves. Note that the shape of a heap is close to that of a complete binary tree, according to the definition given earlier. The arrangement of data in a heap supports an efficient sorting method called the *heap sort*. Heaps are also used to implement priority queues.

Expression Trees

In Lesson 14, we showed how to use a stack to convert infix expressions to postfix form. We also showed in Lesson 14 how to use a stack to evaluate postfix expressions. Yet another way to process expressions is to build a data structure called a parse tree during parsing. For a language of expressions, this structure is also called an *expression tree*. Figure 18-6 shows several expression trees that result from parsing infix expressions.

FIGURE 18-6
Some expression trees

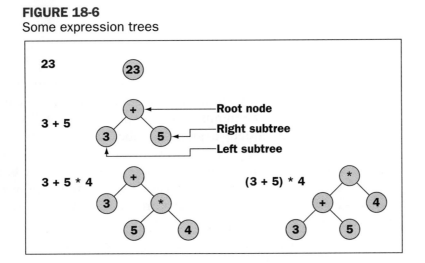

Note that an expression tree consists of either a number or an operator whose operands are its left and right subtrees.

Binary Search Trees

You will remember our use of call trees to trace the execution of recursive methods in Lesson 11. The call tree for a binary search of a typical sorted array is shown in Figure 18-7. The items visited for comparison are shaded.

FIGURE 18-7
A call tree for the binary search of an array

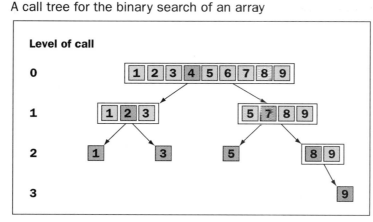

As the figure shows, it requires at most four comparisons to search the entire array of eight items. Because the array is sorted, the search algorithm can reduce the search space by one-half after each comparison.

Now, let us transfer the items that are shaded in the call tree for the binary search to an explicit binary tree structure, as shown in Figure 18-8.

FIGURE 18-8
A binary search tree

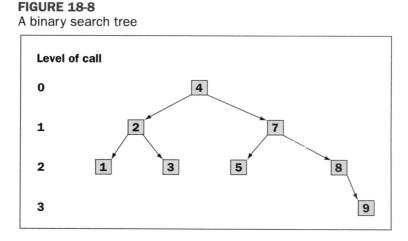

This tree is a *binary search tree*. Note that each node in the tree is greater than or equal to its left child and less than or equal to its right child.

Now, consider the following recursive search process using this tree:

```
If the tree is empty
    Return false
Else if the item in the root equals the target
    Return true
```

```
Else if the item in the root is greater than the target
   Return the result of searching the root's left subtree
Else
   Return the result of searching the root's right subtree
```

Like the binary search of a sorted array, the search of a binary search tree potentially can throw away one-half of the search space after each comparison. We say "potentially" because the efficiency of the search depends in part on the shape of the tree. Figure 18-9 shows three binary search trees that contain the same items but have different shapes.

FIGURE 18-9
Three binary tree shapes with the same data

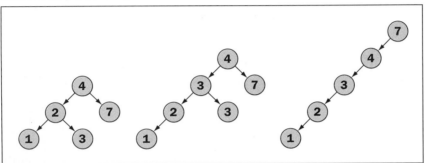

The trees degrade in their support for efficient search from left to right. The leftmost tree is complete, and it is said to be balanced. As such, it supports the most efficient searches. The rightmost tree looks just like a one-way linked list, and as such supports only a linear search. Thus, everything depends on how the data come into the tree. In particular, data coming into the tree in close to sorted order produce a tree whose shape is not optimal for searching.

*E*XERCISE 18.1

1. What are the leaf nodes and the interior nodes in the following tree?

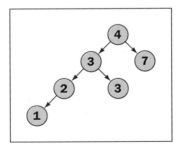

EXERCISE 18.1 Continued

2. Which of the following trees are complete or full?

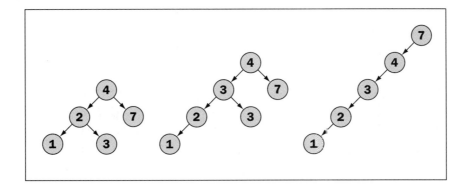

3. What is a heap?

4. What is an expression tree?

18.2 Binary Tree Traversals

In earlier lessons, we saw how to traverse the items in collections using iterators. There are four types of traversals for binary trees: preorder, inorder, postorder, and level order. Each type of traversal follows a particular path and direction as it visits the nodes in the tree.

Preorder Traversal

The preorder traversal algorithm visits the root node, traverses the left subtree, and traverses the right subtree. The path traveled by a preorder traversal is illustrated in Figure 18-10.

FIGURE 18-10
A preorder traversal

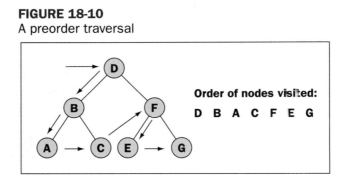

Order of nodes visited:

D B A C F E G

Inorder Traversal

The inorder traversal algorithm traverses the left subtree, visits the root node, and traverses the right subtree. This process has the effect of moving as far to the left in the tree as possible before visiting a node. The path traveled by an inorder traversal is illustrated in Figure 18-11.

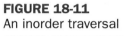

FIGURE 18-11
An inorder traversal

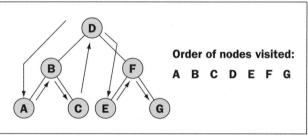

Postorder Traversal

The postorder traversal algorithm traverses the left subtree, traverses the right subtree, and visits the root node. The path traveled by a postorder traversal is illustrated in Figure 18-12:

FIGURE 18-12
A postorder traversal

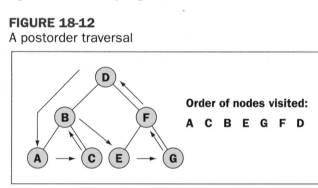

Level Order Traversal

Beginning with level 0, the level order traversal algorithm visits the nodes at each level in left-to-right order. The path traveled by a level order traversal is illustrated in Figure 18-13.

FIGURE 18-13
A level order traversal

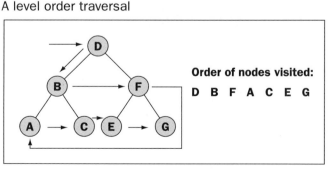

The preorder, inorder, and postorder traversals of an expression tree can be used to generate representations of the expression in prefix, infix, and postfix forms, respectively.

EXERCISE 18.2

1. List the items resulting from the different types of traversals of the tree shown here.
   a. A preorder traversal
   b. An inorder traversal
   c. A postorder traversal

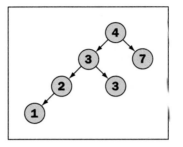

2. What would be an appropriate application of a preorder traversal?

18.3 A Linked Implementation of Binary Trees

Two common implementations of binary trees use an array and a linked structure, respectively. We examine an array implementation in section 18.4. In this section, we explore a linked implementation of a binary search tree. As usual, we develop a prototype interface and a prototype implementation class.

Interface

The interface for a binary search tree should include methods needed to implement sorted sets and sorted maps. In addition, a search tree should support the different types of traversals mentioned in the previous section. These methods, which are coded in the Java interface `BSTPT` (Binary Search Tree ProtoType), are described in Table 18-2.

TABLE 18-2
The methods of the `BSTPT` interface

METHOD	WHAT IT DOES
`Object add(Object obj)`	If the object is not already in the tree, then adds the object to the tree, increasing the tree's size by one, and returns `null`; otherwise, replaces the old object with the new one and returns the old object.
`Object contains(Object obj)`	Returns the node's value if the object is in the tree, else `null`.
`List inorderTraverse()`	Returns a list of items accumulated during an inorder traversal of the tree.
`boolean isEmpty()`	Returns `true` if the tree contains no objects, else `false`.
`Iterator iterator()`	Returns an iterator on the tree. The iterator allows the client to visit the items in alphabetical order. The tree is not used as a backing store, so the method `remove` has no effect.
`List levelorderTraverse()`	Returns a list of items accumulated during a level order traversal of the tree.
`List postorderTraverse()`	Returns a list of items accumulated during a postorder traversal of the tree.
`List preorderTraverse()`	Returns a list of items accumulated during a preorder traversal of the tree.
`Object remove(Object obj)`	If the object is in the tree, removes it and returns the node's value; otherwise, returns `null`.
`int size()`	Returns the number of objects in the tree.
`String toString()`	Returns a string containing the string representations of the items in a format that shows the tree structure.

The Class `LinkedBSTPT`

The linked implementation of a binary search tree has an external pointer to the tree's root node. Each node contains a data element and links to the node's left subtree and right subtree. The following code segment shows the data declarations and constructor method for the class `LinkedBSTPT`:

```
public class LinkedBSTPT{

    private Node root;
    private int size;

    public LinkedBSTPT(){
```

```
        root = null;
        size = 0;
    }

    private class Node{

        private Object value;
        private Node left, right;

        private Node(Node l, Object v, Node r){
            left = l;
            value = v;
            right = r;
        }
    }
}
```

We now develop several operations for this implementation.

Inserting an Item into a Binary Search Tree

The add method inserts an object in its proper place in the binary search tree. Because we will be using a binary search tree to implement sorted sets and sorted maps, this method also replaces a duplicate item with a new item and returns the old item.

In general, an item's proper place will be either the root node (if the tree is already empty) or in a leaf node to the left of the item's natural successor or to the right of the item's natural predecessor, as determined by using the method compareTo. Thus, all items must implement the Comparable interface. The add method uses a loop to advance a temporary pointer until the correct position is found. Following is the code for method add:

```
public Object add(Object obj){
    Node newNode = new Node(null, obj, null);

    // Tree is empty, so the new item goes at the root
    if (root == null){
        root = newNode;
        size++;
        return null;
    }

    // Search for the new item's spot or until a duplicate item is found
    else{
        Node probe = root;
        while (probe != null){
            int relation = ((Comparable)obj).compareTo(probe.value);

            // A duplicate is found, so replace it and return it
            if (relation == 0){
                Object oldValue = probe.value;
                probe.value = obj;
                return oldValue;
```

```
            }

            // The new item is less, so go left until its spot is found
            else if (relation < 0)
               if (probe.left != null)
                  probe = probe.left;
               else{
                  probe.left = newNode;
                  size++;
                  return null;
               }

            // The new item is greater, so go right until its spot is found
            else if (probe.right != null)
               probe = probe.right;
            else{
               probe.right = newNode;
               size++;
               return null;
            }
         }
         return null;    // Never reached
      }
   }
```

Searching a Binary Search Tree

The `contains` method returns the node's value if an object is in the tree and `null` otherwise. We can use a recursive strategy that takes advantage of the recursive structure of the tree nodes. Following is a pseudocode algorithm for this process, where `tree` is a node:

```
if tree is null
   return null
else if the object equals the root item
   return the root item
else if the object is less than the root item
   return the result of searching the left subtree
else
   return the result of searching the right subtree
```

Because the recursive search method requires an extra parameter for the node, we cannot include it as a public method. Instead, we define it as a private helper method that is called from the public `contains` method. Following is the code for the two methods:

```
public Object contains(Object obj){
   return contains(root, obj);
}

private Object contains(Node tree, Object obj){
   if (tree == null)
      return null;
```

```
      else{
         int relation = ((Comparable)obj).compareTo(tree.value);
         if (relation == 0)
            return tree.value;
         else if (relation < 0)
            return contains(tree.left, obj);
         else
            return contains(tree.right, obj);
      }
   }
```

Traversals and the Iterator

As mentioned earlier, there are four ways to traverse the items in a tree. Each type of traversal can use a recursive strategy and can be implemented using a pair of methods as we did with the search operation. Each traversal builds and returns a list of items accumulated.

Inorder Traversal

The inorder traversal uses the following two methods:

1. The private method `inorderTraverse` expects an empty list and a tree's root node as parameters and adds the items from an inorder traversal to the list.

2. The public method `inorderTraverse` returns a list of items accumulated from an inorder traversal of the tree.

Following is the code for these methods:

```
public List inorderTraverse(){
   List list = new ArrayList();
   inorderTraverse(root, list);
   return list;
}

private void inorderTraverse(Node tree, List list){
   if (tree != null){
      inorderTraverse(tree.left, list);
      list.add(tree.value);
      inorderTraverse(tree.right, list);
   }
}
```

Level Order Traversal

The algorithm for a level order traversal starts with level 0 and visits each node from left to right at that level. The algorithm then repeats this process for the next level and so on, until all the nodes have been visited. Clearly, we need some way of constraining the recursive process to march across a tree at each level. A convenient way is to schedule the nodes to be visited on a queue. In the present example, the top-level public method `levelOrderTraverse` creates a queue and a list, the queue for scheduling and the list to return to the client. The method places the root node at the front of the scheduling queue and passes the two collections to the helper method `levelOrderTraverse`:

```
public List levelOrderTraverse(){
   List list = new ArrayList();          // List to accumumate values
   Queue levelsQu = new LinkedQueue();            // Scheduling queue

   if (!isEmpty()){
      levelsQu.enqueue (root);
      levelOrderTraverse (levelsQu, list);
   }
   return list;
}
```

The recursive pattern for a level order traversal dequeues a node for processing and then enqueues the left and right subtrees before the recursive call. Following is the pseudocode for the pattern:

```
If the levels queue is not empty
   Dequeue the node from the levels queue and add
      its value to the values list
   If the node's left subtree is not null
      Enqueue the left subtree on the levels queue
   If the node's right subtree is not null
      Enqueue the right subtree on the levels queue
   Call levelOrderTraverse with the levels queue and the list
```

The order in which the subtrees are enqueued determines the order in which the process moves across each level of the tree. At any given time, the scheduling queue contains the nodes remaining to be visited on one and only one level.

The complete implementation of these and the remaining traversals is left as Project 18-5.

Iterator

Clients using a binary search tree to implement sorted sets and maps would prefer to have an iterator method that allows them to visit items in alphabetical order. The `iterator` method for a binary search tree simply returns an iterator on the list that results from an inorder traversal. Note that the iterator's `remove` method will have no effect on the tree, because the iterator's backing store is the list, not the tree. Following is the code for the iterator:

```
public Iterator iterator(){
   return inorderTraverse().iterator();
}
```

toString

The `toString` method can be implemented with any of the traversals. Because it is used primarily in testing and debugging, it will be useful to return a string that displays the tree's structure as well as its elements. A convenient way to do this for text-only display is to "rotate" the tree 90 degrees counterclockwise and display vertical bars between the interior nodes. The following code builds the appropriate string by first recursing with the right subtree, then visiting an item, and finally recursing with the left subtree.

```java
public String toString(){
   return toString(root, 0);
}

private String toString(Node tree, int level){
   String str = "";
   if (tree != null){
      str += toString(tree.right, level + 1);
      for (int i = 1; i <= level; i++)
         str = str + "| ";
      str += tree.value.toString() + "\n";
      str += toString(tree.left, level + 1);
   }
   return str;
}
```

A Tester Program

The following program tests some of the methods developed thus far. The output of this program is shown in Figure 18-14.

```java
import java.util.*;

public class TestBST{

   public static void main(String[] args){
      LinkedBSTPT tree = new LinkedBSTPT();
      tree.add("D");
      tree.add("B");
      tree.add("A");
      tree.add("C");
      tree.add("F");
      tree.add("E");
      tree.add("G");

      System.out.println("ToString:\n" + tree);

      System.out.println("Iterator (inorder traversal):");
      Iterator iter = tree.iterator();
      while (iter.hasNext())
         System.out.print(iter.next() + " ");

      System.out.println("\nPreorder traversal:");
      List list = tree.preorderTraverse();
      printList(list);

      System.out.println("\nPostorder traversal:");
      list = tree.postorderTraverse();
```

```
        printList(list);

        System.out.println("\nLevel order traversal:");
        list = tree.levelOrderTraverse();
        printList(list);

        System.out.println("\nRemovals:");
        for (char ch = 'A'; ch <= 'G'; ch++)
            System.out.print(tree.remove("" + ch) + " ");
    }

    private static void printList(List list){
        for (int i = 0; i < list.size(); i++)
            System.out.print(list.get(i) + " ");
    }
}
```

FIGURE 18-14
The output of the binary search tree tester program

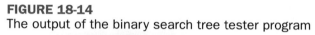

Removing an Item from a Binary Search Tree

You will recall that removing an item from an array causes a shift of items to fill the hole. Removing an item from a linked list requires rearranging a few pointers. Removing an item from a binary search tree can require both. Following is an outline of the strategy for this process:

1. Save a pointer to the root node.

2. Attempt to locate the node to be removed, its parent, and its parent's pointer to this node.

3. If the item is not in the tree, return `false`.

4. Otherwise, if the node has a left child and a right child, replace the node's value with the largest value in the left subtree and delete that value's node from the left subtree.

5. Otherwise, set the parent's pointer to the node to the node's only child.

6. Reset the root node to the saved pointer.

7. Decrement the size and return `true`.

Step 4 in this process is fairly complex, so it can be factored out into a helper method, which takes the node to be deleted as a parameter. The outline for this method follows (we refer to the node containing the item to be removed as the top node):

1. Search the top node's left subtree for the node containing the largest item. This will be in the rightmost node of the subtree. Be sure to track the parent of the current node during the search.

2. Replace the top node's value with the item.

3. If the top node's left child contained the largest item (e.g., that node had no right subtree, so the parent pointer still refers to the top node), set the top node's left child pointer to its left child's left child pointer.

4. Otherwise, set the parent node's right child pointer to that right child's left child pointer.

    The coding of these two methods is left as Project 18-1.

Complexity Analysis of Binary Search Trees

As you might expect, binary search trees are set up with the intent of replicating the $O(\log n)$ behavior for the binary search of a sorted array. Unfortunately, as mentioned earlier, this intent is not always realized. Optimal behavior depends on the shape of the tree. A bushy tree, one that is close to complete in the technical sense defined earlier, supports close to logarithmic searches. In the worst case, when the items are inserted in alphabetical order (either ascending or descending), the tree's shape becomes linear, as does its search behavior. Insertions in random order actually result in a tree with reasonable search behavior.

The run time of insertions is also highly dependent on the shape of the tree. Recall that an insertion involves a search for the item's spot. Thus, the run time of an insertion into a bushy tree is likely to be close to logarithmic.

Removals also require a search for the target item, with behavior similar to that of the other operations.

*E*XERCISE 18.3

1. Write a pseudocode algorithm for a preorder traversal of a binary search tree.

2. Write a constructor method for a binary search tree that expects a collection as a parameter and transfers the items from the collection to the tree.

3. Describe how insertions can have a negative effect on subsequent searches of a binary search tree.

18.4 An Array Implementation of Binary Trees

An array-based implementation of a binary tree is also possible, but is difficult to define and practical only in some special situations. Mapping stacks, queues, and lists to arrays is straight-forward because all are linear and support the same notion of adjacency, each element having an obvious predecessor and successor. But given a node in a tree, what would be its immediate predecessor in an array? Is it the parent or a left sibling? What is its immediate successor? Is it a child or a right sibling? Trees are hierarchical and resist being flattened. Nevertheless, for complete binary trees, there is an elegant and efficient array-based representation.

Consider the complete binary tree in Figure 18-15.

FIGURE 18-15
A complete binary tree

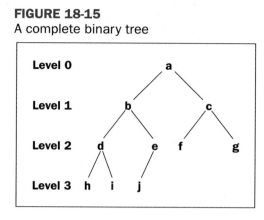

In an array-based implementation, the elements are stored by level, as shown in Figure 18-16.

FIGURE 18-16
An array representation of a complete binary tree

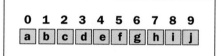

Given an arbitrary item at position *i* in the array, it is easy to determine the location of related items, as shown in the Table 18-3.

TABLE 18-3
The locations of given items in an array representation of a complete binary tree

ITEM	LOCATION
Parent	$(i - 1) / 2$
Left sibling, if there is one	$i - 1$
Right sibling, if there is one	$i + 1$
Left child, if there is one	$i * 2 + 1$
Right child, if there is one	$i * 2 + 2$

Thus, for item d at location 3 we get the results shown in Table 18-4.

TABLE 18-4
The relatives of a given item in an array representation of a complete binary tree

ITEM	LOCATION
Parent	b at 1
Left sibling, if there is one	Not applicable
Right sibling, if there is one	e at 4
Left child, if there is one	h at 7
Right child, if there is one	i at 8

One might naturally ask why the array representation does not work for incomplete binary trees. The reason is not hard to see. In an incomplete binary tree, some levels are not filled above others. But the calculation of a node's relatives in an array is based on being able to multiply or divide its index by 2, which cannot be done when levels are not filled in a top-down manner.

Needless to say, the array representation is pretty rare and is used mainly to implement a heap, which is discussed in the next section.

EXERCISE 18.4

1. Give the formulas for locating a node's parent, a node's left child, and a node's right child in an array representation of a binary tree.

2. What are the constraints on a binary tree that is contained in an array?

18.5 Implementing Heaps

We will use a heap to implement a priority queue, so the heap interface should recognize messages to return its size, add an item, remove an item, and peek at an item (see Table 18-5).

TABLE 18-5
The methods in the interface `HeapPT`

METHOD	WHAT IT DOES
`boolean add(Object obj)`	Inserts the object in its proper place in the heap, increasing the heap's size by one, and returns true.
`Iterator iterator()`	Returns an iterator on the heap. This iterator visits the items from the maximum to the minimum and its remove method has no effect.
`Object peek()`	Precondition: The heap is not empty. Returns the object at the top of the heap.
`Object pop()`	Precondition: The heap is not empty. Removes and returns the topmost item in the heap.
`int size()`	Returns the number of items in the heap.

The two most critical heap operations are `add` and `pop`. The method `add` expects a comparable object as a parameter and inserts the object into its proper place in the heap. That place is generally at a level below an object that is larger and above an object that is smaller. Duplicate objects are placed below previously entered items. The method `pop` deletes the topmost node in the heap, returns the object contained there, and maintains the heap property. The `peek` operation returns but does not remove the topmost object in a heap.

Implementing add and pop

The methods `add` (insertion) and `pop` (removal), which are used throughout the heap implementation, are defined in the class `ArrayHeapPT`. In the array-based implementation, both methods need to maintain the structure of the heap within the array (we actually use an `ArrayList`, but refer to the structure as an array in the following discussion). This structure is similar to the array representation of a binary tree discussed earlier, with the constraint that each node is greater than either of its children.

Let us consider insertion first. The goal is to find the new item's proper place in the heap and insert it there. Following is our strategy for insertions:

1. Begin by inserting the item at the bottom of the heap. In the array implementation, this will be in the cell after the last item currently in the array.

2. Then, enter a loop that "walks" the new item up the heap while the new item's value is greater than that of its parent. Each time this relationship is true, we swap the new item with its parent. When this process stops (either the new item is less than or equal to its parent or we will have reached the top node), the new item is in its proper place.

Recall that the position of an item's parent in the array is computed by subtracting 1 from the item's position and dividing the result by 2. The top of the heap is at position 0 in the array. In the implementation the instance variable `heap` refers to an instance of `ArrayList`. Following is the code for the method `add`:

```java
public boolean add (Object item){
   int curPos, parent;

   heap.add(item);
   curPos = heap.size() - 1;
   while (curPos > 0){
      parent = (curPos - 1) / 2;
      Comparable parentItem = (Comparable)(heap.get(parent));
      if (parentItem.compareTo ((Comparable)item) >= 0)
         return true;
      else{
         heap.set(curPos, heap.get(parent));
         heap.set(parent, item);
         curPos = parent;
      }
   }
   return true;
}
```

A quick analysis of this method reveals that at most $\log_2 n$ comparisons must be made to walk up the tree from the bottom, so the `add` operation is $O(\log n)$. The method occasionally triggers a doubling in the size of the underlying array. When it occurs, this operation is O(n), but amortized over all additions, the operation is O(1) per addition.

The goal of a removal is to return the item in the root node after deleting this node and adjusting the positions of other nodes so as to maintain the heap property. Following is our strategy for removals:

1. Begin by saving pointers to the top item and the bottom item in the heap and by moving the item from the bottom of the heap to the top.

2. Walk down the heap from the top, moving the largest child up one level, until the bottom of the heap is reached.

Following is the code for the method pop:

```
public Object pop(){
    if (size() == 0)
        throw new NoSuchElementException
            ("Trying to remove from an empty heap");

    int curPos, leftChild, rightChild, maxChild, lastIndex;
    Object topItem = heap.get(0);
    Comparable bottomItem = (Comparable)(heap.remove(heap.size() - 1));
    if (heap.size() == 0)
        return bottomItem;

    heap.set(0, bottomItem);
    lastIndex = heap.size() - 1;
    curPos = 0;
    while (true){
        leftChild = 2 * curPos + 1 ;
        rightChild = 2 * curPos + 2;
        if (leftChild > lastIndex) break;
        if (rightChild > lastIndex)
            maxChild = leftChild;
        else{
            Comparable leftItem  = (Comparable)(heap.get(leftChild));
            Comparable rightItem = (Comparable)(heap.get(rightChild));
            if (leftItem.compareTo (rightItem) > 0)
                maxChild = leftChild;
            else
                maxChild = rightChild;
        }
        Comparable maxItem = (Comparable)(heap.get(maxChild));
        if (bottomItem.compareTo (maxItem) >= 0)
            break;
        else{
            heap.set(curPos, heap.get(maxChild));
            heap.set(maxChild, bottomItem);
            curPos = maxChild;
        }
    }
    return topItem;
}
```

Once again, analysis shows that the number of comparisons required for a removal is at most $\log_2 n$, so the pop operation is $O(\log n)$. The method pop occasionally triggers a halving in the size of the underlying array. When it occurs, this operation is $O(n)$, but amortized over all removals, the operation is $O(1)$ per removal.

EXERCISE 18.5

1. How do the run times of the heap operations differ from their counterparts in binary search trees?

2. What is the advantage of using an array list over an array to implement a heap?

3. Implement a method to sort a list using a heap.

4. What is the run time complexity of the heap sort?

18.6 Using a Heap to Implement a Priority Queue

You may recall the discussion of priority queues in Lesson 14, where we implemented a priority queue ADT with an array of queues. Another common implementation of priority queues uses a heap. Items with the highest priority are located near the top of the heap. The enqueue operation wraps the item and its priority number in an object called a *priority node* before inserting the node into the heap. The dequeue operation removes the topmost node from the heap, extracts the item, and returns it. The following code segment shows the public methods of the class HeapPriorityQueue and the implementation of the class PriorityNode:

```
import java.util.*;

public class HeapPriorityQueue implements PriorityQueue{

    private HeapPT heap;        // A heap of items

    public HeapPriorityQueue(){
        heap = new ArrayHeapPT();
    }

    public int size(){
        return heap.size();
    }

    public Object dequeue(){
        if (heap.size() == 0)
            throw new NoSuchElementException
                ("Trying to dequeue an empty priority queue");

        return ((PriorityNode)(heap.pop())).value;
    }

    public void enqueue(Object item){
```

```java
        enqueue (item, 1);
    }

    public void enqueue(Object item, int priority){
        if (priority < 1)
            throw new IllegalArgumentException
                ("Priority must be >= 1 ");

        heap.add (new PriorityNode (item, priority));
    }

    public Iterator iterator(){
        return heap.iterator();
    }

    public Object peekFront(){
        if (heap.size() == 0)
            throw new NoSuchElementException
                ("Trying to peek at an empty priority queue");

        return ((PriorityNode)(heap.peek())).value;
    }

    public String toString()
    {
        if (heap.size() == 0) return "[]";

        Iterator iter = heap.iterator();
        String str = "";
        PriorityNode next;
        int currentPriority = -1;
        while (iter.hasNext()){
            next = (PriorityNode)(iter.next());
            if (currentPriority == next.priority)
                str += ", " + next.value;
            else{
                if (currentPriority != -1)
                    str += "]\n";
                currentPriority = next.priority;
                str += "Priority " + currentPriority + ": [" + next.value;
            }
        }
        return str + "]";
    }

// =============================== Inner Classes =========================

    private static int subpriorityCounter = 0;
    private class PriorityNode implements Comparable {

        private Object      value;      // Value stored in this item
        private int         priority;   // Priority of item
```

```
private int          subpriority;  // Subpriority of item, assigned
                                   // by constructor

private PriorityNode()
{
    throw new IllegalArgumentException
        ("Trying to create a null priority item");
}

private PriorityNode(Object value, int priority)
{
    this.value = value;
    this.priority = priority;
    subpriority = subpriorityCounter;
    subpriorityCounter++;        // Warning: Jumps from +2G to -2G
}

public int compareTo (Object item)
{
    int prior    = ((PriorityNode)item).priority;
    int subprior = ((PriorityNode)item).subpriority;
    if (priority != prior)
        return priority - prior;
    else
        return subprior - subpriority;
}

public String toString()
{
    return "(" + value + "," +
            priority + "," + subpriority + ")";
}
    }

}
```

HeapPriorityQueue does have a compensating space advantage if the range of priorities is large compared to the number of items being queued. One other point that might be made in its favor is that the number of priorities does not have to be fixed ahead of time. LinkedPriorityQueue could be modified to avoid this restriction by allowing it to grow, however.

SUMMARY

In this lesson, you learned:

■ There are various types of trees or hierarchical collections, such as general trees, binary trees, binary search trees, and heaps.

■ The terminology used to describe hierarchical collections is borrowed from biology, genealogy, and geology.

- The four different types of tree traversals are the preorder traversal, the inorder traversal, the postorder traversal, and the level order traversal.

- A binary search tree preserves a natural ordering among its items and can support operations that run in logarithmic time. Binary search trees are useful for implementing sorted sets and sorted maps.

- A heap is useful for ordering items according to priority. A heap also guarantees logarithmic insertions and removals. Heaps are useful for implementing priority queues.

- Binary search trees typically have a linked implementation, whereas heaps typically have an array representation.

VOCABULARY *Review*

Define the following terms:

binary search tree	heap property	parse tree
binary tree	interior node	priority node
expression tree	leaf	right subtree
general tree	left subtree	root
heap		

REVIEW *Questions*

FILL IN THE BLANK

Complete the following sentences by writing the correct word or words in the blanks provided.

1. The node with no predecessor in a tree is called its _____ node.

2. A node in a binary tree has at most _____ children.

3. To visit the items in a binary search tree in alphabetical order, we use a(n) _____ traversal.

4. The number of levels in a full binary tree is _____ times the number of items.

5. Each item in a heap is generally _____ than its parent and _____ than either of its children.

6. The worst-case behavior of the search and insertion operations on a binary search tree is _____.

7. A tree node with no children is called a(n) _____ node.

8. A tree node with at least one child is called a(n) _____ node.

9. A binary search tree that supports optimal searches is called a(n) _____ tree.

10. Each node in a(n) _____ tree can have zero or more children.

PROJECTS

PROJECT 18-1

Write a `remove` method for the binary search tree.

PROJECT 18-2

Write the implementation of a sorted set class using a binary search tree. Your solution should consist of an interface, `SortedSetPT`, an implementing class, `TreeSetPT`, and a tester program. You should decide which methods should be included in the sorted set's interface. Be sure to throw an appropriate exception if a client's item is not comparable.

PROJECT 18-3

Write the implementation of a sorted map class using a binary search tree. Your solution should consist of an interface, `SortedMapPT`, an implementing class, `TreeMapPT`, and a tester program. You should decide which methods should be included in the sorted map's interface. Be sure to throw an appropriate exception if a client's key is not comparable. Also, you should include a private inner class called `MapEntryPT` to contain a key and the associated value. This class should implement the `Comparable` interface and include a `compareTo` method. The binary search tree should receive instances of this class. The methods `get`, `put`, and `removeKey` should create a map entry that contains the key for processing by the tree. When the tree returns an object, it will be an entry, so the map methods should extract the appropriate parts to return to the client.

PROJECT 18-4

Modify the emergency room scheduler case study program from Lesson 14 so that it uses a heap priority queue.

PROJECT 18-5

Add the remaining traversal methods to the binary search tree class. Each of these methods should return a list of items accumulated during the traversal.

PROJECT 18-6

Define a class for representing expression trees. Interior nodes should contain operators (strings) and leaf nodes should contain integers (instances of class `Integer`). A `toString` method should return the result of an inorder traversal. Test this class with a tester program.

PROJECT 18-7

Write a program that evaluates expression trees and also generates expressions from them in infix, prefix, and postfix forms. The evaluation algorithm should traverse a tree and return its value. The other traversals should return strings. All of these operations should be methods included in the ExpressionTree class.

CRITICAL *Thinking*

Jack thinks that binary search trees could be used to implement sorted lists. Jill disagrees, claiming that some list operations would be difficult or impossible to support. Discuss the issues in this debate.

IMPLEMENTING ABSTRACT DATA TYPES

REVIEW *Questions*

TRUE/FALSE

Circle T if the statement is true or F if the statement is false.

T   F   1. The linked implementation of a list allows the size of a list to grow indefinitely, whereas an array implementation does not.

T   F   2. Insertions into a linked list are generally faster than insertions into an array list.

T   F   3. A singly linked structure is a wise choice for implementing a positional list.

T   F   4. A doubly linked structure is a wise choice for implementing a queue.

T   F   5. Hashing guarantees constant-time access.

T   F   6. A list is a wise choice for implementing a set.

T   F   7. A node in a general tree can have zero or more children but at most one parent.

T   F   8. A node in a heap is generally smaller than either of its two children.

T   F   9. A complete binary tree has a complete set of nodes at each level.

T   F   10. All access operations in a binary search tree are logarithmic in the worst case.

FILL IN THE BLANK

Complete the following sentences by writing the correct word or words in the blanks provided.

1. A circular linked list often has a(n) _____ node.

2. The appropriate linked structure for a stack implementation is a(n) _____ linked structure.

3. The hierarchical structure used to implement a priority queue is a(n) _____.

4. The _____ method of hashing resolves collisions by simply searching the array for the next available slot.

5. The _____ method of hashing resolves collisions by taking the square of an incremental distance until an empty slot is found.

6. The _____ method of hashing resolves collisions by associating a linked structure with each slot in the array.

7. A tree node that has no children is called a(n) _____.

8. A(n) _____ traversal returns a binary search tree's items in alphabetical order.

9. A heap most often uses a(n) _____ implementation of a tree.

10. The number of levels in a full binary tree is equal to _____ the number of nodes.

WRITTEN QUESTIONS

Write a brief answer to the following questions or problems.

1. Discuss the issues involved in using a linked structure to implement a queue.

2. In the context of hashing, what are collisions and how can they be resolved?

3. Write the pseudocode algorithm for an inorder traversal of a binary search tree. You can assume that its root node is named `tree`.

4. Jill proposes to use an array to implement a binary search tree. Discuss the costs and benefits of this proposal.

5. Describe how a heap can be used to sort a list of items.

CRITICAL *Thinking*

The stack and queue ADTs have many implementations. Discuss the ways in which the code could be simplified by creating abstract classes for stacks and queues.

GRAPHICS, FILES, APPLETS, AND SWING

Unit 6

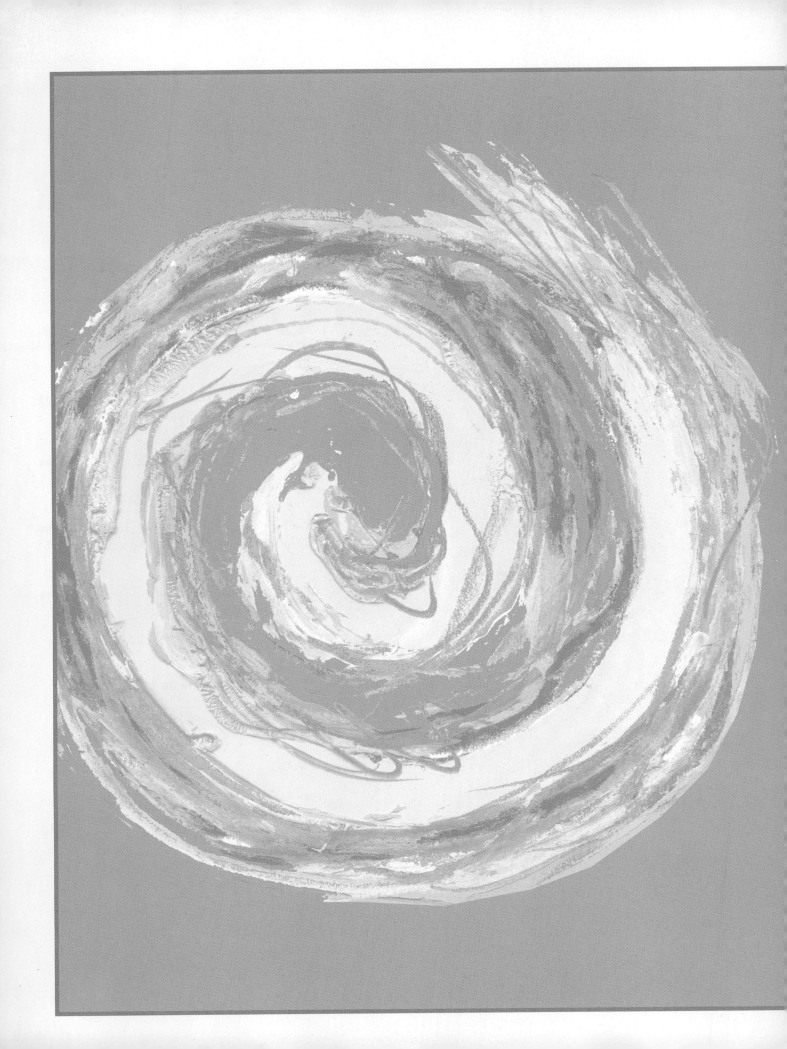

SIMPLE TWO-DIMENSIONAL GRAPHICS

OBJECTIVES

Upon completion of this lesson, you should be able to:

■ Understand the difference between Cartesian coordinates and screen coordinates.

■ Use methods to draw images in two-dimensional graphics.

■ Understand the transient image problem and how to solve it.

■ Create a program that graphs data with charts.

■ Implement methods to handle mouse events.

■ Work with color and text properties.

Estimated Time: 3.5 hours

VOCABULARY

c-curve

coordinate system

fractal object

fractals

graphics context

horizontal bar graph

line graphs

origin

paint mode

panel

refreshable image

screen coordinate system

transient image problem

vertical bar graph

XOR mode

In earlier lessons you used a turtle graphics package to draw simple images in a graphics window. Turtle graphics allowed you to work with standard Cartesian coordinates and to manipulate a pen to draw the images. However, the graphics features of most programming languages do not provide these conveniences, but instead use a different coordinate system and offer a wide range of more primitive, general-purpose operations. Indeed, the turtle graphics package is implemented in terms of these lower-level graphics features in Java. This lesson gives a survey of the support for two-dimensional graphics in Java. Along the way, we will draw geometric shapes; graph data using line, bar, and pie charts; detect and respond to mouse events; manipulate fonts; and implement new graphics classes.

19.1 The Conceptual Framework for Computer Graphics

Underlying every graphics application is a *coordinate system*. Positions in this system are specified in terms of points. Points in a two-dimensional system have x and y coordinates. For example, the point (10, 30) has an x coordinate of 10 and a y coordinate of 30.

The *x* and *y* coordinates of a point express its position relative to the system's ***origin*** at (0, 0). Figure 19-1 presents some examples of points in the familiar Cartesian coordinate system, the one used in earlier lessons with turtle graphics. In this system, two perpendicular lines define an *x* axis and a *y* axis. The point of intersection is labeled (0, 0). Increasing values of *x* are to the right and increasing values of *y* are up.

FIGURE 19-1
A Cartesian coordinate system

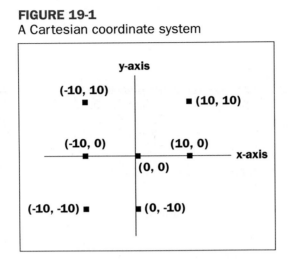

In Java and most other programming languages, the coordinate system is oriented as shown in Figure 19-2. Note that the only quadrant shown is the one that defines the coordinates of the computer's screen. In the positive direction, it extends downward and to the right from the point (0, 0) in the upper-left corner. The other three quadrants exist, but the points in them never appear on the screen. This is called a ***screen coordinate system***.

FIGURE 19-2
Orientation of Java's coordinate system

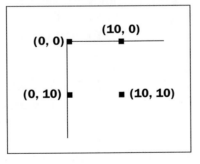

In a window-based application, each window has a coordinate system whose origin is located at the upper-left outside corner of the window. Each integer point in this coordinate system, extending from the origin to the window's lower-right corner, locates the position of a pixel, or picture element, in the window. By an integer point, we mean a point both of whose coordinates are integers. You also can create rectangular regions within a window called ***panels***. Each panel has its own coordinate system that is similar in form to the window's coordinate system. In fact, Java programmers usually draw images on panels and almost never on the window itself. Therefore, in the discussion that follows, we assume that we are drawing images on panels.

The Graphics Class

The package `java.awt` provides a `Graphics` class for drawing in a panel. A panel maintains an instance of this class, called a ***graphics context***, so that the program can access and modify the panel's bitmap. The program sends messages to the graphics context to perform all graphics operations. Hereafter, we refer to the graphics context using the variable name g. Some commonly used `Graphics` drawing methods are listed in Table 19-1. The table also shows the results of running these methods in a window that has a single panel.

TABLE 19-1
Common methods in the `Graphics` class

GRAPHICS METHOD	EXAMPLE CALL AND OUTPUT	WHAT IT DOES

`drawLine(`
`  int x1,`
`  int y1,`
`  int x2,`
`  int y2)`
	`g.drawLine(10, 25, 40, 55)`	Draws a line from point $(x1, y1)$ to $(x2, y2)$.

`drawRect(`
`  int x,`
`  int y,`
`  int width,`
`  int height)`
	`g.drawRect(10, 25, 40, 30)`	Draws a rectangle whose upper-left corner is (x, y) and whose dimensions are the specified width and height.

`drawOval(`
`  int x,`
`  int y,`
`  int width,`
`  int height)`
	`g.drawOval(10, 25, 50, 25)`	Draws an oval that fits within a rectangle whose origin (upper-left corner) is (x, y) and whose dimensions are the specified width and height. To draw a circle, make the width and height equal.

TABLE 19-1 continued
Common methods in the `Graphics` class

GRAPHICS METHOD	EXAMPLE CALL AND OUTPUT	WHAT IT DOES

`drawArc(`
`    int x,`
`    int y,`
`    int width,`
`    int height,`
`    int startAngle,`
`    int arcAngle)`
	`g.drawArc(10, 25, 50, 50, 0, 90)`	Draws an arc that fits within a rectangle whose upper-left corner is (x, y) and whose dimensions are the specified width and height. The arc is drawn from `startAngle` to `startAngle + arcAngle`. The angles are expressed in degrees. A start angle of 0 indicates the 3 o'clock position. A positive arc indicates a counterclockwise rotation, and a negative arc indicates a clockwise rotation from 3 o'clock.

`drawPolygon(`
`    int x [],`
`    int y [],`
`    int n)`
	`int x [] = {10, 40, 60, 30, 40};`
	`int y [] = {25, 25, 50, 60, 40};`
	`g.drawPolygon(x, y, 5);`
		Draws a polygon defined by n line segments, where the first $n-1$ segments run from $(x[i-1], y[i-1])$ to $(x[i], y[i])$, for $1 \le i < n$. The last segment starts at the final point and ends at the first point.

`drawRoundRect(`
`    int x,`
`    int y,`
`    int width,`
`    int height,`
`    int arcWidth,`
`    int arcHeight)`
	`g.drawRoundRect(10, 25, 40,`
	`                 30, 20, 20)`
		Draws a rounded rectangle.

TABLE 19-1 continued
Common methods in the Graphics class

GRAPHICS METHOD	EXAMPLE CALL AND OUTPUT	WHAT IT DOES
drawString(String str, int x, int y)	g.drawString("Java rules!", 10, 50) Java rules!	Draws a string. The point (x, y) indicates the position of the base line of the first character.

In addition, there are the methods `fillArc`, `fillRect`, and `fillOval`, which draw filled shapes.

Adding a Panel to a Window

As mentioned earlier, panels are rectangular areas within a window. Each panel has its own coordinate system and graphics context for drawing images. BreezySwing provides the class GBPanel for defining panels. To write a graphics application, one should do two things:

1. Define a subclass of GBPanel. This class accesses the graphics context to create the drawing. The panel can draw images "on its own" or in response to messages sent to it from the main window.

2. Create an instance of the panel class and add this object to the application's window, in much the same manner as other window objects are added.

Let us assume that someone has defined a panel class named ExamplePanel. The following application adds an instance of this class to a window. Note that the panel is the only window object added, so it stretches across the entire width and height of the window below its title bar.

```
import BreezySwing.*;

public class GraphicsExamples extends GBFrame{

   private GBPanel panel;

   public GraphicsExamples(){
      panel = addPanel(new ExamplePanel(), 1,1,1,1);
   }

   public static void main (String[] args){
      GraphicsExamples theGUI = new GraphicsExamples();
      theGUI.setSize (200, 200);
      theGUI.setVisible(true);
   }
}
```

The form of the method for adding a panel to a window is

```
<variable name> = addPanel(<panel object>,
                           <row>, <col>, <width>, height>);
```

where `<panel object>` is an instance of a subclass of `GBPanel` or of `GBPanel` itself. The latter is rarely the case, because new panels normally have behavior that is specific to an application. More often than not, we will use code such as

```
private ExamplePanel panel;
private GBPanel p;

public SomeConstructor(){
   panel = new ExamplePanel();
   p = addPanel(panel, 1,1,1,1);
}
```

This code provides a variable of the specific panel type so that messages can be sent to it without casting. The variable p, although it refers to the same object as `panel`, is then never used. Alternatively, you could omit the variable p altogether and simply run `addPanel` without assigning the result.

Implementing a Panel Class and the Method `paintComponent`

The responsibilities of a panel class are to draw images in response to messages from an application and also to redraw images whenever the window is refreshed. We discuss the refresh process in this section and examine how a panel receives messages from an application in a later section.

When a window opens, the JVM sends the message `paintComponent` to each window object. If the object has any images to draw, its `paintComponent` method accomplishes this. Thus, for example, when a window containing a button opens at program start-up, the button's `paintComponent` method draws the image of the button on the screen. This process also occurs whenever the window is refreshed—for instance, after it is minimized and restored. The important point here is that the application never calls `paintComponent` directly; it is triggered automatically by the JVM in response to certain events. `paintComponent` receives the window object's graphics context as a parameter, so this object is accessible for drawing. The method also is implemented in a superclass of the class `GBPanel`, so the programmer can override it to draw the appropriate images.

Following is the code for the implementation of the `ExamplePanel` class used earlier. Its `paintComponent` method draws a line segment when the window opens and whenever it is refreshed. The resulting window was shown in the first figure of Table 19-1.

```
import BreezySwing.*;        // Needed for GBPanel
import java.awt.*;           // Needed for Graphics

public class ExamplePanel extends GBPanel{

   public void paintComponent (Graphics g){
      super.paintComponent(g);
      g.drawLine(10, 25, 40, 55);
   }
}
```

Note that the method first calls the same method in the superclass. The reason is that the method in the superclass paints the background of the component. This effectively clears any images in the panel before they are redrawn.

Finding the Height and Width of a Panel

Occasionally, it is useful to know the width and height of a panel. For instance, one might want to center an image in a panel and keep the image centered when the user resizes the window. The methods `getWidth()` and `getHeight()` return the current width and height of a panel, respectively. The following code would maintain a display of a panel's current width and height near the center of the panel:

```
public void paintComponent (Graphics g){
   super.paintComponent(g);
   g.drawString("(" + getWidth() + "," + getHeight() + ")",
            getWidth() / 2, getHeight() / 2);
}
```

EXERCISE 19.1

1. Describe the difference between a screen coordinate system and the Cartesian coordinate system.

2. What is a graphics context?

3. Explain the meaning of the parameters for the method `drawOval`.

4. Write method calls with the `Graphics` object g to draw the following items:
   a. A rectangle at position (40, 30) with a width of 100 pixels and a height of 300 pixels
   b. A rectangle whose upper-left corner is at (40, 30) and whose lower-right corner is at (150, 160)
   c. A circle with a center point at (100, 100) and a radius of 25 pixels
   d. The statement "Graphics is easy in Java!" at position (200, 200)

5. Describe how the method `paintComponent` is used in a Java program.

19.2 The Method `repaint`

Before reapplying drawing commands, we normally want to erase the current drawing. The `repaint()` method provides the needed capability. This method, which also is implemented in one of `GBPanel`'s superclasses, first erases the current drawing in the panel and then calls `paintComponent`.

`repaint` is also implemented in one of `GBFrame`'s superclasses. When sent to a window rather than a panel, this message does more. It tells all the window objects (text fields, labels, buttons, panels, and so forth) to redisplay themselves. We illustrate the use of `repaint` in Case Study 1: Drawing Different Shapes.

EXERCISE 19.2

1. Explain what happens when you call the method `repaint`.

Case Study 1: Drawing Different Shapes

We are now ready to write a complete graphics program. We start with something very simple.

Request

Write a program that allows the user to draw different shapes.

Analysis

The application allows the user to enter the corner point, width, and height of the shape's bounding rectangle in integer fields. When the user selects a shape (**Oval** or **Rectangle**) from the **Shape** menu, the program draws the selected shape in the area to the right of the data fields, after erasing the currently visible shape. The menu option **Shape/Clear** simply erases the current shape in the drawing area. The drawing area is clear at program start-up. The proposed interface is shown in Figure 19-3.

FIGURE 19-3
Interface for the shape drawing program

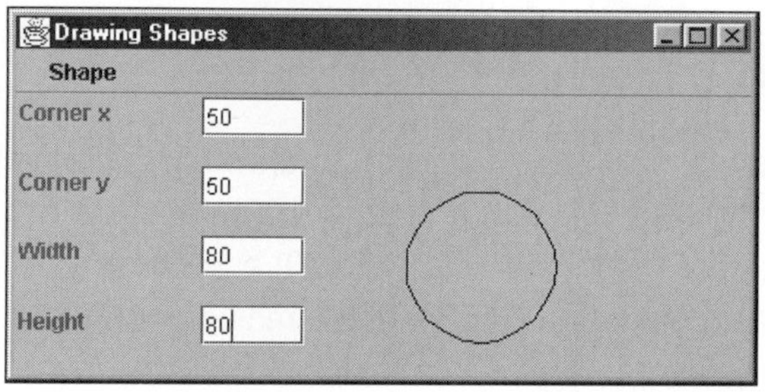

Classes

The program defines two classes: `ShapeApp` and `ShapePanel`. `ShapeApp` sets up the window objects and responds to the user's selection of menu options. `ShapePanel` draws the selected image or clears the panel.

Design

When the user selects a menu option, the `menuItemSelected` method in the `ShapeApp` class

■ Extracts the data from the input fields.

■ Sends the message `drawShape` with these data and the menu option's name to the panel.

The method `drawShape` is in the `ShapePanel` class

■ Sets the panel's instance variables to the shape's type, corner point, width, and height (all parameters).

■ Calls `repaint` to refresh the panel.

The method `paintComponent` in the `ShapePanel` class determines the type of shape to be drawn and calls the appropriate drawing method with the corner point, width, and height. If the type of shape is "clear," `paintComponent` does nothing, with the result that the panel is left empty.

Implementation

Following is the code for the two classes:

```
/* ShapeApp.java
Draw different shapes in a panel
*/
import javax.swing.*;
import BreezySwing.*;

public class ShapeApp extends GBFrame{

    private JLabel xLabel, yLabel, widthLabel, heightLabel;
    private IntegerField xField, yField, widthField, heightField;

    // Must have a variable of type ShapePanel so one can
    // send the drawShape message
    private ShapePanel shapePanel;
    private GBPanel panel;

    private JMenuItem ovalMI, rectangleMI, clearMI;

    public ShapeApp(){
        setTitle("Drawing Shapes");
        // Set up the data fields for the size and position
        // of the shape
        xLabel          = addLabel("Corner x", 1,1,1,1);
        yLabel          = addLabel("Corner y", 2,1,1,1);
        widthLabel      = addLabel("Width",    3,1,1,1);
        heightLabel     = addLabel("Height",   4,1,1,1);
        xField      = addIntegerField(0,    1,2,1,1);
        yField      = addIntegerField(0,    2,2,1,1);
        widthField  = addIntegerField(0,    3,2,1,1);
        heightField = addIntegerField(0,    4,2,1,1);

        shapePanel = new ShapePanel();
        panel = addPanel(shapePanel, 1,3,1,4);

        // Set up the menu options
        ovalMI      = addMenuItem("Shape", "Oval");
        rectangleMI = addMenuItem("Shape", "Rectangle");
        clearMI     = addMenuItem("Shape", "Clear");
    }

    public void menuItemSelected(JMenuItem mi){
        int x = xField.getNumber();
        int y = yField.getNumber();
        int width = widthField.getNumber();
        int height = heightField.getNumber();
```

```
        shapePanel.drawShape(mi.getText(), x, y, width, height);
    }

    public static void main (String[] args){
        ShapeApp theGUI = new ShapeApp();
        theGUI.setSize (400, 200);
        theGUI.setVisible(true);
    }
}
```

```
import BreezySwing.*;
import java.awt.*;

public class ShapePanel extends GBPanel{

    private String shape = "clear";
    private int x, y, width, height;

    public void paintComponent (Graphics g){
        super.paintComponent(g);
        if (shape.equalsIgnoreCase("oval"))
            g.drawOval(x, y, width, height);
        else if (shape.equalsIgnoreCase("rectangle"))
            g.drawRect(x, y, width, height);
    }

    public void drawShape(String shape, int x, int y,
                          int width, int height){
        this.shape = shape;
        this.x = x;
        this.y = y;
        this.width = width;
        this.height = height;
        repaint();                      // Clear panel and call paintComponent
    }
}
```

19.3 The Method getGraphics

The program in Case Study 1 draws just one image at a time, and it erases that image before drawing the next one. Suppose, however, that you want to draw several images that remain in the panel. The program's policy of calling repaint to refresh the window with the new image will not work because the previous image is erased each time. Fortunately, Java provides another method, getGraphics(), which allows the programmer to access a panel's graphics object to draw without repainting. You use this method as follows:

```
Graphics g = getGraphics();
<send messages to g to draw images>
```

The class `ShapePanel` can be modified to draw multiple shapes by

- Omitting the method `paintComponent`

- Placing the code to draw a shape in the method `drawShape`, which uses `getGraphics` to access the graphics object

To clear the panel, `drawShape` calls `repaint`, which clears the panel and calls the `paintComponent` method in a superclass that does nothing. Following is the code for the modified class:

```
import BreezySwing.*;
import java.awt.*;

public class ShapePanel extends GBPanel{

   // No instance variables are needed
   // No paintComponent method is needed
   // All drawing or clearing is done in drawShape

   public void drawShape(String shape, int x, int y,
                         int width, int height){
      Graphics g = getGraphics();
      if (shape.equalsIgnoreCase("oval"))
         g.drawOval(x, y, width, height);
      else if (shape.equalsIgnoreCase("rectangle"))
         g.drawRect(x, y, width, height);
      else
         repaint();                    // Clear panel and call paintComponent
   }
}
```

Graphics Methods and Constructors

We now need to mention a word of caution about using graphics methods. The graphics context of a window or window object is not available until after that component opens and is displayed. Therefore, the programmer should not attempt to use methods such as `repaint` and `getGraphics`, which rely on the graphics context, before this happens. In particular, you should not use these methods in constructor methods. Those who ignore this warning will be treated to a run-time exception.

The Transient Image Problem

The policy of using `getGraphics` instead of `paintComponent` works well for multiple images and is also more efficient because the entire panel is not repainted every time an image is drawn. Suppose a user resizes or hides the window in some way, however. When that happens, the images in the panel disappear! The reason for this unpleasant event, called the *transient image problem*, is that no `paintComponent` method is available to redraw the images during a refresh. It seems that we now have a dilemma: either use `paintComponent` to draw one persistent image only or use `getGraphics` to draw multiple images that are transient. We will examine a way out of this dilemma that uses both methods in a later section of this lesson.

EXERCISE 19.3

1. Explain why one would use the method `getGraphics` for drawing images.

2. Describe the transient image problem and give an example of how it arises.

19.4 Color

In Lesson 5, you saw how to change the color of a pen with turtle graphics. A Java programmer can control the color of images by using the `Color` class, which is included in the package `java.awt`. The `Color` class provides the class constants shown in Table 19-2. For instance, the expression `Color.red` yields the `Color` constant for red. The `Graphics` class includes two methods for examining and modifying an image's color (Table 19-3). Images are drawn in the current color until the color is changed. Changing the color does not affect the color of previously drawn images.

TABLE 19-2
Constants in the `Color` class

COLOR CONSTANT	COLOR
`public static final Color red`	red
`public static final Color yellow`	yellow
`public static final Color blue`	blue
`public static final Color orange`	orange
`public static final Color pink`	pink
`public static final Color cyan`	cyan
`public static final Color magenta`	magenta
`public static final Color black`	black
`public static final Color white`	white
`public static final Color gray`	gray
`public static final Color lightGray`	light gray
`public static final Color darkGray`	dark gray

TABLE 19-3
Two methods in the `Graphics` class for manipulating an image's color

METHOD	WHAT IT DOES
`Color getColor()`	Returns the current color of the graphics context.
`void setColor(Color c)`	Sets the color of the graphics context to c.

The following code segment draws a string in red and a line in blue in the graphics context g:

```
g.setColor (Color.red);
g.drawString ("Colors are great!", 50, 50);
g.setColor (Color.blue);
g.drawLine (50, 50, 150, 50);
```

Java allows the programmer finer control over colors by using RGB (red/green/blue) values. In this scheme, there are 256 shades of red, 256 shades of green, and 256 shades of blue. The programmer "mixes" a new color by selecting an integer from 0 to 255 for each color and passing these integers to a Color constructor as follows:

```
new Color (<int for red>, <int for green>, <int for blue>)
```

The next code segment shows how to create a random color with RGB values:

```
// Create a random color from randomly generated RGB values
int r = (int) (Math.random() * 256);
int g = (int) (Math.random() * 256);
int b = (int) (Math.random() * 256);
Color randomColor = new Color (r, g, b);
```

The value 0 indicates the absence of a color in the mixture, and the value 255 indicates the maximum saturation of that color. Thus, the color black has RGB (0, 0, 0), and the color white has RGB (255, 255, 255). There are 256 * 256 * 256 = 2^{24} possible colors in this scheme.

Setting a Panel's Background Color

In some applications, it is useful to see the area represented by a panel. For example, you could lay out a grid for several types of board games using panels, alternating white and black. A panel recognizes the message setBackGround(aColor), which changes its background color to the given color. The following short program displays a 2 × 2 grid of panels of four different colors, as shown in Figure 19-4.

```
import javax.swing.*;
import BreezySwing.*;
import java.awt.*;

public class TestPanel extends GBFrame{

    private GBPanel northWest, southWest, northEast, southEast;

    public TestPanel(){
        northWest = addPanel(new GBPanel(), 1,1,1,1);
        southWest = addPanel(new GBPanel(), 1,2,1,1);
        northEast = addPanel(new GBPanel(), 2,1,1,1);
        southEast = addPanel(new GBPanel(), 2,2,1,1);
        northWest.setBackground(Color.red);
        southWest.setBackground(Color.green);
```

```
      northEast.setBackground(Color.blue);
      southEast.setBackground(Color.yellow);
   }

   public static void main (String[] args){
      TestPanel theGUI = new TestPanel();
      theGUI.setSize (200, 200);
      theGUI.setVisible (true);
   }
}
```

FIGURE 19-4
Setting the background color of panels

When the panel is a user-defined class, the background's color can be set in its constructor method. Case Study 2: Fractals shows how to do this.

EXERCISE 19.4

1. Describe two ways to create a new color in Java.

2. How does the RGB system work?

3. Write a method `randomColor` that returns a randomly generated color using the RGB system.

Case Study 2: Fractals

Fractals are highly repetitive or recursive patterns. A *fractal object* appears geometric, yet it cannot be described with ordinary Euclidean geometry. Strangely, a fractal curve is not one-dimensional, and a fractal surface is not two-dimensional. Instead, every fractal shape has its own fractal dimension.

An ordinary curve has a precise finite length between any two points. By contrast, a fractal curve has an indefinite length between any two points. The apparent length depends on the level of detail considered. As we zoom in on a segment of a fractal curve, we can see more and more details, and its length appears greater and greater. Consider a coastline. Seen from a distance, it has many wiggles but a discernible length. Now put a piece of the coastline under magnification. It has many similar wiggles, and the discernible length increases. Self-similarity under magnification is the defining characteristic of fractals and is seen in the shapes of mountains, the branching patterns of tree limbs, and many other natural objects.

One example of a fractal curve is a ***c-curve***. Figure 19-5 shows c-curves of the first seven degrees. The level-0 c-curve is a simple line segment. The level-1 c-curve replaces the level-0 c-curve with two smaller level-0 c-curves meeting at right angles. The level-2 c-curve does the same thing for each of the two line segments in the level-1 c-curve. This pattern of subdivision can continue indefinitely.

FIGURE 19-5
The first seven degrees of the c-curve

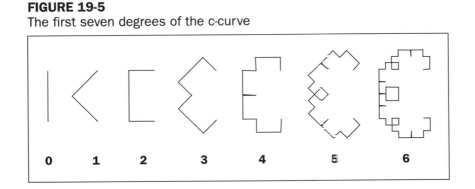

Request

Write a program that allows the user to draw a particular c-curve in varying degrees.

Analysis

The proposed interface is shown in Figure 19-6. The user enters the level in a data field. The initial window displays a c-curve of level 0. The end points of this line segment are (150, 50) and (150, 150). This line segment is a good starting point for higher degree curves, all of which fit nicely within the initial window boundaries. The program has two menus:

1. The **Draw** menu has one selection, **Draw**. When the user selects **Draw**, the program clears the current image and draws a new one.

2. The **Color** menu has three selections, **Red**, **Blue**, and **Black**, which allow the user to change the color of the c-curve.

When the user resizes the window, the program refreshes the current image. Note that the drawing panel's background is white.

FIGURE 19-6
Interface for the c-curve program

Classes

As usual, we define a main window class to handle user input and menu selections and a panel class to do the drawing. We name these classes `FractalApp` and `FractalPanel`, respectively.

Design

We want the program to refresh the c-curve when the user resizes or hides the window. Consequently, the panel must use `paintComponent` and `repaint` to perform the drawing.

The `menuItemSelected` method performs these tasks:

- Sets the current level to the value in the input field.

- Sets the current color to the color indicated by a color selection.

- Sends the `drawCurve` message to the panel with this information.

The `drawCurve` method performs these tasks:

- Sets the color and level of the panel to the current values.

- Calls `repaint`.

The `paintComponent` method performs these tasks:

- Sets the color of the graphics context to the current color.

- Passes the level, the initial line segment (150, 100), (150, 200), and the graphics context to the `cCurve` method.

The `cCurve` method does the actual drawing and depends on the following recursive definition:

- A level 0 c-curve is a line segment $(x1, y1)$, $(x2, y2)$.

- Otherwise, a level n c-curve consists of two level $n - 1$ c-curves constructed as follows:

  - Let xm be $(x1 + x2 + y1 - y2) / 2$.

  - Let ym be $(x2 + y1 + y2 - x1) / 2$.

  - The first level $n - 1$ c-curve uses the line segment $(x1, y1)$, (xm, ym), and level $n - 1$.

  - The second level $n - 1$ c-curve uses the line segment (xm, ym), $(x2, y2)$, and level $n - 1$.

In effect, as we showed in an earlier diagram, we replace each line segment by two shorter ones that meet at right angles.

Implementation

The following code shows the implementation of the class `FractalPanel`. The code for the class `FractalApp` is available from your instructor.

```
import BreezySwing.*;
import java.awt.*;

public class FractalPanel extends GBPanel{

    private Color color = Color.black;
    private int level = 0;

    public FractalPanel(){
```

```
            setBackground(Color.white);
    }

    public void paintComponent (Graphics g){
        super.paintComponent(g);
        g.setColor (color);
        cCurve (150, 100, 150, 200, level, g);
    }

    public void drawCurve(int level, Color color){
        this.color = color;
        this.level = level;
        repaint();
    }

    private void cCurve (int x1, int y1, int x2, int y2,
                         int level, Graphics g){
        if (level == 0)
            g.drawLine (x1, y1, x2, y2);
        else{
            int xm = (x1 + x2 + y1 - y2)/2;
            int ym = (x2 + y1 + y2 - x1)/2;
            cCurve (x1, y1, xm, ym, level - 1, g);
            cCurve (xm, ym, x2, y2, level - 1, g);
        }
    }
}
```

19.5 Graphing Data

A major application of graphics is the display of data in charts and graphs. Some common forms are line graphs, bar graphs, and pie charts.

Line Graphs

Line graphs are the easiest to conceptualize and implement. The data to be plotted might be listed in a table. For example, Table 19-4 lists the numbers of students receiving the letter grades A, B, C, D, and F in a programming course.

TABLE 19-4
Distribution of student grades

LETTER GRADE	NUMBER OF STUDENTS
A	5
B	7
C	10
D	6
F	2

A line graph of these data might look like the one shown in Figure 19-7.

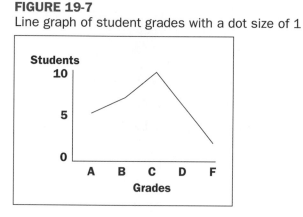

FIGURE 19-7
Line graph of student grades with a dot size of 1

To construct this line graph, we did the following:

- Placed the letter grades along the x axis

- Placed the numbers of these grades along the y axis

- Drew a dot at the coordinates formed by each number/grade pair

- Connected these dots

The major difficulty in drawing line graphs is figuring out the scale; that is

- The number of pixels that lie between each value on the x axis

- The number of pixels that lie between each value on the y axis

The problem is solved by matching the range of values to the pixel dimensions of the graph. Suppose we plot grades on a 200 pixel-wide graph. Because there are five letter grades, there are 40 pixels between each value on the x axis. The general formula for calculating this increment is

```
x increment = width in pixels / number of values to plot
```

The increment for the y axis is calculated as follows:

```
if largest value to plot on the y axis equals 0
   y increment = 0
else
   y increment = total y pixels / largest value to plot on the y axis
```

A second problem is determining the point in the panel corresponding to the origin of the graph. Because this point will lie at the lower-left corner of the panel, the actual x coordinate will be zero, and the actual y coordinate will be the height of the panel minus one. For now, we simply assume that these values are given by the constants X_LEFT and Y_BOTTOM, respectively.

Now we can define two methods that convert data values in the table to pixel coordinates. The method getXCoordinate uses the position of the data value in the array (numbering from 1) and returns the x coordinate of the point to plot. In the code that follows

- xIncrement is the number of pixels between data points on the x axis.

- i is a number from 1 to the number of values to plot, in this example, 5.

- **X_LEFT** is the *x* coordinate of the graph's origin.

```
private int getXCoordinate (int i, int xIncrement){
   return X_LEFT + xIncrement * i;
}
```

The method getYCoordinate returns the *y* coordinate of the point to plot. In the code that follows

- **yIncrement** is the number of pixels per data unit.

- **numStudents** is the number of students being plotted at the current grade.

- **Y_BOTTOM** is the *y* coordinate in the window of the bottommost point on the *y* axis.

```
private int getYCoordinate (int numStudents, int yIncrement){
   return Y_BOTTOM - yIncrement * numStudents);
}
```

This method takes into account the fact that positive *y* coordinates extend downward rather than upward on a computer screen.

Let us assume that the array grades contains the data in Table 19-4's second column—that is, the column labeled **Number of Students**. The letter grades A, B, C, D, and F correspond to the index positions 0 through 4 of the array.

A	0	5
B	1	7
C	2	10
D	3	6
F	4	2

The following code segment plots these data in a dotted line graph:

```
int i, x, y, largestNumber, xIncrement, yIncrement;

// Compute the x and y increments.

largestNumber = findLargest(grades);
xIncrement = totalXPixels / grades.length;
if (largestNumber == 0)
   yIncrement = 0;
else
   yIncrement = totalYPixels / largestNumber;

// Compute and plot the data points.

for (i = 0; i < grades.length; i++){
   x = getXCoordinate (i + 1, xIncrement);
   y = getYCoordinate (grades[i], yIncrement);
   g.fillOval (x, y, 5, 5);
}
```

Note that we add 1 to the value of i before passing it to getXCoordinate because that method expects numbers from 1 to the size of the array.

To connect the dots, we draw line segments between them. We also can add a line segment between the graph's origin and the first dot. Because a line segment has two endpoints, the code requires an extra pair of int variables:

```
int i, x1, y1, x2, y2, largestNumber, xIncrement, yIncrement;

// Compute the x and y increments.

largestNumber = findLargest(grades);
xIncrement = totalXPixels / grades.length;
if (largestNumber == 0)
   yIncrement = 0;
else
   yIncrement = totalYPixels / largestNumber;

// Set the initial end point.

x1 = X_LEFT;
y1 = Y_BOTTOM;

// Compute and plot the data points.

for (i = 0; i < grades.length; i++){
   x2 = getXCoordinate (i + 1, xIncrement);
   y2 = getYCoordinate (grades[i], yIncrement);
   g.fillOval (x2, y2, 5, 5);                       //The dot size can be varied
   if (x1 != X_LEFT)
      g.drawLine (x1, y1, x2, y2);
   x1 = x2;
   y1 = y2;
}
```

In addition to the actual plot, we must take care of such details as drawing the axes, labeling them, and displaying any other information required by the users.

Bar Graphs

A *vertical bar graph* shows the values as rectangular bars extending up from the *x* axis. A *horizontal bar graph* shows the bars as extending to the right from the *y* axis. In this section, we consider bars that are positioned vertically (Figure 19-8).

FIGURE 19-8
Vertical bar graph of student grades

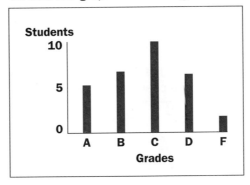

We continue with the student grades example. To construct a bar graph, we must answer the following questions:

■ How many bars are there? Our example needs five.

■ How wide is a bar? The answer to this question usually depends on how many bars there are. The bar width in this example is 10 pixels.

■ How far apart are the bars? We use the same formula to calculate this increment as we did for the *x* increment of line graphs. We then center the bar on this value.

■ How many pixels per unit of data are there? We use the same formula to calculate this increment as we did for the *y* increment of line graphs.

The following code segment brings these ideas together to display a bar graph of the student grades:

```
int i, x, y, height, largestNumber, xIncrement, yIncrement;


// Compute the x and y increments.

largestNumber = findLargest (grades);
xIncrement = totalXPixels / grades.length;
if (largestNumber == 0)
    yIncrement = 0;
else
    yIncrement = totalYPixels / largestNumber;


// Draw the bars.

for (i = 0; i < grades.length; i++){
    x = getXCoordinate (i + 1, xIncrement);
```

```
    y = getYCoordinate (grades[i], yIncrement);
    x = x - BAR_WIDTH / 2;
    height = BOTTOM_Y - y + 1;
    g.fillRect (x, y, BAR_WIDTH, height);
}
```

Pie Charts

A pie chart shows the relative sizes of the data as wedges of a pie (Figure 19-9). The size of a sector's central angle in a pie chart corresponds to a bar's height in a bar graph.

FIGURE 19-9
Pie chart of student grades

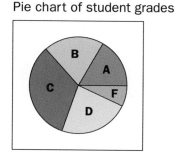

We continue with the student grades example. The angles for the data in our example are listed in Table 19-5. Because there are 30 students, 12 degrees (360 / 30) represents one student. Thus, the central angle for representing the 5 As is 5 * 12, or 60 degrees. In general, the expression for computing the degree increment for each unit of data is

```
if (totalUnits == 0)
    unitAngleSize = 0;
else
    unitAngleSize = 360.0 / totalUnits;
```

where `totalUnits` is the total number of units of data. We will assume that a method `sum(int[] a)` is available to compute this value.

TABLE 19-5
Angles needed for each portion of the student grades pie chart

DATA ITEM	NUMBER OF ITEMS	SECTOR SIZE IN DEGREES
A	5	60
B	7	84
C	10	120
D	6	72
F	2	24

The central angle corresponding to each kind of grade is then

```
centralAngle = (int) Math.round(unitAngleSize * grades[i]);
```

Next we must determine how to start and end each sector. We set the starting angle for the first sector at 0 degrees, which is at 3 o'clock in the pie graph:

```
startAngle = 0;
```

After each sector is drawn, the starting angle of the next sector is computed by setting it to the current ending angle:

```
startAngle = startAngle + centralAngle;
```

We use the method `fillArc` to draw a filled arc in the current color of the graphics context. Before each call to `fillArc`, we set its color to a color generated by a programmer-defined method `intToColor`.

Finally, before we calculate the pie slices, we determine how large the pie will be and where it will be positioned in the panel. In this example, the radius of the pie will be slightly less than half of the panel's width. The pie will be positioned slightly above and to the left of the panel's center. To determine the center point of the window, we use the methods `getWidth()` and `getHeight()`.

A complete code segment to draw the pie chart follows:

```
int totalUnits, centerX, centerY, radius, startAngle, i;
double unitAngleSize;

// Set up center point and radius of the pie, and the unit angle size.

totalUnits = sum(grades);
centerX = getWidth() / 2;
centerY = getHeight() / 2;
radius = centerX - centerX / 3;
centerX = radius;
centerY = centerY - centerY / 3;
if (totalUnits == 0)
   unitAngleSize = 0;
else
   unitAngleSize = 360.0 / totalUnits;
startAngle = 0;

// Draw the wedges in the pie.

for (i = 0; i < grades.length; i++){
   int centralAngle = (int) Math.round(unitAngleSize * grades[i]);
   g.setColor (intToColor(i));
   g.fillArc (centerX, centerY, radius, radius, startAngle, centralAngle);
   startAngle = startAngle + centralAngle;
}
```

Case Study 3: Multiple Views Of Data

We now combine the previous techniques for graphing data into one program.

Request

Write a program that allows the user to enter the numbers of students receiving the grades A, B, C, D, and F and to view these data in a line graph, a bar graph, and a pie chart.

Analysis

The proposed interface is shown in Figure 19-10. To the left of the graph display area are entry fields labeled with each letter grade. The default value for the number of students receiving each grade is 0. The user can display the graphs by clicking the **Graph** button. The data in the fields are transferred to an array of grades, and the three types of graphs are displayed in panels to the right of the data fields.

Note that we omit labels for the data in the graphs.

FIGURE 19-10
Three graphs of student grades

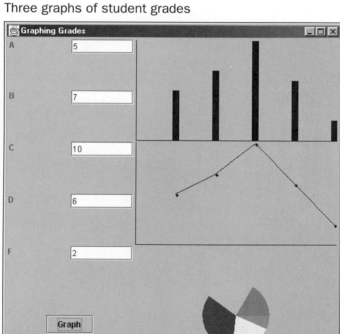

Classes

The program defines four classes. The class `GraphApp` is responsible for getting the inputs, responding to the button click, and sending messages to the graphing panels to draw the graphs. The classes `BarPanel`, `LinePanel`, and `PiePanel` are responsible for drawing bar, line, and pie graphs of the data, respectively.

Design

The method `buttonClicked` extracts the data from the fields and sends these in an array with the `drawGraph` message to the three graphing panels. Each graphing panel implements the `drawGraph` method, which transfers the array to an instance variable and calls `repaint`. The `paintComponent` method in turn uses the code developed earlier to draw the graph.

Implementation

We provide the code for the `GraphApp` class and leave the completion of the graphing panels as a programming project. These are all straightforward adaptations of the code presented in the previous section.

```java
/* GraphApp.java
Draw different graphs of data
*/
import javax.swing.*;
import BreezySwing.*;
import java.awt.*;

public class GraphApp extends GBFrame{

    private JLabel aLabel, bLabel, cLabel, dLabel, fLabel;
    private IntegerField aField, bField, cField, dField, fField;
    private JButton graphBTN;

    private BarPanel barPanel;
    private LinePanel linePanel;
    private PiePanel piePanel;

    private GBPanel p1, p2, p3;

    public static final int MAX_GRADES = 5;

    public GraphApp(){
        setTitle("Graphing Grades");

        // Set up the data fields and command button
        aLabel      = addLabel ("A",      1,1,1,1);
        aField = addIntegerField (0, 1,2,1,1);
        bLabel      = addLabel ("B",      2,1,1,1);
        bField = addIntegerField (0, 2,2,1,1);
        cLabel      = addLabel ("C",      3,1,1,1);
        cField = addIntegerField (0, 3,2,1,1);
        dLabel      = addLabel ("D",      4,1,1,1);
        dField = addIntegerField (0, 4,2,1,1);
        fLabel      = addLabel ("F",      5,1,1,1);
        fField = addIntegerField (0, 5,2,1,1);

        graphBTN    = addButton("Graph",  6,1,2,1);

        // Set up the graphing panels
        barPanel = new BarPanel();
```

```
        linePanel = new LinePanel();
        piePanel = new PiePanel();

        p1  = addPanel(barPanel, 1,3,1,2);
        p2  = addPanel(linePanel, 3,3,1,2);
        p3  = addPanel(piePanel, 5,3,1,2);
    }

    public void buttonClicked (JButton buttonObj){
        int[] grades = new int[MAX_GRADES];
        grades[0] = aField.getNumber();
        grades[1] = bField.getNumber();
        grades[2] = cField.getNumber();
        grades[3] = dField.getNumber();
        grades[4] = fField.getNumber();
        barPanel.drawGraph(grades);
        linePanel.drawGraph(grades);
        piePanel.drawGraph(grades);
    }

    public static void main (String[] args){
        GraphApp theGUI = new GraphApp();
        theGUI.setSize (500, 500);
        theGUI.setVisible (true);
    }
}
```

19.6 Responding to Mouse Events

Until now, we have limited our use of the mouse to clicking on command buttons and selecting menu options. Everyone who has used a drawing program knows that much more can be done with the mouse, and in this section, we show how. Drawing applications usually detect and respond to the following mouse events: button clicks, mouse movement, and dragging the mouse (i.e., moving the mouse while a button is depressed). In addition, a program can respond to the mouse's entry into and exit from a given region. The GBPanel class includes methods for handling these events as described in Table 19-6. Notice that no distinction is made between the left and right mouse button.

Each method has two parameters:

1. the *x* coordinate of the mouse when the event occurs

2. the *y* coordinate of the mouse when the event occurs

TABLE 19-6
Methods for handling mouse events

METHOD	IT IS CALLED
void mouseClicked (int x, int y)	When a mouse button is clicked
void mouseDragged (int x, int y)	When the mouse is moved while a button is depressed
void mouseEntered(int x, int y)	When the mouse enters a given region
void mouseExited(int x, int y)	When the mouse exits a given region
void mouseMoved (int x, int y)	When the mouse is moved
void mousePressed (int x, int y)	When a mouse button is pressed
void mouseReleased (int x, int y)	When a mouse button is released

To detect and handle mouse input, a subclass of GBPanel implements one or more of these methods. A mouse-handling method typically transfers the values of the mouse coordinates to the panel's instance variables, performs some action, and updates the display with the results. For example, the following panel class tracks the position of a mouse press by displaying the mouse's coordinates. The mousePressed method stores the mouse coordinates in the instance variables mouseX and mouseY and then repaints the panel. paintComponent displays the values of mouseX and mouseY at that position.

```
import BreezySwing.*;
import java.awt.*;

public class MousePanel extends GBPanel{

    private int mouseX = 10, mouseY = 10;

    public void paintComponent (Graphics g){
        super.paintComponent(g);
        g.drawString("(" + mouseX + "," + mouseY + ")", mouseX, mouseY);
    }

    public void mousePressed(int x, int y){
        mouseX = x;
        mouseY = y;
        repaint();
    }
}
```

EXERCISE 19.6

1. List the different mouse events that GBPanel recognizes.

2. What does GBPanel do when a mouse event occurs?

3. One way to draw a rectangle with a mouse is to detect and respond to two clicks. One click designates the position of one corner and the other click designates the position of the opposite corner. Describe the problems with implementing this strategy using the mouseClicked method.

4. An alternative way to draw a rectangle is to press the mouse at one corner, drag it to the opposite corner, and then release the mouse. Describe how this process can be implemented with the GBPanel mouse-tracking methods.

Case Study 4: A Very Primitive Drawing Program

Drawing programs allow the mouse to be used as a pencil, paintbrush, or spray can. These programs range from the simple paint programs preinstalled on most computers to the sophisticated and expensive applications used by professional artists. All these programs have a common basis, the ability to draw a small dot at a location selected by the user. In this case study, we show how this is done and in the process implement a very unspectacular drawing program.

Request

Write a program that allows the user to draw a figure by repeatedly clicking a mouse button.

Analysis

The panel class, called sketchpad1, supports the simplest kind of drawing. When the user presses the mouse button in the panel, the program draws a pellet-sized dot on the screen at the current mouse position. The user constructs a figure by repeated applications of the process. The proposed interface, with drawing included, is in Figure 19-11.

FIGURE 19-11
Interface for a very primitive pellet-based drawing program

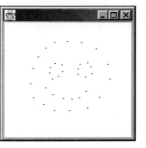

Design

Because a single black pixel does not show up very well, we will represent each dot as a 2 ×2 block of pixels. The program's mousePressed method will draw such a block each time the user presses a mouse button.

Implementation

Following is the code:

```
import BreezySwing.*;
import java.awt.*;

public class Sketchpad1 extends GBPanel{

    public Sketchpad1(){
        setBackground(Color.white);
    }

    public void mousePressed (int x, int y){
        Graphics g = getGraphics();
        g.fillOval (x, y, 2, 2);
    }
}
```

Version 2

A slight modification to the program produces a big improvement in the results. The program now draws dots in response to mouse-dragged events rather than mouse-pressed events. This means that the user does not have to press and release a mouse button for each dot. Instead, at the beginning of a drawing stroke, the user depresses a mouse button, and a trail of dots is drawn as the user drags the mouse. The stroke ends when the user releases the button. Figure 19-12 shows the results.

FIGURE 19-12
An improved pellet-based drawing program

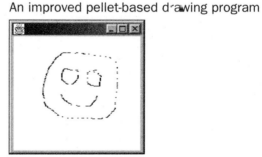

Following is the code:

```
import BreezySwing.*;
import java.awt.*;

public class Sketchpad2 extends GBPanel{

    public Sketchpad2(){
        setBackground(Color.white);
    }
```

```
public void mouseDragged(int x, int y){
    Graphics g = getGraphics();
    g.fillOval (x, y, 2, 2);
}

}
```

Version 3

The preceding pellet-drawing program leaves gaps in the strokes if the user drags the mouse too quickly. A simple line drawing program remedies the problem. As the user drags the mouse, line segments are drawn between successive mouse locations, thereby eliminating gaps in the stroke. Figure 19-13 illustrates the improvement (in everything except the author's artistry). A stroke begins with a mouse-pressed event, continues through a succession of mouse-dragged events, and ends when the user releases the button.

FIGURE 19-13
A simple line drawing program

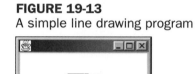

```
import BreezySwing.*;
import java.awt.*;

public class Sketchpad3 extends GBPanel{

    private int oldX, oldY;     //The beginning of a line segment

    public Sketchpad3(){
        setBackground(Color.white);
    }
    //Mark the beginning of a stroke's first line segment
    public void mousePressed (int x, int y){
        Graphics g = getGraphics();
        oldX = x;
        oldY = y;
    }

    //Draw line segments to connect successive locations within a stroke
    public void mouseDragged (int x, int y){
        Graphics g = getGraphics();
        g.drawLine (oldX, oldY, x, y);

        //Get ready for the next line segment
```

```
            oldX = x;
            oldY = y;
        }


        //Draw the last line segment in a stroke
        public void mouseReleased (int x, int y){
            Graphics g = getGraphics();
            g.drawLine (oldX, oldY, x, y);
        }
    }
```

19.7 Transient and Refreshable Images

Our sketchpad application suffers from the transient image problem. To draw a permanent or *refreshable image*—one that reappears when the window is resized—the application must maintain a record of the image and redraw it when necessary. As an illustration, we now modify Sketchpad2 as follows:

1. When the mousePressed method is invoked, the *x* and *y* coordinates are stored in two parallel arrays.

2. We implement a paintComponent method that loops through all the points stored in the arrays and draws the corresponding pellets.

The application handles the details of saving and displaying points in two new methods: savePoint(int x, int y) and displayPoints(Graphics g). Following is the modified program, called Sketchpad4:

```
import BreezySwing.*;
import java.awt.*;


public class Sketchpad4 extends GBPanel{

    private static int MAX_POINTS = 500;
    private int numPoints;
    private int[] xArray;
    private int[] yArray;

    public Sketchpad4(){
        setBackground(Color.white);
        numPoints = 0;
        xArray = new int[MAX_POINTS];
        yArray = new int[MAX_POINTS];
    }

    public void paintComponent (Graphics g){
        super.paintComponent(g);
        displayPoints (g);
    }
```

```
public void mouseDragged (int x, int y){
   if (numPoints < xArray.length){
      Graphics g = getGraphics();
      g.fillOval (x, y, 2, 2);
      savePoint (x, y);
   }else
      new GBFrame().messageBox ("Sorry: cannot draw another pellet.");
}

private void displayPoints (Graphics g){
   int i;
   for (i = 0; i < numPoints; i++){
      g.fillOval (xArray[i], yArray[i], 2, 2);
   }
}

private void savePoint (int x, int y){
   xArray[numPoints] = x;
   yArray[numPoints] = y;
   numPoints++;
}
}
```

Although this version of the program behaves correctly, there is still a problem. When the arrays of coordinates become full, the program can no longer accept mouse clicks, so the user sees a message box. There are several ways to deal with this problem. One way, which we leave as Project 19-6, is to resize the arrays when they become full, perhaps by adding 50 new cells each time this happens. Another way is to use lists to hold the coordinates.

The technique just shown also can be applied with slight modification to Sketchpad3, the version that draws line segments. The trick is to insert in the arrays a special number that marks the boundary between strokes, for instance, -999.

EXERCISE 19.7

1. How does one solve the transient image problem for a set of images?

19.8 Defining and Using a Geometric Class

Many applications implement classes to represent geometric objects such as points, lines, and circles. In this section, we develop a `Circle` class. A circle object has a center, a radius, and a color. Instances of class `Circle` recognize messages to access and modify these attributes and to draw themselves in a given graphics context. Table 19-7 lists the methods.

TABLE 19-7
Methods in Class `Circle`

METHOD	WHAT IT DOES
`Circle(int x, int y, int r, Color c)`	Constructor. Creates a circle with center point (x, y), radius r, and color c.
`int getX()`	Returns the x coordinate of the center.
`int getY()`	Returns the y coordinate of the center.
`int getRadius()`	Returns the radius.
`Color getColor()`	Returns the color.
`void setX(int x)`	Modifies the x coordinate of the center.
`void setY(int y)`	Modifies the y coordinate of the center.
`void setRadius(int r)`	Modifies the radius.
`Color setColor(Color c)`	Modifies the color
`void draw(Graphics g)`	Draws the circle in the graphics context. The circle is filled with its color.
`void drawOutline(Graphics g)`	Draws an outline of the circle in the graphics context.
`boolean containsPoint(int x, int y)`	Returns true if the point (x, y) lies in the circle.
`void move(int xAmount, int yAmount)`	Moves the circle by `xAmount` horizontally to the right and `yAmount` vertically downward. Negative amounts move to the left and up.

Following is an example of a `paintComponent` method that creates and draws a circle with center point (100, 100), radius 50, and color red:

```
public void paintComponent (Graphics g){
   super.paintComponent(g);
   Circle circle = new Circle (100, 100, 50, Color.red);
   circle.draw (g);
}
```

Implementation of the `Circle` Class

For the most part, the implementation of the `Circle` class is trivial. We focus on just two methods: `draw` and `containsPoint`. The `draw` method uses `fillOval` to draw the circle. The `drawOval` method expects the position and extent of the circle's bounding rectangle, which can be derived from the circle's center and radius as shown in the following code:

```
public void draw (Graphics g){
    // Save the current color of the graphics context
    // and set color to the circle's color.
    Color oldColor = g.getColor();
    g.setColor(color);

    // Translate the circle's position and radius
    // to the bounding rectangle's top left corner, width, and height.
    g.fillOval(centerX - radius, centerY - radius, radius * 2, radius * 2);

    // Restore the color of the graphics context.
    g.setColor(oldColor);
}
```

To determine if a point is in a circle, we consider the familiar equation for all points on the circumference of a circle:

$$(x - xc)^2 + (y - yc)^2 = r^2 \qquad \text{(Eq. 1)}$$

or

$$(x - xc)^2 + (y - yc)^2 - r^2 = 0 \qquad \text{(Eq. 2)}$$

where (xc, yc) is the circle's center and r is its radius. A point (x, y) is then in the circle if the left side of Equation 2 is less than or equal to 0. For example, given a circle of radius 2 and center $(0, 0)$, the point $(1, 1)$ produces the result

$$1^2 + 1^2 - 2^2 = -2$$

implying that point is in the circle.

Following is the method that results from this design:

```
public boolean containsPoint (int x, int y){
    int xSquared = (x - centerX) * (x - centerX);
    int ySquared = (y - centerY) * (y - centerY);
    int radiusSquared = radius * radius;
    return xSquared + ySquared - radiusSquared <= 0;
}
```

Case Study 5: Dragging Circles

We now present an application that uses our new Circle class in a program that responds to mouse events.

Request

Write a program that allows the user to drag circles in a window.

Analysis

The application draws some randomly generated circles at start-up. When the user presses the mouse button in a circle, she can drag the circle to another position in the window. The proposed interface is shown in Figure 19-14. The application is based on three classes: the `Circle` class described in the previous section, a drawing panel class called `DragCirclesPanel`, and an application class called `DragCirclesApp`.

FIGURE 19-14
Interface for a circle-dragging program

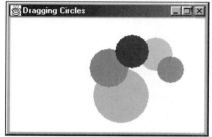

Design

The program maintains an array of the circle objects that appear in the drawing panel. When the user drags a circle, one of these objects is modified and redrawn. At all times, the program keeps track of the currently selected circle and the previous mouse position. During dragging, the program determines how far to move the selected circle by comparing the mouse's previous and current positions.

The design and implementation of the `Circle` class already have been discussed in the previous section. The two principal methods in the `DragCirclesPanel` class are `mousePressed` and `mouseDragged`. The `mousePressed` method begins by searching the array of circles to determine if the user has pressed the mouse button inside a circle. If she has, then

- A `Circle` variable, `selectedCircle`, is set to the circle that was selected.
- The variables `previousX` and `previousY` are set to the mouse's current position.

The `mouseDragged` method

- Determines the incremental amount by which the mouse has just moved by comparing the mouse's current position (`currentX`, `currentY`) to its previous position (`previousX`, `previousY`).
- Calls the `move` method to move the circle by this amount.
- Invokes the `repaint` method, which clears the window and then calls `paint` to redraw all the circles.
- Saves the new mouse position in the variables `previousX` and `previousY`.

Implementation

Following is the code:

```
/* DragCirclesPanel.java
First draw five randomly generated circles. Thereafter, the user can use
the mouse to drag any circle around the window.
*/

import BreezySwing.*;
import java.awt.*;

public class DragCirclesPanel extends GBPanel{

   //Constants that control the characteristics of the randomly generated
   //circles.
   private final static int MAX_CIRCLES  = 5;     //Number of circles
   private final static int MIN_CENTER_X = 50;    //Range of x values for
   private final static int MAX_CENTER_X = 150;   //circle centers
   private final static int MIN_CENTER_Y = 50;    //Range of y values for
   private final static int MAX_CENTER_Y = 150;   //circle centers
   private final static int MIN_RADIUS   = 10;    //Range of values for the
   private final static int MAX_RADIUS   = 50;    //circle radii

   //Instance variables
   private int previousX, previousY;    //Previous mouse position
   private     Circle selectedCircle;   //The selected circle or null if
                                        //none.
   private     Circle[] circles = new Circle[MAX_CIRCLES];
                                        //The array of circles

   //Constructor -- initialize instance variables
   public DragCirclesPanel(){
      int i;
      setBackground(Color.white);
      selectedCircle = null;

      //Generate random circles
      for (i = 0; i < MAX_CIRCLES; i++){
         int centerX = randomInt(MIN_CENTER_X, MAX_CENTER_X);
         int centerY = randomInt(MIN_CENTER_Y, MAX_CENTER_Y);
         int radius = randomInt(MIN_RADIUS, MAX_RADIUS);
         Color color = randomColor();
         Circle circle = new Circle(centerX, centerY, radius, color);
         circles[i] = circle;
      }
   }

   //Redraw the circles. The last circle drawn appears topmost.
   public void paintComponent (Graphics g){
      super.paintComponent(g);
      int i;
      for (i = 0; i < MAX_CIRCLES; i++)
```

```
                circles[i].draw(g);
    }


    //Respond to the mouse-pressed event by recording its position and by
    //determining if a circle has been selected.
    public void mousePressed (int x, int y){
       previousX = x;
       previousY = y;
       selectedCircle = findCircle(x, y);
    }


    //Respond to the mouse-released event by indicating that no circle
    //is currently selected.
    public void mouseReleased (int x, int y){
       selectedCircle = null;
    }


    //Respond to the mouse-dragged event by determining if a circle is
    //currently selected. If a circle is selected, then
    //   move it by an amount equal to the amount the mouse has moved,
    //   repaint the panel, and
    //   record the mouse's position in previousX and previousY.
    public void mouseDragged (int currentX, int currentY){
       if (selectedCircle != null){
          selectedCircle.move(currentX - previousX, currentY - previousY);
          repaint();
          previousX = currentX;
          previousY = currentY;
       }
    }


    //Return the topmost circle containing the point (x, y) or null if no
    //circle contains the point
    private Circle findCircle(int x, int y){
       int i;
       for (i = MAX_CIRCLES - 1; i >= 0; i--)
          if (circles[i].containsPoint(x, y)){
             return circles[i];
          }
       return null;
    }


    //Return a random integer between low and high inclusive.
    private int randomInt (int low, int high){
       return (int) (low + Math.random() * (high - low + 1));
    }


    //Return a random color.
    private Color randomColor(){
       Color color;
       int number = randomInt (1, 5);
       switch (number){
          case 1:
```

```
                        color = Color.red;
                        break;
                    case 2:
                        color = Color.blue;
                        break;
                    case 3:
                        color = Color.green;
                        break;
                    case 4:
                        color = Color.magenta;
                        break;
                    case 5:
                        color = Color.cyan;
                        break;
                    default: color = Color.orange;
                }
                return color;
            }
        }
```

Getting Rid of Flicker

This program has a problem. As we drag a circle around, the window seems to flicker. The cause lies in the `mouseDragged` method. Every time we move a circle, the `repaint` method is called. This method clears the window and then calls `paintComponent` to redraw the circles. Unless the computer is very fast, the human eye experiences the cycles of clear and redraw as flicker. Fortunately, there is a way to overcome the problem. Java allows drawing to be done in two different modes. In the default mode, which we have been using exclusively so far, images (lines, text, shapes) overwrite whatever happens to be underneath them. This mode is called **paint mode**. The second mode is called **XOR mode**. The result of drawing an image in XOR mode depends on two colors—the current color and the XOR color. Wherever the image overlays the XOR color, it is drawn in the current color, and vice versa. A consequence of this strange convention is that if an image is redrawn on top of itself, it disappears, and the window returns to its original appearance before the image was first drawn. Pixels of a different color (neither the current color nor the XOR color) underneath the image are changed in a manner too complex to explain here. However, redrawing over these pixels returns them to their original color, too.

In the code that follows, we use the XOR mode to solve the flicker problem. When a circle is selected, we draw an outline of it in XOR mode. Then, as the user drags the mouse, we redraw the outline using XOR (restoring the pixels covered by the outline) and draw another outline in XOR mode at the mouse's new location. Drawing an outline involves so few pixels that the user sees no flicker and believes the outline is smoothly following the mouse around the window. When the user finally releases the mouse, we repaint the window. Following are the modifications to the program:

```java
public void mousePressed (int x, int y){
    previousX = x;
    previousY = y;
    selectedCircle = findCircle(x, y);
    if (selectedCircle != null)
        selectedCircle.drawOutline(getGraphics());
}
```

```
    public void mouseReleased (int x, int y){
       selectedCircle = null;
       repaint();
    }

    public void mouseDragged (int x, int y){
       if (selectedCircle != null){
          Graphics g = getGraphics();
          selectedCircle.drawOutline (g);                        // Old location
          selectedCircle.move (x - previousX, y - previousY);
          selectedCircle.drawOutline (g);                        // New location
          previousX = x;
          previousY = y;
       }
    }
```

To complete the modifications, we must add a drawOutline method to the circle class. Following is the code:

```
public void drawOutline (Graphics g){
   Color oldColor = g.getColor();
   g.setColor (Color.black);
   g.setXORMode (Color.white);
   g.drawOval (centerX - radius, centerY - radius, radius * 2, radius * 2);
   g.setColor (oldColor);
   g.setPaintMode();
}
```

19.9 Text Properties

From the perspective of a bitmapped display, text is drawn like any other image. A text image has several properties, as shown in Table 19-8. These are set by adjusting the color and font properties of the graphics context in which the text is drawn. In this section, we first provide an overview of Java's Font class and then show some examples of its application.

TABLE 19-8
Text properties

TEXT PROPERTY	EXAMPLE
Color	Red, green, blue, white, black, etc.
Font style	Plain, **bold**, *italic*
Font size	10 point, 12 point, etc.
Font name	Courier, Times New Roman, etc.

The Font Class

An object of class Font has three basic properties: a name, a style, and a size. The following code creates one Font object with the properties **Courier bold 12** and another with the properties *Arial bold italic 10*:

```
Font courierBold12    = new Font("Courier", Font.BOLD, 12);
Font arialBoldItalic10 = new Font("Arial", Font.BOLD + Font.ITALIC, 10);
```

The Font constants PLAIN, BOLD, and ITALIC define the font styles. The font size is an integer representing the number of points, where one point equals 1/72 of an inch. The available font names depend on your particular computer platform. To see what they are, run the code segment

```
String fontNames[] = Toolkit.getDefaultToolkit().getFontList();
int i;
for (i = 0; i < fontNames.length; i++)
    System.out.println (fontNames[i]);
```

This code

- Declares the variable fontNames as an array of strings.

- Runs the Toolkit class method getDefaultToolkit, which returns the default toolkit for the particular computer platform.

- Runs the method getFontList on the toolkit. This method returns a list of the available font names.

- Sets the array fontNames to this list.

- Executes a loop that displays the contents of fontNames in the terminal window.

    Table 19-9 lists the principal Font methods.

TABLE 19-9
The principal Font methods

FONT METHOD	WHAT IT DOES

public Font(String name,
              int style,
              int size)
	Creates a new Font object with the specified properties; style must be PLAIN, BOLD, ITALIC, or a combination of these using +.

public String getName()	Returns the current font name.
public int getStyle()	Returns the current font style.
public int getSize()	Returns the current font size.

Setting the Color and Font Properties of Text

The programmer sets the color and font properties of text by setting the color and font properties of the GUI object's graphics context. For example, assume that we want to display the text "Hello world!" in green and in the font Courier bold 14. The following code would do this:

```
Font ourFont = new Font ("Courier", Font.BOLD. 14);
Color ourColor = Color.GREEN;
Graphics g = getGraphics();
g.setColor (ourColor);
g.setFont (ourFont);
g.drawString ("Hello world!", 100, 100);
```

Changing the font and color of a graphics context affects all subsequent graphics operations in that context but does not alter the font or color of existing images.

Design, Testing, and Debugging Hints

- Computer screen coordinates are not the same as conventional Cartesian coordinates. Computer screen coordinates place the origin (0, 0) in the upper-left corner and get larger as they move to the right and to the bottom of the screen.

- The repaint method always clears the graphics context. Thus, any displayed images will be erased when repaint is invoked. This will occur automatically when the window is resized, unless you override the paintComponent method to redraw the images.

- Remember to call super.paintComponent(g) whenever you implement the method paintComponent. This guarantees that the window objects' background will be painted, thus clearing any images drawn in it.

- Never call a method that accesses a graphics context in a constructor method. This context is not yet available, and you will receive a run-time exception.

SUMMARY

In this lesson, you learned:

- Java uses a screen coordinate system to locate the positions of pixels in a window or panel. The origin of this system is in the upper-left corner of the drawing area and the x and y axes increase to the right and downward, respectively.

- Each window or panel maintains a graphics object, to which the programmer can send messages to draw images, alter the color, and so forth.

- Java does not maintain a permanent bitmap of a graphics object. To refresh a window's or a panel's images, the programmer must repaint the window or panel. The programmer does this by placing drawing commands in the method paintComponent, which the JVM automatically runs whenever a window or panel must be refreshed, or which is invoked when the programmer sends the message repaint to the panel or the window.

■ The graphing of data with bar graphs, line graphs, or pie charts provides an informative way to present them.

■ Each panel tracks mouse events, such as mouse presses, releases, clicks, drags, entries, and exits. The programmer can implement methods to obtain the mouse's coordinates when an event occurs and take the appropriate actions.

■ The programmer can modify the color with which images are drawn and the properties of text fonts for a given graphics object.

VOCABULARY *Review*

Define the following terms:

c-curve	horizontal bar graph	refreshable image
coordinate system	line graphs	screen coordinate system
fractal object	origin	transient image problem
fractals	paint mode	vertical bar graph
graphics context	panel	XOR mode

REVIEW *Questions*

FILL IN THE BLANK

Complete the following sentences by writing the correct word or words in the blanks provided.

1. The origin of a screen coordinate system is in the _____ of the drawing area.

2. A(n) _____ is a smaller rectangular drawing area within a window.

3. A(n) _____ is an object to which drawing messages are sent.

4. The method _____ is run automatically whenever a drawing area needs to be refreshed.

5. The programmer can send the message _____ to a drawing area to force a refresh of that drawing area.

6. The _____ color scheme uses three integer values to specify each one of over 16 million colors.

7. The _____ problem arises because the JVM does not maintain a permanent bitmap of the images in a window or panel.

8. The coordinates of the mouse can be tracked during a(n) _____ event.

9. The three attributes of a font are _____, _____, and _____.

10. The technique used to move images without flicker is called _____ mode.

PROJECTS

PROJECT 19-1

Write a program that allows the user to change the pen color and the background color of the application window and to view its size. The program should provide two menus of colors. When the user selects a color from the **Pen** menu, the program sets the window's graphics context to that color. When the user selects a color from the **Background** menu, the program sets the window's background to that color. The program also displays the height and width of the window's graphics context at the center of the window. These values should be updated whenever the user resizes the window. *Hint*: Send all messages to a single panel in the window.

PROJECT 19-2

The twentieth-century Dutch painter Piet Mondrian developed a style of abstract painting that exhibited simple recursive patterns. For example, an "idealized" pattern from one of his paintings might look like that shown in Figure 19-15.

FIGURE 19-15

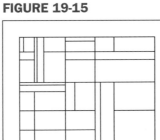

To generate such a pattern with a computer, an algorithm would begin by drawing a rectangle, and then repeatedly draw two unequal subdivisions, as shown in Figure 19-16.

FIGURE 19-16

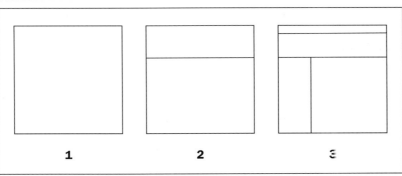

1   2   3

As you can see, the algorithm continues this process of subdivision for a number of levels, until an "aesthetically right moment" is reached. In this version, the algorithm appears to divide the current rectangle into portions representing one-third and two-thirds of its area, and it appears to alternate the subdivisions randomly between the horizontal and vertical axes. Design, implement, and test a program that uses a recursive method to draw such patterns. The user should be able to draw several pictures with different levels, say, 2, 4, 8, and 16.

PROJECT 19-3

Modify the program from Project 19-2 so that it fills the rectangular areas in the picture with randomly generated colors.

PROJECT 19-4

The programs in Projects 19-2 and 19-3 always place the smaller rectangular area to the left or at the top of a subdivision. Modify the program from Project 19-3 so that the smaller rectangular area is randomly placed.

PROJECT 19-5

Complete the program code for Case Study 3: Multiple Views of Data.

PROJECT 19-6

In the Sketchpad4 program from Section 19.7, saving the points in arrays causes a problem: The size of the arrays is fixed when they are created, so the number of pellets the user can draw is limited. Modify the program so that the arrays can accommodate any number of points. The program should use instances of ArrayList to store the points. Test the program thoroughly.

PROJECT 19-7

Sketching programs typically allow users to draw lines, rectangles, and ovals by selecting an item from a menu and clicking the mouse in the desired area of the sketchpad. Write a program that supports this kind of drawing. The program should have a **Shape** menu and a **Color** menu. When the user selects **Shape/Line,** for example, a mouse press and a mouse release in the drawing area will establish the endpoints of a line. Other lines can then be drawn until the user selects a different shape. This program does not have to refresh the images when the window size is modified.

PROJECT 19-8

Modify the program from Project 19-7 so that it can refresh the images. To do this, define the abstract class Shape and the classes Line, Circle, and Rect and maintain a list of shapes. Each of these classes should have a draw method.

PROJECT 19-9

A *scattershot diagram* allows a user to visualize data as points in a two-dimensional graph. In a simple case, we might plot integer values from an array along the y axis and their index positions along the x axis. This image allows us to visualize the movement of data in an array as it is being sorted. Modify the sorting program case study from Lesson 11 so that it displays the data in this manner as they are being sorted. When the user enters a new number of data values, the program refreshes the window by displaying a scattershot of these data. When a sort algorithm exchanges two values in the array, the program redraws these values in the scattershot. The program should not have to repaint the entire scattershot when only two values are exchanged. You may omit the output of statistics on comparisons and exchanges performed during the sorts.

CRITICAL *Thinking*

As you probably know, the game of tic-tac-toe is played with a 3 × 3 grid of squares and each player takes turns marking an X or a O until three letters line up in a row, column, or diagonal. Write a program that plays this game with a user. The program makes the first move, at random. The user places a mark by selecting a square with the mouse. The program should prevent entries in squares already occupied and should make its own entries at random. The program displays a message box announcing the winner when a game is over and allows the user to reset the board by selecting a menu item.

> **Hot Tip**
>
> Use an array of panels to represent the board.

FILES

OBJECTIVES

Upon completion of this lesson, you should be able to:

■ Understand the use of the classes for processing files in the `java.io` package.

■ Open and use input file streams for reading one character, one line, or one word at a time from text files.

■ Understand how to catch exceptions that can occur when opening files and reading from them.

■ Use data input and output streams for the transfer of specific types of data to and from files.

■ Work with object input streams and output streams to serialize objects.

■ Understand the classes used to perform terminal input and output.

■ Use file dialogs to open connections to input and output files.

Estimated Time: 3.5 hours

VOCABULARY

buffer

data flow diagram

exception-driven loop

flushing

input stream

output stream

random access

sequential access

serialization

text file

D ata stored in variables are temporary, existing for the lifetime of an application at most. Data that must last longer are saved in files on secondary storage devices, such as magnetic disks, optical disks (CDs), and magnetic tapes. When needed again later, the data are read from the files back into variables. Dealing directly with directory structures and file layouts on disk is a complex process, so operating systems provide a layer of software to hide the messy details. In addition, Java has built a hierarchy of classes on top of this layer to give it an object-oriented interface. When working with files, a program deals with these Java classes, which in turn manage the actual transfer of data between memory and secondary storage. In Figure 20-1, the boxes labeled "Input file" and "Output file" represent instances of these Java classes.

FIGURE 20-1
File objects and the movement of data between memory and secondary storage devices

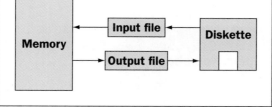

Java supports two types of file access: sequential and random. If we imagine a file as a long sequence of contiguous bytes, then *random access* allows a program to retrieve a byte or group of bytes from anywhere in a file. *Sequential access* forces a program to retrieve bytes sequentially starting from the beginning of a file. Thus, to retrieve the 100th byte, a program must first retrieve the preceding 99. Despite this restriction, sequential file access is extremely useful and is the topic of this lesson.

20.1 File Classes

At the lowest level, Java views the data in files as a stream of bytes. A stream of bytes from which data are read is called an *input stream*, and a stream of bytes to which data are written is called an *output stream*. Java provides classes for connecting to and manipulating data in a stream. The classes are defined in the package `java.io` and are organized in a large complex hierarchy, a small portion of which is shown in Figures 20-2 and 20-3. The concrete classes are shown in light blue boxes and the abstract classes are shown in dark blue boxes.

FIGURE 20-2
A portion of the hierarchy for stream classes

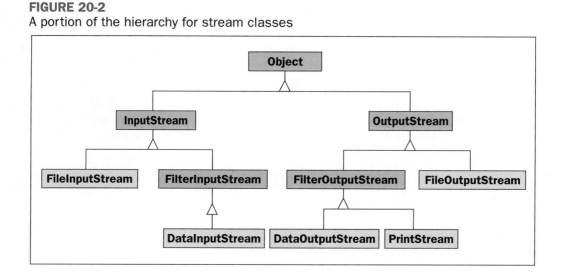

FIGURE 20-3
A few other I/O-oriented classes

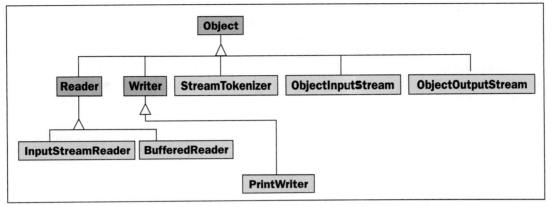

Although the number of these classes looks intimidating, we will use them in a few simple combinations as summarized in Table 20-1. The rest of the lesson is devoted to explaining how to use these combinations.

TABLE 20-1
Combinations of classes used in several common I/O situations

TASK	COMBINATION OF CLASSES USED
Read one character at a time from a text file	`InputStreamReader` on `FileInputStream`
Read one line at a time from a text file	`BufferedReader` on `InputStreamReader` on `FileInputStream`
Read one word at a time from a text file	`StreamTokenizer` or `BufferedReader` on `InputStreamReader` on `FileInputStream`
Write `int`, `double`, `char`, `String`, etc. to a text file	`PrintWriter` on `FileOutputStream`
Write `int`, `double`, `char`, `String`, etc. to a nontext file	`DataOutputStream` on `FileOutputStream`
Read `int`, `double`, `char`, `String`, etc. from a nontext file	`DataInputStream` on `FileInputStream`
Write a complete object to a file	`ObjectOutputStream` on `FileOutputStream`
Read a complete object from a file	`ObjectInputStream` on `FileInputStream`
Read keyboard input	`System.in`, which is a `BufferedReader` on `InputStreamReader` on `InputStream`
Write console output	`System.out` and `System.err`, which are `PrintStream` objects

The table's second column requires some explanation. For instance, the entry

```
InputStreamReader on FileInputStream
```

means that an `InputStreamReader` object is wrapped around a `FileInputStream` object. As indicated in the table, nearly all input operations involve a `FileInputStream`; however, an object of this type has the rather limited capability of reading raw bytes from a file. To treat this stream of raw bytes as characters or lines or words, we must pass it through objects that translate it appropriately. Thus, an `InputStreamReader` object translates raw bytes into characters in some designated encoding scheme. In a similar manner, nearly all output operations involve a `FileOutputStream` in combination with other classes that translate data in various forms to the raw bytes processed by a `FileOutputStream`.

To help you better understand this approach, the following list provides short summaries of some of the classes taken verbatim from Sun's Java documentation. The documentation is downloadable from Sun's Web site (see Appendix A).

- `InputStream`—This abstract class is the superclass of all classes representing an input stream of bytes.

- `FileInputStream`—Obtains input bytes from a file in a file system.

- `Reader`—This is the abstract class for reading character streams.

- `InputStreamReader`—A bridge from byte streams to character streams: It reads bytes and translates them into characters according to a specified character encoding. The encoding that it uses may be specified by name, or the platform's default encoding may be accepted.

- `BufferedReader`—Reads text from a character-input stream, buffering characters so as to provide for the efficient reading of characters, arrays, and lines.

- `StreamTokenizer`—Takes an input stream and parses it into "tokens," allowing the tokens to be read one at a time.

- `OutputStream`—This abstract class is the superclass of all classes representing an output stream of bytes. An output stream accepts output bytes and sends them to some device.

- `FileOutputStream`—This is an output stream for writing data to a File.

- `Writer`—This is the abstract class for writing to character streams.

- `PrintWriter`—Prints formatted representations of objects to a text-output stream.

*E*XERCISE 20.1

1. Why are file classes needed?

2. How does Java represent data to be transferred to and from a file?

3. Why are so many file classes needed?

20.2 File Input

$\mathbf{W}$e begin our discussion of file input by writing a program that reads a text file, converts all alphabetical characters to uppercase, and displays the result in a text area (Figure 20-4). To use the program, type a file name in the text field and click the **Display the Contents** button. On a PC and on some other systems, a text file name commonly has a **.txt** extension, which we use here. We will present four versions of this program. In the first, a stub replaces the method for reading and processing the file. In the other three versions, we show how to read the file one character, one line, and one word at a time.

FIGURE 20-4
Interface for the text conversion program

A typical file input process is described in the following pseudocode algorithm:

```
Open an input connection to a file
Read the data from the file and process them
Close the input connection to the file
```

Following is the program with a stub taking the place of the method `readAndProcessData`:

```
import javax.swing.*;
import java.io.*;
import BreezySwing.*;

public class ConvertText extends GBFrame{

    //Window objects
    private JLabel nameLabel;
    private JTextField nameField;
    private JButton displayButton;
    private JTextArea output;

    //Constructor
    public ConvertText(){
        nameLabel     = addLabel ("File Name:"               ,1,1,1,1);
        nameField   = addTextField (""                       ,1,2,1,1);
        displayButton = addButton ("Display the Contents",2,1,2,1);
```

```
    output         = addTextArea (""                      ,3,1,2,6);
    nameField.requestFocus();                //Move cursor to nameField
    output.setEditable(false);        //Prevent user from modifying output
    setTitle("Convert Text to Uppercase");     //Give the window a title
}


//Respond to the command button
public void buttonClicked(JButton buttonObj){

    //Get the name of the text file
    String fileName = nameField.getText();

    try{

        //Open an input connection on the file, read and process the file,
        //close the file.
         FileInputStream stream = new FileInputStream(fileName);
        readAndProcessData(stream);
        stream.close();

    }catch(IOException e){

        //If cannot open the file, then inform the user.
        messageBox("Error in opening input file:\n" + e.toString());

    }

    //Get ready for the user's next input
    nameField.requestFocus();        //Move cursor to nameField
    nameField.selectAll();           //and select all text in the field
}


//Read and process the data (this is a stub)
private void readAndProcessData(FileInputStream stream){
    messageBox("Running readAndProcessData\n" +
            "File opened successfully");
}

public static void main (String[] args){
    ConvertText tpo = new ConvertText();
    tpo.setSize(300, 300);
    tpo.setVisible(true);
}
}
```

In the following sections, we explain the details of this program.

Exception Handling

Java responds to run-time errors by throwing exceptions. In earlier lessons, we saw examples of divide by 0 exceptions and array subscript exceptions. When these exceptions occurred, the JVM displayed system-defined error messages in a terminal window and stopped. The `try-catch` statement provides a mechanism for handling exceptions under program control without forcing the program to stop. In the discussion that follows, we are concerned only with exceptions related to files, and Java requires all of these exceptions to be caught by the application.

Opening and Closing a `FileInputStream`

The `buttonClicked` method in our previous example program

■ Opens a file input stream on the user's file name

■ Passes the stream to a method for reading and processing the data

■ Closes the stream

As mentioned in Lesson 9, code embedded in a `try-catch` statement consists of two parts:

■ A `try` clause: A block of code is included in this part of the statement. If a run-time error occurs in this block, Java throws an exception and control passes immediately to a `catch` clause.

■ One or more `catch` clauses: Each `catch` clause is qualified by a particular kind of exception that might be thrown in the `try` statement. In this case, an `IOException`, such as a failure to find the file, can occur. Our example has just one `catch` clause, which expects an instance of `IOException`, here named e, as a parameter. When the `catch` clause is invoked, the code in our example sends the `toString` message to the object e, thus obtaining information about the error. Our example then displays this information in a message box.

The code for opening and closing a file stream is always embedded in a `try-catch` statement; otherwise, there is a compile-time error.

Reading Data from a Text File

After a file input stream has been successfully opened, we can read data from it. Now we examine the input of data from text files. A *text file* is one that contains nothing but characters. Java provides several ways to read characters from a file:

■ One character at a time, using the class `InputStreamReader`

■ One line at a time, using the class `BufferedReader`

■ One word at a time, using the class `StreamTokenizer`

To utilize the desired type of input, the Java programmer uses the appropriate class and methods. In the following paragraphs, we show how this is done in the context of our example program.

Reading Data One Character at a Time

The following code segment shows how the method `readAndProcessData` is coded to read text from a file one character at a time:

```
private void readAndProcessData (FileInputStream stream){
   InputStreamReader reader = new InputStreamReader (stream);
   int asciiValue;
   char ch;
   try{
      output.setText("");
      asciiValue = reader.read();                    //read returns an int
      while (asciiValue != -1){                      //-1 indicates end of stream
         ch = Character.toUpperCase ((char)asciiValue);  //cast and convert
         output.append (String.valueOf(ch));  //convert a char to a  String
         asciiValue = reader.read();
      }
   }catch(IOException e){
      messageBox ("Error in file input:\n" + e.toString());
   }
}
```

First the method instantiates an `InputStreamReader` on a `FileInputStream` object. The result is shown in Figure 20-5.

FIGURE 20-5
Combination of objects needed to read text one character at a time

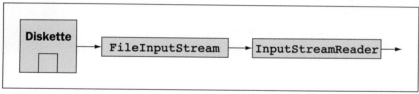

The method uses a `try-catch` statement to read data from the stream. The form of the input loop is fairly general:

```
get the first datum from the stream
while (the datum does not indicate that the end of stream has been reached)
   process the datum
   get the next datum from the stream
}
```

Note three other points:

- The `read` method returns −1 on reaching the end of the stream.

- The `read` method returns a value of type `int`, which corresponds to the ASCII value of the character in the file. This value is cast to `char` before further processing.

- The `catch` clause handles any `IOException` that might occur as the stream is read.

Reading Data One Line at a Time

The next version of the `readAndProcessData` method reads text from a file one line at a time:

```
private void readAndProcessData (FileInputStream stream){
    InputStreamReader iStrReader = new InputStreamReader (stream);
    BufferedReader reader = new BufferedReader (iStrReader);
    String line;
    try{
        output.setText("");
        line = reader.readLine();
        while (line != null){                    //null indicates end of stream
            line = line.toUpperCase();
            output.append (line + "\n");
            line = reader.readLine();
        }
    }catch(IOException e){
        messageBox ("Error in file input:\n" + e.toString());
    }
}
```

To set up the reader, we proceed as before by first connecting an input stream reader to the file input stream. We then connect an instance of `BufferedReader` to the input stream reader. The result is shown in Figure 20-6.

FIGURE 20-6
Combination of objects needed to read text one line at a time

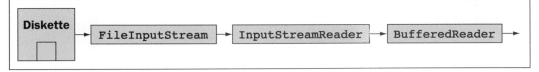

Once again, the method uses a `try-catch` statement. The structure of the input process is the same as before. However, note the following differences:

- We now call the method `readLine` to obtain a string representing the next line of text in the stream.

- When this string has the value `null`, we have reached the end of the stream.

- We use the `String` instance method `toUpperCase` to convert the entire string to uppercase.

- The newline character is not part of the string obtained from `readLine`, so we append a newline to the string before outputting it.

The use of a `BufferedReader` not only allows us to work with whole lines of text, but also can improve the speed at which the data are input. When the programmer uses a `BufferedReader` for input, Java uses an area of memory called a *buffer* to read large chunks of text from the file rather than single characters.

Reading Data One Word at a Time

Sequences of characters separated by white space characters (blanks, tabs, newlines) can be processed as words or *tokens*. For example, suppose a file contains the sequence "16 cats sat on 4 mats." It contains the separate tokens

16

cats

sat

on

4

mats

Java provides a `StreamTokenizer` class for reading tokens from a file. The following code segment revisits our example program to show how tokens are read from a file stream:

```
private void readAndProcessData (FileInputStream stream){
    InputStreamReader iStrReader = new InputStreamReader (stream);
    BufferedReader bufReader = new BufferedReader (iStrReader);
    StreamTokenizer reader = new StreamTokenizer (bufReader);

    //Add periods, commas, semicolons, and exclamation marks to the
    //standard set of white space characters.
    reader.whitespaceChars  ('.', '.');
    reader.whitespaceChars  (',', ',');
    reader.whitespaceChars  ('!', '!');
    reader.whitespaceChars  (';', ';');

    String token = "";
    try{
        output.setText("");
        reader.nextToken();
        while (reader.ttype != StreamTokenizer.TT_EOF){
            if (reader.ttype == StreamTokenizer.TT_WORD){
                token = reader.sval;
                token = token.toUpperCase();
            }else if (reader.ttype == StreamTokenizer.TT_NUMBER)
                token = reader.nval + "";
            output.append (token + "\n");
            reader.nextToken();
        }
    }catch (IOException e){
        messageBox ("Error in file input:\n" + e.toString());
    }
}
```

The setup of the stream extends our previous setup by connecting an instance of StreamTokenizer to a buffered reader. The combination is illustrated in Figure 20-7.

FIGURE 20-7
Combination of objects needed to read text one token at a time

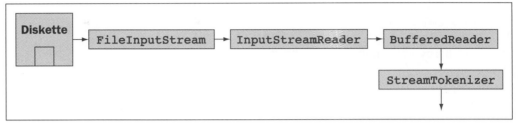

The code uses three instance variables in the class StreamTokenizer. These are described in Table 20-2.

TABLE 20-2
Instance variables in the class StreamTokenizer

INSTANCE VARIABLE	DESCRIPTION
ttype	An int variable containing the type of the current token. Tokens can be of four types: end of file, end of line, word, and number, represented by the constants TT_EOF, TT_EOL, TT_WORD, and TT_NUMBER, respectively.
sval	A String containing the current token if it is a word
nval	A double containing the current token if it is a number

The method nextToken() reads the next token from the input stream and updates the tokenizer's instance variables with information about the type and value of the token. The nextToken method skips white space between words and numbers. Notice that it is possible to treat additional characters as white space.

*E*XERCISE 20.2

1. List the specific stream classes from which you can read the following items:
   a. individual characters
   b. individual lines of text
   c. individual words of text

2. Write the code that is necessary to open a file for the input of individual characters, using the file name "myfile."

3. Assume that an appropriate stream has been set up for input. Write the pseudocode form of the loop for reading the following items from the input stream:

a. individual characters

b. individual lines of text

4. How does a `try-catch` statement work with file streams?

5. Explain how the instance variables `ttype`, `sval`, and `nval` are used with a `StreamTokenizer`.

Case Study 1: A Text Analyzer

To illustrate the use of input streams, we write a simple text analyzer.

Request

Examine a text file and determine the word count, the longest word, and the length of the longest word.

Analysis

The program uses essentially the same interface as our previous text conversion program (see Figure 20-8). When the user clicks the Analyze button, the program opens the indicated text file, counts the number of words, and determines which word is the longest. The program then displays the word count, the longest word, and the length of the longest word in the text area.

FIGURE 20-8
Interface for a text analyzer program

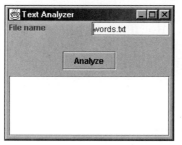

For example, assume that the file **words.txt** contains the following text:

This is a short file. There

are only a few words in it. The

longest word has 7 letters.

The analysis produces the results shown in Figure 20-9.

FIGURE 20-9
Analysis of a sample text

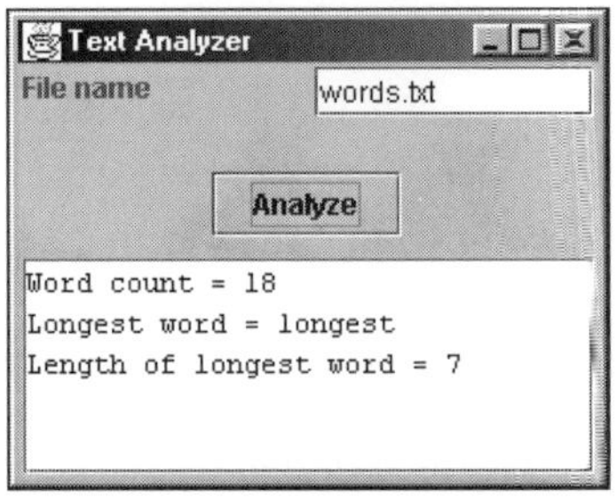

These special considerations are included in the program:

■ If the file name provided by the user is not on disk, the program displays a message box with an error message.

■ A default file name, **words.txt**, appears in the text field initially.

■ Numbers in the file will be ignored.

Design

The following pseudocode describes the operations performed in the `buttonClicked` method:

```
Open a file input stream with the file name provided by the user
Initialize the counter to 0 and the longest word to the empty string
Call the method analyzeFile to read and process the words in the file
Close the file input stream
Call the method printStatistics to display the statistics
```

The `analyzeFile` method reads words and computes statistics as follows:

```
Open an input stream reader on the file input stream
Open a stream tokenizer on the input stream reader
Read the first token
While (there are more tokens){
   If (the token is a word){
       Increment the word count
       If (the length of the word is greater than the longest word)
          Set the longest word to the word just input
   }
   Read the next token
}
```

The structure chart shown in Figure 20-10 illustrates the program's design.

FIGURE 20-10
Structure chart for the text analyzer program

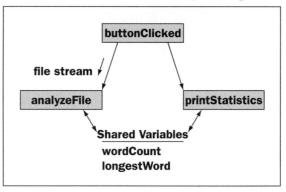

Implementation

Following is the code:

```
/* TextAnalyzer.java
Analyze a text file and determine the number of words, the longest word,
and the length of the longest word. Ignore numbers.
*/

import javax.swing.*;
import BreezySwing.*;
import java.io.*;

public class TextAnalyzer extends GBFrame{

    //Window objects
    private JLabel fileLabel;
    private JTextField fileField;
    private JButton doReport;
    private JTextArea outputArea;

    //Instance variables
    private int wordCount;          //The number of words in the text
    private String longestWord;     //The longest word in the text

    //Constructor
    public TextAnalyzer() {
        fileLabel     = addLabel ("File name",1,1,1,1);
        fileField = addTextField ("words.txt",1,2,1,1);
        doReport      = addButton ("Analyze"  ,2,1,2,1);
        outputArea = addTextArea (""           ,3,1,2,3);
        setTitle("Text Analyzer");
    }

    //Analyze the text
    public void buttonClicked (JButton buttonObj){
```

```
    //Get the file name and initialize the instance variables
    String fileName = fileField.getText();
    wordCount = 0;
    longestWord = "";

    try{

        //Instantiate a file stream on the text file, analyze, and
        //print the results
        FileInputStream fileStream = new FileInputStream(fileName);
        analyzeFile(fileStream);
        fileStream.close();
        printStatistics();

    }catch (IOException e){

        //Report error conditions
        messageBox("File not opened\n" + e.toString());

    }
}

//Instantiate a stream tokenizer on the file stream, process the stream
//one token at a time, count the tokens, and identify the longest token.
private void analyzeFile(FileInputStream fileStream){

    //Declare and initialize local variables
    int tokenType = 0;
    String word = "";

    //Instantiate the stream tokenizer
    InputStreamReader reader = new InputStreamReader(fileStream);
    StreamTokenizer tokens = new StreamTokenizer(reader);

    //Treat periods as white space
    tokens.whitespaceChars  ('.', '.');

    try{

        //Read and process the tokens
        tokens.nextToken();
        while (tokens.ttype != StreamTokenizer.TT_EOF){

            if (tokens.ttype == StreamTokenizer.TT_WORD){
                word = tokens.sval;
                wordCount++;
                if (word.length() > longestWord.length())
                    longestWord = word;
            }
            tokens.nextToken();

        }
```

```
      }catch (IOException e){
         messageBox("Data not read properly " + e.toString());
      }
   }

   //Print the results of the analysis
   private void printStatistics(){
      outputArea.setText("");
      outputArea.append ("Word count = " + wordCount + "\n");
      outputArea.append("Longest word = " + longestWord + "\n");
      outputArea.append("Length of longest word = "
                        + longestWord.length() + "\n");
   }

   public static void main (String[] args){
      TextAnalyzer tpo = new TextAnalyzer();
      tpo.setSize (250, 200);
      tpo.setVisible(true);
   }
}
```

20.3 *File Output*

We now turn our attention to file output. The file output process conforms to the following pattern:

```
Open an output connection to a file
Write data to the file
Close the output connection to the file
```

The details of the file output process are discussed in the following sections.

Opening and Closing a `FileOutputStream`

The code segment shown performs the following actions:

- Opens a file output stream on a file named test.txt
- Passes the stream to a method for writing the data
- Closes the stream

```
try{
   FileOutputStream stream = new FileOutputStream ("test.txt");
   writeData (stream);
   stream.close();
}catch(IOException e){
   messageBox ("Error opening output file " + e.toString());
}
```

Writing Data to a `PrintWriter`

The class `PrintWriter` writes data to a file output stream as encoded characters. The resulting file can be read with a text editor or an input stream reader. The `PrintWriter` methods `print` and `println` each take a single parameter, which can be an `int`, a `double`, a `String`, or any other data type. If the parameter is an object, then the string representation of the object is printed as determined by the object's `toString` method. The `println` method appends a newline character (`'\n'`) to the print stream. Figure 20-11 shows the flow of data from memory to a print writer to a file output stream to disk.

FIGURE 20-11
Combination of objects needed to write data as text

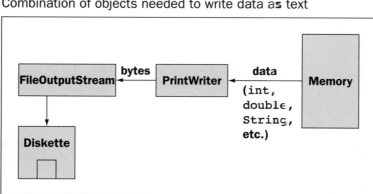

The code shown implements the `writeData` method invoked in the previous code segment. This method performs the following actions:

- Opens a print writer on the file output stream

- Writes a header message followed by a newline to the print writer

- Writes 10 random integers between 1 and 10, separated by spaces, to the print writer

```
void writeData(FileOutputStream fileOutputStream){
    int i;
    PrintWriter printWriter = new PrintWriter (fileOutputStream, true);
    printWriter.println ("Here are 10 random integers: ");

    for (i = 1; i <= 10; i++)
        printWriter.print ((int) (1 + Math.random() * 10) + " ");
}
```

The preferred constructor for a print writer takes a Boolean parameter that indicates whether or not the application desires the output stream to be flushed. *Flushing* sends any data left in the output buffer to the disk. A print writer throws no exceptions, so a `try-catch` statement is not necessary.

*E*XERCISE 20.3

1. List the steps required for writing string data to an output stream.

2. What type of data can be output with the method `println`?

3. What does it mean to flush an output stream?

Case Study 2: Employees and Payroll

There are many situations in which it is necessary to read several files in synchronization and simultaneously write results to an output file. We illustrate a problem of this type in this case study.

Request

Write a program that reads two text files and writes a third. The first file contains employee names and pay rates, the second contains hours worked by each employee during the last payroll period, and the third has each employee's wage for the period. There is a one-to-one correspondence between lines in the employee and hours files. Thus, the hours worked by the *i*th employee in the employee file are recorded in the *i*th line of the hours file.

Analysis

Programs of this type are often accompanied by a ***data flow diagram*** that shows the flow of information into and out of the program. The inputs can come from the console, files, and other programs. Likewise outputs can go to the console, files, and other programs. In a complex application involving many programs, these diagrams are quite involved; however, that is not the case in the current situation (Figure 20-12). In accordance with the standard conventions for data flow diagrams, file names are sandwiched between parallel lines, and program names are placed in ellipses. Keyboard inputs and screen outputs are not enclosed in any manner. Arrows indicate the direction in which information flows—for instance, from a file into a program, or vice versa. Thus, Figure 20-12 indicates that there are two input files, **Employees** and **Hours**, and an output file for the payroll report. The program, called EmployeePayroll, obtains the actual file names from the console at run time.

FIGURE 20-12
Data flow diagram for the payroll program

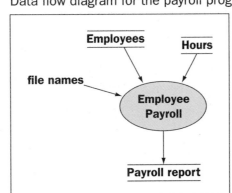

Before writing the program, we must agree on file formats. The text in each file is broken into lines, and the lines are formatted as follows:

Employee File

<last name> <first name> <number of dependents> <hourly rate>

Hours File

<last name> <first name> <regular hours> <overtime hours>

Payroll Report

<employee name> <dependents> <regular pay> <overtime pay> <gross pay> <tax> <net pay>

When the payroll report is printed, it needs to be highly readable. For this reason, we organize the names and numbers in formatted columns. Following are sample data that conform to the described file formats:

Employee File

```
Lambert Ken 7 5.50
Osborne Martin 3 6.75
```

Hours File

```
Lambert Ken 40 4
Osborne Martin 40 6
```

Report File

Employee Name	Dependents	Reg. Pay	O.T. Pay	Gross Pay	Tax	Net Pay
Lambert, Ken	7	220.00	33.00	253.00	2.53	250.47
Osborne, Martin	3	270.00	60.75	330.75	29.77	300.98

Notice that report file begins with explanatory column headers. Lesson 7 describes techniques for achieving the report's neat appearance.

There are a few remaining details to establish. Figure 20-13 shows the proposed interface for the program. An `Employee` class represents employees, and an `Employee` object is responsible for reading an employee's name and hours worked, computing his or her pay, and writing the results to the report file. Overtime hours are paid at 1.5 times the regular hourly rate. The base tax rate is 15 percent of the gross pay with a 2 percent deduction in the tax rate for each dependent. Net pay equals gross pay less tax.

FIGURE 20-13
Interface for the payroll program

Design

We use stream tokenizers for input and a print writer for output. The interface class, `EmployeePayroll`, follows the usual format. Following is pseudocode for the two principal methods:

```
buttonClicked
    Open a file input stream on the employee file
    Open a file input stream on the hours worked file
    Open a file output stream on the report file
    Call the method processFiles with the streams as parameters
    Close the files
processFiles
    Open a stream tokenizer on the employee file stream
    Open a stream tokenizer on the hours worked file stream
    Open a print writer on the report file stream
    Write the header to the report file
    While (a next line is read successfully from the employee file){
        If (a matching line is NOT read from the hours file){
            display an error message
            and break out of the loop
        }
        compute and print an employee's pay
    }
```

In the preceding method, the reading, calculating, and writing is done by methods in the Employee class. Following is a summary of the class:

```
Class:
   Employee extends Object
Private Class Constant:
   static final double TAX_RATE = 0.15
   static final double DEDUCTION = 0.02
Private Instance Variables:
   String firstName
   String lastName
   int dependents
   double hourlyRate
   int regularHours
   int overtimeHours
Public Methods:
   String toString()
   boolean readEmployee(StreamTokenizer stream)
   boolean readHoursWorked(StreamTokenizer stream)
   void computeAndPrintPay(PrintWriter stream)
   void printHeader(PrintWriter stream)
```

The method readEmployee attempts to read a line of data from the employee file and returns a Boolean indicating if it succeeded. Similarly, the method readHoursWorked attempts to read a line of data from the **hours** file. In addition, this method checks to see if the name read from the **hours** file matches the employee's name.

Implementation

Following is the code for the two classes:

```
/* EmployeePayroll.java
Create a payroll report file by reading an employee file and a
corresponding hours file.
*/

import javax.swing.*;
import BreezySwing.*;
import java.io.*;

public class EmployeePayroll extends GBFrame{

   //Window objects
   private JLabel employeeLabel, hoursLabel, reportLabel;
   private JTextField employeeField, hoursField, reportField;
   private JButton doReport;

   //Constructor
   public EmployeePayroll(){
      employeeLabel    = addLabel ("Employee file",1,1,1,1);
```

```
        employeeField = addTextField ("employee.txt" ,1,2,1,1);
        hoursLabel      = addLabel ("Hours file"     ,2,1,1,1);
        hoursField    = addTextField ("hours.txt"    ,2,2,1,1);
        reportLabel     = addLabel ("Report file"    ,3,1,1,1);
        reportField   = addTextField ("report.txt"   ,3,2,1,1);
        doReport         = addButton ("Compute Pay"   ,4,1,2,1);
        setTitle("Employee Payroll");
    }


    //Compute the payroll.
    public void buttonClicked (JButton buttonObj){

        //Read the names of the files
        String employeeFileName = employeeField.getText();
        String hoursFileName    = hoursField.getText();
        String reportFileName   = reportField.getText();

        //Open streams on the files, process the data, close the files.
        try{
            FileInputStream employeeFile = new FileInputStream
                                            (employeeFileName);
            FileInputStream hoursFile    = new FileInputStream(hoursFileName);
            FileOutputStream reportFile  = new FileOutputStream
                                            (reportFileName);
            processFiles(employeeFile, hoursFile, reportFile);
            employeeFile.close();
            hoursFile.close();
            reportFile.close();
        }catch (IOException e){
            messageBox("File not opened\n" + e.toString());
        }
    }


    //Process the files.
    private void processFiles(FileInputStream  employeeFile,
                              FileInputStream  hoursFile,
                              FileOutputStream reportFile){

        //Attach tokenizers to the input streams and a print writer to the
        //output stream.
        InputStreamReader employeeReader = new InputStreamReader
                                            (employeeFile);
        StreamTokenizer   employeeStream = new StreamTokenizer
                                            (employeeReader);
        InputStreamReader hoursReader  = new InputStreamReader(hoursFile);
        StreamTokenizer   hoursStream  = new StreamTokenizer(hoursReader);
        PrintWriter       reportStream = new PrintWriter(reportFile, true);

        //Write the column headers to the report file
        Employee employee = new Employee();
        employee.printHeader(reportStream);
```

```java
        //Process each line of the employee file
        while (employee.readEmployee(employeeStream)){

            //Read a corresponding line from the hours file
            if (!employee.readHoursWorked(hoursStream)){
                messageBox ("Matching data missing from the\n" +
                            "hours file for " + employee.getName());
                break;
            }

            //Compute and print an employee's pay
            employee.computeAndPrintPay(reportStream);
        }

        messageBox ("Processing completed");
    }

    public static void main (String[] args){
        EmployeePayroll tpo = new EmployeePayroll();
        tpo.setSize (300, 200);
        tpo.setVisible(true);
    }
}


/* Employee.java
 An employee knows how to
 1) read his name and basic payroll information from an employee file,
 2) read his hours worked from an hours file,
 3) write column headers to a report file, and
 4) compute and write the wages to the same report file.
*/

import java.io.*;
import BreezySwing.Format; //Import just the Format class from Breezy Swing

public class Employee extends Object{

    private static final double TAX_RATE  = 0.15; //Base tax rate
    private static final double DEDUCTION = 0.02; //Deduction per dependent
    private String firstName = "";                //First name
    private String lastName = "";                 //Last name
    private int    dependents;                    //Number of dependents
    private int    regularHours;                  //Regular hours worked
    private int    overtimeHours;                 //Overtime hours worked
    private double hourlyRate;                     //Hourly pay rate


    //Get the employee's name
    public String getName(){
        return firstName + " " + lastName;
    }
```

```java
            //Return a string representation of an employee.
            public String toString(){
               return lastName      + " "
                   + firstName      + " "
                   + hourlyRate     + " "
                   + dependents     + " "
                   + regularHours + " "
                   + overtimeHours;
            }

            //Read an employee's name, dependents, and pay rate.
            //Return true if the data are read successfully else return false.
            public boolean readEmployee(StreamTokenizer stream){
               try{
                  stream.nextToken();   lastName   = stream.sval;
                  stream.nextToken();   firstName  = stream.sval;
                  stream.nextToken();   dependents = (int) stream.nval;
                  stream.nextToken();   hourlyRate = stream.nval;
                  return (stream.ttype != StreamTokenizer.TT_EOF);
               }catch (Exception e){
                  return false;
               }
            }

            //Read an employee's name and hours.
            //Return true if data are read successfully else return false.
            //The name read from the file must match the employee's name.
            public boolean readHoursWorked(StreamTokenizer stream){
               String tempFirstName = "", tempLastName = "";
               try{
                  stream.nextToken();   tempLastName  = stream.sval;
                  stream.nextToken();   tempFirstName = stream.sval;
                  stream.nextToken();   regularHours  = (int) stream.nval;
                  stream.nextToken();   overtimeHours = (int) stream.nval;
                  if (stream.ttype == StreamTokenizer.TT_EOF)
                     return false;
                  return (tempLastName.equals(lastName) &&
                          tempFirstName.equals(firstName));
               }catch(Exception e){
                  return false;
               }
            }

            //Compute and print the employee's pay.
            //Net pay = gross pay - taxes.
            //Gross pay = hourly rate times regular hours + one and half the hourly
            //            rate for overtime hours.
            //The tax rate equals TAX_RATE less DEDUCTION per dependent.
            public void computeAndPrintPay(PrintWriter stream){
               double regPay = hourlyRate * regularHours;
               double overPay = hourlyRate * 1.5 * overtimeHours;
               double grossPay = regPay + overPay;
               double tax =
```

```
            Math.max (0, grossPay * (TAX_RATE - dependents * DEDUCTION));
        double netPay = grossPay - tax;
        stream.println(
            Format.justify('l', lastName + ", " + firstName, 15)
          + Format.justify('r', dependents            , 12)
          + Format.justify('r', regPay                 , 10, 2)
          + Format.justify('r', overPay                , 10, 2)
          + Format.justify('r', grossPay               , 11, 2)
          + Format.justify('r', tax                    ,  7, 2)
          + Format.justify('r', netPay                 ,  9, 2));
    }

    //Write column headers to the report file.
    public void printHeader(PrintWriter stream){
        stream.println(
            Format.justify('l', "Employee Name", 15)
          + Format.justify('r', "Dependents"   , 12)
          + Format.justify('r', "Reg. Pay"    , 10)
          + Format.justify('r', "O.T. Pay"    , 10)
          + Format.justify('r', "Gross Pay"   , 11)
          + Format.justify('r', "Tax"         ,  7)
          + Format.justify('r', "Net Pay"     ,  9));
        stream.println(
            Format.justify('l', "---------", 15)
          + Format.justify('r', "------"   , 12)
          + Format.justify('r', "-----"    , 10)
          + Format.justify('r', "-----"    , 10)
          + Format.justify('r', "------"   , 11)
          + Format.justify('r', "--"       ,  7)
          + Format.justify('r', "------"   ,  9));
    }
}
```

20.4 Other Input/Output Situations

We have now covered the basics of file I/O, but there are several other common situations to discuss.

Data Input and Output Streams

When print and println methods write a number to a PrintWriter, they transform the number to its humanly readable character string representations. If the number needs to be read later by another program, the string representing the number is first read and then converted back to the appropriate numeric data type. Data input and output streams avoid the need for conversion. A primitive type or string written to a DataOutputStream

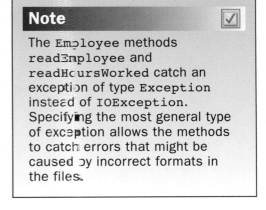

Note ☑

The Employee methods readEmployee and readHoursWorked catch an exception of type Exception instead of IOException. Specifying the most general type of exception allows the methods to catch errors that might be caused by incorrect formats in the files.

is represented in binary format that is not humanly readable, but which can be read back into a program using a `DataInputStream` without conversion. Table 20-3 lists several useful methods in these two classes.

TABLE 20-3

Methods in the classes `DataInputStream` and `DataOutputStream`

METHOD	WHAT IT DOES
`char readChar()`	Reads a char from a `DataInputStream`
`double readDouble()`	Reads a double from a `DataInputStream`
`int readInt()`	Reads an int from a `DataInputStream`
`String readUTF()`	Reads a `String` from a `DataInputStream`
`void writeChar (char ch)`	Writes a char to a `DataOutputStream`
`void writeDouble (double d)`	Writes a double to a `DataOutputStream`
`void writeInt (int i)`	Writes an int to a `DataOutputStream`
`void writeUTF (String s)`	Writes a `String` to a `DataOutputStream`

A program reading from a data input stream must know the order and types of data expected at each moment. To illustrate, we present a sample program that

- Generates a user-specified number of random integers (the number is entered as a parameter in the command line)

- Writes these integers to a data output stream

- Reads them back in from a data input stream

- Outputs the integers to the terminal window

```
/* TestDataStreams.java
1) Write randomly generated integers to a data output stream. A command
line parameter specifies the number of integers to generate.
2) Read them back in using a data input stream and display them in
   the terminal window.
*/

import java.io.*;

public class TestDataStreams{

   public static void main (String[] args){

      //Obtain the number of ints from the command line parameters.
      int number = Integer.valueOf(args[0]).intValue();

      //Generate random ints and write them to a data output stream.
      try{
         FileOutputStream foStream = new FileOutputStream("ints.dat");
```

```
        DataOutputStream doStream = new DataOutputStream(foStream);
        int i;
        for (i = 0; i < number; i++)
            doStream.writeInt((int) (Math.random() * number + 1));
        doStream.close();
    }catch(IOException e){
        System.err.println("Error during output: " + e.toString());
    }

    //Read the ints from a data input stream and display them in
    //a terminal window.
    try{
        FileInputStream fiStream = new FileInputStream("ints.dat");
        DataInputStream diStream = new DataInputStream(fiStream);
        while (true){
            int i = diStream.readInt();
            System.out.println(i);
        }
    }catch(EOFException e){
        System.out.println("\nAll done.");
    }catch(IOException e){
        System.err.println("Error in input" + e.toString());
    }
  }
}
```

A data input stream is processed within an *exception-driven loop*. Using the expression while (true), the loop continues until an EOFException occurs. This exception is not viewed as an error but rather as a good reason to exit the loop. The catch statement in this example prints a reassuring message.

Now that we have seen two different ways to handle file input and output, it is natural to ask when to use each one. Here are two rules of thumb:

1. It is appropriate to use a print writer for output and a stream tokenizer for input when the file must be viewed or created with a text editor or when the order and types of data are unknown.

2. It is appropriate to use a data input stream for input and a data output stream for output when the file need not be viewed or created with a text editor and when the order and types of data are known.

Serialization and Object Streams

Until now we have focused on reading and writing primitive data types and strings. Java also provides methods for reading and writing complete objects. This makes it easy to save a program's state before closing it and to restore the state when the program is run again. Objects that are saved between executions of a program are said to be *persistent*, and the process of writing them to and reading them from a file is called *serialization*. To use serialization, a programmer must do two things:

1. Make classes serializable. (We will explain how this is done momentarily.)

2. Write objects using an ObjectOutputStream and read them later using an ObjectInputStream.

For example, consider the second version of the student test scores program in Lesson 8. This program was written using a model/view pattern in which the model encapsulates the program's data requirements and the view manages the user interface. The data model in turn consists of the two classes Student and StudentTestScoresModel. To serialize these classes, we import the package java.io and add the qualifier implements Serializable to each class's definition. The changes are shown in blue type in the following code:

```
import java.io.*;

public class StudentTestScoresModel implements Serializable{

    // Instance variables
    private Student[] students = new Student[10];
    private int       indexSelectedStudent;
    private int       studentCount;

    . . .

}
```

```
import java.io.*;

public class Student implements Serializable{

    // Instance variables
    private String name;
    private int[] tests = new int[NUM_TESTS];

    . . .

}
```

The interface for the program declares an object called model that is of type StudentTestScoresModel. Saving and restoring the program's data involves nothing more than serializing this single object, which we do in the methods saveModel and loadModel. These methods are activated when the user selects the menu options **File/Save** and **File/Open**, respectively. The additions to the view are shown in blue type in the following code:

```
import java.io.*;
import javax.swing.*;
import BreezySwing.*;

public class StudentTestScoresView extends GBFrame{
    . . .

    private JMenuItem saveModelMI, loadModelMI;
    . . .
    private StudentTestScoresModel model;
    . . .
```

```
    public StudentTestScoresView(){
        saveModelMI = addMenuItem ("File","Save");
        loadModelMI = addMenuItem ("File","Open");

        . . .
    }

    public void menuItemSelected (JMenuItem menuItemObj){
        . . .
        else if (menuItemObj == saveModelMI)
            saveModel();
        else if (menuItemObj == loadModelMI)
            loadModel();
        . . .
    }

    . . .


    private void saveModel(){
        String outputFileName;
        . . . use a file dialog to ask the user for the name
            of the output file as explained soon . . .
        try{
            FileOutputStream foStream = new FileOutputStream (outputFileName);
            ObjectOutputStream ooStream = new ObjectOutputStream (foStream);
            ooStream.writeObject (model);
            foStream.flush();
            foStream.close();
        }catch (IOException e){
            messageBox ("Error during output: " + e.toString());
        }
    }

    private void loadModel(){
        String inputFileName;
        . . . use a file dialog to ask the user for the name
            of the input file as explained soon . . .
        try{
            FileInputStream fiStream = new FileInputStream (inputFileName);
            ObjectInputStream oiStream = new ObjectInputStream (fiStream);
            model = (StudentTestScoresModel) oiStream.readObject();
            fiStream.close();
        }catch (Exception e){
            messageBox ("Error during input: " + e.toString());
        }
    }

    . . .

}
```

In this code, the method `writeObject` outputs the `model` object to the object output stream, which in turn triggers automatic serialization of the array of students and each individual student in the array. Likewise, the method `readObject` inputs the `model` object and all its constituent parts from the object input stream. Note that

■ The method `readObject` returns an `Object`, which is cast to a `StudentTestScoresModel` before it is stored in the variable.

■ The methods `readObject` and `writeObject` can throw several different types of exceptions. To catch all of these in a single `catch` clause, we use the generic `Exception` object as a parameter.

The methods `readObject` and `writeObject` can be used with objects of any type, such as strings, arrays, or user-defined objects. When reading an object, the programmer must be aware of its type and its position in the input stream and must cast and store it in the appropriate type of variable. As you can see, object streams and serialization are powerful and convenient tools for managing persistence.

Terminal Input and Output

We are finally in a position to explain previously hidden details involved in terminal I/O. The stream object `System.out` is an instance of the class `PrintStream`. Another instance of this class, `System.err`, is used to display error messages in a terminal window (which, by default, is the same as the terminal window used by `System.out`). The stream object `System.in` is an instance of the class `InputStream` and is used to read input from the keyboard. The two output streams understand the easy-to-use `print` and `println` methods; however, using the terminal input stream is quite complicated and usually involves the following steps:

1. Open an `InputStreamReader` on the object `System.in`.

2. Open a `BufferedReader` on the resulting input stream reader.

3. Use the method `readLine()` to read a line of text (a `string`) from the buffered reader.

4. Convert this string to a primitive data type as appropriate.

The following program uses the three terminal streams in a brief interaction with the user:

```
/* TestTerminal.java
A simple demonstration of terminal I/O.
*/

import java.io.*;

public class TestTerminal{

    public static void main (String[] args){
        String name;
        int age;
        double weight;

        while (true){
            try{
                //Instantiate a buffered reader on System.in
                InputStreamReader reader = new InputStreamReader(System.in);
                BufferedReader buffer = new BufferedReader(reader);
```

```
                    //Prompt the user for a name.
                    //Read the name and save it in a string variable.
                    System.out.print("\nEnter your name or \"quit\": ");
                    name = buffer.readLine();

                    //Break if name equals "quit"
                    if (name.equals ("quit")) break;

                    //Prompt the user for an age.
                    //Read the age as a string, convert it to an integer, and
                    //store it in an int variable.
                    System.out.print("Enter your age: ");
                    age = (Integer.valueOf(buffer.readLine())).intValue();

                    //Prompt the user for a weight.
                    //Read the weight as a string, convert it to a double,
                    //and store it in a double variable.
                    System.out.print("Enter your weight: ");
                    weight = (Double.valueOf(buffer.readLine())).doubleValue();

                    //Output the results
                    if (age <= 15)
                        System.err.println
                        ("Sorry: use of this program is restricted to those over 15!
                        ");
                    else
                        System.out.println
                        (name + ", age " + age + ", weight " + weight);

                }catch(Exception e){

                    //Flag input errors
                    System.err.println("Input error -- " + e.toString());

                }
            }

        System.out.println("Done");
    }
}
```

A sample session with this program is shown in Figure 20-14.

FIGURE 20-14
A sample session with the `TestTerminal` program

From this example, we get a fair indication of the coding needed to support the `KeyboardReader` class.

File Dialogs

Until now in this lesson, file names have been hard coded into the programs or have been entered into a text field. Problems can arise if the specified file does not exist or if the user cannot remember a file's name. These problems are avoided if a file dialog is used. The user can then browse through the computer's directory structure to find a desired file name or can back out by canceling the dialog. Figure 20-15 shows a typical file dialog as supported by Swing's `JFileChooser` class. Table 20-4 lists important `JFileChooser` methods.

FIGURE 20-15
A typical file dialog

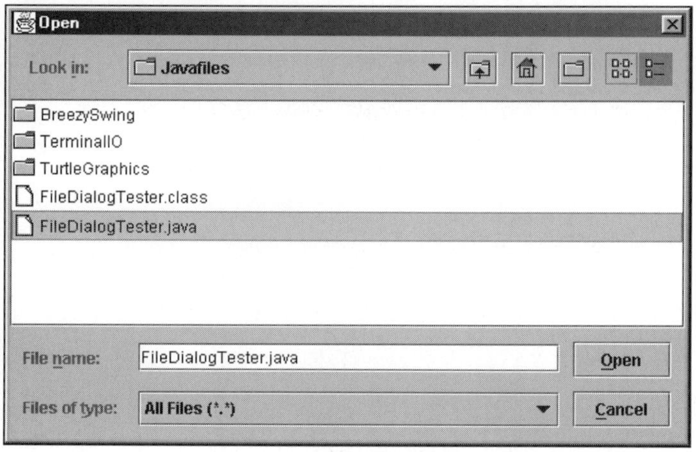

TABLE 20-4
Important `JFileChooser` methods

METHOD	WHAT IT DOES
`JFileChooser()`	Constructor that creates a file dialog that is attached to the user's home directory
`JFileChooser(String directoryPathName)`	Constructor that creates a file dialog that is attached to the specified directory
`int showOpenDialog(JFrame parent)`	Opens a file dialog for an input file and returns the JFileChooser constant APPROVE_OPTION if the user has selected a file or the constant or CANCEL_OPTION if the user has canceled
`int showSaveDialog(JFrame parent)`	Opens a file dialog for an output file and returns the JFileChooser constant APPROVE_OPTION if the user has selected a file or the constant or CANCEL_OPTION if the user has canceled
`File getSelectedFile()`	Returns the selected file

The following code segment displays a file dialog for an input file. After the dialog closes, the code displays the file name if the user did not cancel the dialog; otherwise, the code displays a message saying the dialog was canceled. At instantiation, the dialog is attached to the directory **c:\Javafiles** (on a PC). The parent frame passed to the method `showOpenDialog` is the variable `this`, which refers to the application's view class.

```
JFileChooser chooser = new JFileChooser("c:\\Javafiles");
int result = chooser.showOpenDialog(this);
if (result = JFileChooser.CANCEL_OPTION)
   messageBox ("The dialog was cancelled.");
else
   try{
       File file = chooser.getSelectedFile();
       messageBox ("File name: " + file.getName());
   }catch(Exception e){
       messageBox("Error opening input file " + e.toString());
   }
```

As usual, we must use a `try-catch` statement when opening a file. Following is a segment that combines opening the file and processing its data:

```
JFileChooser chooser = new JFileChooser("c:\\Javafiles");
int result = chooser.showOpenDialog(this);
if (result == JFileChooser.APPROVE_OPTION)
   try{
       File file = chooser.getSelectedFile();
       FileInputStream stream = new FileInputStream (file);
       processData (stream);
       stream.close();
```

```
}catch (IOException e){
    messageBox ("Error opening input file " + e.toString());
}
```

Programming Skills

PROGRAMMING LANGUAGE TRANSLATION

Each time you compile and run a program many software tools come into play. Two programs in particular, a compiler and a run-time interpreter, play the most significant roles.

The compiler's primary task is to translate the expressions in a source program to a form that can be evaluated by the run-time interpreter. A compiler for a full-blown programming language must analyze many different kinds of expressions (loops, conditionals, assignments, function calls, declarations, etc.) and report specific syntax errors to the programmer.

In addition to a large variety of expressions, a compiler must deal with a complex vocabulary and must be capable of generating target expressions that will execute efficiently at run time. A compiler delegates the task of recognizing words in the source program to a module called the *scanner*, and it delegates the task of generating efficient object code to a module called the *code generator*. The work of syntax analysis and error checking falls to a module called the *parser*. Most parsers make use of a table of syntax rules and a pushdown stack to handle backtracking during the processing of expressions.

Most of the real work in compiler design now focuses on the so-called "back end" or code generator. Aside from the task of producing the most efficient code (code that is not only fast but also small), designers face the challenge of generating code for multiple hardware platforms. As you know, a Java compiler generates platform-independent code called *byte code*. Each major hardware platform is then responsible for providing an interpreter that understands byte code.

When the executable program is in the machine language of the computer, the computer executes the program's instructions directly; when the executable program is in an intermediate language, such as byte code, the interpreter must decode the program's instructions and invoke the appropriate machine operations. Most interpreters access a program's data in an area of memory called a *run-time stack*. This stack is also used to store intermediate values of expressions and data belonging to function calls that are currently being evaluated.

Two other software tools that enable compiled programs to be executed are a linker and a loader. The linker combines the code from different modules, such as libraries, into a single executable program. This work usually includes verifying that the functions called in one module have unique definitions in the system. After successful linkage, the loader prepares the run-time system for execution by formatting memory into segments for the program's instructions and for the run-time stack.

Recent advances in programming language translation have led to advances in hardware design. For example, the design of a reduced instruction set chip (RISC) for microprocessors was made possible by new methods of compiler optimization. Thus, programming language translation is an important area of computer science and will become a focus of study as you proceed through upper-level computer science courses.

EXERCISE 20.4

1. When would you use data output and input streams instead of text-based streams?

2. What is serialization? Describe situations that call for serialization.

3. Under what circumstances would serialization be a poor choice?

4. Describe the steps required to create a stream for terminal input.

SUMMARY

In this lesson, you learned:

■ File stream objects for the input and output of data can be opened by instantiating the appropriate classes from the `java.io` package.

■ Input operations exist to read individual characters, lines, or words from text files. Output operations exist to write data of any primitive type or strings to text files.

■ Exceptions can occur when opening a file stream for input or output and when reading from an input file stream. The programmer must catch these exceptions.

■ Data input and output streams allow the programmer to transfer data of specific types, such as primitive types and strings, to and from files.

■ Serialization allows the programmer to transfer object models to or from disk without worrying about conversions to text format.

■ Terminal I/O uses many of the same classes and methods as file I/O.

■ File dialogs provide a means of browsing directories for files.

VOCABULARY *Review*

Define the following terms:

buffer	input stream	sequential access
data flow diagram	output stream	serialization
exception-driven loop	random access	text files
flushing		

REVIEW *Questions*

FILL IN THE BLANK

Complete the following sentences by writing the correct word or words in the blanks provided.

1. The classes used to create connections to files on disk are _____ for input and _____ for output.

2. A Java file stores data as a sequence of _____.

3. The class used to read strings one line at a time from a text file is called _____.

4. The class used to read strings or floating-point numbers one token at a time from a text file is called _____.

5. The class used to output data to a text file using the print message is called _____.

6. File input operations require the programmer to catch a(n) _____.

7. _____ allows the programmer to transfer objects to and from files.

8. The classes _____ and _____ allow the programmer to transfer different types of data to and from non-text files.

9. A(n) _____ is a window that allows users to select an input or output file with a mouse.

10. The type of loop used with data input streams is called a(n) _____ loop.

PROJECTS

PROJECT 20-1

Write a program that reads names from a text file. The names are separated by newline characters, are in sorted order, and some are duplicate names. The program should write the names to a different text file without the duplicate names. Allow the user to specify the file names in text fields.

PROJECT 20-2

A text file contains a list of salespersons and their total annual sales amounts. Each line of the file contains one person's last name, followed by a blank space, followed by a floating-point number. Write a program that reads the data from such a file, sorts them according to name (ascending order) and then according to sales amount (descending order), and outputs the results of the sorts to two different text files. Allow the user to specify the file names in text fields.

PROJECT 20-3

Merging the contents of two files is a common operation. Write a program that reads words from two text files. You may assume that the words in each input file are sorted in ascending order. Write all of these words to a third file so that the contents of this file also are sorted in ascending order.

PROJECT 20-4

Add a command to the program in Project 20-3 that concatenates two files. This operation should place the results in a third file.

PROJECT 20-5

Assume that a text file of names has each name on a separate line and that the names are in random order. Write a program that inputs the names, sorts them, and writes them back to the same file.

PROJECT 20-6

Add a **File** menu to the shape drawing program from Project 19-8. The menu should have the options **New, Open,** and **Save**. When the user selects **New**, the drawing area is cleared and a new data model is created. When the user selects **Open**, the program clears the drawing area, reads the data model from a file, and updates the view. When the user selects **Save**, the program writes the data model to a file. *Hint*: Use object serialization and file dialogs to solve this problem.

CRITICAL *Thinking*

Compare the costs and benefits of using text files and object serialization for maintaining data on secondary storage.

INTRODUCTION TO HTML AND APPLETS

21.1 Hypertext, Hypermedia, and the World Wide Web

In 1945, Vannevar Bush, a scientist at MIT, published a prophetic essay, "As We May Think," in the *Atlantic Monthly*. According to Bush, although computers were already wonderful for number crunching, they would soon be used for data storage, data manipulation, and logical reasoning. These predictions came to pass in the 1950s and 1960s, with the advent of such branches of computer science as database management and artificial intelligence.

Bush also raised and attempted to answer the following question: How could we improve the way in which we consult our information sources during research? The traditional researcher used indexing schemes, such as card catalogs, but this method restricts the user to a linear or binary search. By contrast, the human mind uses association to search its own memory bank. For example, when I hear the word "wife," I instantly think of a particular person, namely, my own wife. My mind does not go through a complex search process to retrieve the associated information. Somehow, it just gets it.

Bush proposed to use computer technology to link chunks of information associatively. The keyed list or map structure that we discussed in Lesson 15 uses associative indexing. Now imagine that the entries in such a table also contain embedded links to other entries in other tables. Bush called his imaginary machine a *memex*. Each individual would have a desktop memex, as a virtual extension of his or her memory. The memex would receive chunks of information from a photocopy machine, a keyboard, or a stylus. The information would be stored on microfilm. The user would establish links between chunks of information by means of a few simple keystrokes.

The computer would maintain these *associative links* and also traces of the user's explorations of them. The user could come back to that trail or give it to another user to link into a more general trail. Research would involve following the trails blazed by the masters, not just the examination of their end products.

Hypertext and Hypermedia

By the late 1960s, the technology for realizing Bush's dream became available. In 1967, Theodor Holm Nelson coined the term *hypertext* to refer to Bush's machine. A hypertext is a structure consisting of nodes and the links between them. Each node is a document or chunk of text. Normally, links to other nodes are displayed to the user as embedded, highlighted terms within a given chunk of text. The user moves to a node by using an arrow key or mouse to select an associated term.

Early hypertext systems were

- Douglas Englebart's NLS/Augment (1968)
- Cognetics Corporation's Hyperties (mid-1980s)

In 1987, Apple Computer released Hypercard, one of the first hypermedia platforms. *Hypermedia* is like hypertext, but adds

- GUIs
- Images
- Sound
- Animation
- Applications

For example, a link might appear as an icon or image rather than as highlighted text. The targeted chunk of information might be a full-screen image, a movie, a musical recording, or a computer application, such as a database program.

Networks and the World Wide Web

All of the early hypertext systems ran on separate stand-alone machines, which maintained data storage for the individual user. With the development of the Internet, people began to think of sharing hypertext across a network of communicating machines. Chunks of information, or pages as they are now called, could be stored on many different physical machines around the world. Each page would be linked in a gigantic hypermedia system, the World Wide Web. The Web is now a reality, taken for granted by millions of users.

The Web consists of two kinds of machines:

- Servers, on which pages of information reside
- Clients, which run browsers to access information on the servers

In some cases the client and server reside on the same machine.

When you open a browser, you are presented with an initial page of information. Embedded in this page are links to other nodes. When you select a link, the following sequence occurs:

- The browser sends a message to the node's machine, requesting a transfer of its information.
- If the request is successful, the information at the node is downloaded to the user's browser.

Because there are different types of computers, a networked hypermedia system requires a uniform means of:

- Representing information using a machine-independent hypertext markup language
- Assigning node addresses using machine-independent uniform resource locators (URLs)
- Transmitting information from site to site using machine-independent network transmission protocols
- Displaying information with browsers from different vendors, subject to the restriction that all the browsers behave in a similar manner

EXERCISE 21.1

1. Describe the basic ideas underlying hypertext.

2. What is the difference between hypertext and hypermedia?

3. What is a URL?

21.2 Overview of the Hypertext Markup Language

The **hypertext markup language** (HTML) was developed as a machine-independent way of representing information in a networked-based hypermedia system. Early word processing systems such as WordStar bracketed text with codes that specified print formats. For example, the code ^I (control I) indicated italics and ^B indicated bold. To illustrate, the text

```
Bush, Vannevar, ^BAs We May Think^B, ^IAtlantic Monthly^I, July, 1945.
```

would have been printed as

```
Bush, Vannevar, As We May Think, Atlantic Monthly, July, 1945.
```

HTML uses a similar scheme. Codes, called *markup tags*, can indicate the format of textual elements or links to other nodes. Browsers interpret these codes as commands and display the text in the desired format. Figure 21-1 shows the relationship between authors and users of HTML documents.

FIGURE 21-1
The Internet

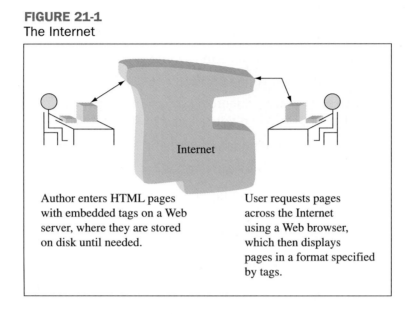

Author enters HTML pages with embedded tags on a Web server, where they are stored on disk until needed.

User requests pages across the Internet using a Web browser, which then displays pages in a format specified by tags.

A Short Example

As a first example of using HTML, we will show you how to create the Web page shown in Figure 21-2.

FIGURE 21-2
A simple Web page

The page includes markup tags for

- A title
- A heading
- Two paragraphs of text

The author of the page had to write an HTML document that looks like this:

```
<html>
<head>
<TITLE>A Short HTML Document</TITLE>
</head>
<body>
<H1>This is a first heading</H1>
<P>You probably thought that Java applications were fun. Wait until
you get going with HTML and applets!</P>
<P>You will learn to write simple Web pages as platforms
for launching Java programs.</P>
</body>
</html>
```

When a browser displays the document, the title appears at the top of the browser's window.

There is a blank line between the heading and the first paragraph and between the two paragraphs. The browser uses word wrap to fit the text within the window's boundaries. A typical HTML document consists of multiple HTML pages.

The document must be stored in a file having the extension .**html** on a UNIX system and .**htm** on a Windows system. Pages can be any size, from a few lines to many hundreds of lines. We now turn to a discussion of the tags that define the HTML protocol

Markup Tags

A markup tag in HTML begins with a left angle bracket (<) and ends with a right angle bracket (>), for example, <title>. Tags are not case sensitive For instance, the tags <title>, <TITLE>, and< TiTlE> are equivalent, though not equally readable. Tags usually occur in pairs, for example, <title> and </title>. The start tag tells the browser where to begin the format, and the end tag, which includes a slash (/), tells the browser where to end the format.

Tags can include attributes. For example, the tag <P ALIGN=CENTER> tells the browser to align the next paragraph in the center of the window. In this example, ALIGN is the attribute's name and CENTER is the attribute's value. Some commonly used markup tags are listed in Table 21-1.

TABLE 21-1
Basic HTML markup tags

MARKUP TAG	WHAT IT DOES
HTML	Designates an HTML document.
HEAD	Designates the head of the document.
BODY	Designates the contents of the document.
TITLE	Designates the title that appears in the browser's window.
P	Designates a paragraph of text.
H1, H2, etc.	Designates a heading. There are six levels of headings.
PRE	Designates text to be formatted literally.
BR	Indicates a line break.
UL	Designates a bulleted list.
OL	Designates a numbered list.
LI	Indicates an item within a list.

Minimal Document Structure

Every HTML document should have the following minimal structure:

```
<HTML>
<HEAD>
<TITLE> the title goes here </TITLE>
</HEAD>
<BODY>
the text for the document goes here
</BODY>
</HTML>
```

Note the following points:

- The HTML tag informs the browser that it is dealing with an HTML document.

- The HEAD tag identifies the first part of the document.

- The TITLE tag identifies the document's title. The title is displayed at the top of the browser's window and is used during searches for the document. The title is also displayed in bookmark lists (a list of the user's favorite links). We recommend short descriptive titles.

Hot Tip

The markup tags for lists can easily be remembered if you note that "UL" stands for "Unordered List," "OL" stands for "Ordered List" (i.e., 1, 2, 3, etc.), and "LI" stands for "List Item."

■ The BODY tags enclose the information provided by the HTML document.

■ The browser ignores extra white space, such as blank lines and tab characters.

Commenting an HTML Document

Authors often add comments to HTML documents. The browser does not interpret comments or show them to the reader. The form of a comment is

```
<!-- text of comment -->
```

In the following example, we have modified the first example by inserting blank lines and comments to make it more readable. However, a browser will display this page exactly as before.

```
<html>
<!-- Authors: Kenneth A. Lambert and Martin Osborne
     Last update: November 30, 2000                -->

<head>
<TITLE>A Short HTML Document</TITLE>
</head>

<body>
<H1>This is a first heading</H1>

<P>You probably thought that Java applications were fun. Wait until
you get going with HTML and applets!</P>

<P>You will learn to write simple Web pages as platforms
for launching Java programs.</P>

</body>
</html>
```

EXERCISE 21.2

1. What does HTML stand for?

2. What is the purpose of HTML tags?

3. Write an HTML code segment that shows the minimal HTML document structure for a Web page.

4. What is an HTML comment? Give an example.

21.3 Simple Text Elements

There are several basic elements for formatting text in a Web page.

Headings

HTML provides six levels of document headings, numbered H1 through H6. The form of a heading is

```
<Hnumber>Text of heading</Hnumber>
```

Headings are displayed in a different font size and style from normal text. The browser inserts a blank line after each heading.

Paragraphs

The end tag </P> may be omitted. The browser then ends the paragraph at the beginning of the next paragraph or heading tag. The browser uses word wrap to fit a paragraph within the borders of the browser's window. Most browsers insert a blank line after the end of each paragraph; however, they ignore blank lines within a paragraph.

The browser recognizes the following alignment attributes:

- LEFT (the default)

- RIGHT

- CENTER

This next example uses headings of several sizes and paragraphs with different alignments:

```
<H1>The first level heading</H1>
<P ALIGN=RIGHT>The first paragraph.</P>
<H2>The second level heading</H2>
<P ALIGN=CENTER>The second paragraph.</P>
<H3>The third level heading</H3>
<P>The third paragraph.</P>
```

The results of this example are shown in Figure 21-3.

FIGURE 21-3
Headings and paragraphs coded with HTML

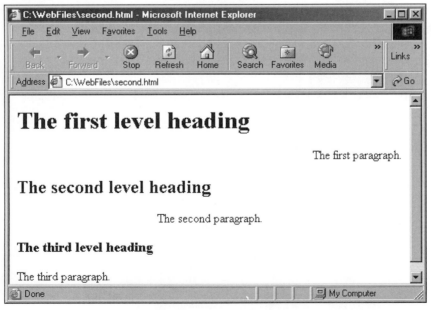

Forced Line Breaks

Occasionally, a Web page author or designer wants to display several lines of text without word wrap. The line break tag, <BR>, is used for this purpose. For example, the following HTML segment would display an address:

```
Department of Computer Science<BR>
Washington and Lee University<BR>
Lexington, VA 24450<BR>
```

Because a line break tag tells the browser where to break a line, no other end tag is required.

Preformatted Text

Suppose you want the browser to display text "as is," with line breaks, extra spaces, and tabs. The <PRE> tag accomplishes this. For example, the following HTML segment displays some Java program code with the indicated indentation and line breaks:

```
<PRE>
   public static void main (String[] args){
      Frame frm = new FahrenheitToCentigrade();
      frm.setSize (200, 150);
      frm.setVisible (true);
   }
</PRE>
```

In general, you should not use other markup tags within a chunk of preformatted text.

*E*XERCISE 21.3

1. When does the HTML programmer need to use forced line breaks?

2. When do we use preformatted text in an HTML document?

3. Write an HTML code segment that shows a level 1 heading and a level 2 heading.

21.4 Character-Level Formatting

In addition to the format of headings and paragraphs, HTML provides some control over the format of characters. Table 21-2 lists some of the commonly used tags and their effects:

TABLE 21-2
Some character format tags

MARKUP TAG	WHAT IT DOES	EXAMPLE HTML	DISPLAYED TEXT
EM	Emphasis, usually italics	<EM>Italics</EM>, for emphasis	*Italics*, for emphasis
STRONG	Strong emphasis, usually bold	<STRONG>Bold</STRONG>, for more emphasis	**Bold**, for more emphasis
CITE	Used for titles of books, etc., usually italics	Plato's <CITE>Republic</CITE>	Plato's *Republic*
B	Bold text	<B>Bold</B> text	**Bold** text
I	Italic text	<I>Italic</I> text	*Italic* text
TT	Typewriter text, a fixed-width font	<TT>Typewriter</TT> text	`Typewriter` text

Escape Sequences

HTML treats <, >, and & as special characters. For example, the characters < and > are treated as the delimiters of an HTML tag. If you want the browser to display these characters rather than interpret them, you must use the escape sequences listed in Table 21-3.

Hot Tip

The escape sequences for < and > are easy to remember if you remember that "lt" stands for "less than" and "gt" stands for "greater than".

TABLE 21-3
Some escape sequences

CHARACTER SEQUENCE	ESCAPE	EXAMPLE HTML	DISPLAYED TEXT
<	&lt;	The character < begins an HTML markup tag.	The character < begins an HTML markup tag.
>	&gt;	The character > ends an HTML . markup tag.	The character > ends an HTML markup tag
&	&amp;	& is an ampersand.	& is an ampersand.

*E*XERCISE 21.4

1. What happens if you forget to close the markup tag for italic on a piece of text?

2. What is the purpose of the escape sequences in HTML? Give an example.

21.5 Lists

There are three kinds of lists that can be displayed in a Web page:

- Unordered (bulleted) lists—tag UL
- Numbered (ordered) lists—tag OL
- Definition (association) lists—tag DL

For bulleted and numbered lists, you perform the following steps:

1. Start with the desired list tag (UL or OL).
2. For each item, enter the LI (list item) tag followed by the text of the item. No closing tags are needed for the items.
3. End with the desired list tag.

An Unordered List Example

The next HTML segment displays a bulleted list of courses that one of the authors taught last year.

```
<UL>
<LI>Fundamentals of Data Structures
<LI>Programming Language Design
<LI>Operating Systems
<LI>Artificial Intelligence
</UL>
```

Figure 21-4 shows the page resulting from this HTML segment.

FIGURE 21-4
An unnumbered list

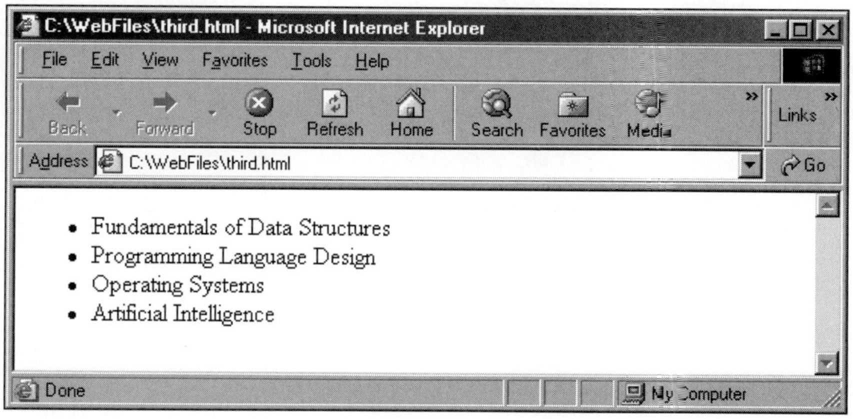

A Definition List Example

A *definition list* displays terms and their associated definitions. Several tags are used with these lists:

■ The tag <DL> begins the definition list and ends it.

■ The tag <DT> precedes each term in a definition list.

■ The tag <DD> precedes each definition in a definition list.

The following example uses a definition list to add course numbers to the course list.

```
<DL>

<DT>CSCI111
<DD>Fundamentals of Data Structures

<DT>CSCI312
<DD>Programming Language Design

<DT>CSCI330
<DD>Operating Systems

<DT>CSCI315
<DD>Artificial Intelligence

</DL>
```

Figure 21-5 shows the page resulting from this HTML segment.

FIGURE 21-5
A definition list

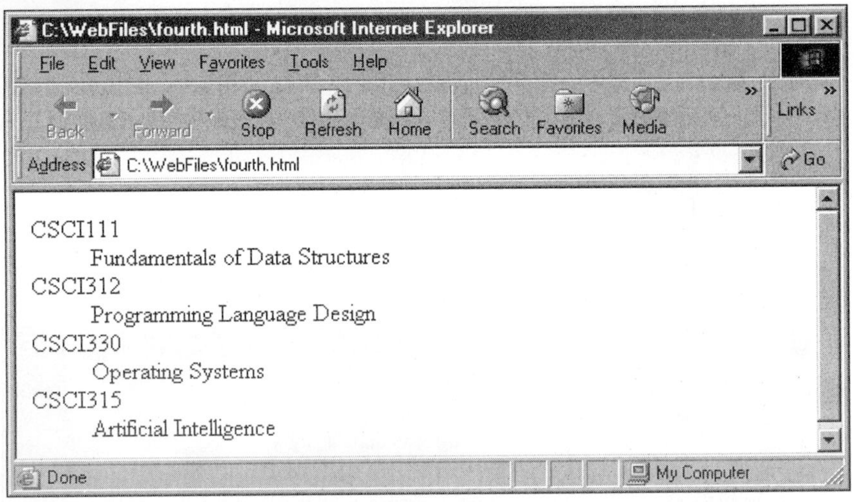

A Nested List Example

Lists can be nested within other lists to any depth, but more than three levels deep can be difficult to read. The following HTML segment nests a numbered list within an unordered one:

```
<UL>
<LI>Fundamentals of Data Structures

<!--The nested, numbered list begins here. -->
<OL>
<LI>Analysis of algorithms
<LI>Collections
<LI>Linked lists
<LI>Stacks
<LI>Queues
<LI>Recursion
<LI>Binary search trees
</OL>
<!--The nested list ends here. -->

<LI>Programming Language Design
<LI>Operating Systems
<LI>Artificial Intelligence
</UL>
```

Figure 21-6 shows the page resulting from this HTML segment.

FIGURE 21-6
A nested list

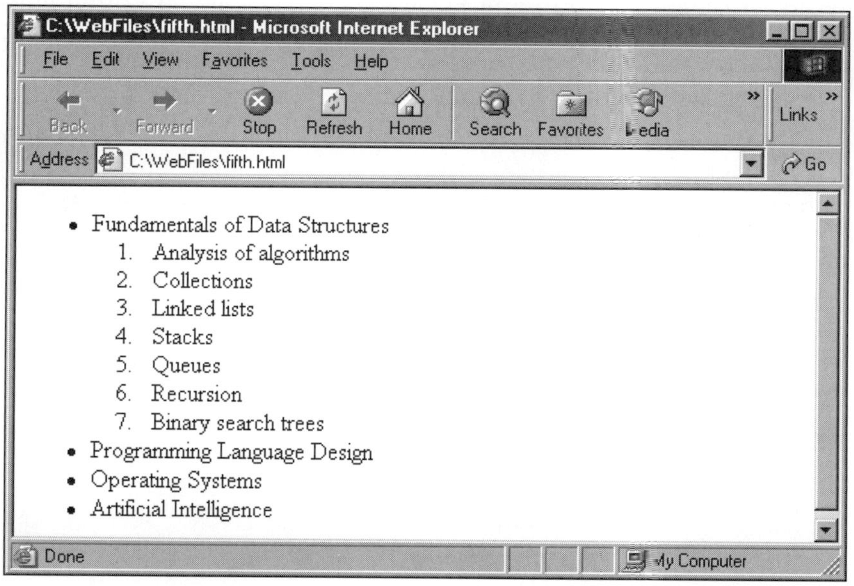

EXERCISE 21.5

1. List three types of HTML lists and describe their characteristics.

2. Write an HTML code segment that uses a list to display the names of your grandparents and your parents. The list should be organized to show the relationships clearly.

21.6 Linking to Other Documents

Links, also called *hyperlinks* or hypertext references, allow readers to move to other pages in the Web. The markup tag for a link is <A>, which stands for anchor. Placing a link in an HTML document involves the following steps:

1. Identify the target document that will be at the other end of the link. This identifier should be a path name or a URL (see the discussion in the following subsections).

2. Determine the text that labels the link in the browser.

3. Place this information within an anchor, using the following format:

```
<A HREF=target document identifier>text of link</A>
```

For example, the next HTML anchor sets up a link to the file **courses.html** and labels the link "courses last year":

```
<A HREF="courses.html">courses last year</A>
```

Links or anchors can appear within any HTML element. They are often embedded as items in a list or as terms in a paragraph. For example, the following segment displays a link to the file **courses.html** in a sentence that mentions the author's courses:

```
<P>
My <A HREF="courses.html">courses last year</A> were Fundamentals of Data S
tructures, Programming Language Design, Operating Systems, and Artificial I
ntelligence.
</P>
```

When the user browses this page, the link is highlighted in some fashion (i.e., a different color text) and usually underlined, as in Figure 21-7.

FIGURE 21-7
A link to another page

When the user clicks on the link, the browser retrieves and displays the target document, provided that the document has been placed at the appropriate location.

Path Names

Note the path name in the Address field in the header portion of Figure 21-7. The path name specifies the path to the file **sixth.html** on the author's computer. This file contains the page currently being displayed. The path name is said to be an *absolute path name* because it specifies the exact or absolute position of the file in the computer's directory structure.

In HTML anchors, we can use absolute or *relative path names* to specify the location of a target document. A relative path name specifies a document's position relative to that of the currently displayed document. Table 21-4 shows some examples of the relative path name to **MyPage.html**.

TABLE 21-4
Relative path names to **MyPage.html**

POSITION OF `MYPAGE.HTML` RELATIVE TO CURRENT PAGE	RELATIVE PATH NAME
In the same directory	`MyPage.html`
Below, in a subdirectory called **Sub1**	`/Sub1/MyPage.html`
In the directory immediately above	`../MyPage.html`
In the directory two levels above	`../../MyPage.html`
In a directory **Twin1**, which is up one and then down one from the current directory	`../Twin1/MyPage.html`

In general, relative path names are easier to use than absolute path names, because

- They are shorter and require less figuring out and typing.

- They need not be changed when a group of documents is moved, even to another computer, provided the documents retain their relative positions.

URLs

When a target document resides on another server in the network, a path name no longer suffices to locate the document. Instead, we use a *uniform resource locator* (URL) to locate the document on another machine. A URL to another Web site (called a host) has the following format:

```
http://server name/document path name
```

For instance, the URL for author Ken Lambert's home page is

```
<A HREF="http://www.wlu.edu/~lambertk">Ken Lambert</A>
```

Please feel free to visit.

EXERCISE 21.6

1. Write the form of the markup tag for links.

2. What is an absolute path name? Give an example.

3. What is a relative path name? Give an example.

4. Write the format of a URL to another Web site.

21.7 Multimedia

As a true hypermedia language, HTML supports the presentation of a range of nontextual information such as images, sounds, and movies.

Inline Images

Inline images are graphical images that are displayed when the user opens a page. The form of the markup tag for an inline image is

```
<IMG SRC=ImageLocation>
```

where *ImageLocation* is a URL or path name. Images can be encoded in the GIF or JPEG format and are stored in files with extensions of **.gif**, **.jpg**, or **.jpeg**.

Several parameters can be used with the markup tag of an inline image:

- Size attributes: These specify the height and width of the image in pixels. Example:

```
<IMG SRC="mypicture.gif" HEIGHT=100 WIDTH=100>
```

- Alignment attribute: This specifies the position of text relative to the image. By default, text that follows an image starts at the image's lower right corner. The text moves to the top right or to the center right of the image when TOP or CENTER are specified. For example:

```
<IMG SRC="mypicture.gif" ALIGN=CENTER>
```

To detach an image from surrounding text, place the image in a separate paragraph. For instance:

```
<p ALIGN=CENTER>
<IMG SRC="mypicture.gif">
</p>
```

External Images

Inline images increase a document's size and slow its transfer across the Net. For that reason, documents sometimes provide links to *external images*, which are not displayed until the user clicks on a link. The following HTML segment shows two ways of linking to an external image. The first link is a string of text. The second link is a smaller version of the image (sometimes called a thumbnail):

```
<A HREF="mypicture.gif">Sample picture</A>

<A HREF="mypicture.gif"><IMG SRC="mythumbnail.gif"></A>
```

This kind of strategy is also used with other media, such as sound recordings and movies.

Colors and Backgrounds

Browsers normally display black text on a gray background with links highlighted in blue. However, an HTML author can easily change the colors of these elements. Background, text, and link colors are controlled by the BGCOLOR, TEXT, and LINK attributes of the BODY tag. For example, the following tag sets the background to black, text to white, and links to red:

```
<BODY BGCOLOR="#000000" TEXT="#FFFFFF" LINK="#FF0000">
```

A string of three two-digit hexadecimal numbers specifies a color by indicating the RGB (red, green, blue) components of the color. The first two digits represent the red component, the second the green, and the third the blue. Thus, a total of 2^{24} colors are possible. The string "#000000" indicates black, a total absence of any color, whereas "#FFFFFF" represents white, a total saturation of all colors. Bright red is "#FF0000" and bright green is "#00FF00". There are many useful Web sites that show how to use colors. One good example is at http://software.ktc.lt/colormanager/HTMLColorManager.html.

Another way to customize a background is to display an image on it. The following tag shows how to use an image as a background:

```
<BODY BACKGROUND="mybackground.jpg">
```

If the image is small, the browser fills the window with the image by a process called *tiling*, which repeatedly displays the image across and down the screen, thus creating a wallpaper-like effect.

Other Media

Table 21-5 shows file name extensions for some typical media used in HTML documents.

TABLE 21-5
Some hypermedia file name extensions

FILE NAME EXTENSION	TYPE OF MEDIUM
.au	AU sound file
.wav	WAV sound file
.mov	QuickTime movie
.mpeg or .mpg	MPEG movie

*E*XERCISE 21.7

1. What is the difference between an inline image and an external image?

2. Write the simplest version of the format of the markup tag for an inline image.

3. Write a markup tag that loads an inline image of the file **image.gif**, centers the image, and scales its size to 200 pixels x 200 pixels.

4. What are two ways of tagging an external image? Give an example of each.

21.8 Tables

It is often useful to organize information in tables. The page in Figure 21-8 uses a table to display the first two weeks of topics in a data structures course.

FIGURE 21-8
A table

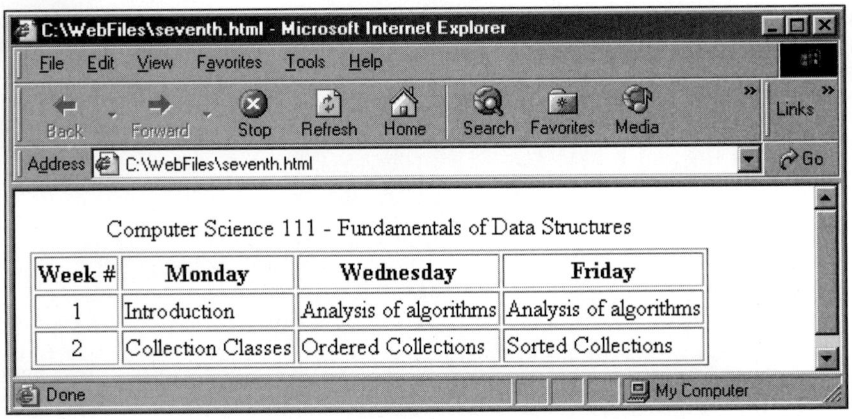

As you have seen in earlier lessons, tables provide a highly structured way of accessing information. This is true of tables in user interfaces as well.

Tables usually contain the following elements:

■ A caption or title, normally at the top of the table.

■ A first row containing column headers. Each header describes the kind of data contained in the column beneath it.

■ Several rows of data. The cells in a row can contain any HTML elements (text, images, links, etc.).

Table 21-6 provides a list of the HTML markup tags used with tables.

TABLE 21-6
Table format tags

TABLE MARKUP TAG	WHAT IT DOES
<TABLE>	Defines a table
<CAPTION>	Defines the title of the table (The default position of the title is at the top of the table, but ALIGN=BOTTOM can also be used.)
<TR>	Defines a row within a table
<TH>	Defines a table header cell
<TD>	Defines a table data cell

The table markup tags accept the attributes shown in Table 21-7.

TABLE 21-7
Table attributes

ATTRIBUTE	TAG	WHAT IT DOES
BORDER	<TABLE>	Display a border
ALIGN (LEFT, CENTER RIGHT)	All	Horizontal alignment of elements in cells
VALIGN (TOP, MIDDLE, BOTTOM)	All except <CAPTION>	Vertical alignment of cells
ROWSPAN=n	<TD>	The number of rows that a cell spans
COLSPAN=n	<TD>	The number of columns that a cell spans
NOWRAP	All except <CAPTION>	Turn off word wrap within a cell

Cell attributes override row attributes, and row attributes override table attributes.

Typical Table Format

The format of a typical table follows. The blank lines between rows increase readability but do not affect the manner in which the table is displayed:

```
<TABLE>
<CAPTION> title of the table </CAPTION>
```

```
<TR>
<TH> header of first column </TH>
.
.
<TH> header of last column </TH>
</TR>

<TR>
<TD> contents of first data cell in first row </TD>
.
.
<TD> contents of last data cell in first row </TD>
</TR>
.
.
<TR>
<TD> contents of first data cell in last row </TD>
.
.
<TD> contents of last data cell in last row </TD>
</TR>
</TABLE>
```

A Simple Example

The table shown in Figure 21-8 at the beginning of this section was created using the following HTML code:

```
<TABLE BORDER>

<CAPTION ALIGN=CENTER>
Computer Science 111 — Fundamentals of Data Structures
</CAPTION>

<TR>
<TH>Week #</TH>
<TH>Monday</TH>
<TH>Wednesday</TH>
<TH>Friday</TH>
</TR>

<TR>
<TD ALIGN=CENTER>1</TD> <TD>Introduction</TD>
<TD>Analysis of algorithms</TD> <TD>Analysis of algorithms</TD>
</TR>

<TR>
<TD ALIGN=CENTER>2</TD> <TD>Collection Classes</TD>
<TD>Ordered Collections</TD> <TD>Sorted Collections</TD>
</TR>

</TABLE>
```

EXERCISE 21.8

1. Describe how you create a table using the HTML table tags.

2. Write an HTML code segment that displays a 3 x 3 table with rows that are numbered as follows:
1 2 3
4 5 6
7 8 9

21.9 Applets

An *applet* is a Java application that runs in a Web page. Two components are needed to run an applet:

1. An HTML document that contains an applet markup tag

2. A byte code file for the applet—that is, a compiled Java applet in a **.class** file

An applet markup tag has the following form:

```
<APPLET CODE=byte code file name WIDTH=width HEIGHT=height></APPLET>
```

The width and height are the width and height, respectively, of the applet's screen area in pixels.

Example

Let us assume that the Fahrenheit/Celsius temperature converter from Lesson 5 has already been rewritten as a Java applet. It might appear in a Web page as shown in Figure 21-9.

FIGURE 21-9
An applet within a Web page

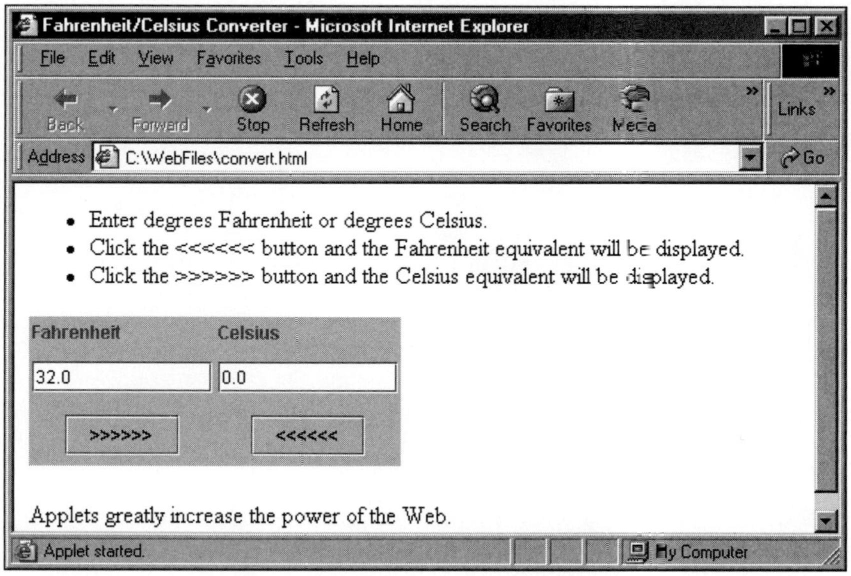

Following is the HTML code for the example:

```
<html>
<head>
<TITLE>Fahrenheit/Celsius Converter</TITLE>
</head>

<body>

<UL>
<LI>Enter degrees Fahrenheit or degrees Celsius.
<LI>Click the <STRONG><<<<<<</STRONG> button and the
Fahrenheit equivalent will be displayed.
<LI>Click the <STRONG>>>>>>></STRONG> button and the
Celsius equivalent will be displayed.
</UL>

<APPLET CODE="ConvertWithGUI.class" WIDTH=250 HEIGHT=100>
</APPLET>

<P>
Applets greatly increase the power of the Web.

<body>
</html>
```

Converting an Application to an Applet

Throughout this text, we have used the class GBFrame to provide the framework for GUI-based applications. We now show how to use a similar class, GBApplet, to write GUI-based applets. To convert Java applications to applets, we must do four things:

1. Replace the name GBFrame with the name GBApplet at the beginning of the class definition.

2. Delete the method main.

3. Eliminate any use of the setTitle method.

4. Replace the constructor, if any, by the method init:

```
public void init(){
    ...
}
```

The following listing shows these changes to the original conversion program and interface in blue:

```
/* ConvertWithGUI.java
A GUI-based temperature conversion program that converts from
Fahrenheit to Celsius and vice versa.
*/

import javax.swing.*;
import BreezySwing.*;
```

```
public class ConvertWithGUI extends GBApplet{

    // Declare variables for the window objects.
    private JLabel       fahrenheitLabel;
    private JLabel       celsiusLabel;
    private DoubleField fahrenheitField;
    private DoubleField celsiusField;
    private JButton      fahrenheitButton;
    private JButton      celsiusButton;

    // Init method - works like a constructor
    public void init(){
        // Instantiate and add window objects to the window.
        fahrenheitLabel  = addLabel        ("Fahrenheit" ,1,1,1,1);
        celsiusLabel     = addLabel        ("Celsius"    ,1,2,1,1);

        fahrenheitField  = addDoubleField (32.0          ,2,1,1,1);
        celsiusField     = addDoubleField (0.0           ,2,2,1,1);
        fahrenheitButton = addButton       (">>>>>>"     ,3,1,1,1);
        celsiusButton    = addButton       ("<<<<<<"     ,3,2,1,1);
    }

    // Respond to button click events
    public void buttonClicked (JButton buttonObj){
        // Local variables
        Thermometer thermo = new Thermometer();

        // Determine which button was clicked.
        if (buttonObj == fahrenheitButton){

            // Convert from Fahrenheit to Celsius
            thermo.setFahrenheit(fahrenheitField.getNumber());
            celsiusField.setNumber (thermo.getCelsius());

        }else{

            // Convert Celsius to Fahrenheit
            thermo.setCelsius(celsiusField.getNumber());
            fahrenheitField.setNumber (thermo.getFahrenheit());
        }
    }

    // No method main is necessary

}
```

Using the Applet Viewer

Sun's JDK comes with a tool called an *applet viewer*. This tool allows the programmer to run an applet and view just its GUI, without the surrounding Web page. To use the applet viewer, you must

1. Compile the Java source program as usual.

2. Create an HTML file with at least the minimal applet tag for the applet.

3. At the command line prompt, run the following command:

```
appletviewer <html file name>
```

Figure 21-10 shows the converter applet running within the applet viewer.

FIGURE 21-10
An applet within the applet viewer

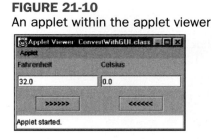

Constraints on Applets

There are several major differences between applets and applications:

■ Although applets generally support drop-down menus, BreezySwing applets do not.

■ To ensure security on the user's machine, applets cannot access files. Imagine how dangerous it would be to download applets across the Web if the applets could trash the files on your computer.

■ Applets and the HTML documents that use them should be placed in the same directory. This rule can be violated, but doing so is beyond the scope of this book. Java programs, whether they are stand-alone applications or applets, frequently utilize classes in addition to those in the standard Java libraries. These classes, which might include the BreezySwing package, should be in the same directory as the applet.

■ The programs in this book use Java 2, so only Web browsers that support Java 2 can run the applets in this lesson. One such browser is available from www.sun.com.

■ The technique for defining dialogs to use in applications, as described in Lesson 10, applies to applets, with three qualifications:

■ The parameter of the dialog's constructor should not be the applet, but instead an anonymous frame. Thus, the value passed to the constructor could simply be new JFrame().

■ You will see a warning message at the bottom of the dialog.

■ The dialog does not prevent you from returning to the Web page. Once there, you cannot interact with the applet, but you can browse to other pages, quit the browser, and perhaps hang up (or lock up) the computer.

Passing Parameters to Applets

It is possible to send information from an HTML page to an applet. The information is passed in HTML parameter tags and is retrieved in the applet's code. In the following example, a parameter tag binds the string "5" to the name "numberOfCourses." The parameter tag must appear between the opening and closing applet tag:

```
<APPLET CODE="Courses.class" WIDTH=150 HEIGHT=100>
<PARAM NAME=numberOfCourses VALUE="5">
</APPLET>
```

At any point within the applet, the method getParameter can retrieve the parameter's value, but always as a string:

```
String str = getParameter ("numberOfCourses");
int num = (new Integer(str)).intValue();
```

A common location for such code is in the init method.

If there are several parameters, each requires its own tag.

*E*XERCISE 21.9

1. Describe the simplest format of an HTML applet tag. Give an example.

2. How is an application converted to an applet using BreezySwing?

3. What can an application do that an applet cannot do?

> **Net Tip**
>
> For a fairly complete reference on HTML and Web page design, enter the following URL in your Web browser:
>
> http://www.ncsa.uiuc.edu/
> General/Internet/WWW/
> HTMLPrimer.html

SUMMARY

In this lesson, you learned:

- The World Wide Web is a hypermedia system that allows users to navigate among and use various resources in a nonlinear manner.

- HTML tags can be used to format text for Web pages. Other markup tags can be used to organize information in lists and tables in a Web page.

- Links to other pages using absolute or relative path names also can be included in HTML elements.

- Web pages also can contain applets, or Java applications that are downloaded from a Web server and run in the user's Web browser.

- There are a few simple steps to convert a Java application to an applet. Applets have most of the functionality of applications, including the GUI, but they lack file access to the user's disks.

VOCABULARY *Review*

Define the following terms:

absolute path name	hypermedia	markup tag
associative link	hypertext	memex
definition list	hypertext markup language	relative path name
external image	(HTML)	uniform resource locator
hyperlinks	inline image	(URL)

REVIEW *Questions*

FILL IN THE BLANK

Complete the following sentences by writing the correct word or words in the blanks provided.

1. _____ generalizes hypertext to include images, sound, video, and embedded applications.

2. HTML stands for _____.

3. The three markup tags that any HTML document usually contains are _____, _____, and _____.

4. The _____ markup tag is used to display text in its original format.

5. A(n) _____ markup tag is used to lay out elements in a two-dimensional grid.

6. The _____ method serves a similar role to a constructor for applets.

7. Two program features that are not allowed in applets are _____ and _____.

8. The JDK's _____ allows the programmer to run an applet without a Web browser.

9. URL stands for _____.

10. A(n) _____ path name is used to obtain a resource from a remote server.

PROJECTS

PROJECT 21-1

If you have not done so already, create a home page on your local Web server. Include a title, a brief paragraph that states who you are, and a picture of your favorite pastime.

PROJECT 21-2

Add a list of courses you are currently taking to the home page created for Project 21-1.

PROJECT 21-3

Make each item in the list from Project 21-2 a link to a page that describes that item. Create these pages and test your hypertext thoroughly.

PROJECT 21-4

Add links to each of the pages created in Project 21-3 that return the user to your home page.

PROJECT 21-5

Write an applet that plays the game tic-tac-toe with the user. The interface should display a 3 x 3 grid of empty buttons at the beginning of a new game. The applet also selects the two letters used by the players at random. When the user selects an empty button, the applet displays the user's letter on that button and displays its own letter on a randomly selected empty button. After each button is selected, the applet determines if there is a winner. If so, the applet displays a message box and then clears the buttons for a new game. You should use the methods `getText` and `setText(String)` to examine and change the label of a button.

CRITICAL *Thinking*

Write a short essay that compares the advantages and disadvantages of using Java applications and applets.

SWING AND AWT

Applications with a graphical user interface are based ultimately on Java's *Abstract Windowing Toolkit* (*AWT*) and *Swing Toolkit*. However, for the sake of simplicity, we have avoided using them until now. Instead, we have made all of our stand-alone programs subclasses of GBFrame and our applets subclasses of GBApplet. These are two of the major classes in the BreezySwing package. Although BreezySwing makes it easy to create GUI-based programs, it blocks access to the full power of Java's GUIs. Fortunately, we have not noticed the deprivation, but with an eye to your future as Java programmers, we now present Swing and AWT in some detail.

22.1 The Swing and AWT Philosophy

Traditional programming languages such as Pascal and C++ provide no standard features for programming graphical user interfaces, so GUI code often must be rewritten when GUI applications are ported to different machines. Moreover, the GUI features themselves may vary from platform to platform. Java's originators developed Swing and the Abstract Windowing Toolkit to solve these problems.

The toolkits are abstract in two senses:

1. They provide classes and methods that are platform independent. Write once, run anywhere.

2. They create user interfaces whose look and feel are platform independent. Run anywhere, look similar.

Applications that use Swing and AWT involve the use of four categories of classes. Table 22-1 briefly describes each category. Later we will explore the categories in detail and show how they work together to support a graphical user interface. Most of the layout managers are in AWT. Event classes and *listener* classes are in both Swing and AWT. AWT and Swing have similar *component* classes, and we explore the Swing versions in this lesson.

TABLE 22-1
Classes used in GUI-based applications

CATEGORIES	WHAT THEY DO
GUI component classes	GUI components include such basic window objects as buttons, text fields, and menu items. Also included in this category are frames, applets, and dialogs, which act as containers for the basic window objects.
Layout manager classes	When objects, such as buttons, are added to a window, their placement is determined by a layout manager. For instance, GBFrame and GBApplet use a grid bag layout. The other layout managers are flow, border, grid, and card.
Event classes	Event classes define the events that are triggered when users do such things as click buttons, select menu items, and move the mouse.
Listener classes	Listener classes contain methods that are activated when events occur.

We use these classes to define a graphical user interface as follows:

1. Add window objects to the interface under the control of a layout manager.

2. Decide which events each object should handle by adding listeners for the event to the object.

We can get a feel for all of this by revisiting the Fahrenheit to Celsius conversion program of Lesson 7 and comparing how it is implemented with GBFrame versus directly with Swing and AWT.

*E*XERCISE 22.1

1. In what two senses are Swing and AWT abstract?

2. What are the four types of classes used in building GUIs, and what are their roles and responsibilities?

22.2 *Conversion Program Implemented with* GBFrame

Figure 22-1 shows a version of the following program implemented with GBFrame:

FIGURE 22-1
The conversion program with GBFrame

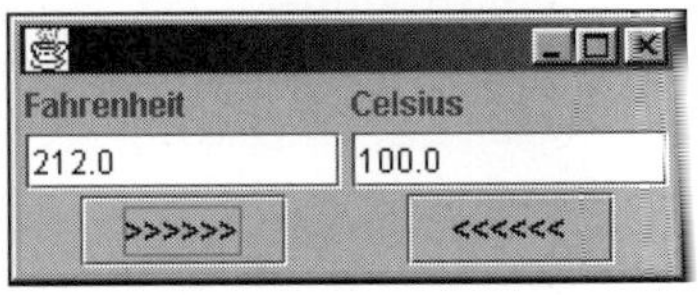

```
/* ConvertWithGUI.java
A GUI-based temperature conversion program that converts from
Fahrenheit to Celsius and vice versa.
*/

import javax.swing.*;
import BreezySwing.*;

public class ConvertWithGUI extends GBFrame{

    // Declare variables for the window objects.
    private JLabel       fahrenheitLabel;
    private JLabel       celsiusLabel;
    private DoubleField  fahrenheitField;
    private DoubleField  celsiusField;
    private JButton      fahrenheitButton;
    private JButton      celsiusButton;

    // Constructor
    public ConvertWithGUI(){
        // Instantiate and add window objects to the window.
        fahrenheitLabel  = addLabel        ("Fahrenheit" ,1,1,1,1);
        celsiusLabel     = addLabel        ("Celsius"    ,1,2,1,1);

        fahrenheitField  = addDoubleField (32.0          ,2,1,1,1);
        celsiusField     = addDoubleField (0.0           ,2,2,1,1);
        fahrenheitButton = addButton       (">>>>>>"     ,3,1,1,1);
        celsiusButton    = addButton       ("<<<<<<"     ,3,2,1,1);
    }

    // Respond to button click events
    public void buttonClicked (JButton buttonObj){
        // Local variables
        Thermometer thermo = new Thermometer();

        // Determine which button was clicked.
```

```
        if (buttonObj == fahrenheitButton){

            // Convert from Fahrenheit to Celsius
            thermo.setFahrenheit(fahrenheitField.getNumber());
            celsiusField.setNumber (thermo.getCelsius());

        }else{

            // Convert Celsius to Fahrenheit
            thermo.setCelsius(celsiusField.getNumber());
            fahrenheitField.setNumber (thermo.getFahrenheit());
        }
    }

    // Execution begins in the method main as usual.
    public static void main (String[] args){
        ConvertWithGUI theGUI = new ConvertWithGUI();
        theGUI.setSize (250, 100);   //Set the window's size in pixels
                                     //  width = 250, height = 100
        theGUI.setVisible (true);    //Make the window visible
    }
}
```

From the perspective of this lesson, there are several points to notice about the code:

1. The program extends GBFrame.

2. The window objects, or GUI components, are instantiated and laid out in the window.

3. The program responds to events that are triggered by the user. In this example, the events of interest are

   ■ Clicking on the >>>>>> button

   ■ Clicking on the <<<<<< button

   ■ Closing the window by clicking on the X button in the window's top right corner

4. There is code to respond to the events. The underlying Java framework activates this listener code when an event occurs. The listener code for the click button event is in the method buttonClicked, whereas that for handling the window close event is handled out of sight inside GBFrame.

22.3 Conversion Program Implemented with Swing and AWT

Now, in contrast, let's look at the program implemented using Swing and AWT without GBFrame. The program is spread out over four files that are listed in Table 22-2.

TABLE 22-2
Files for the conversion program

FILE NAME	WHAT IT DOES
ConversionWithSwing.java	This file contains the program's main class. It defines the GUI and contains code that does the conversion between Fahrenheit and Celsius.
FahrenheitButtonListener.java	This file defines the listener for the >>>>>> button.
CelsiusButtonListener.java	This file defines the listener for the <<<<< button.
GenericWindowListener.java	This file defines the listener for closing the window when the **X** button is clicked.

The Interface

The interface (Figure 22-2) appears essentially the same as it did earlier when we used GBFrame. The cause of the minor differences will become clear when we discuss layout managers later in this lesson.

FIGURE 22-2
The conversion program with Swing

The File ConversionWithSwing.java

The listing is broken by extensive comments that must be read carefully for a proper understanding of how the Swing/AWT classes work together to support a GUI.

We begin as usual by importing the swing package:

```
import javax.swing.*;
```

Because we are now dealing directly with layouts and listeners, we also import the awt package:

```
import java.awt.*;
```

We then extend `JFrame` rather than `GBFrame`:

```
public class ConversionWithSwing extends JFrame {
```

The variables that reference the window objects are declared next:

```
private JLabel     fahrenheitLabel;
private JTextField fahrenheitField;
```

Swing/AWT has no integer fields, so in the preceding line, we use a text field instead.

```
private JLabel     celsiusLabel;
private JTextField celsiusField;
private JButton    fahrenheitButton;
private JButton    celsiusButton;
```

There are a number of tasks that must be performed in the constructor:

```
public ConversionWithSwing(){
```

First, instantiate the window objects:

```
fahrenheitLabel  = new JLabel ("Fahrenheit");
fahrenheitField  = new JTextField ("212", 6);    // 6 columns wide
celsiusLabel     = new JLabel ("Celsius");
celsiusField     = new JTextField ("100", 6);    // 6 columns wide
fahrenheitButton = new JButton (">>>>>>");
celsiusButton    = new JButton ("<<<<<<");
```

Second, before adding and positioning window objects, we must instantiate the layout:

```
FlowLayout layout = new FlowLayout();
```

Third, we must get the frame's content pane and set its layout:

```
Container mainWindow = getContentPane();
mainWindow.setLayout (layout);
```

Fourth, we add the window objects under the influence of the layout, which controls their actual placement. There are several different types of layouts, flow layout being the simplest. A flow layout displays components in the order in which they are added. As many components as possible are displayed on each line. Those that do not fit on a given line wrap around onto the next line.

```
mainWindow.add (fahrenheitLabel);
mainWindow.add (celsiusLabel);
mainWindow.add (fahrenheitField);
mainWindow.add (celsiusField);
mainWindow.add (fahrenheitButton);
mainWindow.add (celsiusButton);
```

Fifth, it is necessary to tell the buttons where their listener code is located. This is done by instantiating listener objects and associating them with the buttons. The Java framework sends messages to the listener objects when the buttons are clicked. The listener object for the first button is an instance of the class `FahrenheitButtonListener`, and for the second button it is an instance of the class `CelsiusButtonListener`. The need for the parameter `this` will be explained soon.

```
fahrenheitButton.addActionListener
                        (new FahrenheitButtonListener (this));
celsiusButton.addActionListener
                        (new CelsiusButtonListener (this));
```

Sixth, a listener is needed to close the window. The listener is activated when the user clicks the **X** in the window's top right corner. We call the listener class `GenericWindowListener`. Following we instantiate the listener object and associate it with the window:

```
addWindowListener (new GenericWindowListener());
    }
```

The conversion from Celsius to Fahrenheit is done in the method that follows. The `FahrenheitButtonListener` object calls this method. We will see the details soon. Note that the method's code is straightforward:

■ The code instantiates a Thermometer.

■ The code then retrieves a string from the Celsius field and converts it to a number.

■ The code then sends this number to the thermometer, retrieves its Fahrenheit equivalent, converts that back to a string, and displays the string in the Fahrenheit field.

The conversions between strings and numbers are necessary because Swing/AWT does not include the numeric fields that are part of `GBFrame` and `GBApplet`. Instead, we must use Swing's `JTextField`:

```
public void computeFahrenheit(){
    Thermometer thermo = new Thermometer();
    String str = celsiusField.getText().trim();
    double celsius = (new Double(str)).doubleValue();
    thermo.setCelsius(celsius);
    double fahrenheit = thermo.getFahrenheit();
    fahrenheitField.setText ("" + fahrenheit);
}
```

The conversion from Fahrenheit to Celsius is handled by the next method. It is similar to the preceding one:

```
public void computeCelsius(){
    Thermometer thermo = new Thermometer();
    String str = fahrenheitField.getText().trim();
    double fahrenheit = (new Double(str)).doubleValue();
    thermo.setFahrenheit(fahrenheit);
    double celsius = thermo.getCelsius();
    celsiusField.setText ("" + celsius);
}
```

The method main is similar, but the window is made a bit narrower:

```
public static void main (String[] args){
   JFrame frm = new ConversionWithSwing();
   frm.setSize (150, 150);
   frm.setVisible (true);
}
}
```

That ends the code for ConversionWithSwing.java. We now examine the code for the listener classes.

The File FahrenheitButtonListener.java

When a user clicks on the button to compute Celsius, the Java framework sends the actionPerformed message to the FahrenheitButtonListener object that we saw instantiated in the earlier code. Following is an annotated listing of the class.

We begin by importing the package java.awt.event:

```
import java.awt.event.*;
```

The class FahrenheitButtonListener implements the ActionListener interface. The ActionListener interface declares just one method, namely, actionPerformed, and the FahrenheitButtonListener class must provide code to define this method. A button would be nonfunctional if the main GUI class failed to associate it with an ActionListener object.

```
public class FahrenheitButtonListener implements ActionListener{
```

Listeners often need to send messages back to the main GUI class. This listener is designed to send a message back to the view, an instance of the class ConversionWithSwing. To do so, it must declare a variable of type ConversionWithSwing:

```
private ConversionWithSwing theGUI;
```

In the constructor that follows, we assign a value to the variable theGUI. The value being assigned corresponds to the word "this" in the main GUI class. Following is the line of code, copied from the previous main GUI class, that activates the constructor:

```
fahrenheitButton.addActionListener
   (new FahrenheitButtonListener (this));
```

And now following is the constructor itself:

```
public FahrenheitButtonListener (ConversionWithSwing gui){
   theGUI = gui;
}
```

As already mentioned, the Java framework sends the actionPerformed message to the FahrenheitButtonListener object when the button to compute Celsius is clicked. An event object is passed to the method as a parameter. The event object contains information about the event, such as the identity of the button that triggered the event, which in this case we already know is the button to compute Celsius.

```
public void actionPerformed (ActionEvent e){
```

Listener code is often very simple. In this example, all it does is send a message back to the main GUI class, requesting the main GUI class to compute and display the degrees Celsius:

```
        theGUI.computeCelsius();
    }
}
```

The File `CelsiusButtonListener.java`

This file is so similar to the listener just discussed that we present the listing without further discussion.

```
import java.awt.event.*;

public class CelsiusButtonListener implements ActionListener{

    private ConversionWithSwing theGUI;

    public CelsiusButtonListener (ConversionWithSwing gui){
        theGUI = gui;
    }

    public void actionPerformed (ActionEvent e){
        theGUI.computeFahrenheit();
    }
}
```

The File `GenericWindowListener.java`

A window listener's principal task is to close the window when the user clicks the window's **X** button, which in turn triggers the window's closing event. However, there are several other window events that can be handled in a window listener class. These include iconifying and de-iconifying the window and activating and deactivating the window. The listener has a separate method for handling each type of window event. When one of these events occurs, the Java framework sends the appropriate message to the window listener object. As in many applications, this window's closing event is the only one of concern. All the methods, however, must be included in the listing, even if some have no code. Following is the listing:

```
import java.awt.event.*;

public class GenericWindowListener implements WindowListener{

    public void windowClosing (WindowEvent e){
        System.exit(0);
    }
```

```
      public void windowActivated (WindowEvent e){}
      public void windowClosed (WindowEvent e){}
      public void windowDeactivated (WindowEvent e){}
      public void windowDeiconified (WindowEvent e){}
      public void windowIconified (WindowEvent e){}
      public void windowOpened (WindowEvent e){}
   }
```

As you can readily see, the difference between writing a GUI application with and without `GBFrame` is dramatic.

EXERCISE 22.3

1. Describe the roles and responsibilities of the different classes written in the `ConversionWithSwing` program.

2. Which parts of the `ConversionWithSwing` program are hidden in the version that uses `BreezySwing`?

22.4 Variations on Implementing with Swing and AWT

The preceding example illustrates one of several different ways to implement the conversion program using Swing and AWT. In this section, we explore several variations. Each variation has pros and cons, and the variation you think best for the conversion program might not be best in another situation. Just remember that, when you write programs, you want to strive for simplicity, clarity, and maintainability.

Simplifying the `GenericWindowListener` Class

The `GenericWindowListener` class listed earlier included a number of empty methods. The need to include the empty methods can be avoided if the `GenericWindowListener` extends the `WindowAdapter` class instead of implementing the `WindowListener` interface. The `WindowAdapter` class is part of the package `java.awt.event`. Its code is shown following. As you can see, its code implements the `WindowListener` interface and consists of nothing but empty methods:

```
   public abstract class WindowAdapter implements WindowListener {
      public void windowOpened(WindowEvent e) {}
      public void windowClosing(WindowEvent e) {}
      public void windowClosed(WindowEvent e) {}
      public void windowIconified(WindowEvent e) {}
      public void windowDeiconified(WindowEvent e) {}
      public void windowActivated(WindowEvent e) {}
      public void windowDeactivated(WindowEvent e) {}
   }
```

The `WindowAdapter` class belongs to a category of classes known as *adapter classes*. An adapter class implements an interface by providing stub methods. Clients then can avoid implementing all the methods in an interface by extending the corresponding adapter class.

Following is the `GenericWindowListener` written as an extension of the `WindowAdapter` class. Only one method now needs to be implemented.

```
import java.awt.event.*;

public class GenericWindowListener extends WindowAdapter{

    public void windowClosing (WindowEvent e){
       System.exit(0);
    }
}
```

Altogether there are 11 listener interfaces in AWT. We have seen two, `ActionListener` and `WindowListener`, and will examine most of the remaining ones soon. Listeners with more than one method have a corresponding adapter, thus providing programmers with the convenience of extending the adapter rather than implementing the interface.

Incorporating the Listeners into the Main GUI Class

Listeners do not have to be in separate classes but can be incorporated into the main GUI class. This is achieved by having the main GUI class implement the desired listeners in addition to extending the `JFrame` class. We illustrate the process by incorporating the button and window listeners. We will, of course, need to implement all the methods in the `ActionListener` and the `WindowListener` interfaces. By the way, a class can extend only one other class but can implement any number of interfaces. Following is the code broken by some comments:

```
import javax.swing.*;
import java.awt.*;
import java.awt.event.*;

public class ConversionWithSwing extends JFrame
                                 implements ActionListener,
                                            WindowListener{

    private JLabel     fahrenheitLabel;
    private JTextField fahrenheitField;
    private JLabel     celsiusLabel;
    private JTextField celsiusField;
    private JButton    fahrenheitButton;
    private JButton    celsiusButton;


    public ConversionWithSwing(){
       fahrenheitLabel  = new JLabel ("Fahrenheit");
       fahrenheitField  = new JTextField ("212", 6);    // 6 columns wide
       celsiusLabel     = new JLabel ("Celsius");
       celsiusField     = new JTextField ("100", 6);    // 6 columns wide
```

```
      fahrenheitButton = new JButton (">>>>>>");
      celsiusButton    = new JButton ("<<<<<<");

      FlowLayout layout = new FlowLayout();
      Container mainWindow = getContentPane();
      mainWindow.setLayout (layout);
      mainWindow.add (fahrenheitLabel);
      mainWindow.add (celsiusLabel);
      mainWindow.add (fahrenheitField);
      mainWindow.add (celsiusField);
      mainWindow.add (fahrenheitButton);
      mainWindow.add (celsiusButton);
```

We still need to associate the buttons and the window with listener objects. But now the only listener object is the application itself, namely, `this`.

```
      fahrenheitButton.addActionListener (this);
      celsiusButton.addActionListener (this);
      addWindowListener (this);
   }
```

A class that implements the `ActionListener` must include the method `actionPerformed`.

```
   public void actionPerformed (ActionEvent e){
      String str;
      double fahrenheit, celsius;
      JButton btn = (JButton)e.getSource();
      Thermometer thermo = new Thermometer();

      if (btn == celsiusButton){
         str = celsiusField.getText().trim();
         celsius = (new Double (str)).doubleValue();
         thermo.setCelsius(celsius);
         fahrenheit = thermo.getFahrenheit();
         fahrenheitField.setText ("" + fahrenheit);
      }
      else{
         str = fahrenheitField.getText().trim();
         fahrenheit = (new Double (str)). doubleValue ();
         thermo.setFahrenheit(fahrenheit);
         celsius = thermo.getCelsius();
         celsiusField.setText ("" + celsius);
      }
   }
```

A class that implements the `WindowListener` must include the seven methods that follow, even if most of them are empty.

```
   public void windowClosing (WindowEvent e){
      System.exit(0);
   }
```

```
public void windowActivated (WindowEvent e){}
public void windowClosed (WindowEvent e){}
public void windowDeactivated (WindowEvent e){}
public void windowDeiconified (WindowEvent e){}
public void windowIconified (WindowEvent e){}
public void windowOpened (WindowEvent e){}
```

Fortunately, some things never change. Following is the familiar method main:

```
public static void main (String[] args){
    JFrame frm = new ConversionWithSwing();
    frm.setSize (150, 150);
    frm.setVisible (true);
}
}
```

Once again, there are many ways to structure the code of a GUI-based application. We explore one more in the case study in this lesson. This, however, completes our overview of the workings of Swing and AWT. In the next section we turn to some of the details, beginning with a discussion of GUI components and layouts.

EXERCISE 22.4

1. What is an adapter class? Give an example.

2. Describe the structure of an application that incorporates listeners into the main GUI class.

22.5 GUI Components

The first category of classes used in developing windows-based applications is that of the GUI components. The visible objects that constitute a window fall into this category. These objects include buttons, text fields, text areas, lists, menu items, and so forth. You can find complete documentation for all of the GUI component classes at the Java Web site, as described in Appendix A.

The Component Class Hierarchy

All of the GUI component classes, whether in Swing or AWT, are subclasses of an abstract class in AWT called Component. This class specifies the most basic attributes and behavior of all GUI objects. For example, every component has attributes that define its size (width and height in pixels), background color, foreground color, text font, and visibility. Commonly used methods for modifying these attributes are shown in Table 22-3.

TABLE 22-3
Some commonly used Component methods

COMPONENT METHOD	WHAT IT DOES
void setBackground(Color c)	Sets the background color of the component.
void setEnabled(boolean b)	Enables or disables the component.
void setFont(Font f)	Sets the font of the component.
void setForeground(Color c)	Sets the foreground color of the component.
void setSize(int w, int h)	Sets the width and height of the component.
void setVisible(boolean b)	Displays or hides the component.

The Component class also includes methods for adding listener objects to a component, as illustrated earlier in the conversion program.

Figure 22-3 shows a portion of the Swing branch of the Component class hierarchy.

FIGURE 22-3
A portion of the Swing classes in the Component hierarchy

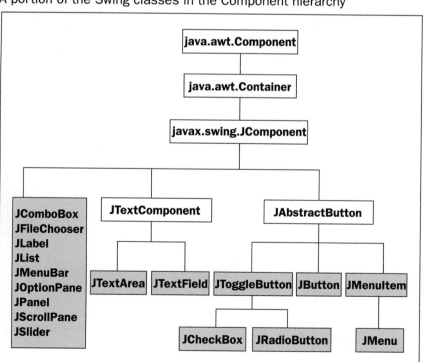

Note the following points about the figure:

■ The two classes at the top of the hierarchy are in `java.awt`, whereas the rest of the classes are in `javax.swing`.

■ The concrete classes are shaded, whereas the abstract classes are not.

The classes `DoubleField` and `IntegerField`, which we have defined in the `BreezySwing` package, are subclasses of the `JTextField` class, and thus understand all `JTextField` messages. You are already familiar with the capabilities and behavior of many of the component classes, but several deserve further explanation. In the following sections we discuss panels, scroll bars, sliders, menu components, option panes, and container classes.

Panels

`JPanel` is the parent class of the `BreezySwing` class `GBPanel`. As we saw in Lesson 19, a panel represents a rectangular area within a window. This area can be painted and repainted independently of the rest of the window.

Scroll Bars

You have seen *scroll bars* along the sides of list box and text area components. Scroll bars are not automatically provided for these components, however. To add scroll bars to a list box or text area, you must wrap an instance of `JScrollPane` around it, as shown in the following code segment:

```
Container c = getContentPane();
TextArea ta = new JTextArea();    // Create a text area
c.add(new JScrollPane(ta));       // Wrap it in scroll bars and add to GUI
```

Sliders

A *slider* is used to enter an input value, usually a number, by dragging the mouse along a ticked ruler. Sliders are instances of the class `JSlider`. The case study later in the lesson uses sliders and a panel to create a color meter for your computer.

Menu Components

In earlier lessons, `BreezySwing` hid the details of menu setup. For example, the following code segment uses `BreezySwing` to set up a **File** menu and an **Edit** menu with appropriate options:

```
JMenuItem newFileItem   = addMenuItem("File", "New");
JMenuItem openFileItem   = addMenuItem("File", "Open");
JMenuItem saveFileItem   = addMenuItem("File", "Save");

JMenuItem cutEditItem    = addMenuItem("Edit", "Cut");
JMenuItem copyEditItem   = addMenuItem("Edit", "Copy");
JMenuItem pasteEditItem  = addMenuItem("Edit", "Paste");
```

To perform the equivalent task without `BreezySwing`, the programmer must do the following:

1. Create new menu items with the appropriate labels.

2. Create new menus with the appropriate labels.

3. Create a new menu bar.

4. Add the menu items to their respective menus.

5. Add the menus to the menu bar.

6. Add the menu bar to the application window.

These steps are performed in the following code segment:

```
// Create the menu items.
JMenuItem newFileItem    = new JMenuItem ("New");
JMenuItem openFileItem   = new JMenuItem ("Open");
JMenuItem saveFileItem   = new JMenuItem ("Save");
JMenuItem cutEditItem    = new JMenuItem ("Cut");
JMenuItem copyEditItem   = new JMenuItem ("Copy");
JMenuItem pasteEditItem  = new JMenuItem ("Paste");

// Create the menus and the menu bar.
JMenu fileMenu = new JMenu ("File");
JMenu editMenu = new JMenu ("Edit");
JMenuBar menuBar = new JMenuBar();

// Add the menu items to the menus.
fileMenu.add (newFileItem);
fileMenu.add (openFileItem);
fileMenu.add (saveFileItem);
editMenu.add (cutEditItem);
editMenu.add (copyEditItem);
editMenu.add (pasteEditItem);

// Add the menus to the menu bar.
menuBar.add (fileMenu);
menuBar.add (editMenu);

// Add the menu bar to the application window.
setJMenuBar (menuBar);
```

The menu classes also support the creation of submenus. To create a submenu, you simply add one menu as an item to another.

The programmer sets up listeners for menu events in the same way as shown earlier for button events, by implementing the interface ActionListener. In this case, an action listener is added to each menu item.

Option Panes

Option panes provide a set of commonly used dialogs, such as prompters, message boxes, and confirmation dialogs. They are created by sending messages to the class JOptionPane. Table 22-4 lists some typical messages.

TABLE 22-4
Some JOptionPane methods

JOptionPane METHOD	WHAT IT DOES
int showConfirmDialog(Component parent, String message)	Pops up a confirmation dialog with the options Yes, No, and Cancel and the title "Select an Option." Returns the JOptionPane constants YES_OPTION, NO_OPTION, and CANCEL_OPTION.
String showInputDialog(Component parent, String message)	Pops up a prompter dialog with the message. Returns null if cancelled; otherwise, returns the string entered.
void showMessageDialog(Component parent, String message)	Pops up a message dialog with the message and the title "Confirm."

There are several variations of each method that allow the client to specify the title, the type of message (error, warning, etc.), and so forth. The following code segment shows the use of a confirmation dialog:

```
int choice = JOptionPane.showConfirmDialog(this, "Want to quit?");
if (choice == JOptionPane.YES_OPTION)
   System.out.println("Yes");
else if (choice == JOptionPane.NO_OPTION)
   System.out.println("No");
else if (choice == JOptionPane.CANCEL_OPTION)
   System.out.println("Cancel");
```

Container Classes

Container objects are so called because they contain other window objects, including other containers. Figure 22-4 shows Swing's primary container classes, and Table 22-5 describes their uses.

FIGURE 22-4
The primary Swing container classes

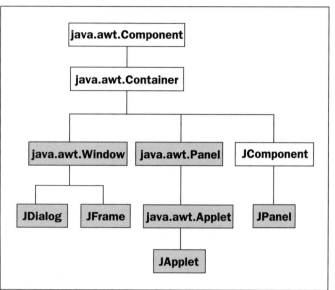

TABLE 22-5
The uses of Swing's container classes

CONTAINER CLASS	WHAT IT DOES
JFrame	Displays components in an application window. All stand-alone GUI applications must extend JFrame (or GBFrame when using BreezySwing).
JApplet	Displays components in a Web browser. Applets have neither a menu bar nor a border. All Web-based applications must extend JApplet (or GBApplet when using BreezySwing).
JDialog	Displays components in a dialog window. Dialogs are used as auxiliary windows in stand-alone applications and applets. They can be either modal or nonmodal. Until it is dismissed, a modal dialog blocks user interaction with the rest of an application. Dialogs extend JDialog (or GBDialog when using BreezySwing).
JPanel	Organizes a set of components as a group. Panels can factor complex interfaces into modular chunks. An applet, frame, or dialog can contain several panels, which in turn can contain buttons, text fields, lists, and so forth, and even other panels. Panels extend JPanel (or GBPanel in BreezySwing).

A container must use a layout manager that determines the arrangement of the components within it. The different types of layouts are discussed in the following section.

EXERCISE 22.5

1. Write a code segment that uses a `JOptionPane` method to prompt the user for her name.

2. What are container classes? Give three examples.

22.6 Layouts

In many programming environments, one must specify the location and size of window objects in terms of pixel positions and pixel dimensions. Although this approach provides precise control over a window's appearance, it has a drawback. When a window is resized, its components remain fixed in position and size. Consequently, if the window is too small, some of the components cannot be seen, and if it is too large, the components seem to huddle in the window's top left corner. In contrast, components in a Java window distribute themselves to fill the available space. The exact manner of this distribution depends on what is called the window's layout, as defined by one of Java's layout manager classes. Although you have had no way of knowing it, `GBFrame` and `GBApplet` use the layout manager `GridBagLayout`. Table 22-6 lists the layout manager classes with an illustration and overview of each.

TABLE 22-6
The layout manager classes in AWT

LAYOUT MANAGER	ILLUSTRATION	OVERVIEW
`BorderLayout`		A border layout divides a window into five regions, positioned as shown. Each region can contain one component. This is the default layout for frames and dialogs.
`CardLayout`		A card layout consists of a stack of components. Only one component can be seen at a time, but it is possible to switch between components.
`FlowLayout`		A flow layout displays components in the order in which they are added. As many components as possible are displayed on each line. Those that do not fit on a given line wrap around onto the next line. This is the default layout for panels and applets.

A more detailed description of each layout manager is given in the following subsections.

Border Layouts

The default layout for frames and dialogs is BorderLayout. The layout of Figure 22-5 divides a container into five regions.

FIGURE 22-5
A border layout

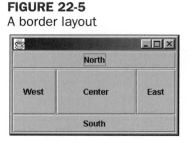

A region's size is based on several factors. First, it depends on the preferred size of the component placed in it. Second, regions North and South are expanded horizontally to fill the container's width, and regions East and West are expanded vertically. Third, the Center region expands to fill the remaining space. Not all regions need to be present. If the Center region is omitted, it leaves an empty space in the container; however, if any of the other regions are omitted, the central region expands to fill the vacated space (Figure 22-6).

FIGURE 22-6
Border layouts that are not filled

A component is added to a region using the add method:

```
add (<component>, <region>)
```

where <region> is one of the strings "North," "South," "East," "West," and "Center."

For example, the following code segment creates the border layout shown in Figure 22-5, which includes all five regions. The usual place for this sort of code is in a constructor.

```
// Create and set the layout
BorderLayout layout = new BorderLayout();
Container mainWindow = getContentPane();
mainWindow.setLayout (layout);

// Add components under control of the layout
mainWindow.add (new JButton("North"), "North");
mainWindow.add (new JButton("East"), "East");
mainWindow.add (new JButton("South"), "South");
```

```
mainWindow.add (new JButton("West"), "West");
mainWindow.add (new JButton("Center"), "Center");
```

In the code, the first two lines can be omitted when using a frame or a dialog.

Flow Layouts

The default window layout for panels and applets is FlowLayout. A flow layout displays components in horizontal lines in the order in which they are added. Components that do not fit on a line wrap around onto the next (Figure 22-7).

FIGURE 22-7
A flow layout

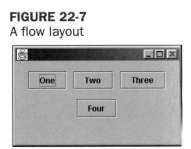

When a user resizes a window, the wrapping points shift, and the appearance of the window changes dramatically. For instance, the two windows in Figure 22-8 were created by the same program.

FIGURE 22-8
Two views of the same program with a flow layout

By default, a flow layout centers the components in each row and separates them horizontally and vertically by five pixels. The flow layout shown in Figure 22-7 can be created as follows:

```
FlowLayout layout = new FlowLayout();
Container mainWindow = getContentPane();
mainWindow.setLayout (layout);

mainWindow.add (new JButton("One"));
mainWindow.add (new JButton("Two"));
mainWindow.add (new JButton("Three"));
mainWindow.add (new JButton("Four"));
```

The first two lines are optional in panels and applets. The programmer has some minor control over a flow layout. One can align the components to the left, center, or right using the constants

```
FlowLayout.LEFT
FlowLayout.CENTER
FlowLayout.RIGHT
```

For instance, to align the components at the left (Figure 22-9), the programmer writes

```
FlowLayout layout = new FlowLayout (FlowLayout.LEFT);
Container mainWindow = getContentPane();
mainWindow.setLayout (layout);

// Now add the components
```

FIGURE 22-9
A flow layout with components aligned to the left

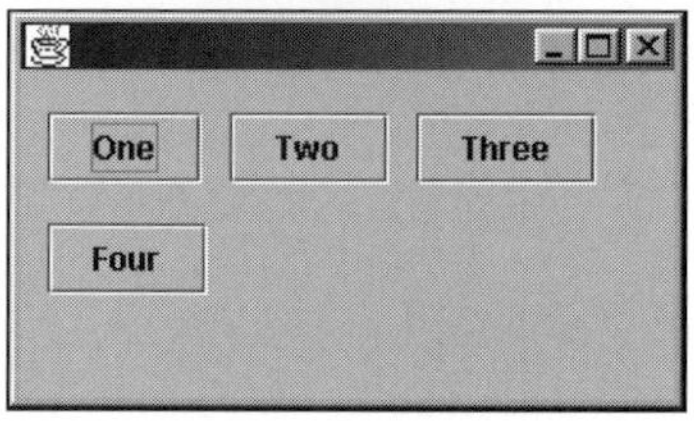

The programmer can control the horizontal and vertical spacing between components. The following example centers window objects with horizontal gaps of 10 pixels and vertical gaps of 15 pixels (see Figure 22-10):

```
FlowLayout layout = new FlowLayout (FlowLayout.CENTER, 10, 15);
Container mainWindow = getContentPane();
mainWindow.setLayout (layout);

// Now add the components
```

FIGURE 22-10
A flow layout with fixed spacing and components aligned to the center

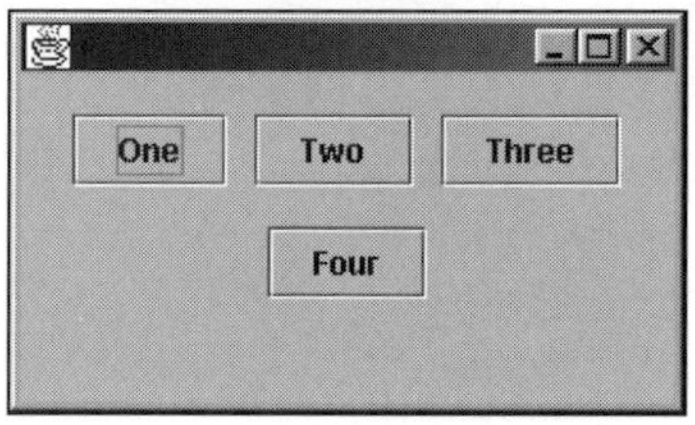

Grid Layouts

A regular pattern of objects, such as a table of buttons, is easily displayed with a grid layout. To use a grid layout:

1. Create a new instance of class GridLayout with the desired number of rows and columns.

2. Set the container's layout to this instance.

3. Add the components to the container.

The components are positioned in the grid from left to right and top to bottom, in the order added, and each cell in the grid is the same size. The following code segment creates the grid layout displayed in Figure 22-11:

```
mainWindow.setLayout (new GridLayout(2, 2));
mainWindow.add (new JButton("One"));
mainWindow.add (new JButton("Two"));
mainWindow.add (new JButton("Three"));
mainWindow.add (new JButton("Four"));
```

FIGURE 22-11
A grid layout

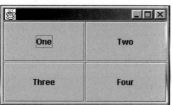

Grid Bag Layouts

The **grid bag layout** is the most versatile and most complex layout manager. It treats the display area as a grid of cells. The grid begins with no cells and adds cells as needed to accommodate the components. Components occupy rectangular blocks of cells called display areas. Cells can be empty, and their size can vary. In Figure 22-12, a grid has been superimposed on the window. The button One occupies two cells. Each of the other buttons occupies a single cell. The remaining cells are empty. Notice that the cells differ markedly in size, and the components fill their display areas in varying degrees. The classes GBFrame, GBApplet, and GBDialog use a grid bag layout.

FIGURE 22-12
The grid within a grid bag layout

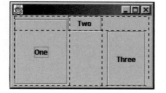

Class `GridBagLayout` must always be used in conjunction with another class: `GridBagConstraints`. A constraints object specifies the manner in which a component occupies the grid. This is done by assigning values to the constraints object's public instance variables. Following is an illustrative code segment:

```
GridBagLayout layout = new GridBagLayout();
Container mainWindow = getContentPane();
mainWindow.setLayout (layout);

constraints = new GridBagConstraints();
constraints.gridy = 0;           // row 0
constraints.gridx = 0;           // column 0
constraints.gridheight = 2;
constraints.fill = GridBagConstraints.BOTH;
constraints.insets = new Insets (6,4,3,0);
constraints.weightx = 100;

JButton button1 = new JButton ("One");
layout.setConstraints (button1, constraints);
mainWindow.add (button1);
```

The public instance variables are described in Table 22-7.

TABLE 22-7
The grid bag constraints

PUBLIC INSTANCE VARIABLE	DESCRIPTION
anchor	When a component is smaller than its display area, an anchor specifies how to position the component in the area. The valid values are CENTER (the default), NORTH, NORTHEAST, EAST, SOUTHEAST, SOUTH, SOUTHWEST, WEST, and NORTHWEST. These values must be preceded by the name of the class—for instance, `GridBagConstraints.NORTH`.
fill	When a component's requested size is smaller than its display area, the fill attribute can be used to stretch the component. The valid values are NONE Do not stretch the component. This is the default. HORIZONTAL Stretch the component as much as possible horizontally. VERTICAL Stretch the component as much as possible vertically. BOTH Stretch the component as much as possible horizontally and vertically. These values must be preceded by the name of the class—for instance, `GridBagConstraints.VERTICAL`.

TABLE 22-7 continued
The grid bag constraints

PUBLIC INSTANCE VARIABLE	DESCRIPTION
gridx, gridy	Use gridx and gridy to specify the top left cell in a component's display area. Numbering begins at 0. The value GridBagContraints.RELATIVE (the default value) can be used instead of a number. This value indicates that a component is to be positioned relative to the last component added, to the right for gridx and below for gridy.
gridwidth, gridheight	These variables specify the width and height of a component's display area, as measured in cells. The default value is 1. The values REMAINDER and RELATIVE can be used to specify that the component is the last or next to last, respectively, in a row or column.
ipadx, ipady	These variables are used to increase a component's minimum size by the specified number of pixels on the left and right (ipadx) and on the top and bottom (ipady). The default values are 0.
insets	Insets specify how much empty space, as measured in pixels, should be placed between a component and the edges of its display area. The default is 0. Following is an example: `constraints.insets = new Insets (top,left,bottom,right);` where top, left, bottom, and right are nonnegative integers.
weightx, weighty	In a grid bag layout, not all cells need to be the same size. Their sizes can vary depending on values assigned to weightx and weighty. These values do not specify absolute dimensions for a cell, merely a relative size. Thus, all things being equal, a cell with weightx = 100 is twice as wide as one with weightx = 50, whereas a cell with weightx = 0 is just wide enough to display its component. Of course, all things are seldom equal. The algorithm used for determining a cell's dimensions is not described in Java's online documentation, so one must acquire an intuitive sense for what happens through experimentation. By the way, if all the weights are 0 (the default), the components huddle together in the center of the container.

Following is code to create the grid bag layout shown in Figure 22-12:

```
// Create and set the layout
   GridBagLayout layout = new GridBagLayout();
   Container mainWindow = getContentPane();
```

```
   mainWindow.setLayout (layout);

// Create a constraints object
   GridBagConstraints constraints;

// Create three button objects
   JButton button1 = new JButton ("One");
   JButton button2 = new JButton ("Two");
   JButton button3 = new JButton ("Three");

// Set the constraints object for button1, indicating that
// button1
//    starts in row 0, column 0
//    has a height of 2 cells
//    fills its display area in both directions
//    is inset within its display area by 6, 4, 3, and 0
//    has a horizontal weighting factor of 100
// with the remaining constraints taking their default values
   constraints = new GridBagConstraints();
   constraints.gridy = 0;          // row 0
   constraints.gridx = 0;          // column 0
   constraints.gridheight = 2;
   constraints.fill = GridBagConstraints.BOTH;
   constraints.insets = new Insets (6,4,3,0);
   constraints.weightx = 100;
   layout.setConstraints (button1, constraints);
   mainWindow.add (button1);

// Set the constraints object for button2, indicating that
// button2
//    starts in row 0, column 1
// with the remaining constraints taking their default values
   constraints = new GridBagConstraints();
   constraints.gridy = 0;          // row 0
   constraints.gridx = 1;          // column 1
   layout.setConstraints (button2, constraints);
   mainWindow.add (button2);

// Set the constraints object for button3, indicating that
// button3
//    starts in row 1, column 2
//    fills its display area in the vertical directions
//    has a horizontal weighting factor of 50
//    has a vertical weighting factor of 100
// with the remaining constraints taking their default values
   constraints = new GridBagConstraints();
   constraints.gridy = 1;          // row 1
   constraints.gridx = 2;          // column 2
   constraints.weightx = 50;
   constraints.weighty = 100;
   constraints.fill = GridBagConstraints.VERTICAL;
   layout.setConstraints (button3, constraints);
   mainWindow.add (button3);
```

Card Layouts

A card layout consists of a stack of components. Only one component can be seen at a time, but it is possible to switch between components. When a card layout is created, the top component is visible. Figure 22-13 illustrates a card layout, and following is the code that created it:

FIGURE 22-13
A card layout

```
CardLayout layout = new CardLayout();
Container mainWindow = getContentPane();

setLayout (layout);
mainWindow.add ("One", new JButton("One"));
mainWindow.add ("Two", new JButton("Two"));
mainWindow.add ("Three", new JButton("Three"));
mainWindow.add ("Four", new JButton("Four"));
```

Several methods are used to move between components. These are `first`, `last`, `next`, `previous`, and `show`. Following is some code that demonstrates these methods in action. The word this refers to the container in which the code is running, a frame in this example. At other times, this might be replaced by a variable name that refers to the container associated with the layout.

```
layout.first (this);
layout.next (this);
layout.previous (this);
layout.last (this);
layout.show (this, "Three");
```

Panels

For the sake of simplicity, all of the components in the preceding discussion were buttons. We could equally well have used lists, text areas, and even panels. A panel is a container that can contain other components, including other panels. Fancy graphical user interfaces can be built by combining panels and other components in an imaginative manner. Figure 22-14, for instance, shows an example that is plenty fancy and more than a bit silly.

FIGURE 22-14
The use of panels

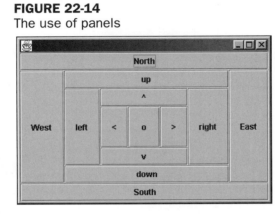

Following is the code that laid out the GUI in Figure 22-14:

```
BorderLayout layout = new BorderLayout();
Container mainWindow = getContentPane();
mainWindow.setLayout (layout);

mainWindow.add (new JButton ("North"), "North");
mainWindow.add (new JButton ("East"), "East");
mainWindow.add (new JButton ("South"), "South");
mainWindow.add (new JButton ("West"), "West");

JPanel panel = new JPanel();
mainWindow.add (panel, "Center");

BorderLayout layout2 = new BorderLayout();
panel.setLayout (layout2);
panel.add (new JButton ("up"), "North");
panel.add (new JButton ("down"), "South");
panel.add (new JButton ("left"), "West");
panel.add (new JButton ("right"), "East");

JPanel panel2 = new JPanel();
panel.add (panel2, "Center");

BorderLayout layout3 = new BorderLayout();
panel2.setLayout (layout3);
panel2.add (new JButton ("^"), "North");
panel2.add (new JButton ("v"), "South");
panel2.add (new JButton ("<"), "West");
panel2.add (new JButton (">"), "East");
panel2.add (new JButton ("o"), "Center");
```

EXERCISE 22.6

1. What is a panel? Give an example of its use.

2. List the major layout manager classes and their primary features.

3. What are the default layouts of frames, applets, and dialogs?

22.7 Events

When developing a graphical user interface, the programmer is concerned not only with the layout of the window objects but also with handling the events they trigger. If we use `BreezySwing`, then we handle events very easily in methods such as `buttonClicked` and `menuItemSelected`. But life becomes complicated when we use Java's GUI packages directly, as illustrated in the conversion program earlier in the lesson. In this section, we give a brief overview of the relationships between events, listeners, and components. For an exhaustive survey of all of the events, listeners, and components supported by Swing and AWT, see Sun's documentation.

Events and Components

From our work with the conversion program, we know that certain events can be associated with certain components. For instance, action events can be associated with buttons, and keyboard events can be associated with text fields. Table 22-8 (on page 760) lists

■ Three different classes of events

■ Their associated components

■ The conditions that trigger the events

   For example, the table indicates that the `ActionEvent`

■ Is limited to buttons, lists, menu items, and text fields

■ Can be triggered by clicking a button, double-clicking an item in a list, selecting a menu item, or pressing the **Enter** key in a text field

TABLE 22-8
Some events and their associated components

EVENT CLASS	ASSOCIATED COMPONENTS	TRIGGERED WHEN
ActionEvent	JButton	The button is clicked.
	JList	An item in the list is double-clicked.
	JMenuItem	The menu item is selected.
	JTextField	The user presses the **Enter** key in the field.
MouseEvent extends InputEvent	Component	A mouse button is pressed in the extends component.
		A mouse button is released in the component (provided it was pressed in the same component). A mouse button is clicked in the component (i.e., pressed and then released).
		The mouse enters the component.
		The mouse exits the component.
		The mouse is dragged in the component (i.e., moved while a button is depressed).
		The mouse is moved in the component.
WindowEvent	Window	The window is activated.
		The window is closed.
		The window is closing.
		The window is deactivated.
		The window is deiconified.
		The window is iconified
		The window is opened.

Events and Listeners

An event is ignored unless the originating component has added a listener to handle the event. In the conversion program we used the addActionListener method to add listeners to buttons. Table 22-9 lists some events in AWT, their associated listeners, and how to add/remove these listeners. We did not have any reason to remove a component's listener in the conversion program, but the table shows that we could have done so. Table 22-9 also lists the methods included in each listener interface.

TABLE 22-9

Some events and their associated listeners

EVENT CLASS	ASSOCIATED LISTENER INTERFACE	IS THERE AN ADAPTER CLASS?	METHODS TO ADD/REMOVE LISTENER	LISTENER INTERFACE METHODS
Action Event	Action Listener	No	addActionListener () removeActionListener()	actionPerformed (ActionEvent)
Mouse Event extends InputEvent	Mouse Listener	Yes	addMouseListener() removeMouseListener()	mousePressed (MouseEvent) mouseReleased (MouseEvent) mouseClicked (MouseEvent) mouseEntered (MouseEvent) mouseExited (MouseEvent)

	Mouse
	
	Motion
	Listener
		Yes	AddMouse
			
			    MotionListener()
			removeMouse
			    MotionListener()
				mouseDragged
				(MouseEvent)
				
				mouseMoved
				(MouseEvent)

Window Event	Window Listener	Yes	addWindowListener() removeWindowListener()	windowActivated (WindowEvent) windowClosed (WindowEvent) windowClosing (WindowEvent) window Deactivated (WindowEvent) window Deiconified (WindowEvent) windowIconified (WindowEvent) windowOpened (WindowEvent)

Events and Their Methods

When an event occurs, the event object, e, is passed as a parameter to the appropriate listener method, and the listener method can then send messages to the event object. For instance, consider the following code segment:

```
JButton btn = (JButton) e.getSource();
```

The getSource message is understood by all events and returns the object in which the event originated—a button in the preceding example. Table 22-10 lists several different classes of events and the most useful methods in each class.

TABLE 22-10
Some events and their associated methods

EVENT CLASS	EVENT METHODS	DESCRIPTION
All events	Object getSource()	Gets the object in which the event originated.
	String toString()	Returns a string representation of the event.
MouseEvent extends InputEvent	int getClickCount()	Returns the number of mouse clicks associated with the event. Could be 0, 1, or 2.
	Point getPoint()	Returns the x, y position of the mouse where the event occurs relative to the top left corner of the component in which the event occurs.
	int getX()	Returns the x position of the mouse where the event occurs relative to the top left corner of the component in which the event occurs.
	int getY()	Returns the y position of the mouse where the event occurs relative to the top left corner of the component in which the event occurs.
	boolean isPopupTrigger ()	Returns true if this mouse event triggers the pop-up menu, else false.
Window Event	getWindow()	Returns the window in which the event occurred.

EXERCISE 22.7

1. Describe how components, listeners, and events cooperate in an application.

22.8 Dialogs

In Lesson 10, we examined how to construct dialogs with the BreezySwing class GBDialog. In a real Java application or applet, you would use the Swing class JDialog. Like the JFrame class, which is used to implement application windows, JDialog is a subclass of the Window class. Thus, dialogs are like frames in many ways, but with two important exceptions:

1. A dialog can be *modal*; that is, it can prevent the user from accessing the rest of the application before quitting the dialog.

2. A dialog must have a parent—that is, a frame to which it can refer after it is created.

A dialog also can have a title. There are several constructors that allow the programmer to specify these attributes:

```
public JDialog (JFrame parent, String title, boolean modal)
public JDialog (JFrame parent, String title)
public JDialog (JFrame parent, boolean modal)
public JDialog (JFrame parent)
```

Dialogs are not modal by default. The reference to the parent frame allows a dialog to send messages to the application.

The programmer must use Swing and AWT to lay out a dialog's window objects and set up their listeners, just as with frames. To show how this is done, we redo the dialog example presented in Lesson 10. The interface of the revised dialog is shown in Figure 22-15.

FIGURE 22-15
A sample dialog

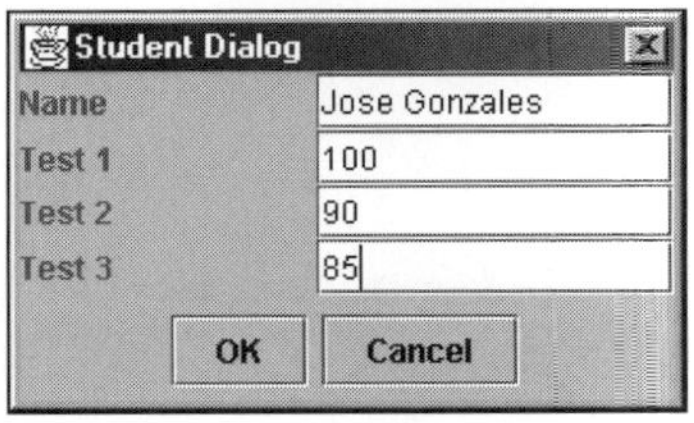

Following is the portion of the of the application's main interface class that involves the use of the dialog:

```
private void add(){
//Adds a new student
//   Preconditions  -- none
//   Postconditions -- if the user cancels the dialog, then no change
//                  -- else the new student is selected
//                        she is added to the end of the student list
//                        her name is added to the end of the name list
//                        her info is displayed
//                        she becomes the selected item in both lists
```

```
        Student tempStu = new Student();
        StudentDialog studentDialog
                    = new StudentDialog (this, tempStu);
        studentDialog.show();
        if (studentDialog.getDlgCloseIndicator().equals ("OK")){
            String message = model.add (tempStu);
            if (message != null){
                messageBox(message);
                return;
            }
            model.setCurrentStudent(tempStu.getName());
            displayCurrentStudent();
        }
    }
}
```

Following is a listing of the revised dialog class. We use Swing and AWT directly.

```
/*  StudentDialog.java

1) This is the dialog for the student test scores program.
2) It displays the student passed to it.
3) The user can then change the data in the dialog's window.
4) If the user clicks the OK button, the student is updated with
   the data in the window.
5) If the user clicks the Cancel button, the dialog closes and returns
   without modifying the student.
*/


import javax.swing.*;
import java.awt.*;
import java.awt.event.*;

public class StudentDialog extends JDialog
                                implements ActionListener{

    //Window objects
    private JLabel nameLabel, test1Label, test2Label, test3Label;

    private JTextField nameField, test1Field, test2Field, test3Field;

    private JButton btnOK, btnCancel;

    //Instance variables
    private Student student;        //The student being modified
    private String closeIndicator;  //The dialog close indicator

    public StudentDialog (JFrame f, Student stu){
    //Constructor
    //  Preconditions  -- the input parameters are not null
    //  Postconditions -- the dialog's window is initialized
```

```
//                 -- the student variable is set
//                 -- the student's data are displayed in the
//                    dialog's window

    //Housekeeping required in every modal dialog
    super (f, true);

    //Set the dialog's size and title
    setSize (250,150);
    setTitle ("Student Dialog");

    //Set the dialog's default value for the close indicator to Cancel.
    //If the user closes the dialog without clicking either the OK or
    //Cancel button, the default takes effect.
    setDlgCloseIndicator ("Cancel");

    //Save the student reference and display the student data in the
    //dialog's window.
    student = stu;

    // Instantiate the window objects
    nameLabel  = new JLabel("Name");
    test1Label = new JLabel("Test 1");
    test2Label = new JLabel("Test 2");
    test3Label = new JLabel("Test 3");
    nameField  = new JTextField(12);
    test1Field = new JTextField(3);
    test2Field = new JTextField(3);
    test3Field = new JTextField(3);
    btnOK     = new JButton("OK");
    btnCancel = new JButton("Cancel");

    // Add the window objects to the appropriate layout
    JPanel labelPanel = new JPanel(new GridLayout(4, 1));
    JPanel fieldPanel = new JPanel(new GridLayout(4, 1));
    JPanel buttonPanel = new JPanel();
    Container mainWindow = getContentPane();
    mainWindow.add("West", labelPanel);
    mainWindow.add("East", fieldPanel);
    mainWindow.add("South", buttonPanel);
    labelPanel.add(nameLabel);
    labelPanel.add(test1Label);
    labelPanel.add(test2Label);
    labelPanel.add(test3Label);
    fieldPanel.add(nameField);
    fieldPanel.add(test1Field);
    fieldPanel.add(test2Field);
    fieldPanel.add(test3Field);
    buttonPanel.add(btnOK);
    buttonPanel.add(btnCancel);
```

```
        // Add the action listeners to the buttons
        btnOK.addActionListener(this);
        btnCancel.addActionListener(this);

        // Display the student's information
        nameField.setText (student.getName());
        test1Field.setText("" + student.getScore(1));
        test2Field.setText("" + student.getScore(2));
        test3Field.setText("" + student.getScore(3));
    }

    public void actionPerformed (ActionEvent e){
    //Responds to the OK and Cancel buttons.
    //  Preconditions  -- one of the two buttons has been clicked
    //  Postconditions -- if the Cancel button then
    //                      the student is not modified
    //                      the close indicator equals Cancel
    //                      the dialog is closed
    //                      control returns to the caller
    //                   -- if the OK button then
    //                      the student is modified
    //                      the close indicator equals OK
    //                      the dialog is closed
    //                      control returns to the caller

        //Get the data from the screen
        String name = nameField.getText();
        int score1 = new Integer(test1Field.getText()).intValue();
        int score2 = new Integer(test2Field.getText()).intValue();
        int score3 = new Integer(test3Field.getText()).intValue();
        String   validationErrors;

        // Get the button in which the click occurred
        JButton buttonObj = (JButton) e.getSource();

        if (buttonObj == btnCancel)                      //Cancel button

            //Close the dialog and return to the caller
            dispose();

        else{                                            //OK button

            //Update the student with the screen data
            student.setName(name);
            student.setScore(1, score1);
            student.setScore(2, score2);
            student.setScore(3, score3);

            //Set the close indicator to OK, close the dialog, and
            //return to the caller.
            setDlgCloseIndicator ("OK");
```

```
            dispose();
        }
    }

    public void setDlgCloseIndicator(String s){
        closeIndicator = s;
    }

    public String getDlgCloseIndicator(){
        return closeIndicator;
    }
}
```

The critical code to notice in the main interface class is

```
StudentDialog studentDialog
            = new StudentDialog (this, tempStu);
studentDialog.show();
if (studentDialog.getDlgCloseIndicator().equals ("OK")){
    String message = model.add (tempStu);
    if (message != null){
        messageBox(message);
        return;
    }
    model.setCurrentStudent(tempStu.getName());
    displayCurrentStudent();
}
```

The dialog is activated in line 2, at which point the main interface is blocked until the user closes the dialog. After the dialog is closed, execution resumes at line 3. Here the application determines the manner in which the user closed the dialog and then in line 4 takes the appropriate action.

You have seen similar code for the action listener earlier in this lesson. Note the following points, however:

1. The constructor method calls the JDialog constructor (super) with the parent and the title parameters.

2. A dialog's default layout is BorderLayout.

3. This particular dialog sets its own size.

EXERCISE 22.8

1. Why bother to define a dialog class when you can use a JOptionPane?.

22.9 The Model/View/Controller Pattern

In Lesson 8, we introduced the idea of separating an application into a model and a view. Now we take the idea one step further and show how to divide an application into a model, a view, and a controller, where the controller represents all the application's listener classes. This division of responsibilities is well suited to handling the complexities of large applications, although it will appear a little awkward in the small case study that we present next.

In the *model/view/controller pattern*, also called the MVC pattern, it is the view's responsibility to

■ Instantiate the window objects, position them in the interface, and attach listeners to them as needed

■ Instantiate and initialize the model

■ Accurately represent the model to the user

The responsibilities of the model are to

■ Define and manage the application's data (which usually requires coordinating the activities of several programmer-defined classes)

■ Respond to messages from the listeners

■ Inform the view of changes to the model's internal state

The responsibilities of controller are to

■ Implement the necessary listeners

■ Send messages to the model in response to user-generated events

EXERCISE 22.9

1. Explain the purpose of a controller.

Case Study: A Color Meter Application

Request

Create an application that allows the user to view a color by mixing red, green, and blue (RGB) values.

Analysis

The proposed interface is shown in Figure 22-16.

FIGURE 22-16
The interface for the color meter application

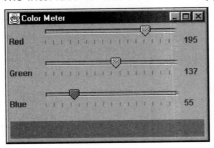

A color has three components (red, green, blue). The user manipulates each component separately by means of one of the sliders. Each slider takes on values in the range 0..255. The rectangular patch below the sliders changes color in response to changes in the sliders. In addition, the RGB values are displayed to the right of the sliders.

The application uses the seven classes listed in Table 22-11.

TABLE 22-11
Classes used in the color meter application

CLASS	ROLE IN THE PROGRAM
ColorMeterView	The view class defines the window's layout, associates listeners with the sliders, instantiates the model, and redisplays the color when requested by the model.
ColorMeterModel	The model knows the current color, changes the color in response to messages from the listeners, and informs the view when the color display needs to be changed.
GenericWindowListener	The controller contains one instance of the GenericWindowListener encountered earlier in the lesson. This listener closes the application's window when the user clicks the **X** button.
SliderListener	The controller contains three slider listeners, one attached to each slider. The listeners detect changes in the sliders and inform the model. The listener classes are organized in a hierarchy whose abstract class is SliderListener and whose concrete classes follow.
RedSliderListener	The listener for red slider
BlueSliderListener	The listener for blue slider
GreenSliderListener	The listener for green slider

Design and Implementation of `ColorMeterView`

The constructor has these tasks to perform:

- Instantiates the model, passes it a pointer back to the view, and initializes the color to pure red

- Instantiates the window objects and adds them to a grid bag layout

- Initializes the appearance of the view to match the model

- Attaches listeners to the sliders and to the window

  The method `public void update (Color color)`

- Is called by the model whenever the color changes

- Redisplays the color patch and the numbers beside the sliders to reflect the latest color

```java
import javax.swing.*;
import java.awt.*;

public class ColorMeterView extends JFrame{

    // Declare variables for the window objects
    private JLabel        redLabel;
    private JLabel        greenLabel;
    private JLabel        blueLabel;
    private JSlider       redSlider;
    private JSlider       greenSlider;
    private JSlider       blueSlider;
    private JLabel        redValue;
    private JLabel        greenValue;
    private JLabel        blueValue;
    private JPanel        colorPanel;

    // Declare a variable for the model
    private ColorMeterModel model;

    // Constructor
    public ColorMeterView(){

        // Set the title
        setTitle ("Color Meter");

        // Instantiate the model
        model = new ColorMeterModel (this, new Color (255,0,0));

        // Instantiate the window objects
        redLabel    = new JLabel("Red");
        greenLabel  = new JLabel("Green");
        blueLabel   = new JLabel("Blue");
        redSlider   = createSlider();
        greenSlider = createSlider();
        blueSlider  = createSlider();
        redValue    = new JLabel("    ");
```

```
      greenValue  = new JLabel("    ");
      blueValue   = new JLabel("    ");
      colorPanel  = new JPanel();
      //colorPanel.setSize(100, 50);

      // Instantiate and set a grid bag layout
      GridBagLayout layout = new GridBagLayout();
      getContentPane().setLayout(layout);

      // Add the window objects to the layout
      //                         row,col,width,height
      addComponent(layout, redLabel    , 0, 0, 1, 1);
      addComponent(layout, greenLabel  , 1, 0, 1, 1);
      addComponent(layout, blueLabel   , 2, 0, 1, 1);
      addComponent(layout, redSlider   , 0, 1, 1, 1);
      addComponent(layout, greenSlider , 1, 1, 1, 1);
      addComponent(layout, blueSlider  , 2, 1, 1, 1);
      addComponent(layout, redValue    , 0, 2, 1, 1);
      addComponent(layout, greenValue  , 1, 2, 1, 1);
      addComponent(layout, blueValue   , 2, 2, 1, 1);
      addComponent(layout, colorPanel  , 3, 0, 3, 10);

      // Initialize the appearance of the view to match the model
      redSlider.setValue (255);
      greenSlider.setValue (0);
      blueSlider.setValue (0);
      update (new Color (255,0,0));

      // Add listeners to three scrollsliders
      redSlider.addChangeListener
           (new RedSliderListener(model));
      greenSlider.addChangeListener
           (new GreenSliderListener(model));
      blueSlider.addChangeListener
           (new BlueSliderListener(model));

      // Add a listener to the window
      addWindowListener(new GenericWindowListener());
   }

   private JSlider createSlider(){
      JSlider slider = new JSlider(SwingConstants.HORIZONTAL, 0, 255, 16);
      slider.setBackground(getBackground());
      slider.setPaintTicks(true);
      slider.setPaintTrack(true);
      slider.setMajorTickSpacing(16);
      return slider;
   }
```

```
// Add a component to the layout in the indicated row and column
// with the indicated height and width
private void addComponent(GridBagLayout layout,
                          Component component,
                          int row, int col,
                          int width, int height){

    GridBagConstraints constraints = new GridBagConstraints();

    constraints.fill = GridBagConstraints.BOTH;
    constraints.insets.bottom = 2;
    constraints.insets.top    = 2;
    constraints.insets.left   = 2;
    constraints.insets.right  = 2;
    constraints.weightx = 100;
    constraints.weighty = 100;

    constraints.gridx = col;
    constraints.gridy = row;
    constraints.gridwidth = width;
    constraints.gridheight = height;
    layout.setConstraints(component, constraints);
    getContentPane().add (component);
}


// The model calls this method whenever the model wants
// to update the view. It updates the number to the right of
// each slider and repaints the canvas in the current color.
public void update(Color color){
    redValue.setText("" + color.getRed());
    greenValue.setText("" + color.getGreen());
    blueValue.setText("" + color.getBlue());
    colorPanel.setBackground(color);
}


public static void main (String[] args){
    JFrame frm = new ColorMeterView();
    frm.setSize (300, 200);
    frm.setVisible (true);
}
}
```

Design and Implementation of `ColorMeterModel`

Two instance variables are needed:

1. `color`, which indicates the current color

2. `view`, which points back to the view class, thus allowing the model to send messages to the view

The constructor

- Initializes the variable that points back to the view
- Initializes the variable that holds the color

  The method `public void setRedValue(int value)`

- Is called by the red slider listener
- Has a parameter that indicates the red component's new value
- Sets the specified component to the value indicated and tells the view to update itself

  The methods `setGreenValue(anIt)` and `setBlueValue(anInt)` are similar.

```java
import java.awt.*;

public class ColorMeterModel{

    private Color color;
    private ColorMeterView view;

    public ColorMeterModel(ColorMeterView vw, Color initialColor){
        view = vw;
        color = initialColor;
    }

    // Change the red component of the color.
    // value -- indicates the new red component.
    public void setRedValue(int value){

        // Get the current component colors;
        int greenValue = color.getGreen();
        int blueValue = color.getBlue();

        // Reset the meter's color
        color = new Color(value, greenValue, blueValue);

        // Update the view to reflect the change in color
        view.update (color);
    }

    // Change the green component of the color.
    // value -- indicates the new green component.
    public void setGreenValue(int value){

        // Get the current component colors;
        int redValue = color.getRed();
        int blueValue = color.getBlue();

        // Reset the meter's color
        color = new Color(redValue, value, blueValue);

        // Update the view to reflect the change in color
```

```
        view.update (color);
    }


        // Change the blue component of the color.
        // value -- indicates the new blue component.
    public void setBlueValue(int value){

        // Get the current component colors;
        int redValue = color.getRed();
        int greenValue = color.getGreen();

        // Reset the meter's color
        color = new Color(redValue, greenValue, value);

        // Update the view to reflect the change in color
        view.update (color);
    }
}
```

Design and Implementation of the Listener Classes

The abstract sliderListener class implements the ChangeListener interface. A slider listener object declares the protected instance variable model that refers to the model. Following is the code:

```
// SliderListener

import javax.swing.event.*;

abstract public class SliderListener implements ChangeListener{

    protected ColorMeterModel model;

}
```

When the user interacts with a slider, a ChangeEvent occurs. This event is passed to the stateChanged method, which is implemented in the subclasses RedSliderListener, GreenSliderListener, and BlueSliderListener. The stateChanged method

■ Extracts the integer value from the slider's event

■ Runs the model's method for changing the appropriate color with this integer as a parameter

Following is the code for the class RedSliderListener:

```
// RedSliderListener

import javax.swing.*;
import javax.swing.event.*;

public class RedSliderListener extends SliderListener{

   public RedSliderListener(ColorMeterModel cmmdl){
      model = cmmdl;
   }

   public void stateChanged(ChangeEvent e) {
      JSlider slider = (JSlider)e.getSource();
      int value = Math.min (255, slider.getValue());
      model.setRedValue(value);
   }
}
```

22.10 Applets, Swing, and AWT

We have already seen how to convert stand-alone programs into applets when GBFrame and GBApplet are used. The conversion process follows the same pattern when Swing/AWT is used. Following are a few points to remember:

- Window objects are created and added to the interface in an init() method rather than in a constructor.

- There is no method main.

- Because applets are embedded in Web pages, the Web browser handles the applet's closing. Thus, there is no need for a WindowListener.

- Like stand-alone applications, applets need listeners to detect and handle events in components.

- Applets can be split between a view and a model in the same manner as applications.

To illustrate the conversion process, following is the second version of the ConversionWithSwing program from the beginning of the lesson rewritten as an applet:

```
import javax.swing.*;
import java.awt.*;
import java.awt.event.*;

public class ConversionWithSwing extends JApplet
                                 implements ActionListener{

   private JLabel     fahrenheitLabel;
   private JTextField fahrenheitField;
   private JLabel     celsiusLabel;
   private JTextField celsiusField;
   private JButton    fahrenheitButton;
   private JButton    celsiusButton;
```

```java
public void init(){
    fahrenheitLabel  = new JLabel ("Fahrenheit");
    fahrenheitField  = new JTextField ("212", 6);      // 6 columns wide
    celsiusLabel     = new JLabel ("Celsius");
    celsiusField     = new JTextField ("100", 6);      // 6 columns wide
    fahrenheitButton = new JButton (">>>>>>");
    celsiusButton    = new JButton ("<<<<<<");

    Container mainWindow = getContentPane();
    mainWindow.setLayout(new FlowLayout());
    mainWindow.add (fahrenheitLabel);
    mainWindow.add (celsiusLabel);
    mainWindow.add (fahrenheitField);
    mainWindow.add (celsiusField);
    mainWindow.add (fahrenheitButton);
    mainWindow.add (celsiusButton);

    fahrenheitButton.addActionListener (this);
    celsiusButton.addActionListener (this);
}

public void actionPerformed (ActionEvent e){
    String str;
    double fahrenheit, celsius;
    JButton btn = (JButton)e.getSource();
    Thermometer thermo = new Thermometer();

    if (btn == celsiusButton){
        str = celsiusField.getText().trim();
        celsius = (new Double (str)).doubleValue();
        thermo.setCelsius(celsius);
        fahrenheit = thermo.getFahrenheit();
        fahrenheitField.setText ("" + fahrenheit);
    }
    else{
        str = fahrenheitField.getText().trim();
        fahrenheit = (new Double (str)). doubleValue ();
        thermo.setFahrenheit(fahrenheit);
        celsius = thermo.getCelsius();
        celsiusField.setText ("" + celsius);
    }
}
}
```

EXERCISE 22.10

1. Why do applets not need a window listener?

22.11 *Setting the Look and Feel*

As mentioned in Lesson 7, the programmer can set the look and feel of a GUI-based program written with Swing. BreezySwing users accomplish this by calling the method setLookAndFeel within a subclass of GBFrame, GBDialog, or GBApplet. Following is the code for the method, which you can place in any subclass of JFrame, JDialog, or JApplet as well:

```
public void setLookAndFeel(String type){
    int value = 0;
    UIManager.LookAndFeelInfo[] looks;
    looks = UIManager.getInstalledLookAndFeels();
    if (type.equalsIgnoreCase("METAL"))
        value = 0;
    else if (type.equalsIgnoreCase("MOTIF"))
        value = 1;
    else
        value = 2;
    try{
        UIManager.setLookAndFeel(looks[value].getClassName());
        SwingUtilities.updateComponentTreeUI(this);
    }catch(Exception e){
        messageBox("Error: \n" + e.toString());
    }
}
```

SUMMARY

In this lesson, you learned:

■ The user interface of a GUI-based program consists of components, layout managers, listeners, and events. Component, listener, and event classes are included in the package javax.swing; layout manager, listener, and event classes are included in the package java.awt.

■ Container classes are special types of components that represent application windows, panels, applets, and dialogs.

■ The programmer lays out a graphical user interface, adding components to a container under the influence of a layout manager. Layout managers include the flow layout, border layout, grid layout, grid bag layout, and card layout.

■ A listener is an interface that specifies methods for responding to events in a component. The programmer can customize a listener by defining a class that implements the interface with methods to perform the desired tasks. The programmer then attaches listeners to the component to handle the corresponding events.

■ An adapter is a class that implements a listener interface with method stubs.

■ The model/view/controller pattern is the preferred way of structuring GUI-based programs.

VOCABULARY *Review*

Define the following terms:

Abstract Windowing Toolkit (AWT)	container	option panes
	grid bag layout	scroll bar
adapter class	listener	slider
component	model/view/controller pattern	Swing Toolkit

REVIEW *Questions*

FILL IN THE BLANK

Complete the following sentences by writing the correct word or words in the blanks provided.

1. A(n) _____ is a special type of component to which other components are added for display.

2. _____ is the default layout manager of frames and dialogs.

3. _____ is the default layout manager of applets and panels.

4. _____ is a layout manager that allows grid cells to extend through multiple rows or columns.

5. _____ are objects that respond to events in components.

6. The _____ pattern is a framework for dividing the responsibilities of a software system among three categories of classes.

7. _____ provides a ticked ruler that allows the user to specify a quantity by dragging the mouse.

8. The class _____ provides a set of static methods for displaying commonly used dialogs.

9. The class _____ allows the programmer to organize components within a rectangular area of a window.

10. To allow the user to quit a window or a dialog using the close box, the programmer must implement a(n) _____ .

PROJECTS

PROJECT 22-1

Redo the Fahrenheit to Celsius temperature conversion application with Swing/AWT so that your program adheres to the model/view/controller pattern as described in the case study.

PROJECT 22-2

Redo the shapes drawing program in Project 19-8 using Swing/AWT.

PROJECT 22-3

Modify the shapes drawing program in Project 22-2 so that the user can select the color from a dialog that displays a color meter.

PROJECT 22-4

Develop a double field class that behaves in a similar manner to the double field class of `BreezySwing`.

CRITICAL *Thinking*

Discuss the advantages and disadvantages of having the main application class implement the listeners for the window and window objects.

GRAPHICS, FILES, APPLETS, AND SWING

REVIEW *Questions*

TRUE/FALSE

Circle T if the statement is true or F if it is false.

T F 1. A stream of bytes from which data are read is called an input stream.

T F 2. Java lets you read characters from a file one character at a time, one word at a time, or one line at a time.

T F 3. A file dialog is a window that displays as the result of an event.

T F 4. Hypertext and hypermedia are both ways to jump from page to page on the Web.

T F 5. The HEAD markup tag designates the title that appears in the browser's window.

T F 6. You can code six types of lists using HTML tags.

T F 7. The .wav extension designates an inline image.

T F 8. The coordinate system in Java and other programming languages is the Cartesian coordinate system.

T F 9. Listener objects tell buttons where the listener code is located.

T F 10. The flow layout displays objects in the order in which they are added.

FILL IN THE BLANK

Complete the following sentences by writing the correct word or words in the blanks provided.

1. The set of classes used to connect a program to a file stream are defined in Java's _____ package.

2. A(n) _____ statement provides a way to locate and respond to run-time errors.

3. Sequences of characters separated by white-space characters and processed as words are called _____.

4. A stream of bytes to which data are written is called a(n) _____.

5. The World Wide Web consists of two kinds of machines: _____ and _____.

6. HTML codes called _____ indicate the format of text elements or links to other nodes.

7. To convert a Java application to an applet, you must replace the name GBFrame with the name _____.

8. Java provides the _____ class for drawing in components.

9. A(n) _____ is a rectangular area within a window that can be painted independently of the rest of the window.

10. _____ objects are so called because they contain other window objects.

WRITTEN QUESTIONS

Write a brief answer to each of the following questions or problems.

1. Assume that the data for a student have been saved in a binary file. These data include the student's ID number, name, and five grades. The types of data are positioned in the file as follows:

   ```
   <int> <String> <5 doubles>
   ```

   Write a Java code segment that opens a data input stream on this file and reads the student's data into the appropriate variables.

2. Describe how to convert an application written with BreezySwing to an applet.

3. Explain how a Web browser accesses and runs an applet.

4. A programmer is designing an application that writes integer data from an array to a file. Which Java classes would be appropriate for this kind of output operation? Write a pseudocode algorithm that describes the task.

5. Explain what happens when your program calls the method `repaint`.

6. Explain the difference between an ordinary window object and a container object.

PROJECTS

SCANS **PROJECT U6-1**

Modify the Fahrenheit to Celsius conversion program in Lesson 7 so that it displays the degrees Fahrenheit and degrees Celsius in parallel vertical bars.

SCANS **PROJECT U6-2**

A text file of student grades has the following format:

<name> <newline>

<grade1> <space> <grade2> <space> <grade3> <newline>

Write a program that inputs data from this file and displays the class average, the students with the highest grade, and the students with the highest average grade (display all ties).

SCANS PROJECT U6-3

Write an applet that allows the user to convert decimal numbers to numbers in other bases and back again. The applet should have three fields (decimal, other number, and other base) and two buttons (**To Decimal** and **From Decimal**). The enclosing Web page should contain instructions for the use of the applet. Use the method `Integer.parseInt(aString, aBase)` to convert a string of digits in a given base to an `int`. Use the method `Integer.toString(anInt, aBase)` to convert an `int` to a string of digits in a given base.

SCANS PROJECT U6-4

Convert the program in Project U6-3 from a `BreezySwing` applet to a Swing applet.

CRITICAL*Thinking*

The programmer who does file I/O with arrays must deal with the problem of not knowing how many data objects need to be read during file input. Discuss this problem and propose a solution.

APPENDIX A

Java Resources

Java Documentation and the JDK

Sun Microsystems maintains an excellent Web site where programmers can find complete documentation for the Java API (Application Programming Interface) and download a free JDK (Java Development Kit). The following sections discuss some of the items that you can access on the Web.

SUN'S TOP-LEVEL JAVA PAGE (http://www.javasoft.com)

This page contains news about events in the Java world and links to documentation, Java-related products, program examples, and free downloads of the JDK.

PRODUCTS AND API (http://www.javasoft.com/products/)

This page allows you to select the version of JDK that matches your computer and to begin the download process. You also can download the documentation if you do not want to access it on the Web.

DOCUMENTATION AND TRAINING (http://developer.java.sun.com/developer/infodocs/)

This page introduces you to the documentation for the Java API and describes the most effective ways to browse this documentation.

PACKAGE INDEX (http://java.sun.com/j2se/1.3/docs/api/)

This page has links to all of the packages in JDK 1.3.

We suggest that you bookmark all of these links and use the last one on a daily basis. You might even bookmark the links to the most commonly used packages, such as `java.lang`, `java.awt`, and `javax.swing`. When you visit a package, you can browse all of the classes in that package. When you visit a class, you can browse all of the variables and methods defined in that class. There are numerous cross-references to superclasses and related classes in a given package. You also can download the JDK documentation for quicker browsing on your hard drive.

If you decide to download the JDK, be sure to select JDK 1.3 (`BreezySwing` cannot be used with versions earlier than JDK 1.2). Note that at the time of this writing, the most current version of JDK was JDK 1.3. After downloading, you install the JDK on your computer by running the installation program. You should print the **Readme** file for further reference. The installation will leave the directory JDK1.3 on your disk.

THE BREEZYSWING PAGE (http://www.wlu.edu/~lambertk/hsjava)

The I/O packages used in the book, BreezySwing, TerminalIO, and TurtleGraphics, as well as the source code and information about their use, can be obtained from your instructor or downloaded from the BreezySwing page.

Installation of I/O Packages with JDK and DOS Command Prompt

In this appendix we provide installation instructions for using the I/O packages with JDK and a DOS command prompt. Installation instructions for other programming environments can be found on the book's Web site at http://www.wlu.edu/~lambertk/hsjava/.

Let's assume you have installed JDK 1.3 on the C: drive of your PC. You should copy the files **BreezySwing.jar, TerminalIO.jar,** and **TurtleGraphics.jar** to the directory **C:\jdk1.3\jre\lib\ext.** You also should copy these files to the directory **C:\Program Files\JavaSoft\JRE\1.3\lib\ext.**

Place the following command in the **autoexec.bat** file and restart your machine:

```
path=%path%;c:\;c:\jdk1.3\bin
SET CLASSPATH=c:\jdk1.3\classes;.
```

Be sure to terminate CLASSPATH with a semicolon.

Before you use JDK, make sure that all of your Java source program (**.java**) files are in the current directory (this can be any directory on your computer). You can define more than one class in a source file, but the usual procedure is to have one source file for each class. Each source file should begin with the same name as the class that it contains and should end with **.java.** Remember that Java class names and file names are case sensitive. If you want to run an applet, the appropriate **html** file also should be in this directory.

Using the Basic JDK Tools

You can then do the following at the system command prompt:

- **Compile a program.** The basic syntax is javac <filename>, where <filename> is a Java source file name (ending in **.java**). Java locates and compiles all of the files required by your program. Any syntax error messages are displayed in the command window, and a byte code (**.class**) file is generated for each class defined in your program. The command javac *.java is a quick way to compile a program that consists of several source files.

- **Run an application.** The basic syntax is java <filename>, where <filename> is the name of the class that defines the main method of your program. Note that the **.class** extension must be omitted. Run-time error messages are displayed in the command window.

- **Run an applet.** The basic syntax is appletviewer <filename>, where <filename> is the name of an **html** file that links to your applet.

Java Language Elements

This appendix covers some extra non-GUI features of Java that are useful. We make no attempt to provide a complete description of Java. For a full reference, consult the documentation at Sun's Web site.

Reserved Words

The words shown in bold are not discussed in this book. For a discussion of them, see the references on Sun's Web site.

abstract	double	import	private	**throws**
boolean	else	**inner**	protected	**transient**
break	extends	instanceof	public	try
byte	final	int	**rest**	**var**
case	**finally**	interface	return	void
catch	float	long	short	**volatile**
char	for	**native**	static	while
class	**future**	new	super	
const	**generic**	null	switch	
continue	**goto**	operator	**synchronized**	
default	if	**outer**	this	
do	implements	**package**	throw	

Data Types

Java supports two kinds of data types: primitive types and reference types. Primitive types represent numbers, characters, and Boolean values. The numeric data types are listed in Table B-1.

TABLE B-1
Java's primitive data types

TYPE	STORAGE REQUIREMENTS	RANGE
byte	1 byte	−128 to 127
short	2 bytes	−32,768 to 32,767
int	4 bytes	−2,147,483,648 to 2,147,483,647
long	8 bytes	−9,223,372,036,854,775,808L to 9,223,372,036,854,775,807L
float	4 bytes	−3.40282347E+38F to 3.40282347E+38F
double	8 bytes	−1.79769313486231570E+308 to 1.79769313486231570E+308

Type `char` represents the Unicode character set, consisting of 65,536 values. These values include those of the traditional ASCII set and other international characters. A table listing the ASCII character set appears in Appendix D.

Character literals are enclosed in single quotation marks (for example, `'a'`). Table B-2 lists some commonly used escape sequences for nonprinting characters.

TABLE B-2
Some escape sequences

ESCAPE SEQUENCE	MEANING
\b	backspace
\t	tab
\n	newline
\"	double quotation mark
\'	single quotation mark
\\	backslash

The type `boolean` represents the Boolean values `true` and `false`. `boolean` is the type of all expressions that serve as conditions of `if` statements and loops.

Reference types represent objects, such as strings, arrays, other built-in Java objects, and user-defined objects.

Casting Numeric Types

The numeric types from least to most inclusive are

```
byte  short  int  long  float  double
```

The cast operator converts a more inclusive type to a less inclusive one. The form of the operator is

```
(<less inclusive type name>) <more inclusive value>
```

For instance, following is a sequence of assignment statements in which we begin with a `double`, cast to an `int`, and finally cast to a `char`:

```
double d;
int i;
char c;

d = 65.57;
i = (int) d;          // i contains 65, due to truncation.
c = (char) i;         // c contains 'A'.
writer.println(c);    // Displays 'A'.
```

As we notice in this example, the cast operation can destroy information. In general, the fractional part of a `double` or `float` is thrown away when cast to `byte`, `short`, `int`, or `long`. In addition, if the number being cast is outside the range of the target type, unexpected values can result. Thus,

```
(int)8.88e+009   becomes     290065408
```

The cast operator also can be used within expressions. Normally, when an operator involves mixed data types, the less inclusive type is automatically converted to the more inclusive before the operation is performed. For instance

```
2 / 1.5                becomes    2.0 / 1.5
2 + 1.5                becomes    2.0 + 1.5
aByte  / aLong         becomes    aLong   / aLong
aFloat - anInt         becomes    aFloat  - aFloat
aFloat % aDouble       becomes    aDouble % aDouble
```

We could present other examples in a similar vein. Sometimes, though, we want to override this automatic conversion and, for instance, to treat

```
aFloat / anInt     as     anInt / anInt
```

This can be achieved by using the cast operation again, as illustrated next:

```
(int)aFloat * anInt            becomes    anInt * anInt
aByte       / (byte)aLong      becomes    aByte / aByte
aFloat      + (float)aDouble   becomes    aFloat + aFloat
```

In these expressions, the unary cast operator has higher precedence than the binary arithmetic operators.

Control Statements

COMPOUND STATEMENT

A compound statement consists of a list of zero or more declarations and statements enclosed within braces, {}. A semicolon must terminate each statement, except for the compound statement itself. Following is the form:

```
{
    <declaration or statement-1>
    .
    .
    <declaration or statement-n>
}
```

DO-WHILE STATEMENT

do-while statements have the following form:

```
do
    <statement>
while (<boolean expression>)
```

SWITCH STATEMENT

The switch statement handles a selection among cases, where each case is a constant of a primitive type. Following is an example:

```
switch (ch){
    case 'a':
    case 'A': doSomething1();
            break;
    case 'b':
    case 'B': doSomething2();
            break;
    case 'c': doSomething3();
            break;
    default:  doSomething4();
}
```

The break statements are optional in this example, but they are required if the case lists are to be considered mutually exclusive. The default statement is also optional but highly recommended.

Math Class Methods

The Math class includes many static methods that allow clients to perform trigonometric functions and so forth. For example, the code

```
System.out.println(Math.sqrt(2));
```

outputs the square root of 2. Table B-3 lists most of these methods.

TABLE B-3
Math class methods

Math Class METHOD	DESCRIPTION
`double abs(double a)`	Returns the absolute value of a double value. Similar methods exist for `float`, `int`, and `long`.
`double acos(double a)`	Returns the arc cosine of an angle, in the range of 0.0 through pi.
`double asin(double a)`	Returns the arc sine of an angle, in the range of −pi/2 through pi/2.
`double atan(double a)`	Converts rectangular coordinates (b, a) to polar (r, theta).
`double atan2(double a, double b)`	Converts rectangular coordinates (b, a) to polar (r, theta).
`double ceil(double a)`	Returns the smallest (closest to negative infinity) double value that is not less than the argument and is equal to a mathematical integer.
`double cos(double a)`	Returns the trigonometric cosine of an angle.
`double exp(double a)`	Returns the exponential number e (i.e., 2.718...) raised to the power of a double value.
`double floor(double a)`	Returns the largest (closest to positive infinity) double value that is not greater than the argument and is equal to a mathematical integer.
`double log(double a)`	Returns the natural logarithm (base e) of a double value.
`double max(double a, double b)`	Returns the greater of two double values. Similar methods exist for `float`, `int`, and `long`.
`double min(double a, double b)`	Returns the smaller of two double values. Similar methods exist for float, int, and long.
`double pow(double a, double b)`	Returns the value of the first argument raised to the power of the second argument.
`double random()`	Returns a double value with a positive sign, greater than or equal to 0.0 and less than 1.0.
`double rint(double a)`	Returns the double value that is closest in value to a and is equal to a mathematical integer.
`long round(double a)`	Returns the closest `long` to the argument.
`double sin(double a)`	Returns the trigonometric sine of an angle.
`double sqrt(double a)`	Returns the correctly rounded positive square root of a double value.
`double tan(double a)`	Returns the trigonometric tangent of an angle.
`double toDegrees(double angrad)`	Converts an angle measured in radians to the equivalent angle measured in degrees.
`double toRadians(double angdeg)`	Converts an angle measured in degrees to the equivalent angle measured in radians.

The Character and Integer Classes

The Character and Integer classes allow char and int values to masquerade as objects when included in collections. These classes also include several static methods that are useful in processing numeric data. For example, Character methods exist for converting between single digits and the numbers they represent, and Integer methods exist for the conversion of strings of digits to numbers. Tables B-4 and B-5 list some of these methods.

TABLE B-4
Some Character class methods

Character METHOD	DESCRIPTION
int digit(char ch, int radix)	Returns the numeric value of the character ch in the specified radix.
char forDigit(int digit, int radix)	Determines the character representation for a specific digit in the specified radix.
int getNumericValue(char ch)	Returns the Unicode numeric value of the character as a nonnegative integer.
boolean isDigit(char ch)	Determines if the specified character is a digit.
boolean isLetter(char ch)	Determines if the specified character is a letter.
boolean isLowerCase(char ch)	Determines if the specified character is a lowercase character.
boolean isUpperCase(char ch)	Determines if the specified character is an uppercase character.
boolean isWhiteSpace(char ch)	Determines if the specified character is white space according to Java.
char toLowerCase(char ch)	The given character is mapped to its lowercase equivalent; if the character has no lowercase equivalent, the character itself is returned.
char toUpperCase(char ch)	Converts the character argument to uppercase.

TABLE B-5
Some `Integer` class methods

`Integer` METHOD	DESCRIPTION
`int parseInt(String s)`	Parses the string argument as a signed decimal integer.
`int parseInt(String s,` `    int radix)`	Parses the string argument as a signed integer in the radix specified by the second argument.
`String toString(int i)`	Returns a new `String` object representing the specified integer.
`String toString(int i,` `            int radix)`	Creates a string representation of the first argument in the radix specified by the second argument.
`Integer valueOf(String s)`	Returns a new `Integer` object initialized to the value of the specified `String`.
`Integer valueOf(String s,` `            int radix)`	Returns a new `Integer` object initialized to the value of the specified `String`.

The Class `java.util.Arrays`

Common operations on arrays include searching, sorting, comparing two arrays for equality, and filling an array's cells with a default value. The class `java.util.Arrays` includes many static methods that perform these functions. Most of them are overloaded for arrays of different element types, including all the primitive types and the class `Object`. Table B-6 lists one example of each type of operation; we refer the reader to Sun's documentation for descriptions of the others.

TABLE B-6
Some `Arrays` methods

`Arrays` METHOD	DESCRIPTION
`static int binarySearch(int[]a,` `                    int key)`	Searches the array a for the integer key using the binary search algorithm.
`static Boolean equals(int[] a,` `                int[] a2)`	Returns true if the two specified arrays of `ints` are *equal* to one another.
`static void fill(int[] a, int val)`	Assigns the specified `int` value to each element of the specified array of ints.
`static void sort(int[] a)`	Sorts the specified array of `ints` into ascending numerical order.

The Class `java.util.ArrayList`

The package `java.util` includes several list classes, each of which implements the `List` interface. The class `ArrayList` provides the basic behavior of an array (including random access of elements) but also allows clients to add or remove elements. An array list tracks the number of elements currently available and also allows the client to set an initial capacity or trim the capacity to the number of elements. Table B-7 describes the `ArrayList` methods.

TABLE B-7
The `ArrayList` methods

`ArrayList` METHOD	DESCRIPTION
`ArrayList()`	Constructs an empty list.
`ArrayList(Collection c)`	Constructs a list containing the elements of the specified collection, in the order they are returned by the collection's iterator.
`ArrayList(int initialCapacity)`	Constructs an empty list with the specified initial capacity.
`void add(int index,` `        Object element)`	Inserts the specified element at the specified position in this list.
`boolean add(Object o)`	Appends the specified element to the end of this list.
`boolean addAll(Collection c)`	Appends all of the elements in the specified `Collection` to the end of this list, in the order that they are returned by the specified `Collection's Iterator`.
`boolean addAll(int index,` `               Collection c)`	Inserts all of the elements in the specified `Collection` into this list, starting at the specified position.
`void clear()`	Removes all of the elements from this list.
`Object clone()`	Returns a shallow copy of this `ArrayList` instance.
`boolean contains(Object elem)`	Returns `true` if this list contains the specified element.
`void ensureCapacity(` `   int minCapacity)`	Increases the capacity of this `ArrayList` instance, if necessary, to ensure that it can hold at least the number of elements specified by the minimum capacity argument.
`Object get(int index)`	Returns the element at the specified position in this list.
`int indexOf(Object elem)`	Searches for the first occurence of the given argument, testing for equality using the `equals` method.
`boolean isEmpty()`	Tests if this list has no elements.
`int lastIndexOf(Object elem)`	Returns the index of the last occurrence of the specified object in this list.
`Object remove(int index)`	Removes the element at the specified position in this list.

TABLE B-7 (Continued)
The `ArrayList` methods

ArrayList METHOD	DESCRIPTION
`protected  void removeRange(` `   int fromIndex, int toIndex)`	Removes from this list all of the elements whose index is between `fromIndex`, inclusive and `toIndex`, exclusive.
`Object set(int index,` `          Object element)`	Replaces the element at the specified position in this list with the specified element.
`int size()`	Returns the number of elements in this list.
`Object[] toArray()`	Returns an array containing all of the elements in this list in the correct order.
`Object[] toArray(Object[] a)`	Returns an array containing all of the elements in this list in the correct order.
`void trimToSize()`	Trims the capacity of this `ArrayList` instance to be the list's current size.

Three-Dimensional Arrays

Java does not limit the number of dimensions for arrays. Following is the declaration and initialization of a three-dimensional array:

```
int[][][] threeD = {{{ 1, 2, 3}, { 4, 5, 6}},
                    {{ 7, 8, 9}, {10,11,12}},
                    {{13,14,15}, {16,17,18}}};
```

The array's elements fill a box whose dimensions are 3 by 2 by 3. To refer to an element, we indicate its position in the box, remembering as usual to start counting at 0. Thus, element 8 is at position (1,0,1) and is referred to as follows:

```
threeD[1][0][1]
```

Operator Precedence

Table C-1 shows the operator precedence. The operators shown in bold are not discussed in this book. For a discussion of them, see the references on Sun's Web site.

TABLE C-1
Operator precedence

OPERATOR	FUNCTION	ASSOCIATION
()	Parentheses	Left to right
[]	Array subscript	
.	Object member selection	
++	Increment	Right to left
- -	Decrement	
+	Unary plus	
-	Unary minus	
!	Boolean negation	
~	**Bitwise negation**	
(*type*)	Type cast	
*	Multiplication	Left to right
/	Division	
%	Modulus	
+	Addition or concatenation	Left to right
-	Subtraction	
<<	**Bitwise shift left**	**Left to right**
>>	**Bitwise shift right**	
>>>	**Bitwise shift right, sign extension**	
<	Less than	Left to right
<=	Less than or equal to	
>	Greater than	
>=	Greater than or equal to	
instanceOf	Class membership	

TABLE C-1 (Continued)
Operator precedence

OPERATOR	FUNCTION	ASSOCIATION
==	Equal to	Left to right
!=	Not equal to	
&	**Boolean AND (complete)**	**Left to right**
	Bitwise AND	
^	**Boolean exclusive OR**	**Left to right**
	Bitwise exclusive OR	
|	**Boolean OR (complete)**	**Left to right**
	Bitwise OR	
&&	Boolean AND (partial)	Left to right
||	Boolean OR (partial)	Left to right
?:	**Ternary conditional**	**Right to left**
=	Assign	Right to left
+=	Add and assign	
-=	Subtract and assign	
*=	Multiply and assign	
/=	Divide and assign	
%=	Modulo and assign	
<<=	**Shift left and assign**	
>>=	**Shift right, sign extension, and assign**	
>>>=	**Shift right, no sign extension, and assign**	
&=	**Boolean or bitwise AND and assign**	
|=	**Boolean or bitwise OR and assign**	
^=	**Boolean or bitwise exclusive OR and assign**	

ASCII Character Set

Table D-1 shows the ordering of the ASCII character set. The digits in the left column represent the leftmost digits of the ASCII code, and the digits in the top row are the rightmost digits. Thus, the ASCII code of the character R at row 8, column 2, is 82. The printable characters range from ASCII 33 to ASCII 126. The values from ASCII 0 to ASCII 32 and ASCII 127 are associated with white-space characters, such as the horizontal tab (HT), or nonprinting control characters, such as the escape key (ESC).

TABLE D-1
Ordering of the ASCII character set

	0	1	2	3	4	5	6	7	8	9
0	NUL	SOH	STX	ETX	EOT	ENQ	ACK	BEL	BS	HT
1	LF	VT	FF	CR	SO	SI	DLE	DC1	DC2	DC3
2	DC4	NAK	SYN	ETB	CAN	EM	SUB	ESC	FS	GS
3	RS	US	SP	!	"	#	$	%	&	`
4	(	)	*	+	,	-	.	/	0	1
5	2	3	4	5	6	7	8	9	:	;
6	<	=	>	?	@	A	B	C	D	E
7	F	G	H	I	J	K	L	M	N	O
8	P	Q	R	S	T	U	V	W	X	Y
9	Z	[	\	]	^	_	`	a	b	c
10	d	e	f	g	h	i	j	k	l	m
11	n	o	p	q	r	s	t	u	v	w
12	x	y	z	{	|	}	~	DEL		

APPENDIX E

Number Systems

When we make change at the store, we use the decimal (base 10) number system. The digits in this system are the characters 0 through 9. Computers represent all information in the binary (base 2) system. The digits in this system are just the characters 0 and 1. Because binary numbers can be very long strings of 1s and 0s, programmers also use the octal (base 8) and hexadecimal (base 16) number systems, usually for low-level programming in assembly language. The octal digits range from 0 to 7, and the hexadecimal digits include the decimal digits and the letters A through F. These letters represent the numbers 10 through 15, respectively.

To identify the system being used, one can attach the base as a subscript to the number. For example, the following numbers represent the quantity 414 in the binary, octal, decimal, and hexadecimal systems:

```
414 in binary notation          110011110₂
414 in octal notation           636₈
414 in decimal notation         414₁₀
414 in hexadecimal notation     19E₁₆
```

Note that as the size of the base grows, either the number of digits or the digit in the largest position might be smaller.

Each number system uses positional notation to represent a number. The digit at each position in a number has a positional value. The positional value of a digit is determined by raising the base of the system to the power specified by the position. For an n-digit number, the positions (and exponents) are numbered 0 through $n - 1$, starting with the rightmost digit and moving to the left. For example, as Figure E-1 illustrates, the positional values of a three-digit decimal number are 100 (10^2), 10 (10^1), and 1 (10^0), moving from left to right in the number. The positional values of a three-digit binary number are 4 (2^2), 2 (2^1), and 1 (2^0).

FIGURE E-1
Positional values of base 10 and base 2 numbers

base 10				base 2			
positional values	100	10	1	positional values	4	2	1
positions		2	1	0	positions	2	1	0

The quantity represented by a number in any system is determined by multiplying each digit (as a decimal number) by its positional value and adding the results. The following examples show how this is done for numbers in several systems:

```
414 base 10 =

4 * 10² + 1 * 10¹ + 4 * 10⁰ =

4 * 100 + 1 * 10 + 4 * 1 =

400      + 10      + 4 = 414
```

```
110011110 base 2 =

1 * 2⁸ + 1 * 2⁷ + 0 * 2⁶ + 0 * 2⁵ + 1 * 2⁴ + 1 * 2³ + 1 * 2² + 1 * 2¹ + 0 * 2⁰ =

1 * 256 + 1 * 128 + 0 * 64 + 0 * 32 + 1 * 16 + 1 * 8 + 1 * 4 + 1 * 2 + 0 * 1 =

256      + 128      + 0       + 0       + 16      + 8      + 4      + 2      + 0 = 414
```

```
636 base 8 =

6 * 8² + 3 * 8¹ + 6 * 8⁰ =

6 * 64 + 3 * 8 + 6 * 1 =

384      + 24      + 6 = 414
```

```
19E base 16 =

1 * 16² + 9 * 16¹ + E * 16⁰ =

1 * 256 + 9 * 16 + 14 * 1

256      +  144    + 14 = 414
```

Each of these examples appears to convert from the number in the given base to the corresponding decimal number. To convert a decimal number to a number in a given base, we use division and remainder rather than multiplication and addition. The process works as follows:

1. Find the largest power of the given base that divides into the decimal number.

2. The quotient becomes the digit at that power's position in the new number.

3. Repeat steps 1 and 2 with the remainder until the remainder is less than the number.

4. If the last remainder is greater than 0, the remainder becomes the last digit in the new number.

5. If you must skip a power of the base when performing step 3, then put a 0 in that power's position in the new number.

To illustrate, let us convert the decimal number 327 to the equivalent binary number.

The highest power of 2 by which 327 is divisible is 256 or 2^8. Thus, we'll have a nine-digit binary number, with 1 in position 8:

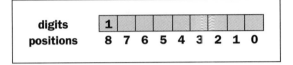

digits	1								
positions	8	7	6	5	4	3	2	1	0

The remainder of the first division is 71. The highest power of 2 by which 71 is divisible is 64 (2^6). Thus, we have skipped 128 (2^7), so we write 0 in position 7 and 1 in position 6:

digits	1	0	1						
positions	8	7	6	5	4	3	2	1	0

The remainder of the second division is 7. Thus, as you can see, we skip 3 more powers of 2 — 32, 16, and 8—on the next division in order to use 4. So, we place 0s at positions 5, 4, and 3, and 1 at position 2 in the new number:

digits	1	0	1	0	0	0	1		
positions	8	7	6	5	4	3	2	1	0

The remainder of the third division is 3. This is divisible by the next power of 2, which is 2, so we put 1 at position 1 in the new number. The remainder of the last division, 1, goes in position 0:

digits	1	0	1	0	0	0	1	1	1
positions	8	7	6	5	4	3	2	1	0

One reason that programmers prefer to use octal or hexadecimal notation instead of binary notation is that octal and hexadecimal are more expressive (one can say more with less). Another reason is that it is very easy to convert an octal number or a hexadecimal number to the corresponding binary number. To convert octal to binary, you assume that each digit in the octal number represents three digits in the corresponding binary number. You then start with the rightmost octal digit and write down the corresponding binary digits, padding these to the left with 0s to the count of 3, if necessary. You proceed in this manner until all of the octal digits have been converted. The following examples show such conversions:

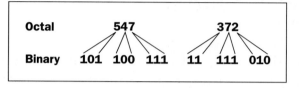

The conversion of hexadecimal numbers to binary numbers works in a similar way, except that each hexadecimal digit translates to four binary digits.

APPENDIX F

Java Exception Handling

Java divides run-time errors into two broad categories: errors and exceptions. Errors are serious run-time problems that usually should not be handled by the programmer. For example, if a method gets stuck in an infinite recursion, Java will throw a StackOverflowError. Java defines a separate class for each type of error. You can browse through these in Sun's Web site, as described in Appendix A, starting with the class Error in the package java.lang.

Exceptions come in two varieties: those that Java requires the programmer to handle, such as IOException, and those that the programmer may or may not handle, such as ArithmeticException and ArrayIndexOutOfBoundsException. To explore Java's Exception class hierarchy on Sun's Web site, select the desired package in the package index and scroll to the bottom of the page. Most of the exception classes are defined in java.lang, but several important ones also are defined in java.io and java.util

The following code segments show how you might handle exceptions in the cases of division and array subscripting:

```
// Catch an attempt to divide by zero

try{
    quotient = dividend / divisor;
    System.out.println("Successful division");
}
catch (ArithmeticException e){
    System.out.println("Error1: " + e.toString());
}
```

```
// Catch an attempt to use an array index that is out of range

try{
    a[x] = 0;
    System.out.println("Successful subscripting");
}
catch (ArrayIndexOutOfBoundsException e){
    System.out.println("Error2: " + e.toString());
}
```

When Java detects an error and throws an exception, control is immediately transferred from the offending instruction in the try statement to the catch statement. Thus, the output of the first message would be skipped if an exception occurs in either of the preceding code segments. If the try statement completes successfully, the catch statement is not executed.

A `try` statement can be followed by more than one `catch` statement. For example, the following code segment combines the exception handling of the previous two segments:

```
// Catch an attempt to divide by zero and to use an array index
// that is out of bounds

try{
    quotient = dividend / divisor;
    System.out.println("Successful division");
    a[x] = quotient;
    System.out.println("Successful subscripting");
}
catch (ArithmeticException e){
    System.out.println("Error1: " + e.toString());
}
catch (ArrayIndexOutOfBoundsException e){
    System.out.println("Error2: " + e.toString());
}
```

The same two exceptions are possible in this example, but Java will get to throw only one of them. When this occurs, control shifts to the first `catch` statement following the `try` statement. If the class of the exception thrown is the same as or is a subclass of the class of that `catch` statement's parameter, then the code for the `catch` statement executes. Otherwise, Java compares the exception thrown to the parameter of the next `catch` statement and so on.

It is possible (and often desirable) to define new kinds of exceptions that can be thrown by methods in user-defined classes. The complete rules for doing this are beyond the scope of this book but can be found on Sun's Web site.

Java Packages

A Java package is a name that stands for a set of related classes. For example, the package `java.io` stands for all of the Java file stream classes. Exceptions and interfaces also can be parts of a package.

The package `java.lang` contains many commonly used classes, such as `Math` and `String`. This package is implicitly imported into every Java program file, so no `import` statement is required. To use any other package, such as `java.io`, in a program file, the programmer must explicitly import the package with an `import` statement.

Programs can import all of the classes in a given package, using the form

```
import <package name>.*;
```

It is also possible to import selected classes from a given package and omit others. For example, the following line imports just the `ArrayList` class from the `java.util` package and omits the others:

```
import java.util.ArrayList;
```

This statement has the effect of making the `ArrayList` class visible to the program file, but leaves the rest of the classes in the `java.util` package invisible.

Occasionally, a program uses classes that have the same name but are defined in different packages. For example, the `List` class in `java.awt` implements a scrolling list box (similar to `javax.swing.JList`), whereas the `List` interface in `java.util` specifies operations for Java's list collections. To avoid ambiguity in these programs, you must prefix the class name with its package wherever the class name is used. Following is an example:

```
import java.util.*;
import java.awt.*;

   .
   .

   // Instantiate a scrolling list box to display the data
   javB.awt.List listView = new java.awt.List();

   .
   .

   // Instantiate an array list to contain the data
   java.util.List listModel = new ArrayList();
```

To define and compile a package, perform the following steps:

1. Create three directories on your disk. Name the first directory **testbed** and the second directory **sources**. The third directory should have the name of the package you are defining, such as **mypackage**. The **sources** and **mypackage** directories should be contained as subdirectories in the **testbed** directory.

2. Place a tester program (say, **Tester.java**) for your package in the **testbed** directory.

3. Open a DOS window and move to the **mypackage** directory.

4. Place the Java source files (**.java** extension) for your package in the **mypackage** directory. Each source file in the package should have the line

```
package mypackage;
```

at the beginning of the file.

5. Compile the Java files using the DOS command **javac *.java.** If all goes well, the byte code files (**.class** extension) should be in the **mypackage** directory.

6. Move up to the **testbed** directory and compile the tester program.

7. Run the tester program using the DOS command **java Tester.** If all goes well, your package is ready for release. Before distributing your package, move the source (**.java**) files to the **sources** directory. A package should have just **.class** files.

Go back to Step 5 each time you need to modify a source file in the package.

APPENDIX H

I/O Packages

T his appendix provides a quick reference to open-source packages that support terminal-based I/O, GUI-based I/O, and turtle graphics. These packages are called `TerminalIO`, `BreezySwing`, and `TurtleGraphics`. Methods that are part of AWT and Swing are so noted. For more details, byte code, source code, a tutorial, and a related package, `BreezyGUI`, that uses only AWT components, see the Web site at http://www.wlu.edu/~lambertk/hsjava/.

BreezySwing

Programs that use `BreezySwing` should import the package as follows:

```
import BreezySwing.*;
```

`BreezySwing` provides the following features:

1. A grid bag layout and methods for creating and positioning window objects.
2. Abstract methods for handling typical events, such as button selections, menu item selections, list item selections, and mouse events. The programmer overrides these methods for use in particular applications.
3. Specialized data entry field classes for integers and floating-point numbers.
4. Methods for displaying message boxes.
5. A class for formatting strings and numbers as centered, left justified, or right justified.

To use `BreezySwing` in a Java application, define the application class as an extension of the class `GBFrame`. To use `BreezySwing` in a Java applet, define the applet class as an extension of `GBApplet`. Applets do not have a method `main`, and they use an `init` method instead of a constructor method. `GBApplet` provides the same functionality as `GBFrame`, but without menus. To use `BreezySwing` in a dialog, define the dialog class as an extension of `GBDialog`.

Methods to Initialize a Window

There are three methods to set up almost every application window. They are part of AWT.

void setSize(int width, int height)

Action: Adjusts the size of the window to the specified width and height in pixels.

Example: `theGUI.setSize(200, 200);`

void setTitle(String title)

Action: Adds the specified title to the title bar of the window.

Example: `theGUI.setTitle("Shape Drawing program");`

```
void setVisible(int width, int height)
```

Action: Makes the window visible or invisible.

Example: `theGUI.setVisible(true);`

Method Specifications for Classes `GBFrame`, `GBApplet`, and `GBDialog`

The following methods are used in classes that extend `GBFrame`, `GBApplet`, and `GBDialog`. When adding window objects to a window, the `row` and `col` parameters specify a row and a column in the window's underlying grid bag layout (counting from 1). The `width` and `height` parameters specify the number of columns and rows through which a window object extends. Window objects include labels, buttons, lists, menu items, and data entry fields. A window automatically adjusts the size and spacing between objects when it is resized.

Methods That Add Window Objects to a Window

```
JLabel addLabel(String text, int row, int col, int width, int height)
```

Action: Creates a new label with the given text, places the label in the framework at the given location, and returns the label.

Example: `JLabel radiusLabel = addLabel("Radius", 1, 1, 1, 1);`

```
JButton addButton(String label, int row, int col, int width, int height)
```

Action: Creates a new button with the given label, places the button in the framework at the given location, and returns the button.

Example: `JButton calculateButton = addButton("Calculate", 1, 1, 1, 1);`

```
IntegerField addIntegerField(int number, int row, int col, int width, int
                             height)
```

Action: Creates a new integer field with the given number, places the integer field in the framework at the given location, and returns the integer field.

Example: `IntegerField radiusField = addIntegerField(0, 1, 1, 2, 1);`

```
DoubleField addDoubleField (double number, int row, int col, int width, int
                            height)
```

Action: Creates a new double field with the given number, places the double field in the framework at the given location, and returns the double field.

Example: `DoubleField areaField = addDoubleField(0.0, 1, 1, 2, 1);`

```
JTextField addTextField(String text, int row, int col, int width, int height)
```

Action: Creates a new text field with the given text, places the text field in the framework at the given location, and returns the text field.

Example: `JTextField nameField = addTextField("Sandy", 1, 1, 3, 1);`

```
JTextArea addTextArea(String text, int row, int col, int width, int height)
```

Action: Creates a new text area with the given text, places the text area in the framework at the given location, and returns the text area.

Example: `JTextArea resultArea = addTextArea("", 1, 1, 5, 2);`

`JList addList(int row, int col, int width, int height)`

Action: Creates a new list, places the list in the framework at the given location, and returns the list.

Example: `JList nameList = addList(1, 1, 5, 1);`

`JCheckBox addCheckBox (String text, int row, int col,`
`                       int width, int height)`

Action: Creates a new check box with the given text, places the checkbox in the framework at the given location, and returns the checkbox.

Example: `JCheckBox marriedBox = addCheckBox ("Married", 1, 1, 1, 1);`

`JMenuItem addMenuItem(String menuLabel, String itemLabel)`

Action: Creates a menu with the specified label if one does not exist, then creates a menu item with the specified label, adds the menu item to the menu, and returns the menu item. *Note:* Not available for `GBApplet` and `GBDialog`.

Example: `JMenuItem saveFileItem = addMenuItem("File", "Save");`

`JRadioButton addRadioButton (String text, int row, int col, int width, int`
`                             height)`

Action: Creates a new radio button with the given text, places the radio button in the framework at the given location, and returns the radio button.

Example: `JRadioButton marriedBTN = addRadioButton ("Married", 1, 1, 1, 1);`

`GBPanel addPanel (GBPanel p, int row, int col, int width, int height)`

Action: Creates a new panel with the given panel, places the panel in the framework at the given location, and returns the panel.

Example: `GBPanel testPanel = addPanel (new GBPanel(), 1, 1, 1, 1);`

Methods That Display Message Boxes

Message boxes are used to pop up messages. They are typically used to display short text outputs such as error messages.

`void messageBox(String message)`

Action: Displays a message box with the specified string.

Example: `messageBox("Computation completed.");`

`void messageBox(Double number)`

Action: Displays a message box with the specified number.

Example: `messageBox(3.14);`

`void messageBox(Object obj)`

Action: Displays a message box with the string representation of the object.

Example: `messageBox(new Student());`

```
void messageBox(String message, int width, int height)
```

Action: Displays a message box with the specified string in a window with the specified dimensions.

Example: `messageBox("Computation completed.", 200, 50);`

```
void messageBox(Double number, int width, int height)
```

Action: Displays a message box with the specified number in a window with the specified dimensions.

Example: `messageBox(3.14, 50, 50);`

```
void messageBox(Object obj, int width, int height)
```

Action: Displays a message box with the string representation of the object in a window with the specified dimensions.

Example: `messageBox(new Student(), 300, 300);`

Methods for Handling Events in Window Objects

When an event (e.g., a button click, menu selection, list selection, mouse move, etc.) occurs, the JVM calls one of the following methods.

```
void buttonClicked(JButton buttonObj)
```

Action: The framework invokes this method when a button is selected. The application should override this method to take the appropriate action. The parameter is the button where the event occurred.

```
void listDoubleClicked(JList listObj, String itemClicked)
```

Action: The framework invokes this method when a list item is double-clicked. The application should override this method to take the appropriate action. The parameters are the list and the list item where the event occurred. *Note*: this method is invoked *after* the method `listItemSelected` (see next method).

```
void listItemSelected(JList listObj)
```

Action: The framework invokes this method when a list item is selected with a single click or a double click. The application may or may not override this method to take the appropriate action. The parameter is the list in which the item was selected. The programmer can use the `JList` methods `getSelectedValue()` and `getSelectedIndex()` to determine the selected item and its position.

```
void menuItemSelected(JMenuItem mI)
```

Action: The framework invokes this method when a menu item is selected. The application should override this method to take the appropriate action. The parameter is the menu item where the event occurred. *Note*: Not available for GBApplet and GBDialog.

Method Specifications for Class `GBDialog`

The following messages are unique to class `GBDialog` and are not shared by classes `GBFrame` or `GBApplet`.

`GBDialog(JFrame f)`

Action: This is the constructor. Its use is required in the constructor of a `GBDialog` subclass, and it is invoked by calling `super`. The constructor's parameter is the parent frame of the dialog. When the dialog is used by an application, the parent frame is a reference to the application. When the dialog is used by an applet or by another dialog, the parent frame is an anonymous frame.

`String getDlgCloseIndicator()`

Action: Returns the dialog's closing indicator. The value of this indicator is "Cancel" by default.

Example: `String indicator = theDialog.getDlgCloseIndicator();`

`void setDlgCloseIndicator(String s)`

Action: Sets the dialog's closing indicator to the given string.

Example: `theDialog.setDlgCloseIndicator("OK");`

Method Specifications for Class `GBPanel`

`GBPanel` is a `BreezySwing` extension of `JPanel`. `GBPanel` provides several default methods for handling mouse events.

`void mouseClicked(int x, int y)`

Action: The framework invokes this method when a mouse button is clicked. The panel should override this method to take the appropriate action. The parameters represent the panel coordinates of the mouse when the event occurred.

`void mousePressed(int x, int y)`

Action: The framework invokes this method when a mouse button is pressed. The panel should override this method to take the appropriate action. The parameters represent the panel coordinates of the mouse when the event occurred.

`void mouseReleased(int x, int y)`

Action: The framework invokes this method when a mouse button is released. The panel should override this method to take the appropriate action. The parameters represent the panel coordinates of the mouse when the event occurred.

`void mouseMoved(int x, int y)`

Action: The framework invokes this method when the mouse is moved. The panel should override this method to take the appropriate action. The parameters represent the panel coordinates of the mouse when the event occurred.

`void mouseDragged(int x, int y)`

Action: The framework invokes this method when the mouse is dragged (i.e., moved while a button is pressed). The panel should override this method to take the appropriate action. The parameters represent the panel coordinates of the mouse when the event occurred.

```
void mouseEntered(int x, int y)
```

Action: The framework invokes this method when the mouse enters the panel. The panel should override this method to take the appropriate action. The parameters represent the panel coordinates of the mouse when the event occurred.

```
void mouseExited(int x, int y)
```

Action: The framework invokes this method when the mouse exits the panel. The panel should override this method to take the appropriate action. The parameters represent the panel coordinates of the mouse when the event occurred.

Method Specifications for Class `Format`

The class `Format` allows a programmer to center, left justify, or right justify data within a number of columns.

```
static String justify(char justification, String text, int width)
static String justify(char justification, char ch, int width)
static String justify(char justification, long number, int width)
static String justify(char justification, double number, int width,
                      int precision)
```

Action: Formats and returns the string representation of the given data, where justification is `'l'`, `'r'`, or `'c'`. The data are centered, left justified, or right justified within the given width. If the width cannot accommodate the data, asterisks (*) are displayed.

Examples:
```
String strOutput  =  Format.justify('r', "Hi there!", 34);

String charOutput =  Format.justify('c', 'A', 10);

String intOutput  =  Format.justify('l', 21, 80);

String dollars    =  Format.justify('r', 3.1416, 10, 2);
```

Method Specifications for Window Objects

All the classes described in this section are defined in `javax.swing` except for `IntegerField` and `DoubleField`, which are `BreezySwing` extensions of Java's `JTextField` class. Additional information can be found in Sun's standard Java documentation.

Methods Common to All Window Objects

The method `setVisible(aBoolean)` (described in the `BreezySwing` section at the beginning of this appendix) also works with any window object to make it appear or disappear. The method `setEnabled(aBoolean)` works with such window objects as buttons, menu items, and fields. This method enables or disables the actions of a button or the input or output of fields. The method `requestFocus()` sends the cursor to a field or makes a button ready to be pressed.

Method Specifications for Classes `JLabel` and `JButton`

The method `setText(aString)` modifies the text associated with a label or a button. The method `getText()` returns this text.

Method Specifications for Class `JTextField`

`String getText()`

    Action: Returns the text field's contents.

    Example: `String data = theField.getText();`

`void setText(String str)`

    Action: Replaces the contents of the text field with the given string.

    Example: `theField.setText("Jane Roe");`

`void setEditable(boolean)`

    Action: Enables or disables editing of the field.

    Example: `theField.setEditable(false);`

Method Specifications for Class `JTextArea`

`void append(String str)`

    Action: Appends the given string to the text already displayed in the text area.

    Example: `theArea.append("A string with a newline\n");`

`String getText()`

    Action: Returns the text area's contents.

    Example: `String data = theArea.getText();`

`void setText(String str)`

    Action: Replaces the contents of the text area with the given string.

    Example: `theArea.setText("Jane Roe");`

`void setEditable(boolean)`

    Action: Enables or disables editing of the text area.

    Example: `theArea.setEditable(false);`

Method Specifications for Class `IntegerField`

`IntegerField` is a `BreezySwing` extension of `JTextField`.

`int getNumber()`

Action: Returns the integer currently stored in the integer field or 0 if the integer is malformed.

Example: `int radius = radiusField.getNumber();`

`void setNumber(int number)`

Action: Displays the specified number in the integer field.

Example: `radiusField.setNumber(2316);`

`boolean isValid()`

Action: Returns true if the integer in the field is well formed and false otherwise.

Example: `if (radiusField.isValid())`

Method Specifications for Class `DoubleField`

`DoubleField` is a `BreezySwing` extension of `JTextField`.

`double getNumber()`

Action: Returns the floating-point number currently stored in the `double` field or 0 if the number is malformed.

Example: `double velocity = velocityField.getNumber();`

`void setNumber(double number)`

Action: Displays the specified number in the `double` field.

Example: `areaField.setNumber(527.32);`

`boolean isValid()`

Action: Returns true if the floating-point number in the field is well formed and false otherwise.

Example: `if (velocityField.isValid())`

`void setPrecision(double number)`

Action: Sets the number of digits to be displayed after the decimal point in the `double` field.

Example: `salaryField.setPrecision(2);`

`int getPrecision()`

Action: Returns the number of digits to be displayed after the decimal point in the `double` field.

Example: `System.out.println("Precision = " + salaryField.getPrecision());`

Method Specifications for Check Boxes, Radio Buttons, and Button Groups

Check boxes and radio buttons support the methods setText(aString) and getText(), for changing and examining their labels, and the methods setSelected(aBoolean) and isSelected(), for selecting, deselecting, and examining their selection status. To group radio buttons in a manner that allows only one at a time to be selected, you add them to an instance of JButtonGroup with the method add(aRadioButton).

Method Specifications for the Classes `JList` and `DefaultListModel`

To manipulate the contents of scrolling lists, you must use methods from the JList and DefaultListModel classes. Table H-1 describes the JList methods.

TABLE H-1
The JList methods

JList METHOD	DESCRIPTION
ListModel getModel()	Returns the model for the list. You should cast the result to a DefaultListModel.
int getSelectedIndex()	Returns the position of the selected item.
Object getSelectedValue()	Returns the selected item.
void setSelectedIndex(int index)	Selects the item at the given index.
void setSelectedValue(Object obj, boolean shouldScroll)	Selects the given item.

Table H-2 describes the DefaultListModel methods.

TABLE H-2
The DefaultListModel methods

DefaultListModel METHOD	DESCRIPTION
add(int index, Object obj)	Inserts an item at the given position.
addElement(Object obj)	Adds an item to the end of the list.
void clear()	Makes the list empty.
Object get(int index)	Returns the item at the given position.
Object remove(int index)	Removes the item at the given position.
boolean removeElement(Object obj)	Removes the first instance of the given item.
Object set(index i, Object obj)	Replaces the item at the given position with the given item.
int size()	Returns the number of items in the list.
Object[] toArray()	Returns an array of the items.

TerminalIO

Programs that use `TerminalIO` should import the package as follows:

```
import TerminalIO.*;
```

The package provides objects and methods for reading from the keyboard and writing to the terminal window.

Method Specifications for the Class `KeyboardReader`

This class provides methods for reading user input entered at the keyboard. Such input is automatically echoed in the terminal window. In what follows, assume that `reader` is an instance of the class `KeyboardReader`.

void pause()

Action: Prompts the user to press Enter and waits for the user to do so. This method can be used to pause output in the terminal window and to keep the terminal window from closing in non-GUI programs.

Example: `reader.pause();`

char readChar(String userPrompt)

Action: Displays `userPrompt` in the terminal window and waits for the user's input. Returns a character that represents the user's input from the terminal window.

Example: `char letter = reader.readChar("Please enter a letter: ");`

char readChar()

Action: Same as the preceding except there is no prompt.

double readDouble(String userPrompt)

Action: Displays `userPrompt` in the terminal window and waits for the user's input. Returns a `double` that represents the user's input as echoed in the terminal window. Throws a `NumberFormatException` if the user's input does not represent a `double`.

Example: `double d = reader.readDouble("Please enter a real number: ");`

double readDouble()

Action: Same as the preceding except there is no prompt.

double readInt(String userPrompt)

Action: Displays `userPrompt` in the terminal window and waits for the user's input. Returns an `int` that represents the user's input as echoed in the terminal window. Throws a `NumberFormatException` if the user's input cannot represent an int.

Example: `int i = reader.readInt("Please enter an integer: ");`

double readInt()

Action: Same as the preceding except there is no prompt.

```
String readLine(String userPrompt)
```

Action: Displays userPrompt in the terminal window and waits for the user's input. Returns a string that represents the user's input as echoed in the terminal window.

Example: String name = reader.readLine("Please enter your name: ");

```
String readLine()
```

Action: Same as the preceding except there is no prompt.

Method Specifications for the Class ScreenWriter

This class provides methods for writing program output to the terminal window. Its behavior is similar to that of System.out. Following is a list of the methods. We omit explanations.

```
void print(boolean x)
void print(char x)
void print(char[] x)
void print(double x)
void print(float x)
void print(int x)
void print(long x)
void print(Object x)
void print(String x)
void println()
void println(boolean x)
void println(char x)
void println(char[] x)
void println(double x)
void println(float x)
void println(int x)
void println(long x)
void println(Object x)
void println(String x)
```

TurtleGraphics

Programs that use `TurtleGraphics` should import the package as follows:

```
import TurtleGraphics.*;
```

The package provides classes and methods for manipulating a pen in a graphics window. The pen or turtle is an invisible device, initially positioned at the center of a sketchpad. This center point, also called home, is at the origin of a Cartesian coordinate system. The programmer draws images with the pen by sending it messages. There are several types of pens, as listed in Table H-3. All implement the `Pen` interface, as described in the following section.

TABLE H-3
The `Pen` classes

Pen CLASS	FEATURES
StandardPen	Draws with a straight line in the pen's current color.
BackwardPen	Moves in the opposite direction of a standard pen.
RainbowPen	Draws with a straight line in randomly generated colors.
WigglePen	Draws with a wiggly line in the pen's current color.
WiggleRainbowPen	Draws with a wiggly line in randomly generated colors.

The `Pen` Interface

The `Pen` interface specifies the methods that all of the types of pens support. A pen is initially positioned at the home position (the origin or center of the sketchpad), faces due north, and is placed down on the sketchpad's surface. A nonrainbow pen's default color is blue. When placed down and moved, the pen draws; when picked up and moved, the pen simply moves without drawing. Following are the methods:

void home()

Action: The pen jumps to the center of the graphics window without drawing and points north.

Example: `pen.home();`

void setDirection(double degrees)

Action: The pen points in the indicated direction. Due east corresponds to 0 degrees, north to 90 degrees, west to 180 degrees, and south to 270 degrees. Because there are 360 degrees in a circle, setting the direction to 400 would be equivalent to 400 − 360 or 40 and setting it to −30 would be equivalent to 360 − 30 or 330.

Example: `pen.setDirection(90);    // Make the pen point due north`

void turn(double degrees)

Action: The pen adds the indicated degrees to its current direction. Positive degrees correspond to turning counterclockwise. The degrees can be an integer or floating-point number.

Example: `pen.turn(-45); // Rotate the pen 45 degrees clockwise`

void down()

Action: The pen lowers itself to the drawing surface.

Example: `pen.down();`

void up()

Action: The pen raises itself from the drawing surface.

Example: `pen.up();`

void move(double distance)

Action: The pen moves the specified distance in the current direction. The distance can be an integer or floating-point number and is measured in pixels (picture elements). The size of a pixel depends on the monitor's resolution. For instance, when we say that a monitor's resolution is 800 by 600, we mean that the monitor is 800 pixels wide and 600 pixels high.

Example: `pen.move(100);`

void move(double x, double y)

Action: Moves the pen to the position (x, y).

Example: `pen.move(50, 50);`

void drawString(String string)

Action: Draws the string at the pen's position.

Example: `pen.drawString("Here is the turtle!");`

void setColor(Color color)

Action: Sets the pen's color to the specified color.

Example: `pen.setColor(Color.red);`

void setWidth(int width)

Action: Sets the pen's width to the specified width.

Example: `pen.setWidth(8);`

Pens, Sketchpads, and Sketchpad Windows

Three classes cooperate to implement a turtle graphics program. They are one of the pen classes mentioned earlier, the `SketchPad` class, and the `SketchPadWindow` class. `SketchPadWindow`, a subclass of `GBFrame`, provides the application window for turtle graphics. `SketchPad`, a subclass of `GBPanel`, provides the drawing area within a sketchpad window. Associated with each sketchpad is a pen. Thus, the programmer can manipulate several pens in a single sketchpad window by creating several sketchpads and adding them to the window. In the remaining sections of this appendix, we describe three ways to create turtle graphics applications using these classes.

METHOD 1: CREATE JUST A PEN

The simplest way to create a turtle graphics program is to instantiate a pen and start sending it messages. The framework automatically associates a pen with a sketchpad, places this panel in a window that is 150 pixels by 150 pixels, and opens the window. Following is an example code segment:

```
import TurtleGraphics.*;


public class TestTurtleGraphics{
   public static void main(String [] args) {
      Pen pen = new StandardPen();
      pen.move(100, 100);
   }
}
```

The constructors for `WigglePen` and `WiggleRainbowPen` require the user to specify the number of wiggles and a wiggle angle as parameters. The following code creates a `WigglePen` with 10 wiggles and a wiggle angle of 45:

```
Pen pen = new WigglePen(10, 45);
```

The user can manipulate a sketchpad window like any other window. Any images that the pen has drawn will automatically be refreshed. Note, however, that the programmer has no control over the window and there is only a single drawing area with one pen.

METHOD 2: CREATE A SKETCHPAD WINDOW WITH A PEN

To give the programmer control over a pen's window, you can create it before associating it with a pen. The process consists of two steps:

1. Instantiate a `SketchPadWindow`. Its width and height can be passed as optional parameters, or you get a default size of 150 by 150.

2. Instantiate a pen with the `SketchPadWindow` as a parameter. The window is opened at this point.

Following is an example code segment:

```
import TurtleGraphics.*;


public class TestTurtleGraphics{
   public static void main(String [] args) {
      SketchPadWindow win = new SketchPadWindow(400, 400);
      Pen pen = new StandardPen(win);
      pen.move(100, 100);
   }
}
```

METHOD 3: CREATE A SKETCHPAD AND A PEN

To give programmer control over a pen's sketchpad or drawing area, to work with multiple drawing areas and pens in a single window, or to associate a sketchpad with any application window, an applet, or a dialog, you can create a sketchpad before associating it with a pen. The process consists of three steps:

1. Instantiate a SketchPad.

2. Instantiate a pen with the SketchPad as a parameter.

3. Add the SketchPad to the window. You can use the addPanel method if you are implementing an application, dialog, or applet with GBFrame, GBDialog, or GBApplet. Alternatively, you can instantiate a SketchPadWindow with the SketchPad as a parameter.

The following code segment shows the first option of Step 3. The program creates two sketchpads, sets their background colors, associates them with different types of pens, adds them to an application window, and draws similar images in them.

```java
import TurtleGraphics.*;
import BreezySwing.*;
import java.awt.Color;

public class TestTurtleGraphics extends GBFrame{

    private SketchPad leftPad, rightPad;
    private Pen leftPen, rightPen;

    public TestTurtleGraphics(){
        leftPad = new SketchPad();
        rightPad = new SketchPad();
        leftPad.setBackground(Color.pink);
        rightPad.setBackground(Color.yellow);
        leftPen = new StandardPen(leftPad);
        rightPen = new WigglePen(rightPad, 10, 45);
        addPanel(leftPad, 1,1,1,1);
        addPanel(rightPad, 1,2,1,1);
    }

    public static void main(String [] args) {
        TestTurtleGraphics theGUI = new TestTurtleGraphics();
        theGUI.setSize(400, 400);
        theGUI.setVisible(true);
        theGUI.leftPen.move(100, 100);
        theGUI.rightPen.move(100, 100);
    }
}
```

AP Correlations

This textbook covers all of the required features of Java for the AP A exam and the AP AB exam, as well as other features potentially relevant to the first and second courses in programming but not tested. Table I-1 provides a reference to these features in the book.

TABLE I-1

AP exam features covered in this text

TESTED IN A, AB EXAM	TESTED IN AB EXAM ONLY	POTENTIALLY RELEVANT TO CS1/CS2 COURSE BUT NOT TESTED
`int, double, boolean` (p. 54, 98, 173)		`short, long, byte, char, float` (p. B-2)
+ ,-, *, /, %, ++, — (p. 58, 92)		
=, +=, -=, *=, /=, %= (p. 57, 91–92)		
==, !=, <, <=, >, >= (p. 100)		
&&, ||, ! and short-circuit evaluation (p. 172, 175)		
`(int)`, `(double)` (p. 62)		Other numeric casts such as (`char`) or (`float`) (p. B-3)
String concatenation (p. 63)		
Escape sequences \" \\ \n inside strings (p. 64)		Other escape sequences (\' \t \unnnn) (p. B-2)
`System.out.print,` `System.out.println` (p. 31, 39)		System.in, Stream input/output, GUI input/output, parsing input, formatted output (p. 665)
		`public static void main(String args)` (p. 273)
1-dimensional arrays, 2-dimensional rectangular arrays (p. 235)		arrays with 3 or more dimensions, ragged arrays (p. B-9)
`if, if/else, while,` `for, return` (p. 97, 101, 105, 150)		`do/while, switch, break` (p. B-4)
Modify existing classes (p. 131)	Design classes (p. 404)	

TABLE I-1 (Continued)
AP exam features covered in this text

TESTED IN A, AB EXAM	TESTED IN AB EXAM ONLY	POTENTIALLY RELEVANT TO CS1/CS2 COURSE BUT NOT TESTED
`public` classes, `private` instance variables, `public` or `private` methods or constants (p. 131)		`protected` or package visibility (p. 284)
`final` local variables, `static final` class variables (p. 270)		`final` instance variables, methods or classes (p. 293)
`static` methods (p. 270)		`static non-final` variables (p. 270)
`null`, `this`, `super` (p. 137, 284)	`super.method (args)` (p. 284)	`this.var`, `this.method(args)`, `this(args)` (p. 284)
Constructors and initialization of static variables (p. 270)		default initialization of instance variables, initialization blocks (p. 242)
Understand inheritance hierarchies, modifying subclass implementations and implementations of interfaces (p. 282)	Design an implement subclasses (p. 404)	
Understand the concepts of abstract classes and interfaces (p. 274, 286)	Design and implement abstract classes and interfaces (p. 404)	
Understand `equals`, `==` and `!=` comparison of objects (p. 308)	`Comparable. compareTo` (p. 321)	clone, implementation of `equals` (p. 308, 310)
Conversion to supertypes and `(Subtype)` casts (p. 285, 301, 334)		`instanceof` (p. 334)
		Inner classes (p. 541)
Package concept, `import x.y.Z;` (p. 68)		`import x.y.Z`, defining packages, class path (p. G-1)
Exception concept, common exceptions, throwing standard unchecked exceptions (p. 305)		
`String`, `Math`, `Random`, `Object`, `ArrayList` (p. 93, 94, 309, 352)	`Comparable`, `List`, `Set`, `Map`, `Iterator`, `ListIterator`, `LinkedList`, `HashSet`, `TreeSet`, `HashMap`, `TreeMap` (p. 321, 437, 457, 501)	
	Wrapper classes (`Integer`, `Double`) (p. 354)	
	Sorting methods in `Arrays & Collections` (p. 522, B-7)	

GLOSSARY

A

absolute path name A string that specifies the location of a resource, such as an HTML file, on a Web server.

abstract Simplified or partial, hiding detail.

abstract class A class that defines attributes and methods for subclasses but is never instantiated.

abstract data type (ADT) A class of objects, a defined set of properties of those objects, and a set of operations for processing the objects.

abstract method A method that is specified but not implemented in an abstract class. The subclasses must implement this method.

Abstract Windowing Toolkit (AWT) A Java package that contains the definitions of all of the classes used to set up graphical user interfaces.

abstraction A simplified view of a task or data structure that ignores complex detail.

accessor A method used to examine an attribute of an object without changing it.

accumulator A variable used for the purpose of summing successive values of some other variable.

activation record An area of computer memory that keeps track of a method call's parameters, local values, return value, and the caller's return address. *See also* **run-time stack**.

actual parameter A variable or expression contained in a method call and passed to that method. *See also* **formal parameter**.

adapter class A Java class that allows another class to implement an interface class without implementing all of its methods. *See also* **interface**.

address An integer value that the computer can use to reference a location. Often called address of a memory location. *See also* **value**.

algorithm A finite sequence of effective statements that, when applied to a problem, will solve it.

alias A situation in which two or more names in a program can refer to the same memory location. An alias can cause subtle side effects.

analysis The phase of the software life cycle in which the programmer describes what the program will do.

applet A Java program that can be downloaded and run on a Web browser.

application software Programs that allow human users to accomplish specialized tasks, such as word processing or database management.

argument A value or expression passed in a method call.

arithmetic expression A sequence of operands and operators that computes a value.

arithmetic/logic unit (ALU) The part of the central processing unit that performs arithmetic operations and evaluates expressions.

arithmetic overflow A situation that arises when the computer's memory cannot represent the number resulting from an arithmetic operation.

array A data structure whose elements are accessed by means of index positions.

array index The relative position of the components of an array.

ASCII character set The American Standard Code for Information Interchange ordering for a character set (See Appendix D).

assembly language A computer language that allows the programmer to express operations and memory addresses with mnemonic symbols.

assertion Special comments used with if statements and loops that state what you expect to happen and when certain conditions will hold.

assignment operator The symbol =, which is used to store a value in a variable.

assignment statement A method of putting values into memory locations.

association A pair of items consisting of a key and a value.

association list A collection of items that can be accessed by specifying key values. *See also* **keyed list.**

associative link A means of recognizing and accessing items in a network structure, such as the World Wide Web.

attribute A property that a computational object models, such as the balance in a bank account.

B

backing store A storage area, usually a collection, that holds the data accessed by an iterator.

base address The memory address of the first cell in an array.

behavior The set of actions that a class of objects supports.

big-O notation A formal notation used to express the amount of work done by an algorithm or the amount of memory used by an algorithm.

binary digit A digit, either 0 or 1, in the binary number system. Program instructions are stored in memory using a sequence of binary digits. *See also* **bit.**

binary search The process of examining a middle value of a sorted array to see which half contains the value in question and halving until the value is located.

binary search algorithm A method of searching a collection of items with a natural ordering that allows the search to discard ½ of the elements on each pass.

binary search tree A binary tree in which each node's left child is less than that node and each node's right child is greater than that node.

binary tree A tree in which each node has at most two children.

bit A binary digit.

bitmap A data structure used to represent the values and positions of points on a computer screen or image.

block An area of program text, enclosed in Java by the symbols {}, that contains statements and data declarations.

Boolean expression An expression whose value is either true or false. *See also* **compound Boolean expression** and **simple Boolean expression.**

border layout A Java layout class that allows the programmer to place window objects in five areas (north, south, west, east, and center) of a window. Border layout is the default layout for Java applications.

bottom-up implementation A method of coding a program that starts with lower-level modules and a test driver module.

boundary condition A value at which two equivalence classes meet.

bubble sort A sorting algorithm that swaps consecutive elements that are out of order to bubble the elements to the top or bottom on each pass.

bucket The location in an array to which an item is hashed using the chaining method of collision processing. A bucket also holds a linked list of items.

buffer A block of memory into which data are placed for transmission to a program, usually with file or string processing.

buffered file input The input of large blocks of data from a file.

button object A window object that allows the user to select an action by clicking a mouse.

byte A sequence of bits used to encode a character in memory. *See also* **word.**

byte code The kind of object code generated by a Java compiler and interpreted by a Java virtual machine. Byte code is platform independent.

C

call Any reference to a method by an executable statement. Also referred to as **invoke.**

call stack The trace of method calls that appears when Java throws an exception during program execution.

cancellation error A condition in which data are lost because of differences in the precision of the operands.

card layout A Java layout class that allows the programmer to manipulate the window as a stack of cards.

cast An operator that is used to convert a value of one type to a value of a different type (e.g., `double` to `int`).

c-curve A fractal shape that resembles the letter C.

central processing unit (CPU) A major hardware component that consists of the arithmetic/logic unit and the control unit.

chaining A strategy of resolving collisions in which the items that hash to the same location are stored in a linked structure.

chains The linked structures used in the chaining method of resolving collisions.

character set The list of characters available for data and program statements.

check box A window object that allows the user to check a labeled box.

children Elements that directly succeed a given element in a hierarchical collection.

choice list A window object that allows the user to select from a pull-down list of options.

circular linked list A linked structure in which the next pointer of the last node is aimed at the first node.

class A description of the attributes and behavior of a set of computational objects.

class constant A constant that is visible to all instances of a class and, if public, is accessed by specifying the class name. For example, `Math.PI` is a class constant.

class constructor A method used to create and initialize an instance of a class.

class diagram A graphical notation that describes the relationships among the classes in a software syatem.

class (static) method A method that is invoked when a message is sent to a class. For example, `Math.sqrt` is a class method. *See also* **message**.

class (static) variable A variable that is visible to all instances of a class and, if public, is accessed by specifying the class name.

client A computational object that receives a service from another computational object.

client/server relationship A means of describing the organization of computing resources in which one resource provides a service to another resource.

clustering A phenomenon in which several items are placed in adjacent array locations during hashing.

coding The process of writing executable statements that are part of a program to solve a problem. *See also* **implementation**.

cohesive method A method designed to accomplish a single task.

collaboration diagram A graphical notation that describes the manner in which objects communicate in a software system.

collection A group of data elements that can be treated as one thing. A collection tracks a number of elements, which can be added or removed.

collision A situation that takes place when two items hash to the same array location.

combinatorial explosion A multiplicative growth.

comments Nonexecutable statements used to make a program more readable.

compatible type Expressions that have the same base type. A formal parameter and an actual parameter must be of compatible type, and the operands of an assignment statement must be of compatible type.

compilation error An error detected when the program is being compiled. *See also* **design error, run-time error,** and **syntax error.**

compiler A computer program that automatically converts instructions in a high-level language to machine language.

complete code coverage A set of tests in which every line in a program is executed at least once.

complexity analysis The process of deriving a formula that expresses the rate of growth of work or memory as a function of the size of the data or problem that it solves. *See also* **big-O notation.**

component An object that supports the display of an image, such as a button, menu item, or window, in a graphical user interface.

compound assignment An assignment operation that performs a designated operation, such as addition, before storing the result in a variable.

compound Boolean expression Refers to the complete expression when logical connectives and negation are used to generate Boolean values. *See also* **Boolean expression** and **simple Boolean expression.**

compound statement A statement that uses the symbols { and } to group several statements and data declarations as a unit. *See also* **block.**

concatenation An operation in which the contents of one data structure are placed after the contents of another data structure.

concrete class   A class that can be instantiated. *See also* **abstract class**.

conditional statement   *See* **selection statement**.

conjunction   The connection of two Boolean expressions using the logical operator && (AND), returning false if at least one of the expressions is false or true if they are both true.

constant   A symbol whose value cannot be changed.

constructor   A method that is run when an object is instantiated, usually to initialize that object's instance variables.

contained class   A class that is used to define a data object within another class.

container   A Java class that allows the programmer to group window objects for placement in a window.

content-based operation   An operation that involves a search for a given element irrespective of its position in a collection.

contiguous memory   Computer memory that is organized so that the data are accessible in adjacent cells.

control structure   A structure that controls the flow of execution of program statements.

control unit   The part of the central processing unit that controls the operation of the rest of the computer.

coordinate system   A grid that allows a programmer to specify positions of points in a plane or of pixels on a computer screen.

counter   A variable used to count the number of times some process is completed.

count-controlled loop   A loop that stops when a counter variable reaches a specified limit.

current position indicator   The pointer in a positional list that locates the item about to be accessed with a next or a previous operation.

D

data   The particular characters that are used to represent information in a form suitable for storage, processing, and communication.

data flow diagram   A graphical depiction of the communication between program components that share data.

data input stream   A Java class that supports the input of data from a binary file.

data output stream   A Java class that supports the output of data to a binary file.

data type   A formal description of the set of values that a variable can have.

data validation   The process of examining data prior to its use in a program.

debugging   The process of eliminating errors, or "bugs," from a program.

decrement   To decrease the value of a variable.

default constructor   A method that Java provides for creating objects of a class. The programmer can override this method to do extra things.

definition list   An HTML structure that allows an author to display a keyed list on a Web page.

density ratio   A measure of the degree to which an array is filling with items, computed by dividing the number of items by the array's capacity.

design   The phase of the software life cycle in which the programmer describes how the program will accomplish its tasks.

design error   An error such that a program runs, but unexpected results are produced. Also referred to as a logic error. *See also* **compilation error, run-time error,** and **syntax error**.

dialog   A type of window that pops up to display information or receive it from the user.

dictionary   A data structure that allows the programmer to access items by specifying key values. *See also* **association list**.

DOS development environment   A set of software tools that allows you to edit, compile, run, and debug programs using the DOS operating system.

double   A Java data type used to represent numbers with a decimal point, e.g., a real number or a floating-point number.

double field object   A non-standard window object or component which supports the input and output of floating-point numbers.

doubly linked structure   A linked structure in which each node has a pointer to the previous node and a pointer to the next node.

do-while loop   A posttest loop examining a Boolean expression after causing a statement to be executed. *See also* for loop, loops, and while loop.

driver   A method used to test other methods.

dynamic memory   Memory allocated under program control from the heap and accessed by means of pointers. *See also* **heap** and **pointer**.

dynamic structure   A data structure that may expand or contract during execution of a program. *See also* **dynamic memory**.

E

element   A value that is stored in an array.

empty link   *See* **null value**.

empty statement   A semicolon used to indicate that no action is to be taken. Also referred to as a **null statement**.

encapsulation   The process of hiding and restricting access to the implementation details of a data structure.

end-of-file marker   A special marker inserted by the machine to indicate the end of the data file.

end-of-line character   A special character (`'\n'`) used to indicate the end of a line of characters in a string or a file stream.

entrance-controlled loop   *See* **pretest loop**.

enumeration   A Java class that allows the programmer to process a sequence of objects.

equivalence class   All the sets of test data that exercise a program in the same manner.

error   *See* **compilation error, design error, logic error, run-time error,** and **syntax error**.

event   An occurrence, such as a button click or a mouse motion, that can be detected and processed by a program.

event-driven loop   A process, usually hidden in the operating system, that waits for an event, notifies a program that an event has occurred, and returns to wait for more events.

exception   An abnormal state or error that occurs during run time and is signaled by the operating system.

exception-driven loop   The use of exceptions to implement a normal loop, usually for file input.

execute   To carry out the instructions of a program.

exit-controlled loop   *See* **posttest loop**.

expanding capabilities implementation   A coding strategy that begins with a running but incomplete program and gradually adds features until the program is complete.

explicit type conversion   The use of an operation by a programmer to convert the type of a data object.

exponential form   *See* **floating-point**.

expression tree   A tree in which each leaf node contains a number and each interior node contains an operator.

extended `if` statement   Nested selection in which additional `if-else` statements are used in the `else` option. *See also* **nested `if` statement**.

external image   An image displayed when the user selects a link on a Web page.

external pointer   A special pointer that allows users to access the nodes in a linked list.

extreme condition   Data at the limits of validity.

F

Fibonacci numbers   A series of numbers generated by taking the sum of the previous two numbers in the series. The series begins with the numbers 1 and 2.

field width   The number of columns used for the output of text. *See also* **formatting**.

file   A data structure that resides on a secondary storage medium.

file input stream   A Java class used to connect a program to a file for input.

file output stream   A Java class used to connect a program to a file for output.

final method   A method that cannot be implemented by a subclass.

fixed-point   A method of writing real numbers in which the decimal is placed where it belongs in the number. *See also* **floating-point**.

floating-point   A method for writing numbers in scientific notation to accommodate numbers that may have very large or very small values. *See also* **fixed-point**.

flow layout   A Java layout class that allows the user to place window objects in wrap-around rows in a window. Flow layout is the default layout for applets.

flowchart A diagram that displays the flow of control of a program. *See also* **control structure**.

flushing The process of clearing an output buffer before closing an output file stream.

font The kind of typeface used for text, such as Courier and Times Roman.

for loop A structured loop consisting of an initializer expression, a termination expression, an update expression, and a statement.

formal parameter A name, introduced in a method definition, that is replaced by an actual parameter when the method is called.

formal specification The set of preconditions and postconditions of a method.

formatting Designating the desired field width when displaying text. *See also* **field width**.

fractal geometry A theory of shapes that are reflected in various phenomena, such as coastlines, water flow, and price fluctuations.

fractal object A type of mathematical object that maintains self-sameness when viewed at greater levels of detail.

frame A Java class that defines the window for an application. *See also* **application software**.

free list An area of memory used to allocate storage for objects.

front The end of a queue from which elements are removed.

G

garbage collection The automatic process of reclaiming memory when the data of a program no longer need it.

general tree A tree in which each node can have zero or more children.

global identifier A name that can be used by all of the methods of a class.

global variable *See* **global identifier**.

graph collection A collection whose elements may have zero or more predecessors and successors.

graphical user interface (GUI) A means of communication between human beings and computers that uses a pointing device for input and a bitmapped screen for output. The bitmap displays images of windows and window objects such as buttons, text fields, and pull-down menus. The user interacts with the interface by using the mouse to directly manipulate the window objects. *See also* **window object**.

graphics context In Java, an object associated with a component where the images for that component are drawn.

grid bag layout A Java layout class that allows the user to place window objects in a two-dimensional grid in the window and to have control over how the window objects occupy the cells in that grid.

grid layout A Java layout class that allows the user to place window objects in a two-dimensional grid in the window.

H

hacking The use of clever techniques to write a program, often for the purpose of gaining access to protected resources on networks.

hardware The computing machine and its support devices.

has-a relationship A relationship between two classes in which one class contains an instance of the other class.

hash code A number that is used to determine the location of an item in an array.

hash function A method of generating a hash code in constant time.

hashing A method by which the position of an item in a collection is related to the item's content and can be determined in constant time.

head The first element in a list.

heap A tree in which each node is greater than either of its children.

heap An area of computer memory in which storage for dynamic data is available.

heap property The relationship that characterizes nodes and their children in a heap, e.g., each node is greater than either of its children.

heap underflow A condition in which memory leakage causes dynamic memory to become unavailable.

helper method A method used within the implementation of a class but not used by clients of that class.

hierarchical collection A collection whose elements may have zero or more successors but at most one predecessor.

high-level language Any programming language that uses words and symbols to make it relatively easy to read and write a program. *See also* **assembly language** and **machine language.**

hyperlinks An item in a hypertext document that allows the user to navigate to another document.

hypermedia A data structure that allows the user to access different kinds of information (text, images, sound, video, applications) by traversing links.

hypertext A data structure that allows the user to access different chunks of text by traversing links.

hypertext markup language (HTML) A programming language that allows the user to create pages for the World Wide Web.

I

identifiers Words that must be created according to a well-defined set of rules but can have any meaning subject to these rules.

identity The property of an object that it is the same thing at different points in time, even though the values of its attributes might change.

if-else statement A selection statement that allows a program to perform alternative actions based on a condition.

immutable object An object whose internal data or state cannot be changed.

implementation The phase of the software life cycle in which the program is coded in a programming language.

increment The process of increasing a number by 1.

index *See* **array index.**

index-based operation An operation that accesses an element by specifying its position in a collection. For lists, the position is specified as an integer ranging from 0 to the size of the collection minus 1.

infinite loop A loop in which the controlling condition is not changed in such a manner to allow the loop to terminate.

infinite recursion The state of a running program that occurs when a recursive method cannot reach a stopping state.

infix form The form of an expression in which the operator is surrounded by its operands.

information hiding A condition in which the user of a module does not know the details of how it is implemented, and the implementer of a module does not know the details of how it is used.

inheritance The process by which a subclass can reuse attributes and behavior defined in a superclass. *See also* **subclass** and **superclass.**

initializer list A means of expressing a set of data that can be assigned to the cells of an array in one statement.

inline image An image that is loaded when the user accesses a Web page.

input Data obtained by a program during its execution.

input assertion A precondition for a loop.

input device A device that provides information to the computer. Typical input devices are a mouse, keyboard, disk drive, microphone, and network port. *See also* **I/O device** and **output device.**

input stream A data object that allows a program to input data from a file or the keyboard.

insertion sort A sorting algorithm that locates an insertion point and takes advantage of partial orderings in an array.

instance A computational object bearing the attributes and behavior specified by a class.

instance method A method that is called when a message is sent to an instance of a class. *See also* **message.**

instance variable Storage for data in an instance of a class.

instantiation The process of creating a new object or instance of a class.

integer arithmetic operations Operations allowed on data of type `int`. These include the operations of addition, subtraction, multiplication, division, and modulus to produce integer answers.

integer field object A non-standard window object or component which supports the input and output of whole numbers.

integer overflow A condition in which an integer value is too large to be stored in the computer's memory.

integrated development environment (IDE) A set of software tools that allows you to edit, compile, run, and debug programs within one user interface.

interface A formal statement of how communication occurs between the user of a module (class or method) and its implementer.

interface A Java file that simply specifies the methods to be implemented by another class. A class that implements several interfaces can thus adopt the behavior of several classes.

interior node A node that has at least one child.

invariant expression An assertion that is true before the loop and after each iteration of the loop.

invoke *See* **call**.

I/O device Any device that allows information to be transmitted to or from a computer. *See also* **input device** and **output device**.

is-a relationship A relationship between two classes in which one class is a subclass of the other class.

iteration *See* **loops**.

iterative process A running program that executes a loop.

iterator An object that allows clients to navigate a collection by tracking a current position indicator. Basic operations are visiting the next element, testing for the presence of a next element, and removing the element just visited.

J

Java virtual machine (JVM) A program that interprets Java byte codes and executes them.

just-in-time compilation (JIT) A feature of some Java virtual machines that first translates byte codes to the machine's code before executing them.

justification The process of aligning text to the left, the center, or the right within a given number of columns.

K

key An item that is associated with a value and is used to locate this value in a collection.

keyed list A data structure that allows the programmer to access items by using key values. *See also* **association list**.

keywords *See* **reserved words**.

knows-a relationship A relationship between two classes in which one class neither has the other class nor is the other class but instead carries it or displays it or eats it or some other such thing.

L

label object A window object that displays text, usually to describe the roles of other window objects.

leaf A node without children.

left subtree The node and its descendants to the left of a given node in a binary tree.

library A collection of methods and data organized to perform a set of related tasks. *See also* **class** and **package**.

lifetime The time during which a data object or method call exists.

linear An increase of work or memory in direct proportion to the size of a problem.

linear collection A collection whose elements have at most one predecessor and at most one successor.

linear collision processing A strategy of resolving collisions that searches the array for the next available empty slot for an item.

linear search *See* **sequential search**.

linked structure A structure in which each item is linked to the next one by means of a pointer. *See also* **recursive data structure**.

list iterator An object that extends an iterator to allow insertions, replacements, and removals of elements from a list.

listener A Java class that detects and responds to events.

literal An element of a language that evaluates to itself, such as 34 or "hi there."

load factor A measure of the degree to which an array is filling with items, computed by dividing the number of items by the array's capacity.

loader A system software tool that places program instructions and data into the appropriate memory locations before program start-up.

local identifier A name whose value is visible only within a method or a nested block.

local variable *See* **local identifier.**

logarithmic An increase of work in proportion to the number of times that the problem size can be divided by 2.

logic error *See* **design error.**

logical operator Either of the logical connective operators (&&, ||) or the negation operator(!).

logical size The number of data items actually available in a data structure at a given time. *See also* **physical size.**

logical structure The organization of the components in a data structure, independent of their organization in computer memory.

long A Java data type used to represent large integers.

loop invariant An assertion that expresses a relationship between variables that remains constant throughout all iterations of the loop.

loop variant An assertion whose truth changes between the first and final execution of the loop.

loop verification The process of guaranteeing that a loop performs its intended task.

loops Program statements that cause a process to be repeated. *See also* do-while **loop,** for **loop,** and while **loop.**

low-level language *See* **assembly language.**

M

machine language The language used directly by the computer in all its calculations and processing.

main (primary) memory The high-speed internal memory of a computer, also referred to as random access memory (RAM). *See also* **memory** and **secondary memory.**

main unit A computer's main unit contains the central processing unit (CPU) and the main (primary) memory; it is hooked to one or more **input devices** and one or more **output devices.**

mainframe Large computers typically used by major companies and universities. *See also* **microcomputer** and **minicomputer.**

mantissa/exponent notation A notation used to express floating-point numbers.

map An unordered collection in which each value is associated with a unique key.

markup tag A syntactic form in the hypertext markup language used to create different elements displayed on a Web page.

mathematical induction A method of proving that parts of programs are correct by reasoning from a base case and an induction hypothesis to a general conclusion.

matrix A two-dimensional array that provides range checking and can be resized.

megabyte Shorthand for approximately 1 million bytes.

memex A hypothetical machine proposed by Vannevar Bush that would allow users to store and retrieve information via associative links.

memory The ordered sequence of storage cells that can be accessed by address. Instructions and variables of an executing program are temporarily held here. *See also* **main memory** and **secondary memory.**

memory location A storage cell that can be accessed by address. *See also* **memory.**

menu item A window object that displays as an option in a pull-down menu or pop-up menu.

merge The process of combining lists. Typically refers to files or arrays.

message A symbol used by a client to ask an object to perform a service. *See also* **method.**

message box A window object used to display text to a user, allowing the user to close the box by pressing a button.

method A chunk of code that can be treated as a unit and invoked by name. A method is called when a message is sent to an object. *See also* **class method** and **instance method**.

method heading The portion of a method implementation containing the function's name, parameter declarations, and return type.

microcomputer A computer capable of fitting on a laptop or desktop, generally used by one person at a time. *See also* **mainframe** and **minicomputer**.

minicomputer A small version of a mainframe computer. It is usually used by several people at once. *See also* **mainframe** and **microcomputer**.

mixed-mode Expressions containing data of different types; the values of these expressions will be of either type, depending on the rules for evaluating them.

modal A state in which the computer user cannot exit without explicitly signaling the computer, usually with an "Accept" or "Cancel" option.

model/view/controller pattern A design plan in which the roles and responsibilities of the system are cleanly divided among data management (model), user interface display (view), and user event handling (controller) tasks.

modem A device that connects a computer to a telephone system to transmit data.

module An independent unit that is part of a larger development. Can be a method or a class (set of methods and related data).

module specifications In the case of a method, a description of data received, information returned, and task performed by a module. In the case of a class, a description of the attributes and behavior.

multidimensional array An array whose elements are accessed by specifying more than one index.

mutator A method used to change the value of an attribute of an object.

mutually comparable A property of two items such that they can be related by less than, greater than, or equal to.

N

negation The use of the logical operator ! (not) with a Boolean expression, returning true if the expression is false, and false if the expression is true.

nested `if` statement A selection statement used within another selection statement. *See also* **extended `if` statement**.

nested loop A loop as one of the statements in the body of another loop.

nested selection Any combination of selection statements within selection statements. *See also* **selection statement**.

network A collection of resources that are linked together for communication.

node A component of a linked list, consisting of a data item and a pointer to the next node.

null statement *See* **empty statement**.

null value A special value that indicates that no object can be accessed.

O

object A collection of data and operations, in which the data can be accessed and modified only by means of the operations.

object code *See* **object program**.

object heap An area of memory used to allocate storage for objects.

object-oriented programming The construction of software systems that use objects.

object program The machine code version of the source program.

off-by-one error Usually seen with loops, this error shows up as a result that is one less or one greater than the expected value.

offset The quantity added to the base address of an array to locate the address of an array cell.

one-dimensional array An array in which each data item is accessed by specifying a single index.

one-way list A list that supports navigation in one direction only.

operating system A large program that allows the user to communicate with the hardware and performs various management tasks.

option panes Window objects which provide standard services, such as prompting for input values, yes/no queries, and message boxes.

ordinal data type A data type ordered in some association with the integers; each integer is the ordinal of an associated value of the data type.

origin The point (0,0) in a coordinate system.

output Information that is produced by a program.

output assertion A postcondition for a loop.

output device A device that allows you to see the results of a program. Typically, it is a monitor, printer, speaker, or network port. *See also* **input device** *and* **I/O device.**

output stream A data object that allows a program to output data to a file or the terminal screen.

overflow In arithmetic operations, a value may be too large for the computer's memory location. A meaningless value may be assigned or an error message may result. *See also* **underflow.**

overloading The process of using the same operator symbol or identifier to refer to many different functions. *See also* **polymorphism.**

overriding The process of re-implementing a method already implemented in a superclass.

P

package A group of related classes in a named directory.

paint mode The default state of a graphics context in which images are drawn.

panel A window object whose purpose is to contain other window objects.

parallel arrays Arrays of the same length but with different component data types.

parameter *See* **argument.**

parameter list A list of parameters. An actual parameter list is contained in a method call. A formal parameter list is contained in a method heading.

parent The immediate superclass of a class.

parent A given node's predecessor in a tree.

parse tree A tree that contains the structure of a sentence.

peripheral memory *See* **memory** *and* **secondary memory.**

persistence The property of a data model that allows it to survive different runs of an application. *See also* **serialization**

physical size The number of memory units available for storing data items in a data structure. *See also* **logical size.**

pivot A data item around which an array is subdivided during the quicksort.

pixel A picture element or dot of color used to display images on a computer screen.

pointer A reference to an object that allows you to access it.

polymorphism The property of one operator symbol or method identifier having many meanings. *See also* **overloading.**

pop The operation that removes an element from a stack.

portable Able to be transferred to different applications or computers without changes.

positional list A list in which a client navigates by moving a current position indicator.

position-based operation An operation performed with respect to a current position indicator in a collection.

postcondition A statement of what is true after a certain action is taken.

postfix form The form of an expression in which the operator follows its operands.

posttest loop A loop in which the control condition is tested after the loop is executed. A `do-while` loop is a posttest loop. Also referred to as an **exit-controlled loop.**

precondition A statement of what is true before a certain action is taken.

pretest condition A condition that controls whether or not the body of the loop is executed before going through the loop.

pretest loop A loop in which the control condition is tested before the loop is executed. A `while` **loop** is a pretest loop. Also referred to as an **entrance-controlled loop.**

primary memory *See* **main memory** and **memory.**

priming input statement An input statement that must be executed before a loop control condition is tested.

primitive data type A data type such as `char`, `int`, `double`, or `boolean` whose values are stored directly in variables of that type. Primitive data types are always passed by value when they are parameters in Java and copied during assignment statements.

print stream A Java class that sends text output to the terminal window.

priority queue A collection in which the items are ordered according to priority.

private inner class A class that is defined as a helper class within another class.

private method A method that is accessible only within the scope of a class definition.

private variable A variable that is accessible only within the scope of a class definition.

procedural programming A style of programming that decomposes a program into a set of methods or procedures.

program A set of instructions that tells the machine (the hardware) what to do.

program proof An analysis of a program that attempts to verify the correctness of program results.

program walk-through The process of carefully following, using pencil and paper, steps the computer uses to solve the problem given in a program. Also referred to as a **trace.**

programming language Formal language that computer scientists use to give instructions to the computer.

protected variable A variable that is accessible only within the scope of a class definition, within the class definition of a subclass, or within the class's package.

prototype A trimmed-down version of a class or software system that still functions and allows the programmer to study its essential features.

pseudocode A stylized half-English, half-code language written in English but suggesting Java code.

public method A method that is accessible to any program component that uses the class.

public variable A variable that is accessible to any program component that uses the class.

pull-down menu A window object that allows the user to pull down and select from a list of menu items. *See also* **menu item.**

push The operation that adds an element to a stack.

Q

quadratic An increase of work or memory in proportion to the square of the size of the problem.

quadratic collision processing A strategy of resolving collisions that searches the array for the next available empty slot for an item, using the square of an incrementally increasing distance to leapfrog potential clusters.

quality assurance The ongoing process of making sure that a software product is developed to the highest standards possible subject to the ever-present constraints of time and money.

query-controlled input A style of taking multiple user inputs and asking the user if she wants to continue after each one.

queue A data structure that allows the programmer to insert items only at one end and remove them from the other end.

quicksort A sorting technique that moves elements around a pivot and recursively sorts the elements to the left and the right of the pivot.

R

radio button A type of check box that permits the user to select only one check box in the group. *See also* **check box.**

ragged array A two-dimensional array in which each row may have a different length.

random access data structure A data structure in which the time to access a data item does not depend on its position in the structure.

random walk   A process in which positions in a structure are visited at random; for example, visiting points in two-dimensional space at random.

range bound error   The situation that occurs when an attempt is made to use an array index value that is less than 0 or greater than or equal to the size of the array.

rear   The end of a queue to which elements are added.

recursion   The process of a subprogram calling itself. A clearly defined stopping state must exist. Any recursive subprogram can be rewritten using **iteration**.

recursive data structure   A data structure that has either a simple form or a form that is composed of other instances of the same data structure. *See also* **linked structure**.

recursive method   A method that calls itself.

recursive step   A step in the recursive process that solves a similar problem of smaller size and eventually leads to a termination of the process.

recursive subprogram   *See* **recursion**.

reference type   A data type such as array, String, or any other Java class, whose instances are not stored directly in variables of that type. References or pointers to these objects are stored instead. References to objects are passed when they are parameters in Java, and only the references, not the objects, are copied during assignment statements.

refreshable image   An image that is redisplayed when the user resizes or minimizes a window.

relational operator   An operator used for comparison of data items of the same type.

relative path name   A string that specifies the location of a resource without mentioning the Web server.

repetition   *See* **loops**.

representational error   A condition in which the precision of data is reduced because of the order in which operations are performed.

reserved words   Words that have predefined meanings that cannot be changed. A list of reserved words for Java is in Appendix B.

return type   The type of value returned by a method.

right subtree   The node and its descendants to the right of a given node in a binary tree.

robust   The state in which a program is protected against most possible crashes from bad data and unexpected values.

root   The node in a tree that has no predecessor.

round-off error   A condition in which a portion of a real number is lost because of the way it is stored in the computer's memory.

round-robin scheduling   The use of a queue to rotate processes for access to a resource.

run-time error   An error detected when, after compilation is completed, an error message results instead of the correct output. *See also* **compilation error, design error, exception,** and **syntax error**.

run-time stack   An area of computer memory reserved for local variables and parameters of method calls.

S

scanning   The process of picking words or tokens out of a stream of characters.

scope of identifier   The largest block in which the identifier is available.

screen coordinate system   A coordinate system used by most programming languages in which the origin is in the upper left corner of the screen, window, or panel, and the y values increase toward the bottom of the drawing area.

scroll bar   A window object that allows the user to select a value from a continuous range.

scrolling list   A window object that displays a selectable list of strings.

secondary memory   An auxiliary device for memory, usually a disk or magnetic tape. *See also* **main memory** *and* **memory**.

selection   The process by which a method or a variable of an instance or a class is accessed.

selection sort   A sorting algorithm that sorts the components of an array in either ascending or descending order. This process puts the smallest or largest element in the top position and repeats the process on the remaining array components. *See also* **quicksort**.

selection statement A control statement that selects some particular logical path based on the value of an expression. Also referred to as a **conditional statement.**

self-documenting code Code that is written using descriptive identifiers.

semantics The rules for interpreting the meaning of a program in a language.

sentinel node A special node in a linked structure that contains no data but instead marks the beginning or end of the structure.

sentinel value A special value that indicates the end of a set of data or of a process.

sequential access A situation in which access to a data item depends on its position in the data structure.

sequential search The process of searching a list by examining the first component and then examining successive components in the order in which they occur. Also referred to as a **linear search.**

sequential traversal The process of visiting each data item in an array or a linked list from beginning to end.

serialization A mechanism that maintains the persistence of objects in a data model. *See also* **persistence.**

server A computational object that provides a service to another computational object.

set An unordered collection of unique items.

short A Java data type used to represent small integers.

short-circuit evaluation The process by which a compound Boolean expression halts evaluation and returns the value of the first subexpression that evaluates to true, in the case of ||, or false, in the case of &&.

side effect A change in a variable that is the result of some action taken in a program, usually from within a method.

simple Boolean expression An expression in which two numbers or variable values are compared using a single relational operator. *See also* **Boolean expression** and **compound Boolean expression.**

singly linked structure A collection of items in which each item except the last has a link or reference to the next item in the structure.

software Programs that make the machine (the hardware) do something, such as word processing, database management, or games.

software development life cycle (SDLC) The process of development, maintenance, and demise of a software system. Phases include analysis, design, coding, testing/verification, maintenance, and obsolescence.

software engineering The process of developing and maintaining large software systems.

software reuse The process of building and maintaining software systems out of existing software components.

sorted map A type of map that allows clients to visit its keys in sorted order.

sorted set A type of set that allows clients to visit its items in sorted order.

source code The program text as viewed by the human who creates or reads it, prior to compilation.

source program A program written by a programmer.

stack A dynamic data structure in which access can be made from only one end. Referred to as a LIFO (last-in, first-out) structure.

stack overflow error A situation that occurs when the computer runs out of memory to allocate for its call stack. This situation usually arises during an infinite recursion.

stand-alone program A Java program that runs directly on a computer without the aid of a Web browser.

state The set of all the values of the variables of a program at any point during its execution.

statement An individual instruction in a program.

statement block (synonym compound statement) A form by which a sequence of statements and data declarations can be treated as a unit.

stepwise refinement   The process of repeatedly subdividing tasks into subtasks until each subtask is easily accomplished. *See also* **structured programming** *and* **top-down implementation.**

stopping state   The well-defined termination of a recursive process.

stream   A channel in which data are passed from sender to receiver.

stream tokenizer   A Java class that allows the programmer to input text from a file one word at a time.

string   An abbreviated name for a string literal.

string buffer   A Java class that allows the programmer to modify the contents of a string and efficiently increase its size.

string literal   One or more characters, enclosed in double quotation marks, used as a constant in a program.

string tokenizer   A Java class that allows the programmer to access text in a string one word at a time.

structure chart   A graphical method of indicating the relationship between modules when designing the solution to a problem.

structured programming   Programming that parallels a solution to a problem achieved by top-down implementation. *See also* **stepwise refinement** and **top-down implementation.**

stub programming   The process of using incomplete functions to test data transmission among the functions.

subclass   A class that inherits attributes and behavior from another class.

subscript   *See* **array index.**

substring   A string that represents a segment of another string.

superclass   The class from which a subclass inherits attributes and behavior. *See also* **inheritance** *and* **subclass.**

Swing Toolkit   A set of Java classes used to create programs with graphical user interfaces.

syntax   The rules for constructing well-formed programs in a language.

syntax error   An error in spelling, punctuation, or placement of certain key symbols in a program. *See also* **compilation error, design error,** *and* **run-time error.**

system software   The programs that allow users to write and execute other programs, including operating systems such as Windows and MacOS.

T

tail   The last element in a list.

tail-recursive   The property that a recursive algorithm has of performing no work after each recursive step. *See also* **recursion.**

task-controlled loop   A type of loop that terminates when it is finished performing some task.

terminal I/O interface   A user interface that allows the user to enter input from a keyboard and view output as text in a window.

text area object   A window object that provides a scrollable region within which the user can view or enter several lines of text.

text field object   A window object in which the user can view or enter a single line of text.

text files   Files that contain characters and are readable and writable by text editors.

token   An individual word or symbol.

top   The end of a stack where elements are added or removed.

top-down implementation   A method for coding by which the programmer starts with a top-level task and implements subtasks. Each subtask is then subdivided into smaller subtasks. This process is repeated until each remaining subtask is easily coded. *See also* **stepwise refinement** and **structured programming.**

trace   *See* **program walk-through.**

transient image problem   A problem that occurs when an image is lost when the user resizes or minimizes a window.

truth table   A means of listing all of the possible values of a Boolean expression.

turtle graphics   A set of methods that manipulate a pen in a graphics window.

two-dimensional array   An array in which each data item is accessed by specifying a pair of indices.

two-way list   A list that supports navigation in both directions.

type   *See* **data type.**

type promotion The process of converting a less inclusive data type, such as `int`, to a more inclusive data type, such as `double`.

U

underflow A value that is too small to be represented by a computer; it is automatically replaced by its negation. *See also* **overflow.**

Unicode A character set that uses 16 bits to represent over 65,000 possible characters. These include the ASCII character set as well as symbols and ideograms in many international languages. *See also* **ASCII character set.**

Unified Modeling Language (UML) A graphical notation for describing a software system in various phases of development.

uniform resource locator (URL) The address of a page on the World Wide Web.

unordered collection A collection whose elements are in no particular order from the client's perspective.

user-defined class A new data type introduced and defined by the programmer.

user-defined method A new function introduced and defined by the programmer.

user-friendly Describes an interactive program with clear, easy-to-follow messages for the user.

V

value An item that is associated with a key and is located by a key in a collection.

variable A memory location, referenced by an identifier, whose value can be changed during execution of a program.

vector A one-dimensional array that supports resizing, insertions, and removals.

virtual machine A software tool that behaves like a high-level computer.

virus A program that can enter a computer and perhaps destroy information.

visibility modifier A symbol (`public`, `protected`, or `private`) that specifies the kind of access that clients have to a server's data and methods.

void method A method that returns no value.

W

waterfall model A series of steps in which a software system trickles down from analysis to design to implementation. *See also* **software development life cycle.**

while loop A pretest loop that examines a Boolean expression before causing a statement to be executed.

window A rectangular area of a computer screen that can contain window objects. Windows typically can be resized, minimized, maximized, zoomed, or closed. *See also* **frame.**

window object A computational object that displays an image, such as a button or a text field, in a window and supports interaction with the user.

word A unit of memory consisting of one or more bytes. Words can be addressed.

wrapper class A class designed to contain a primitive data type so that the primitive type can behave like a reference type. *See also* **primitive data type** and **reference type.**

X

XOR mode The state of a graphics context that allows images to be drawn free of flicker.